# *Baedeker's*

# SCANDINAVIA

172 colour photographs
66 maps and plans
1 large road map

Text:
Waltraud Andersen
Dr Johannes Gamillscheg
Reiner Gatermann
Gerald Sawade (Climate)
Dr Walter Thauer (Geography, etc.)
Christine Wessely (Art)

Editorial work:
Baedeker Stuttgart
English language: Alec Court

Cartography:
Ingenieurbüro für Kartographie,
Huber & Oberländer, Munich
Georg Schiffner, Lahr

Design and layout:
Creativ Verlagsgesellschaft mbH
Stuttgart
Ulrich Kolb,

Conception and general direction:
Dr Peter Baumgarten,
Baedeker Stuttgart

English translation:
James Hogarth

© Baedeker Stuttgart
Original German edition

© Jarrold and Sons Ltd
English language edition worldwide

© Prentice-Hall, Inc, US and Canada

© The Automobile Association, 57354
United Kingdom and Ireland

Licensed user:
Mairs Geographischer Verlag GmbH & Co.,
Ostfildern-Kemnat bei Stuttgart

Reproductions:
Gölz Repro-Service GmbH,
Ludwigsburg

The name *Baedeker* is a registered trademark

Printed in Great Britain by Jarrold & Sons Ltd,
Norwich

0–13–056085–5 US and Canada
0 86145 100 7 UK

Source of illustrations:

Many of the coloured illustrations were provided by
the Danish Tourist Board in Copenhagen, Hamburg
and Munich, the Norway Travel Association in Oslo
and Hamburg, the Swedish Tourist Board in Stockholm and Hamburg and the Finnish Tourist Board in
Helsinki and Hamburg. Others:

Allianz-Archiv (p. 292)
Ragner Andersson, Falun (pp. 34, 90, 234, 235, 331).
Anthony-Verlag, Starnberg (pp. 46, 47; 60, top left;
127, 159, 238; 245, top).
Christian Baedeker, Stuttgart (pp. 73, 86, 129, 130,
144, 147, 254, 256, 265; 272, left).
Bavaria-Verlag, Gauting (pp. 185, 190, 244; 276,
right; 284, 294).
Timo Byckling, Espoo (p. 16).
Pär Domeij, Sweden (pp. 23, 184).
Gullersproduktion, Göteborg (p. 103).
Husmo-foto, Oslo (pp. 58–9).
Topi Ikäläinen, Kuopio (pp. 165; 320, right).
Dr W. Jenninger, Tübingen (pp. 81, 84, 210, 227,
255).
Värmland Turisttrafikförbund, Karlstad (p. 158).
Wasavarvet/Sjöhistoriska museet, Stockholm (p.
250).
Zentrale Farbbild Agentur (ZEFA), Düsseldorf (cover
picture; pp. 303, 304).

# How to use this Guide

The principal towns and areas of tourist interest are
described in alphabetical order. The names of other
places referred to under these general headings can be
found in the very full Index. (For the convenience of
the English-speaking reader the letters æ, ä, ø, ö and å,
which in Scandinavia come at the end of the alphabet,
appear in English alphabetical order.)

Note that geographical terms like "lake", "street", etc.
(see list on p. 319), are usually suffixed to the
place-name and do not appear as separate words. A
suffix ending in *n* or *t* is the definite article
(Stortorget=the Stortorg or main square); a suffix
ending in *r* marks the plural.

Following the tradition established by Karl Baedeker
in 1844, sights of particular interest and hotels or
restaurants of particular quality are distinguished by
either one or two asterisks.

In the lists of hotels b.=beds, SP=outdoor swimming
pool and SB=indoor swimming bath.

The symbol ⓘ at the beginning of an entry or on a
town plan indicates the local tourist office or other
organisation from which further information can be
obtained. The post-horn symbol on a town plan
indicates a post office.

Only a selection of hotels and restaurants can be
given: no reflection is implied, therefore, on establishments not included.

This guidebook forms part of a completely new series of the world-famous Baedeker Guides to Europe.

The English editions are now published for the first time in this country. Each volume is the result of long and careful preparation and, true to the traditions of Baedeker, is designed in every respect to meet the needs and expectations of the modern traveller and holiday-maker.

The name of Baedeker has long been identified in the field of guidebooks with reliable, comprehensive and up-to-date information, prepared by expert writers who work from detailed, first-hand knowledge of the country concerned. Following a tradition that goes back over 150 years to the date when Karl Baedeker published the first of his handbooks for travellers, these guides have been planned to give the tourist all the essential information about the country and its inhabitants: where to go, how to get there and what to see. Baedeker's account of a country was always based on his personal observation and experience during his travels in that country. This tradition of writing a guidebook in the field rather than at an office desk has been maintained by Baedeker ever since.

Lavishly illustrated with superb colour photographs and numerous specially drawn maps and street plans of the major towns, the new Baedeker Guides concentrate on making available to the modern traveller all the information he needs in a format that is both attractive and easy to follow. For every place that appears in the gazetteer, the principal features of architectural, artistic and historic interest are described, as are the main scenic beauty-spots in the locality. Selected hotels and restaurants are also included. Features of exceptional merit are indicated by either one or two asterisks.

A special section at the end of each book contains practical information to ensure a pleasant and safe journey, details of leisure activities and useful addresses. The separate road map will prove an invaluable aid to planning your route and your travel within the country.

# Contents

# Introduction to Scandinavia

## Denmark
## Norway
## Sweden
## Finland

The midnight sun in northern Norway

## Scandinavia
**Denmark**
**Norway**
**Sweden**
**Finland**

Hammerfest
Kirkenes
Tromsø
Narvik
Kiruna
Arctic Circle
Rovaniemi
Luleå
Oulu
SWEDEN
SVERIGE
FINLAND
SUOMI
Vaasa
Trondheim
Sundsvall
Tampere
HELSINKI
ÅLAND
ISLANDS
Turku
NORWAY
NORGE
Bergen
OSLO
STOCKHOLM
Karlstad
Stavanger
Gothenburg
GOTLAND
DENMARK
DANMARK
Ålborg
ÖLAND
Århus
COPEN-
HAGEN
Malmö
Odense
BORNHOLM

The name "Scandinavia" embraces the countries of Denmark, Norway and Sweden (also, strictly speaking, Iceland). It only came into general use in the 18th c. In practice, Finland is also counted as a Scandinavian country.

**Denmark** (with the Færoes and Greenland), **Norway** (with Svalbard, Jan Mayen and its Antarctic possessions) and **Sweden** are demo-cratic parliamentary monarchies; **Finland** is a republic.

All four countries are members of the United Nations, and together with Iceland meet in the *Nordic Council.* Denmark, Norway and Sweden belong to the Council of Europe, and Denmark is a member of the European Community.

Although the Scandinavian countries cannot claim the impressive tourist statistics of some other European countries, they are attracting steadily increasing numbers of visitors – drawn perhaps by the varied natural beauties of the four countries, but also an interest in the way of life of these northern nations, their social and economic pattern, their historical and artistic treasures and the opportunities for relaxing or active holidays they offer. A visit to any of the countries described in this Guide, or to all of them, will be a memorable experience and will lead to a better understanding of the Scandinavian countries and their peoples.

The terms Scandinavia and Scandinavian have arisen in the last few centuries from the name given to the magnificently formed peninsula which extends for some 1900 km (1180 miles) from Skåne in the south to the North Cape, separating the Baltic from the North Atlantic. Nowadays it is occupied by the two countries of **Norway** and **Sweden**, but from the Treaty of Kalmar in 1397 until 1814, Norway was part of the Kingdom of Denmark. The southern half of Sweden (Skåne) remained Danish for nearly three centuries and Finland was an integral part of Sweden until 1809 when she was ceded to Russia, in exchange for which Norway was handed over to Sweden and remained Swedish until 1904. Iceland, originally settled by Norwegians, remained Danish until 1940 when the occupation of Denmark by Germany meant that she had, in a matter of days almost, to assume independence which was formally agreed to by Denmark in 1944. Although Finland and Denmark are not part of this Scandinavian peninsula, there is good reason to include them as Scandinavian countries.

**Finland** was shaped by the same natural forces as Sweden; in many ways it shows the topographical forms moulded by the last Ice Age more markedly than Sweden. Its coastal regions bear the strong imprint of Sweden in their history and culture, and the busy shipping traffic on the Gulf of Bothnia has bound the two countries closely together.

Jutland, the largest province of **Denmark**, is the only area of Scandinavia which is conjoined to the mainland of Europe. Norway, though, has a brief frontier with Russia in the far north and the whole of Finland's eastern border has a common frontier with Russia. Until 1658 Denmark held extensive territories across the straits on the Scandinavian peninsula, and evidence of Danish influence can still be seen in Skåne.

Thus *Scandinavia in the wider sense* coincides with the geographical conception of NORTHERN EUROPE, a region of clearly marked individuality. If we disregard eastern Europe, there is no other part of the European continent with such a uniform topographical structure. It lacks the fragmented pattern of uplands and mountains found in central and particularly in southern Europe; and although the coasts of Scandinavia are much indented they follow a generally straight line, while there is easy passage from end to end of Sweden, impeded by rivers but without any mountain barriers. Though much broken up by geological action, the Scandinavian mountains form a unified and self-contained complex.

Scandinavia in this wider definition, bounded in the east by the Soviet Union and to the south by Germany, has an area of some 1,150,000 sq. km (444,000 sq. miles), or more than four and a half times that of the United Kingdom. The distance from Gedser to the North Cape is about the same as from Gedser to Tunis, while the distance from Bergen in the west to the shores of Lake Ladoga in the east is about the same as from Paris to Warsaw.

The total population of this large area, however, is only some 22,000,000, and the population of its northern parts is particularly sparse: although the regions north of the 61st parallel account for two-thirds of the total area of Scandinavia they are occupied by only a fifth of its population, at a density of only about 5 to the sq. kilometre (13 to the sq. mile). This relative concentration of population in the southern parts of Scandinavia is, of course, primarily due to climatic conditions; but the northern regions could undoubtedly support a larger population than any other part of the world in the same latitude.

More significant than the inhospitable climate, however – though this, thanks to the Gulf Stream, is milder than in similar territories elsewhere – is the fact of the long winter nights, with their inevitably depressing psychological effect. The variation in the length of the day over the course of a year increases towards the north, so that beyond the Arctic Circle (66°33′) the sun does not set in summer or rise in winter for an increasing number of days (at Kiruna about 45 days, at Hammerfest 72). At the North Pole it appears above the horizon on 21 March and does not set until 21 September, so that in spring it climbs above the horizon in an apparently spiral course and in autumn spirals down again.

The **topographical structure** of Scandinavia appears remarkably simple. Throughout the whole length of Norway and along the Norwegian–Swedish border the Scandinavian mountain chain extends for a distance of some 1700 km (1000 miles) compared with barely 1000 km (600 miles) for the Alps. Its characteristic features are the great expanses of high plateau, partly consisting of peat-bogs and dotted with small lakes, which lie at a fairly uniform altitude between 1000 and 1500 m (3000 and 5000 ft). Above the plateau, particularly around the Sognefjord and in northern Sweden, rear numerous sharply pointed and much glaciated peaks which reach heights of 2468 m (8098 ft) in central Norway (Galdhøpiggen) and 2117 m (6946 ft) in northern Sweden (Kebnekaise); and here and there isolated massifs rise to heights of some 1800 m (5900 ft).

On the Norwegian side of the chain the high plateaux are slashed by numerous valleys, the lower reaches of which are frequently filled by the ends of fjords which cut deeply into the land, and the upper parts by long narrow lakes. The valleys have the typical U-shaped profile gouged out by the mighty glaciers of the Ice Age, extending right down to the Atlantic. Along the west side of the mountains is a relatively flat coastal strip, beyond which the tops of rocky hills worn by ice action emerge from the sea in the form of skerries or rock islets. Where the coastal strip is wider and stands higher above the sea, as for example at the mouth of the Hardangerfjord, we find expanses of attractive green countryside.

On the Swedish side the valleys tend to be broader and the plateau more broken up into separate massifs. Along the eastern fringe of the mountains runs a broad swath of uplands ranging in width between 150 and 250 km (90 and 150 miles), falling from about 600 m (2000 ft) to 200 m (650 ft) near the Gulf of Bothnia. In this region are numerous isolated hills of the type known to geologists as monadnocks (local name *klack*), but these rise barely above 800 m (2600 ft). In Norrland the coastal strip and the girdle of skerries are very narrow indeed.

From the Finnish coast, lying opposite Sweden across the Gulf of Bothnia, the land rises much more gradually to the Finnish Lake Plateau, an extraordinary tangle of lakes, inlets, islands and peninsulas which has its counterpart in Sweden, on a smaller scale, in the Lake Mälar complex. This region – the inland counterpart of the fjords and skerries of the Scandinavian west coast – is brought to an abrupt end by the Salpausselkä ridge of hills, to the south of which the land slopes regularly and gradually down, with only a few lakes of smaller size, to the Gulf of Finland.

The Stockholm skerries

Between the southwest coast of Finland and the western coast of Sweden lies the largest fringe of skerries. Between Turku and the Åland Islands are swarms of these rocky islets, with rounded tops produced by the action of the glaciers, those nearer the coast being higher and wooded, while farther out they are completely bare. There is a similar fringe off Stockholm in which no fewer than 24,000 islands and islets have been counted. From here the Southern Lowlands of Sweden extend westward from Lake Mälar to Lake Vänern, a relic of the sea which once covered this region. To the south is Småland, rising to a height of barely 400 m (1300 ft); and to the southwest both the Southern Lowlands and Småland are bounded by the coast of Bohuslän and Halland with its fringe of skerries.

**Geology.** – Skåne, at the southernmost tip of the Scandinavian peninsula, has a quite different geological structure from the rest of Scandinavia. A narrow ridge of ancient rock does, it is true, emerge from more recent deposits, pointing towards Bornholm; but for the rest the basement rocks match those of the Danish islands, and the coastal forms of Skåne are quite different from those found elsewhere on the Scandinavian peninsula. Here there are neither fjords nor skerries; instead there are projecting spits of land and fringes of dunes. In Denmark massive superficial deposits almost completely cover the basement rocks; only on the east sides of the islands of Falster and Møn and on the southeast coast of Zealand are there chalk cliffs such as are found on the German island of Rügen. Jutland, with coasts of quite different character on its west and east sides (dunes on the one side, coastal inlets on the other), is nevertheless, taken as a whole, an accumulation of superficial deposits, tending to be loamy in the east and sandy in the west.

Everywhere in Scandinavia north of Skåne very ancient rocks predominate in the landscape, though in many places they are overlaid by the most recent geological formations, the morainic deposits of the Ice Age. Mesozoic strata are entirely absent. The western parts of southern and central Sweden are mainly built up of gneisses, while to the east of a line running south through Lake Vättern granites predominate, overlaid in places by flows of porphyry. Horizontally bedded Cambrian and Silurian sediments are found only in the form of remnants of varying size, the Silurian deposits frequently providing the basis for expanses of fertile arable land. At various points, too, volcanic eruptions in the Palaeozoic era have yielded diabases – producing, for example, the prominent Kinnekulle range and the plateau-like hills of Västergötland with their striking rock walls. The islands of Öland and Gotland consist almost entirely of Silurian limestones.

In Silurian times the varied ancient rocks of the Scandinavian mountains were subjected to the Caledonian folding movement and thrust over the horizontally bedded rocks to the east. The southwestern continuation of the range, which is some twenty times older than the Alps, emerges again in Scotland and northern Ireland.

The geological processes of the last Ice Age, however, played a much greater part in shaping the present topography of all the Scandinavian countries. Even when the morainic formations, so common everywhere, and other glacial deposits are lacking, the work of the ice has so radically transformed the earth's surface that all older forms can be only dimly perceived below the surface: only the massive Scandinavian mountain chain has survived. For tens of thousands of years the whole of northern Europe and North Germany was covered with great masses of ice, only the highest peaks of the Scandinavian mountains emerging from the ice in the form of "nunataks"; but while North Germany became ice-free some 20,000 years ago northern Scandinavia was still covered with ice 10,000 years ago. As a result of the gradual retreat of the ice the Baltic, originally only a large lake along the fringe of the ice, had a constantly changing coastline. Only in what is known as the Yoldia Phase did it connect up with the open sea – not through the Danish Sound, as it does now, since that was not yet open, but by way of the "Billingen Gate" in central Sweden when this was opened up by the retreat of the ice. At the same time the Baltic was connected with the White Sea by a channel which ran northeast along the edge of the ice mass, so that the whole of northern Scandinavia now became an island.

The large lakes of central Sweden are relics of the sea which once covered this area; but the abundant flow of water from many rivers has long removed any trace of salt.

The great masses of ice, 2 km ($1\frac{1}{4}$ miles) thick, bore down heavily on the underlying land, and when this pressure was relieved with the melting of the ice the land rose, most markedly in the middle of the area formerly covered by ice. Some 8500 years ago, therefore, the channels traversing central Sweden and Finland were raised above sea level and drained of water; and the Baltic again became a lake – known as Lake Ancylus – which with the continuing retreat of the ice now included the present-day Gulf of Bothnia. Finally, some 7000 years ago, the present channels between the Danish islands opened up and provided a link with the North Sea. Thus there came into being the Litorina Sea, the forerunner of the Baltic as we know it today.

Geologists have been able to establish an absolute time scale for these events with the help of the "varve" deposits, which are particularly well exposed at Uppsala. Just as tree-rings can be dated by the varying pattern they form from year to year, so these clay deposits, varying in colour and grain size, form a pattern which can be dated, and the thickness and quality of each annual layer yield information about meteorological conditions year by year in the post-glacial period.

The land is continuing to rise in Scandinavia, at a rate which around the Gulf of Bothnia amounts to about 1 m (40 in.) in a century, so that towns such as Luleå and Oulu have had to move their harbours steadily farther out to follow the retreating sea. In the Stockholm area the rise is at the rate of about 40 cm (16 in) in a century; and within historical times new skerries have kept emerging from the sea and older channels and inlets of the sea have become dry land.

The action of the glaciers produced a very varied topographical pattern. In the Scandinavian mountains they ground their way over the high plateaux, leaving only the prominent "nunataks" which had always stood out above the mass of the ice. The separate arms of the glaciers gouged out the mighty U-shaped valleys, forming vertical rock faces over which waterfalls now tumble. The valleys often had deeper basins scooped out by the ice or were blocked by morainic deposits, leading to the formation of the lakes so commonly found in them. The fjords, too, were carved out to very great depths: the Sognefjord, for example, is very much deeper (1245 m – 4085 ft) than the North Sea, most of which barely attains a tenth of that depth.

On the east side of the Scandinavian mountains the great fringe of lakes in the Nordland resulted from the fact that the last remains of the ice cover lay not within the mountains but farther east, thus blocking any outflow to the Gulf of Bothnia. In consequence the lakes found a lower overflow westward to the North Atlantic, so carving out the deep valleys

through the mountains which now form convenient passages between the Norwegian coast and the interior. After the disappearance of the last great ice masses these lakes all found an easier outflow to the Baltic, so that the old valleys through the mountains were left high and dry.

The *terminal moraines* marking the different stages in the melting of the ice extend across Sweden and Finland like gigantic ribbons of debris. The traveller constantly encounters these great accumulations of boulders, against which man the cultivator has been able to make little headway. In southern Finland some of these moraines were deposited under the sea and evenly distributed by the action of the waves, producing the regularly shaped Salpausselkä range of hills.

The grinding action of the glaciers is also seen in the lowland areas, for example in the *roches moutonnées* (rocks rounded or smoothed by glacial action) found in the skerries and also inland, where even the hardest rocks have been eroded into a characteristic "whale-backed" shape. Particularly striking are the *eskers* (*oser, singular os*; Swedish *ås*), long stratified gravel ridges which may extend for several hundred miles and sometimes enclose lakes of some size. These were originally sedimentary deposits in the channels carved out by rivers under the ice, and when the ice melted were left as natural causeways which provided convenient traffic routes for man. Stockholm is situated where it is largely because of an esker which helped to close off Lake Mälar and offered a convenient means of passage.

One other notable glacial feature is the "kettlehole", a small depression formed where a mass of ice was covered by drift and, being thus protected from the sun, was slower to melt; then when it did melt the covering of soil fell in and formed a funnel-shaped depression.

The most characteristic features of the coastal regions formerly covered by ice are the *fjords* which are found in Scandinavia in every variety of form. In northern Norway they cut deep into the land, broad and funnel-shaped. In the Lofoten Islands they form a maze of inlets flanked by

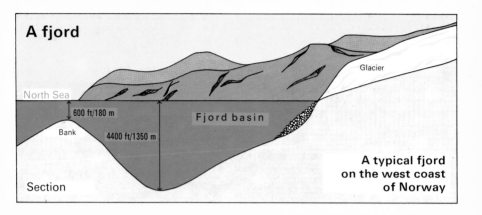

**A fjord**

North Sea

600 ft/180 m

Bank

4400 ft/1350 m

Fjord basin

Glacier

Section

**A typical fjord on the west coast of Norway**

## Formation of the fjords

During the last Ice Age, about 100,000 years ago, the whole of Scandinavia was covered with a massive ice sheet, reducing in thickness towards the coast. The existing river valleys were gouged out by the ice to ever greater depths – often as deep as the rocks rearing above the valley were high.

Since along the coast the ice was thinner the fjords were gouged out to a lesser depth at their mouths. The bank at the mouth of a fjord may be only some 180 m (600 ft) deep, while farther inland depths of up to 1350 m (4400 ft) have been measured.

When the ice retreated the huge fjord basins were filled with sea-water. Thanks to the salt content of the water and to the warming influence of the Gulf Stream the fjords remain ice-free throughout the year except in their innermost branches.

The great icefields in the mountain regions are remnants of the Ice Age glaciers. The melt-water from these surviving glaciers, pouring into the valleys in countless waterfalls, is now harnessed in many places to produce hydroelectric power.

precipitous rock walls. The Trondheim-fjord, on the other hand, occupies a broad drowned longitudinal valley with numerous inlets opening off it. The much ramified fjords in the area of the Norwegian 2000 m (6000 ft) peaks have the appearance of flooded Alpine valleys. In southern Norway and Bohuslän, where the mountains slope down more gently towards the coast and the ice cover was not so thick, the fjords are shorter; only the Oslofjord reaches far inland in a tectonic rift valley (a valley formed by deformation and subsidence of the earth's crust).

In Sweden and Finland the fjords are more intimately intermeshed with the fringe of skerries, with their heads reaching in between the low rounded contours of the roches moutonnées.

The inlets on the east coast of Jutland, like those of Schleswig, reach inland into green and fertile rolling country.

# Climate

Extending as it does for more than 1800 km (1100 miles) from north to south, Scandinavia shows **great climatic variations**. Denmark and southern Sweden, with their cool, temperate maritime climate, lie in a region of transition to the Central European climatic zone (annual rainfall between 400 and 800 mm (160 and 320 in.), maximum rainfall in August, autumn and winter storms in the west, very changeable weather).

Norway, extending far beyond the Arctic Circle, has Arctic climatic features only in those parts of northern Lapland which lie far from the sea, with temperatures occasionally falling as low as about −50 °C (−58 °F) (Karasjok −51·4 °C (−60·5 °F) – and of course in the outlying territory of Spitzbergen in the Arctic Ocean. Most of the country is warmed in winter by the Gulf Stream and by southwest winds. Thus Svolvær in the Lofotens, lying beyond the 68th parallel, has the same mean temperature in January (−1·7 °C (28·9 °F)) as Negotino, 3000 km (1800 miles) farther south near the Yugoslav−Greek border (lat. 41½° N; alt. 147 m (480 ft)). The southwest winds, often stormy in autumn and winter, produce heavy rainfall, reaching an annual 2200 mm (860 in.) on the outermost coastal strip (falling mainly in autumn and winter). The plateau glaciers in southern Norway, like the huge Jostedalsbre (length almost 100 km (65 miles), area 1000 sq. km (385 sq. miles)), owe their great extent to these high precipitations in winter (with annual averages of up to 3000 mm (1180 in.) on particularly exposed mountains). On Kebnekaise, 700 km (440 miles) farther north in Swedish Lapland but in a region with relatively low precipitations, the permanent snow line is considerably higher in spite of the long Arctic night and the much more severe cold in winter. In contrast to the extreme maritime climate of the west coast, with small variations in temperature, the valleys farther east, lying in the rain shadow, show markedly continental climatic features, with great seasonal variations in temperature and less rainfall than in the driest parts of Germany, so that in the upper Gudbrandsdal, for example, artificial irrigation is required. The fall in temperature towards the Arctic latitudes is more marked in Norway in summer, when the relative warming potential of the Gulf Stream is less. The differences in temperature between north and south in the interior of the country are less in summer, since the long period of sunshine in the higher latitudes produces more effect in large land masses. Thus temperatures of over 30 °C (86 °F) have been frequently recorded in Lapland, but temperatures in this range never occur on the west coast.

The continental character of the climate in eastern Norway becomes still more marked in Sweden and Finland. In summer the temperature increases from west to east in consequence of the more rapid warming up of the land masses and the lesser cloud cover in the lee of the west winds. The continental nature of the climate is, however, mitigated to some extent by the cooling effect of the Baltic and the Finnish Lake Plateau; in winter these expanses of water are without influence on the climate, since they are then covered with snow and ice at least as far as the latitude of Stockholm.

The coasts of Denmark and the west coasts of Sweden and Norway usually remain ice-free. Snow usually lies in southern Sweden from December to February, in central Sweden and southern and central Finland from November to March or April, in Lapland from October to May. In Denmark (apart from the west

coast of Jutland) and Skåne and on the south and southwest coasts of Norway there are average temperatures below freezing point for up to 1 month; in the Norwegian and northern Swedish mountains they are found for anything up to 7 months. – Number of days with midnight sun or Arctic night: Kiruna 45, Tromsø 64, Hammerfest 72, North Cape 78, Spitzbergen 127.

**Temperatures** vary very little in Denmark, with its small area. The annual average ranges from 7·2 °C (45 °F) at Rugbjerg (northeast of Tønder) to 7·9 °C (46·2 °F) at Odense, the February average from −1·2 °C (29·8 °F) at Copenhagen to 1·4 °C (34·5 °F) at Skagen, the July average from 15·5 °C (59·9 °F) at Tønder and Rugbjerg to 17·2 °C (63 °F) at Copenhagen, and the annual temperature range from 14·5 °C (58·1 °F) at Tønder to 18·4 °C (65·1 °F) at Copenhagen.

In Norway the annual average ranges from −3·5 °C (25·7 °F) at Sizzajavre in Lapland (−8 °C (17·6 °F) at Grønhavn, south of Barentsburg, Spitzbergen) to 7·6 °C (45·7 °F) at Flekkefjord, between Stavanger and Kristiansand (other figures, from south to north: Oslo 5·4 °C (41·7 °F), Bergen 7·2 °C (45 °F), Dombås 1·3 °C (34·3 °F), Trondheim 4·4 °C (39·9 °F), Svolvær (Lofotens) 4·2 °C (39·6 °F), Tromsø 2·3 °C (36·1 °F), Alta 0·6 °C (33·1 °F), Hammerfest 2·1 °C (35·8 °F), Tana −0·8 °C (30·6 °F), Vardø 1·1 °C (34 °F), Bear Island −5 °C (23 °F), the January or February average from −15 °C (5 °F) at Sizzajavre (−18·2 °C (−0·8 °F) at Grønhavn) to 1·7 °C (35·1 °F) at Bergen and Kristiansund (Oslo −3·8 °C (25·2 °F), Lillehammer −8 °C (17·6 °F), Trondheim −2·1 °C (28·2 °F), Alta −8·2 °C (17·2 °F), Hammerfest −3·5 °C (25·7 °F), Tana −11·3 °C (11·7 °F), Vardø −4·5 °C (23·9 °F), Bear Island −8·2 °C (17·2 °F) in March), the July average from 8·5 °C (47·3 °F) at Vardø (3·8 °C (38·8 °F) at Kvadehuken, near Ny-Ålesund, Spitzbergen) to 16·3 °C (61·3 °F) at Flekkefjord (Oslo 16·2 °C (61·2 °F), Bergen 13·7 °C (56·7 °F), Lillehammer 14 °C (57·2 °F), Trondheim 13·5 °C (56·3 °F), Hammerfest 11·5 °C (52·7 °F), Bear Island 5·5 °C (41·9 °F) in August) and the annual temperature range from 12 °C (53·6 °F) at Bergen to 26·7 °C (80·1 °F) at Sizzajavre (Oslo 20 °C (68 °F), Lillehammer 22·5 °C (72·5 °F), Trondheim 17·9 °C (64·2 °F), Svolvær 13·5 °C (56·3 °F), Tana 23 °C (73·4 °F), Vardø 13 °C (55·4 °F), Bear Island 13·7 °C (56·7 °F), Grønhavn 23·2 °C (73·8 °F), Kvadehuken 18·8 °C (65·8 °F)).

In Sweden the annual average ranges from −2·3 °C (27·9 °F) at Karesuando in Lapland to 7·7 °C (45·9 °F) at Malmö and Göteborg (Stockholm 5·9 °C (42·6 °F), Östersund 2·4 °C (36·3 °F), Haparanda 1 °C (33·8 °F), Abisko −1 °C (30·2 °F)), the January or February average from −13·8 °C (7·2 °F) at Karesuando to 0 °C (32 °F) at Malmö (Stockholm −2·5 °C (27·5 °F), Östersund −7·8 °C (18 °F), Haparanda −11·6 °C (11·9 °F), Abisko −11·2 °C (11·8 °F)), the July average from 11·2 °C (52·2 °F) at Abisko to 17·3 °C (63·1 °F) at Karlstad (Stockholm 16·2 °C (61·2 °F), Östersund 13·8 °C (56·8 °F), Haparanda 15·2 °C (59·4 °F)) and the annual temperature range from 16·3 °C (61·3 °F) at Malmö to 28·6 °C (83·5 °F) at Övertorneå, north of Haparanda (Stockholm 18·7 °C (65·7 °F), Östersund 21·6 °C (70·9 °F), Haparanda 26·8 °C (80·2 °F)).

In Finland the annual average ranges from −2·2 °C (28 °F) at Enontekiö in Lapland to 5·5 °C (41·9 °F) at Hanko (Turku 4·6 °C (40·3 °F), Tuusula, near Helsinki, 3·4 °C (38·1 °F), Kotka 4·1 °C (39·4 °F), Kuopio 2·6 °C (36·7 °F), Rovaniemi −0·1 °C (31·8 °F), Inari −2·1 °C (28·2 °F)), the February average from −14·6 °C (5·7

°F) at Enontekiö (absolute minimum at Ivalo, −48·7 °C (−55·7 °F)) to −3·9 °C (25 °F) at Hanko (Turku −6 °C (21·2 °F), Tuusula −7 °C (19·4 °F), Kotka −7·2 °C (19 °F), Kuopio −8·7 °C (16·3 °F), Rovaniemi −12·6 °C (9·3 °F), Inari −14·3 °C (6·3 °F) in January), the July average from 10·8 °C (51·4 °F) at Utsjoki (the most northerly place in Finland) to 16·5 °C (61·7 °F) at Kotka and Lappeenranta (Turku 16·3 °C (61·3 °F), Tuusula 16 °C (60·8 °F), Kuopio 15·7 °C (60·3 °F), Rovaniemi 13·8 °C (56·8 °F), Inari 11·7 °C (53·1 °F)) and the annual temperature range from 20·3 °C (68·5 °F) at Hanko to 27·5 °C (81·5 °F) at Enontekiö (Turku 22·3 °C (72·1 °F), Kuopio 24·4 °C (75·9 °F), Rovaniemi 25·8 °C (78·4 °F)).

The average annual **precipitation** (rainfall) in *Denmark* is 550–650 mm (21·5–25·5 in.) (Copenhagen 579 mm (22·8 in.), Odense 621 mm (24·4 in.), Ålborg 611 mm (24·1 in.), Rønne 559 mm (22 in.)), on some of the eastern islands below 500 mm (20 in.) (Christiansø 419 mm (16·5 in.)) and above this level in western Jutland, particularly in Slesvig (Åbenrå 762 mm (30 in.), Tønder 750 mm (29·5 in.)). The rainiest month is almost invariably August (Copenhagen 75 mm (3 in.), Tønder 98 mm (3·9 in.), Christiansø 52 mm (2 in.)), the driest February (Copenhagen 32 mm (1·3 in.), Tønder 41 mm (1·6 in.), Christiansø 22 mm (0·9 in.)).

In *Norway* the level of precipitation along the coastal strip depends on the degree of exposure to the rain-bringing southwest winds and the nearness to the hills which precipitate the rain. The wettest month in the south and the north is usually October; around Bergen it is January. The driest month is June, in the north usually April (with exceptions, some of which are noted below). The following are the annual figures for places near the coast, from south to north: Kristiansand 1472 mm (58 in.), Flekkefjord 1722 mm (68 in.) (October–December 200 mm (8 in.), July 57 mm (2¼ in.)), Stavanger 1072 mm (42 in.), Josedal (southeast of Bergen) 2152 mm (85 in.) (January 310 mm (12 in.), June 82 mm (3 in.)), Bergen 1895 mm (75 in.) (January 230 mm (9 in.), June 110 mm (4 in.)), Balestrand in the Sognefjord 1895 mm (75 in.), Leikanger (farther up the fjord) only 936 mm (37 in.), Molde 1440 mm (57 in.), Trondheim 821 mm (32 in.), Bodø 867 mm (34 in.), Røst (most southwesterly of the Lofotens) 513 mm (20 in.) (April 27 mm (1 in.)), Svolvær 1561 mm (61 in.) (November 188 mm (7½ in.), April 73 mm (3 in.)), Tromsø 935 mm (37 in.) (September, August), Hammerfest 558 mm (22 in.) (October 63 mm (2½ in.), April 31 mm (1 in.)), Alta 308 mm (12 in.) (July, April), Vardø 600 mm (24 in.) (January, May). Other places, in the lee of the southwest winds: Oslo 736 mm (29 in.) (maximum August 100 mm (4 in.), minimum April 39 mm (1½ in.)), Lillehammer 602 mm (24 in.), Listad (northwest of Lillehammer) 390 mm (15 in.) (August 76 mm (3 in.), February 8 mm (⅓ in.)), Dombås 372 mm (14½ in.) (August 58 mm (2¼ in.), April 9 mm (⅓ in.)). Very low levels are also recorded in Lapland: Sizzajavre 376 mm (15 in.) (maximum July, minimum March), Karasjok 316 mm (12½ in.) (August, March). Bear Island has 384 mm (15 in.) (September 45 mm (1¾ in.), June 18 mm (¾ in.)), Spitzbergen 423 mm (17 in.) at Barentsburg (November 55 mm (2 in.), June 23 mm (1 in.)) and 314 mm (12 in.) at Kvadehuken (August 40 mm (1½ in.), May 11 mm (½ in.) (frequent thick fog)).

In *Sweden* the annual precipitation averages 500–650 mm (20–25 in.), with the maximum almost invariably in August and the minimum in February, more rarely (particularly in Skåne and on the southwest coast) in March, at Visby in May. Examples of average figures are: Stockholm 569 mm (22 in.) (August 79 mm (3 in.), February and March each 28 mm (1 in.)), Malmö 526 mm (21 in.), Lund 616 mm (24 in.), Visby 513 mm (20 in.), Haparanda 532 mm (21 in.). Higher averages are found only in southwestern Sweden at places like Göteborg 738 mm (29 in.), Båstad 764 mm (30 in.) and Borås 903 mm (36 in.); lower figures in the south (Falsterbo 443 mm (17 in.)) and southeast (Kalmar 464 mm (18 in.)), on Öland (Norra Udde 415 mm (16 in.)) and Gotland (Hoburg 423 mm (17 in.)), and in Lapland (Kiruna 453 mm (18 in.), Karesuando 325 mm (13 in.), Abisko 267 mm (11 in.), with 42 mm (1½ in.) in July and 12 mm (½ in.) in April).

In *Finland* the average is 600–700 mm (24–28 in.) in the south and 400–500 mm (16–20 in.) in the north, with a minimum at the north end of the Gulf of Bothnia resulting from the extremely low winter snowfalls. The wettest month is July almost everywhere, the driest February or March, very rarely April. The following are examples: Tuusula (northeast of Helsinki) 695 mm (27 in.) (August 110 mm (4¼ in.), February 29 mm (1 in.)), Lohja (west of Helsinki) 754 mm (30 in.) (August and November each 87 mm (3½ in.), March 20 mm (¾ in.)), Turku 612 mm (24 in.), Kotka 648 mm (26 in.), Tampere 628 mm (25 in.), Kuopio 618 mm (24 in.), Rovaniemi 474 mm (19 in.) (August 79 mm (3 in.), March 18 mm (¾ in.)), Inari 471 mm (19 in.), Utsjoki (almost 70° N) 417 mm (16 in.) (July 74 mm (3 in.), December, January, March and April each 23 mm (1 in.)), Ulkokalla (on Gulf of Bothnia, above 64° N) 348 mm (14 in.) (August 55 mm (2 in.), February 8 mm (¼ in.)).

# Plant and Animal Life

**Plant Life.** – In spite of the climatic differences between the Atlantic coast and the interior, the boundaries between different vegetation zones for the most part cut right across Scandinavia; for the growing period, which is determined by temperatures in spring and autumn, is less affected by differences between east and west and tends rather to become shorter in stages from south to north, while the light conditions which play such an important part in plant growth also vary with latitude. As well as this, of course, the vegetation of the mountain regions is affected by differences in altitude.

The beech is found throughout Denmark and in Skåne, Halland and Blekinge, but does not grow in Småland or farther north. Oaks are still common in central Sweden. In Småland, with its higher altitude, and above all in Norrland, central Norway and Finland coniferous forests (spruce, pine) are predominant, with birches in many places. In Norway, the upper limit of the conifers falls from 900 m (3000 ft) round the Hardangerfjord and in Telemark to 450 m (1500 ft) in Finnmark, these heights being reached only by spruces of notably slender growth and a few scattered pines.

A feature typical of Scandinavia and not found anywhere else is the birch zone which extends for some 200 m (650 ft) above the coniferous zone. The ground cover in the forests consists of numerous berry-bearing shrubs and, in drier situations, lichens. The extensive forest regions of Scandinavia are interrupted by numerous lakes and by stretches of peat-bogs. Areas of mountain pasture are found only in southern Norway; farther north the upper slopes of the mountains are covered with a heath vegetation of dwarf shrubs and low-growing plants extending up to the snow-line.

In spite of the intensive timber-working industry of northern Sweden and Finland the forests – apart from the scattered areas which have been brought into cultivation – have suffered little thinning out, and have largely been preserved in their natural state, though in some areas much timber has been consumed by the busy ironworking industry of past centuries.

**A birch-lined footpath in Finland**

The situation is very different in many parts of Norway, where the character of the mountains has largely confined the forests to the sheltered valleys which have been frequented and developed by man since very ancient times. The Norwegian Atlantic coast is not by nature densely forested, whereas the outer skerries consist of bare rock and, with the high rainfall in this region, are exposed to severe erosion.

Central Sweden consists largely of arable land, though numerous *roches moutonnées* shaped by Ice Age glaciers emerge like inland skerries from the clayey alluvial plain. The distribution of arable land and forest – here confined to the areas of rocky and morainic soil – is mainly determined by this natural mosaic. Only in the Silurian basins are there large expanses of continuous arable land. The most favourable conditions for arable farming, however, are to be found in the lower-lying parts of Skåne and on the Danish islands, where the forest frequently survives only in the carefully tended woodlands in the grounds of country houses.

In eastern Finland

In Jutland a series of vegetation zones runs from north to south, as in the neighbouring German provinces of Schleswig-Holstein. Along the much indented east coast runs a strip of land formed by ground moraines, with occasional patches of beech forest; then comes a swath of terminal moraines of different periods, which have provided the sandy soil of central Jutland, formerly occupied by large expanses of heathland; and beyond this again is the west coast of Jutland, with its numerous coastal spits and its fringes of dunes, areas of fenland like those of Friesland being confined to the southwestern coast.

**Animal Life.** – The animal life of the Scandinavian countries is determined by two climatic and vegetation zones. The forests of the southern parts of Scandinavia are within the Central European temperate zone and are inhabited by much the same species as are – or were – the forests of Germany (red deer, roe-deer, foxes, hares, badgers, etc.). Thanks to the lower population density and to a lesser degree of human intrusion or interference with natural conditions, Scandinavia has preserved a greater variety of species, including animals which in Central Europe have become extinct or been much reduced in numbers.

The rugged cliffs on the Norwegian coast provide sheltered nesting places not only for countless sea-birds, mainly *auks* and *guillemots*, but also for species which have become rare or have died out elsewhere in Europe, such as the white-tailed eagle and the golden eagle – both species which breed only in natural conditions. In the coastal waters of Norway *seals* and several species of *whales* are found; and the rivers and lakes, still largely preserved from harmful environmental influences, are well stocked with *salmon*, *trout*, *carp* and *perch*.

The northern regions, in particular Lapland, belong to the Arctic and Alpine zones. Their animal life is less numerous but excellently adapted to living in these rigorous conditions. The commonest species is the *reindeer*, which roams in huge herds over the sparse grazing to be found on the tundra and is of supreme economic importance to the native population as a supplier of milk, meat and skins. As a result of strict conservation measures there has been a considerable increase in the number of *elks*. Other species characteristic of these regions are the ptarmigan, the blue hare, the glutton (a furry animal similar to a wolverine), the arctic fox and the *lemming*, a small vole-like rodent known for its long migrations in which countless numbers die.

# The Four Countries

The topographical pattern of Scandinavia has been produced by a great variety of factors – geological structure, mountain formation, ice action, climate and vegetation. The boundaries between the different countries and their administrative subdivisions, however, are not always clearly defined by nature: much sharper is the distinction between the rocky and morainic mountains and hills on the one hand and the lower land occupied by lakes and rivers, and it is the intricate intermingling of these different elements that gives the landscape of Scandinavia its pattern. A further element is contributed by the farms, mostly still timber-built, which are scattered about in the countryside, coming together to form villages only in the area round Lake Siljan – though the farms themselves, with their numerous separate buildings serving a variety of functions, look from a distance like little hamlets on their own. In Sweden a characteristic note is given to the landscape by the rust-red "Falu" paint which is used on most of the houses. In a country of progressive attitudes like Sweden, however, the old traditions of the countryside are much less vigorously preserved than in Norway, where the countryfolk are by nature more conservative and the old "log-cabin" type of house, often with carved decoration and a turf roof, has been preserved and cherished. Norway has, too, a more austere natural landscape, with its great expanses of high plateau, its glacier-hewn valleys with their lakes and fjords and its fringe of islands, from the swarms of tiny skerries to the great rock masses of the Lofotens, towering up as if built by a giant's hand.

**DENMARK**, which forms a kind of land bridge leading from continental Europe to the Scandinavian peninsula, is itself linked together by numerous bridges which are among the largest in Europe. On the island of Zealand is **Copenhagen**, the largest city in Scandinavia, with a quarter of the population of Denmark. Its great period of expansion began only in the 19th c., when the fortifications which had cramped its growth were pulled down. It enjoys an excellent situation on the shortest of the three channels leading from the Baltic to the open sea.

Insular Denmark, with its fine marly soil formed by ground moraines, is devoted to

# Denmark
**Kongeriget Danmark**
**Kingdom of Denmark**

| County (*amt*) | Area sq. km | sq. miles | Population | County (*amt*) | Area sq. km | sq. miles | Population |
|---|---|---|---|---|---|---|---|
| 1 Københavns amt | 619 | 239 | 1,185,000 | 9 Ribe amt | 3,131 | 1,210 | 215,000 |
| 2 Frederiksborg amt | 1,347 | 520 | 331,000 | 10 Vejle amt | 2,997 | 1,157 | 327,000 |
| 3 Roskilde amt | 891 | 344 | 205,000 | 11 Ringkøbing amt | 4,853 | 1,873 | 264,000 |
| 4 Vestsjællands amt | 2,984 | 1,152 | 278,000 | 12 Århus amt | 4,561 | 1,761 | 578,000 |
| 5 Storstrøms amt | 3,398 | 1,311 | 259,000 | 13 Viborg amt | 4,122 | 1,591 | 231,000 |
| 6 Bornholm amt | 588 | 227 | 47,000 | 14 Nordjyllands amt | 6,173 | 2,383 | 482,000 |
| 7 Fyns amt | 3,486 | 1,346 | 454,000 | | | | |
| 8 Sønderjyllands amt | 3,930 | 1,517 | 250,000 | Denmark | 43,080 | 16,629 | 5,116,000 |
| | | | | (excluding Færoes and Greenland) | | | |

intensive agriculture, and is also favoured by a usually mild and equable climate. Throughout its development it has been well served by a series of market towns with active processing and canning industries for handling its produce, typical in this respect being Funen with its market town of *Odense*. Zealand is noted for its handsome manor-houses and castles, set in beautiful parks; and large estates are more numerous on Zealand than on the other Danish islands.

The economic focal point of *Jutland* lies on the east side of the peninsula. Small and medium-sized towns, linked by the important Flensburg–Frederikshavn road, have grown up at the head of the various inlets. *Århus*, half-way up the east coast, has developed into a large town with considerable foodstuffs and textile industries. *Esbjerg*, on the west coast, is central to the Danish North Sea (or in Danish "West Sea") fisheries and the principal port for trade with Britain. *Århus* and *Ålborg* have large shipyards.

**SWEDEN.** – Skåne is similar in landscape and economy to the Danish islands. It has a number of considerable ports, chief among them *Malmö*, and an agricultural hinterland devoted mainly to the growing of sugar-beet and wheat. In the middle of this agricultural area is the quiet little university town of *Lund* with its Romanesque cathedral, the finest church in Sweden.

A more distinctively Swedish region begins at the low ridge of hills which runs southeast across Skåne from the rugged and sharply pointed Cape Kullen and re-emerges on the Danish island of Bornholm. The landscape in *Småland*, still in the latitude of Jutland though it is, has an authentically northern stamp. Its rump of gneisses and granites, worn down by Ice Age glaciers, rising to barely 400 m (1300 ft), is still largely a sparsely inhabited expanse of forest and moorland. In earlier times the abundance of timber in this region led to the establishment of a busy glass-making industry; the industrial towns of the present day have developed around the junctions of the extensive railway network.

From the north Lake Vättern thrusts into the Småland hills like a wedge, its straight shoreline reflecting its situation in a tectonic rift valley. At its southern end are *Jönköping* and the smaller town of *Huskvarna*, at the geographical midpoint of Sweden. To the south of Jönköping is the Taberg; high grade iron ore was formerly extracted here by opencast working, but the area is now a popular nature reserve.

Of the coastal regions flanking Småland, *Halland*, to the west, has been particularly favoured economically by the important railway line from Skåne to Göteborg. *Blekinge* to the south and the Kalmar region on the east have extensive morainic deposits, so that the forests usually reach right down to the coast, which is much indented by fjords.

*Central Sweden* is a much more open and hospitable territory and has a milder climate, although its coastal region is less open. **Göteborg** (Gothenburg), on the west coast, has an excellent natural harbour on the funnel-shaped estuary of the Götaälv, but the coastal strip is narrow and rocky, so that the town was compelled to expand on to the surrounding hills and to build its industrial suburbs in the narrow side valleys.

On the east side of central Sweden is **Stockholm**, sheltered by an almost impenetrable girdle of skerries and accessible from the sea only through a labyrinth of concealed channels. This intricate landscape pattern is continued on the inland side of the city by *Lake Mälar* with its thousand inlets and islands, and it is further protected by a dense ring of forest. Still farther inland are extensive areas of open country which the farmers of the Svear were able to develop; and this situation, cut off from the coast, may have helped to determine the independent and apparently aloof disposition of the Swedes.

Central Sweden is very far from being a uniform region with a common focus. No other part of Sweden is so clearly compartmented into small separate units; and areas of level arable land on the Silurian limestones alternate constantly with densely wooded horsts of ancient rocks and bleak moorland plateaux formed of volcanic rocks (particularly diabase) of the Palaeozoic era. Nature thus determined the rigid medieval subdivisions of the territory; and until modern times people of Finnish stock continued to make their way through the impassable stretches of forest between these units into central Sweden.

The variety of landscape pattern is reflected most clearly in the ever-changing shoreline of *Lake Vänern*: now following a straight line along a fault, now fringed by clusters of skerries, now shaped into a delta by alluvial deposits, now extending in a wide bay formed by the action of wind and water.

The towns of central Sweden have their various specialties: *Norrköping* is a textile

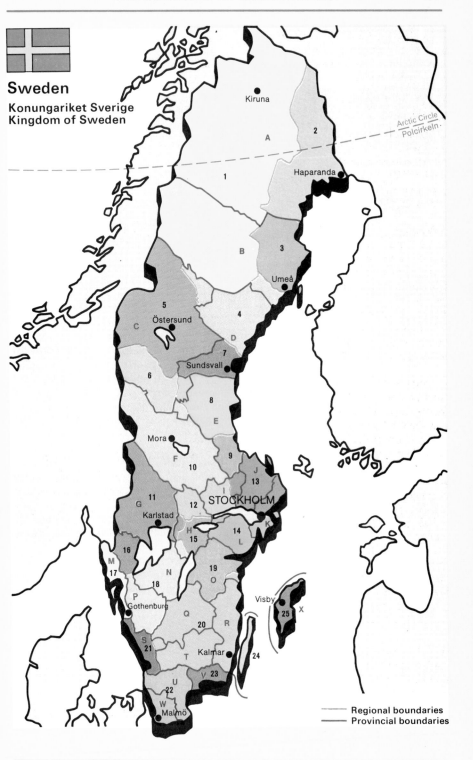

## Sweden
### Konungariket Sverige
### Kingdom of Sweden

Kiruna

Arctic Circle
Polcirkeln

A

2

1

Haparanda

B

3

Umeå

5

Östersund

4

C

D

7

Sundsvall

6

8

E

Mora

F

9

10

J

13

I

G    11

12    STOCKHOLM

Karlstad

H

15    14

K

L

16

M

17

N

19

18

O

P

Gothenburg

Q

Visby

20

R

25    X

S

21

T    Kalmar

24

V    23

U

22

W

Malmö

——— Regional boundaries
——— Provincial boundaries

## The Swedish Regions

| | | | |
|---|---|---|---|
| 1 Lapland | 6 Härjedalen | 13 Uppland | 20 Småland |
| (Northern Lapland, | 7 Medelpad | 14 Södermanland | 21 Halland |
| Southern Lapland) | 8 Hälsingsland | 15 Närke | 22 Skåne |
| 2 Norrbotten | 9 Gästrikland | 16 Dalsland | 23 Blekinge |
| 3 Västerbotten | 10 Dalarna | 17 Bohuslän | 24 Öland |
| 4 Ångermanland | 11 Värmland | 18 Västergötland | 25 Gotland |
| 5 Jämtland | 12 Västmanland | 19 Östergötland | |

## The Swedish Provinces

| Province (län) | Area (excl. water) sq. km | sq. miles | Population | Province (län) | Area (excl. water) sq. km | sq. miles | Population |
|---|---|---|---|---|---|---|---|
| A  Norbottens län | 98,913 | 38,180 | 264,000 | N  Skaraborgs län | 7,938 | 3,064 | 270,000 |
| B  Vasterbottens län | 55,401 | 21,384 | 245,000 | O  Östergötlands län | 10,562 | 4,077 | 393,000 |
| C  Jämtlands län | 49,443 | 19,085 | 135,000 | P  Alvborgslän | 11,395 | 4,398 | 426,000 |
| D  Vasternorrlands län | 21,678 | 8,368 | 263,000 | Q  Jönköpings län | 9,944 | 3,838 | 301,000 |
| E  Gävleborgs län | 18,191 | 7,024 | 290,000 | R  Kalmar län | | | |
| F  Kopparbergs län | 28,193 | 10,883 | 285,000 |    (incl. öland) | 11,170 | 4,312 | 239,000 |
| G  Värmlands län | 17,584 | 6,787 | 280,000 | S  Hallands län | 5,454 | 2,105 | 238,000 |
| H  Örebro län | 8,519 | 3,288 | 271,000 | T  Kronobergs län | 8,458 | 3,265 | 174,000 |
| I  Västmanlands län | 6,302 | 2,433 | 260,000 | U  Kristianstads län | 6,087 | 2,350 | 280,000 |
| J  Uppsala län | 6,989 | 2,698 | 250,000 | V  Blekinge län | 2,941 | 1,135 | 152,000 |
| K  Stockholms län | 6,488 | 2,504 | 1,562,000 | W  Malmöhus län | 4,938 | 1,906 | 747,000 |
| L  Södermanlands län | 6,060 | 2,340 | 250,000 | X  Gotlands län | 3,140 | 1,212 | 56,000 |
| M  Göteborgs och Bohus län | 5,141 | 1,984 | 712,000 | Sweden | 410,929 | 158,619 | 8,343,000 |

town, *Linköping* manufactures machinery and motor vehicles, *Örebro* is devoted primarily to the leather industry, *Karlstad* and its surrounding area have numerous sawmills and large cellulose factories using the vast timber resources of northern Värmland, which are floated down the rivers in rafts or transported by land. The smaller country towns handle the agricultural produce of the surrounding area and perform an important function as market towns – a role which brought them early prosperity, reflected in the imposing secular buildings and old monastic houses to be seen in many of these towns.

Although Göteborg (Gothenburg), situated in western Sweden in convenient proximity to the open sea, has developed into the country's leading international port and its second largest city, **Stockholm**, on the eastern side, is not only the geographical midpoint of Sweden but the focal point of all traffic in the Baltic. It has thus taken over the role once played by Visby (Gotland) in the heyday of the Hanseatic League. The intricate landscape of forests and lakes does not seem at first sight a favourable area for the establishment of a capital city; but the situation had one decisive advantage, since it was only at this point that a road running up the east side of Sweden from south to north could find a means of passage along a ridge between the much indented Lake Mälar and the tangle of skerries off the Baltic coast. Moreover, in the middle of the waterway that had to be crossed here there lay an island which provided not only a defensible situation for a medieval town but a means of watching over traffic both by water and by land.

In the layout of present-day Stockholm the port and industrial installations are agreeably unobtrusive, while the city's extensive new residential districts thrust outwards in all directions into the hilly and wooded surrounding countryside; and out in the Skärgård, the endless scatter of skerries, the people of this great capital city have a magnificent holiday and recreation area where they can find peace and relaxation in the intricately ramified waterways and on a host of lonely little islets.

Immediately north of central Sweden lies *Bergslagen*, a region of rather mixed character, still preserving many relics of the busy mining industry which once brought it prosperity. Elsewhere there are great concentrations of modern heavy industry, including the steelworks of *Sandviken, Domnarvet* and *Kvarnsveden*. Similar contrasts are found in the two neighbouring towns of *Falun* and *Borlänge*. And not far away, in *Dalarna*, is an oasis of prosperous traditional country life, the area around *Lake Siljan* which is also a popular tourist area.

Lake Siljan is less than half-way up the total length of Sweden; but the more northerly parts of the country, Norrland and Lapland, are immense territories with much less differentiation of character than southern Sweden. They are regions of endless forest and tumultuous rivers, formerly used to float down huge quantities of logs to the sawmills. Nowadays extensive areas of forest are served by good roads, so that most of the timber – still felled on an enormous scale – is now transported by truck. The sawmills, formerly all situated on the estuaries of the great rivers, are now also to be found inland, away from the rivers. Large amounts of timber are used by cellulose factories.

*Norrland* is a remote and austere region, with huge unfrequented lakes which in winter are concealed for many months under a thick armour-plating of ice. Far to the north, beyond the Arctic Circle, are numerous hydroelectric power stations – at *Porjus, Harsprånget* and many other places – and more are under construction.

Still farther north, in the zone of birch forest, is *Kiruna*, a town founded only in the early years of this century, with the largest area of any Swedish town. In the immediate vicinity of the town are two "monadnocks" of iron ore with an iron content of 70%, the ore from which is transported to Narvik in Norway on the "ore railway" and shipped from there. The neighbouring double town of *Gällivare-Malmberget* ships its ore from *Luleå* in summer when the Gulf of Bothnia is ice-free.

Lake Kaitum in northern Sweden

These ore towns lie in the heart of *Lapland*. Here the coniferous forests have given place to expanses of open birch forest and great stretches of moorland and bog, with sluggish streams pursuing an uncertain course through the rubble and debris of the last Ice Age. Until quite recently this was the domain of the Lapps' great herds of reindeer, but their possession of the territory is increasingly being disputed by the advance of modern civilisation. In 1986 the reindeer feeding grounds were badly affected by radioactive fallout from the nuclear reactor disaster at Chernobyl in the USSR.

From here it is possible to turn eastward into **FINLAND**. Like Norrland, this is a region of sublime austerity, and from any hill the summit of which rises above the surrounding forest there is an immense prospect of unspoiled natural beauty. The continually repeated but continually varied pattern of woodland and water, now clamorous with the sound of the wind and the rivers, now hushed to silence, reduces man to insignificance and humility and then lifts his heart with the radiance of the sun and the white splendour of the clouds chasing one another across the sky. Finland is called the "land of a thousand lakes", but in reality there are many more than that; and surely nowhere on earth are woodland and water so intimately interwoven. The *Finnish Lake Plateau* slopes gradually down in a north-westerly direction to the Gulf of Bothnia; but there too the ground is stony and the rivers tumble their way down over outcrops of rock. The lakeland region, which seems to extend endlessly northwards, is much more sharply bounded on the south by the Salpausselkä ridge. Beyond this are the most densely populated regions of Finland, in which arable farming and cattle rearing are still the most rewarding occupations; and in the middle of this area, on a rocky promontory, is the capital, **Helsinki**.

After the Second World War Finland was compelled to cede considerable areas of its territory to the Soviet Union. In the southeast it lost Viipuri (Viborg) and the north-western shore of Lake Ladoga, and in the north the important port of Petsamo on the Arctic Ocean, which in spite of its northerly situation was, thanks to an arm of the Gulf Stream which warmed its waters, the only port in Finland which was ice-free throughout the year. Even worse from the Finnish point of view, Karelia, the most loved and most "Finnish" of all areas of Finland, now became part of the Soviet Union.

On the other hand the Finnish *Åland Islands*, at the entrance to the Gulf of Bothnia, have a Swedish-speaking population, and, as Finland was a Swedish province until 1814, there has always been a considerable Swedish element in the Finnish coastal towns, so that on many occasions difficulties arose between the two ethnic groups.

In spite of the obstacles created by nature, the interior of Finland is served by railways and good roads, for the industry and hard work of the Finns have opened up these inhospitable regions for the activities of man. Some 70% of the area of

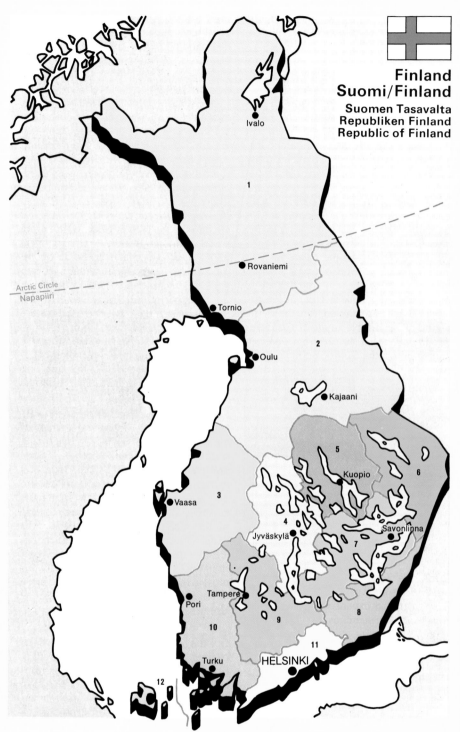

Finland
## Suomi/Finland
Suomen Tasavalta
Republiken Finland
Republic of Finland

| Province (*lääni*) | Area sq. km | sq. miles | Population | Province (*lääni*) | Area sq. km | sq. miles | Population |
|---|---|---|---|---|---|---|---|
| 1 Lapin lääni | 93,057 | 35,920 | 201,000 | 9 Hämeen lääni | 17,010 | 6,566 | 678,000 |
| 2 Oulun lääni | 56,866 | 21,950 | 432,000 | 10 Turun-Porin | | | |
| 3 Vaasan lääni | 26,447 | 10,209 | 444,000 | lääni | 22,170 | 8,558 | 713,000 |
| 4 Keski-Suomen lääni | 16,230 | 6,267 | 248,000 | 11 Uudenmaan lääni | 9,898 | 3,821 | 1,189,000 |
| 5 Kuopion lääni | 16,511 | 6,373 | 256,000 | 12 Ahvenanmaa | | | |
| 6 Pohjois-Karjalan | | | | maakunta (admin. | | | |
| lääni | 17,782 | 6,864 | 178,000 | district) | 1,527 | 589 | 24,000 |
| 7 Mikkelin lääni | 16,342 | 6,308 | 209,000 | | | | |
| 8 Kymen lääni | 10,783 | 4,162 | 341,000 | Finland | 304,623 | 117,584 | 4,913,000 |

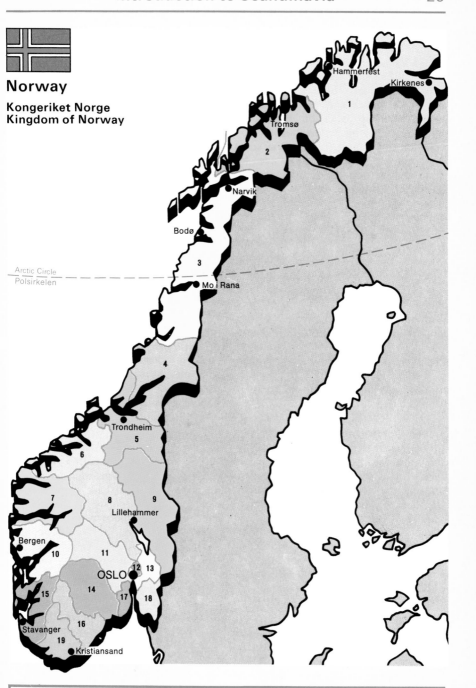

## Norway
### Kongeriket Norge
### Kingdom of Norway

| County (fylke) | Area sq. km | sq. miles | Population | County (fylke) | Area sq. km | sq. miles | Population |
|---|---|---|---|---|---|---|---|
| 1 Finnmark fylke | 48,637 | 18,774 | 77,000 | 11 Buskerud fylke | 14,927 | 5,762 | 219,000 |
| 2 Troms fylke | 25,954 | 10,021 | 147,000 | 12 Oslo fylke | 454 | 175 | 447,000 |
| 3 Nordland fylke | 38,327 | 14,798 | 244,000 | 13 Akershus fylke | 4,917 | 1,898 | 386,000 |
| 4 Nord-Trøndelag | | | | 14 Telemark fylke | 15,315 | 5,913 | 162,000 |
| fylke | 22,463 | 8,673 | 127,000 | 15 Rogaland fylke | 9,141 | 3,529 | 320,000 |
| 5 Sør-Trøndelag | | | | 16 Aust-Agder fylke | 9,212 | 3,557 | 94,000 |
| fylke | 18,831 | 7,271 | 244,000 | 17 Vestfold fylke | 2,216 | 856 | 191,000 |
| 6 Møre og Romsdal | | | | 18 Østfold fylke | 4,183 | 1,615 | 235,000 |
| fylke | 15,104 | 5,832 | 238,000 | 19 Vest-Agder fylke | 7,280 | 2,811 | 140,000 |
| 7 Sogn og Fjordane | | | | | | | |
| fylke | 18,634 | 7,195 | 106,000 | Norway | 323,878 | 125,017 | 4,146,000 |
| 8 Oppland fylke | 25,260 | 9,753 | 182,000 | (excl. Svalbard, Jan | | | |
| 9 Hedmark fylke | 27,388 | 10,575 | 187,000 | Mayen and the Antarctic | | | |
| 10 Hordaland fylke | 15,634 | 6,036 | 398,000 | territories) | | | |

Finland is forest-covered, with pine, spruce and birch predominating and just under 12% is accounted for by lakes, while more than 1440 rapids have been counted on the country's rivers. The wealth of Finland lies in its forests and its never failing supply of water power; but the exploitation of these resources depends on constant and persistent effort. Only some 9% of the country's area can be used for cultivation. In addition to the cultivated plants of central Europe, wild plants bearing berries are a feature of the countryside.

**NORWAY**, in spite of its long land frontiers, stands, as it were, back to back with the other Scandinavian countries. Its capital, **Oslo**, lies in a sheltered situation at the inner end of a fjord which cuts deeply into the land and has the country's longest rivers flowing into it. The long valleys of these rivers lead road traffic to the capital, which has the advantage of a beautiful hilly setting, giving it a privileged situation among the northern capitals.

Around Oslo lies a region of varied and attractive scenery, occupied by an active and industrious population which, particularly on the southern and southeastern slopes of the Norwegian mountains, can look back on long farming and mining traditions. The *Setesdal* is particularly renowned for its trim farmhouses and its rich traditional costumes. The prosperity of the agricultural population of *Telemark* is now based on a highly developed stock-farming system in which the Alpine pastures in the higher areas of the region play an important part.

Some 400 km (250 miles) north of Oslo is the old town of *Trondheim*, which, like Oslo, has round it a region brought into cultivation by peasant farmers, though on a smaller scale. High up in the hinterland of Trondheim is the little mining town of *Røros*, where rich deposits of ore have yielded more than 100,000 tons of pure copper over the past 300 years.

From Stavanger to Kirkenes the Norwegian west coast with its succession of fjords extends for some 2000 km (1250 miles), offering scenery of breathtaking magnificence. On this coast is *Bergen*, the largest town in western Norway, but which has remained a purely coastal town

with no real hinterland. Its economy revolves around fishing, the fish industry and the fish trade. To the west of Bergen are the Norwegian North Sea oilfields, now producing large quantities of oil and natural gas. Bergen is connected to Oslo by a boldly engineered railway line over the mountain plateaux which reaches a height of 1300 m (4265 ft). In recent years industry has been successfully established at a number of points on Norway's long west coast: thus the abundant supplies of water power in the Sognefjord (Høyanger) and Hardangerfjord (Odda) have been harnessed for use in the manufacture of aluminium, and in addition an active smelting industry has grown up around the copper and pyrite mines in the Sulitjelma area in northern Norway.

In *southern Norway* the developing town of *Stavanger* has specialised in the fish-canning industry, and in recent years its shipyards have built drilling rigs and platforms for the North Sea oilfields, while oil refineries have been established to handle the abundant supplies now flowing from the oilfields.

Farther north, enclosed within their skerries, are the little towns of *Ålesund* and *Kristiansund*, which have continued to depend on the fisheries for their living; and the hard conditions of the fisherman's trade are displayed most vividly in the *Lofoten Islands* which lie offshore in the far north of the country.

In the latitude of the Lofotens begins *northern Norway*, with its numerous islands emerging from the sea like the peaks of a submerged mountain range and the alarmingly narrow passages between them. Ensconced in its fjord is *Narvik*, the ice-free port which ships the iron ore of Swedish Lapland, brought from the mines on the "ore railway" over a pass 593 m (1945 ft) high.

In the most northerly part of Norway the fjords, flanked by the sheer rock faces which terminate the featureless mountain plateaux, are rather broader. *Hammerfest*, once called the most northerly town in Europe, is still 100 km (60 miles) short of the North Cape. One of the most interesting places in this area is *Bossekop*, on the Altafjord – almost the only point at which the two elements in the economy of the most northerly part of Europe, fishing and reindeer-herding, are found together.

Everywhere along the much-indented west coast of Norway rear up the *Scandinavian mountains* which extend from the coast of the Skaggerak right up to the North Cape; these mountains, especially towards the north, have many of the characteristics of mountains of lower elevation. Although there are a number of convenient routes through the mountains there are relatively few contacts between the west coast of Norway and the interior of Sweden. Northern Norway is too exclusively turned towards the sea, and the economically unproductive swath of mountain country (parts of which, to the north, are still used as grazing for the Lapps' reindeer herds) is too broad to encourage communication between the two regions.

# Population

The Scandinavian countries enjoy good-neighbourly relations, as reflected for example in the relaxation of controls on travel between the different countries. There is no sign, however, of any trend towards political union: on the contrary they have frequently broken away from such unions in the course of their history. Although all four countries are predominantly of the same Lutheran faith they are psychologically too different to contemplate a closer union.

The NORWEGIAN, turned towards the sea since time immemorial, is impulsive by nature, less given to respectable middle-class virtues. His actions often seem dictated less by logical reasoning than by intuition; and it need cause no surprise, therefore, that this small nation has produced a number of major composers and writers, as well as Arctic explorers such as Nansen and Amundsen.

The SWEDE, on the other hand, seems to attach more importance to respectability and a quiet life, although he is also thoroughly cosmopolitan. Sweden has produced distinguished scientists – mathematicians, physicists, biologists –

---

## Statistics of Population and Religion

**Denmark**

Total population: 5·1 million
(97% Danes)
Minorities: 1·7% Germans
(Northern Schleswig)
0·4% Swedes
Religion: 98% Lutherans
(Evangelical Lutheran Church)
27,000 Roman Catholics
7000 Jews

**Norway**

Total population: 4·1 million
(99% Norwegians)
Minorities: 22,000 Lapps
12,000 Finns
Religion: 94% Lutherans
(Lutheran State Church)
70,000 members of the Pentecostal movement
21,000 Baptists
19,000 members of the Evangelical Lutheran Free Church
18,000 Methodists
11,000 Roman Catholics
1000 Jews

**Sweden**

Total population: 8·3 million
(99% Swedes)
Minorities: 50,000 Finns
8500 Lapps
Religion: 88% Lutherans
(Swedish Lutheran Church)
150,000 Baptists
130,000 members of the Pentecostal movement
81,000 Roman Catholics
32,000 members of the Swedish Mission Covenant Church
13,000 Jews

**Finland**

Total population: 4·9 million
(93·2% Finns)
Minorities: 6·6% Swedes
2200 Lapps
Religion: 92% Lutherans
(Evangelical Lutheran Church)
55,000 Orthodox
8000 members of free churches
7500 Jehovah's Witnesses
3000 Roman Catholics
1500 Jews
1000 Mohammedans

but scarcely a single composer of signifi-cance. A logical and matter-of-fact approach, a tranquil and natural way of life, a subtle and apt sense of humour, a reserved disposition, a strongly individualist line – these are Swedish characteristics.

The FINN is strongly attached to the landscape, the lakes and forests, of his country. His character has been formed by the hard struggle for existence which calls for exertion of both mind and body. The Finnish people have notable achieve-ments to their credit in the scientific and artistic fields, particularly in architecture and design, and their sporting prowess has been no less remarkable; the mystical side of the Finn is exemplified by the music of Sibelius. The individual Finn, however, remains modest and companionable and Finnish hospitality never fails.

It is more difficult to characterise the DANE. Parallels can be found between the Danes and the Dutch, and economi-cally the two countries have much in common; but Holland is more thickly dotted with towns than Denmark, which,

with the exception of Copenhagen, largely consists of open country, so that the Dane still retains something of the countryman in his makeup. He appears more given to philosophising and reflection than the Swede; and Hans Andersen and Kierkegaard, very different from one another though they are, are both typically Danish.

These differences in the character of the Nordic peoples, among whom we must also include the LAPPS, are not of course reflected in every individual, but they do find some kind of expression in the different ways of life of the Scandinavian countries. But at the same time it is legitimate to see them as belonging to the same family of peoples, which have in common a high standard of living, well-organised systems of government, well-developed commercial relations with the rest of the world and – a factor of some importance to the visitor – an excellent transport system with a well-coordinated system of roads, railways, air and boat services, in spite of the great distances and the sparse populations over much of their territory.

# History

Only in quite recent years have detailed studies been published on the settlement of northern Europe (Denmark, Norway, Sweden and Finland) in **prehistoric and early historical times.**

In the *last interglacial period* there were men living on the territory of present-day Denmark, as is shown by the finds of objects made from animal bones.

In the *Stone Age* there were human settlements in the western Baltic region (southern Sweden and Denmark). Hunters and fishermen advanced into Sweden as far as the Dalälv and up the Norwegian coast to the Trondheim area. The inhabitants of the coastal regions lived by fishing and gathering shellfish, leaving evidence of their presence in the shells and kitchen refuse found on their "kitchen middens" (*køkkenmøddinger*) in northern Jutland, Zealand and southern Norway.

It is not until the middle of the 3rd millennium B.C., in the Neolithic period, that we find evidence of the first farming culture (the Trichterbecher or TRB culture, with the first pottery), but this was confined by climatic conditions to a very meagre level. During this period Eastern European tribes from Finland pushed into central Scandinavia but were later driven back.

The northern *Bronze Age* (*c.* 1800–500 B.C.) appears mainly in Denmark and southern Sweden, but material belonging to this period has also been found in southern and western Norway. The bronze was obtained by barter from regions farther south, though what it was exchanged for (perhaps amber) is not clear. From this period date the rock carvings found particularly at Tanum (in Bohuslän, north of Göteborg), on the east coast of Sweden, in the area north of Lake Mälar, on the west side of the Oslofjord and in a band of territory extending eastwards from Trondheim into Sweden, as well as the chambered tomb at Kivik on the southeast coast of Sweden and various solar wheels or solar discs reflecting a cult of the sun.

The northern *Iron Age* (*c.* 500 B.C. to A.D. 500), of which scanty evidence has been found in Denmark and on the Swedish islands of Gotland and Öland, has yielded domestic equipment, ornaments and above all improved weaponry. The area of Germanic settlement in Norway now extended up to the Arctic Circle. Runic inscriptions are found on ornaments and implements from the 2nd c. A.D. onwards, and about the end of the 4th c. runes began to be carved on stone (rock faces, standing stones, gravestones).

The name SCANDINAVIA occurs for the first time in Pliny the Elder (*c.* A.D. 75), and is found also in the name of the Swedish province of Skåne or Scania. There are references in Tacitus to Swedes (Suiones) and Finns (Fenni). The Jutland peninsula was originally occupied by Saxons, Angles and Jutes, the Danish islands and southern Sweden by the Heruli; but during the period of the great migrations these peoples were compelled to withdraw in face of the Danes advancing from the east and north. During these troubled times numerous fortified settlements and ring forts were built. To the north of these various peoples there lived on the Scandinavian peninsula the Goths, separated by dense forests from the Swedes who were to be found still farther north. Forests and mountains, together with Lake Vänern and the Götaälv to the southwest, bounded the territory of the Norwegians, for whom the older songs had no common name: the later term "Norvegr" or "Nordmenn' is probably no more than a reference to the direction in which they lived. Internal conflicts and struggles for power seem to have lain at the origin of the expeditions of these Norsemen, named Vikings after the fjords and inlets (*vikr*) from which they sailed, who ravaged the whole of Europe and are believed to have been the first to reach North America.

## DENMARK

### Emergence of the Danish state; the Viking age

7th and 8th c.    The coming of the Danes.
The Scandinavian Danes occupy southern Sweden, the islands and Jutland, driving back the West Germanic Heruli, Angles, Saxons and Jutes.

9th–11th c.    Formation of the state; Christianisation; Viking expeditions.
804–810 King *Godfred* builds the Danevirke in southern Jutland as a frontier fortification directed against Charlemagne. – The **Christianisation** of Denmark begins in the 9th c. but is not completed until the time of Knut (Canute) the Great. – *Gorm the Old* (*c.* 900–935) and *Harald Bluetooth* (935–985) unify Denmark after fierce fighting with local chieftains.
The **Western Vikings** (Danes and Norwegians) or NORSEMEN ravage northwestern, western and southern Europe in their small but seaworthy ships, in raids directed at booty and conquest. The settlement of ICELAND begins in 874, of GREENLAND in 983; North America may have been reached around 1000 and later the Canadian arctic islands. In 911 the Viking chief *Rollo* is made Duke of Normandy (Robert I) by King Charles III of France.

1000–42    Danish empire.
*Sven (Swein) Forkbeard* (985–1014) and *Knut (Canute) the Great* (1018–35) conquer Norway and England; but this empire falls to pieces after 1042.

### The age of the Valdemars

The age of the Valdemars (1157–1375) brings Denmark internal consolidation, external power, material prosperity and a period of intellectual and artistic flowering, with the development of an urban culture.

*c.*1000–1250    Romanesque architecture.
Monumental stone churches built in the first half of the 12th c. are the cathedrals of Ribe and Viborg. Thereafter brick begins to be used as a building material. To the second half of the century belong the monastic churches of Sorø (Cistercian) and Ringsted (Benedictine) and the five-towered Church of Our Lady in Kalundborg.

1157–82    *Valdemar I, the Great.*
Valdemar re-establishes the unity of Denmark. In 1168 he conquers the island of Rügen, occupied by the Wends. Bishop *Absalon* (1128–1201), a great statesman and military commander, founds Copenhagen.

1202–41    *Valdemar II.*
Valdemar conquers the German-Swedish Baltic territories and in 1214 compels the Emperor Frederick II to give them up; but is forced to abandon them after a defeat at Bornhöved in Holstein. – 1219: crusade against Estonia, which Valdemar conquers in 1238. In the battle of Reval (Tallinn) the "Dannebrog", the Danish flag, is believed to have fallen mysteriously from heaven.

13th–16th c.    Gothic architecture in brick.
13th c. (with later alterations): Roskilde Cathedral; Århus Cathedral; St Knud's Church, Odense. – 14th c.: St Botolph's Church (Budolfi Kirke), Ålborg. – 15th c.: St Nicholas's Church, Køge.

**1340–75** *Valdemar IV Atterdag.*
Valdemar restores the royal authority. – In 1361 he plunders Visby (Gotland), which is allied with Lübeck, but in 1367–70 is defeated by the Hanseatic League and is compelled to recognise their privileges.

## The Union

From 1375 to 1523 the three northern kingdoms are united under Danish rule. Denmark is an elective monarchy; the power of the nobility grows.

**1375–1412** *Margaret, daughter of Valdemar IV.*
Margaret becomes Regent in Denmark for her son Olaf (d. 1387) in 1375, in Norway after the death of her husband Håkon IV in 1380, in Sweden in 1389.

**1397** The **Union of Kalmar** unites Denmark, Norway and Sweden. Eric of Pomerania, Margaret's grand-nephew, is crowned king of the three kingdoms. Norway remains united with Denmark until 1814; Sweden wins its independence between 1433 and 1523.

**1448–81** *Christian I* of Oldenburg, founder of the dynasty which still reigns in Denmark.

**1460** The Estates of Schleswig-Holstein elect Christian as their Duke. This personal union of the two duchies (whose indivisibility is confirmed by Christian) with Denmark holds the seed of the later conflicts of 1848–64.

**1478** Foundation of the University of Copenhagen.

**1513–23** *Christian II.*
Christian attempts to re-establish the Union of Kalmar, conquers Sweden in 1520 and executes 82 leading Swedes, but is driven out of Sweden by Gustavus Vasa 1521 and out of Norway and Denmark in 1523.

### The struggle for supremacy in the Baltic

**1534–59** *Christian III.*
1534–6: Lübeck seeks to intervene in Denmark's internal conflicts in order to establish its commercial dominance, but is defeated in the "Count's War".

**1536** The **Reformation** is established by the Rigsdag. *Johan Bugenhagen* organises the Danish Church.

**1559–88** *Frederik II.*
**Beginning of the conflict with Sweden.** – 1563–70: the "War of the Three Kings" against Sweden brings bitter fighting but no territorial changes. Sweden is compelled, however, to recognise the Sound dues.
1576–97: under Frederik's patronage, *Tycho Brahe* sets up his observatory on the island of Ven in the Øresund and increases the accuracy of astronomical observations.

**1588–1648** *Christian IV*, the most popular of Danish kings.
1625–9: Christian intervenes in Germany during the **Thirty Years War**. His defeat in 1626 at Lutter in the Harz region seriously weakens Denmark.

*c.* 1540–1660 Renaissance architecture.
The buildings of this period, mostly in red brick with sandstone decorative features, show the influence of Dutch architecture: Kronborg Castle (1577–85), Frederiksborg Castle (1602–20), Rosenborg (1608–17), the Exchange in Copenhagen (1619–40).

**1613–15 and 1643–45** Wars with Sweden.
Denmark is obliged to give up large territories on the Scandinavian peninsula.

**1648–70** *Frederik III.*
Between 1657 and 1660 Denmark fights two wars with Sweden. Charles X of Sweden invades Denmark. 1659, heroic defence of Copenhagen and Danish victory at Nyborg. Denmark is finally compelled, however, to give up its possessions in southern Sweden.

### Absolutism

**1660** Denmark becomes an **unlimited hereditary monarchy.** The poor showing of the nobility in the wars with Sweden arouses popular feeling against them. The Rigsdag is summoned by Frederik and grants him absolute power (the "King's Law" of 1665).

**1670–99** *Christian V.*
1671 : establishment of a court and administrative nobility.

**1699–1730** *Frederik IV.*
Frederik mitigates the rigours of the bondage system. Both Christian and Frederik seek to recover the lost territories and to incorporate Holstein in Denmark.

**1675–1720** Wars with Sweden.
The Danish navy wins a number of major victories, in Køge Bugt in 1677 under *Niels Juel*, off Rügen in 1715 and at Marstrand in 1719 under *Tordenskjold*.

*c.* 1660–1730 Baroque architecture.
Charlottenborg Palace, Copenhagen (after 1672); Vor Frelsers Kirke, Copenhagen (after 1682).

**1720–1807** A long period of peace.
Economic and intellectual flowering. Copenhagen increases in importance as an international commercial centre.

**1746–66** *Frederik V.*
Under Frederik's minister Count *J. H. Bernstorff* German influence in Denmark reaches its peak.

*c.* 1730–80 Rococo architecture.
Amalienborg Palace (1740–50), Charlottenlund.

**1766–1808** *Christian VII.*
Count *A. P. Bernstorff* carries through major reforms (1784–97), culminating in the emancipation of the peasants (1786–88).

**1807** British bombardment of Copenhagen.
During the Napoleonic wars Britain seeks to bring Denmark into the war against Napoleon by bombarding Copenhagen and seizing the Danish navy and merchant fleet.

**1808–39** *Frederik VI.*
Frederik acts as Regent from 1784 during the mental incapacity of his father. The British attack of 1807 leads Denmark to ally itself with France and involves it in the Napoleonic wars.

**1814** Treaty of Kiel.
Denmark loses Norway and Heligoland.

*c.* 1780–1840 Neo-classical architecture.
Colonnade at Amalienborg (1795), Church of Our Lady (1811–29), Law Courts (1815), Thorvaldsen Museum (1839–48), all in Copenhagen.

### Denmark as a constitutional monarchy

**1839–48** *Christian VIII.*

**1848–63** *Frederik VII.*
1849: introduction of a constitution.

**1848–64** **Schleswig-Holstein** is separated from Denmark.
In 1848 Denmark proclaims the full incorporation of Schleswig in the Danish kingdom and in 1863 of both duchies. It represses an armed rising by the

people of Schleswig-Holstein in 1850, but is defeated in 1864 by the forces of the German Confederation (Prussia and Austria), to which Holstein belonged, and gives up Schleswig, Holstein and Lauenburg.

**1863–1906** *Christian IX.*
From 1864 Denmark maintains a policy of neutrality in foreign affairs. Internally, conservative, liberal and socialist views compete for predominance.

**1912–47** *Christian X.*
Denmark remains neutral in the **First World War.**
1915: new democratic constitution; women are granted the vote. – 1917: Denmark sells its islands in the West Indies to the United States.

**1918** ICELAND becomes an independent kingdom, in personal union with Denmark (until 1944).

**1920 Northern Schleswig** becomes part of Denmark.
Under the Treaty of Versailles a plebiscite is held, after which Denmark acquires an area of some 4000 sq. km (1500 sq. miles), with a population of over 160,000 (a quarter of whom are Germans).

*c.* 1860–1920 Architecture in 'historicist" styles.
Theatre Royal (neo-Renaissance, 1872–4), Town Hall (neo-Renaissance, 1892–1905), Christiansborg Palace (neo-Rococo, 1907–20), Central Station (1907–11), all in Copenhagen.
The basis of the Danish economy is a strong farming community with highly developed cooperative institutions; the large landowners are now of little significance. Some 80 folk high schools (first founded 1844) give the rural population a good general education. As a result of the fall in world wheat prices Danish farmers switch to stock-farming and build up a large export trade in dairy products and meat.

**1939–45 Second World War.**
Denmark remains neutral. The occupation by German troops (1940–5) is a painful ordeal for the whole country. The Danish government remains in office. Growth of a resistance movement. – In the autumn of 1943 the commander of the German occupation forces takes over executive power, replacing the Danish government. – The German surrender is signed on 4 May 1945. A Social Democrat, *Buhl*, forms a provisional government in Copenhagen.

**1944** ICELAND breaks free of Denmark and becomes a republic.

After its experiences during the war Denmark abandons its strict neutrality and joins the western system of alliances, although in the early post-war years the Communists are a political force to be reckoned with. – 1947: death of Christian X.

**1947–72** *Frederik IX.*
Denmark remains a monarchy.

**1948** The Færoe Islands are granted self-government, but remain under the Danish crown.

**1949** Agreements with the German provincial government of Schleswig-Holstein securing full democratic rights and freedoms for the Danish minority in southern Schleswig.
Denmark joins **NATO.** The United States guarantee to protect Greenland, where there are American bases.

**1951** Denmark becomes a founding member of the Nordic Council (economic and cultural cooperation between the northern countries).

**1953** Constitutional reform (unicameral system),

enabling women to succeed to the throne. Greenland to elect two members of the Folketing.

**1958 Nordic Passport and Customs Union.**

**1960** Denmark becomes a founding member of the European Free Trade Association (EFTA).

**1972** Crown Princess Margrethe is proclaimed queen as *Margrethe II.* Denmark joins the **EEC** and thus relinquishes membership of EFTA.

**1974** Trade agreement with the German Democratic Republic.

**1978** Abolition of the death penalty.

**1979** GREENLAND is given its own administration (government and parliament for domestic matters) but remains under Danish sovereignty. A movement for independence develops.
Elections to the Folketing strengthen the Social Democrats and Conservatives. The Prime Minister in office, *Anker Jørgensen*, forms a new Social-Democrat minority government (October).

**1980** Second UN World Conference of Women meets in Copenhagen. Electoral defeat of the Social-Democrats in the Færoes.

**1981** Dispute between Germany and Denmark over the quota of cod permitted to be caught by West German fishermen off Greenland. Fresh elections to the Folketing in December result in loss of votes for the Social-Democrats, Jørgensen forms another Social-Democrat minority government.

**1982** In a referendum the population of Greenland votes to leave the Common Market. The Jørgensen government, which has not been able to solve the economic problems, resigns. *Paul Schlüter,* the leader of the Conservatives, forms a four-party minority government.

**1983** The Folketing refuses to allow further US medium-range missiles to be stationed in Denmark. Schlüter resigns (December).

**1984** As a result of the elections, which have been brought forward, the four-party minority government, with Paul Schlüter as Prime Minister, is again in power.

**1985** Greenland leaves the EEC and receives the special status of an overseas country or territory (1 February). Industrial unrest in Denmark (March).

**1986** Denmark signs the agreement amending the EEC (extension of the Common Market; February).

## NORWAY

### Early history; the unification of the state

In the Bronze Age Norway is occupied by Germanic peoples. The mountainous nature of the country hampers communications between the different valleys and fjords and leads to the formation of kinship groups ruled by petty kings. By the time of the Viking expeditions, however, there is a form of loose association into four large communities called "things".

**872–930** *Harald Hårfager (the Fair-Haired).*
Harald, scion of an old ruling family in the Oslofjord, defeats the other petty kings, after bitter fighting, and unifies a large part of the country under his rule. Many of his opponents and men whom he had outlawed leave the country (first settlers in Iceland, 874).

**9th–11th c.** Some of the petty kingdoms are re-established. After Harald's death there is no overall royal authority.

During this period the **Vikings** set out on their raiding expeditions to the coastal regions of Europe. On returning from their campaigns, however, the warriors for the most part go back to tilling the soil.

995–1000   *Olav Tryggvason* (Tryggvessøn).
Olav Tryggvason, a great-grandson of Harald Fairhair, having spend all his youth and young manhood in Viking raids and expeditions abroad, was eventually baptised as a Christian by the Bishop of Winchester. He sailed from England to the Trondheim area to claim the throne of Norway and equally anxious to make Norway turn to Christianity. He landed in 995 and was immediately accepted as King of Norway (Olav I) by the people of the area and subsequently by the rest of the country. He founded the city of Trondheim as a capital, building a palace and the first Christian church. Unfortunately, his enforcement of Christianity made him many enemies who joined the Danes and Swedes and together they attacked Olav's very much outnumbered force at the naval battle of *Svolder*. When he saw that the battle was lost, Olav, rather than capitulate, jumped overboard and was drowned. By all accounts he was very good-looking, physically and mentally strong and a great athlete. He clearly appealed very much to the Norwegians of his day and this together with his manner of dying (death rather than dishonour) left a tremendous impression on the national mind, so that for centuries, and to some extent even today, he has been regarded as the prototype of a national hero.

11th and 12th c.   The struggle to establish royal authority.
Frequent conflicts with the Danes during the 11th c. Bergen founded in 1070. – The power of the Church grows during the 12th c.; it claims the power to grant the crown as an ecclesiastical fief.

1066–93   *Olav Kyrre.*
Danish claims abandoned; internal consolidation; growth in the strength of the towns. Establishment of Norwegian bishoprics at Nidaros (Trondheim), Bergen and Oslo.

1177–1202   *Sverre.*
Sverre, leader of the Trondheim party, the Birkebeiners (named after their birch-bark leggings), opposes the pro-Danish Church party, the Baglers ("crozier-men"), who are powerful in southern Norway.

1217–63   *Håkon Håkonsson.*
The great days of chivalry. Håkon, Sverre's grandson, ends the conflict between the parties. Incorporation of ICELAND into Norway.

1263–80   *Magnus Lagaboetir* ("reformer of the laws").
Further constitutional reforms; national system of law; abolition of the old "*things*".

12th and 13th c.   Building of the stave churches.
The native timber architecture of Norway reaches its peak in these old wooden churches, of which some 30 have survived (Heddal, Borgund; Fantoft, near Bergen; Gol, in the National Museum, Oslo).

## Union with Denmark

From 1319 the dynastic policy of the Crown is directed towards bringing about a union of the three northern kingdoms. In 1387 Margaret of Denmark is elected queen of Norway as well. – 1397: Union of Kalmar (see above under Denmark).

1387–1814  **Norway in personal union with Denmark.**
The old nobility has been destroyed in the conflict with the monarchy. The economy is thriving, but is largely in the hands of the Hanseatic League. The Reformation is introduced in 1536, and at the same time Norway becomes a Danish province ruled by a governor. Danish becomes the language of government, the Church and the schools, and Old Norwegian survives only in local dialects. In its wars with Denmark Sweden also attacks Norway, and this arouses Norwegian national feeling, which had been almost extinguished. The development of maritime trade brings new ideas into the country and provides a powerful new intellectual stimulus.

1556–60   Decline of Hanseatic power.
In 1559 the power of the Hanseatic League, which had almost completely dominated Norwegian trade in the 15th and 16th c., is broken in Bergen.

1624  **Mining** begins in Norway, with the help of miners brought in from Germany: silver at Kongsberg in 1624, copper at Røros in 1644.

1807   The **continental blockade**.
Denmark's alliance with France and its involvement in Napoleon's "continental system" leads to a British blockade of the Norwegian coast. Shipping is brought to a standstill and the country suffers acute shortages. Norway seeks to break free from Denmark.

## Union with Sweden

1814   Norway is united with Sweden.
After Napoleon's defeat Denmark is compelled under the treaty of Kiel to cede Norway to Sweden. The Norwegians do not recognise the treaty, declare their country independent and adopt a liberal constitution at Eidsvoll (17 May: now Norway's National Day). They are, however, compelled by the arrival of Swedish troops under Bernadotte and by pressure from the great powers to accept the **personal union with Sweden**, but are allowed to have their own constitution.

1853   Beginning of the "Language Movement".
*Ivar Aasen* publishes samples of the Landsmål, a written language diverging from Danish which he has formed out of local dialects and which now achieves great popularity.

1872–1905   *Oskar II* (d. 1907).
The last king of both Norway and Sweden. Frequent conflicts between the Storting and the Crown.

1905   A national referendum decides in favour of dissolving the union with Sweden, and this is confirmed in the **treaty of Karlstad** on 26 October.

## Norway as an independent kingdom

1905–57   *Håkon VII* (b. 1872).
Prince Karl of Denmark is elected king of Norway and takes the name of Håkon. The constitution is made still more democratic; women get the vote.

1914–18  **First World War.**
Norway remains neutral. Half its merchant fleet, which carries cargo for the Allies, is sunk by German submarines. Popular feeling is hostile to Germany.

1920   Norway joins the League of Nations. It is granted sovereignty over SPITZBERGEN (Svalbard), which is finally incorporated in Norway in 1925.

1920–7   Prohibition (ban on alcohol).

1929   Occupation of the island of JAN MEYEN.

**1939–45 Second World War.**
In 1940 German troops invade and occupy Norway, anticipating an imminent British landing. There is fierce fighting for the possession of Narvik. The king and government flee to London. Norway is ruled by a German commissioner, who is supported by a former Norwegian minister, *Vidkun Quisling*. After the German surrender in May 1945 the Norwegian government in exile returns from Britain.

**1945** The Workers' Party wins a general election. – Norway takes part in the foundation of the United Nations.

**1949** Treaty with the Soviet Union regulating the northern frontier between the two countries. – Norway joins **NATO**.

**1951** Norway becomes a founding member of the Nordic Council (see above under Denmark).

**1957** *Olav V* (b. 1903).
Crown Prince Olav, Håkon VII's only son, succeeds his father.

**1958 Nordic Passport and Customs Union.**

**1960** Norway is a founding member of the European Free Trade Association (EFTA).

**1965** The right-wing parties win a majority in a general election.

**1973** Free trade agreement with the EEC, after a national referendum decides against full membership of the Community.

**1974 Drilling for oil and natural gas** begins in the North Sea.

**1977** An oil pipeline 450 km (280 miles) long from the Ekofisk oilfield, northwest of Stavanger, to Emden in Germany is brought into operation. – The Workers' Party wins 76 seats in the Storting in a general election.

**1979** A huge field of natural gas is discovered 130 km (80 miles) northwest of Bergen.
The Social Democrats fare badly in local government elections.

**1980** Supply platform, the "Alexander Kielland", of the Ekofisk oilfield in the North Sea capsizes on 23 July in a storm with 123 dead and missing. – Agreement on the stationing of US troops on Norwegian soil for defence purposes, if necessary.

**1981** Prime Minister *Odvar Nordli* (Norwegian Workers' Party, DNA) resigns on 30 January on health grounds. The deputy DNA chairman *Gro Harlem Brundtland* becomes the first woman to be Prime Minister of Norway. – Total price freeze until the end of 1981, reduction of income tax.
Fresh elections to the Storting (parliament) on 13 and 14 September bring victory to the Conservative Høvre Party under *Kaare Willoch* who becomes the new Prime Minister and forms a minority government (October).

**1982** With a majority of only one vote Parliament approves the implementation of the NATO double resolution; this is opposed by the Social Democrats in particular.

**1983** The Conservative Prime Minister, Kaare Willoch (Høyre Party) persuades the Christian People's Party and the Centre to support the government; the coalition is supported by a bare majority.

**1984** On 20 January the security police arrest Arne Treholt, who for some time had been Secretary of State for Trade and Maritime Law; he confesses to having been an agent of the KGB.

**1985** An Oslo court sentences Arne Treholt to life

imprisonment (20 June). In the parliamentary elections the existing coalition under Prime Minister Kaare Willoch gains a narrow majority (September).

**1986** Resignation of Kaare Willoch (fall in the price of oil), *Gro Harlem Brundtland* becomes Prime Minister at the head of a Social-Democrat minority government (May)

## SWEDEN

### The early centuries

**1st–5th c.** Settlement of the country.
The oldest inhabitants are probably ancestors of the Finns. Germanic tribes coming from the west and south push northwards as far as the coasts of Finland.

*c.* 500 Skåne, in southern Sweden, is occupied by Danes. To the north are the Goths, who have become wealthy through their trade with the south but have lost much of their population by movement to other regions. Round Lake Mälar and in Uppland are the Svear, who have a productive agriculture and a strict tribal discipline.

**6th–8th c.** Struggle for predominance.
The Svear finally overcome the Goths; the final battle probably takes place around 750. They give their name to the whole country (Svearike, the kingdom of the Svear – Sverige – Sweden).

**8th–11th c.** The **Viking age**.
Swedish Vikings ravage the coasts of the Baltic and, in their light ships, push far into the lowlands of eastern Europe. They found a number of states, beginning with one on Lake Ilmen centred on Holmgard (later Novgorod) and another round Kiev. They reach as far as Constantinople, where they are known as Varangians and form the imperial guard.

**12th–13th c.** Christianity comes to Sweden.
About 830 *St Ansgar* preaches the Christian faith at Birka, on the little island of Björkö in Lake Mälar, which was then the largest trading town in Sweden. In 1008 King *Olof Erikson* is baptised, and in 1164 an archbishop is appointed in Sweden.

### Sweden before the Union

**10th–12th c.** The early monarchy.
The king is elected in Upper Sweden and must then receive homage throughout the country. Alongside the king, however, there is still a powerful and ambitious nobility.

**1150–60** King *Erik IX* (St Erik), ruling in Uppsala.
In order to beat off Finnish incursions Erik undertakes the so called **crusade into south-western Finland**, the first step towards the establishment of Swedish rule in that area.

**1250–1363** The **Folkungs**.
Kings and regents ("stewards of the realm") of the Folkung dynasty consolidate the power of Sweden and complete the **conquest of Finland**.

**1250–66** *Birger Jarl* as Regent.
He strengthens internal security by the so-called "peace laws", founds Stockholm in 1255 as a stronghold against Finnish raids and promotes trade by the grant of extensive privileges to Hanseatic merchants.

**1275–90** *Magnus I Ladulås*.
Magnus protects townspeople and peasants against oppression by the nobility. Around 1280 **mining** begins at Falun with the help of miners from Germany. The excessive privileges granted to Germans arouse hostility among the Swedes.

## The Union

Between 1319 and 1523 Sweden is linked by various forms of personal union with Norway and Denmark. The union with Denmark, however, usually takes on the aspect of domination by foreigners, and on several occasions Sweden fights for, and obtains, de facto independence.

1319–63 *Magnus II Eriksson.*
Magnus, a Folkung, is also king of Norway until 1343. – In 1350 a general (national) code of law replaces the various regional systems of law. – In 1360 Skåne and in 1360 Öland and Gotland are annexed by Denmark. Magnus is deposed.

1363–89 *Albert III.*
The nobility win considerable power.

1389–1412 *Margaret,* daughter of Valdemar IV of Denmark, becomes Regent. – 1397: **Union of Kalmar** (see under Denmark).
Margaret is a strong ruler; she restricts the power of the nobility.

1433–1523 **Swedish resistance to the Union.**
There are constant risings against the kings and their representatives in Sweden, who think only of Danish interests. On several occasions Sweden gains de facto independence as a result of these risings.

1433–6 Peasant rising led by the mine-owner *Engelbrekt Engelbrektsson.*

1448–70 *Karl VIII Knutsson* "anti-king" of Sweden.

1470–1503 *Sten Sture the Elder,* "Guardian of the Realm".
In 1471 he defeats King Christian I of Denmark in a battle on the Brunkeberg. – The University of Uppsala is founded in 1477.

1520 The "**Stockholm Bloodbath**".
Christian II of Denmark defeats *Sten Sture the Younger* and has 82 leading Swedes executed in Stockholm.

## Sweden as a great power; the Reformation

1523–60 **Gustav I Vasa.**
Gustav Vasa, leader of a rising which starts in Dalarna in 1521, drives out the Danes and is elected king of Sweden in 1523. He introduces the **Reformation** in 1527, helps to break the commercial predominance of the "Count's War" (1534–6: see under Denmark) and makes Sweden a **hereditary monarchy** in 1544.

1560–1611 Under Gustav Vasa's sons Sweden finds itself in grave difficulties on a number of occasions, until finally his youngest son *Karl IX* (1599–1611) re-establishes settled government and enhances the standing of the kingdom.

1611–32 **Gustav II Adolf (Gustavus Adolphus).**
Gustavus brings to a successful end the wars which his father had begun against Russia, which is compelled to cede Ingermanland in 1617, and Poland, which cedes Livonia in 1629. He reorganises the administration and promotes trade and industry.

1630 At the request of the German Protestant princes Gustavus enters the **Thirty Years War** and is killed after winning a great victory at Lützen.

1632–54 Queen *Christina,* Gustavus Adolphus's daughter.
Her chief minister is *Axel Oxenstierna.* The Swedish army, under Gustav Horn, Johan Banér and Lennart

Torstensson, successfully continues the war. In 1645 Denmark is forced to give up Jämtland, Gotland and other territories, and in 1648 Sweden acquires the principalities of Bremen and Verden, Stettin and the islands of Rügen, all in Germany.

1654–60 *Karl X Gustav* of Zweibrücken.
Gustav, a cousin of Queen Christina, becomes king after her abdication. He wages war against Poland and Denmark, which is obliged to give up Halland, Skåne and other territories in 1658. His principal aim is to establish the sole authority of Sweden over the Baltic and its coasts.

1660–94 *Karl XI (Charles XI).*
He succeeds his father, Karl X, at the age of four. In the treaty of Oliva (1660) the king of Poland renounces all claims on Sweden. – 1668: foundation of the University of Lund. – Karl joins in Louis XIV's war against Holland, Britain and Brandenburg on the French side. The Swedish army is defeated by Brandenburg in the battle of Fehrbellin in 1675, but Sweden is not compelled to surrender any territory. The king takes advantage of the general discontent with the maladministration of the nobility to take back Crown fiefs which had fallen to nobles and to introduce legislation giving the Crown almost unlimited powers.

1697–1718 *Karl XII (Charles XII).*
This gifted energetic king beats back attacks by Denmark, Poland and Russia (battle of Narva, 1700) and carries the war into the enemy countries. On an adventurous expedition into the Ukraine, however, he is decisively defeated at Poltava in 1709 and flees into Turkey. In 1716, accompanied by two faithful followers, he rides in 16 days to Stralsund. He is killed in 1718 under the walls of the Norwegian fortress of Fredrikssten.
This ends the short period of absolutist rule in Sweden.

## Towards constitutional government and neutrality

1719–72 The "**Era of Liberty**".
After this collapse Sweden is compelled to give up, between 1719 and 1721, the Baltic provinces, Bremen, Verden and other territory in Germany, and ceases to be a European great power. Nevertheless the country makes a rapid economic recovery. The Estates limit the power of the kings (who from 1751 to 1818 belong to the House of Holstein-Gottorp). The war party, known as the "Hattar" ("Hats"), drive Sweden into the Seven Years War.

1771–92 *Gustav III.*
The king recovers control of the government from the Estates by a coup d'état in 1772 and establishes an enlightened despotism. He abolishes torture, introduces the freedom of the press and stabilises the coinage. In 1792 he is assassinated at a masked ball in a conspiracy by the nobility.

1792–1809 *Gustav IV Adolf.*
Moved by his abhorrence for Napoleon, Gustav joins the coalition against France, and loses Pomerania in 1807 and Finland in 1809. He is deposed in 1809.

1809–18 *Karl XIII.*
Since Karl, Gustav IV's uncle, is old and childless, the Riksdag in 1810 elects the French marshal Jean-Baptiste *Bernadotte* as heir to the throne; he is then adopted by the king and takes the name of Karl Johan. In 1812 he leads Swedish troops against Napoleon, and in the treaty of Kiel (1814) he compels Denmark to give up Norway; in return Denmark receives Swedish Pomerania.

**1814 1905 Union with Norway.**
Kings: *Karl IV Johan* (Bernadotte, 1818–44), *Oskar I* (1844–59), *Karl XV* (1859–72), *Oskar II* (1872–1907). Sweden keeps out of the European wars, and receives a new constitution in 1865. This is a period of economic and cultural advance, and industry develops rapidly. There is a change in the country's social structure; the first laws for the protection of workers are passed in 1889; the Social Democratic Party is founded. In 1895 the scientist Alfred Nobel establishes the annual **Nobel Prizes.**
The rise of national awareness revives old hostilities, and in 1905 King Oskar gives up the Norwegian crown and dissolves the Union.

**20th c.** Swedish **neutrality.**
Kings: *Gustav V* (1907–50), *Gustav VI Adolf* (1950–73). *Karl XVI Gustav* (since 1973) Sweden maintains its neutrality in both world wars in spite of considerable difficulties. The Swedish Red Cross serves the cause of humanity (Count Folke Bernadotte, 1895–1948). The constitution is still further democratised. The continued improvement of social conditions and social services involves the heavy financial burdens of the welfare state.

**1946** Sweden becomes a member of the UN.

**1949** Sweden joins the Council of Europe.

**1951** Sweden becomes a founding member of the Nordic Council (see above under Denmark).

**1958 Nordic Passport and Customs Union.**

**1960** Sweden a founding member of EFTA.

**1973** *Karl XVI Gustav.*
Gustav VI Adolf dies; grandson succeeds him as Karl XVI. Free trade agreement with the EEC.

**1974** New constitution: the king's powers are considerably reduced from 1 January 1975.

**1976** Law for workers' participation in industrial management – The right-wing win a general election after 44 years of Social Democratic government.

**1977** Birth of Princess Victoria Ingrid Alice Desirée. – The law of succession to the throne (since 1810 confined to males) is altered.

**1979** A further general election returns a narrow right-wing majority. *Thorbjörn Fälldin*, the leader of the Centre Party forms a right-wing coalition on 11 October. – Parliament votes for primogeniture (right of succession to throne of first-born child).

**1980** As heiress to the throne Princess Victoria receives the title of Duchess of Vestergötland. – By a majority of 58·1% Parliament resolves to increase the provision of atomic power (maximum 12 reactors). – Serious labour troubles (100,000 strikers)).

**1981** The Conservative Party withdraws from the coalition. At the end of May Thorbjörn Fälldin forms a new minority government of the Centre and Liberal parties. – Economic crisis and inflation continue. – On 23 June the actress and singer, Zarah Leander, dies in Stockholm aged 74.
The Soviet submarine U-137 runs aground on the reefs near the Swedish base of Karlskrona. This leads to diplomatic complications with Russia.

**1982** In the parliamentary elections the parties of the Left (Social-Democrats and Communists) gain a majority (September). The Prime Minister elect, *Olof Palme* forms a minority cabinet of Social-Democrats, supported by the Communists. In the inaugural address demands are made for an expanded economic policy and for the creation of a zone in northern Europe free of atomic weapons (October).

**1983** The government passes a law against tax-evasion by "moonlighting" (1 January). Introduction of the so-called trade-union fund (December).

**1984** On 17 January a follow-up Conference of European Co-operation and Disarmament opens in Stockholm; 35 Foreign Ministers take part.

**1985** Industrial unrest accompanied by strikes and lockouts (May). In the elections the Social-Democrats under Olof Palme are the victors (Sept.).

**1986** Opening in Stockholm of the ninth round of negotiations of the Conference of European Security and Co-operation (Jan.). On 28 February Prime Minister Olof Palme is shot dead. Social-Democrat *Ingvar Carlsson* is new Prime Minister (March).

## FINLAND

### Early history

**Around the beginning of the Christian era** The Finns arrive from the east and by sea from the south into territories which are already inhabited.

**1st millennium** A.D. The main occupations are farming and stock-rearing. The settlers establish themselves along the coast and then move inland.

**6th–10th c.** Formation of the ethnic structure. Finland is occupied by three ethnic groups – in the southwest the true Finns, in the southern lake country the people of Häme or Tavaste, in the east the Karelians. – The **fur trade,** carried on by sea with the countries to the west and south, brings a measure of economic wellbeing. A farming nobility comes into being, but there is still no move towards a unified state.

### Finland under Swedish rule

**9th–13th c.** Sweden gains control of Finland and promotes the spread of **Christianity.**
There is evidence of a Christian population on the southwest coast about the year 1000. In a series of "crusades" in 1154, 1249 and 1293 Sweden extends its authority over the country and drives back the influence of Novgorod and the Orthodox Church, which had reached into central Finland. Roman Catholic bishops gain a leading role.

**1323** The treaty of Schlüsselburg divides Karelia between Novgorod and Finnish Sweden.

**14th c.** Finland becomes a **Swedish province** with the same rights as other parts of the country.
In 1362 Finland is given the right to vote in the election of the king, and later it sends representatives to the Swedish Riksdag. – During the period of Swedish rule Finnish national traditions are not suppressed, but neither are they fostered. Swedish is the language of government and of culture. Finland enjoys the advantages of being part of a powerful foreign state.

**1495–1595** Russian incursions.
The areas exposed to invasion are devastated, and maritime towns trade with Hanseatic towns suffers.

**1523** Introduction of the **Reformation.**
*Mikael Agricola's* translation of the New Testament (1548) becomes the foundation of the written language. Beginning of education for all children.

**1596–7** A peasant rising is ruthlessly repressed.

**1611–32** *Gustav II Adolf* (Gustavus Adolphus) king of Sweden. 1611–17: war with Russia; Gustavus Adolphus conquers territory on the shores of Lake

Ladoga. – Finnish troops fight in Germany as part of the Swedish army during the **Thirty Years War.**

1637–40 and 1648–54 Count *Per Brahe* is Swedish governor of Finland.
1640: foundation of the Academy (University) of Åbo (Turku), then capital; teaching is in Swedish.

1696–70 More than 100,000 people die of hunger and epidemics.

1700–1809 Swedish wars with Russia.
Finland is repeatedly devastated. The idea of separation from Sweden comes to the fore from time to time (1788–90, conspiracy by the Anjala association), but is always repressed. – 1808: Russian troops conquer the whole of Finland.

## Finland as part of Russia

1809 Finland becomes the Russian **Grand Duchy of Finland.** At the Diet of Borgå (Porvoo) in March 1809 Tsar *Alexander I* promises to maintain Finnish rights and privileges and receives homage as Grand Duke of Finland. Under the treaty of Fredrikshamn (Hamina), signed on 17 September, Sweden cedes the whole of Finland and the Åland Islands to Russia.

1811–12 The territories lost in 1721 and 1743, including Viborg (Viipuri), are reunited with Finland. Helsingfors (Helsinki) becomes capital.

1835 *Elias Lönnrot* publishes the Finnish national epic "Kalevala"

1880–1912 Suppression of Finnish self-government. 1891: postal services, customs and the currency are taken over by Russia. 1892: an Orthodox bishopric is established in Viborg. 1900: Russian becomes the language of government. 1903: the Finnish army is abolished. 1912: Finnish citizenship granted to Russians.

## Finland as an independent republic

1917 **Declaration of independence** (6 Dec.).
*P. E. Svinhufvud* becomes head of the government.

1918 **War of Liberation.**
In January Finnish Communists and Russian Bolsheviks occupy Helsinki and advance into the rest of the country. A Finnish volunteer army under General *C. G. von Mannerheim* (1867–1951), supported by German troops, defeats these forces in southern Finland in April and May. – General Mannerheim becomes Regent of Finland.

1919 Republican constitution.
*K. J. Ståhlberg* becomes first President of Finland.

1920 Treaty of Tartu (Dorpat).
Finland recognised as an independent state receives the area round Petsamo on the Arctic Ocean.

1919–21 The **Åland Islands** seek reunion with Sweden, but are assigned to Finland by the League of Nations. The islands are granted their own constitution and are demilitarised.

1922 Land reform.

1930–8 Finland's foreign policy is directed towards avoiding involvement in German or Soviet policies.

1939–40 The **Winter War** with the Soviet Union. The Soviet Union demands bases in southern Finland and terminates the non-aggression pact of 1932. War begins at the end of November 1939. Under the treaty of Moscow Finland is obliged to cede important territories to the Soviet Union

(including Viipuri and part of Karelia) and to lease Hanko to the Soviet Union.

1941–4 War renews with Soviet Union. Under the armistice agreement Finland loses the Petsamo area and leases Porkkala to the Soviet Union in place of Hanko. 480,000 Finns have to be resettled.

1944–6 *Marshal Mannerheim* President.

1946–56 *J. K. Paasikivi* President.

1947 The treaty of Paris confirms the agreements reached in the armistice.

1948 Treaty of friendship and mutual assistance with Soviet Union (in the first place for ten years).

1955 Finland becomes a member of the Nordic Council (see above under Denmark) and the UN.

1956 The Soviet base at Porkkala is returned to Finland. – *U. K. Kekkonen* becomes President.

1958 **Nordic Passport and Customs Union.**

1961 Finland becomes an associate member of the European Free Trade Association (EFTA).

1970 The treaty of friendship with the Soviet Union is extended for another 20 years.

1973 Finland establishes full diplomatic relations with Federal Germany and the German Democratic Republic. – Free trade agreements with the EEC.

1975 Final summit of the Conference of European Security and Co-operation in Helsinki (30 July–1 Aug.).

1978 New government of Social Democrats, the Centre Party, Liberals and Communists, excluding the Swedish People's Party.

1979 General election (March). The new government includes Social Democrats, Communists, the Centre (Agrarian) and the Swedish People's Party.

1980 Local elections in October give the Social Democrats 25·6%, the opposing Conservative National Collective Party 23·1% and the Country Party 18·8%, the Communist party suffers losses.

1981 Ratification in April of a "social package" avoids a government crisis. On 27 October the 81-year-old Urko Kaleva Kekkonen resigns as President of Finland on grounds of health. The head of the government (Social Democrat Party), takes over until new elections in January 1982.

1982 On 26 January Mauno Koivisto is officially elected as the new President. In February a government led by *Kalevi Sorsa*, the leader of the Social-Democrat Party, takes office. After a quarrel between the Communists and the four-party coalition about defence the cabinet is reshuffled (December).

1983 As a result of parliamentary elections (20/21 August) a new administration, composed of four parties is announced, with Kalevi Sorsa again at its head. Premature renewal of the Treaty of Friendship and Support with Russia (this was due for renewal in 1990, but will now last until 2003).

1984 The municipal elections result in only minor changes in party support; the dominant political power remains with the Social Democrats.

1985 Meeting of the Foreign Ministers of the 35 countries who signed the final communiqué of the Conference of European Security and Co-operation, on its tenth anniversary (31 July–2 August).

1986 In spring several thousand state employees strike for an increase in salaries and wages.

# Art

## SCANDINAVIA

The **Neolithic period**, during which the transition from a hunting culture to a settled farming culture took place and the pre-Indo-European peoples were steadily thrust back by the advancing Germanic tribes, lasted in Scandinavia until about 1800 B.C. The **Nordic culture**, which later spread into Central Europe, is known to us only through its pottery, of various types and in various styles. The two main groups, Megalithic ware and Single Grave or Corded ware, are founded in many local variations. In the Megalithic ware two broad trends can be distinguished – a Danish and a Swedish style. In Denmark four phases can be identified in the decoration of pottery:

The *Dolmen period*: ribs and scratched vertical lines.

The *early Passage Grave period*: a framework of horizontal and vertical lines formed by deep incisions.

The *late Passage Grave period*: the same type of framework decoration but more delicately executed and occasionally with overall patterns.

The *Stone Cist period*: a rapid decline in the standard of decoration.

To the Neolithic period belong also the realistic (earlier) or schematic (later) rock carvings of the **Arctic culture**, found mainly in Norway, which are ascribed to the pre-Indo-European population (the Arcto-Baltic culture). These carvings, mostly of the animals which were the hunters' prey but more rarely of human figures, were no doubt of magical significance, designed to bring luck in the chase.

The GERMANIC ART of Scandinavia covers a period of some 3000 years (1800 B.C. to A.D. 1200), with a sharp division between the Bronze Age and the early historical period of the first Christian centuries.

The **Bronze Age**, which dates in Scandinavia between 1800 and 600 B.C., offered fresh scope for technical and artistic development through the introduction of the new material, bronze (9 parts copper, 1 part tin). Weapons, implements and ornaments were now cast in stone and clay moulds, and in the Middle Bronze Age the *cire perdue* method came into use. The decoration was either cast in the mould or applied by the use of punches, engraving or hammering. As in the earlier period, pottery was made without the potter's wheel. The Nordic culture of the Bronze Age was undoubtedly developed by Germanic peoples, whose work in bronze was of a high technical and artistic standard. Four stylistic phases can be distinguished:

*Proto-Bronze Age:* rectilinear designs following the Neolithic traditions of the Nordic culture.

*Early Bronze Age:* transition to geometric spiral ornament.

*Middle Bronze Age:* the spiral ornament gives place to star patterns.

*Late Bronze Age:* the star patterns in turn are replaced by spiral whorls and bands of wavy lines; the decoration becomes less rigidly geometric and begins to incorporate vegetable forms (tendrils and foliage).

Rich assemblages of grave goods have been found in burial mounds, particularly at Uppsala and Seddin. The existence of a solar cult is reflected in numerous representations of solar discs, as in the Trundholm "sun chariot", a waggon-shaped cult utensil found in a bog near Nykøbing in 1902; 60 cm (2 ft) long, it dates from between 1500 and 1300 B.C.

Rock carvings at Tanum (southwest Sweden)

The representational art of the Bronze Age is known to us only in the Germanic rock carvings of southern Sweden and Norway – schematic figures of cultic significance, solemn processions, ritual contests, trains of sledges, ships, pilgrims. Although the detailed interpretation of these carvings is still the subject of dispute, they are undoubtedly connected with fertility rites. The Scandinavian carvings are among the finest of the kind to be found anywhere. There are also a number of figural representations on funerary monuments (the "King's Grave" at Kivik in Skåne).

The carvings depict solar wheels, weapons, schematic figures wearing cloaks or bound with chains; here too the interpretation of the figures is disputed.

In the **Iron Age**, which dates in Scandinavia from about 600 B.C. to A.D. 400, the decorative art of the Bronze Age disappears and is replaced by only the most modest attempts at ornament.

The magnificent silver cauldron found in a bog at Gundestrup, near Ålborg in Jutland (National Museum, Copenhagen), with half-length figures of deities on the outside and scenes of sacrifice on the inside, is thought to be a cult vessel of Celtic origin dating from about the beginning of the Christian era.

The second main period of Germanic art in Scandinavia, the **early historical period** of the first Christian centuries, saw a great flowering of artistic achievement, with a development from the simple filigree ornament of the first part of the period through a phase of decoration using inlaid coloured stones to the organic vigour of the animal style of ornament. From the 6th c. figural representations become more frequent. Four stages of development can be distinguished:

The *filigree style* (from the beginning of the Christian era to about A.D. 350): ornaments, particularly fibulas, decorated with gold or silver wire by the techniques of "flushing" or granulation.

The *"coloured" style*, using chip-carved ornament (A.D. 350–550). The Goths adopted decorative techniques of Iranian origin – inlays of precious stones (frequently garnets) and cloisonné enamel work. Chip-carving is a form of decoration in which small chips of triangular profile, meeting at an angle, are cut in the surface of the object. In Scandinavia the chips are usually cut in the body of the metal with a burin. Originally, no doubt, taken over from wood-carving, the technique is still used in folk art.

*Abstract animal ornament* and interlace patterns (A.D. 550–800). The earliest form, **Animal Style I**, is characterised by animal figures so fantastically articulated that they sometimes disintegrate altogether. The heads, often consisting only of semicircular eye apertures, are juxtaposed to form mosaic-like patterns. A later form of the style, **Animal Style II**, incorporating interlace ornament of

South German type, became the main type of animal ornament on the European continent. In **Animal Style III**, which developed in Scandinavia about 700, highly abstract animal figures are used to form elaborate ornamental compositions, producing for example circular whorls or mirror-image pairs. Here again the burin was used.

The *Viking style* or late animal style (A.D. 800–1100). The great Viking expansion was made possible by their keeled boats, with strengthened bottoms to take the mast and keel, like those found in a bog at Nydam in Slesvig (three sea-going boats dating from the 4th c., the largest being an open oared boat 25 m (82 ft) long which could accommodate a crew of 40 men) and at Kvalsund. Other important finds were made in the Nydam bog, in particular 38 silver objects with ornamental birds' and human heads, Anglian products of the 5th c. (Museum of Prehistory, Schloss Gottorf, Schleswig).

An impressive example of the new type of keeled boat is the Oseberg Ship, used as the tomb of a Norwegian princess (Norwegian Folk Museum, Bygdøy, Oslo). This vessel, 22 m (72 ft) long, with carved animal ornament on the prow and stern, contains a timber burial chamber, beside which were found a waggon, several sledges, furniture and remains of clothing and woven carpets. A magnificent animal-head post is decorated with two superimposed ornamental systems in the **"gripping beast"** style, also known as the Oseberg style. The date of the burial is put around 850.

A further example of the type is the Gokstad Ship from the Kongshaugen area in Norway (Norwegian Folk Museum, Oslo). This 24 m (79 ft) long vessel, clinker-built of oak, contained the body of a man lying fully clad on a splendid funeral couch, with rich grave goods.

In contrast to the Oseberg style, which was probably influenced by Carolingian art, is the more abstract **Jelling style** (900–1100), which shows the influence of the Celtic animal ornament of Ireland and later of Anglo-Saxon art. The outstanding example of this style is the runic stone of Harald Bluetooth at Jelling (c. 985), the finest surviving piece of Viking sculpture, which already shows Christian influence in a figure of Christ on one face, with a lion devouring a snake on another.

Also at Jelling is a stone erected for King Gorm (*c.* 980). Of rather later date are the runic stones of Stenkyrka on Gotland (*c.* 1000), Lundagård (Lund) and Tulstorp in Skåne. The characteristic animal is the "great beast", a beast of prey with spiral limbs and a massive mane.

With the final victory of Christianity the animal style disappeared: the last examples date from about 1100 (stave church at Urnes in Norway, *c.* 1090; Swedish runic stones). Figural decoration is relatively rare, and the gold bracteates of the 6th c. (ornamental discs, usually pendants, often decorated only on one side, with figural representations) were an isolated phenomenon. Then in the 7th c. we find small figural representations on helmet mountings (Vendel and Torskinda, Sweden) depicting deities and cultic scenes, such as the figure of Wotan as a horseman carrying a lance (helmet from Vendel).

In ICELAND there was a great flowering of this northern Germanic art. Notable examples are found on the carved doorways of the stave churches, like the one from Valthjofstad (11th–12th c.) in the Reykjavik Museum.

Until the beginning of the Christian period in Scandinavia, however, there is little artistic progress to record. The adoption of Christianity (*c.* 1000) marked the terminal point of Viking art, and the stone churches which were now built displayed the power of the new faith. These churches, the best preserved monuments of the **Romanesque period**, were originally simple buildings in limestone, later in granite. The finest – aisled basilicas with two west towers influenced by the cathedrals of the Rhineland – are the cathedrals of Lund (now in Sweden but architecturally belonging to Denmark), Viborg and Ribe (both in Denmark). Viborg Cathedral, however, was so heavily restored in the 19th c. that it can rank only as a modern copy of the style. The village churches were influenced by the great cathedrals, as can be seen for example in the churches of Tveje Merløse (with beehive-shaped spires on its towers) and Fjenneslev (*c.* 1140). The Swedish churches of the 12th and 13th c. are usually simpler. There are also a number of round churches, particularly on Gotland (Church of the Holy Ghost and St Lars' Church in Visby, both of about 1260) and hall churches influenced by

Borgund stave church (southwest Sweden)

those of Westphalia. Another notable church is that of Varnhem (*c.* 1200).

The **STAVE CHURCHES**, found mainly in Norway, are timber-built structures on a framework of vertical posts which show the influence of shipbuilding techniques. They are not merely an imitation of masonry construction in wood but a deliberately developed architectural form, with a large internal space which may derive from the old royal hall of the Scandinavian kings. The gables with their dragons' heads recall the prows of the Viking ships. Some 30 stave churches have survived in Norway: see the entry "Stave churches" in this Guide.

Brick building came in about 1160. Tradition has it that the Dannevirke, the defensive wall built by Valdemar the Great, was the first purely brick structure in Scandinavia. Roskilde Cathedral (begun about 1160), the burial-place of the Danish kings, was completed in the **Gothic style**, now following French and Spanish rather than German models. After the great burst of building activity in the 12th c. there is relatively little in the way of Gothic architecture in Denmark. Mention should be made of the Cistercian church of Sorø (1161–81) and the Church of Our Lady at Kalundborg, with its five towers and central plan. The influence of the brick-built Gothic churches of northern Germany can be seen in St Peter's (*c.* 1400) in Malmö, St Mary's and St Olaf's in Helsingør, St Knud's (1301) in Odense, with its elegant interior, Århus Cathedral and St Peter's in Næstved (completed about 1370).

Only a very few secular buildings of this period have been preserved; these include the Goose Tower at Vordingborg (*c.* 1350), a remnant of an imposing fortress built by Valdemar Atterdag, and the little castle of Gjorslev (Zealand), on a Greek cross plan.

In Sweden the churches of the Gothic period tend to be rather low and squat. For large-scale buildings foreign masons were brought in, as in the construction of the Gothic choir of Linköping Cathedral (by Master Gerlach of Cologne). The second main work of the Gothic period is Uppsala Cathedral (begun about 1250). Considerably later in date are St Birgitta's Church at Vadstena (1388–1430) and St Peter's in Malmö (*c*. 1400).

In Norway the stone churches of both the Romanesque period (Stavanger Cathedral, *c*. 1130; Lyse Cathedral, begun 1146) and the Gothic period (Trondheim Cathedral, rebuilding begun 1152) follow English models.

The medieval painting of Scandinavia achieves no very distinctive character of its own (altar frontals at Hitterdal, Kinsarvik, Nes, Dale and Årdal, all dating from 1250 to 1350), and is represented mainly by wall and ceiling paintings in churches – at Jelling, Sæby and Hjørlunde (Zealand), Næstved, Roskilde and Århus Cathedrals, Kettinge (Maribo) and Kjeldby (St Andrew's Church) in Denmark, and Vä Vidtskofte, Strängnäs and Härkeberga in Sweden.

Norwegian sculpture is also of no particular distinction: the carving on the stave churches is a survival of older Germanic traditions, and in the later medieval period Norway imported sculpture from the Netherlands, the Lübeck area (winged altarpieces) and England. Danish Romanesque sculpture, on the other hand, is represented by a remarkable variety of work – crucifixes at Åby and Lisbjerg (*c*. 1100), doorways in Ålborg Cathedral (*c*. 1150), tombstones and some 1500 granite fonts (the splendid "lion fonts" of Jutland; a beautifully ornamented font at Åkirkeby on Bornholm bearing the runic signature of the sculptor). Particularly notable are the so called "golden altars" of this period (e.g. an altar of around 1150 at Lisbjerg) – magnificent examples of the goldsmith's craft, with a profusion of figures and ornament.

Gothic sculpture now increasingly finds expression in wood and ivory rather than stone, and it is often difficult to decide whether a particular item is of French or Danish workmanship (crucifix at Herlufsholm, 1250). Later Danish sculpture of the Gothic period is under strong German influence, the most notable examples of this being the altarpiece in Århus Cathedral by *Bernt Notke* (*c*. 1440–1509) and the huge altarpiece by *Claus Berg* (*c*. 1470–after 1532) in the Greyfriars church (now St Knud's) in Odense.

Sweden too imported much sculpture from Lübeck from the end of the 14th c., when English and French influence gave place to that of Germany and the Netherlands. Bernt Notke's masterpiece, the St George group, was created for the Storkyrka in Stockholm. Norway also imported sculpture from Lübeck and later from the Netherlands and England (alabaster reliefs).

During the **Renaissance** and **Baroque** periods little work of significance was produced in Norway, gifted artists, such as the architect L. van Haven and the sculptor M. Berg, being drawn away to the Danish court. In Sweden after the Reformation church building took second place to the building of castles (Gripsholm, 1573; Vadstena, mainly 17th c.). The style of the Lombard Renaissance was brought to Sweden in the 16th c. by German architects. The finest castle built in the 17th c., largely based on Dutch models, was Drottningholm, the royal summer residence, on Lake Mälar. It was begun in 1662 by the Swedish architect *Nicodemus Tessin the Elder* (1616–after 1685). Other notable buildings of this period are the Palace in Stockholm, in Roman High Baroque, begun by *Nicodemus Tessin the Younger* (1654–88), with an 18th c. interior; Kalmar Cathedral, by the two Tessins; and Skokloster Castle, near Uppsala (1654–5).

Trolleholm Castle (originally 16th c.) in Skåne

Danish architecture of the Renaissance and Baroque periods came under Dutch and German influence: Kronborg Castle, Helsingør (1574–84); Frederiksborg Castle on Zealand (1602–22, by H. von Steenwinkel and A. von Opbergen); and, in Copenhagen, Dyvekes Hus (1616), the Exchange (1619–25), the Trinity Church (1632–56) and Christiansborg Palace (1731–40), by *Elias David Häusser* (1687–1745). Copenhagen was planned as a fortified town of the Baroque period, and *Nicolai Eigtved* (1701–54) laid out the Amalienborg quarter, bringing the French **Rococo** style to Denmark but imparting to it his own distinctive note of cool elegance (Prince's Palace, now the National Museum: modelled on the Hôtel de Ville in Paris).

In Sweden and Denmark sculpture was at first largely the work of Dutch sculptors; in the 18th c. the predominance passed to French sculptors. Particularly notable were funerary monuments such as those of Gustavus Vasa (1580) in Uppsala Cathedral and Gabriel Gustafson Oxenstierna in the church at Tyresö (1641) and statues, of which the equestrian statue of Gustavus Adolphus (1796) in Stockholm is a good example.

With *Johan Tobias Sergel* (1740–1814), who was also an excellent draughtsman, the **classical style** established itself; his best works are in the National Museum in Stockholm. In Denmark there were the Dutch sculptor Adriaen de Vries (*c.* 1560–1626: Neptune Fountain, Frederiksborg Castle) and the French sculptors Abraham C. L'Amoureux (d. 1692: equestrian statue of Christian V in Kongens Nytorv, Copenhagen) and Jacques-François Saly (1717–76: Equestrian statue of Frederik V).

Swedish painting is notable particularly for the interior decoration of Kalmar Castle and the Palace in Stockholm (by J. B. van Uther) and the work of *Holger Hansson* (fl. 1586–1619), *Ottomar Elliger the Elder* (1633–79), *Johan Sylvius* (d. 1695), the Hamburg artist David Klöcker von Ehrenstrahl (1629–98), the Flemish family of van Mytens or Meytens, *Alexander Roslin* (1718–93), *Gustaf Lundberg* (1696–1796) and *C. G. Pilo* (1711–93). Among Danish painters were *Jakob Binck* (born *c.* 1500), Hans Knieper (d. 1587) of Antwerp and Karel van Mander (1605–70).

Classical-style architecture left its mark on Copenhagen in the range of buildings linking the Amalienborg palaces, by *Kaspar Fredrik Harsdorff* (1735–99) and his pupil *Christian Fredrik Hansen* (1756–1845). Building took place from 1794 onwards.

*Theophil Hansen* (1813–91), a representative of the school known as **Historicism** (neo-classicism), designed Athens University and some imposing buildings on the Ring in Vienna. *Martin Nyrop* (1849–1921) built the Town Hall in Copenhagen, and together with *Peter Vilhelm Jensen-Klint* (1853–1930: Grundtvig Church, Copenhagen) developed new architectural forms. *M. G. Bindesbøll* (1800–56) designed the Thorvaldsen Museum to house the work of *Bertel Thorvaldsen* (1770–1844), Denmark's greatest sculptor, who ranks with Antonio Canova and Asmus Jakob Carstens as a representative of the ideals of neo-classicism in their purest form but also displays the weaknesses of the style; among his finest works is the figure of Christ in the Church of Our Lady in Copenhagen. Other sculptors of the period were *H. V. Bissen* (1798–1868) and *J. A. Jerichau* (1816–83).

Notable examples of Swedish architecture are the Old Opera House (by F. Adelcrantz, 1716–96), the Exchange (by E. Palmstedt, 1741–1803) and the interior of the Palace (by C. Hårlemann, 1700–53), all in Stockholm. Sculptors included, in addition to J. T. Sergel, *J. N. Byström* (1783–1848), *B. E. Fogelberg* (1786–1854) and *Per Hasselberg* (1850–94).

Norway produced very fine work in the field of folk art, which indeed flourished throughout Scandinavia, notable in the rustic "rose painting". The heyday of rustic painting in southern Sweden was between 1750 and 1850 (Dalarna, Gästrikland, Helsingland). The painted wall hangings produced mainly for festive occasions were mostly of cloth or paper; wall and ceiling painting was practised in the north.

In the 19th c. many Swedish painters went to Düsseldorf and later to Paris for training. Notable among them were the landscape artist *C. J. Fahlcrantz* (1774–1861), Peter Krafft the Younger, a German (1777–1863), *C. Wahlbom*

(1810–58), *A. Wahlberg* (1834–1906) and above all the greatest of modern Swedish painters, *Anders Zorn* (1860–1920), who also produced etchings.

In Denmark, where landscape painting was a favourite genre, impressive and original work was done by *Jens Juel* (1745–1802), *N. A. Abildgaard* (1743–1809) and *Christopher Wilhelm Eckersberg* (1783–1853). Eckersberg in particular influenced the next generation of painters. About 1800 the Copenhagen Academy attracted many German painters, among them the neo-classicist A. J. Carstens and the Romantic artists P. O. Runge and C. D. Friedrich. *Christen Købke* (1810–58) took up the inheritance of C. W. Eckersberg, and among a large number of lesser artists the names of *Vilhelm Marstrand* (1810–73) and *Kristian Zahrtmann* (1843–1917) may be mentioned. Two notable figures at the end of the 19th c. were *Vilhelm Hammershøi* (1864–1916) and *Peter Severin Krøyer* (1851–1909), the latter a practitioner of **Impressionism**. *Joakim Skovgaard* (1856–1916) renewed the art of monumental religious painting (frescoes in Viborg Cathedral).

Scandinavia has played a prominent role in *20th c. architecture*. During the 1920s and 1930s a "close to the earth" style of architecture was popular – family houses, terraced houses, the *bakkehuse* ("hill houses") of the Danish architect *Ivar Bentsen* (1876–1943). The international **Functionalism** of *Gunnar Asplund* (1885–1940), however, made increasing headway, with such buildings as the exhibition halls for the Stockholm Exhibition of 1930 (light, airy structures of glass and steel), Stockholm Municipal Library (1924–7) and an extension of Göteborg (Gothenburg) Town Hall (1934–7). *Sven Markehus* built the Concert Hall in Helsingborg (1936). The ideas of the Swedish Arts and Crafts Association on modern design were the starting point of a distinctive Scandinavian school of interior decoration and the design of everyday articles and utensils.

The basic types of housing developed in Sweden were various forms of tower block (Örebro, 1948–50; Danviksklippen, by S. Backström and L. Reinius, 1945). The best known of Stockholm's satellite towns is Vällingby.

Perhaps the best known Danish architect was *Arne Jacobsen* (1902–71), who was responsible for new town halls at Århus (1941) and Mainz (1969).

Among leading Danish sculptors of the 20th c. are *Robert Jacobsen* (b. 1917), who works in metal; *Kai Nielsen* (1882–1924), creator of a new monumental style; *Bengt Sørensen* (b. 1923), *Gunnar Westmann* (b. 1915) and *Svend W. Hansen* (b. 1922). The youngest generation of sculptors follows current post-war trends.

The leading Swedish sculptor of this century is *Carl Milles* (1875–1955). Others include *Carl Johan Eld* (1873–1954) and *Johannes Collin* (1873–1951). The most recent generation frequently breaks through the boundary between sculpture and painting.

Notable Norwegian sculptors are *Stephan Sinding* (1846–1922) and *Gustaf Vigeland* (1869–1943: sculpture in Frogner Park, Oslo), both trained in France.

Norwegian painters also have impressive achievements to their credit; among them the 19th c. Romantic painter *Johan Christian Dahl* (1788–1857) and his pupil Thomas Fearnley (1802–42). *J. F. Eckersberg* and *Hans Gude* (1825–1903) were associated with the Düsseldorf

Sculpture by Carl Milles in the Millesgård, Stockholm

school; *Gerhard Munthe* (1849–1929), *Erik Werenskiold* (1855–1938) and Christian Krogh followed French models. One Norwegian painter of international importance was *Edvard Munch* (1863–1944), who is regarded as the founder of **Expressionism**, though he did not carry the movement through to its logical conclusion. In his later work he turned away from the gloomier sides of life (*angst*, illness, death, the struggle of the sexes) to more positive themes. He also achieved remarkable effects in his graphic work.

Among the older Danish painters of the present day mention may be made of *Richard Mortensen* (b. 1910), perhaps the richest talent among the abstract artists who show affinities with Expressionism, and *Asger Oluf Jorn* (actually Jørgensen: b. 1914). Painters of the younger generation have an international outlook and are trying to break through the artistic isolation of Denmark, with financial support from the government Art Foundation.

The older generation of modern Swedish painters included, in addition to Anders Zorn, *Carl Larsson* (1853–1919), author of delightful books for children, the animal painter *Bruno Liljefors* (1860–1939), *L. Engström* (1886–1927), *O. Baerteling* and *C. O. Hultén*. About 1930 *O. G. Carlsund* brought abstract art to Sweden; and in the 1950s the Hungarian painter E. Nemes was the leader of the Valand school. The younger generation, which is no longer bound by the traditional laws of art, includes *Olle Kåks* (b. 1941); *J. Franzén* (b. 1942) and *Ola Billgren* (b. 1940), who belong to the school of **Photo-Realism**; *Lars Englund* (b. 1933), who creates "volumes" made of rubber or plastic; *Hans Nordenström* (b. 1927: collages); and *Arne Jones* (b. 1914), who works with mobiles and "light sculpture" (the "Expanderator").

## FINLAND

Although the Finns are not of Germanic origin but moved into Finland from the Baltic area in the early years of the Christian era, driving back the Lapps, the development of their art in the early and medieval periods was closely connected with that of other northern European countries.

The churches, apart from the stave churches, were mostly built of undressed stone with a steeply pitched saddle roof and a separate tower. The interior, with a vaulted roof and usually aisled, was decorated in the late medieval period with wall and ceiling paintings. Examples are the 15th c. church at Lohja, near Helsinki, and Turku Cathedral (begun in the 13th c.; choir 14th c.; enlarged in the 15th c.).

Artists from the Hanseatic towns worked in Finland as in other Scandinavian countries; examples of their work are the 15th c. brasses on St Henry's tomb at Nousiainen and the St Barbara altar by Master Francke (*c*. 1410: National Museum, Helsinki). The Finnish fortified castles are of imposing monumental effect (Viipuri, now in the Soviet Union; Turku, *c*. 1300; Olofsburg, Savonlinna, *c*. 1475).

After the Reformation there was only a very limited amount of church building, mostly wooden churches which either imitated the medieval stone churches with a nave or had a cruciform plan with arms of equal length and a central dome. The interior was decorated in popular style by local artists, as at Salvinen (1632), Padasjoki (1675) and Kanhava (1756).

In the 18th c. there developed alongside this folk art a modest aristocratic and middle-class art (manor-houses and burghers' houses; portrait painting).

Helsinki, capital of Finland from 1812, was given a neo-classical aspect by the Berlin architect Johann Carl Ludwig Engel (1778–1840) in the first half of the 19th c.; but the present city is notable for the buildings designed by contemporary Finnish architects.

Finnish painting also began to develop in the 18th c., at first under German influence (Ekman, 1808–73; Holmberg, 1830–60) and later under French influence (Edelfelt, 1853–1905). Around 1900 a distinctive national style began to develop, particularly in the work of *Axeli Gallén-Kallela* (1865–1931: illustrations for the Finnish national epic "Kalevala") and *Tyko Constantin Sallinen* (b. 1879).

A sculptor of outstanding quality was *Väinö Aaltonen* (1894–1966).

After the romantic "national" architecture at the end of the 19th c. (National Museum, Helsinki) Finnish architecture developed the clear, calm forms which have established its international reputation. In spite of its uncompromisingly progressive approach, however, it has remained in tune with the harshness and austerity of the northern landscape. The pioneer of modern Finnish architecture was *Eliel Saarinen* (1873–1950: Central Station, Helsinki, designed 1904), who, like other Finnish architects, later worked in the United States. No less important was the work of his son, *Eero Saarinen* (1910–61: General Motors Technical Center, Warren, Michigan, 1950; MIT Auditorium, Cambridge, Mass., 1955; Yale University hockey rink, New Haven, Connecticut, 1958; TWA Terminal, Kennedy Airport, New York, 1962; Gateway Arch, St Louis, 1965).

Another architect of international reputation was *Alvar Aalto* (1898–1976), who concerned himself particularly with the effect of colour ("red" and "white" periods). His work in Finland included a sanatorium at Paimio (1930), the Viipuri Library (1927–34: now in the Soviet Union), the Mairea housing estate in Norrmark (1938–9), the Finnish pavilion at the New York International Exposition of 1939, the Palace of Culture in Helsinki (1955–8) and the Town Hall of Säynätsalo (1951–2).

Notable architects of the younger generation are *K.* and *H. Siren* (husband and wife: Forest Church, Otaniemi, 1956–7), *A. Ervi* (b. 1910: Community Complex, Tapiola garden city), *J. Järvi* (Grammar School, Helsinki) and *V. Rewell* (1910–64: nursery school, Tapiola, 1954; Toronto City Hall).

## LAPLAND

The Lapps (Same or Samians), whose ethnic origin is the subject of dispute but who are probably part Mongol, live in northern Sweden, Norway and Finland and in Karelia (part of which is in the Soviet Union). Their semi-nomadic way of life, focused on reindeer herding, which is now gradually being abandoned, has produced a rich and distinctive *folk art*; but this, like folk traditions in other countries, is threatened by the progress of modern life.

# Economy

Reflecting their varied geological and climatic conditions, the economies of the four Scandinavian countries differ considerably from one another.

**DENMARK,** which until the end of the Second World War was typical of an agricultural country with a low degree of industrialisation, has undergone a radical transformation in the last twenty years, particularly since it became a member of the European Community in January 1973. Industrial development, promoted by massive investment programmes, is drawing younger people away from the land into the towns and is leading to a progressively older agricultural population. This trend is accompanied by a sharp reduction in the number of small holdings and in the area under cultivation. Pig breeding has declined significantly in favour of cattle and poultry, while flower-growing and the production of vegetables have considerably increased. There are also about 2500 mink farms in Denmark, most of which are associated with agricultural concerns.

The fishing industry (canned and deep frozen products), once quite prosperous, has been facing growing problems in recent years. The rise in fuel costs, the unilateral extension of fishing zones by some countries, and falling fish stocks in the heavily fished waters of the North Sea and western Baltic, have led to fierce competition. The largest fishing port is Esbjerg on the west coast of Jutland.

Entry into the Common Market has almost doubled Denmark's industrial production. The most significant part of Danish industry, however, is still in the processing of the country's agricultural produce. In the wider industrial field, too, Denmark's lack of raw materials has confined it to the processing industries (machinery, hardware, shipping, furniture, glass, porcelain, textiles, leather, rubber and timber products, chemicals and pharmaceuticals, etc.). The country's main industrial concentrations are around Copenhagen (with some 40% of the total industrial labour force), Odense, Århus and Ålborg-Norresundby.

In communications, Denmark is an important bridge between the Scandinavian countries and continental Europe, though it is hampered in this role by its considerable geographical fragmentation. It depends, therefore, on an excellent network of shipping and ferry services and, in more recent times, air services.

The main arteries of road and rail traffic are, to the west, the north–south route through eastern Jutland and, to the east, the north–south route by way of Lolland and Zealand, which is continued into West Germany by the Fugleflugtslinie ("Bird's Flight Line"). A transverse connection is provided by the west–east route over the Great and Little Belts and island of Funen.

Communications within Denmark depend on a series of major bridges, causeways and tunnels. The most ambitious project is the plan for a bridge or tunnel across the Öresund, a joint Danish-Swedish enterprise which – if carried out – will provide the basis for the largest industrial and commercial concentration in Scandinavia, extending along both sides of the Sound. – The hub of international air traffic in Scandinavia is Copenhagen's Kastrup Airport.

Denmark's principal trading partners are the countries of the European Community, especially West Germany and Great Britain, as well as Sweden, Norway and Finland. The country has an adverse balance of trade. In order to minimise its dependence on foreign sources of energy efforts have been made for some years to provide alternative sources of energy. The Danes have been especially successful in utilising the power of the wind.

In **NORWAY** neither geology nor climate are favourable to agriculture, and only just over 3% of the country's area is suitable for cultivation. In southern Norway corn and potatoes are grown, often unprofitably; farther north cattle-raising predominates, and in the extreme north there is reindeer herding. Goats, formerly reared in large numbers, are now giving way to cattle and pigs, and the traditional method of cattle farming, in which the cattle grazed in summer on the mountain pastures, is being replaced by cooperative dairy farming. A developing branch of agriculture is fur-farming (fox, mink). Arable farming is of relatively little significance in Norway, and is a long way from being able to meet the country's needs.

Approximately a quarter of the country's area is covered by forests producing usable timber (pine, spruce; in the north and at higher altitudes birch). The annual growth of timber is much greater than the rate of felling, so that there is room for expansion in this field.

The Norwegian fisheries have long been of central importance to the country's economy, and the intricately patterned coastline provides excellent fishing grounds. A high proportion of the catch is sold on the international market in the form of canned, dried or deep-frozen fish. The number of small fishing boats has declined sharply in favour of larger and better equipped vessels, and for the "part-time" fishermen whose main source of income lies elsewhere, fishing is a seasonal occupation. The fish-processing industry, as might be expected, is concentrated around the principal fishing ports – Stavanger, Bergen, Ålesund, Kristiansund, Bodø, Harstad, Tromsø and Hammerfest. The excellent salmon caught in Norway's mountain rivers have a world-wide market.

Norway has numerous but relatively small deposits of minerals – silver and copper (worked since the 17th c.), iron, pyrites, titanium, molybdenum, antimony and nickel. The coal required for smelting comes from Spitzbergen.

In 1968 very large fields of oil and natural gas were discovered in the North Sea off the Norwegian coasts, and these are now being worked. Additional large reserves of natural gas – comparable in size, on a conservative estimate, with those of the Arabian peninsula – have been discovered recently 150 km (95 miles) from Bergen. Thanks to these huge resources of energy, and to the large water power resources already available in northern Norway, numbers of new industries have been established, particularly along the coast. A notable achievement associated with the working of North Sea oil is the huge platform in the Ekofisk field known as Ekofiskbyen, with living accommodation and supply facilities, from which there is an oil pipeline to Teesside in the north of England and also a gas pipeline to Emden in West Germany. In 1980 the supply platform "Alexander Kielland" capsized. As a result of the discovery of oil off the coast, Norwegian

Oil rig off Stavanger

shipyards have switched to the construction of giant tankers and drilling rigs.

The building of roads and railways in Norway, with its rocky and mountainous topography, is an expensive process, involving major engineering works (bridges, tunnels, protection against snow), costly maintenance, and the provision of ferry services. The only through road from south to north (interrupted by numerous ferries) is E6, which runs from Oslo via Trondheim and Narvik to Tromsø and Hammerfest. The railway system is adequate only in the south of the country; in the north it is replaced by buses.

Norway's international airport is Fornebu, near Oslo, and there is an extensive and efficient network of domestic air services.

Norway's principal trading partner is Sweden, followed by Britain, West Germany, the United States, Canada and, recently, Japan. As a member of the European Free Trade Association (EFTA), Norway has a customs agreement with the EEC. A good 50% of Norway's total exports consists of oil and gas and approximately one-sixth is in ships and ship fittings. Then come metal ores, metals, wood, paper and paper products, fish and fish products and chemical goods. The main imports are machinery and vehicles, salt for preserving fish, and foodstuffs.

At the beginning of the 1980s the success of the Norwegian oil and gas fields led to a sustained improvement in the economy of the country, which was accompanied by increased investment, a reduction in unemployment and measures to strengthen international competitiveness. However, in the middle of the 80s, there was a drop in the price of oil, caused by the state of the world market, which was to the disadvantage of Norway.

**SWEDEN** is one of the most prosperous nations in the world, and in social terms is perhaps the most progressive. This is the result of a long period of peace which allowed a slow but steady advance and of the country's abundance of mineral resources and water power, which provided the basis for an early and rapid development of industry.

Sweden has large deposits of iron ore in Lapland with a 60–70% iron content as well as zinc, lead, pyrites, copper, manganese, silver and gold. The coalfields in western Skåne, now depleted, led to the development of industries in that region which must now use imported coal. New hydroelectric power stations are being built in northern Sweden, but with the demand for power continually rising, it is necessary to import electricity from Norway. As in other countries there is controversy over the use of nuclear power. The main industrial activity is in the metal-processing, particularly the manufacture of machinery, motor vehicles, aircraft and shipbuilding, followed by the manufacture of timber products, paper and cellulose, glass, textiles and foodstuffs.

Agriculture in Sweden is of subordinate importance, although efforts are being made to develop a substantial measure of self-sufficiency. Barely 10% of the country's area is suitable for cultivation – primarily the low-lying regions in southern and central Sweden which are devoted to the growing of corn, sugar-beet and, increasingly, vegetables. Farther north, as a result of the climatic conditions, arable farming gives place to stock-farming, which in Lapland is confined to reindeer herding. The drift of population from the land continues, but is compensated by the adoption of more efficient farming methods and an increase in the size of holdings.

More than half the country is covered by coniferous forest, at altitudes above 500 m (1650 ft), in the north by birches, and in the south also by mixed forest. The resources of the forests are very far from being fully exploited, since new growth still exceeds felling; but the fierce competition in world markets appears for the present to stand in the way of further expansion.

Swedish fisheries in the North Sea and the Baltic are of no more than regional importance. The fish are sold fresh on the domestic market.

Much attention has been devoted in Sweden to the development of the country's communications. It has long had a high proportion of motor vehicles to population, and has excellent roads reaching far into the north of the country. The railway system has been reduced in recent years by the closing of certain lines. Coastal shipping is of great importance to trade with Sweden's Baltic neighbours, and the country's main concentrations of industry lie around the great ports of Gothenburg, Stockholm, Helsingborg and Malmö.

The principal airports are Arlanda and Bromma (for Stockholm), Torslanda, Gothenburg (Göteborg) and Bulltofta (Malmö).

Swedish glass

Sweden's principal trading partner is West Germany, followed by Britain, Norway, Denmark, the United States, Finland, Holland, France, Belgium and Luxembourg, Italy and the Soviet Union. Trade with the USA has been increased. The main exports are finished products, particularly machinery, ships and motor vehicles (which together account for 40% of total exports), followed by paper, timber and cellulose products (15–20%). The principal imports are raw materials (coal, oil).

Sweden is a member of the European Free Trade Association (EFTA), and has a customs agreement with the EEC.

Growth in the economy has slowed up in Sweden. Priority has been given to exports. By price controls the government has sought on several occasions to keep down the rate of inflation. The unemployment situation has been improved.

Rafts of timber at Joensuu (northern Karelia)

The economy of **FINLAND** depends on its extraordinary wealth of forests. Fully 70% of its area is covered by coniferous forest, which provides the raw material for a flourishing paper, cardboard and cellulose industry, the manufacture of prefabricated houses and furniture and the production of cut timber and plywood. Timber and timber products account for some two-thirds of the total volume of exports and are by far the largest source of revenue.

Only some 8% of the total area of Finland is suitable for cultivation, and all the suitable land lies to the south of a line running southeast from the north end of the Gulf of Bothnia. Because of the severe climate the major form of agriculture is stock-farming. The stock of cattle and pigs is sufficient to meet the country's needs; imports and exports of agricultural produce are roughly in balance.

Finland has some mineral resources, with iron ore (in Lapland and central Finland), copper, chromium, vanadium, sulphur, zinc, cobalt, nickel and uranium on a sufficient scale to be economically workable. The need to pay reparations to the Soviet Union after the Second World War led to the development of an efficient heavy industry using these mineral resources, now concentrated mainly around Helsinki and specialising in the manufacture of machinery for use in polar regions.

The hydroelectric resources of northern Finland are not sufficient to meet the country's needs, so it is necessary to import considerable quantities of oil and electric power. Finland has an oil refinery and two nuclear power stations.

The principal means of transport is boat. Some 90% of the country's freight traffic goes by water, and within Finland rafts are still frequently used as an economical means of transport (although now to some extent being superseded by trucks). The main transhipment points are the new port of Naantali (near Turku), Turku itself, Helsinki and Hamina. There are important ferry services between Helsinki and Stockholm, Turku and Stockholm, Helsinki and Travemünde (Lübeck) in Germany, and Vaasa and northern Sweden.

In southern Finland the road system is dense and of excellent quality, but in the north it is still not fully developed. The railway system, mostly single-track and broad-gauge, is primarily used for traffic with the Soviet Union, but there is also a rail ferry service to Sweden.

Finland has an international airport at Helsinki and an efficient network of domestic services which reach into the remotest parts of the country. Fares are very reasonable.

For a long time Finland's principal trading partners have been Sweden and the Soviet Union, followed by West Germany, Britain, the United States, Holland, France and Denmark. The main exports to the West are timber and timber products (particularly paper), and to the Eastern bloc metal products. Finland's main imports are raw materials and capital and consumer goods.

Finland's economic policies are dictated by its situation between the two economic blocs formed by the EEC and the Communist countries. In an effort to maintain balanced trading relationships with both blocs and to achieve industrial diversification – which in view of Finland's dependence on the timber industry has long been desirable – loose trading agreements have been concluded with both sides. Although the principle of the free market economy is still maintained, the country's key industries have in fact been nationalised through majority government shareholding. Since the government has not subsidised the "old industries", the economy of the country has been able to come to terms relatively quickly with the changed conditions of world trade. The number of unemployed has decreased and taxes are not as high as in Sweden.

**Tourism.** – The state of tourism in the Scandinavian countries is generally satisfactory. Their hotels have a limited bed capacity, and the emphasis of the tourist trade is on holiday villages and camping. In Denmark there are holiday hotels and centres which provide a variety of holiday arrangements.

The summer season is short (July–August), and the weather tends to be uncertain. Popular areas for seaside vacations in Denmark are the entire North Sea coast and northern Zealand, whose dune-fringed coast is already suffering the effects of development. In Sweden there are beach resorts scattered along the west coast from the Kullen hills to the Norwegian hills and also on the islands of Gotland and Öland. The lakes of central Sweden also attract many visitors. In Finland the unspoiled lakeland plains are a particular attraction for nature lovers.

Winter sports areas which used to be frequented almost exclusively by Scandinavians are now becoming increasingly popular with visitors from abroad. They are to be found in the Jotunheim and Rondane regions in Norway and in central Sweden and Lapland.

A popular form of vacation is a cruise up the Norwegian coast to the North Cape, stopping at a succession of beautiful fjords on the way. They generally follow the "Hurtigrute" (express route) of the mail boats which make the 2300 km (1430 mile) long passage between Bergen in the south and Kirkenes in the north.

Timber house in Finnish Lapland

# Scandinavia
# A to Z

Copenhagen – Christiansborg Palace from the air

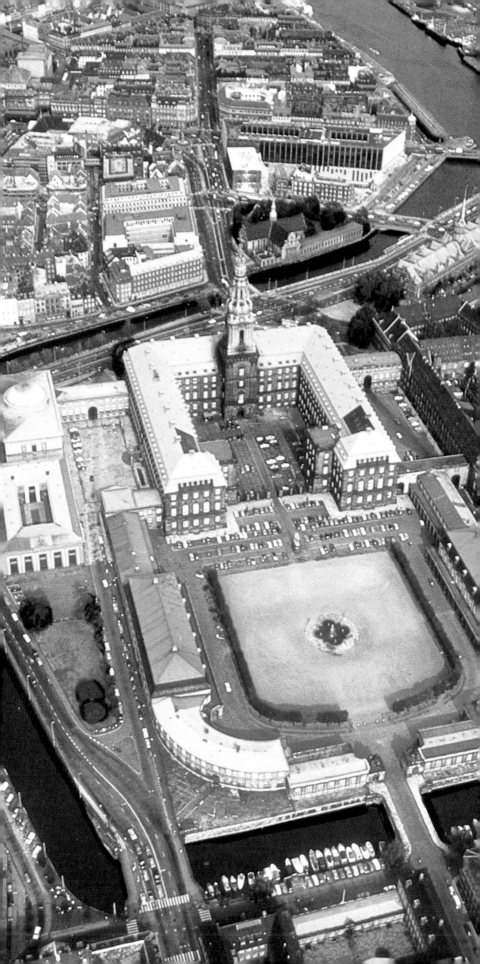

# Abisko

Sweden (Northern).
Province: Norrbottens län. – Region: Lapland.
Altitude: 395 m (1296 ft).
Postal code: S-98024. – Telephone code: 0980.
ⓘ Kiruna Turistbyrå,
   Hj. Lundbomsväj,
   S-98131 Kiruna;
   tel. (09 80) 188 80.

HOTELS. – *Abisko Turiststasjon*, 330 b.; *Gästgarden*, 64 b.

**Abisko lies in the north of Sweden on Lake Torneträsk, a mountain lake 71 km (44 miles) long, up to 9 km (5½ miles) wide and 164 m (540 ft) deep. Abisko can be reached by the Lapland railway between Kiruna and the Norwegian port of Narvik, and also by a road running parallel to the railway. The town lies on the northern edge of the Abisko National Park and is the starting point of the Kungsleden or Royal Trail (see p. 172).**

Abisko depends almost entirely on the tourist trade. From the hotel, situated on a 15 m (50 ft) deep canyon-like gorge on the *Abiskojokk*, there are panoramic views of *Lake Torneträsk and the mountains. The midnight sun is visible from 13 June to 4 July.

SURROUNDINGS. – Trips on Lake Torneträsk in the motorboat belonging to the hotel. – A cableway 1958 m (2140 yds) long and a marked footpath ascend Mt *Njulla* or Nuolja (1199 m – 3934 ft). From the top the midnight sun is visible from 31 May to 18 July. – 15 km (10 miles) S of Abisko are two rather hills which offer rewarding climbs, *Pallemtjåkko* (1740 m – 5709 ft) and *Nissontjårre* (1745 m – 5725 ft). Between Nissontjårre and *Tjuonjatjåkko* (1582 m – 5191 ft), to the E, is the ridge known as the *Lapporten* ("the Lapp Gate").

A trip on the railway to Narvik offers an experience not to be missed (for the best views, sit on the right). The line runs through the longest tunnel in Sweden (1100 m – 1200 yds), passing under Mt *Njulla*, and then crosses the *Rakkasjokk* on a high viaduct.

**Björkliden** (alt. 420 m (1378 ft); hotels: Fjället, 117 b.; Gammelgården, 44 b.) lies in a very beautiful setting. 20 minutes SE is the fine *Rakkaskårtje* waterfall, formed by the Rakkasjokk at its inflow into Lake Torneträsk. The line follows the shores of the lake for another 5 km (3 miles) and then turns W.

After passing through the *Tornehamnstunnel* (536 m – 580 yds) you will come to the *Kopparåsen* station, beyond which the landscape shows the typical scouring effect of glaciers. The line continues via *Vassijaure* to the frontier station of *Riksgränsen* (520 m (1706 ft); Hotel Riksgränsen, 400 b.) in a popular skiing area. The wide expanse of mountain country is almost completely treeless. 2 km (1¼ miles) beyond Riksgränsen station is the Swedish-Norwegian frontier. Beyond this point, see under Narvik p. 195.

# Åland Islands/ Ahvenanmaa

Finland.
Autonomous region of Åland (Ahvenanmaan maakunta).
Area: 1505 sq. km. (580 sq. miles).
Population: 21,000.
Postal code: SF-22100.
Telephone code: 928.
ⓘ Ålands Turistförening,
   Norra Esplanadgatan 1,
   SF-22100 Mareihamn;
   tel. 1 21 40.

TRANSPORTATION. – *Car ferries* from Stockholm, Grisslehamn, Simpnes and Kapellskär (Sweden) and from Turku and Naantali (Finland). – In summer *air services* from Stockholm, Helsinki, Turku and Hamburg.

**The Åland Islands (Finnish Ahvenanmaa) lie between Finland and Sweden at the S end of the Gulf of Bothnia, which they separate from the Baltic Sea. To the W of the islands, towards Sweden, is the Åland Sea, some 40 km (25 miles) across; to the E is the arm of the sea known as Skiftet. The group consists of 6554 islands and columns of rock with a total area of 1505 sq. km (580 sq. miles); only 80 islands are inhabited. They are a popular vacation area, particularly with Swedes.**

The islands became part of Russia in 1809 together with the rest of Finland. After the First World War there was a movement for union with Sweden. But in 1921 the islands were assigned by the League of Nations to Finland, and the population was granted full self-government, permanent demilitarisation and the exclusive use of the Swedish language. The main sources of income are shipping (second largest tonnage in Finland), agriculture and tourism. The islanders are proud of their independence and do not like to be referred to as Finns.

On the main island of **Åland** is the only town in the group, **Mariehamn** (Finnish *Maarianhamina*: pop. 9600; hotels: Adlon, 124 b., SB.; Alandia, 167 b., SB.; Arkipelag, 315 b.; Park, 102 b., SB.; Savoy, 100 b., SB.; Strandnäs, 202 b.,

Mariehamn (Åland Islands)

SB). Mariehamn is a popular seaside resort situated on a promontory at the S end of the island. In Norra Esplanadgata, in the middle of the town, stands the church (1927); at 9 Storgata is the Åland Museum. In the W harbour are the Maritime Museum and the four-masted ship "Pommern", which is also a museum.

23 km (15 miles) NE of Mariehamn by way of *Jomala* (old church) is the stronghold of **Kastelholm** (14th c.), until 1634 the seat of the governor of Åland; it was badly damaged by fire in the mid-18th c. One wing which survived the fire houses the Åland Cultural and Historical Museum. Nearby is the Jan Karlsgården Open-Air Museum. 4 km (2½ miles) N of Kastelholm stands the 13th c. stone church of *Sund* with old sculptures. – The fortress of *Bomarsund*, 11 km (7 miles) E of Kastelholm, was built by the Russians and destroyed by the British and French during the Crimean War (1854).

23 km (15 miles) N of Mariehamn (via Jomala, then road on left before Kastelholm) stands the 15th c. church of *Saltvik*, one of the oldest on the island. – 6 km (4 miles) NE of Saltvik is the **Orrdalsklint** (132 m – 433 ft), the highest point on the island. There is a better view from the *Kasberg* (116 m – 381 ft), 10 km (6 miles) N of Saltvik. – 20 km (12 miles) N of Mariehamn (beyond Jomala continue to

left) lies *Finström*, with a church which contains medieval wall paintings. Another 21 km (13 miles) N is *Geta*, the most northerly parish on the island.

21 km (13 miles) NW of Mariehamn at *Hammerland*, there is a church which may date from the 12th c.

15 km (9 miles) SE of Mariehamn is *Lemland* where, near the ruined *Lemböte Chapel* (13th c.) is to be found a *Viking cemetery*, one of the largest in the Åland group.

# Ålborg/Aalborg

Denmark (Northern Jutland).
County: Nordjyllands amt.
Altitude: 15 m (50 ft). – Population: 155,000.
Postal code: DK-9000. – Telephone code: 08.
ⓘ **Aalborg Turistforening,**
Østerågade 8;
tel. 12 60 22.

HOTELS. – *Hvide Hus*, Vesterbro 2., 364 b., SP; *Central-Hotel*, Vesterbro 38, 119 b.; *Limfjordshotellet*, Ved Stranden 14–16, 360 b.; *Phønix*, Vesterbro 77, 300 b.; *Scheelsminde*, Scheelsmindevej 35, 120 b. YOUTH HOSTEL.

CAMP SITES. – Mølleparken, Strandparken, Østervangen, Lindholm (Nørresundby).

RESTAURANTS. – *Bondestuen*, Vingardsgade 5; *Jomfru Ane*, Jomfru Anesgade 16; *Promenaden*, Kastetvej 12 (Greenland specialties); *Ellen Marsvins Vinhus*, Østerågade 23.

EVENT. Ålborg Festival: concerts, etc. (August).

**Ålborg (Aalborg), Denmark's fourth largest town, lies on the S side of the Limfjord, which links the North Sea with the Kattegat. A road and railway bridge and the Limfjord Tunnel (553 m (600 yds) long, 6 lanes), opened in 1969, lead to Nørresundby on the N side of the fjord, now part of Greater Ålborg.**

Originally a Viking settlement, Ålborg received its municipal charter in 1342 and after the Reformation became a flourishing commercial town. It is now a hub of commerce, industry, education and culture (University founded 1973). The modern harbour handles Danish trade with Greenland, and among the town's principal industries are shipbuilding, cement manufacture, tobacco and the

Evening in the Åland Islands

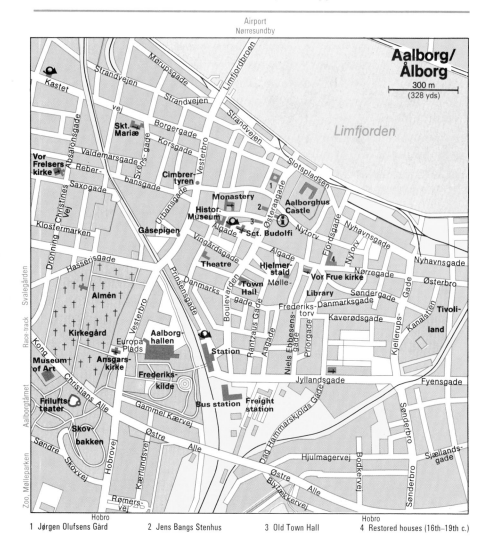

Airport
Nørresundby

**Aalborg/**
**Ålborg**

300 m
(328 yds)

Limfjorden

1 Jørgen Olufsens Gård     2 Jens Bangs Stenhus     3 Old Town Hall     4 Restored houses (16th–19th c.)

production of snaps ("Aalborg Akvavit").
The town has many old buildings and
attractive parks and gardens.

this, in Østerågade, *Jens Bangs Stenhus, the best-preserved and best-
appointed old burgher's house in the

SIGHTS. – In the middle of the old town,
in *Budolfi Plads*, stands the late medieval
**St Botolph's Church** (Sct. Budolfi
Kirke: restored *c.* 1900). The carillon of 18
bells (1970) plays at every hour from 9
a.m. to 10 p.m. A little way NW of the
church, at 48 Algade, is the *Historical
Museum* (prehistoric material; history of
the town; glass and silver). To the NE, in
C. W. Obels Plads, is the well preserved
**Monastery of the Holy Ghost** (founded 1431), Denmark's oldest social
service institution, now a welfare home
(conducted tours by arrangement with
the Tourist Office).

NE of St Botolph's, in Gamle Torv, is the
*Old Town Hall* (1762); and to the N of

Jens Bangs Stenhus, Ålborg

town, built in 1623–4 by a prosperous merchant named Jens Bang. Beyond this, on the W side of Østerågade, is *Jørgen Olufsens Gård*, another merchant's house (1616) with a stone doorway. Opposite is **Aalborghus Castle** (1539), now occupied by local government offices; visitors can see the fortifications.

SE of Budolfi Plads, reached by way of Algade, we come to one of the town's oldest churches, *Vor Frue Kirke* (Church of Our Lady: built *c*. 1100, rebuilt 1879). There are a number of old houses in the neighbourhood, including a historic old *potter's workshop* in Hjelmerstald. In the angle between Nørregade and Fjordsgade nine houses from various parts of the town, all between 150 and 400 years old, have been rebuilt. – To the S of Vor Frue Kirke, on the site of a former monastery, is the *Northern Jutland Library*. Farther E is the **Tivoliland** amusement park.

The old town is bounded on the W by *Vesterbro*, in which are two notable works of sculpture: at the end of Bispegade the *Cimbrian Bull* (Cimbrertyren), by Bundgård, and farther S the *Goose Girl* (Gåsepigen), by Henning, both erected in 1937. Vesterbro runs S to *St Ansgar's Church* (Sct. Ansgar Kirke), on the W side of the street, and opposite this is the **Aalborghallen**, a large conference and cultural complex and theatre with seating for 3400. To the SW, at 50 Kong Kristians Allé, is the *Northern Jutland Museum of Art* (1971), which contains a collection of Danish painting from 1890 and 20th c. foreign art. Immediately S of this is the *Skovbakke* (Forest Hill), with an open-air theatre (Friluftsteater) and a lookout tower 55 m (180 ft) high, *Aalborgtårnet*. 1·5 km (1 mile) SW is the *Møllepark*, with the *Zoo*.

To the E of the town are a new residential district AALBORG-OST and extensive industrial installations.

SURROUNDINGS. – To the N of the Limfjord, near *Nørresundby*, lies the Viking site of *Lindholm Høje*, a large cemetery in which more than 650 graves have so far been found, together with the remains of a village (15 houses, 6 wells).

27 km (17 miles) S of Ålborg (Road A10), in an area of heathland, are the beautiful **Rebild Hills** (*Rebild Bakker*), declared a National Park on the initiative of Danish Americans (great celebrations on Independence Day, 4 July). At the entrance to the park are a restaurant and a museum (local history; the travelling fiddlers of Jutland). In the park is a replica of *Lincoln's Log Cabin*, built in 1934 with logs from America (museum of emigration). On a hill to the NE is the *Cimbrerstenen*, a rock with the carved figure of a bull and the inscription "Cimbrerne drog ut fra disse egne" ("The Cimbri set out from this area"). – 3 km (2 miles) S of the park is the village of **Rebild** (youth hostel; two camp sites; holiday houses). Near the village, on road 10, is the *Tingbæk Limestone Quarry*, with extensive underground workings, now housing a museum of sculpture by Bundgård and Bonnesen. To the S of Rebild extends the **Rold Skov**, one of the largest and most unspoiled areas of forest in Denmark (6400 hectares – 16,000 acres). In the village of Rold is a circus museum containing old equipment, pictures, etc.

# Ålesund

Norway (Central).
County: Møre og Romsdal fylke.
Altitude: sea level. – Population: 40,500.
Postal code: N-6000. – Telephone code: 071.
ⓘ **Ålesund Reiselivslag,**
   Rådhuset;
   tel. 2 12 02.

HOTELS. – *Havly*, R. Ronnebergsgate 4, 90 b.; *Noreg*, Kongensgate 27, 179 b., SB; *Parken Hotel*, Storgate 16, 248 b. – YOUTH HOSTEL – CAMP SITE.

**The busy commercial and port town of Ålesund, in western Norway, lies on the islands of Nørvøy, Aspøy and Heissa, reaching out into the coastal fringe of small islands or skerries. It is Norway's principal fishing port, with fish-processing plants, as well as shipyards and clothing factories. After a great fire in 1904 destroyed almost all the town's old timber houses, it was rebuilt in stone, and still has many Art Nouveau housefronts dating from that period.**

Sunset over Ålesund

The two main islands of Ålesund are linked by a bridge. On **Aspøya** are the *church* (1909: fine frescoes and stained glass) and the *Aquarium*. On **Nørvøya** is the town itself, with hotels, the Post Office and the *Municipal Museum*. The harbour lies between these two islands, facing N and sheltered by Skansen peninsula which projects from Nørvøy. On *Skansenkai* is the dock used by the ships of the "Hurtigrute" ("Fast Coastal Service").

To the E of the town in a beautiful park is a *bauta stone* (standing stone) 7 m (23 ft) high with a carved effigy of Kaiser Wilhelm II, commemorating the help given by Germany after the 1904 fire. Also in the park is a statue of Rollo, conquerer of Normandy, who came from the Ålesund area (this was presented by the town of Rouen in 1911). E of the park is *Aksla*, a hill 189 m (620 ft) high, climbed by a steep path, with a *fjellstue* (mountain hut) at a height of 135 m (443 ft) offering a magnificent overall *view of the town, the sea and the islands, and SE towards the Sunnmøre hills. The hut can also be reached on a road which branches off Borgundvei.

SURROUNDINGS. – Many motor-ships travel to the outer islands and the smaller fjords S of the town. On the W side of **Valderøy** (10 minutes) is *Skjonghelleren* cave, 130 m (140 yds) long, which was occupied in Neolithic times. – On **Giske** (20 minutes) stands a chapel (probably 12th c.), partly built of

white marble. – On the island of **Runde**, SW of Ålesund, is Norway's most southerly seabird cliff, the nesting-place of some 700,000 birds of 40 different species. – It is worth taking the ferry across the *Storfjord* from Solevågen to Festøy (Road 14) for the sake of the magnificent view into the *Hjørundfjord*.

On a peninsula 4 km (2½ miles) E of Ålesund is **Borgund**, with a *church* founded in the 11th c. and restored to its original form after the 1904 fire, and the open-air *Sunnmøre Museum* (old houses, boats and a section devoted to the fishing industry).

# Alsen/Als

Denmark.
County: Sønderjyllands amt.
Area: 315 sq. km (122 sq. miles).
Population: 53,000.
ⓘ **Sønderborg Turistbureau**,
   Rådhustorvet,
   DK-6400 Sønderborg;
   tel. (04) 42 35 55.
   **Augustenborg Turistforening**,
   Storegade 28,
   DK-6400 Augustenborg;
   tel. (04) 47 17 20.

**The Danish island of Alsen (Als) lies at the southern end of the Little Belt, between the mainland of Denmark and the island of Funen. Its beautiful beaches make it a popular vacation spot.**

The chief place on the island is the old town of **Sønderborg** (pop. 30,000; hotels: Ansgar, 75 b.; Baltic, 28 b.; Dybbøl Banke, 28 b.; Scandic, 190 b., SB.; youth

**The Midnight Sun north of the Arctic Circle**
Position of the sun
photographed on the Norwegian island of Loppa
(*c.* 100 km (60 miles) WSW of Hammerfest)
at intervals of an hour
between 7 p.m. on 21 July and 6 p.m. on 22 July

hostel, camp site). It is beautifully situated at the S end of the island on both sides of the Als Sund, which is crossed by a bridge. The medieval castle contains a museum with collections of historical material and art. Town Hall (1936). St Mary's Church (*c.* 1600) has much sculpture. – S of the central town is the modern College of Sport (mosaic and sculpture decoration by Danish artists).

6·5 km (4 miles) NE of Sønderborg is *Augustenborg* (pop. 6600; Slotshotellet, 15 b.), with a castle (1776; now a hospital) located in a large park. – Road 8 runs NE to *Fynshav*, from which there is a ferry to the island of Funen (see p. 96).

# Arctic Circle
## (Polarcirkel/Polcirkeln/ Napapiiri)

Norway, Sweden and Finland.

**The Arctic Circle is an imaginary line around the earth at latitude 66·5° N beyond which the length of the day so increases in summer that the sun never sinks below the horizon and the phenomenon known as the midnight sun can be observed. It also separates the northern temperate zone from the polar climatic zone. – In Norway the Arctic Circle (Polarcirkel) runs just N of Mo i Rana, in Sweden (Polcirkeln) near Jokkmokk, in Finland (Napapiiri) a bit N of Rovaniemi.**

The different lengths of day and night in all latitudes except on the Equator are due to the angle of 23·5° between the earth's equatorial plane and the plane of its orbit.

At the summer solstice (22 June) the apparent course of the sun at the Arctic Circle reaches its greatest northern declination (i.e. its greatest angular distance N of the celestial equator), so that at midnight the sun is still in the sky. In a clear sky this **\*\*midnight sun** is an impressive sight, but even when the sun is obscured by mist or clouds its glowing red ball in the night sky is a memorable spectacle.

Exactly on the Arctic Circle the midnight sun is visible on only one day in the year, but farther N the length of this arctic day steadily increases. At the North Pole the polar day should in theory last exactly half a year, but the refraction of the sun's rays in the earth's atmosphere makes it slightly longer than this. The altitude from which it is observed also affects the length of time during which the midnight sun can be seen, since the published data are calculated for sea level. Thus an observer on a

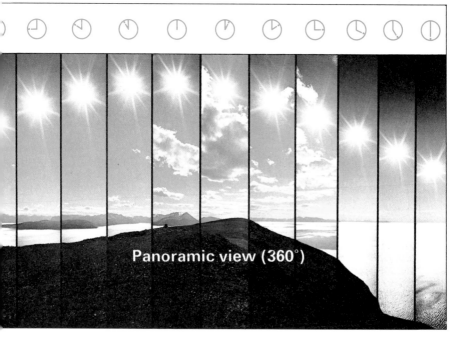

Panoramic view (360°)

Stone marking the Arctic Circle in northern Norway

hill can see the midnight sun some distance S of the Arctic Circle.

The parts of Norway, Sweden and Finland N of the Arctic Circle – the "Land of the Midnight Sun" – are also known in Scandinavia as **Nordkalotten** (Finnish *Pohjoiskalotti*), the "Northern Cap".

The Arctic Circle also marks the approximate southern boundary of the *Nor-thern Lights or Aurora Borealis. This phenomenon is caused by electrically charged particles emitted by the sun being caught up by the earth's magnetic field. These particles produce striking light effects in the thin ionised upper atmosphere at heights between 70 and 1000 km (40 and 600 miles). The sky is lit up by bluish arcs of light, glowing coronas and shimmering curtains of radiance flaring over the sky in constant movement, offering the fortunate spectator an unforgettable experience.

YOUTH HOSTEL. – Ostre Skovvej 2A, in Risskov.

CAMP SITES. – *Århus Nord*, 8·6 km (5 miles) N; *Blommehaven*, 5 km (3 miles) S, near beach, etc.

RESTAURANTS. – *Barberen*, Vestergade 51; *Den gamle By's Restaurant; Den røde Okse*, Klostergade 28–30; *Teater Bodega*, Skolegade 7; *Hyttefadet*, Vesterbrogade 36 (fish specialties). – *Moesgård Skovmølle* (with water-mill), Højbjerg; *Varna*, Marselisborg; *Åkrogen*, Risskov, on beach.

EVENT. – *Festival Week* (theatre, art, sport; historical market in Den gamle By), beginning of September.

**Århus, Denmark's second largest city, lies on the E coast of Jutland in a wide bay of the Kattegat. It first appears in the records in 928 as the see of a bishop, and received its municipal charter in 1441. It is now the cultural and educational hub of Central Jutland, with a University founded in 1928. It is also an industrial town (foodstuffs, machinery, textiles, etc.).**

SIGHTS. – The central feature of the inner city, which is enclosed by a semicircular peripheral boulevard (Ringgade), is *Store Torvet* (the Great Market). On the E side of this square, near the harbour, stands the *Cathedral of St Clement, founded in 1201 but much altered and enlarged in later centuries, so that it now has the appearance of a late Gothic building. Features of the interior are the high altar, with a rich array of figures, by the Lübeck master Bernt Notke (1479; recently restored), the beautifully carved 16th c. pulpit by Mikkel van Groningen and the organ (1730). The vault paintings date from the 15th c. In front of the Cathedral is a *monument to Christian X* (1955). To the S is the *Theatre* (1900).

# Århus

Denmark (Central Jutland).
County: Århus amt.
Altitude: sea level. – Population: 250,000.
Postal code: DK-8000. – Telephone code: 06.
(i) **Århus Turistforening**,
    Rådhuset;
    tel. 12 16 00.

HOTELS. – *Ansgar Missionshotel*, Banegårdsplads 14, 236 b.; *Atlantic*, Europaplads 12–14, 184 b.; *Motel La Tour*, Randersvej 139, 90 b.; *Park Hotel*, Sønder Allé 3, 21 b.; *Marselis*, Strandvejen 25, 160 b.; *Ritz*, Banegårdspladsen 12, 99 b.; *Royal*, Store Torv 4, 208 b. – IN HØJBJERG (5 km/3 miles S): *Scanticon*, 220 b., SP. – IN BRABAND (6 km/4 miles W): *Årslev Kro og Motel*, 81 b. – IN VIBY (6 km/4 miles SW): *Mercur*, 220 b.

Town Hall, Århus

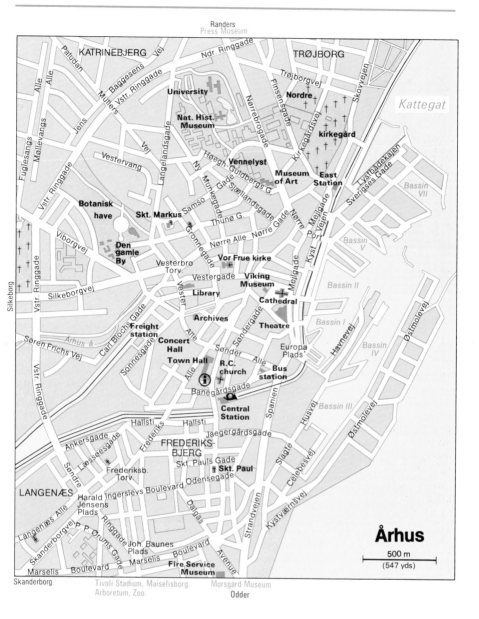

Randers
Press Museum

KATRINEBJERG
TRØJBORG

University

Nat. Hist.
Museum

Nordre
kirkegård

Vennelyst

Museum of Art
East Station

Botanisk have
Skt. Markus

Den gamle By
Vesterbro Torv

Vor Frue kirke

Vestergade
Viking Museum

Library

Cathedral

Archives

Theatre

Freight station
Concert Hall
Town Hall
R.C. church

Europa Plads

Bus station

Banegårdsgade

Central Station

Hallsti

FREDERIKS-BJERG

Frederiksb. Torv

Skt. Pauls Gade
Skt. Paul

LANGENÆS

Harald Ingerslevs Boulevard

Jensens Plads

Joh. Baunes Plads

Fire Service Museum

Marselis Boulevard

Kattegat

**Århus**

500 m
(547 yds)

Skanderborg

Tivoli Stadium, Maiselisborg.
Arboretum, Zoo.

Morsgård Museum
Odder

SW of the Cathedral, at 6 Clemenstorv, is a small *Viking Museum*. Farther SW, on the S side of the busy Rådhus Plads, the hub of the city's traffic, stands the Rådhuset (**Town Hall**) (by A. Jacobsen and E. Møller, 1938–42), with a notably fine interior (conducted tours); from the tower, 60 m (200 ft) high, there is a fine view. On the W side of the square is the attractive *Pig Fountain* (Grisebrønden), by M. Bøggild, and to the S of the Town Hall another fountain, "Agnes and the Triton". From here it is only a few steps to the concert hall, the home of the Århus Symphony Orchestra.

NW of the Cathedral in Vestergade is **Vor Frue Kirke** (Church of Our Lady,

13th–15th c.), with a monastery used since the Reformation as an old people's hospital. The old chapterhouse in the W wing has late medieval wall paintings. There is also a remnant of the Gothic cloister. – A little way W of the church, in the southern half of the *Botanic Garden*, an interesting open-air museum, *Den gamle By (the "Old Town"), consists of a collection of some sixty old houses, shops and workshops with their furnishings, from different parts of Denmark ings, from different parts of Denmark. The central feature is the Burgomaster's House of 1597 containing a collection of furniture.

In a park to the N of the town are the buildings, erected from 1933 on, of the

"Den gamle By", Århus

From Århus A15 serves the southern part of the *Djursland* peninsula, leaving the N side of the town and following the wide arc of *Kalø Bay*.

At *Løgten* a road goes off on the left to the interesting Renaissance castle of *Rosenholm* (16th c.). – 1 km (¾ mile) before Rønde a minor road on the left leads to **Thorsager**, with the only *round church in Jutland (dating in part from *c.* 1200).

The road to Ebeltoft branches off A15 just before Rønde. To the right of this road, on a peninsula reaching out into Kalø Bay, are the ruins of *Kalø Castle* (destroyed in the 17th c.), in which Gustavus Vasa was held prisoner in 1518. Ahead is an attractive view of the *Mols* peninsula.

**Ebeltoft** (pop. 12,000; hotels: Ebeltoft Strand, 136 b.; Hvide Hus, 130 b.; youth hostel; several camp sites) is a charming little country town with a 16th c. Town Hall (now a museum), the Farvergård, an old dyer's workshop, and a glass museum. In the harbour is a 19th c. frigate, the "Jylland". There is also a "windmill park" for producing power.

**University** (founded 1928), including the main block (1946) and Møller's "Book Tower". In the College of Journalism is a *Museum of the Press*. In the southern part of the park we find the *Natural History Museum* and farther S, in Vennelystpark, the *Museum of Art* (1966), with paintings, graphic art and some sculpture, mainly by Danish artists.

To the S of the town are the *Tivoli-Friheden* amusement park, the *Marselisborg Hall* and the *Stadium*. Still farther S, in a park beyond Carl Nielsens Vej, is the little palace of *Marselisborg* (1902), the summer residence of the Queen. To the NE of this, on the far side of Kongevej, a memorial park commemorates Danes who fell in the First World War. – To the SE, in Ørneredevej, is the *Varna Restaurant*, with a view of Århus Bay. From here Strandvej, running alongside the sea, leads N back to the middle of the town. In Dalgas Avenue, which branches off on the left, is the **Danish Fire Service Museum**, with some sixty vehicles.

The **Harbour**, to the E of the town, is protected by breakwaters and has five basins (9·5 km (6 miles) of quays) and a fishing harbour.

SURROUNDINGS. – 9 km (6 miles) S of the town (leaving on Strandvej) is the **Moesgård Prehistoric Museum**, housed in an old manor-house. A particularly notable feature of the museum is the "Grauballe Man", a body dating back some 1600 years, found perfectly preserved in a bog. In the grounds of the museum is a "Prehistoric Trail", which leads past Stone Age and Bronze Age remains and reconstructions of houses of the early historical period.

SE of Århus, in the *Samsø Belt*, is the island of **Samsø** (area 114 sq. km (44 sq. miles), pop. 5200). From the harbour of *Kolby Kås* (Hotel Færgekroen, 20 b.) there are ferry services to and from Århus and Kalundborg. The Manor-house of Brattingsborg is set in a park.

*Ballen*, a fishing village on the E coast, has a yacht harbour and beautiful beaches. – 5 km (3 miles) W is *Brundby*, with a post windmill more than 300 years old.

**Nordby** (pop. 320) is an attractive old-world village. To the N are the *Nordby Bakker* hills, part of which is a nature reserve.

**Tranebjerg** (pop. 660; Hotel Sølyst, 24 b.), the chief place on the island, lies roughly half-way between the E and W coasts. Massive 14th c. church; *Samsø Museum*, a farmhouse of 1800 with a collection of antiquities.

# Bear Island/ Bjørnøya

Norway. – Administrative district: Svalbard.
Area: 178 sq. km (69 sq. miles). – No permanent population.

**Bear Island – almost inaccessible for tourists – lies in the Barents Sea roughly half-way between the mainland of Scandinavia and Spitzbergen. It was discovered in 1596 by the Dutch navigator Willem Barents, who was trying unsuccessfully to find the North-East Passage to China. Since 1925, together with Spitzbergen, it has formed part of the Norwegian administrative district of Svalbard.**

This lonely island lies in latitude 75°25′ N, within the area subject to drift ice, and is a port of call for fishing boats only in the height of summer. Its only activity is a Norwegian weather station with a radio transmitter. The coal-mines formerly worked here were closed in 1925. – Situated at the meeting of a cold current from the NE and the Gulf Stream, Bear Island is almost always shrouded in mist.

On the E coast is the island's highest hill, *Misery-Fjell* (Mt Misery, 536 m – 1759 ft). – To the S is the little port of *Sørhamn*, hemmed in by sheer rock walls. – The steep coastal cliffs are the nesting place of countless Arctic birds, particularly *Fugle-fjell* ("Bird Mountain", 411 m – 1348 ft), at the southern tip of the island. – The interior of the island is covered with large numbers of small lakes.

# Bergen

Norway (Southern).
County: Hordaland fylke. – Population: 207,000.
Postal code: N-5000. – Telephone code: 05.
ⓘ **Bergen Reiselivslag,**
Slottsgaten 1;
tel. 31 38 60.

HOTELS. – *Norge*, Ole Bulls Plass 4, 498 b.; *SAS Royal Hotel*, Bryggen, 500 b.; *Grand Hotel Terminus*, Kong Oscarsgate 71, 220 b.; *Hordaheimen*, C. Sundtsgate 18, 122 b.; *Neptun*, Walckendorffsgate 8, 174 b.; *Orion Royal Hotel*, Bradbenken 3, 220 b., SB; *Rosenkrantz*, Rosenkrantzgate 7, 190 b.; *Scandic Hotel Bergen*, Kokstadflaten 2, 315 b., SB; *Strand*, Strandkaien 24, 100 b. – SUMMER HOTEL: *Fantoft*, in Fantoft, 40 b.

YOUTH HOSTEL. – *Montana*, in Landås.

CAMP SITES. – *Lone*, 19 km (12 miles) E, and *Grimen*, 15 km (9 miles) SE, both with huts.

RESTAURANTS. – *Grand*, Olav Kyrresgate 11; *Bryggen*, Bryggen 6; *Den små hjem*, Engen 25; *Wesselstuen*, Engen 14; *Willies*, Ole Bulls Plass 15; *Bellevue*, Bellevuebakken 9 (with view); *Fløyen*, at the upper station of the cableway (magnificent **view).

EVENT. – *Festival* (music, drama, etc.), May–June.

NOTE. – Drivers of cars passing through the inner town are charged a toll.

**Bergen, situated on the inner reaches of the Byfjord, is Norway's second largest city and principal port on the Norwegian W coast (with a considerable merchant fleet and several large shipyards). It is the**

View of Bergen from the Fjellvei

Bryggen, Bergen

administrative capital of the district of Bergen and the county of Hordaland, the see of the Lutheran bishop of Bjørgvin and has a university and a commercial college. Surrounded by a ring of heights up to 643 m (2110 ft), largely forest-covered, with houses climbing up the lower slopes, Bergen is one of the most attractive towns in Norway. In spite of its northern latitude (60°24′ N − a bit farther N than the southern tip of Greenland), its humid and unusually mild climate enables almost all the usual deciduous trees of Central Europe to flourish and gives it a rich growth of vegetation. Bergen is noted for its high rainfall (over 2000 mm (80 in.) annually, compared with some 750 mm (30 in.) in Oslo); this is a result of its maritime climate and its mountains.

The oldest parts of the town lie around the busy harbour, *Vågen*, and extend up the slopes of the *Fløyfjell* to the NE. Like most Norwegian towns, Bergen has suffered frequently from devastating fires, particularly those of 1702 and January 1916; in the 1916 fire several hundred houses in the timber-built commercial district to the S of Vågen were destroyed. These repeated destructions have left little of the old Bergen, and the pattern of the town is now set by the stone buildings and wider streets of more modern times. The narrow lanes known to the local people as *smug* have all but disappeared, and only in the northern districts of Skuteviken and Sandviken are there still a few of the old warehouses on the seafront (*søgårder*) once so characteristic of Bergen − large wooden buildings with a crane, on the harbour front. Unfortunately many of the still surviving old warehouses were destroyed in great fires in 1955 and February 1958.

HISTORY. − About 1070 Olav Kyrre granted municipal status to *Bjørgvin* ("hill pasture"), then a port settlement of some importance on the E side of Vågen. The town developed rapidly as an occasional royal residence. In 1233 Håkon Håkonsson's hereditary right to the throne was recognised at a general assembly here, and by 1240 Bergen was formally declared the capital of Norway in place of Trondheim. − As early as 1236 there were permanent German trading establishments in Bergen, but the town's rise to prosperity began with the establishment of a "counting-house" of the Hanseatic League, first recorded in 1343. By virtue of a privilege granted by the Danish kings, under which the people of the northern territories were required to bring the produce of their fisheries to Bergen and to no other port, the German merchants soon gained control of all Norwegian trade. Their employees lived in a special quarter of the town on the "German Bridge" (Tyskebryggen), with sixteen long narrow houses which doubled as warehouses. Each house was controlled by a *bygherre* and was divided into several *stuer* ("rooms"), each of which belonged to a particular owner. − In 1599 the power of the

Hanseatic League was broken by the feudal lord Kristofer Valkendorf, but the counting-house remained in existence for another 200 years, until in 1764 the last *stue* was sold to a Norwegian.

Throughout its history the prosperity of Bergen has been based on shipping and commerce, especially fish and fish products. In the 17th c. Bergen was still of much greater commercial importance than Copenhagen, and even at the beginning of the 19th c. it had a larger population than Kristiania (Oslo). Right into the 20th c. it remained Norway's principal fishing port, and fish and fish products still figure importantly in its trade. In more recent years the establishment of large fishing companies and numerous canning and preserving plants nearer the fishing grounds has promoted the development of other fish marketing towns; but in spite of this Bergen's outgoing trade (including steel and machinery among much else) is exceeded only by that of Oslo. – During the Second World War Bergen suffered considerable damage, and among the buildings destroyed was the old Theatre in Sverres Gate – Norway's first theatre – which was founded in 1851 by the famous fiddler Ole Bull, and of which Ibsen (1851–7) and Bjørnson (1858–60) were directors.

SIGHTS. – At the SE end of the principal harbour, Vågen, is the *Market Square* (Torget). Here are the docks where the fishing boats moor when they come in with their catches in the morning (interesting fish market). On the SE side of the square is a statue (by John Børjeson, 1883) of the writer Ludvig Holberg (b. 1684 in Bergen, d. 1754 in Copenhagen), creator of the Danish-Norwegian comedy. Behind it stands the *Exchange*. – At the upper end of the Vetrlidsalmenning, which runs NE from the square, is the lower station of the Fløybanen (funicular).

From the market square **Bryggen** (formerly *Tyskebryggen*, "German Bridge") runs along the NE side of the harbour. Here once stood the houses of the German merchants, later steadily replaced by stone-built warehouses in a style characteristic of the Hanseatic period. Only one of these houses, the early 18th c. *Finnegård*, at the near end of the quay, has been preserved in its original condition; since 1872 it has housed the * **Hanseatic Museum**.

The INTERIOR of the Museum gives a good impression of the internal arrangement of the Hanseatic warehouses, and displays weapons, domestic furnishings and equipment, most dating from the final phase of the Hanseatic counting-house. The ground floor was used for the storage of goods; on the first floor were the office of the Hanseatic merchant, the dining room and bedroom, and on the second the bedrooms of apprentices and assistants.

The *Bryggen Museum* displays material uncovered by excavation between 1955 and 1968. – NW of this rises the twin-towered Romanesque and Gothic **St Mary's Church** (*Mariakirke*, 12th and 13th c.; pulpit and altar 17th c.), which belonged to the Hanseatic merchants from 1408 to 1766 and in which the service was in German until 1868. In the churchyard are a number of German graves. Opposite the church, at 50 Øvregate, is the *Schøtstue*, a meeting-place of the Hanseatic merchants.

Bryggen is continued to the NW by the *Festningskai*, on the N side of which is the old fortress of **Bergenhus**, formerly commanding the entrance to the harbour. At the S end of the fortress, on the quay, is the *Rosenkrantz Tower*, built by Erik Rosenkrantz in 1562–7 around an earlier 13th c. structure (severely damaged by the explosion of a German munition ship in 1944 but later rebuilt). Beyond it is *Håkonshallen* (the hall of Håkon), begun in English Gothic style by King Håkon Håkonsson in 1247, which, after falling into a state of dilapidation, was restored in 1880–95 and again in 1957–61. Above the Bergenhus fortress are the walls of the *Sverresborg*, built about 1660 on the remains of a castle of King Sverre. – To the N extend the old districts of SKUTEVIKEN and SANDVIKEN. In Sandviken is the **Open-Air Museum of Old Bergen** (*Gamle Bergen*), with old Bergen houses.

From the N end of the market square Kong Oscarsgate runs SE past the *Korskirke* (Holy Cross Church, founded 1170, present building 1593) to the **Cathedral** (*Domkirke*), originally built as a monastic church in 1248, rebuilt in 1537 and restored in 1870 (fine doorway in tower, beautiful Gothic windows). Kong Oscarsgate ends a little way E of the railway station at a *town gate* dating from 1628. Outside the gate, on the right, is an old cemetery, with the grave of Ole Bull, identified by a large black urn. – SW of the Cathedral, in Rådstuplass, stands the small *Old Town Hall* (16th c.). A little way S of this beyond a lake, *Lille Lungegårdsvann*, to the SW of the station, is the *Municipal Library*; a short way SW, in Strømgate, the *Grieg-Halle* (concerts, ballet). On the S side of the lake the excellent little *Rasmus Meyer Collection*, bequeathed to the city in 1923 by the businessman of that name, includes pictures by Norwegian artists from 1814 to 1914 (J. C. Dahl, H. Gude, Edvard

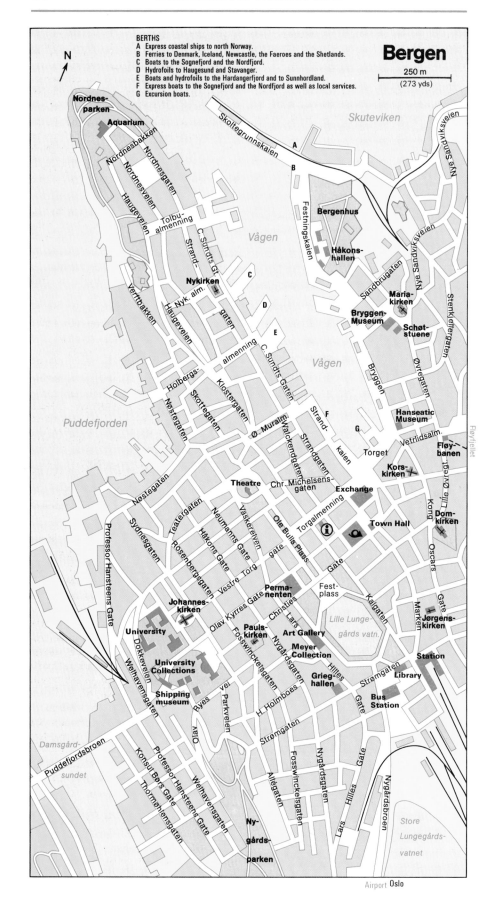

BERTHS
A  Express coastal ships to north Norway.
B  Ferries to Denmark, Iceland, Newcastle, the Faeroes and the Shetlands.
C  Boats to the Sognefjord and the Nordfjord.
D  Hydrofoils to Haugesund and Stavanger.
E  Boats and hydrofoils to the Hardangerfjord and to Sunnhordland.
F  Express boats to the Sognefjord and the Nordfjord as well as local services.
G  Excursion boats.

# Bergen

250 m
(273 yds)

Munch, G. Munthe). Some 200 m (200 yds) NW, at the S end of the Municipal Park, is a building (*Permanentan*) housing the *Vestlandske Kunstindustrimuseum* (applied and decorative art, furniture, carpets, porcelain, etc.), the *Fishery Museum,* which gives a good general picture of the Norwegian fishing industry, and the *Municipal Museum of Art,* with a collection of work by Norwegian painters of the 19th and 20th c. (J. C. Dahl, H. Gude, E. Munch, etc.). From here Christies Gate runs S past *St Paul's Church* (Paulskirker, R.C.) to the hill of *Sydneshaugen,* on which are the **University** and, adjoining the *Botanic Garden,* the *University Collections* : in the old building natural history, in the new building cultural history and a *Shipping Museum.* – To the SE extends the beautiful *Nygårdspark,* in the southern part of which is Vigeland's Unicorn Fountain. – From the Museum the *Puddefjord Bridge* runs towards the southern districts of the town.

To the N of the Vestlandske Kunstindustrimuseum is the small *Municipal Park,* in the northern part of which can be seen a statue (by J. Vik, 1917) of the Bergen-born composer Edvard Grieg (1843–1907). – To the W of the park is the elongated *Ole Bulls Plass,* with a monument (by Stephen Sinding, 1901) to another native of Bergen, the "king of fiddlers" Ole Bull (1810–80). At the W end of the square is the handsome **Theatre,** the *Nasjonale Scene* (1906–9). In the gardens stands a bronze statue (by G. Vigeland, 1917) of the dramatist Bjørnson (1832–1910). – In the NW of the town, at the tip of a promontory between Vågen and the Puddefjord, we find the *Nordnespark,* with a beautiful view and an interesting *Aquarium (1960).

SURROUNDINGS. – To the NE of the town rises the **Fløyfjell** (319 m – 1047 ft), from which there are magnificent views of Bergen and its surroundings, particularly beautiful in the early morning or at sunset. The hill can be climbed either on foot (about 3 km – 2 miles) or by means of the funicular (Fløybanen) from the Vetrlidsalmenning (10 minutes: the line passes through a tunnel 150 m (160 yds) long and then, after the Fjellveien station, another tunnel 75 m (80 yds) long). At the upper station is the *Fløyen Restaurant* (313 m – 1027 ft), from which there are splendid **views of the town and the coastal scenery, extending as far as the open sea. – From the upper station a road (30 minutes' walk) runs NE over the plateau, which becomes steadily more barren, to the foot of the **Blåmann** (551 m – 1808 ft). There is a footpath to the top of this hill, from which there are fine panoramic views, particularly by evening light.

The somewhat higher peak behind it is not worth the extra climb. The road continues to the radio station on the *Rundemann* (556 m (1824 ft): half-hour's walk). – The *Fjellvei,* half-way up the Fløyfjell, affords a number of attractive viewpoints. At the SE end of this path, some 25 minutes' walk from the intermediate station of the funicular, is a restaurant.

To the SE of the town is another summit offering far-ranging views, **Ulrikken** (643 m – 2110 ft), reached by a cableway from Haukeland, on the SE outskirts. On foot it takes approximately two hours to reach the top. – 6 km (4 miles) from the middle of the town is the *Fantoft stave church,* brought here from Fortun in 1884 and extensively restored.

*Sognefjord, *Hardangerfjord, *Nordfjord and Hardangervidda: see the entries for these places.

# Bodø

Norway (Central).
County: Nordland fylke.
Altitude: sea level. – Population: 32,000.
Postal code: N-8000. – Telephone code: 0 81.
ⓘ **Bodø Reiselivslag,**
Tourist Information,
Storgate 16;
tel. 2 12 40.

HOTELS. – *SAS Royal Hotel*, Storgate 2, 373 b.; *Central*, Prof. Schyttesgate 6, 75 b.; *Grand Hotel*, Storgate 3, 68 b.; *Norrøna* (no rest.), Storgate 4, 200 b. – YOUTH HOSTEL: *Flatvoll*, Rønvikrykset, 132 b.

CAMP SITE. – *Bodøsjøen Camping*, 3 km (2 miles) from the middle of the town (with huts).

RECREATION and SPORTS. – Fishing; motorboat rental for game fishing; riding.

**The Norwegian port of Bodø, chief town of the county of Nordland, lies in the Saltfjord, N of the Arctic Circle. The sun does not set here between the beginning of June and the middle of July. The town received its municipal charter in 1816, but its development was slow until the second half of the 19th c., when the herring fisheries gave it a boost. – During the Second World War, Bodø suffered severe damage in the fighting of May 1940 and almost the whole central area of the town was destroyed by fire. Rebuilt in modern style, it is now a lively commercial town, with a number of factories, a shipyard and several technical colleges.**

Bodø is linked by road to Fauske, on the important European highway E6. There are two trains daily to Bodø on the Nordland railway from Trondheim, extended to here in 1962. The fast ships of the

Harbour and SAS Royal Hotel, Bodø

**Løpsfjell** (603 m – 1978 ft). Here is a good view of the Lofoten Islands 100 km (60 miles) away. To the E can be seen the glacier-covered Sulitjelma (1913 m – 6277 ft), 90 km (55 miles) away on the Swedish frontier, and to the left of this the Blåmannsis with its snowfields rising to 1571 m (5154 ft).

40 km (25 miles) NE of Bodø (bus: Road 834, with one ferry) is the old trading post of **Kjerringøy**, with an open-air museum (old buildings, with furnishings).

An expedition of some 35 km (22 miles) can be made S from Bodø to the *Saltstraumen, a strait 2·5 km (1½ miles) long, some 150 m (160 yds) wide and up to 50 m (165 ft) deep between the islands of Straumen and Straumøy. It links the Saltfjord with the Skjerstadfjord. The movement of the tide forces some 370 million cubic metres (80,000 million gallons) of water through this narrow passage, creating whirlpools and eddies. Good fishing.

Bodø is also one of the ports providing access to the **Lofoten Islands** (see p. 179).

"Hurtigrute" from Bergen to Kirkenes dock at Bodø; and there is an air-strip linking the town with the Scandinavian network of air services.

SIGHTS. – In Rådhusplassen is the *Town Hall*, completed in 1959, from the tower of which there are panoramic views. The nearby **Cathedral** (*Domkirke*, 1956), with a separate tower, contains fine stained glass by Aagen Storstein. To the S of the Cathedral is the *Nordland County Museum* (Nordland Fylkesmuseum), with sections devoted to agriculture, local crafts and the fisheries as well as prehistoric and medieval material.

SURROUNDINGS. – 3 km (2 miles) E of the town centre is the old stone-built church of **Bodin** (12th c.), with a Baroque altarpiece (1670). Louis-Philippe, Duke of Orleans (king of France 1830–48), stayed in the presbytery on his journey to the North Cape in 1796.

4 km (2½ miles) N is the *Rønvikfjell* (155 m (509 ft): mountain hut), with panoramic views. From here it is a two hours' walk on a marked footpath to the top of the

# Bohuslän

Sweden (Southern).
Province: Göteborgs och Bohus län.
ⓘ **Bohus Turist,**
Postfach 56,
S-45115 Uddevalla;
tel. (0522) 1 40 55.

**The region of *Bohuslän extends N from Gothenburg along the coast of the Skagerrak to the Norwegian frontier. It is the most westerly province of Sweden, to which it has belonged since the treaty of Roskilde in 1658. The traditional fisheries which were for long the region's only significant source of income have been supplemented in recent years by a growing tourist trade, so that during the summer Bohuslän sometimes tends to be overcrowded.**

The much indented coastal regions with their innumerable skerries, worn smooth by wind and water, their delightfully colourful wooden houses and their clean and strongly saline water, have been a popular holiday area for more than a century. In addition Bohuslän is rich in remains of the past, particularly rock carvings of the Stone and Bronze Ages and Viking stone-settings.

**Tour of Bohuslän.** – The main traffic artery is the E6, which runs N from Gothenburg to Svinesund on the Norwegian frontier, continuing to Oslo.

**Bodø**

200 m
(219 yds)

Salten

Station

Fauske

Hurtigrute

Sjøgata

Storgata

Torget

Drohningens gate

Kongens gate

Library

Prof. Schyttes gata

Town Hall

Prinsens gate

Customs

Bankgata

Bus station

Rådhus-plassen

Cathedral

Museum

Rensåsgata

Fredensborgveien

Parkveien

Moloveien

People's House

Airfield

Numerous attractive excursions can be made from this road, particularly in the southern part, going W towards the coast.

From Gothenburg the road runs N under the *Götaälv* and then follows the valley of the river (here canalised).

**Kungälv** (pop. 29,000; Fars Hatt Hotel, 230 b.; Lökebergs Pensionat, 106 b.; youth hostel; camp site), the oldest town in Bohuslän, known in the Middle Ages as *Kongahälla*, has a wooden church of 1679 with fine ceiling paintings. In the southern outskirts of the town E6 crosses the *Nordre Älv*: on an island to the right can be seen the large ruined castle of **Bohus** (magnificent view), built by King Håkon V of Norway in 1310, and which has given its name to the region.

Sailing boats at Marstrand (Bohuslän)

From Kungälv a road runs W to the coast (18 km – 11 miles) and continues over bridges and a ferry to the seaside resort of *Arvidsvik* on **Koø** ("Cow Island"). From here there is a ferry service to the popular resort of **Marstrand** (Alphyddan Hotel, 70 b.; Båtellet, 103 b.; Villa Maritime, 200 b.), situated on a small island and dominated by the 17th c. Carlsten Castle. St Mary's Church dates from 1640. An international sailing regatta is held at Marstrand in mid July.

Beyond Kungälv E6 leaves the canal and passes the old church of *Kareby*. Soon afterwards it comes to the *Ingetorpssjö* (on right), with an Iron Age cemetery.

At **St Höga** an attractive trip can be made on Road 160, which runs to Uddevalla by way of the islands of **Tjörn** and **Orust**. The Stenungsund was formerly spanned by a massive bridge 600 m (650 yds) long. After the old bridge was rammed by a ship in January 1980 causing its collapse, the new suspension bridge was brought into use in November 1981. – On the W coast of Tjörn is *Skarhamn*, a fishing town and also a port for the export of cars.

Road 160 continues over another bridge on to the island of Orust, the third largest in Sweden (336 sq. km – 130 sq. miles), with numerous little fishing villages and places for swimming. Off Orust lies the little island of **Gullholmen**, on which is a very ancient fishing village. – From here we can return to the

mainland by the Nötesundsbro (603 m (660 yds) long); then either left for Fiskebäckskil or right for Uddevalla.

Beyond St Höga E6 runs inland for some distance and then comes to the popular seaside resort of *Lyckorna* (founded 1876) and the commercial town and resort of **Ljungskile** (Hotel Åh Stiftsgård, 57 b.; Motel Backamo, 150 b.), on a bay of the same name in the *Havstensfjord*. – 5 km (3 miles) beyond this, to the left of the road, is the church of *Resteröd* (partly dating from the 12th c.; restored 1919–20), one of the oldest in Bohuslän.

**Uddevalla** (pop. 47,000; hotels: Carlia, 100 b.; Centralhotell, 36 b.; Bohusgården, 200 b.; Gyldenlöwe, 74 b), a busy industrial town lies near the outflow of the *Bäveå* into the Byfjord. In Kungstorg stands an equestrian statue of King Karl X Gustav (1908), and to the E of this, on an adjoining hill, the early 19th c. church with a separate tower (1751). The town has large shipyards and dock installations. – From here Road 44 runs E to Lake Vänern (see p. 283), passing in 2·5 km (1½ miles) the Skalgrusbänkar (extensive deposits of fossil sea-shells).

E6 continues NW. At *Torp* Road 161 goes off on the left and runs via *Bokenäs* (12th c. church) to the old fishing village and bathing resort of *Fiskebäckskil*, on the island of **Skaftö** in the beautiful *Gullmarsfjord*. It then continues over a ferry to the attractive seaside resort of *Lysekil* (pop. 15,000; hotels: Fridhem, 30 b.; Lysekii, 65 b.; several camp sites), at the southern tip of the Stångenäs peninsula (fish preserving). Near the fine Gothic church is a rocky crag, the Flaggberg, from which there are good views. From here continue along the coast via *Tanumshede* to rejoin E6.

At *Dingle* a road branches off E6, cuts across the coast road and comes to the seaside resorts of *Hunne-bostrand* (Gästis Hotel, 70 b.) and *Kungshamn* (Kungshamn Hotell, 150 b.; Snäckan, 40 b.). Kungshamn has a large modern fishing harbour. Offshore lies the island of **Smögen**, with a seaside resort.

On the island of Smögen (Bohuslän)

**Fjällbacka**, a fishing village and popular seaside resort, can also be reached from either of these roads. On the uninhabited island of *Stensholm*, 2 km (1¼ miles) S, is the grave of the German writer Hans Kinau, known as Gorch Fock (b. 1880), who was killed in the battle of Jutland (1916).

E6 continues to *Greby*, with a cemetery of 200 burial mounds and numerous standing stones, probably dating from the 4th c. A.D., which legend associates with the defeat of a Scottish invading force. – At *Hällevadsholm* Road 165 branches off on the right to *Lake Bullaren* (29 km (18 miles) long, the largest lake in Bohuslän), and continues to the Norwegian frontier.

E6 now follows the western edge of the parish of *Tanum*, with numerous prehistoric rock carvings (*hällristningar*), and comes to **Tanum**, with one of the largest churches in Bohuslän. Opposite the church are a runic stone and an orientation table. 2 km (1¼ miles) S, at *Vitlycke*, are large *rock carvings (ships, warriors, figures blowing lurs). There are other carvings at *Litsleby* and *Fossum*.

At *Vik* a road runs W from E6 to **Strömstad** (pop. 9500; hotels: Centralhotell, 46 b.; Krabban, 27 b.; Laholmen, 200 b.; youth hostel; camp sites), the oldest swimming resort in Sweden (established 1781).

An attractive coastal promenade runs round the *Laholmen* peninsula. 5 km (3 miles) NW are the vacation spots of *Vette* and *Capri*. – 10 km (6 miles) SW (boat trips from Strömstad) are the **Kosta Islands**, Sweden's most westerly island group, notable for their rich plant life.

At *Norrhede* Road 163 goes off on the left, also leading to Strömstad. A little way N is a large prehistoric *stone-setting in the form of a ship, known as *Blomsholmsskeppet* (42 m (140 ft) long, 9 m (30 feet) across). Nearby are an old place of judgment (11 blocks of stone) and several burial mounds.

E6 continues through rocky and wooded country to *Svinesund*, the Swedish customs post. The road then crosses the narrow Svinesund, which here forms the frontier between Sweden and Norway, on a reinforced concrete *bridge 420 m (450 yds) long and 60 m (200 ft) high (magnificent views) and continues along the shores of the *Oslofjord* (p. 216) to **Oslo** (p. 208).

# Borås

Sweden (Southern).
Province: Älvsborgs län. – Region: Västergötland.
Altitude: 120 m (394 ft). – Population: 100,000.
Postal code: S-500 . . . –505 . . .
Telephone code: 0 33.
(i) **Borås Turistbyrå,**
    Torggatan 19;
    tel. 16 70 87.

HOTELS. – *Boras*, Sandgärdsgatan 25, 107 b.; *City*, Allégatan 32, 88 b.; *Grand*, Hallbergsgatan 14, 281 b.; *Mark*, Yxhammarsgatan 1, 92 b., SB; *Scandic*, Hultasjögatan 7, 205 b.; *Vävaren*, Allégatan 21, 140 b. – IN BORÅS-BRÄMHULT: *Motel Lage*, 70 b. – YOUTH HOSTEL. – CAMP SITE.

**The lively town of Borås in southern Sweden, between Gothenburg and Jönköping, straddles the River Viska. Founded in 1622, it has a busy textile industry and several large mail order businesses.**

SIGHTS. – In the Market Square stands the imposing *Town Hall* (1908–10), with a carillon. In front of it is the attractive *Sjuhäradsbrunn*, a fountain by Nils Sjögren (1941), and to the N the *Caroli Kyrka* (1660, restored 1941), with a fine interior. The **House of Culture** (1975) contains the *Museum of Art*, the *Municipal Theatre* and a library. In the *Ramnapark* is the open-air **Borås Museum**, with old peasants' houses and a 16th c. church.

In *Borås Park* are the interesting *Zoo* and recreation facilities. Adjoining is the Alideberg swimming pool, with a restaurant.

SURROUNDINGS. – 8 km (5 miles) NE, on the Ulricehamn road (No. 40), the commandingly situated church of *Brämhult*, has 18th c. paintings. – 25 km (15 miles) SE, on the shores of *Lake Åsund*, is *Torpa Castle*, containing a fine Renaissance Knights' Hall and a Baroque chapel of 1699.

**Jönköping** and *Gothenburg* : see pages 146 and 102.

# Bornholm

Denmark.
County: Bornholms amt.
Area: 587 sq. km (227 sq. miles).
Population: 47,000.
(i) **Samvirkende Bornholmske Turistforeningers Bureau** (*SBT*),
    Havnen (the Harbour),
    DK-3700 Rønne;
    tel. (03) 95 08 10.

Round church, Østerlars (Bornholm)

RECREATION and SPORTS. – Hire of bicycles; riding, tennis, golf, fishing, scuba diving, windsurfing, sailing.

The Baltic island of *Bornholm, lying 37 km (23 miles) off the Swedish coast and 150 km (95 miles) from Copenhagen, has belonged to Denmark since 1522. In medieval times it was an important trading post. The present-day population lives mainly by fishing, fish-processing and farming; but the island's mild climate and good bathing beaches have also promoted the development of a lively holiday and tourist trade.

ACCESS. – Ferry services to Rønne on Bornholm from Copenhagen, Ystad in southern Sweden, Lübeck-Travemünde (German Federal Republic) and Sassnitz (German Democratic Republic). – Air services between Copenhagen and Rønne.

The island consists of a great mass of granite, much of it with only a thin coating of soil, bounded on the N by fine steep cliffs and on the SE and W by dunes. The interior is partly wooded, partly heathland. Its most notable remains of the past are four fortified *round churches of the 12th and 13th c.

Tour of the island. – The capital of Bornholm is **Rønne** (pop. 15,300; Fredensborg Hotel, 132 b.; Griffen, 284 b., SB; Badehotel Ryttergården, 224 b., SB, SP; youth hostel; camp site), which also has the island's airfield and its principal harbour. In the oldest part of the town stands St Nicholas's Church (originally 14th c., largely rebuilt 1918).

At 29 Sct.-Mortens-Gade are the Bornholm Museum, with good natural history collections and material of local interest, and the Museum of Art. The *Castle*, to the S of the town, was built about 1650, and has a massive round tower (military area).

8 km (5 miles) NE of Rønne is the round church of *Nyker* (1287), the only two-storeyed church on the island. – 9 km (5½ miles) N of Rønne we come to the *Brogårdssten*, the most important runic stone on Bornholm, and 2 km (1¼ miles) beyond this *Hasle* (pop. 6900; Herring Festival at beginning of July), with a massive stone church (14th c.). 7 km (4½ miles) farther N the road reaches the imposing granite cliffs on the coast, with the 40 m (130 ft) high crag known as *Jons Kapel* ("John's Chapel"). The road then continues to the double village of **Allinge-Sandvig** (pop. 2100; Abilgård, 250 b., SP; Allinge, 40 b.; Boes-Vang, 68 b.; Friheden, 70 b.; Hammersø, 90 b.; Pepita, 68 b.; Sandvig, 86 b.; Strandhotel, 76 b.; several holiday apartments; youth hostel; four camp sites), one of the most attractive swimming resorts on the island. There is a pleasant walk to the *Hammeren* lighthouse, to the N, passing the highest crag on the island, the *Stejleberg* (84 m – 276 ft), and on from there to the ruins of *Hammershus Castle*, to the SE of the lighthouse. The castle was built about 1250 and fiercely contested on many occasions; thereafter it was used as a quarry for building stone until it was scheduled as a historic monument in 1822. From the 74 m (240 ft) high crag on which it stands there are magnificent views. There are interesting boat trips to be made from Hammershus Hotel, for example to the *Våde Ovn*, a cave 55 m (60 yds) long by 12 m (40 ft) high.

4 km (2½ miles) S of Allinge is the round church of *Ols* (built in the 12th c., restored 1948–50), the tallest on the island (30 m – 100 ft). – 11 km (7 miles) SE of Allinge are the *Helligdom cliffs*, and 6 km (4 miles) farther on lies the fishing village of **Gudhjem** (hotels: Feriegården, 62 b.; Stammershalle, 70 b., SP; Helligdommen, 41 b., SP; youth hostel; camp site), with a harbour blasted out of the rock. To the S is **Østerlars** which has the largest * round church on the island (11th c., with wall paintings of about 1350). – S of Østerlars extends the state forest of **Almindingen**, planted between 1800 and 1830, the

scene of a "forest run" at the end of September; the forest contains a number of small lakes and the island's highest hill, *Rytterknægten* (162 m (530 ft): outlook tower). 20 minutes N are the ruins of *Lilleborg Castle*, which ranked with Hammershus as one of the two strongest fortresses on Bornholm.

7 km (4½ miles) SE of Gudhjem, on the coast, are the wild *Randkløveskår* cliffs, and 8 km (5 miles) beyond this is the picturesque little fishing town of **Svaneke** (pop. 1200; hotels: Siemsens Gård, 89 b.; Østersøen, 56 b.; youth hostel; camp sites), with old houses and a post-mill of 1634. "Festival of the Springs" at the end of June. – 3 km (2 miles) SW is the *Brændesgårdshaven* amusement park.

The road S runs past the beautiful *Paradisbakkerne* ("Paradise Hills") to the port of **Neksø** or *Nexø* (pop. 8950; Harbour Festival at beginning of August). 3 km (2 miles) S is *Balka*, with a beach of fine sand, and 7 km (4½ miles) beyond this the southern tip of the island is reached; here are the *Dueodde* lighthouse, gently rolling dunes and a beautiful beach.

15 km (10 miles) inland we find the only town on Bornholm not on the coast, **Åkirkeby** (pop. 7380; Kanns Hotel, 50 b.; Dams på Bakken, 44 b.; Limensgade Mølle, 12 b.; holiday apartments; camp site), with a handsome 12th c. stone church (font with carved decoration and a runic inscription). The Church of the Rosary (Rosenkranskirken, 1932: R.C.) is one of the most attractive modern churches in Denmark. – The road to Rønne (16 km – 10 miles) runs via *Nylars*, with the latest and best preserved of Bornholm's round churches (12th c.).

It is well worth taking a boat trip from Allinge, Gudhjem or Svaneke to *Ertholmene* ("Pea Islands"). The principal island is **Christiansø** (pop. 118), with fortifications of 1684. The neighbouring island of *Frederiksø* was formerly notorious as a place of exile. *Græsholmen* is a bird sanctuary.

# Copenhagen (København)

Denmark (Zealand).
County: Københavns amt.
Altitude: sea level.
Population: 638,000 (with suburbs 1,400,000).
Postal code: DK-1000-2900.
Telephone code: 01, 02 (suburbs).

(i) **Danmarks Turistråd**
*(Danish Tourist Board)*,
H. C. Andersens Boulevard 22,
DK-1553 København V;
tel. (01) 11 14 15.
*Hotelbooking København*,
Hovedbanegården,
Kiosk P,
DK-1570 København V;
tel. 2 28 80.
**Forenede Danske Motorejere** (*FDM:
Federation of Danish Motorists*),
FDM-Huset, Blegdamsvej 124,
DK-2100 København Ø;
tel. (01) 38 21 12.
*Youth Information Centre* (*Use It*),
Magstræde 14,
DK-1204 København K;
tel. (01) 15 65 18.

EMBASSIES. – *United Kingdom*: Kastelevej 36–40, DK-2100 København Ø, tel. 26 46 00. – *USA*: Dag Hammerskjölds Allé 24, tel. 42 31 44. – *Canada*: Kr. Bernikowsgade 1, DK-1105 København K, tel. 12 22 99.

HOTELS. – CITY CENTRE: *Astoria*, Banegårdspladsen 4, 153 b.; *Codan*, Sankt Annae Plads 21, 250 b.; *Cosmopole*, Colbjørnsensgade 11, 203 b.; *Hotel D'Angleterre*, Kongens Nytorv 34, 249 b.; *Kong Frederik*, Vester Voldgade 23–27, 221 b.; *Labroke Palace*, Rådhuspladsen 57, 293 b.; *Plaza*, Bernstorffsgade 4, 156 b.; *Richmond*, Vester Varimagsgade 33, 237 b.; *Royal*, Hammerichsgade 1, 453 b.; *Scandinavia*, Amager Boulevard 70, 875 b.; *Sheraton Copenhagen*, Vester Søgade 6, 840 b.; *Absalon*, Helgolandsgade 15, 423 b.; *Alexandra*, H. C. Andersens Boulevard 8, 116 b.; *Missionshotellet Ansgar*, Colbjørnsensgade 29, 150 b.; *Centrum*, Helgolandsgade 14, 125 b.; *City*, Peder Skramsgade 24, 161 b.; *Copenhagen Admiral*, Toldbodgade 24–28, 815 b.; *Grand Hotel*, Vesterbrogade 9A, 204 b.; *Missionshotellet Hebron*, Helgolandsgade 4, 216 b.; *Imperial*, Vester Farimagsgade 9, 301 b.; *Merkur*, Vester Farimagsgade 17, 210 b.; *Missionshotellet Nebo*, Istedgade 6, 145 b.; *Nyhavn Hotel*, Nyhavn 71, 110 b.; *Østerport*, Oslo Plads 5, 136 b.; *Park Hotel*, Jarmers Plads 3, 107 b.; *Triton*, Helgolandsgade 7–11, 236 b.; *Viking*, Bredgade 65, 165 b.; *Webers Hotel*, Vesterbrogade 11B, 141 b. – IN THE NORTH: *Gentofte*, Gentoftegade 29, 132 b.; *Hellerup Parkhotel*, Hellerup, Strandvejen 203, 128 b. – IN THE WEST: *Tre Falke*, Falkoner Allé 9, 280 b.; *Broadway*, Vesterbrogade 97, 70 b.; *Glostrup Park Hotel*, Glostrup, Hovedvejan 41, 94 b.; *Wittrup Motel*, Albertslund, Roskildevej 251, 104 b. – IN THE SOUTH: *Bel Air*, Løjtegårdsvej 99, 420 b., SP; *Danhotel*, Kastruplundgade 15, 511 b.; *Globetrotter*, Engvej 171, all near Kastrup Airport; *Motel Amager*, Kongelundsvej 232, 20 b.

YOUTH HOSTELS. – *Copenhagen Hostel*, Sjælland-sbroen 55, DK-2300 København S; *Københavns Vandrerhjem "Bellahøj"*, Herbergvejen 8, DK-2700 Brønshøj; *Vesterbro Ungdomsgård*, Absalonsgade 8, DK-1658 København V.

CAMP SITES. – *Absalon*, Korsdalsvej, DK-2160 Rødovre; *Bellahøj*, Hvidkildevej, DK-2400 København NV; *Nærum*, Ravnebakken, DK-2850 Nærum; *Strandmøllen*, Strandmøllevej, DK-2942 Skodsborg.

RESTAURANTS. – * LUXURY RESTAURANTS: *H. C. Andersens Eventyrrestaurant*, Gyldenløvesgade 54; *Reine Pédauque*, Kongens Nytorv 34; *Langelinie Pavillonen*, Langelinie; *Hellerup Park Hotel*, Strandvejen 203; *Skt Gertruds Kloster*, Hauser Plads 32. – GOURMET RESTAURANTS: *Anatole*, Gothersgade 35; *Børskælderen*, Børsgade; *Den Sorte Ravn*, Nyhavn 14; *Pakhuskælderen*, Nyhavn 71; *Skovshoved Hotel*, Strandvejen 267. – FISH SPECIALTIES: *Fiskekælderen*, Ved Stranden 18; *Fiskehusets Restaurant*, Gammel Strand 34; *Krogs Fiskerestaurant*, Gammel Strand 38. – VEGETARIAN: *Den Grønne Køkken*, Larsbjørnsstræde.

THEATRES and CONCERTS. – Drama, opera and ballet in the *Kongelige Teater*, Kongens Nytorv (closed in summer); many small private theatres with performances in Danish; regular concerts in the *Royal Conservatoire*, Niels Brocksgade 1, the *Radio Concert Hall*, Julius Thomsensgade, and the *Louisiana Museum*. In summer there are numerous concerts in churches and in the open air. In **Tivoli** (open beginning of May to mid-September) there are concerts in the concert hall and a variety of performances (pantomime, variety, puppets, concerts) in the open air.

JAZZ, FOLK, POP. – *Montmartre*, Nørregade 41; *Vingården*, Nikolaj Plads 21; *Vognporten*, Magstræde 14; *Musikkaféen*, Magstræde 14; *Vognhjulet*, Thorsgade 67.

BARS, DISCOTHEQUES, FLOOR SHOWS. – *Kakadu Bar*, Colbjørnsensgade 6; *Valencia*, Vesterbrogade 32; *Wonder Bar*, Studiestræde 69; *Club de Paris*, Kompagnistræde 21; *No. 1*, Amagertorv 23.

SHOPPING. – Copenhagen's main shopping area is the long pedestrian precinct known as **Strøget**, with its numerous side streets. Here are found not only large department stores but numerous small shops and boutiques offering a wide variety of wares. Particularly tempting buys are *porcelain* (Kongelige Porzellanfabrik, Bing & Grøndahl), *furniture and furnishings* (Den Permanente display of Danish design, Town Hall Square; Illum Bolighus), *furs* (Birger Christensen, A. C. Bang), *silver* (Georg Jensen), *pewter* (Just Andersen) and knitwear. – When goods are despatched to addresses outside Denmark (make sure that they are insured!) the Danish value-added tax (MOMS) is deducted.

*Art auctions:* Arne Bruun Rasmussen, Bredgade 33. – Numerous *antique shops* in the "Latin quarter" around the University and in Nyhavn. – *Flea-market* on Saturday mornings in Israels Plads.

The Chinese Tower, Tivoli

**⁎⁎Copenhagen, capital of the kingdom of Denmark, lies on the E side of the island of Zealand, on the shores of the Øresund. Denmark's intellectual and cultural hub, it combines Scandinavian elegance with European joie de vivre. It is a city pulsating with life, particularly in the summer, and it draws visitors not only to see particular sights and features of interest but also to enjoy its own very distinctive atmosphere.**

In addition to being the seat of the government and the residence of the monarch, Copenhagen is an important commercial, business and industrial city. Its port, once of major importance, has now been outstripped by Gothenburg and Hamburg. Its airport at Kastrup, however, plays a central role in air traffic between Scandinavia and other European and overseas countries.

Visitors to Copenhagen will enjoy the opportunity it offers of seeing the sights and doing their shopping within a relatively small area. In central Copenhagen it is best to do without a car and see the city on foot. But this pedestrian sightseeing should be supplemented by longer trips into the modern and fashionable suburbs of the city and into the beautiful surrounding country, which can be easily reached with the help of the suburban railway (*S-tog*, operating from 5 a.m. to half an hour after midnight).

HISTORY. – First mentioned in 1043 under the name of *Havn*, after the building of the Slotsholmen fortress by Bishop Absalon of Roskilde (remains still visible under Christiansborg), the settlement rapidly developed into a considerable trading town. King Christopher of Bavaria made Copenhagen his capital and royal residence in 1445, and under the popular King Christian IV (1588–1648) the town acquired handsome new buildings and stronger fortifications. Its walls withstood attacks by the Swedes in 1658 and 1659, by Anglo-Dutch and Swedish fleets in 1700 and by the British in 1801 and 1809 (bombardment of Copenhagen), but were pulled down in the 19th c. and replaced by parks and gardens. Copenhagen University was founded in 1479.

# Museums, Galleries, etc.

## CITY

### Amalienborg Palace
(*Amalienborg*),
Frederiksgade 22;
not open to public.

### Applied Art, Museum of
(*Kunstindustrimuseet*),
Bredgade 68;
throughout the year, Tues.–Sun. 1 to 4 p.m.; 1 September to 31 May and 1 September to 30 November, Tues. 1 to 9 p.m.

### Arsenal Museum
(*Tøjhusmuseet*),
Tøjhusgade 3;
1 May to 30 September, Mon.–Sat. 1 to 4 p.m., Sun. 10 a.m. to 4 p.m.; 1 October to 30 April, Mon.–Sat. 1 to 3 p.m., Sun. 11 a.m. to 4 p.m.

### Astronomical Clock, Town Hall
(*Jens Olsens Verdensur*);
throughout the year, Mon.–Fri. 10 a.m. to 4 p.m., Sat. 10 a.m. to 1 p.m.

### Bakkehus Literary Museum
(*Bakkehusmuseet*),
Rahbeks Allé 23;
throughout the year, Wed., Thurs., Sat. and Sun. 11 a.m. to 3 p.m.

### Botanic Garden
(*Botanisk Haves*),
Gothersgade 130;
throughout the year, daily 8.30 a.m. to 4 p.m.; *Palm House* daily 10 a.m. to 3 p.m.

### Brøste Collection
(*Brøstes Samling*),
Christianshavn,
Overgaden oven Vandet 10;
throughout the year, daily 10 a.m. to 4 p.m.

### Carlsberg Brewery Museum,
Valby Langgade 1;
1 May to 31 October, Mon.–Fri. 10 a.m. to 4 p.m.; 1 November to 30 April, Mon.–Fri. 12 noon to 3 p.m.

### Christiansborg Palace
(*Christiansborg Slot*),
Christiansborg Slotsplads.
*State Apartments and Knights' Hall:* 1 June to 31 August, conducted tours in English daily except Mon. at 12 noon, 1 and 3 p.m.; 1 September to 31 May, conducted tours in English daily except Mon. and Sat. at 2 p.m.
*Medieval remains* (Bishop Absalon's castle of 1167): 1 June to 31 August, daily 10 a.m. to 4 p.m.; 1 September to 31 May, daily except Sat. 9.30 a.m. to 4 p.m.
*Parliamentary chambers*: throughout the year, Sun. 10 a.m. to 4 p.m.; June to September, conducted tours Mon.–Fri., except when Parliament is sitting, 10 a.m. to 4 p.m., on the hour.

### David Collection
(*C. L. Davids Samling, European and Oriental handicrafts*),
Kronprinsessegade 30;
throughout the year, Tues.–Sun. 1 to 4 p.m.

### Film Museum
(*Det Danske Filmmuseum*),
Store Søndervolstræde;
throughout the year, Mon.–Fri. 12 noon to 4 p.m.; 1 September to 31 May, Tues. and Thurs. also 6.30 to 9 p.m.

### Freedom Museum
(*Frihedsmuseet, Denmark's memorial to the Resistance, 1940–5*),
Churchillparken;
1 May to 15 September, Tues.–Sat. 10 a.m. to 4 p.m., Sun. 10 a.m. to 5 p.m.; 16 September to 30 April, Tues.–Sat. 11 a.m. to 3 p.m., Sun. 11 a.m. to 4 p.m.

### Fyrskib XVII
(*Lightship XVII*),
Nyhavn 2;
throughout the year, open when flag is raised and gangway down.

### Geological Museum
(*Geologisk Museum*),
Øster Voldgade 7;
throughout the year, Tues.–Sun. 1 to 4 p.m.

**Glyptotek:** see Ny Carlsberg Glyptotek.

### Grundtvig Church
(*Grundtvigs Kirke, modern cathedral in the style of a Danish village church*),
På Bjerget;
throughout the year, Mon.–Fri. 9 a.m. to 4.45 p.m.; 15 May to 15 September, Sun. 12 noon to 4 p.m.; 16 September to 14 April, Sun. 12 noon to 1 p.m.

### Hirschsprung Collection
(*Hirschsprungske Samling, 19th c. Danish art*),
Stockholmsgade 20;
throughout the year, Wed.–Sun. 1 to 4 p.m., 1 October to 30 April, also Wed. 7 to 10 p.m.

### Holmen Church
(*Holmens Kirke, the Church Royal*),
Holmens Kanal;
15 May to 15 September, Mon.–Fri. 9 a.m. to 2 p.m., Sat. 9 a.m. to 12 noon; 16 September to 14 May, Mon.–Sat. 9 a.m. to 12 noon.

### Kastellet,
Langelinie;
throughout the year, daily 6 a.m. to 10 p.m.

**Marble Church/Frederick Church**
(*Marmorkirken/Frederikskirken*),
Frederiksgade 1;
1 May to 30 September, Mon.–Fri. 9 a.m. to 4 p.m., Sat
9 a.m. to 12.30 p.m.; 1 October to 30 April, Mon.–Fri.
9 a.m. to 3 p.m., Sat 9 a.m. to 12.30 p.m.

**Medical History, Museum of**
(*Medicinsk-historisk Museum*),
Bredgade 62;
throughout the year, Tues., Thurs. and Sun. 11 a.m. to
2 p.m., conducted tours in English 12 noon and 2 p.m.

**Motor Ship Museum**
(*B & W Museum*),
Strandgade 4;
throughout the year, Mon.–Fri. 10 a.m. to 1 p.m.; first
Sun. in month 10 a.m. to 1 p.m.

**Municipal Museum and Kierkegaard Collection**
(*Bymuseum og Søren-Kierkegård-Samlingen*),
Vesterbrogade 59;
1 May to 30 September, Tues.–Sun. 10 a.m. to 4 p.m.;
1 October to 30 April, Tues.–Sun. 1 to 4 p.m.

**Musical History Museum and Carl Claudius Collection**
(*Musikhistorisk Museum og Carl Claudius' Samling*),
Åbenrå 34;
throughout the year, Tues. and Fri.–Sun. 1 to 3.50
p.m., Wed. 10 a.m. to 1 p.m.

**National Museum**
(*Nationalmuseet*),
Frederiksholms Kanal 12,
*Danish prehistory, Middle Ages, Renaissance and Baroque, classical antiquity and coin collection:* 16
June to 15 September, Tues.–Sun. 10 a.m. to 4 p.m.;
16 September to 15 June, Tues.–Fri. 11 a.m. to 3 p.m.,
Sat. and Sun. 12 noon to 4 p.m.
*Danish folk culture:* 16 June to 15 September,
Tues.–Sat. 1 to 4 p.m., Sun. 10 a.m. to 4 p.m.; 16
September to 15 June, Tues.–Sat. 1 to 3 p.m., Sun. 12
noon to 4 p.m.
*Ethnographical collection:* 16 June to 15 September,
Tues.–Sun. 10 a.m. to 4 p.m.; 16 September to 15
June, Tues.–Fri. 11 a.m. to 3 p.m., Sat. and Sun. 12
noon to 4 p.m.
*Town and manor culture:* 16 June to 15 September,
Sat. and Sun. 10 a.m. to 4 p.m.; 16 September to 15
June, Sat. and Sun. 12 noon to 4 p.m.

**Naval Museum**
(*Orlogsmuseet*),
Qvinti Lynette, Refshalevej.

**Ny Carlsberg Glyptotek,**
Dantes Plads;
1 May to 30 September, Tues.–Sun. 10 a.m. to 4 p.m.;
1 October to 30 April, Tues. – Sat. 12 noon to 3 p.m.,
Sun. 10 a.m. to 4 p.m.

**Postal and Telegraph Museum**
(*Post- og Telegrafmuseet*),
Valkendorfsgade 9;
1 May to 31 October, Thurs. and Sun. 10 a.m. to 4 p.m.

**Puppet Theatre Museum**
(*Dukketeatermuseet*),
Købmagergade 52;
throughout the year, Mon.–Fri. 12.30 to 5.30 p.m.

**Railway Museum**
(*Jernbanemuseet*),
Sølvgade 40;
1 April to 31 October, Wed. 12 noon to 4 p.m., Sat.
12 noon to 3 p.m.

**Rosenborg Castle** (*Crown Jewels*)
(*Rosenborg Slot*),
Østervoldgade 4A;
1 May to 31 May and 1 September to 19 October, daily
11 a.m. to 3 p.m.; 20 October to 30 April, Tues. and Fri.
11 a.m. to 1 p.m., Sun. 11 a.m. to 2 p.m.; 1 June to
31 August, daily 10 a.m. to 3 p.m.

**Round Tower**
(*Rundetårn*),
Købmagergade;
1 November to 31 March, Mon.–Sat. 11 a.m. to
3.45 p.m., Sun. 12 noon to 3.45 p.m.; 1 April to
31 May, Mon.–Fri. 10 a.m. to 4.45 p.m., Sun. 12 noon
to 3.45 p.m.; 1 June to 31 August, Mon.–Sun. 10 a.m.
to 4.45 p.m. and 7 to 9.45 p.m.; 1 September to
31 October, Mon.–Sat. 10 a.m. to 4.45 p.m., Sun.
12 noon to 3.45 p.m.
*Observatory*
15 September to 15 April, Wed., 7 to 9.45 p.m.

**Royal Library**
(*Kongelige Bibliotek*),
Christians Brygge 8;
throughout the year, Mon.–Sat. 9 a.m. to 7 p.m.

**Royal Stables**
(*Kongelige Stalde og Kareter*),
Christiansborg Ridebane;
1 May to 31 October, Fri.–Sun. 2 to 4 p.m.; 1
November to 30 April, Sat. and Sun. 2 to 4 p.m.

**St Ansgar's Church Museum**
(*Museet ved Skt. Ansgars Kirke*),
Bredgade 64;
Sat. 11 a.m. to 3 p.m., Sun. 11 a.m. to 4 p.m., also by
appointment (tel. 13 37 62).

**St Peter's Church**
(*Skt. Petri Kirke*),
Nørregade/Sankt Peders Stræde;
throughout the year, conducted group visits Tues. and
Wed. 10 to 11 a.m. (tel. 13 38 34), 1 June to 31
August, Fri. and Sat. 10 a.m. to 12 noon, Sun. 11 a.m.
to 12 noon.

**State Museum of Art**
(*Statens Museum for Kunst*),
Sølvgade;
throughout the year, Tues.–Sun. 10 a.m. to 5 p.m.

**Theatre Museum**
(*Teatermuseet*),
Christiansborg Ridebane 18;
June to September, Wed., Fri. and Sun. 2 to 4 p.m.;
October to May, Wed. and Sun. 2 to 4 p.m.

**Thorvaldsen Museum**
(*Thorvaldsens Museum*),
Slotsholmen, beside Christiansborg Palace;
2 May to 30 September, daily 10 a.m. to 4 p.m.;
1 October to 30 April, daily except Tues. 10 a.m. to
3 p.m.

**Tivoli,**
main entrance in Vesterbrogade;
1 May to 16 September, daily 10 a.m. to midnight.

**Tobacco Museum**
(*Tobaksmuseet*),
Amagertorv 9;
throughout the year, Mon.–Fri. 10 a.m. to 4 p.m., Sat.
10 a.m. to 1 p.m.

**Town Hall**
(*Rådhus*),
Rådhuspladsen;
throughout the year, Mon.–Fri. 10 a.m. to 4 p.m., Sat.
10 a.m. to 1 p.m.; several conducted tours daily.
*Tower*
ascents: throughout the year, Mon.–Fri. 11 a.m. and
2 p.m., Sat. 11 a.m.

**Toy Museum**
(*Legetøjsmuseet*),
Teglgårdstræde 13;
throughout the year, daily 10 a.m. to 4 p.m.

**Tussaud's Wax Museum**
(*Louis Tussauds Voksmuseum*),
H. C. Andersens Boulevard 22;
1 May to 14 September, daily 10 a.m. to midnight;
15 September to 30 April, daily 10 a.m. to 4.30 p.m.

**Vor Frelsers Kirke**
(*Church of Our Saviour*),
Prinsessegade;
1 May to 30 September, Mon.–Sat. 10 a.m. to 3.40
p.m., Sun. 12 noon to 3.40 p.m.; 1 October to 30 April,
Mon.–Sat. 10 a.m. to 1.40 p.m., Sun. 12 noon to
1.40 p.m.

**Vor Frue Kirke**
(*Church of Our Lady*),
Nørregade 6;
1 May to 30 September, Mon.–Sat. 9 a.m. to 5 p.m.;
1 October to 30 April, 9 a.m.–12 noon.

**Zoological Garden**
(*Zoologisk Have*),
Roskildevej 32;
throughout the year, daily 9 a.m. to sunset (not later
than 6 p.m.).

**Zoological Museum**
(*Zoologisk Museum*),
Universitetsparken 15;
1 May to 30 September, daily 10 a.m. to 5 p.m.;
1 October to 30 April, Mon.–Fri. 1 to 5 p.m., Sat. and
Sun. 10 a.m. to 5 p.m.

## SURROUNDINGS

**Amager Museum**
(*Amagermuseet*),
Hovedgaden 4 and 12, Store Magleby;
1 June to 31 August, Wed.–Sun. 11 a.m. to 3 p.m.;
1 September to 31 May, Wed. and Sun. 11 a.m. to
3 p.m.

**Aquarium**
(*Danmarks Akvarium*),
Strandvejen, Charlottenlund;
1 March to 31 October, daily 10 a.m. to 6 p.m.;
1 November to 28 February, Mon.–Fri. 10 a.m. to
4 p.m.; Sat. and Sun. 10 a.m. to 5 p.m.

**Dragør Museum**,
Havnepladsen, Dragør;
1 May to 30 September, Tues.–Fri 2 to 5 p.m., Sat. and
Sun. 12 noon to 6 p.m.

**Mølsted Museum**,
Blegerstræde 1, Dragør;
1 May to 30 September, Sat. and Sun. 2 to 5 p.m.

**National Museum** (Brede section),
I. C. Modesvegsvej, Brede;
Special exhibitions: 16 May to 20 October,
Mon.–Tues. and Thurs.–Fri. 10 a.m. to 4 p.m.,
Sat.–Sun. 10 a.m. to 5 p.m.

**Open-Air Museum**
(*Frilandsmuseet*),
Kongevejen 100, Sorgenfri, Lyngby;
15 April to 30 September, Tues.–Sun. 10 a.m. to 5
p.m.; 1–14 October, Tues.–Sun. 10 a.m. to 3 p.m.; 15
October to 14 April, Sun. 10 a.m. to 3 p.m.

**Ordrupgaard Collection** (French Impressionists)
(*Ordrupgaardsamlingen*),
Vilvordevej 110, Charlottenlund;
throughout the year, Tues.–Sun. 1 to 5 p.m., Wed. also
7 to 10 p.m.

# Sightseeing in Copenhagen

The OLD TOWN of Copenhagen is traversed by a pedestrian precinct 1·8 km (a mile) long, *Strøget, a series of streets extending from Rådhuspladsen (Town Hall Square) to Kongens Nytorv. A good starting point for a walk round the old town is Nytorv (not to be confused with Kongens Nytorv), in the middle of the pedestrian precinct. In this square are the former *Law Courts*, in neo-classical style. Going N from here by way of Gammel Torv and Nørregade, we come to **Vor Frue Kirke** (Church of Our Lady). The present church is the sixth on this site, a neo-classical building designed by C. F. Hansen and built between 1811 and 1829 after the destruction of the previous church during the bombardment of Copenhagen in 1807. The church (two-storeyed, with a vaulted roof) contains numerous sculptures by Thorvaldsen – his well-known figure of Christ behind the altar, the twelve Apostles along the walls, a font with a figure of a kneeling angel. The characteristic square tower, with a flat roof, is topped by a gleaming cross. To the N of the church, beyond Bispetorv, is the main building of the **University**, founded by Christian I in 1478 and reorganised in 1537. The present building (1831–6), in a style influenced by the Oxford and Cambridge colleges, shows a mingling of neo-classical, neo-Gothic and late Roman forms. In the entrance hall are mythological frescoes by Constantin Hansen. Adjoining the University building, to the right, is the old *University*

Town Hall Square, Copenhagen

*Library*. – On the other side of Nørregade stands *St Peter's Church*, the oldest in Copenhagen (originally late Gothic; restored 1816), with a tower 78 m (255 ft) high (1756). Since 1586 St Peter's has been the church of the German community in Copenhagen. Attractive "herb garden", with graves.

From Nørregade a number of narrow lanes lead into *Fiolstræde*, a parallel street with many bookshops and antique dealers. In Krystalgade is the *Synagogue*, built in yellow brick. Passing this we come into *Købmagergade* (pedestrians only), a busy shopping street, with the *Regensen* (1623), a students' residence with an attractive arcade. Opposite it is the **Round Tower** (*Rundetårn*), 36 m (120 ft) high and 15 m (50 ft) in diameter, which was built as an observatory and contains a small collection of material relating to the 16th c. Swedish astronomer Tycho Brahe. The platform on the top, from which there are magnificent views of the green roofs of Copenhagen, is reached on a wide spiral ramp 209 m (685 ft) long, up which Peter the Great rode in 1716 and the Empress Catherine later drove in a carriage. The tower is the one referred to in Hans Andersen's tale, "The Tinder-Box": "eyes as big as the Round Tower". It is actually part of *Trinity Church* (1656; roof turret of 1728). – To the S of the Round Tower, by way of

Skindergade and Kejsergade, is **Gråbrødretorv** (Greyfriars' Square), one of Copenhagen's most charming squares, with brightly coloured old houses, some of them dating from the 18th c. On fine summer days the square is a favourite resort of students, daydreamers and others with time on their hands. From here it is a short distance back to Nytorv by way of Strøget.

The busy **Town Hall Square** (*Rådhuspladsen*) is dominated by the **Town Hall** (*Rådhus*, 1892–1905) with a 106 m (350 ft) high tower, is built partly in Italian Renaissance style, partly modelled on medieval Danish architecture. The building is richly adorned with sculpture and painting. Above the main entrance is a figure of Bishop Absalon in gilded copper, and in the Great Hall are busts of the architect who designed the building, M. Nyrop (d. 1921), the sculptor Thorvaldsen (1770–1844), Hans Christian Andersen (1805–75) and the physicist Niels Bohr (1885–1962). The *World Clock* at the main entrance, which was designed and constructed by Jens Olsen (1955), shows not only the time and the date but various astronomical constellations. – On the Town Hall Square are the *Dragon Fountain*, a monument to Hans Christian Andersen (1914 by S. Wagner) and the *Lur-Players* (two bronze figures on a stone column 12 m (40 ft) high).

# Tivoli Amusement Park

| AMUSEMENTS | 8 Glass House | 17 "Little Flyers" |
|---|---|---|
| 1 Flying Carpet | 9 "Traffic Roundabout" | 18 Roundabout |
| 2 "Ladybird" | 10 Woodland Roller | 19 Odin Expressway |
| 3 Children's Giant | 11 Vintage Cars | 20 Merry-go-round |
|    Wheel | 12 "Red Dragon" swing | 21 Galleys |
| 4 "Caterpillar" | 13 Haunted House | 22 Tub track |
| 5 The Viking | 14 Tram, line 8 | 23 Balloon Swing |
| 6 Boating pool | 15 Dodgems | 24 Slide |
| 7 "Mini Go-go" | 16 Blue Cars | 25 "Devil's Fire" |

Crossing H. C. Andersens Boulevard, we come first to the new *Union of Industrialists* building (with the well-known exhibition of Danish design, *Den Permanente*). Beyond this is the famous amusement park, \*Tivoli (main entrance in Vesterbrogade), which is best visited in the evening. This festively decorated park, the meeting-place of Copenhageners of all ages, from children to pensioners, and of thousands of visitors, has a unique carefree atmosphere of its own. This cheerful whirl of activity generates a genuine joie de vivre, but without vulgarity or bad taste.

The Tivoli Concert Hall is open throughout the year, the park itself only from May to mid-September. Its attractions include lakes, concerts, variety shows, pantomime, restaurants, cafés, shooting galleries and a great range of other entertainments. Firework displays usually on Wednesdays at 11.45 p.m., Saturdays and Sundays at 11.45 p.m. The park closes at midnight.

Going along H. C. Andersens Boulevard, we pass *Tussaud's Wax Museum* and come to Copenhagen's finest art collection, the \*\*Ny Carlsberg Glyptotek, in Dantes Plads. In front of the building is the *Dante Column*, an antique column presented by the city of Rome. The collection was assembled by Carl Jacobsen, a brewer, who bequeathed it to the nation in 1888, together with a substantial sum of money which was used to extend it. The building was erected in two stages, the first part, with three wings and a richly decorated brick façade on Dantes Plads, in 1892–7, the second part in

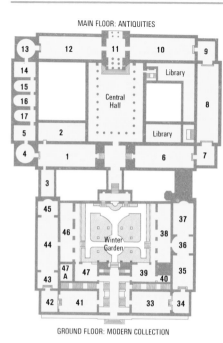

MAIN FLOOR: ANTIQUITIES

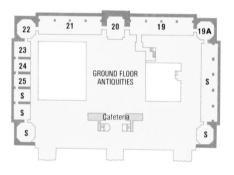

GROUND FLOOR: MODERN COLLECTION

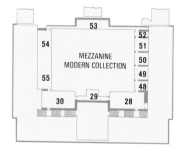

# Ny Carlsberg Glyptotek, Copenhagen

**MAIN FLOOR: ANTIQUITIES**
Entrance through Winter Garden

| | |
|---|---|
| 1–4 | Egyptian art |
| 5 | Ancient Oriental art |
| 6–9 | Greek archaic, classical and Hellenistic art |
| 10 | Greek portraits |
| 11–17 | Roman portraits |

**GROUND FLOOR: MODERN COLLECTION**
Entrance through Entrance Hall or Winter Garden

| | |
|---|---|
| 33–37 | French sculptors (Carpeaux and Rodin) |
| 38 | Cafeteria |
| 39 | Catalogues, postcards |
| 40 | Lift |
| 41–42 | Danish sculptors of 19th and 20th c. (H. V. Bissen, J. A. Jerichau) |
| 47 and | |
| 47A | Works by G. Henning |

**GROUND FLOOR: ANTIQUITIES**
Entrance through Central Hall

| | |
|---|---|
| 19–23 | Etruscan art |
| 24–25 | Palmyra collection |
| S | Study collections |

**MEZZANINE: MODERN COLLECTION**
Stairs from Entrance Hall or lift from Room 40

| | |
|---|---|
| 28–30 | French Impressionists and their followers (29 Degas bronzes) |
| 48–52 | Danish painting from J. Juel (early 19th c.) |
| 53 | Sculpture by H. E. Freund |
| 54–55 | Danish painting and sculpture from T. Philipsen to N. L. Stevns and E. Weie, K. Isakson (19th–20th c.) |

**UPPER FLOOR: MODERN COLLECTION**
Stairs from Entrance Hall or lift from Room 40

| | |
|---|---|
| 26 | French painting from David to Manet |
| 27 | French sculpture |
| 31–32 | French painting from Gauguin to Toulouse-Lautrec |

Gammel Strand, Copenhagen

1901–6. The central feature is a pillared marble hall in the style of an ancient temple court, lit from the roof.

INTERIOR. – The front building contains the **modern collection**. To the left of the entrance hall are rooms containing works by Danish sculptors, in particular by two of Thorvaldsen's pupils, H. W. Bissen (1798–1868) and J. A. Jerichau. (1816–83). The rooms to the right are devoted to French sculpture, with a collection of Rodin's work which for completeness is unequalled anywhere outside France. The mezzanine and upper floor of the front building contain further sculpture (including an important collection of bronzes by Degas) and a collection of pictures by French and Danish artists of the 19th and 20th c. (Impressionists). – In the Winter Garden are further sculptures, including a fountain group, the "Mother of Waters and her Children", by Kai Nielsen (1882–1924).

The **collection of antiquities** in the rear building is one of the finest of its kind N of the Alps; and its assemblage of Roman portrait statues and busts is not surpassed even in Rome itself. The Egyptian and Etruscan collections are also very fine. Every period of Egyptian sculpture is represented in the collection; and the Greek sculpture includes outstanding examples of 6th and 5th c. archaic art and some of the best sculpture of the time of Phidias, Polycletus, Praxiteles and Lysippus.

The street opposite the Glyptotek, *Ny Vester Gade*, leads to the *National Museum, finely situated on the Frederiksholms Kanal. This has a very remarkable *Danish Collection, with important prehistoric material as well as exhibits dating from historical times (interesting items from Greenland); a fine *Ethnographical Collection, giving an excellent impression of the life of the peoples of the Polar regions; a collection of antiquities; and another of coins and medals. From time to time there are also exhibitions on special themes. Incorporated in the National Museum is the *Prince's Palace* (1741–4), the earliest Danish Rococo palace, influenced by the French style of the period.

From here we cross the canal to the island of **Slotsholmen**, on which stands **Christiansborg Palace**, seat of the Danish government and Parliament (*Folketing*). The remains of the oldest fortified castle on this site, built by Bishop Absalon in 1167, can be seen under the present building.

The foundation stone of the first palace erected on the site of the original castle was laid by Christian VI in 1733, but this was not completely finished when it was destroyed by fire in 1794. Of the huge palace of four wings in Viennese Baroque style there survives only the Riding School (Ridebane). A new palace was built by Frederik VI in the first twenty years of the 19th c., but was only rarely used as a royal residence; in 1849 it became the home of the new Parliament. This palace in turn was burned down in 1884, among the parts which survived the fire being the palace church. The third Christiansborg Palace was built in 1907–16 to the design of Thorvald Jørgensoen. Reflecting the Danish conception of the state, the building was intended to house the royal residence, the Supreme Court and the Danish Parliament, then consisting of two chambers; but, since the king preferred to occupy Amalienborg Palace, the accommodation thus set free was taken over by the Foreign Ministry.

INTERIOR. – In the courtyard is an equestrian statue of Frederik VII. There are conducted tours of the state apartments and the Folketing. The *palace church* (1826), in a restrained neo-classical style, has a dome with figures of angels by Thorvaldsen. Within the Riding School complex (where the royal horses are exercised every morning) is the old court theatre, now the Theatre Museum; in the middle of the Riding School is a monument to Christian IX.

On the other side of Tøjhusgade from Christiansborg is the old **Arsenal** (*Tøjhus*), now housing a military museum, and adjoining it the **Royal Library** (1,700,000 volumes, 52,000 manu-scripts: temporary special exhibitions), and a small park. This area was once occupied by a harbour basin.

Immediately NW of Christiansborg Palace is the **Thorvaldsen Museum**, with works by the greatest Danish sculptor, Bertel Thorvaldsen (1770–1844). The building, in neo-classical style, was designed by Gottlieb Bindesbøll (1839–48). On the exterior wall facing the canal are frescoes depicting Thorvaldsen's return from Rome in 1838. In addition to Thorvaldsen's works the museum contains his own art collection and displays illustrating his method of working. – In *Gammel Strand*, on the opposite side of the canal, is a statue of an old fishwife; and in front of the statue can be seen every morning her living repre-sentatives – the fishwives who have the privilege of selling their wares here.

SE of Christiansborg, facing the harbour, is the *Exchange (Børsen*, 1619–20), a

The Exchange, Copenhagen

picturesque building in Dutch Renais-sance style with a spire 54 m (177 ft) high formed of the intertwined tails of four dragons. On the opposite side of the canal is the early 17th c. **Holmen Church**, originally built as an anchor forge, with a Baroque altar of unpainted oak by Abel Schrøder, who also carved the pulpit. The "Royal Doorway" was brought here from Roskilde Cathedral. Organ recitals are given in the church. In a side chapel are the tombs of Nils Juel (d. 1697) and Peder Tordenskjold.

From here the *Knippelsbro*, a bascule bridge with a span of 29 m (95 ft), leads into the CHRISTIANSHAVN district. The older part of this district, traversed by a number of canals, has something of the atmosphere of Amsterdam. In Skt. Annæ Gade is the **Church of Our Saviour** (*Vor Frelsers Kirke*), with a splendid Baroque altar, a beautiful font and a richly carved organ. The characteristic spire, with an external spiral staircase and a figure of Christ standing on a globe, affords extensive views. In Strandgade are attractive old houses and the *Christians Kirke*, flanked by two pavilions.

In an old barracks in Bådsmandsstræde is the "free state of Christiania", which proclaimed its independence in 1971, received a measure of official recognition as a social experiment from 1973 to 1975, and since then has continued to exist, although the authorities could, legally, evict the occupants – an unconventional example of the famous Danish tolerance, which does not always stretch as far as this.

From Town Hall Square the pedestrian precinct known as *Strøget, a suc-cession of short streets running into one another, extends E to Kongens Nytorv, lined by shops, boutiques and street cafés. A little way E of Town Hall Square the street opens out to form two squares, *Gammel Torv* and *Nytorv*. In Nytorv are old patrician houses dating from about 1800. Farther along Strøget, on the left, is the *Church of the Holy Ghost* (Hel-ligåndskirken), with the *Helligåndshus*, the only medieval building in Copen-hagen, originally belonging to a monas-tery. In *Amager Torv* (No. 6) is what is believed to be the oldest private house in the city, built by Burgomaster Hansen in 1616 (Dutch Baroque style, with a fine

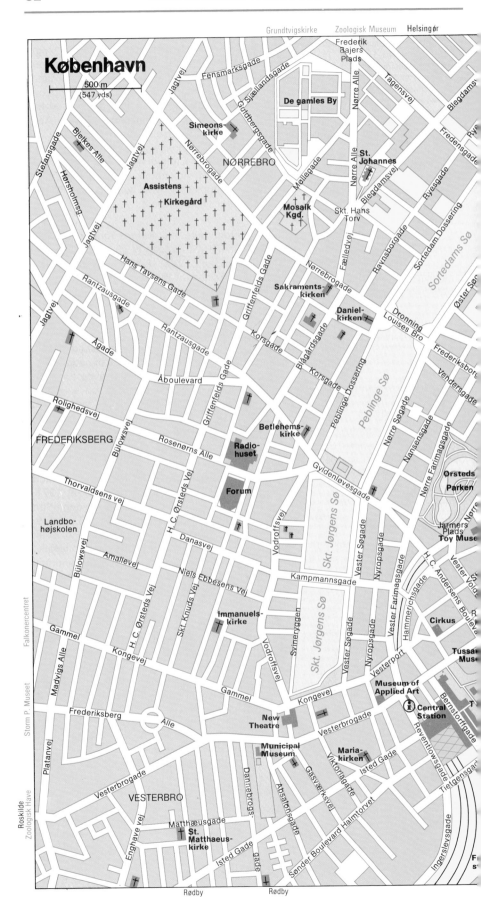

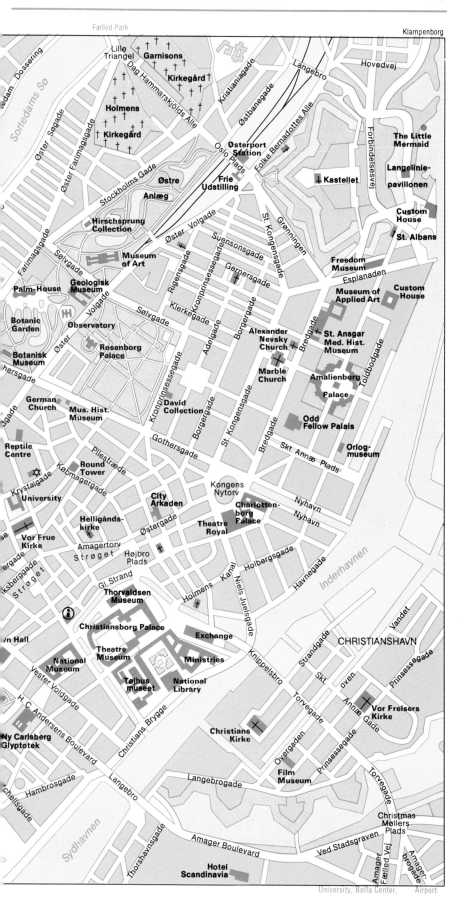

sandstone doorway), and now occupied by the showroom and shop of the Royal Porcelain Manufactory. At No. 10 is Illums Bolighus, a large department store selling fine Danish craft goods. After passing the *Stork Fountain* we come into *Kongens Nytorv, a large square (3·3 hectares – 8¼ acres) laid out towards the end of the 17th c., with an equestrian statue of Christian V in the middle. On the S side of the square is the **Theatre Royal** (*Kongelige Teater*, 1872–4), in late Renaissance style. In front of the entrance are bronze statues of the Danish dramatists Ludwig Holberg (author of comedies) and Adam Oehlenschläger (tragedies).

On the E side of Kongens Nytorv stands *Charlottenborg Palace*, since 1754 occupied by the Royal Academy of Art. Beyond the palace can be seen **Nyhavn** ("New Harbour"), flanked by old-world gabled houses. At the upper end is a gigantic anchor, commemorating Danish seamen who lost their lives in the last war. Nyhavn, from which boats leave for tours of the city, was once a disreputable quarter of the city: it is now a very charming part of Copenhagen, with its numerous brightly coloured little houses on the left-hand side of the canal and its restaurants, bars and tattooists' parlours. From Nyhavn there is a hydrofoil service to Malmö in Sweden (35 minutes) and also boat cruises on the canals. – At the upper end of Nyhavn is Bredgade. Going along this street, we pass a number of old mansions and come to the **Marble Church** (*Marmorkirken, Frederikskirken*), begun in 1749 but not completed until 1894 because of shortage of funds. The church has a dome 84 m (275 ft) high, and the façade is decorated with statues of great figures in Biblical and ecclesiastical history, including St Ansgar, the Apostle of the North, and Bishop Grundtvig, the 19th c. religious reformer. Features in the interior include an ivory crucifix, a German carving in oak of the Descent from the Cross and Grundtvig's seven-branched gold candelabrum. – Frederiksgade, opposite the church, leads to *Amalienborg Palace, residence of the Queen. The spacious octagonal * Palace Square is surrounded by the four wings of the palace, originally separate noble mansions. In the middle of the square is an *equestrian statue of Frederik V* (1771). On the SE side of the square stands the palace of Christian IX, now the

home of the royal family (with state apartments); adjoining it is the palace of Frederik VIII, now occupied by Queen Ingrid the Queen Mother; beyond this is the palace of Christian VIII (Crown Prince Knud); and on the SW side of the square is the palace of Christian VII, with the main state apartments and reception rooms. The ceremonial changing of the guard takes place daily at noon in front of the palace, with a military band when the Queen is present. The soldiers of the royal guard, with their blue uniforms and tall black fur caps, are one of the familiar sights of Copenhagen.

Returning to Bredgade, we continue past the Russian *Alexander Nevsky Church*, with three gilded onion domes, and the *District Court*, originally the Opera House, which later served as a military academy, a barracks, and from 1884 to 1918 (after the destruction of Christiansborg by fire) as the home of the Danish Parliament. On the opposite side of the street is *St Ansgar's Church*, Copenhagen's oldest Roman Catholic church and, since 1942, of cathedral status (fine statue of St Ansgar on façade). Adjoining the church is the *Museum of Applied Art* (Kunstindustrimuseet), with international collections of applied and decorative art of the past and present (notable 16th and 17th c. wood-carving). – Bredgade now joins *Esplanaden*, along which to the right is the old citadel, Kastellet. Before visiting this it is well worth while going a short

The Little Mermaid, Copenhagen

distance along the street to the left to see *Nyboder*, a settlement of characteristic old 17th and 18th c. houses – low yellow terraced houses in uniform style – built to accommodate sailors of the Danish fleet. The 17th c. houses at 20–40 Skt. Pauls Gade are the oldest.

The oldest parts of the Citadel (*Kastellet*), formerly known as Frederikshavn Citadel, date from 1625. When Denmark lost its possessions E of the Øresund (now southern Sweden) in 1658 and Copenhagen thus became a frontier town, the fortifications of the Citadel were strengthened. The buildings within the Citadel have been preserved, including its two handsome gates. In the large park adjoining are the *Freedom Museum*, commemorating the Danish Resistance movement against the Nazis (1940–5), the elegant *English Church* (St Alban's) and the *Gefion Fountain* (1908), which shows the goddess Gefion with her oxen ploughing the island of Zealand out of the soil of Sweden. Beyond the fountain is *Langelinie, with the famous bronze figure of Hans Andersen's *Little Mermaid* (*Den lille Havfrue*) by Edvard Eriksen. Langelinie is the quay where cruise ships and ships of the Royal Danish Navy lie at anchor.

At the W corner of the Citadel grounds is the *Østerport* station, and opposite this the *Free Art Exhibition* (Den frie Udstilling). To the left is a park, the *Østre Anlæg*, along the NW side of which runs Stockholmsgade (at No. 20 the *Hirschsprung Collection* of 19th c. Danish art). Continuing along Dag Hammarskjölds Allé, we come to the *Fælled Park* (Stadium), to the W of which (Universitetsparken) is the modern *Zoological Museum*.

To the N and W of the old town are a number of large parks which are well worth a visit. NW of the Town Hall Square is the romantic *Ørsteds Park*, laid out over the remains of the old fortifications and therefore hilly. From here Rømersgade runs past *Israels Plads* (Saturday flea-market) to the **Botanic Garden**, with the Botanic Museum, the Palm-House, the Geological Museum and the Technical College. To the SE, along Gothersgade, is **Kongens Have** (the King's Garden) or *Rosenborg Have*, much frequented by sun-bathers in summer; it contains a number of statues and the *Hercules Pavilion* (puppet theatre in summer). In

the upper part of the park is *Rosenborg Palace**, a country house built by Christian IV between 1610 and 1626 which was the spring and autumn residence of the royal family until the mid-18th c. In 1833 it became a royal family museum and was opened to the public as the *Chronological Collections of the Danish Kings*. Features of particular interest are Frederik III's *Marble Room, the Crown Jewels and royal insignia, and the *Banqueting Hall or Knights' Hall.

Immediately N of the King's Park, beyond a street intersection, is another large park, the *Østre Anlæg*, in which is the *State Museum of Art** (*Statens Museum for Kunst*, 1891–6).

The **collection of pictures** presents a cross-section of European art from the 13th to the 18th c. The *Italian section* includes a number of important works, including pictures by Titian and Tintoretto. The *Dutch and Flemish schools* are represented by Rubens and Rembrandt. The *German collection* includes works by Lucas Cranach the Elder, his studio and his followers. The gallery also has a rich collection of 19th c. Danish painting of the Biedermeier period and some work produced in the early decades of the 20th c., but little in the way of modern art. There is also a notable private collection of works by Braque, Matisse, Picasso and others which was presented to the Museum. The *Print Collection*, which has been separated from the Royal Library, contains some 100,000 items.

In the western district of FREDERIKS-BERG (reached by way of Vesterbrogade and Frederiksberg Allé) is another extensive park, **Frederiksberg Have**, in the southern part of which stands Frederiksberg Palace, an Italian-style building with an ochre-yellow façade. To the W of the palace is the *Zoological Garden*, with a children's zoo and a lookout tower. In the district of VALBY, to the S, is the large complex of the *Carlsberg Breweries* (conducted tours). In Ny Carlsberg Vej the **Elephant Tower**, a cooling tower borne on four massive granite elephants, is an unusual example of Danish industrial architecture.

In *Bispebjerg*, 6 km (4 miles) NW of the mid-city (by way of the Botanic Garden, Sølvgade and Tagensvej), we find the *Grundtvig Church* (by P. V. Jensen-Klint, 1921–40), one of the major achievements of 20th c. Danish architecture. Standing on high ground, this is a massive structure in yellow brick modelled on a typical Danish country church. The W front resembles a gigantic organ. The church, with a high, light interior, is used for concerts and recitals; the organ is one of the largest in Scandinavia.

SURROUNDINGS. – The SE part of Copenhagen lies on the island of **Amager**, which is linked to Zealand by bridges. On Amager are the *Bella Center*, a modern exhibition hall, and *Kastrup Airport*. On the E coast of the island the little fishing town of **Dragør**, a popular bathing resort, has some well-preserved 18th c. houses. There are attractive walks through the town, whose inhabitants are concerned to preserve its character unspoiled.

The *Lyngbyvej* (motorway) runs N from Copenhagen to *Kongens Lyngby*, *Sorgenfri* with the little palace of Sorgenfri, the outstation of the National Museum in *Brede* (temporary exhibitions) and the very interesting **Open-Air Museum** (*Frilandsmuseet*), a park of 36 hectares containing old farmhouses, cottages and mills from all over Denmark (including the Færoes). Every building has authentic old furniture and furnishings.

Another attractive trip to the N of Copenhagen is by way of Østerbrogade and Strandvejen, passing the *Tuborg Brewery* (with the largest beer bottle in the world, 26 m (85 ft) high, holding as much as 1,425,000 normal bottles); then through *Hellerup* and *Charlottenlund* (Aquarium, with 3000 fish from all over the world; trotting track) to the *Dyrehave*, an extensive wild deer-park in which visitors can see red deer and roe-deer grazing, look for mushrooms, cycle, ride, drive in a horse-carriage or merely ramble about on foot. In the beautiful beech forest of some 860 hectares is the *Eremitage*, a royal hunting lodge which is still in use; magnificent views over the Øresund to Sweden. To the S of the park lies **Bakken**, a very popular and noisy fairground and amusement park. At the SE corner of the park is the residential suburb and bathing resort of **Klampenborg**. – The coast road continues to the elegant residential towns of *Skodsborg*, *Vedbæk* and *Rungsted*. – To the *Louisiana* art gallery and **Helsingør**, see p. 128.

S of Copenhagen the highway passes residential districts (modern apartments) of Albertslund, Brøndby Strand and Ishøj and then through flat and treeless country of no particular attraction to **Køge** (pop. 35,000; Hvide Hus Hotel, Strandvejen 111, 224 b.; youth hostel; two camp sites), a port in *Køge Bay* with many attractive old timber-framed houses (the oldest dating from 1527) and St Nicholas's Church, which has a beautiful carved pulpit and altar (1624) – 7 km (4½ miles) S is the Renaissance mansion of *Vallø* (1586), which since 1738 has housed an institution for ladies of the nobility. An elegant three-storeyed building with two massive towers, one round and one square, it was ravaged by a fire in 1893 which destroyed the whole of the interior. The house is surrounded by a broad moat and a beautiful park.

# Dalarna

Sweden (Central).
Province: Kopparbergs län.

(i) **Dala Tour**,
Tullkammaregatan I,
S-79131 Falun;
tel. (0 23) 1 06 30

The little wooden horses of Dalarna

*Dalarna, also known in English as Dalecarlia, lies NW of Stockholm, extending to the Norwegian frontier. It is one of Sweden's principal tourist regions, and is undoubtedly one of the most attractive parts of the country – a wooded upland region watered by the rivers Västerdalälv and Österdalälv, with fertile valleys, the beautiful Lake Siljan in the middle of the area and rugged rocky hills to the NW. Dalarna is also popular for skiing (particularly cross-country skiing). It is noted for the brightly coloured little wooden horses which are a traditional local craft.*

Towards the Norwegian frontier the land rises to some 1200 m (3900 ft). Some 20,050 hectares (50,000 acres) – 72% of the total area of Dalarna – are covered with forest. In addition to agriculture and forestry (woodworking industry) there are also mines in the SW of the province (iron-smelting, steel works). The old mining town of Falun produces the Falu red paint (originally a by-product of copper-mining) with which many Swedish houses are painted. – The attractions of Dalarma for the tourist include walking, fishing, water sports and, in winter, skiing. – The distance from Stockholm to Lake Siljan is about 260 km (160 miles).

The people of Dalarna are noted for their bravery and love of freedom. In 1434 Engelbrekt Engelbrektsson led a peasant rising against the ruler of the region, Eric of Pomerania. In 1520 Gustav Eriksson called on his countrymen to rise against King Christian II of Denmark, and in 1523 he was crowned as King Gustav I Vasa of Sweden (his portrait still appears on Swedish 5-kr. notes). His flight towards Norway at the beginning of the rising is commemorated in the Vasa Run (Vasaloppet), a cross-country ski run of 85·8 km (53 miles) between Sälen and Mora which is held every year at the beginning of March (first run 1922; in 1985 some 10,000 participants). – By the middle of the 19th c. Dalarna was already a popular tourist region. The celebrations of Midsummer Night are carried on particularly enthusiastically on Lake Siljan, the "heart of Sweden". Unfortunately, however, these old customs have lost much of their original charm: visitors are likely to see them at their best in the smaller towns and villages.

*Tour of Dalarna. – Visitors coming from the S can reach Dalarna either on Road 60 from Örebro or Road 70 from Stockholm. The starting point of the tour is the town of Avesta, 170 km (105 miles) NW of Stockholm.

Avesta (alt. 84 m (276 ft); pop. 26,900; Star Hotel, 126 b.), on the Dalälv (two waterfalls), has been a considerable industrial town since the 14th c. The largest copper coin in the world, weighing almost 20 kg (45 lb), was once minted here; and the town now has a large steel-works producing high-grade steel. The Gamla By (Old Town) in the middle of Avesta still has all the atmosphere of the 17th c.; park, with a large herd of bison.

6 km (4 miles) SE of Avesta is **Karlbo**, with the house (Tolvmannagård) in which the poet Erik Axel Karlfeldt (1864–1931) was born. His grave is in Folkärna cemetery, 11 km (7 miles) NE.

20 km (12 miles) beyond Avesta on Road 70 is **Hedemora** (alt. 107 m (351 ft); pop. 17,000; Stadshotellet, 55 b.), the oldest town in Dalarna (chartered 1446). In the main square, Stora Torget, are the Town Hall (1761) and a red timber-built pharmacy of 1779. The Theatre (1820) formerly also served as a granary. The church dates from 1441. To the N of the town, on a small lake, is an open-air museum with old houses (Hedemora Gammelgård).

12 km (7½ miles) NE (Road 270), on the Dalälv, is the village of **Näsgård**, from which an interesting circuit of some 35 km (22 miles) can be made (the "Husbyring"): *Husby Kungsgård*, where the first mining rights in the Falu mines (see p. 90) were granted in 1347. The church has retained its original medieval interior. – **Stjärnsund**, on *Lake Grycken*. There was an iron foundry in operation here until 1942. Manufacture of Stjärnsund clocks, once made by Christopher Polhem (1661–1751); museum. Old craftsmen's houses – *Silvhytteå*, with an old iron foundry (restored). – *Högsta-Weg* (1·1 km – ¾ mile), with ancient stone-settings. – *Kloster* has the ruins of the Cistercian monastery of Gudsberga (1477–1538). – **Näsgård**.

From Hedemora Road 70 continues to **Säter** (alt. 157 m (515 ft); pop. 10,360), with the interesting Åsgårdarnas Hof (houses dating from the last four centuries; workshop for making tiled stoves).

To the N extends the charming *Säterdal*, a deeply indented valley some 6 km (4 miles) long; open-air theatre. From the old mining settlement of *Bispberg*, 3 km (2 miles) NE, there is a path to the top of *Bispbergs Klack* (314 m – 1030 ft), which affords extensive views. – Soon afterwards the 86 m (280 ft) high spire of the church at *Stora Tuna* comes into sight in the distance (church built 1486; paintings; crucifix 6 m (20 ft) high).

The road then comes to **Borlänge** (alt. 139 m (456 ft); pop. 46,000; hotels: Borlänge, 37 b., SP; Brage, 153 b.; Galaxan, 185 b.; Gustav Wasa, 150 b., SB; youth hostel), a considerable industrial town with iron and steel works, rolling mills and a paper-mill. From the *Forssa Klack*, 2 km (1¼ miles) N, there are far-ranging views. 20 km (12½ miles) NE is Falun (p. 90), 45 km (28 miles) S Ludvika.

Road 70 follows the *Dalälv*, which is formed at **Djurås** by the junction of the Öster- and Västerdalälv. From Djurås it runs N through the old village of *Gagnef* (alt. 183 m (600 ft); 16th c. church, fine stained glass), which is famous for its beautiful lace, and the little industrial town of *Insjön* (alt. 183 m – 600 ft), to the N of which is the 15th c. church of *Ål* (local museum adjoining the church), and comes to Leksand, on the S side of *Lake Siljan (26 km (16 miles): see p. 234).

Immediately N of Lake Siljan is *Lake Orsa* (alt. 161 m (528 ft); area 56 sq. km (22 sq. miles), greatest depth 97 m – 320 ft). At the N end of this lake is **Orsa** (alt. 171 m (561 ft); pop. 5000; Orsa Hotel, 68 b.; youth hostel), the industrial and commercial capital of northern Dalarna. The church, originally dating from the 14th c., has fine 16th c. frescoes. Extensive recreational facilities at the mouth of the *Oreälv*.

12 km (7½ miles) NW of Orsa is the recreation complex of *Fryksås* (Fryksås Hotell, 36 b.; winter sports), with magnificent *views of Lakes Orsa and Siljan. – 17 km (11 miles) NE of Orsa (Road 296), situated some 100 m (330 ft) above the Oreälv, we come to the village of *Skattungsbyn*. At the W end of the village stands a birch-tree ("Skattungsbjörken") which retains its leaves until the new shoots appear in spring. – The tourist resort of **Furudal** (alt. 205 m – 673 ft), another 20 km (12 miles) E between *Lake Skattung* to the NW and *Lake Ore* to the SE, originally grew up round a chain-making forge. 12 km (7½ miles) N are the summer grazings of *Ärteråsen* (468 m – 1535 ft). 20 km (12 miles) S (Road 300), at Boda, is a waterfall 36 m (120 ft) high, the *Styggfors*.

From Orsa Road 81 runs N into an inhospitable region, the *Orsa Finnmark*, which was settled by Finnish immigrants in the 17th c. and still has many villages and mountains with Finnish names, such as Pilkalampinoppi (644 m (2113 ft): extensive views) and Korpimäki (706 m – 2316 ft). Both of these, together with *Lake Fågel*, are in **Hamra National Park** (27 hectares (70 acres); natural forest).

**Djurås to Särna** (260 km (160 miles) without detours). – Take Road 71, which runs W, parallel to the Västerdalälv, to *Dala-Floda*, where Sweden's oldest suspension bridge can be seen. Pleasant excursions to the surrounding mountain pastures (*views). – At *Björbo* Road 247 branches off on the left, going S.

Road 247 runs past an expanse of protected natural forest at *Skärlacken* and comes in 27 km (17 miles) to the ancient little mining town of **Nyhammar**. 5 km (3 miles) NW is the *Gasenberg* (417 m – 1368 ft), and 8 km (5 miles) NE the *Grangärde-Hästberg*, with numerous rock carvings and a fine viewpoint, the *Hästbergsklack* (419 m – 1375 ft). – 3 km (2 miles) beyond Nyhammar is the village of *Grangärde*, situated between two lakes (alt. 160 m (525 ft); Saxenborg Hotel, 80 b.). – The road continues, skirting *Lake Västman* (alt. 155 m – 509 ft) at one point, and comes in another 21 km (13 miles) to **Ludvika** (alt. 157 m (515 ft); pop. 32,750; Stadshotell, 55 b.), once an important mining town (first ironworks established 1555) but now dominated by the electrical industry (transformer testing plant of the ASEA company). To the W of the town is an old 16th c. mining settlement (Gammelgård: eight houses, old equipment), with a mining museum; mine-owner's house of 1720. – 16 km (10 miles) SW of Road 60, near the border of the province of Västmanland, the little mining town of **Grängesberg** (alt. 273 m (896 ft); Grängesbergs Värdhus, 48 b.) has given its name to the great Grängesberg iron and steel corporation. In this area are the largest reserves of iron ore in Sweden outside Lapland, worked since the 16th c. and now exploited to a depth of 600 m (2000 ft) (conducted tours). – A detour can be made to the *Fjällberg* (469 m – 1539 ft), 5 km (3 miles) NW.

Road 71 continues W from Björbo and comes in 17 km (11 miles) to *Nås*, probably the oldest parish in western Dalarna. Here Selma Lagerlöf found the theme of her novel "Jerusalem", and a play by Rune Lindström based on the novel is performed every year at the beginning of July. 17 km (11 miles) S is the old iron foundry of *Lindesnäs*, now closed down. – In another 28 km (17 miles) Road 71 reaches **Vansbro**, where a "Vasa Run for swimmers" is held in the Västerdalälv at the beginning of July (3 km (2 miles), in water which is usually still quite cold). – 45 km (28 miles): **Malung** (alt. 302 m (990 ft); pop. 12,000;

Skinnargården Hotel, 116 b.), chief town of a district and the focus of the Swedish leather industry (midsummer celebrations in which leather features prominently); 13th c. church, with a 15th c. figure of St Olof; open-air museum (Gammelgård), with old houses.

From here Road 297 runs N up the Västerdalälv valley, passing through the villages of *Lima* and *Transtrand*. – 65 km (40 miles): **Sälen** (Hasses Hotel, 36 b.; Wardshuset Gammelgården, 75 b.; Lindvallen i Sälen holiday village with chalets), a tourist area below the E side of the *Transtrandsfjäll*, the most southerly of Sweden's mountains (Storfjäll, 923 m (3028 ft); Sälens Högfjällhotell, 800 m (2625 ft), 396 b.). Excellent walking country. On the banks of the river is a monument to Gustavus Vasa, who reached this point in his flight from the Danes. It is now the starting point of the Vasa Run to Mora (see p. 234). – Another 69 km (43 miles) N, on the *Österdalälv*, here dammed to form a lake 70 km (44 miles) long, *Trängsletsjön*, is the village of **Särna** (alt. 440 m (1444 ft); Knappgårdens Kurs o Friluftsgård, 60 b.), which until 1644 was in Norway; wooden church of 1690 (restored 1766).

3 km S is *Mickeltemplet* (624 m (2047 ft): lookout tower), with a magnificent *view of the **Fulufjäll** (1044 m – 3425 ft) to the SW. On the N side of this hill is the *Njupeskärfall*, Sweden's highest waterfall (125 m (410 ft), with a sheer drop of 70 m – 230 ft), which can be reached on a footpath (3 km – 2 miles) from the village of Mörkret, 26 km (16 miles) W of Särna.

Road 295 continues to the Norwegian frontier (customs post at Flötningen, 70 km – 43 miles). 32 km (20 miles) from Särna is **Idre**, a tourist resort on the Österdalälv (which is dammed at this point). From here the highest road in Sweden passable for motors runs N to the **Nipfjäll** (1191 m (3908 ft); parking place at about 1000 m – 3280 ft). Another road, running NW from Idre, climbs in 45 km (28 miles) to the *Grövelsjö* tourist station on the western slopes of the *Långfjäll*, which rises to over 1200 m (3900 ft).

# Esbjerg

Denmark (SW Jutland).
County: Ribe amt.
Altitude: sea level. – Population: 80,000.
Postal code: DK-6700. – Telephone code: 05.

ⓘ **Esbjerg Turistbyrå,**
    Skolegade 33;
    tel. 12 55 99.
    *British Consulate,*
    Grimsbyvej;
    tel. 13 08 11.

HOTELS. – *Ansgar Missionhotel*, Skolegade 36, 90 b.; *Bangs Hotel*, Torvet 21, 137 b.; *Britannia*, Torvet, 121 b.; *Esberg*, Skolegade 31, 58 b.; *E.S.A.*, Spangsbjerg Kirkevej 110, 112 b.; *Palads Hotel*, Skolegade 14, 77 b.; *Scandic Hotel*, Olympic, Strandbygade 3, 174 b. – YOUTH HOSTEL. – CAMP SITE.

RESTAURANTS. – *Sands Restaurant*, Skolegade 60; *Den røde Okse*, Tarphagevej 9.

**The life of Esbjerg, Denmark's fifth largest town, revolves around its harbour, the construction of which was begun in 1868. It is the most important Danish North Sea port (export of agricultural produce, passenger and vehicle ferry connections with Britain and the Færoes) and the country's largest fishing port. It is now also the base of Danish exploration for oil and natural gas in the North Sea. The town received its municipal charter only in 1898.**

On the island of Fanø

SIGHTS. – From the *Water-Tower* in the public gardens overlooking the harbour there are fine views. Adjoining the tower is the *Art Gallery* (1962: modern Danish art). On the quay of the fishing harbour stands the **Fish Auction Hall**, 225 m (740 ft) long (first auction at 7 a.m. on weekdays). Along the seafront to the NW is the interesting **Fishery and Shipping Museum** (1968), with a salt-water aquarium and a seal pool (1976). – To the N of the mid-town is the modern *Trinity Church* (1961), with a large mosaic window. Beyond it lies the idyllic *Vognsbølpark* and to the E, on Kirkevej (A1), is *Jerne* church, which is mentioned in the records in 1306.

SURROUNDINGS. – From the harbour it is a 20 minutes' trip in the car ferry to the offshore island of **Fanø** (area 55 sq. km (21 sq. miles), pop. 2800). The chief place on the island is the fishing village of **Nordby** on the E coast (Krogården, 19 b.; Nordby, 24 b.), with a local museum and an 18th c. church (models of ships). – 3 km (2 miles) SW is the attractive swimming resort of **Vesterhavsbad** (Hotel Kongen ag Danmark, 90 b.; Golf Hotel, 30 b.; Kellers, 26 b.; Fanø Bad, 90 b.; Vesterhavet holiday resort, with

houses for 6–8 persons, SP and SB; several camp sites). It has a beautiful sandy beach, on which it is possible to drive to the picturesque village of **Sønderho** (Sønderho Kro, 14 b.; Sønderho, 14 b.; camp site), 17 km (10 miles) away at the southern tip of the island. The village has well-preserved old houses and a modest little church with many old models of boats.

# Falster

Denmark. – County: Storstrøms amt.
Area: 514 sq. km (198 sq. miles).
Population: 50,000.
ⓘ **Nykøbing Turistbyrå,**
Østergade 2,
DK-4800 Nykøbing F;
tel. (03) 85 13 03.
**Gedser Turistbyrå,**
Langgade 61,
DK-4874 Gedser;
tel. (03) 87 90 41.

**The Danish island of Falster lies between the two larger islands of Lolland and Zealand. On the E coast it has beautiful sandy beaches. Gedser Odde, the southern tip of the island, is the most southerly point in Denmark.**

From Lolland the Frederik IX Bridge crosses the Guldborg Sound to the largest town on Falster, **Nykøbing**, beautifully situated on the E side of the sound (pop. 26,000; Baltic Hotel, 135 b.; Teaterhotellet, 38 b.; Liselund Motel, Sundby, 50 b.; camp site). Founded in the Middle Ages and now a busy industrial town (sugar-refining, tobacco-processing), Nykøbing has some well-preserved old streets and half-timbered houses (Store Kirkestræde, Langgade, Slotsgade). A notable feature is the Franciscan church (Gråbrødrekirke), a Gothic building of 1532, containing a picture (1540) by Lucas Cranach the Elder. The Falster Museum is housed in a building of 1700, known as the Czarens Hus, in which Peter the Great lived in 1716.

Nykøbing (Falster)

25 km (15 miles) SE is the little port of **Gedser** (Gedser Hotel, 35 b.; Højvangs Petit Motel, 22 b.), from which there are ferry services to Lübeck-Travemünde in the Federal Republic of Germany (3 hours) and Rostock-Warnemünde in the German Democratic Republic (1½ hours).

A2 runs NW from Nykøbing through fertile arable country and pastureland. At *Nørre Alslev* (15 km – 10 miles) a road branches off on the right to **Stubbekøbing** (pop. 7300; Elverkroen 80 b.; camp site), an ancient little town beautifully situated on the Grønsund, with the oldest church on the island (*c.* 1200); attractive views from the tower. A ferry crosses in 12 minutes to Bogø, from which a bridge leads on to the island of Møn (see p. 193).

N of Nørre Alslev the **Storstrøm Bridge** leads to the island of Masnedø and from there over a bascule bridge to the island of Zealand. To the NE of Nørre Alslev the E4, coming from Lolland, traverses the first section of the **Farø Bridges** on to the island of Farø and from there crosses the second section to Zealand.

# Falun

Sweden (Central).
Province: Kopparbergs län. – Region: Dalarna.
Altitude: 113 m. – Population: 49,150.
Postal code: S-791 . . . – Telephone code: 023.

ⓘ **Falu Turistbyrå,**
Stora Torget,
S-79183 Falun;
tel. 8 36 38.

HOTELS. – *Bergmästaren*, 160 b., SB; *Birgittagården*, 35 b.; *Grand Hotel*, 320 b.; *Kåre*, 29 b.; *Samuelsdals Herrgårdspensionat*, 50 b., SB; *Scandic Hotel*, 223 b. – YOUTH HOSTEL. – CAMP SITE.

EVENTS. – *Swedish Ski Games* (February).

**The old mining town of Falun, chief town of the province of Kopparberg, lies NW of Stockholm in Dalarna (central Sweden). It is situated on both banks of the River Falun between Lake Varpa and Lake Runn.**

Although Falun's deposits of copper, discovered before the year 1000, have been of immense economic and financial importance to Sweden, the town received its municipal charter only in 1614, when its great days were nearing their end,

though it was still the second largest town in Sweden. E. T. A. Hoffman wrote the story "The Mines of Falun" (1818).

SIGHTS. – In the middle of the town old and new buildings rub shoulders with one another. In the main square, *Stora Torg*, which has a monument to Engelbrekt Engelbrektsson, leader of the 15th c. peasant rising, are the *Old Town Hall* (1764), the new *Local Government Offices* (1968), the *Kristine Church* (1642–55; tower, 1865; fine interior) and the headquarters of the mining corporation, the Stora Kopparbergs Bergslags AB. Here, too, is the house in which Selma Lagerlöf (1858–1940) lived while writing "The Wonderful Journey of Nils Holgersson" and other works. To the W, on the far side of the river, are the *Dalarna Museum* and *Art Gallery* (local costumes, painting, crafts, etc.). Beside the Northern Station is the *Kopparberg Church* (14th c.), the oldest building in Falun.

Opencast copper workings, Falun

In the districts of Östanfors, Gamla Herrgården and Elsborg there are numbers of old wooden houses dating from the 17th–19th c. – On the E side of the town is the *Skiing Stadium* (1973), with ski-jumping towers up to 52 m (170 ft) high (lift; fine views). Nearby is a large *Sports Hall* (90 by 45·5 m – 295 by 150 ft).

The town is bounded on the SW by the **Falu Coppermine** (*Falu Gruva*), which is reached by way of Gruvgata. The opencast workings cover an area of 400 by 350 m (430 by 380 yds) and are up to 95 m (310 ft) deep; and below this underground workings extend to a depth of 450 m (1475 ft). In the mid-17th c. the mine produced some 3000 tons of crude copper, representing about two-thirds of world output; its total output to date amounts to some 500,000 tons. The collapse of underground galleries in 1687,

1833 and 1876 led to the decline of this "treasurehouse of the realm" and to the development of the present opencast workings, the *Stora Stöten*, which yield mainly iron pyrites, zinc and lead (annual output of ore some 150,000 tons). – The mine belongs to the Stora Kopparbergs Bergslags AB, probably the oldest industrial company in the world (its predecessor being referred to in an episcopal letter of 1288 and a royal charter of 1347). The Stora Kopparberg became a limited company (AB) in 1888, and is now one of Sweden's largest industrial corporations, its main interests being in metals and woodworking. – *Conducted tours of the mine daily from May to the end of August. Close to the workings is the *Stora Kopparbergs Museum*, housed in the old mine offices (1771–85), with models of the mines, minerals and a collection of copper coins.

SURROUNDINGS. – 14 km (9 miles) NE of Falun, on the S side of *Lake Tofta* (alt. 119 m – 390 ft), is **Sundborn**. The Swedish painter *Carl Larsson* (1853–1919: "The House in the Sun", a series of watercolours) lived here from 1901 until his death. His grave is near the red chapel (1755), which contains pictures by him (as does the commune office). Larsson's house, preserved as it was in his lifetime, is now a *museum (conducted visits: waiting may be necessary at height of season). – From Sundborn an excursion can be made to the beautiful *Svärdsjö*, at the E end of Lake Tofta.

# Finnish Lake Plateau
## (Järvi-Suomi/ Finska Sjöplatån)

Finland (Central).
Provinces: Hämeen lääni (Tavastehus län/Häme), Kymen lääni (Kymmene län/Kymi), Mikkelin lääni (Sankt Michels län/Mikkeli), Keski-Suomen lääni (Mellersta Finlands län/Central Finland), Kuopion lääni (Kuopios län/Kuopio) and Pohjois-Karjalan lääni (Norra Karelens län/Northern Karelia).

**The *Finnish Lake Plateau, with its intricately patterned lakes and thousands of islands, covers almost a third of Finland's total area, earning it the name of the "Land of 60,000 Lakes". To the E the lakes extend to the Soviet frontier; on the S they are bounded by the massive terminal moraines of Salpausselkä, and on the N by the barrier of Suomenselkä, which forms the watershed be-tween the Gulf of Bothnia and the Gulf of Finland. The harmonious mingling of woodland and water makes this region a paradise for nature-lovers and boating enthusiasts.**

Within this extensive area there are three main drainage basins, loosely connected with one another. To the W, N of Tampere, is the smallest of the three, *Näsijärvi*; in the middle the long straggling *Lake Päijänne*; and to the E the large *Lake Saimaa*, which is drained into the Soviet Union by the Vuoksen. All these lake systems lie some 76–78 m (250–255 ft) above sea level.

The Finnish Lake Plateau is traversed from S to N by three important roads, linked by a number of transverse connections. E4 runs along the western edge of the lake region from Lahti by way of Jyväskylä and Kärsämäki to Oulu; Road 5 runs through the middle of the region from Lahti to Mikkeli and Kuopio; and Roads 6 and 18 run in a wide arc round the eastern edge of the plateau via Lappeenranta and Joensuu to Kajaani and Oulu.

**Lahti to Oulu via Jyväskylä (E4). –** **Lahti** (see p. 167) lies at the southern tip of *Vesijärvi* (area 113 sq. km – 44 sq. miles), which forms the S end of Lake Päijänne. In the northern outskirts of the town Road 5 branches off E4 on the right and runs NE to Mikkeli on Lake Saimaa. E4 continues through hilly and wooded country to the little town of *Vääksy* (Tallukka Hotel, 288 b., SB), where there is a swing bridge over the *Vääksy Canal*, constructed in 1871 to link Vesijärvi with **Lake Päijänne**, 4 m (13 ft) lower (lock). The road now follows the western shore of this lake.

Lake Päijänne, lying 78 m (255 ft) above sea level, is 140 km (87 miles) long and up to 28 km (17 miles) wide, with an area of some 1111 sq. km (430 sq. miles) and a maximum depth of 93 m (305 ft). Its shores are wooded and for much of the way rocky and rugged. Immediately beyond the swing bridge, Road 314 goes off on the right to *Arsikkala* (pop. 7600), continuing over the narrow isthmus of *Pulkkilanharju*, 6·5 km (4 miles) long, to the E side of Lake Päijänne and then running N alongside the lake to *Sysmä* (pop. 7000; Hotel Uoti, 19 b.; camp site), which has a stone-built 15th c. church.

20 km (12 miles) beyond the turning for Arsikkala E4 reaches the village of *Padasjoki* (pop. 4800; Nelosmutka Hotel, 18 b.; camp site; two holiday bungalow villages), and then continues via *Kuhmoînen* to *Jämsä* (pop. 12,000; Motelli Martin, 50 b.; Monrepos Hotel, 45 b.; camp site), an industrial town (papermill) at an important road junction, where Road 9 (E80) goes off on the left to Tampere (see p. 262). – E4 continues via the beautifully situated village of *Korpilahti*, (Turistikeidas Pyhimys Hotel, 24 b.; camp site) to *Muurame*, which has a church designed by Alvar Aalto. A short distance beyond this, off the road to the right, is the village of *Säynätsalo*, with communal offices by Alvar Aalto. E4 then comes to **Jyväskylä** (see p. 153), beautifully situated on the northern shore of *Jyväsjärvi*. From here Road 9 runs E to Kuopio. E4 continues N, past a side road (No. 13) to the attractively situated village of *Saarijärvi*, on to the recently developed little town of **Äänekoski**, 1·5 km (1 mile) on right (pop. 11,000; Hirvi Hotel, 50 b.; youth hostel; camp site): woodworking industry, hydroelectric power station on the river flowing out of *Lake Keitele*. 8 km (5 miles) SE is the busy little industrial town of *Suolahti* (pop. 6200; Keitele Hotel, 40 b.).

E4 continues via *Konginkangas* (a little way off the road) to *Viitasaari* (Pikhuri Hotel, 72 b.; Rantasipi Ruuponsaari, 212 b.; youth hostel; several camp sites), on an island at the N end of the much ramified *Lake Keitele* (over 80 km (50 miles) long). To the N of the village, which is reached on a causeway, is a lookout tower. Pleasant boat trips on the lake (good fishing).

**Pihtipudas** (Niemenharjun Lomakeskus Motelli, 70 b.; SB) lies at the NW end of Kolimajärvi, on the northern boundary of Central Finland. – *Pyhäsalmi* is a mining village (iron ore, precious metals), a short way off the road on Pyhäjärvi (alt. 141 m – 463 ft). E4 now leaves the Lake Plateau and continues via *Kärsämäki* and *Leskelä* to **Oulu** (p. 219) on the Gulf of Bothnia.

**Lahti to Kajaani via Mikkeli and Kuopio** (Road 5). – This route through the central part of the plateau also starts from **Lahti** (p. 167). On the N side of the town take Road 5, which runs NE. Off the road to the right, in a beautiful setting, is

*Vierumäki*, with the *National Sports College* (main building 1937: can be visited). – Road 5 then crosses the *Kyminjoki*, which drains Lake Päijänne into the Gulf of Finland, on an arched bridge (beautiful view).

**Heinola** (pop. 16,000; hotels: Kumpeli, 154 b.; Seurahuone, 38 b.; youth hostel), situated on the N side of the *Jyrängönvirta*, a stretch of rapids on the Kyminjoki, received its municipal charter in 1776. It is now a popular holiday resort and also an educational and industrial town of some consequence. The finely situated wooden church (1811) has a separate tower built in 1843 by the Berlin architect Carl Ludwig Ehgel.

From *Lusi* Road 59 runs N to Jyväskylä (p. 153), while Road 5 continues NE through extensive forests and past numerous lakes to Mikkeli (p. 190) on Lake Saimaa.

40 km (25 miles) NE of **Mikkeli** Road 14 diverges to the right to Savonlinna. Road 5 continues through wooded country via the village of *Joroinen* (Joronjälki Hotel, 106 b.) to the important industrial town of **Varkaus** (pop. 25,000; Keskus Hotelli, 120 b.; Taipale, 93 b., SP; youth hostel; camp site), with sawmills, a paper and cellulose factory, an engineering plant and large shipyards where boats for service on the lakes are built. An interesting feature is the nine-storey water tower (1954) which is also an apartment house (fine view; art museum on ground floor). From Varkaus there are boat services to Kuopio and Savonlinna. (Savonlinna can also be reached on an attractive minor road which runs along the E bank of the *Haukivesi*.)

From here a rewarding visit can be made to the only two Orthodox religious houses in Finland. Road 70 runs NE from Varkaus to *Karvio* (55 km – 35 miles), where a road goes off on the left to the nunnery of **Lintula**, in the commune of Palokki (open to visitors; café; overnight accommodation). 8 km (5 miles) farther along Road 70 another road on the left leads to the monastery of **Uusi Valamo** (commune of Papinniemi), at the S end of Juojärvi. A community of Orthodox monks found a new home here when they were compelled to leave their monastery of Valamo on Lake Ladoga in consequence of the Soviet occupation of the area in winter 1940. They were able to bring with them numerous icons and valuable church furnishings. Uusi Valamo, with a church consecrated in 1976, is the largest Russian Orthodox monastery outside the Soviet Union.

Road 5 continues to the village of Leppävirta (Kantakievari Leppäkerttu Hotel, 120 b., SP; camp site), on the N shore of *Lake Unnukka*, which is dotted with numerous islands. Stone-built church (1846).

**Kuopio** (p. 165) lies on a peninsula in the **Kallavesi**, which the road crosses N of the town on a causeway with several bridges. On the far side, to the left, is a monument to General Sandel, who resisted the Russian advance in 1808. 2·5 km (1½ miles) farther on, Road 17 goes off on the right to Joensuu. Road 5 continues via *Siilinjärvi* (Siilinjärven Spa Kuntoutumiskeskus Hotel, 275 b., SP) to the industrial town of **Iisalmi** (pop. 22,000; hotels: Koljonvirta, 61 b.; Runni Spa, 108 b.; Seurahuone, 85 b.; camp site), on the N bank of the Porovesi. This was the birthplace of the writer Juhani Aho (1861–1921), who founded the realist literary school in Finland at the time when industry was beginning to develop. To the N of the town is the wooden church of Iisalmi-Land.

4 km (2½ miles) N of Iisalmi Road 19 branches off on the left to Oulu. Road 5 continues to **Kajaani** (p. 154), from where Road 77 runs along the N side of Oulujärvi to **Oulu** (p. 219).

**Helsinki to Kajaani via Lappeenranta and Joensuu.** – This route traverses the eastern part of the Finnish Lake Plateau. In the southern part of the route the road in places runs close to the Soviet frontier.

From **Helsinki** (p. 131) to Lappeenranta on Lake Saimaa there are two alternative routes. The first is on E4 to Lahti, and from there E on Road 12 to Kouvola.

**Kouvola** (pop. 30,000; hotels: Cumulus, 330 b.; Hilppa, 26 b.; Kymenhovi, 45 b.; Matkahovi, 32 b.; Turisthovi, 63 b.; youth hostel; camp site) is the main town of the province of Kymen lääni; it has an Academy of Music. – 6·5 km (4 miles) NW, on the *Kymenjoki*, is situated the little industrial town of *Kuusankoski*, with large paper-mills. – 47 km (29 miles) N of Kouvola, on *Vuohinjärvi*, we reach the recreation spot of *Orilampi* (water sports, indoor swimming pool, tennis courts, etc.). – At Kouvola, Road 15, coming from Kotka on the Gulf of Finland, joins Road 6, which continues NE to Lappeenranta.

The alternative route from Helsinki to Lappeenranta leaves on Road 7, which skirts the Gulf of Finland at some distance from the shore. After passing through

**Porvoo** (p. 222), *Loviisa* (Zilton Hotel, 22 b.), where there are remains of the old town walls, and **Kotka** (pop. 35,000; hotels: Koskisoppi, 82 b.; Ruotsinsalmi, 54 b.; Seurahuone, 252 b.; two youth hostels), with a large harbour (export trade), it comes to the junction with Road 15, which runs NW to Kouvola.

*Anjala* is a small village with a manor-house of 1790, now a museum, and a wooden church of 1756. – The road then continues via the industrial town of *Myllykoski* (paper-mill) to Kouvola, from which Road 6 runs E along the N side of the *Salpausselkä* ridge to **Lappeenranta** (p. 173), at the S end of *Lake Saimaa* (p. 231). 7 km (4½ miles) beyond this, at *Lauritsala*, the road crosses the Saimaa Canal.

*Imatra* (p. 174), only 6·5 km (4 miles) from the Soviet frontier, has large wood-working plants. – At *Särkisalmi* Road 14 goes off on the left, offering an attractive drive to Savonlinna.

Punkaharju nature reserve

Road 14 runs NW through beautiful scenery to the village of *Punkaniemi*, on the *Punkasalmi* river, which links the *Puruvesi*, to the N, with the *Väistönselkä*. The road continues alongside the railway on a narrow causeway and along the *Punkaharju* ridge (7 km (4½ miles) long, up to 25 m (80 ft) high: nature reserve). The ridge, deposited by the melt-waters of the last Ice Age, falls steeply down on both sides and is covered with pine, larch and birch forest, with a number of attractive footpaths. – At *Antolla*, where Road 14 continues to **Savonlinna** (p. 231), turn right into Road 71 for Kerimäki.

**Kerimäki** (Herttua Hotel, 138 b.; SB), on the E bank of the Puruvesi, is noted for its huge wooden church (seating for 5000), built in 1847 at the expense of a local man who had emigrated to America. The large size of the church is said to be due to the fact that the measurements on the plan, in feet, were interpreted as metres. Some of the events in the Savonlinna musical festival (see p. 233) take place in the church. – At *Puhos* we rejoin Road 6, coming from the E bank of the Puruvesi.

The road continues via *Onkamo* and *Pyhäselkä* to **Joensuu** (p. 145), capital of northern Karelia. From here Road 17 runs W to Kuopio. Road 18 continues N to a junction at *Uura*.

Here Road 73 goes off on the right via *Eno* (Pihkanokka Hotel, 18 b.) to *Uimaharju*, at the S end of **Lake Pielinen** (area 1095 sq. km – 423 sq. miles), and continues along the E side of the lake, through beautiful scenery.

**Lieksa** (Hopeakettu Hotel, 60 b.; Aigabriha Motel, 50 b., SB.; youth hostel; camp site), popular for water sports, has an open-air museum (60 old buildings). – From here an attractive trip can be made to the *Ruuna* rapids, 25 km (15 miles) NE.

Road 73 continues along the shores of Lake Pielinen, and beyond *Nurmes* rejoins Road 18.

From Uura Road 18 runs N to the *Karjajanselkä* ridge, which is bounded on the SW by Lake Pielinen. At *Ahmovaara* a road goes off on the right to the *Koli Hills** (p. 162).

*Juuka*, a straggling village on the W side of Lake Pielinen, has a wooden church with a separate tower. Here the *Pielisjoki* provides a link between Lake Pielinen and Lake Saimaa (several locks).

The road continues NW, crossing the Suomenselkä, to **Kajaani** (p. 154); then on Road 77 to **Oulu** (p. 219).

# Frederikshavn

Denmark (N Jutland).
County: Nordjyllands amt.
Altitude: sea level. – Population: 35,000.
Postal code: DK-9900. – Telephone code: 08.
(i) **Turistbureau,**
　　Brotorvet I;
　　tel. 42 32 66.

HOTELS. – *Hoffmans Hotel*, Tordenskoldsgade 3, 127 b.; *Jutlandia*, Havnepladsen 1, 202 b.; *Motel Lisboa*, Sondergade 248, 90 b.; *Mariehønen*, Danmarksgade 40, 72 b.; *Park Hotel*, Jernbanegade 7, 63 b.; *Turist-hotellet*, Margrethevej 5, 55 b. – YOUTH HOSTEL: Buhlsvej 6. – CAMP SITE: Apholmenvej 40.

**The busy Danish port and industrial town (shipyards, engineering) of Frederikshavn in northern Jutland was known as Fladstrand until 1818, when it received its municipal charter. From its fortified natural harbour there are ferry services to Gothenburg, Larvik, Fredrikstad and Oslo.**

SIGHTS. – In the middle of the town, by the harbour, stands the old *Powder Tower* (Krundttårnet, 1688), which now houses a collection of weapons dating from about 1600 onwards. To the N of the fishing harbour is the oldest part of the

Church tower at Skagen, half buried by sand

town, *Fiskerklyngen*, with many well-preserved 17th c. houses. 4 km (2½ miles) from the mid-town, by way of Gærumvej and Brønderslevvej, is a 58 m (190 ft) high observation tower, *Cloostårnet* (alt. 165 m – 540 ft) from which there are attractive views. Close by, in Gærumvej are the *Iron Age Cellars* (Jernalder-kældrene), with material of the Early Iron Age found in the locality. – 3 km (2 miles) SW by way of Møllehus Allé, set in 50 hectares (125 acres) of wooded parkland, is the manor-house of *Bangsbo* (1750), now a museum, with models of ships, figureheads and a collection of more than 1000 stones with carvings or inscriptions, the oldest of them dating from prehistoric times. – To the S of the town lies *Pikkerbakken*, a small range of very low hills, from which there are magnificent views of Frederikshavn, the surrounding countryside and the sea.

SURROUNDINGS. – The ferry takes 1 hour 40 minutes to reach the island of **Læsø**, in the Kattegat (area 116 sq. km (45 sq. miles), pop. 2800; in Vesterø Havn Carlsens Hotel, 20 b., Sømandshjem, 18 b., youth hostel, camp site; in Østerby Havn: Østerby Somandshjem Hotel, 16 b.; camp site). Two-thirds of the island is uninhabited; at the N end is *Højsand*, a dune up to 28 m (90 ft) high. The main town on the island, **Byrum**, has a local museum in a 200-year-old farmhouse. At low tide it is possible to drive in a horse carriage to the little island of *Hornfiskrøn*.

12 km (7½ miles) S of Frederikshavn on E3 (A10) is the fishing port and seaside resort of **Sæby** (pop. 17,500; Viking Hotel, 50 b.; Motel Oda, 10 b.; youth hostel; several camp sites). Near the beach is St Mary's Church which is richly decorated with fescoes (*c.* 1500), and which originally belonged to a monastery founded in 1469.

N of Frederikshavn A10 runs through a region of fields, woodland, heath and dunes. In 38 km (24 miles) (2·5 km (1½ miles) before Skagen) a road (signposted) goes off on the right to a parking place 0·5 km (500 yds) E, from which a sandy footpath leads in 10 minutes to the *tower* of the old Skagen church, half buried in blown sand; the nave was demolished in 1795.

2·5 km (1½ miles) farther on A10 comes to **Skagen**, in English traditionally the *Skaw*, Denmark's most northerly town, situated on the tip of Jutland (pop. 14,000; Brøndums Hotel, 86 b.; Hotel Dommergården, 23 b.; Foldens Hotel, 37 b.; Hotel Norden, 50 b.; Hotel Skagen, 110 b., SP; holiday houses; youth hostel). Skagen is a resort much favoured by artists. The newer part of the town extends along the Kattegat among the dunes; it has a fishing harbour (fish auction hall), a small museum of art (painting and sculpture), an open-air museum and a town hall built in 1968. The older part of the town, Gamle Skagen, lies on the Skagerrak.

The road continues 3 km (2 miles) beyond Skagen and ends at a parking place in the dunes (restaurant) to the rear of the *Grenen* lighthouse (44 m – 145 ft high; museum). Near here is the grave of the Danish poet and novelist Holger Drachmann (1846–1908), the "singer of the sea". From the parking place visitors can drive in a "sand-worm" (*sandorm* – a tractor drawing a passenger-carrying trailer) or in dry weather in their own car (to the left), or, best of all, can walk (15 minutes) to the northern tip of Jutland, where the waters of the Skagerrak and Kattegat surge against one another (swimming highly dangerous).

# Funen (Fyn)

Denmark.
County: Fyns amt.
Area: 3486 sq. km (1346 sq. miles).
Population: 444,000.

(i) **Odense Turistforening,**
Rådhuset,
DK-5000 Odense;
tel. (09) 12 75 20.
**Middelfart Turistbureau,**
Havnegade 10,
DK-5500 Middelfart;
tel. (09) 41 17 88.
**Fåborg Turistbureau,**
Havnegade 2,
DK-5600 Fåborg;
tel. (09) 61 07 07.
**Svendborg Turistbureau,**
Møllergade 20,
DK-5700 Svendborg;
tel. (09) 21 09 80.
**Nyborg Turistbureau,**
Torvet 9,
DK-5800 Nyborg;
tel. (09) 31 02 80.

**Funen (Fyn), Denmark's second largest island, lies between Jutland and the island of Zealand. Its fertile soil has earned it the name of the "garden of Denmark", but it also has much of historical and artistic interest to offer, in particular its**

**beautiful old manor-houses. The administrative and cultural capital of the island is Hans Andersen's town of Odense.**

Funen can be reached from Jutland on one or other of the two large bridges spanning the **Little Belt**. The older of the two (1935), to the S, is a reinforced concrete structure (1178 m (1300 yds) long; clear height above the water 33 m – 108 ft); the newer one (1970), within sight of the old one to the N, is Denmark's first suspension bridge (1080 m (1200 yds) long; span 600 m (650 yds); clear height 42 m – 138 ft), and affords fine views. Immediately beyond the bridge is **Middelfart** (pop. 18,000; Stavrby Skov Hotel, 80 b.; Melfar, 67 b.; camp site), of which the main feature of interest is the old royal castle of Hindsgavl on the peninsula of the same name (W of the town). The main building, erected in 1784, stands in a beautiful park; also of interest are the local museum in Henner Frisers Hus (1600) and the church, with a beautiful interior.

From Middelfart to **Odense** (see p. 201) there are two routes – the A1 motorway (45 km – 28 miles) and the scenically more attractive old road (51 km – 32 miles). The two roads cross one another 12 and 24 km (7½ and 15 miles) from Middelfart and unite 10 km (6 miles) before Odense.

From Middelfart it is 40 km (25 miles) to **Assens** (pop. 11,000; Marcussens Hotel, 13 b.; Hotel Phønix, 10 b.), an old town on the Little Belt with many 16th and 17th c. half-timbered houses and a church of 1488, 60 m (195 ft) long, with a fine interior. From here there are boat services to the islands of *Bågø* (30 minutes) and *Brandsø* (1¼ hours), NW of Assens in the Little Belt.

From Assens it is 39 km (25 miles) NE to Odense. 8 km (5 miles) from Assens, to the left, is the *Øksnebjerg* (85 m – 279 ft), with a memorial to Johan Rantzau, who defeated a force from Lübeck and a peasant army in 1535; there is also a windmill of 1859. To the right is the *Skovsbjerg* (97 m – 318 ft). A pleasant detour can be made to the left of the road, taking in *Glambsbjerg*, *Krengerup* and *Frøbjerg*, with the highest hill on Funen (131 m (430 ft): fine view; parking place).

Nyborg Castle, Funen

Funen can also be reached from the island of Als. The ferry across the Little Belt from *Fynshav* to *Bøjden* (Funen) takes 45 minutes. Half-way between Bøjden and the Assens road junction lies *Horne* where there is possibly the best round, fortified church in Denmark, the interior of which is most attractive. The main road (A8) comes in 9 km (5½ miles) to the town of **Fåborg**, 1·5 km (1 mile) off the road to the S (pop. 18,000; Feriehotel Klinten, holiday houses, SB; Fåborg Fjord, 80 b.; Steensgaard Herregårdspension, 7 km (4¼ miles) outside the town; youth hostel; camp sites). Fåborg has well-preserved old houses and streets (W gate), a belfry with the largest carillon on Funen and a museum housing a large collection of pictures by the Funen school of painters, and sculpture by the sculptor Kai Nielsen (1882–1924), a native of Svendborg. – 2 km (1¼ miles) E is the *Kaleko Mølle* (museum), a 600-year-old watermill which was renovated in 1968. – There is a ferry service from Fåborg to Gelting (2 hours), and boats to the island of **Ærø** (Søby).

Beyond Fåborg the road to Nyborg (48 km (30 miles), A8) runs through the hills known as the "Funen Alps". To the left of the road is the *Lerbjerg* (126 m – 413 ft). 9 km (5½ miles) from Fåborg, on the right, is *Brahetrolleborg* Castle (partly 12th c.), with a large park, at the entrance to which

is the "Humlehave", a restaurant with a gallery of modern art and antiques. – 9 km (5½ miles) farther on, to the left of the road, the handsome mansion of *Eges-kov (1524–54), built on piles in a lake, is one of the best preserved moated houses in Europe. The house, set in a beautiful park, contains a museum of cars, aircraft, etc. – From here it is 25 km (15 miles) to Nyborg.

The "green" road from Fåborg to Svend-borg (26 km – 16 miles) follows the curve of S Fyn, never more than 5–6 km (3–4 miles) from the shores of Fåborg Bay, and comes in 22 km (14 miles) to the manor-house of *Hvidkilde*, to the left of the road (central range of buildings c. 1560: not open to public). – Then on to **Svendborg** (pop. 37,450; hotels: Christiansminde, 180 b., SB; Royal, 45 b.; Svenborg, 100 b.; Tre Roser, 140 b., SP; Troense, 68 b.; youth hostel; camp site), finely situated on the Svendborg Sound (tobacco manufacture, packaging, shipbuilding). There is a pleasant walk along the beach to Christiansminde Wood, to the SW (fine views over the sound to the island of Tåsinge). – Fine Romanesque church of St Nicholas (1220; restored 1892), with a beautiful interior. The Municipal Museum occupies two houses, one of which, Anne Hvides Gård, is the oldest secular building in the town (1560; restored 1978). At various points in the town are sculptures by the local artist Kai Nielsen (at St Nicholas's Church, the Library, the swimming pool, etc.).

From Svendborg a large bridge (1966: 1200 m (1300 yds) long, clear height 33 m – 108 ft) crosses the Svendborg Sound to Vindeby on the island of **Tåsinge** (area 70 sq. km (27 sq. miles)). 3 km (2 miles) SE lies the village of *Troense* (Motel Troense, 14 b.), with a picturesque main street. 1 km (¾ mile) S we come to *Valdemarsslot*, one of the finest Late Baroque buildings in Denmark. Today Waldemar's Castle is a manor-house museum (exhibitions of Funen). – From the tower of the village church (alt. 74 m – 243 ft) in *Bregninge* there are panoramic *views. The museum contains a section devoted to the tragic love affair of Count Sparre and Elvira Madigan, who are buried in Landet cemetery, 3 km (2 miles) S.

From the SE side of the island of Tåsinge a causeway and a bridge (1962: 1700 m (1850 yds) long), lead by way of the little islet of *Siø* to the island of **Langeland** in the Great Belt (area 184 sq. km (71 sq. miles); 52 km (32 miles) long, 3–11 km (2–7 miles) across: noted for its magnificent beech trees), which attracts many visitors. Its main town is **Rudkøbing**, on the W coast (pop. 7000; Rudkøbing Hotel, 12 b.; Skandinavien, 15 b.; youth hostel; camp site), which has an interesting church, the oldest part of which is late Romanesque (c. 1100; tower 1621). and many old houses and streets. Langeland Museum has a notable

Viking grave. – From *Bagenkop*, at the S end of the island (Bagenkop Kro, 12 b.; two camp sites), there is a ferry service to Kiel in Germany (2¼ hours), and from *Lohals*, in the NW of the island (Tom Knudson's Safari Museum), boats leave for Korsør (1½ hours).

From Svendborg there are ferry services to the island of **Ærø** (area 88 sq. km – 34 sq. miles), SW of the town in the Little Belt. On the N coast is **Ærøskøbing** (pop. 490; Ærøhus Hotel, 66 b.; Phønix, 19 b.; camp site and resort), an old-world little place with thirty-six 17th and 18th c. houses protected as ancient monuments, and a shipping museum (750 ship models and ships in bottles). – 13 km (8 miles) from Ærøskøbing, on the E coast lies the busy port and fishing town of **Marstal** (pop. 4000; hotels: Danmark, 35 b.; Marstal, 10 b.; youth hotels; camp site). Museum (100 ship models); church of 1737 (tower 1920); 17th c. houses.

A causeway to the E of the Svendborg bridge leads on to the island of **Thurø** (Røgeriet Hotel, no rest., 27 b.; camp sites), which offers excellent swimming.

The fast motorway from Svendborg to Nyborg is the A9 which leaves from the E side of the town running N to Kvaerudrup where it joins the A8 (Fåborg–Nyborg), but the scenic coastal road is much more attractive and affords scope for a variety of pleasant detours. In 12 km (7½ miles) a minor road branches off on the right (4 km – 2½ miles) to the seaside resort of *Lundeborg*, and in another 2 km (1¼ miles) a road (1·5 km – 1 mile) leads to the manor-house of *Hesselagergård* (1538: no admission). 6 km (4 miles) beyond this, at the village of *Langå*, a side road on the left of the main road leads (2 km – 1¼ miles) to the 16th c. manor-house of *Rygård*, built on piles. – 1 km (¾ mile) N of Langå another road on the left leads to still another 16th c. manor-house, *Glorup*, in a beautiful park (open Saturdays, Sundays and Thursdays). – 11 km (7 miles) farther on, to the right of the main road, stands the Renaissance mansion of *Holckenhavn* (1580–1630), with a richly appointed chapel. The park (12 hectares – 30 acres) is open to the public every day. – In another 3 km (2 miles) the road comes to **Nyborg** (pop. 18,000; Hesselet Hotel, 92 b., SB; Nyborg Strand, 400 b.; camp site), a finely situated port town on the Great Belt channel which was a royal capital from 1200 to 1430. The royal castle was built in the 12th c. to control the Great Belt (restored 1917–23), and has imposing defences. Other features of interest in the town are a 15th c. Gothic church and the Landport, an old town gate (1666). – From Nyborg it is another 4·5 km (3 miles) to *Knudshoved*, from which a ferry

(50 minutes) crosses the Great Belt to *Halsskov* on Zealand.

From Odense there is a choice between the direct road to Nyborg and Knudshoved (29 and 33·5 km – 18 and 21 miles) and the road via Kerteminde, 12 km (7½ miles) longer. For the first 9 km (6 miles) the two routes coincide (A1); then the road to Kerteminde forks left off the main road, which continues to Nyborg. 9 km (6 miles) along the Kerteminde road is the village of *Ladby*, 1·5 km (1 mile) N of which (signposted "Ladbyskibet") is the Ladby Ship, a Viking ship 22 m (72 ft) long which was discovered here in 1935 and is now displayed in a museum specially built to house it. – 5 km (3 miles) farther on we come to **Kerteminde** (pop. 10,000; Tornøes Hotel, 27 b.; youth hostel; two camp sites), an old fishing port beautifully situated in Kerteminde Bay with many old houses; Municipal Museum, in a half-timbered house of 1630; church, thought to date from about 1200. – An interesting excursion can be made to the *Hindsholm* peninsula, which has a somewhat harsher climate than the rest of Funen. Beautiful scenery, at first hilly, then falling away to the flat northern tip of the peninsula, *Fyns Hoved*. The road ends in 16 km (10 miles) at the village of *Nordskov*; beautiful beaches.

From Kerteminde a road runs SE, skirting the bay, and then turns inland to *Avnslev* (13 km – 8 miles), where it joins A1: turn left for Nyborg. In another 3 km (2 miles) the motorway goes off on the left and skirts the N side of the town to *Knudshoved* (8·5 km – 5 miles).

# Gällivare

Sweden (Northern).
Province: Norrbottens län. – Region: Lapland.
Altitude: 359 m (1178 ft). – Population: 25,000.
Postal code: S-97200. – Telephone code: 0970.
ⓘ **Gällivare Turistbyrå,**
  Storgatan 16;
  tel. 1 86 63.

HOTELS. – *Dundret*, Per Högströmsgatan 1, 29 b.; *Nex Hotel*, Lasarettsgatan 1, 131 b. – Holiday villages of *Dundret* and *Tjuonajokk* (anglers' camp). – YOUTH HOSTEL. – CAMP SITE.

The town of Gällivare in northern Sweden owes its existence to the local deposits of iron ore. It lies on the Vásarajärvi ("Hammer Lake"), 70 km (44 miles) N of the Arctic Circle. The midnight sun is visible here from 2 June to 12 July.

ACCESS. – Gällivare can be reached either on Road 97 via Jokkmokk (96 km – 60 miles), which passes the Muddus National Park (to E) and continues via Porjus, at the southern tip of the Stora Lulevatten lake; or from Luleå on E4 to Töre (54 km – 34 miles), then on Road 98 to Överkalix (51 km – 32 miles), from which it is another 128 km (80 miles) to Gällivare.

The deposits of iron ore round Gällivare have been known since the 18th c. A British company began to work them in 1869 and built a railway line to Luleå in 1884. Six years later it sold the workings to the Swedish government, which in 1957 also took over another private mining company, the Luossavaara-Kiirunavaara AB (LKAB). The reserves of ore are estimated at 400 million tons, with an iron content of 62–70%. Only in high summer can the ore be exported from Luleå; during most of the year it is carried by train through Kiruna on the "iron-ore railway" to the ice-free Norwegian port of Narvik; only a small proportion is processed in Luleå by the Svenska Stål AB, another state-owned company associated with LKAB, or in other Swedish steelworks.

SIGHTS. – There is a romantic **wooden church** (1881), known as the "one öre church" because every taxpayer had to contribute one öre towards its cost. *Lapp boarding school* (used in summer as a youth hostel); in the upper classes of the secondary school there are special subjects for Lapps.

SURROUNDINGS. – 5 km (3 miles) SW is the hill of *Dundret (823 m (2700 ft): magnificent views), with the Dundret recreation area. The hill can be climbed in 1½ to 1¾ hours (hut); attractive skiing spot. – 6 km (4 miles) N is the ore mountain of **Malmberget**, with three peaks, *Välkomman* (617 m – 2024 ft), *Kungsryggen* (580 m – 1903 ft) and *Kaptenshöjden* (518 m – 1700 ft). From the mining settlement of *Malmberget* (Malm Hotell, 46 b.) at the foot of the hill there are beautiful views towards Dundret. All Saints Church (1944) had to be moved some years ago, since it was in danger of sinking into a mine shaft. The altar consists of a block of Malmberg ore. In the LKAB offices is a mining museum. Visits to the workings (c. 250 km (150 miles) of underground galleries and tunnels) can be arranged. – 4 km (2½ miles) NE of Malmberget are the *Koskullskulle* iron-mines.

# Gävle

Sweden (Central).
Province: Gävleborgs län. – Region: Gästrikland.
Altitude: sea level. – Population: 87,500.
Postal code: S-800 . . . -805 . . .
Telephone code: 026.

(i) **Gävle Turistbyrå,**
Stortorget,
S-80103 Gävle;
tel. 10 16 00.

HOTELS. – *Aveny*, Södre Kungsgatan 31, 60 b.; *Gävle*, Staketgatan 44, 93 b.; *Grand Central*, Nygatan 45, 350 b.; *Scandic Hotel*, Johanneslotsvägen 6, 475 b., SB; *Triangeln*, Nygatan 8, 152 b.; *Winn*, Norra Slottsgatan 19, 407 b. – YOUTH HOSTEL.

The busy commercial and industrial town of Gävle, between Stockholm and Sundsvall, is the administrative capital of the province of Gävleborgs län, which consists of the regions of Gästrikland and Hälsingland. The town lies on both banks of the Gävleå, which here flows into the Gulf of Bothnia.

Gävle is the largest and oldest town in Norrland, and with its modern port installations plays an important part in the export of timber and metal ore. It is also important and the main E–W junction for road and rail to Dalarua and Norway. After a fire in 1869 which destroyed the districts N of the river the town was rebuilt.

SIGHTS. – In the Town Hall Square (Rådhustorget), immediately N of the river, are the *Town Hall* (18th c.) and the *Town House* (Stadshuset, 1803–5). From here two broad parallel streets, Rådmansgata and Norra Kungsgata, lead to the finely situated *Theatre*.

From Town Hall Square *Drottninggata* leads SW to the *Trinity Church*, the oldest building in the town after the Castle (1654; restored 1936–8 and 1954). Farther along the N bank of the river is the beautiful *Municipal Park* (Stadsträdgården).

A little way S of the Town Hall, on the other bank of the river, the **Castle**, built by King Johan III in 1583–93 and renovated in 1792, is now the governor's residence. To the E of the Castle, on the far side of Södra Kungsgata, is the interesting **Museum**, with material on the history of the town, modern pictures and sculpture; there is also a prehistoric collection which includes a boat of about A.D. 100, of the type described by Tacitus in his "Germania'', found at Björke in 1948, and a small Persian lamp brought here by the Vikings. – S of the Museum, in Södra Centralgata, is the *Folkets Hus* (People's House, 1946). On the southern outskirts of the town is the carefully renovated district of GAMLA GÄVLE (Old Gävle), with many 18th c. wooden houses, the homes of artists and craftsmen. – 1 km (about a ½ mile) W of the Castle is the *Museum Silvanum* (Museum of Forestry), with an interesting park.

SURROUNDINGS. – 3 km (2 miles) SE is the *Järvsta* cemetery, with a runic stone. To the E of this, in Gävle Bay, we find the little resort of *Furuvik* (sandy and rocky beach), with an amusement and animal park. – From here the road continues through the port and industrial town of *Skutskär* (woodworking) and crosses the *Dalälv*. Situated on the three arms of this river the town of **Älvkarleby** (pop. 10,000; Turist Hotell, 100 b.; Pensionat Kronsäter, 27 b.; camp site) has a 15th c. church with fine wall paintings and a salmon hatchery. The once imposing waterfalls have lost much of their charm through the construction of a hydroelectric power station. Above the power station, opposite the island of Flakö, is a hydraulic laboratory with models of hydroelectric systems. – 8 km (5 miles) NE is Sweden's first wind-operated power station, an experimental unit with a tower 23 m (95 ft) high.

From Gävle Road 80 runs W to Falun (p. 90). 3 km (2 miles) along this road is *Valbo*, with a 14th c. church and a runic stone of about A.D. 100. Beyond this are *Mackmyra* (iron foundry of 1885, now closed down) and **Sandviken**, an industrial town on the northern shore of the Storsjö (alt. 71 m (233 ft); pop. 71,000; Eos-Car Hotel, 120 b.; Hotel Hammaren, 60 b.). The dominant feature of the town is a large steelworks established in 1862, the oldest Bessemer works in Sweden. – On the S side of the Storsjö is *Årsunda* church (c. 1450), with wall paintings and a medieval altar of Flemish workmanship.

# Geirangerfjord

Norway (Central).
County: Møre og Romsdal fylke.

The ** **Geirangerfjord and surrounding area offer some of the finest scenery in the whole of Norway. The fjord is the eastward continuation of the Sunnlyvsford, which in turn branches off the Storfjord. The shores of the Geirangerfjord are notable for their numerous waterfalls and beautiful views.**

The narrow and winding road to the village of Geiranger at the head of the fjord turns N off Road 15 (Gudbrandsdal to the Nordfjord) to the W of Grotli.

**Grotli** (alt. 870 m (2854 ft); Høyfjells-hotell, 107 b.), an important road junction, frequently has snow until well into the summer. Some 15 km (10 miles) W of the town the Geiranger road (No. 58) turns off. The first stretch of the road runs through bare mountainous country on the northern shore of the *Breidalsvann* (alt. 880 m – 2887 ft), which is enclosed between the *Breidalsegga* on the N and the *Vassvendegga* on the S, and then skirts two smaller lakes (on left). After 18 km (11 miles) the road passes, also on the left, the *Djupvann* (1004 m – 3294 ft), which is frequently frozen until August, and in another 2 km (1¼ miles) comes to the highest point on the road (1038 m – 3406 ft), which is open for traffic from 1 June to 15 October. On the S side of the lake are the sheer rock faces of the *Grasdalsegga* (1570 m – 5151 ft). At the W end of the lake is the *Djupvashytta* hotel (1020 m (3347 ft); 30 b.), which is frequented by summer skiers (ski race at end of June).

Here the road known as the *Nibbevei* (normally open 1 June to 1 October; toll) branches off on the right and climbs (5 km (3 miles); gradients up to 12·5%; 10 hairpin turns) to the summit of the **Dalsnibba** (1495 m – 4905 ft), from which there are superb ** views of the mountains and the Geirangerfjord far below.

Soon after Djupvashytta, beyond the watershed between the Skagerrak and the Atlantic, an impressive stretch of mountain road begins. The * *road to Geiranger* (opened 1885) descends some 1000 m (3280 ft), with gradients of up to 8%, 20 sharp turns (some of them very narrow indeed) and several bridges, to reach Geiranger in 17 km (10 miles) (distance as the crow flies 7 km – 4½ miles). Travellers on this road experience a sudden transition from the severe climate of the mountain regions to the warmer and milder air of the sheltered valley. – 2 km (1¼ miles) along the road, on the left, is the *Blåfjell*, with the *Jettegryte* (''Giant's Pot''), a cavity 2·2 m (7 ft) across and 9·5 m (30 ft) deep gouged out by glacier action.

Beyond the *Øvre Blåfjellbro* (bridge) there is a magnificent * view: to the left the *Flydalshorn*, to the right the *Vindåshorn*, beyond it the *Såthorn* (1779 m – 5837 ft), and the *Grindalshorn* (1534 m – 5033 ft), and straight ahead the ''Eagles' Road'' which winds its way up from Geiranger to Eidsdal. The road crosses the *Nedre Blå-fjellbro*, with the falls on the *Kvandalselv*

The Geirangerfjord from the Flydal gorge

to the right, and then descends into the next stage of the valley, the **Flydal**: to the left the Flydalshorn, to the right the Blåhorn (1738 m – 5702 ft). Beyond *Ørjeseter* is the * **Flydalsjuv** (300 m – 330 yds), a gorge from which there is another superb view (parking place). From *Hole,* a short distance beyond this, a rewarding detour can be made to *Vesterås* and from there on a marked footpath to the *Storseterfoss,* a waterfall 30 m (100 ft) high. – The main road continues to the *Utsikten Bellevue Hotel* (72 b.) and beyond this (on left, before a bridge) a standing stone commemorating the adoption of the Norwegian constitution of 1814.

**Geiranger** (Geiranger Hotell, 125 b.; Grande Fjord Motell, 100 b.; Meroks Fjordhotel, 107 b.; Union Turisthotel, 243 b., SP; several camp sites) is a popular little tourist resort and port in a beautiful setting at the E end of the * * **Geiranger-fjord.**

During the season very attractive *sightseeing cruises* by motor-ship (2 hours) are run several times daily, giving visitors an excellent opportunity of seeing the impressive scenery of the fjord, with its sheer rock walls and numerous waterfalls. High up on the left can be seen the abandoned farm of *Skageflå;* then on the right the *Syv Søstre* (Seven Sisters) waterfall, which forms seven separate falls when it is swollen by melt-water in spring. To the left of this is the *Friar* ("Suitor"), to the right the *Brudeslør* ("Bridal Veil"). – To the W the Geirangerfjord runs into the * **Sun-nylvsfjord,** to the S of which is the village of *Hellesylt* (ferry to Geiranger); at the N end of the fjord, on the left, is *Stranda.*

From Geiranger Road 58 runs along the N side of the fjord, coming in 3 km (2 miles) to a group of houses over 200 years old, *Møllgårdene,* the starting point of the "Eagles' Road".

The * "**Eagles' Road**" runs from the Geirangerfjord to the Norddalsfjord. It climbs with eleven hairpin turns, with beautiful views of the fjord and the waterfalls, to *Korsmyra* (624 m – 2047 ft), where the road reaches its highest point, and then descends past the *Eidsvann* to **Eidsdal** on the *Norddalsfjord,* a village with woodworking and clothing factories and an octagonal church of 1782. Ferry to *Linge,* on the N side of the fjord, from which Road 63 runs W to Ålesund (p. 57) and E to Åndalsnes (p. 226).

# Göta Canal

Sweden (Southern).
Provinces: Göteborgs och Bohus län, Älvsborgs län, Skaraborgs län, Östergötlands län, Södermanlands län, Stockholms län.
Regions: Bohuslän, Västergötland, Östergötland, Södermanland, Uppland.

(i)   **Rederi AB Göta Kanal,**
     Hotellplatsen 2,
     S-40124 Göteborg;
     tel. (0 31) 17 76 15.
     Skeppsbron 20,
     S-10316 Stockholm;
     tel. (08) 24 04 79 and 24 04 78.

**The three-day trip in one of the old passenger boats on the * Göta Canal from Gothenburg to Stockholm (or vice versa) is one of the most memorable tourist experiences which Sweden has to offer. The total distance is 560 km (350 miles), of which 87 km (55 miles) are in canals. To overcome a difference in height of 91·5 m (300 ft) there are 65 locks on the route. The service operates from mid-May to the beginning of September.**

The three boats which ply on the Göta Canal are old but have been modernised to bring them into line with modern

A passenger boat in the Göta Canal

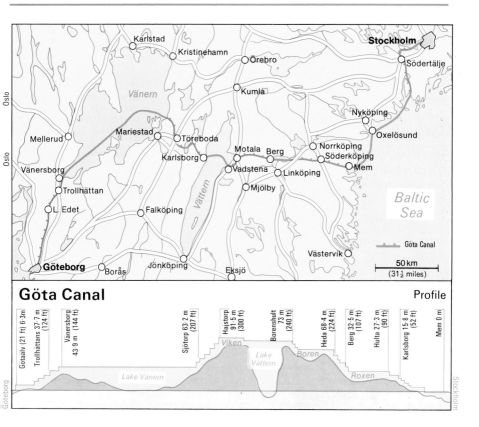

**Göta Canal**                                                    Profile

requirements. They do not carry cars, but the shipping company can arrange for the transport of passengers' cars by land. Early booking is advisable, since these trips are very popular. It is possible to return by rail if desired.

HISTORY. – The construction of a waterway between Stockholm and Gothenburg so as to link the Kattegat with the Baltic was contemplated by Gustavus Vasa, but the first steps towards realising the project were not taken until the time of *Charles XII* (1716). Two engineers, *Swedenborg* and *Polhem*, sought to bypass the Trollhätten falls by the construction of locks, but the levee was destroyed by driftwood in 1755, and thereafter the project hung fire until 1793. In 1810 work began on the section of the canal between Lakes Vänern and Vättern, in Västergötland (61·5 km – 38 miles) long, with 21 locks). The Östergötland section, between Motala and the Baltic, is 92·5 km (57 miles) long, with 37 locks. The construction of the canal is particularly associated with the names of Baron *Baltzar Bogislaus von Platen* and *Daniel Thunberg*. By 1832 the whole length of the canal from Gothenburg to Mem on the Baltic was open for traffic. In those days the canal was an important industrial transport route; nowadays it is used almost exclusively by tourist traffic.

*Along the Göta Canal. – Starting from Gothenburg (p. 102), the boat sails up the *Götaälv*, passing the ruins of *Bohus Castle*, and comes in some 5 hours to **Trollhättan** (alt. 38 m – 125 ft). While the boat is passing through the locks

(height difference 32 m – 105 ft) there is time to look around the power station. By the time (about 4 p.m.) the boat enters **Lake Vänern** at *Vänersborg* (alt. 44 m – 144 ft) it has passed through 6 locks.

On Lake Vänern, the largest lake in Sweden, can be seen on the right * **Läckö Castle** and the wooded hill of *Kinnekulle* (307 m – 1007 ft). On the E side of the lake, at *Sjötorp*, is the beginning of the Västergötland section of the canal, where during the night and early morning the boat climbs 47 m (154 ft) over a distance of 36 km (22 miles) by means of 20 locks, to reach *Tåtorp* on Lake Viken (which serves as a reservoir of water for this part of the canal). At *Lyrestad* the canal is crossed by E5, and at *Stora Lanthöjden* it reaches its highest point (91·5 m (300 ft) above sea level).

The boat continues through *Lake Viken* (area 46 sq. km (18 sq. miles), depth 25 m – 82 ft) and the adjoining *Lake Botten* (13 sq. km – 5 sq. miles), with the *Vaberg* (226 m – 742 ft) on the right, to enter * **Lake Vättern** at *Karlsborg*. The passage across the northern part of the lake takes 4 hours. The boat reaches the eastern shore at **Vadstena** (time to drive around the town and see the castle), and then skirts the shore to **Motala**, where the main office and works of the canal are to be found and the Östergötland section of the canal begins. – On the N bank of the canal can be seen the tomb of Baron von Platen. A series of 6 locks leads down into *Lake Boren* (alt. 74 m – 243 ft), and the boat reaches *Borensberg*, at the E end of the lake, in the late afternoon. Over the next 22·2 km (14 miles), until the canal enters Lake Roxen at *Berg* (alt. 32·5 m – 107 ft), it descends another 41·5 m (136 ft), passing through 16 locks. (Passengers travelling in the opposite direction can make a very early morning visit to *Vreta Abbey*, 20 minutes SE.)

Then follows a stretch of 26 km (16 miles) through *Lake Roxen* (alt. 32·5 m – 107 ft) and the narrow *Lake Asplång* (27 m – 89 ft), 5 km (3 miles) long. After this the canal descends (15 locks) to the old town of *Söderköping*, which is reached about 5 a.m. (starting from Stockholm about 9 p.m.). From here it is 5 km (3 miles) to *Mem*, where the canal reaches *Slätbaken*, a 15 km (10 mile) long inlet on the Baltic. On its S side can be seen the tower of the ruined *Stegeborg Castle*.

From here the boat turns N through the skerries and the open **Baltic**, passing the inlet of *Bråvik* and the steel town of *Oxelösund*, and enters the long narrow *Himmerfjärd*, which leads into the fjord-like *Hallsfjärd* and the 5 km (3 mile) long *Södertälje Canal* (constructed 1806–19, widened 1917–24) linking the Baltic with Lake Mälar.

At the industrial town of **Södertälje** the boat passes through its last lock and continues for another 39 km (25 miles) along the E end of **Lake Mälar** to reach **Stockholm** (p. 247) about 6 p.m. on the evening of the third day.

# Gothenburg

Sweden (Southern).
Province: Göteborgs och Bohus län.
Region: Bohuslän
Altitude: sea level. – Population: 424,000.
Postal code: S-400 . . . – Telephone code: 0 31.
ⓘ **Göteborgs Turistbyrå,**
Kungsportsplatsen 2,
S-41110 Göteborg;
tel. 10 07 40.

HOTELS. – *Europa*, Köpmansgatan 38, 907 b., SB, pedestrian underpass to Central Hotel; *Park Avenue Hotel*, Kungsportsavenyn 36–38, 530 b., SB; *Sheraton Göteburg*, Södra Hamngatan 59–65, 680 b., SB, SP; *Eggers*, Drottningtorget 1, 170 b.; *Ekoxen*, Norra Hamngatan 38, 120 b.; *Excelsior*, Karl Gustavsgatan 9, 120 b.; *Kung Karl*, Nils Ericsonsgatan 23, 130 b.; *Liseberg Heden*, Sten Sturegatan, 310 b.; *Lorensberg*, Berzeliigatan 15, 205 b.; *Onyxen*, Sten Sturegatan 23, 48 b.; *Opalen*, Engelbrektsgatan 73, 330 b.; *Örgryte*, Danska Vägen 68–70, 140 b.; *Panorama*, Ekladagatan 51–53, 500 b., SB; *Ramada*, Gamla Tingstadsgatan 1, 260 b., SB; *Ritz*, Burggrevegatan 25, 200 b.; *Riverton*, Stora Badhusgatan 26, 580 b., SB; *Royal*, Drottninggatan 67, 120 b.; *Rubinen*, Kungsportsavenyn 24, 270 b.; *Sara Hotel Gothia*, Mässansgatan 24, 600 b., SB; *Scandinavia*, Kustgatan 10, 650 b., SB, SP; *Tre Kronor*, Norra Kustbanegatan 15–17, 300 b.; *Vasa*, Viktoriagatan 6, 91 b.; *West Side Hotel*, Stora Badhusgatan 28, 77 b.; *Windsor*, Kungsportsavenyn 6, 133 b.

YOUTH HOSTELS. – *Studentenheim Ostkupan*, in Kallebäck, about 200 b.; *Vandrarhem*, in Partille, 120 b.; *Torrekulla Turiststation*, in Kållered near Mölndal, 60 b.

CAMP SITE. – *Karralunds Camping*, Olbergsgatan.

RESTAURANTS. – *Johanna*, Södra Hamngatan 47; *Fiskekrogen*, Lilla Torget 1, *Valand*, Kungsportsavenyn; *Henriksberg* (fish specialties), Stigbergsgatan 7, with view of harbour; *White Corner/Pajazzo*, Vasagatan 43; *Trädgårdsföreningen*, Liseberg Huvudrestaurant, both with cabaret and floor show.

EVENT. – Antique Market.

SPORTS and RECREATION. – Swimming, sailing, golf, fishing, sea angling.

**\*Gothenburg (in Swedish Göteborg), lying on the shores of the Kattegat on both banks of the Götaälv, is Sweden's second largest city and its leading port and commercial town. The administrative capital of the province of Göteborgs och Bohus län, it has a university and a college of technology and is the see of a bishop. Its economy is largely dependent on major industrial activities, including shipbuilding, motor vehicles (Volvo), the manufacture of ball-bearings and the chemical industry. There are ferry services to England, to Denmark, Holland and Norway, and to Kiel and Lübeck-Travemünde in Germany.**

HISTORY. – Gothenburg is a relatively young town, having received its charter from King Gustav II Adolf (Gustavus Adolphus) only in 1621 to open Swedish trade to the W and counteract the punishing tolls exacted by the Danes on all shipping passing through the Öresund. There had been four earlier settlements in the area, but all had been destroyed either by war or fire. Settlers from Holland had great influence on the early development of the town: the membership of the first town council comprised ten Dutchmen, seven Swedes and one Scot. Gothenburg quickly grew into a major port, involved particularly in the shipment of timber and iron. During Napoleon's continental blockade (1806) it was the focal point for British trade with northern Europe. This period saw the rise of the merchant aristocracy from whose munificence the city frequently benefited.

Gothenburg's heyday as an international port began in the early years of the 20th c. as a result of the development of transatlantic traffic, and roughly a quarter of the Swedish merchant fleet is now based there. With over 20 km (12 miles) of quays, the port (almost always ice-free) is the largest in northern Europe, and can accommodate tankers of up to 225,000 GRT (Gross Register Tonnage). The people of Gothenburg are open-minded and liberally disposed and have always looked towards the West: in their eyes Stockholm is in Siberia. A favourite Swedish joke declares that when it rains in London the people of Gothenburg unfurl their umbrellas.

SIGHTS. – Following the Dutch pattern, the main traffic arteries of Gothenburg were once canals, most of which have been filled in and are now streets (e.g. Ostra and Västra Hamngatan). Only the central canal, the *Stora Hamnkanal*, and the old defensive moat which runs round the S side of the old town have been preserved. By the Stora Hamnkanal is **Gustav Adolfs Torg**, a large square which until 1854 was known as Stora Torget. In that year the *statue of Gustav II Adolf* (by B. E. Fogelberg) which stands in the square was erected. It is the second copy of the statue: the original was acquired by Bremen after the ship carrying it ran aground and the citizens of Gothenburg refused to pay the salvage money demanded by the men of Heligoland. On the N side of the square is the **Exchange** (*Börsen*, 1849), which also houses the city's Council Chamber and a museum devoted to the Czech composer Smetana, who lived in Gothenburg from 1856 to 1861. On the W side of the square is the **Town Hall** (*Rådhus*, 1762), designed by Nicodemus Tessin the Elder, with a beautiful inner courtyard. The N wing was designed by E. G. Asplund (1935–7); the relief, "The Winds", was the work of Eric Grates. Behind the Town Hall to the W, in Norra Hamngata, stands the *Kristine Kyrka* or *German Church* (rebuilt 1748–83), with the octagonal burial vault of Field Marshal Rutger von Ascheberg (1693), governor of Skåne, Halland, Göteborg and Bohuslän. Farther along, at 12 Norra Hamngata, the former headquarters (1750) of the East India Company now houses the **Historical Museum**, with material of historical and ethnographic interest, particularly from western Sweden and the Gothenburg region. In the same building are the *Archaeological Museum* and the *Museum of Ethnography*, with interesting collections of the Lapps and Eskimos among much else. To the N, in Kronhusgata, is the **Kronhus** (1643–53), Gothenburg's oldest building, used in the past as a warehouse, an arsenal and a garrison church. In the great hall (Rikssalen) the five-year-old Charles XI was proclaimed king in 1660. Part of the building is now occupied by the Municipal Museum. Adjoining are the *Kronhusbodarna* (1756–9), converted into shops and workshops at the end of the 19th c. in the style of that period. – Across the Stora Hamnkanal from the Historical Museum, to the right, is the *Lilla Torg*, with a statue of the textile manufacturer Jonas Alströmer (1685–1761) by Börjesson (1904). Farther to the right, at the end of Södra Hamngata, stands the 17th c. *Governor's Residence* (rebuilt and enlarged about 1850). Along Västra Hamngata, at the intersection with Kungsgata (on left), is the *Cathedral* (Domkyrka), built in 1815 on the ruins of two earlier churches which had been destroyed by fire.

Kungsportsavenyn, Gothenburg

Between Gustav Adolfs Torg and Drottningtorg (to the E along Norra Hamngata) lies the ÖSTRA NORDSTAN district, in which the old houses have been replaced by modern functional buildings. from the parking garage a tunnel leads to the **Central Station** in Drottningtorg, with the *Head Post Office* (1924) opposite it. Nils Ericsonsgata runs N to the Götaälv and the *Gullbergskaj*, with the four-masted barque "Viking" (1907: now a school of seamanship), the lightship "Fladen" (1915) and a boat which formerly sailed on Lake Vänern, "Valborg II" (1902). To the right the *Götaälv Bridge* (1939: view of port and shipyards) gives access to the *Hisinge* peninsula. 1 km (¾ mile) upstream is the *Tingstad Tunnel*, which also leads to Hisinge (E6 to Kungälv and Oslo).

From the NE side of Gustav Adolfs Torg, Östra Hamngata runs S to Kungsportsplats, with an equestrian statue of Charles IX (by Börjesson, 1903). Between here and Västra Hamngata are a number of business and shopping streets. To the S of the square, beyond the old moat, is the **Grand Theatre** (*Stora Teatern*, 1859), on the E side of the *Kungspark*. Past it runs **Kungsportsavenyn** (*Avenyn*, "the Avenue", for short), Gothenburg's finest street, on the far side of which is a sculpture by Molin, "Bältespännare" ("The Wrestlers"), and beyond this lies the beautiful *park* of the

Gothenburg

Horticultural Society (Trädgardsförenin-gen), with a large palm-house and a restaurant (main entrance in Nya Allé). In the Aveny, between Nya Allé and Parkgatan, can be seen a statue (by I. Fallstedt, 1899) of the engineer *John Ericsson* (1803–89), who after emigrating to the United States perfected the screw propeller for steamships and built the warship "Monitor".

At the SE end of the Aveny is *Götaplats*, the cultural hub of the city, with the imposing *Poseidon Fountain* by Carl Milles (1931). A broad flight of steps leads up to the *Museum of Art* (*Konstmuseet*, 1921–3), with the finest collection of Scandinavian art and works by Italian, French and Dutch masters (Rembrandt, "*The Falconer*", *c*. 1665, and "*Adoration of the Kings*", *c*. 1631; Rubens, van Gogh, etc.) and modern French artists (Picasso, Cézanne, etc.). Adjoining the Museum is the *Art Gallery* (exhibitions).

On the E side of Götaplats is the *Municipal Theatre* (Stadsteatern, 1934), and on the W side the *Concert Hall* (Konserthuset, 1935). NW of the theatre stands the *Municipal Library* (Stadsbiblioteket), with an interesting Doll Museum. To the SE of Götaplats (main entrance in Örgrytevägen) is the **Liseberg** amusement park, opened in 1923. On the opposite side of the street we find the *Trade Fair*

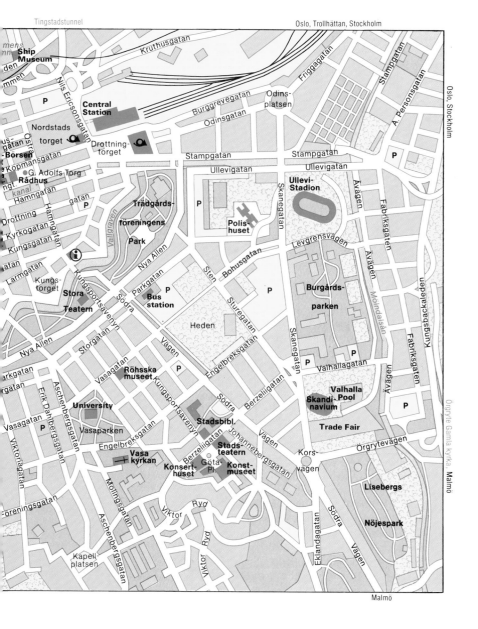

*grounds* (Svenska Mässan), adjoining which are the *Skandinavium* (1971), the largest arena in northern Europe, with seating for up to 12,000 spectators, and the *Valhalla Swimming Pool*. Farther N, in Skånegatan, is the large *Ullevi Stadium*. E of the Skandinavium are the *Industrial Museum* and the *Örgryte Old Church* (Gamla Kyrka: built in 13th c.).

In Vasagatan (Nos. 37–39), which cuts across the Aveny, the *Museum of Applied Art* (*Röhsska Konstslöjdmuseet*: by Carl Westman, 1916), houses ancient and modern gold and silver, textiles, furniture, glass and porcelain. At the entrance are two Chinese marble lions of the Ming dynasty (1386–1644). – On the S side of Vasagatan, in the Vasa Park, is the *University*, and to the S of this the *Vasa Church* (1909). At the W end of Vasagatan, at the intersection with Haga Kyrkogatan, is the *Commercial College*, and to the N of this the *Haga Kyrka* (1859). On a hill to the SW is a remnant of the old fortifications, *Skansen Kronan*, from which there are fine views. The massive tower (1697) houses a *Military Museum*, with a collection of historical weapons and Swedish uniforms from the 17th c. to the present day. Around the hill extends a working-class district developed from 1850 onwards.

To the N, at the W end of Södra Allégatan, is the *Järntorg*, with a fountain by Tore Strindberg (1927); on the outside of the basin are old iron stamps. From here Första Langgatan runs W to *St John's Church* (1866), to the S of which, on a plateau, stands the *Masthuggskyrka* (1914: fine views of town and harbour). Then by way of Stigbergsgatan and Stigbersplatsen, with the well-preserved *Gathenhielmska Hus* (1710), to the **Shipping Museum** (*Sjöfartsmuseet*), which shows the development of shipping, shipbuilding and fishing from the Viking period to today; aquarium. Adjoining the Museum is the *Seamen's Tower* (49 m – 160 ft), topped by Ivar Johnsson's sculpture, "Woman by the Sea"; the tower was built to commemorate the seamen who lost their lives in the First World War (good views). To the W the *Älvborg Bridge* (1966), 933 m (1020 yds) long and 45 m (148 ft) high, leads on to the Hisinge peninsula. Near the Shipping Museum is the *fishing harbour* (interesting auctions from 7 a.m.

on weekdays). It is also well worth visiting the fish market (*feskekörka*) on the Rosenlundskanal.

Gothenburg's largest park, the *Slottsskog* (Castle Wood), lies S of the Shipping Museum on Dag Hammarskjöldsled. It is a beautifully wooded area (oaks and conifers), with lakes (seals), a deer-park, attractive footpaths and roads, and two restaurants; from the lookout tower there are extensive views. At the NE corner of the park is the *Natural History Museum* (the whales being of particular interest). To the SE, beyond Dag Hammarskjöldsled, is the *Botanic Garden* (Botaniska Trädgården), on the NE side of which is the *Sahlgren Hospital*, one of the largest in Sweden. – Between the Slottsskog and the Götaälv lies the MAJORNA district, formerly a working-class quarter, with the *Landshövdingehus* ("governor's houses") of about 1875, in typical Gothenburg style. Since timber-built houses were not allowed to have more than two storeys the ground floor was built of stone.

SURROUNDINGS. – From Lilla Bommen it is a half-hour trip by motorboat to the fortress of *Nya Elfsborg* (1670; restored 1971), on an island off the mouth of the river. There are also attractive trips to the skerries, particularly popular being one of the outer islands, *Styrsö* (swimming). – 9 km (5 miles) SW at the mouth of the Götaälv is **Långedrag**, formerly a fishing village and now a popular resort (summer restaurant) and attractive residential suburb. – *Landvetter*, Gothenburg's airport, is 18 km (11 miles) from mid-city on the Borås road (No. 40).

7 km (4½ miles) S of E6 is the industrial town of **Mölndal**, now almost fused with Gothenburg (pop. 47,300; hotels, see under Gothenburg). 2 km (1¼ miles) E stands *Gunnebo Castle* (1796), in a beautiful English-style park; to the W is *Åby* racecourse. – 7 km (4½ miles) farther S on E6 is *Kållered*, which has a church dating in part from the 13th c., with a beautifully painted wooden ceiling. At *Lindome* the road leaves the province of Bohuslän and continues to *Halland* and **Kungsbacka** (pop. 40,900; Hotel Carlsons Rum, 16 b.; Halland Hotel, 121 b.; Gillet, 25 b.): Town Hall of 1935 with library and theatre, open-air museum in the beautiful natural park of Kungsbacksskog. – 5 km (3 miles) E, on a peninsula in the Rolfså, is *Gåsevadsholm Castle*. – 11 km (7 miles) NW of Kungsbacka we come to the idyllic island of *Särö*, now linked with the mainland and increasingly being drawn into the orbit of Gothenburg. 10 km (6 miles) SW, on a road which runs along the shore of the Kungsbackafjord, we reach *Onsala* which has a richly painted church (17th–18th c.; restored 1918–19). In the octagonal burial vault are two massive marble sarcophagi containing the remains of the Swedish naval hero and privateer Lars Gathenhielm (1689–1718) and his wife Ingela. In the adjoining church stables is a Carriage Museum. – 4 km (2½ miles) beyond Onsala is the resort of *Gottskär* (Marinhotellet, 20 b.).

8 km (5 miles) S of Kungsbacka a road branches off E6 on the left and runs 3 km (2 miles) E to the *Fjärås Bräcka*, a morainic ridge several miles long which skirts the W end of Lake Lyngern (18 km (11 miles) long). At the W end of the ridge are a large Iron Age cemetery and 103 standing stones, the largest of which is 4·75 m (15$\frac{1}{2}$ ft) high. – Returning to the main road, turn off almost at once into a road on the right signposted to Åsa. 3·5 km (2 miles) SW of Torpa, on a peninsula on the S side of the Kungsbackafjord, is the imposing *Tjolöholm Castle*, a mansion in English Renaissance style built by the Gothenburg business- man James Frederik Dickson between 1898 and 1904 (conducted tours in summer). – 6 km (4 miles) farther S on the main road is the little seaside resort of *Åsa* (motel, 40 b.). Beyond this, at *Frillesås*, we rejoin E6. At Backa a road goes off on the right to the *Ringhals* nuclear power station; at *Åskloster* E6 crosses the River *Viska*, which flows into the *Klosterfjord*; and in another 10 km (6 miles) a road goes off on the left (No. 41) to Borås (see p. 70). From this point it is 2 km (1$\frac{1}{4}$ miles) to **Varberg** (pop. 43,550; hotels: Bergklinten, 222 b.; City, 39 b.; Gästis, 55 b.; Statt, 214 b.; Strandgården, 52 b.; Varberg, 43 b.; youth hostel; two camp sites), a town with a history dating back to the Middle Ages but now known mainly as an attractive seaside resort. There are more than 6 km (4 miles) of cliff-fringed sandy beaches, with varied and beautiful scenery in the surrounding area. This is an important area for sea fishing (several boat trips daily). The town's most prominent feature is the 13th c. fortress (with later alterations) on a rocky promontory to the W, which came into Swedish hands in 1645. It now houses a local museum, notable in particular for the clothes found on a body dating from medieval times which was discovered in 1936 in a bog at Bocksten, to the E of the town. In the fortifications is a café with a superb view of the sea. To the N of the town are the ruins of the parish church, dating in part from the 14th c. In the Old Harbour Magazine is a glass-works (open to visitors). – Off the coast to the W lies the island of *Getterö*, linked with the mainland by a causeway. – Car ferry to Grenå in Denmark (4$\frac{1}{2}$ hours). – 7 km (4$\frac{1}{2}$ miles) S of Varberg is the largest fishing village in Halland, *Träslövsläge* (wooden church with interesting paintings).

47 km (30 miles) NE of Gothenburg on E3 is the beautifully situated town of Alingsås. Ascending the valley of the Säveå, the road comes to *Jonsered* (13 km – 8 miles), where it enters the *Västergötland* region, and then continues along the S side of *Lake Aspen* to *Lerum* (church with ceiling of 1750). Then, after passing through *Floda*, along the E side of *Lake Sävelång* to *Nääs*, where there is a 19th c. castle set in a beautiful park. The castle is situated on a peninsula and now houses a College of Arts and Crafts (founded 1868: open to visitors).

**Alingsås** (alt. 64 m (210 ft); pop. 28,550; Hotel Gripen, 20 b.; Scandic Hotel, 139 b.), on the N side of *Lake Mjörn*, is an old court and industrial town (weaving mills). In 1724 Jonas Alströmer and Christoffer Polhem established a textile mill here and thus founded the Swedish textile trade. In the market square are a bust of Alströmer (1685–1761) and an old warehouse of 1631, now a museum. In the park of Nolhaga Castle (deer-park, lakes, old beech trees) Alströmer grew the first potatoes and tobacco in Sweden. – 9 km (6 miles) NW, at *Brobacka*, the river which links Lake Anten and Mjörn flows between steep rock walls. 2 km (1$\frac{1}{4}$ miles) away is *Anten*, with an old-time railway (engine and coaches dating from

the turn of the 19th c.) which runs trains to Gräfsnäs (12 km – 7$\frac{1}{2}$ miles) on Sundays in summer

*Marstrand:* see p. 69.

*Gota Canal: see p. 100.

# Gotland

Sweden.
Province: Gotlands län.
Area: 3140 sq. km (1212 sq. miles).
Population: 54,000.

ⓘ Gotlands Turistförening,
Strandgaten 9;
S-62101 Visby;
tel. (0498) 1 90 10.

EVENT. – *Miracle play*, "Petrus de Dacia" (Visby).

*Gotland is the largest island in the Baltic, 125 km (78 miles) long and 55 km (35 miles) across at its widest point. It lies some 90 km (60 miles) from the mainland of Sweden and is separated from the island of Öland to the SW by an arm of the sea 55 km (35 ft) wide and up to 200 m (650 ft) deep. Once a famous Viking strong- hold, the island has numerous important remains from the past in- cluding not only the famous stand- ing stones (*raukar*) and Viking sites, but also the magnificent town walls of Visby and 92 churches, none of which were built later than 1350. For centuries the island played a major part in the Baltic trade, but with the founding of Visby by the Hansa League on the site of an early settle- ment the town became not only the greatest Swedish town, but the greatest and richest of all the towns in the Baltic. As a result, though it remained, for the most part, firmly Swedish, its authority was claimed and frequently held from time to time by Germans, Danes, Norwe- gians and the Dutch. The tourist trade is now one of its main sources of income: during the main summer season, therefore, it is advisable to book accommodation and passages on the car ferry in plenty of time.**

ACCESS. – The *ferry service* between the island and the mainland of Sweden is run by the Gotland Company (Gotlandsbolaget, Box 2003, S-62102 Visby, tel. 04 98 1 1 9 00). The shortest connection is between *Västervik* or *Grankullavik* (Öland) and Visby (June to August only; 3$\frac{1}{2}$ hours or 2 hrs. 50 mins.). There are services throughout the year between Visby and *Oskarshamn* (about 4¼ hours) and *Nynäshamn* (55 km (35 miles) S of Stockholm: about 5 hours). In summer only there are connections between Stockholm and Visby (Rederi AB Gotland). – *Air services* by Linjeflyg, the Swedish domestic airline, between Gotland and 25 airports in mainland Sweden; the flight from Stockholm to Visby takes only 35 minutes.

> Foreign visitors to Gotland should note that the northern part of the island and the two small islands of Fårö and Gotska Sandö are restricted military areas. Foreigners may visit Fårö only on excursions organised by the Gotlandsresor or Reso firms. For a stay of more than 72 hours in the other restricted areas it is necessary to obtain a permit from the police or the military authorities in Visby.

Gotland is a limestone plateau lying at an altitude of between 20 and 30 m (65 and 100 ft) with no lakes of any size and no rivers or river valleys, since the water seeps away quickly into the soil. The coasts are fringed by long sandy beaches or steep limestone cliffs, which often take the form of bizarrely shaped free-standing crags known as *raukar* (singular *rauk*). The Ice Age left its mark on Gotland in the shape of numerous erratic blocks of gneiss, granite and porphyry. – Thanks to its mild climate the island has a varied and abundant plant life. It has large expanses of lush meadowland and arable fields; rather less than half its area is forest-covered. Even orchids flourish here. Sheep-farming is enjoying a new upsurge of prosperity. The only industries are cement works and the assembly of electronic apparatus. Prospecting for oil began in 1979.

HISTORY. – Gotland, with its capital Visby, was long an important staging point on the trade route between Asia and Europe. Until the early 12th c. it remained firmly in the hands first of the Vikings and then of the Goths, who had also established a settlement at Novgorod in Russia. Thereafter its growing trade passed increasingly to Russians and to an even greater extent to Germans. In 1161 the Goths obtained a licence to trade with German territories, and in 1280 Visby and Lübeck formed a defensive alliance against piracy, which was also joined by Riga. The predominance of Visby in the Baltic trade was broken in 1293 when the Hanseatic League resolved that the German settlement in Novgorod should be allowed only to deal direct with Lübeck. Further difficulty was caused by armed conflicts between peasants and townspeople. In 1361 the island was conquered by the Danish King Valdemar Atterdag (betrayed, according to legend, by the lovesick daughter of a Visby goldsmith), and four years later it fell into the hands of the Vitalienbrüder, a band of pirates supported by the duchy of Mecklenburg, who remained in possession until they were driven out by the Teutonic Knights in 1398. The Knights later (1408) sold Gotland to Eric of Pomerania, heir to Margaretha and ruler of the united Scandinavian kingdoms. From 1449 it was again under Danish sovereignty. In 1524 the Swedes and a year later Lübeck made unsuccessful attempts to conquer the island, and it did not become Swedish again until 1645, under the treaty of Brömsebro. Thereafter it underwent two further periods of foreign rule – from 1676 to 1679 by the Danes and in 1803, for 23 days, by the Russians. Little of the island's former splendour and wealth has been preserved.

The island's capital is **Visby**, on the NW coast (pop. 20,000; hotels: Donnersplats, 50 b.; Gute, 71 b.; Nya Hotel Solhem, 151 b.; Snäck, 428 b., SB; Strand, 104 b.; Villa Borgen, 34 b.; Visby, 160 b.; holiday vil-

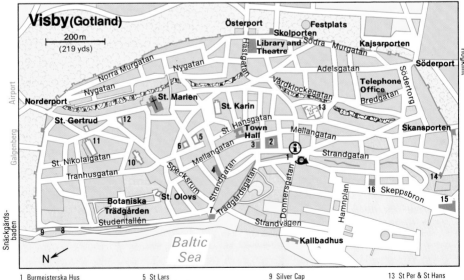

**Visby** (Gotland)

200 m
(219 yds)

Baltic Sea

N

| | | | |
|---|---|---|---|
| 1 Burmeisterska Hus | 5 St Lars | 9 Silver Cap | 13 St Per & St Hans |
| 2 Museum of Antiquities | 6 Drotten church | 10 St Clement | 14 Visborg Castle |
| 3 Liljehornska Hus | 7 Powder Tower | 11 St Nicholas | 15 Harbour Office |
| 4 Old Pharmacy | 8 Maiden's Tower | 12 Church of Holy Ghost | 16 Custom House |

lages; youth hostel; camp sites), the "city of ruins and roses", seat of the governor of the province of Gotland and the see of a bishop. Within its enclosing walls it has preserved much of its medieval atmosphere. Of its seventeen churches ten survive only as ruins, and services are still held in only one of them (St Mary's). From the beginning of July to the middle of August the miracle play (with music) by Friederich Mehler, "Petrus de Dacia", is performed about every other day in the ruins of St Nicholas's Church.

Miracle play, Visby (Gotland)

SIGHTS. – The most notable feature of Visby is the 3·5 km (2 miles) long circuit of **town walls**, built of limestone towards the end of the 13th c. and strengthened about 1300. At regular intervals in the walls are 44 towers standing between 15 and 20 m (50 and 60 ft) high. At two points there are large breaches in the walls – one on the E side, probably the result of the Swedish attack in 1524, and the other caused by the insurgents from Lübeck a year later. On the seaward side is the *Powder Tower* (Kruttornet), probably dating from the 11th c. and incorporated in the later walls. Near the N end stands the *Maiden's Tower* (Jungfrutornet), in which legend has it that the daughter of a goldsmith of Visby was walled up alive for betraying the town to king Valdemar Atterdag of Denmark. The adjoining corner tower is known as the "*Silver Cap*" (Silverhättan). From here the walls run E to the line of cliffs, turn S at the main gateway (Norderport) and follow the edge of the cliffs to the Söderport at the S end of the town, and finally turn W to end at the ruins of *Visborg Castle*, overlooking the harbour.

From the harbour Hamngata leads to *Donnersplatsen*, with the *Burmeisterska Hus*, built in 1652 by a Lübeck merchant named Burmeister, and which now houses the Tourist Information Office. Obliquely opposite is the *Post Office*. To the N, along Strandgatan, we come to the *Museum of Antiquities* (Gotlands Fornsal), with a fine collection of Viking and medieval material, tombstones and runic stones, arms and armour, furniture and religious art. Close by is the *Liljehornska Hus*. Beyond Packhusplatsen, on the right, is the *Clematishus*, and then (No. 28) the *Old Pharmacy* (Gamla Apoteket), a 13th c. house with a crow-stepped gable (exhibition of arts and crafts).

The Labska Gränd leads to the market square. (*Stora Torg*), on the S side of which are the ruins of *St Catherine's Church* (St Karin), built about 1230, which originally belonged to a Franciscan friary. To the N, in St Hansgatan, are the ruined churches of *Drotten* (or the Trinity) and *St Lars* (13th c.), with a massive towers which served for purposes of defence. To the W, uphill, stands **St Mary's Church**, the **Cathedral**, built by the Hanseatic League (consecrated 1225; much altered in later centuries; restored 1899–1907 and 1945), the only one of the old churches of Visby which is still in use; in earlier times it was used as a warehouse and as a place of safe keeping for valuables. The church has three towers, a massive square one on the W front and two more slender octagonal towers at the E end. The S chapel commemorates the burgomaster of Visby, Swerting, executed in 1350. The church contains a fine carved pulpit of walnut wood and ebony from Lübeck (1684) and a 13th c. font of red Gotland marble.

From St Mary's the Norra Kyrkogata runs N to the ruins of the Romanesque *Church of the Holy Ghost* (Helgeandskyrka), which dates from the first half of the 13th c. This two-storeyed octagonal structure, of a type unusual in Scandinavia, shows the influence of the double churches of Germany. There was probably a bridge linking the upper storey of the church with a hospital which stood close by. From here a side street passes the remains of the little 15th c. *St Gertrude's Chapel* and comes to the ruined *St Nicholas's Church*, the largest in Visby, where the play "Petrus de Dacia" is performed. The church, which originally belonged to a Dominican monastery, was begun about 1230 and was destroyed by Lübeck forces in 1525. Beautiful rose window in gable. – To the S, among houses, are the remains of the Romanesque *St Clement's Church*, built in the mid 13th c. Excavations have brought to light the foundations of three other churches, the oldest of which (12th c.) was probably one of the earliest stone churches in Visby; fine S doorway. To the right of the church is an old weapon-house, in which the men deposited their arms before entering the church.

On the NW side of the town is the *Botanic Garden* (Botaniska Trädgården), at the S end of which are the ruins of *St Olof's Church* (Romanesque, c. 1200). – A little way SE of Donnersplatsen are the scanty remains of two adjoining churches, *St Per* and *St Hans*. Excavations in 1917 revealed the foundations of three other churches below St Per, the older and smaller of the two.

SURROUNDINGS of Visby. – A very attractive *walk leads through the Norderport and past the ruins of *St Göran's Church* (13th c.), which originally belonged to a leper hospital, to the *Galgenberg* (Gallows Hill: 30 minutes), a medieval place of execution with three tall stone pillars 6 m (20 ft) high (magnificent view of the town and the sea). At the foot of the hill to the N is the *Trojeborg*, a stone maze which was probably a very ancient cult site. Its name recalls the ancient Roman "Troy game" (*Trojae ludus* – a sham fight on horseback). – To the SE of the town by way of the Österport is the *Korsbetning* (Cross Meadow), with the ruins of *Solberga monastery* (1246) and *Valdemar's Cross* (Valdemarskors: 2·5 m (8 ft) high, with a Latin inscription), at the burial place of the Gotland peasants who fell in 1361. Excavations in 1905 brought to light between 300 and 400 skeletons together with arms and armour. – 4 km (2½ miles) SW, near the camp site and holiday villages of Kneippby and the Villa Villekulla, is a children's playground with numerous delights. 4 km (2½ miles) farther on from a rugged crag, the *Högklint* (45 m – 148 ft), there are extensive views of the sea and the town of Visby; below the top are the limestone spur known as *Getsvältan* and a cave. Nearby is the *Villa Fridhem*, which belonged to Prince Oskar Bernadotte (boarding school), with a large park. – 4 km (2½ miles) NE of Visby on a road skirting the beach we reach the popular resort of *Snäckgärdsbad*.

EXCURSIONS. – Remains of the past are to be seen everywhere on Gotland: no other part of Sweden has so many ancient monuments covering a wide range of periods, prehistoric and historical. The Gotland Tourist Agency (Gotlandsresor AB) runs numerous excursions during the summer to the island's main features of interest. Gotland is also a paradise for the cyclist (with facilities for rental of bicycles), and the Tourist Agency rents bicycles and tents and offers cycling packages.

**Visby to Lickershamn** (27 km – 17 miles). – Leave Visby on Road 149, via the Norderport. In 4 km (2½ miles) a side road goes off to the resort of Snäckgärdsbad, and 6 km (4 miles) beyond this is the *Herb Garden* (Krusmyntargården), on the Brissund road (200 types of medicinal herbs). Another 4 km (2½ miles) along Road 149, at *Lummalunda*, there is a stalactitic cave system which was discovered only in recent years. In the immediate neighbourhood are a wildlife park, a mink farm, the remains of an old iron foundry (closed down 1712) and a huge mill-wheel 10 m (33 ft) in diameter. Another 4 km (2½ miles) N on Road 149 is *Lummelunda church* (late 13th c.; restored 1960). 9 km (6 miles) beyond this lies the fishing port of **Lickershamn** (holiday village, 12 chalets). A narrow path 600 m (650 yds) long runs along the cliffs to the imposing *rauk* known as the *Jomfru* (Maiden), 11·5 m (38 ft) high (fine views).

**Visby to Fårösund** (55 km – 35 miles). – Leave by the Norderport and Road 148, which continues past the airport to **Bro** (12 km – 7½ miles), which has a *church in Romanesque and Gothic style (early 13th c.) with a Baroque interior; bell (15th c.) with an inscription in Low German. Built into the external wall are numerous stones with representations of animals and symbolic devices from an earlier church (perhaps 5th c.). – 12 km (7½ miles): *Tingstäde*, on the NW shore of a lake, the *Tingstäde Träsk* (alt. 45 m – 148 ft). The engineer and inventor Christoffer Polhem was born here in 1661. Fine 13th c. church. Beneath the waters of the lake are the remains of a pile-built defensive structure of the Iron Age known as the Bulverk. – 10 km (6 miles) beyond Tingstäde Road 147 branches off on the right and comes in 9 km (5½ miles) to the port and industrial town of *Slite* (Slite-badens Hotell, 19 b.; Slite holiday village, 50 chalets), the heart of the Gotland cement industry. From the church (1960) there is an attractive view. – Road 148 continues to *Lärbro* (3 km – 2 miles), which has a 14th c. church with an unusual octagonal tower; it contains numerous sculptures and paintings. Adjoining the church is a 12th c. defensive tower. 3 km (2 miles) NW are the ruins of *Gann church* (13th c.). – From Lärbro the road continues past *Rute church* (c. 1260) and through a military restricted area to **Bunge** (13 km – 8 miles), with an early 14th c. fortified church richly

*Raukar*, Gotland

decorated with sculpture and painting. To the E of the church is an open-air museum with some fifty old buildings. **Fårösund**, 2 km (1¼ miles) beyond this, has a small harbour on the Fårö Sound (1·5 km (1 mile) wide), which separates Gotland from the island of **Fårö** (ferry). Fårö ("Sheep Island") has a number of beautiful sandy beaches (Sudersandsvik, Ekevik, Norsta Auren) and large assemblages of *rauker*, in groups of up to 80 rocks 8–10 m high.

**Visby to Roma and Dalhem** (17 or 24 km – 10 or 15 miles). – Leave by the Söderport and Road 143, which runs past *Follingbo church* to **Roma**, with a church built about 1250. 2 km (1¼ miles) SE are the ruins of *Roma monastery*, a Cistercian house founded in 1164 which was pulled down after the Reformation and used as a quarry of building material for the nearby royal palace. – 7 km (4½ miles): **Dalhem**. Above the village stands a \*church of about 1250 (restored in the early 20th c.) which is one of the most interesting on Gotland and is notable in particular for its wall paintings and stained glass. 300 m (328 yds) S of the church is the old railway station, now a Railway Museum. – From here it is 17 km (10 miles) to the holiday village of *Åminne* (10 chalets, camp site), at the mouth of the River Gothemå.

**Visby to Burgsvik** (81 km – 50 miles). – Leave by the Söderport and Road 140. In 3 km (2 miles) a road goes off on the right to *Kneippby* and the *Högklint*. 13 km (8 miles) farther on is *Tofta church* (13th c.), and the Tofta bathing station to the right of the road. – 26 km (16 miles) from Visby we reach the little resort of *Västergarn*, with a church which was originally the choir of a larger building. Kronholmen golf-course, on the sea. – 7 km (4½ miles): *Klintehamn* (hotels: Klintehamns, 18 b.; Mattsarve Sommergård, 75 b.; Gannarve Gård, 20 b.), a port and seaside resort. Motorboats ply from here past the island of *Lilla Karlsö*, inhabited only by sheep of the old Gotland breed, to the larger island of **Stora Karlsö** (alt. 51 m – 167 ft), 12 km (7½ miles) SW, which is noted for its abundance of bird life (250 species recorded, including razorbills, peregrine falcons, eiders and guillemots) and its many rare plants (orchids). Numerous *raukar* and caves, the largest of which, the Stora Förvar, was occupied by man in Stone Age times. Both islands are nature reserves.

From Klintehamn continue either on Road 140, which runs nearer the coast via *Fröjel* (12th c. church with an old wooden crucifix; to the N an old castle affording magnificent views) to Burgsvik (39 km – 25 miles), or by the 9 km (5 mile) longer route on Road 141.

2 km (1¼ miles) along Road 141, on the right, is *Klinte church* (13th c.). 20 km (12½ miles): *Hemse*, once a considerable trading town, with a Romanesque church (c. 1200; 14th and 15th c. paintings). From here continue S of Road 142, which comes from Visby. In 2 km (1¼ miles) is seen Smiss Slott, an old fortified castle. Then another 10 km (6 miles) to the fine church of *Grötlingbo* (1340), with well-preserved medieval stained glass; the pulpit was originally made for Visby Cathedral. – 12 km (7½ miles): **Burgsvik**, a port and holiday resort on the S side of the inlet of the same name (Björklunda guest-house, 70 b.; Holmhällar guest-house, 110 b.; camp site). 2 km (1¼ miles) E is *Öja church* (13th c.), with a very fine \*triumphal crucifix dating from the second half of the 13th c.

From Burgsvik a road runs S, past the old southern Gotland farm of **Bottarvegården** (5 km – 3 miles), now a museum, and *Vamlingbo church* to the hill of *Hoburgen* (37 m (121 ft): lighthouse), at the southern tip of the island.

Curious cliff formations (four "castles"), and the impressive *rauk* known as Hoburgsgubben (4·5 m (15 ft) high); old quarries and caves. – An alternative route to Hoburgen is on a narrow road which turns right off the main road 9·5 km (6 miles) S of Burgsvik for *Gervalds*, continuing close to the coast, through ruggedly beautiful cliff scenery, to Hoburgen. Abandoned quarries. – 13 km (8 miles) SE of Burgsvik is *Holmhällar*, with imposing *raukar*. On the beach are old stone fishermen's cottages. 400 m ($\frac{1}{4}$ mile) offshore lies the island of *Heligholmen*, with a "Silver Cave" which is the subject of many legends.

Situated on the SE coast of Gotland (48 km (30 miles) SE of Visby) and second only to Visby in its attraction to visitors, is the port and seaside resort of **Ljugarn** (Hotel Lövängen, 70 b.; Ljugarns Badpensionat, 44 b.; Vitvär holiday village, 22 chalets; youth hostel; camp site), with a small Customs Museum. 2·5 km (1$\frac{1}{2}$ miles) NE are the *raukar*, extending for some 500 m (550 yds), of *Folhammar*. – 7·5 km (5 miles) SW of Ljugarn stands *Garde church* (11th c.), with wall paintings in Byzantine style, and 4 km (2$\frac{1}{2}$ miles) SE, on *Lau Hill*, we find a fine 13th c. church. – at *Guffride*, 6 km (4 miles) S of Ljugarn, are Bronze Age *stone-settings in the form of ships, the largest on Gotland. – 16 km (10 miles) NW by way of *Ala* is *Kräklingbo*, with a 14th c. church. Some 4·5 km (3 miles) S, in forest country, is the *Torsburg*, the oldest prehistoric fortified settlement on Gotland, probably dating from the 5th c. It occupies a steep-sided limestone crag (68 m – 223 ft), with a wall 1·5 km (1 mile) long and 4–7 m (13–23 ft) high along the S side; lookout tower.

# Gudbrandsdal

Norway (Southern).
County: Oppland fylke.
(i) **A/L Oppland Reiseliv,**
   Kirkegate 74,
   N-2600 Lillehammer;
   tel. (0 62) 5 57 00.
   **Nord-Gudbrandsdal Reiselivslag,**
   N-2670 Otta;
   tel. (0 62) 0 03 65.
   **Midt-Gudbrandsdal Reiselivslag,**
   N-2640 Vinstra;
   tel. (0 62) 9 01 66.

The *Gudbrandsdal, known as "the valley of valleys", extends NW of Lillehammer for some 200 km (125 miles) up the valley of the River Lågen, lying between the Rondane and Dovrefjell chains to the E and the imposing mountain region of the Jotunheim to the W. It is one of the most popular tourist regions of Norway, both in summer and in winter. The people of the valley have preserved many of their ancient customs. The region has a mild inland climate with long periods of dry weather.

From **Lillehammer** (alt. 180 m (590 ft): see p. 175) E6 follows the River Lågen upstream through the *Gudbrandsdal. 6 km (4 miles) from Lillehammer is *Fåberg* (alt. 148 m – 486 ft), where the Lågen flows into Lake Mjøsa; to the right is a steep-sided hill, *Balbergkamp* (660 m – 2165 ft). From here Road 255 runs NW into the Gausdal and Espedal (Peer Gynt Road, Espedal Road). The main road continues to *Hunder* and beyond this to the *Hunderfoss power station* (conducted tours). The station is supplied with water by an artificial lake 7 km (4 miles) long formed by a dam (road along top) 280 m (300 yds) long and 16 m (50 ft) high. Fish-ladder and trout-breeding station (some 20,000 fish annually). The road along the dam leads to a beautifully situated camp site (huts). To the right lies *Åsletta*, from which a private road (toll) leads NE to *Nermo Fjellstue* (56 b.), 8 km (5 miles) away, and Hornsjø. 6 km (4 miles) from Hunder, on the hill to the right, stands *Øyer church* (1725: interior in pleasant Baroque style). On the other side of the Lågen (bridge) is *Øyer* (alt. 181 m (594 ft); Gjestgård, 64 b.; two camp sites, with huts). 12 km (7$\frac{1}{2}$ miles) beyond this we reach **Tretten** (alt. 191 m (627 ft); pop. 750; hotels: Austlid Feriesenter, 375 b.; Bådstø Gjestgiveri & Camping, 90 b.; Glomstad Gård og Pensjonat, 20 b.; Optun Gård og Pensjonat, 35 b.; two camp sites; Mageli holiday village, 6 km (4 miles) N), at the S end of *Lake Losna* (alt. 182 m (597 ft); 17 km (10 miles) long; good fishing), which was formed by the widening of the River Lågen. Church of 1728 with old ceiling paintings. Road 254, to the W, joins the Peer Gynt Road. – E6 continues along the eastern shore of Lake Losna. In 15 km (10 miles) it comes to the *Kirkestuen* road junction, with *Fåvang church*, originally a stave church but rebuilt in the 17th c. as a cruciform church (restored 1951). 4 km (2½ miles) farther on is the village of *Fåvang* (alt. 188 m (617 ft); camp site). In another 7 km (4½ miles), at *Elstad*, a road on the right branches off to the *Ringebu stave church* (2 km – 1¼ miles). The church, originally built about 1200 and enlarged about 1630 (restored 1921), contains a carved altarpiece of 1688. From here it is 3 km (2 miles) to *Ringebu* (alt. 197 m (646 ft); pop. 1100; hotels: Fagerhøi Fjellskole, 98 b.; Ringebu, 61 b.; Spidsbergseter Fjellstue, Venabygd, 22 km (14 miles) N, 40 b.; Venabu Fjellshotell, 18 km (11 miles) N, 110 b.; camp site, with huts).

The Rondane hills from Folldal

From here an excursion can be made on Road 220, which runs N to *Enden* (38 km – 24 miles), then on No. 27 and from *Folldal* (50 km – 31 miles) on No. 29, alongside the beautiful **Rondane** chain, Norway's third highest range of hills, part of which is a National Park (Rondeslottet, 2183 m (7162 ft); *Høgronden*, 2114 m – 6936 ft), to *Hjerkinn* (28 km – 17 miles), where we rejoin E6.

Beyond Ringebu E6 follows the course of the Lågen, coming in 10 km (6 miles) to the village of *Hundorp* (alt. 193 m – 633 ft), with the Gudbrandsdal Folk High School. In the school grounds are graves and standing stones of the Viking period. The octagonal *Sør-Fron church* (1800) has an electronic carillon. – From here it is 8 km (5 miles) to *Harpefoss* (alt. 223 m – 732 ft), where there is an exhibition of furniture and applied art. Hydroelectric power station (dam 125 m (140 yds) long and 16 m (52 ft) high; the water has a fall of 33 m – 108 ft). – 7 km (4½ miles) farther on is **Vinstra** (alt. 241 m (791 ft); pop. 2500; Fefor Hoifjellshotell, 220 b., SB; Sulseter Fjellstugu, 45 b.; Sødorp Gjest-givergård, 93 b.; Wadahl Høgfjellshotell, 170 b.; two groups of chalets), opposite

the junction of the Vinstra with the Lågen. Features of interest are *Sødorp* wooden church (1752) and the Peer Gyntgård, with 18 old houses (private property). – Beyond Vinstra the scenery becomes still grander. 10 km (6 miles) farther on is *Kvam* (alt. 253 m (830 ft); hotels: Kvamshytta, 36 b.; Sinclair Vertshuset, 24 b.), where the decisive battle for the Gudbrandsdal was fought in 1940. The church (1952) contains a 400-year-old Bible; the old church was destroyed in 1940. 14 km (9 miles) N (part of the way on a private road, with toll) are the *Rondane Høyfjellshotell* (alt. 900 m (2950 ft); 140 b.) and the *Rondablikk* (view). To the S of Kvam is the mountain of *Teigkamp* (1027 m – 3370 ft). – In another 9 km (5 miles) the main road comes to *Sjoa* (alt. 285 m (935 ft); youth hostel; three camp sites, with chalets), with the mountain of *Torgeirkamp* (1186 m – 3891 ft) to the right.

From here Road 257 runs W into the **Heidal**. 15 km (10 miles) along this road, beyond the village of *Heidal* (many old houses and farms protected as ancient monuments), is the church, rebuilt in 1938 on the model of the previous church (1752), which was burned down in 1933. Close by, on the beautiful farm of Bølstad, is a chapel of about 1600; parts of doorway from an 11th c. stave church and a crucifix of about 1200.

In another 8 km (5 miles) E6 comes to *Kringen* (camp site), with a memorial commemorating a victory won by the local peasants in 1612 over a band of Scottish mercenaries (said, erroneously, to have been commanded by a certain Captain Sinclair) which was on its way to Sweden. NW of the village is *Pillarguri-kamp* (849 m – 2786 ft), from which legend has it that one Pillarguri warned

The River Gjende (Gudbrandsdal)

the peasants of the approach of the Scots. From here it is 3 km (2 miles) to **Otta** (alt. 288 m (945 ft); pop. 2500; Müllerhotel Otta, 175 b.; Rapham Høyfjellshotell, 100 b., SB; six camp sites, with chalets), an important road junction at the confluence of the River Otta and the Lågen. It is possible to drive to a point 1 km (¾ mile) below the summit of Pillargurikamp, from which there is a magnificent view. Here Road 15 branches off to the left, going via Vågåmo and Lom to the Nordfjord. A minor road runs 13 km (8 miles) NE to the Mysuseter Høyfjellspensjonat (50 b.). – E6 continues to follow the course of the Lågen, coming in 3 km (2 miles) to *Sel*, with a church of 1782. An area of some 500 hectares (1250 acres) between the church and the station has been transformed within the last 20 years from moorland to fertile arable land. The farm of Romundgård nearby, though it was built some 300 years later than the story, was used by Sigrid Undset (1882–1949), the Nobel prize-winner, as the model for Jörungård, the homestead which plays so large a part in the trilogy "Kristin Lavransdatter". She also wove the story of "Laurgård" and the "Sinclair hut", in which a Scottish captain is said to have spent the night before his death, into the fabric of her tale.

A road on the right (8 km (5 miles); toll) leads to *Mysuseter*. In 3 km (2 miles) a short path goes off to the curious *Kvitskriuprestinn*, pyramids of morainic gravel deposits up to 6 m (20 ft) high. From Mysuseter there is a footpath (10 km – 6 miles) to the *Rondvassbu hut*, on the edge of the **Rondane National Park** (area 570 sq. km – 220 sq. miles), a good base for walkers and climbers.

Over the next 14 km (9 miles) the valley becomes steadily narrower and the scenery wilder. – At *Rosten* a narrow road (10 km – 6 miles) leads to a group of summer grazing stations (*seter*) at *Høvringen*, which attracts many visitors in both summer and winter (alt. 960 m (3150 ft); Haukeliseter Fjellstue, 54 b.; Høvringen Høgfjellshotell, 100 b.; Smuksjøseter Fjellstue, 45 b.). – E6 comes in another 8 km (5 miles) to *Brennhaug* (alt. 449 m – 1473 ft). From here there are views to the NE of *Storkuven* (1452 m – 4764 ft) and to the S of the *Jetta* range, with the commanding *Blåhø* (1618 m (5309 ft): road from Vågåmo).

9 km (5½ miles) farther on is *Dovre* (alt. 485 m (1591 ft); pop. 400; Toftemo Turiststasjon, 115 b.; two camp sites, with chalets), in the commune of Dovre (pop. 3150), with a wooden church of 1740. Off the road to the right is the former royal property of *Tofte* (17th and 18th c.). – 13 km (8 miles) beyond this is **Dombås** (alt. 659 m (2162 ft); pop. 1200; Dombås Turisthotell, 200 b.; Dovrefjell Hotell, 170 b., SB; youth hostel; six camp sites, with chalets), an important road junction. From here E69 descends the valley of the Lågen to Åndalsnes (see p. 226).

E6 continues NE through the *Hinddal* and climbs up into the **Dovrefjell** (highest point *Snøhetta*, 2286 m – 7500 ft). Here the coniferous forest gives way to stunted birch trees, which in turn soon disappear. E6 follows the line of the old "Royal Road" (Kongsvei), along which for several centuries kings travelled to be crowned in Trondheim. In 10 km (6 miles) the road comes to *Fokstua* (alt. 982 m – 3222 ft). To the left is the beginning of the high moorland region of *Fokstumyren*, the haunt of many birds (nature reserve). To the right is a view of *Fokstuhø* (1716 m – 5630 ft), which can be climbed in 2½–3 hours. E6 continues over the moor, with the *Falketind* (1684 m – 5525 ft) to the right and, in another 8 km (5 miles), a long lake, the *Valasjø*, on the left. At the end of the lake a short side road leads to *Dovregubbens Hall* (food and accommodation). After passing the *Avsjø* on the right the road comes in another 10 km (6 miles) to **Hjerkinn** (alt. 956 m (3137 ft); Fjellstue, 70 b.), situated in a wide high valley in the Dovrefjell – the driest place in Norway, with a rainfall of only some 217 mm (8½ in.) a year. To the W is a military area closed to the public (firing range). The *Eystein Church* was built in 1969 to commemorate King Eystein Magnussen, who had the first hut built here in the 12th c. Stone marking the Royal Road, travelled by 41 reigning monarchs. 1 km (¾ mile) farther N is the highest point on the road (1025 m – 3366 ft). In the Tverfjell to the W are the Folldal mines (iron ore, pyrites, copper). An hour and a half's walk to the NE is the *Hjerkinnhø* (1282 m – 4206 ft), with superb views of Snøhetta, the Rondane range and the Jotunheim. – Road 29 goes off on the right to Folldal (27 km – 17 miles), from which it is possible either to turn S on Road 27 or to continue via Røros to the Swedish frontier (174 km – 108 miles).

After reaching its highest point N of Hjerkinn E6 runs down the *Driva* valley through the **Dovrefjell National Park** (rich mountain plant life; musk-oxen and wild reindeer). In 12 km (7½ miles) it comes to the *Kongsvoll Fjellstue* (alt. 887 m (2910 ft); inn) the newest of the *fjellstuer* in the Dovrefjell. 750 m (½ mile) farther on, off the road, is a Botanic Garden. – Kongsvoll is the base from which to climb the *Søndre Knutshø* (1690 m (5545 ft): 3–5 hours), to the E, and the starting point of a footpath (4–5 hours) to the *Reinheim hut* (key in Kongsvoll), from which Snøhetta (2286 m – 7500 ft) can be climbed in some 4 hours.

Farther down the Driva valley stretches of the road have had to be blasted from the rock. In 9 km (5 miles) the *Vårstig*, a section of the old Royal Road (first mentioned in 1182: now a footpath, offering magnificent views), branches off on the E. – 4·5 km (3 miles) farther on, to the right, is the *Drivstua* (alt. 680 m (2230 ft): accommodation). Beyond this, on the left, is a view into the *Amotsdal*. The scanty stands of birches now give way to coniferous forest. – 9·5 km (6 miles) beyond the Drivstua *Magalaupet*, a gorge through which the Driva tumbles and foams for a distance of some 100 m (110 yds) is reached on the old E6, which branches off on the left (camp site). – Then comes *Rise*, with an Iron Age cemetery. Close by are the *Smedgården* camp site and *Driva* railway station. A road on the right (toll) leads into the beautiful mountain scenery of *Loseter* (1100 m – 3600 ft). To the NE rears up the *Sisselhø* (1621 m (5319 ft): climbed from Oppdal in 3 hours). The road then reaches **Oppdal**, a vacation resort and road junction. E6 continues NE towards Trondheim (122 km – 76 miles). Road 16 branches off on the left and descends the Sunndal (p. 261) to *Kristiansund* (165 km – 103 miles).

The **Peer Gynt Road** (91 km – 57 miles) offers an attractive alternative to E6 between Lillehammer and Vinstra (7 km (4½ miles) longer; tolls). – From *Lillehammer* take E6 as far as *Fåberg* (6 km – 4 miles), and then turn left into Road 255. In 3 km (2 miles) it comes to the *Fåberg church* (1727: runic stone), and 11 km (7 miles) beyond this to *Aulestad*, with an old Viking homestead which was acquired by Bjørn-stjerne Bjørnson in 1874. The property now belongs to the state and is managed by Bjørnson's grandson (open May–September: museum). – At *Segalstad* (2 km – 1¼ miles) Road 255 continues W to Vestre Gausdal: the Peer Gynt Road runs N on Road 254. In 5 km (3 miles) it comes to *Østre Gausdal*, with a stone medieval church. Nearby is the presbytery (now uninhabited), the largest in Norway.

At *Svingvoll* (alt. 480 m (1575 ft); camp site) Road 254 goes off on the right to *Tretten* (8 km – 15 miles). The Peer Gynt Road runs NW (8 km – 5 miles) to *Skeikampen* and *Gausdal* (alt. 800 m (2625 ft); Skeikampen Høifjellshotell, 105 b.; Gausdal Høif-jellshotell, 240 b.; camp site), at the foot of *Skeikampen* (1123 m (3685 ft): chair-lift, magnificent views). Then on via *Frøysehøgda* (970 m (3183 ft): beautiful view of the Gausdal) and *Fagerhøy* (1018 m – 3340 ft) to *Rauhagen*, at the highest point on the road (1053 m – 3455 ft): extensive views, with the Rondane range and the Dovrefjell (Snøhetta) to the N and the Jotunheim to the NW. In another 8 km (5 miles) the road comes to *Skærvangen*, where a private road (10 km – 6 miles) goes off on the right to Hundorp on E6. Then, 5 km (3 miles) farther on, the tourist resort of *Golå* and *Wadahl* (Golå Høifjellshotell, 70 b., SB), 930 m (3050 ft) above the Golåvann (lookout tower). From *Vollsdammen* it is worth making a detour W to Dalseter (21 km – 13 miles). The main road continues to *Fefor* (Høifjellshotell, 220 b., SB), with Lake Fefor to the left and *Feforkampen* (1175 m (3855 ft): the climb takes ¾ hour and offers wide views of the Dovrefjell and Jotunheim). From Vollsdammen it is 10 km (6 miles) to *Vinstra*.

The **Espedal Road** (117 km – 73 miles) is another attractive, rather longer, alternative to E6 between Lillehammer and Vinstra. As far as *Segalstad* (22 km – 14 miles) it coincides with the Peer Gynt Road, and from there runs W to *Vestre Gausdal* (pop. 400), which has a wooden cruciform church of 1784. From here a road (open only in summer) runs SW through beautiful and varied scenery, with numerous bends and fine viewpoints (at altitudes of up to 1000 m – 3300 ft), to *Fagernes* (84 km – 52 miles). – The Espedal Road now continues for 22 km (14 miles) through the Svatsumdal to *Svatsum* (octagonal wooden church of 1860). 13 km (8 miles) farther on, at the S end of the *Espedalsvatn* (on left), is the remarkable cave system

known as *Helvete* ("Hell"): the largest chamber measures 100 by 40 m (330 by 130 ft). 2 km (1¼ miles) beyond this is the abandoned nickel mine of *Vassen-den*, and 3 km (2 miles) beyond this again the *Strand Fjellstue* (alt. 730 m (2395 ft); inn; beautiful view of the lake). In another 5 km (3 miles) the road comes to *Megrund Gård*, the oldest farm in the Espedal (c. 1785). From here it is 4 km (2½ miles) to the *Espedalen Fjellstue* (730 m (2395 ft); inn; camp site; good fishing), with a church of 1974. There was a nickel mine here until 1874. At *Dalseter*, 4 km (2½ miles) farther on (Høyfjellshotell, 130 b., SP, SB), the side road from Vollsdammen on the Peer Gynt Road comes in. To the right there is a view of *Ruten* (1513 m – 4964 ft). 3 km (2 miles) beyond this the road reaches its highest point (972 m – 3189 ft): to the W are the *Sikkilsdalshø* (1783 m – 5850 ft) and the *Heimdalshø* (1848 m – 6063 ft), to the N the *Gråhø* (1156 m – 3793 ft). To the left of the road is the artificial lake of *Olstappen*. At *Kamfoss* is a dam; and when the water is high the overflow forms a beautiful waterfall. – 10 km (6 miles) from Dalster, at *Skåbu*, the Espedal Road joins Road 255. The Jotunheim road (private: toll) goes off on the left to *Bygdin*; Road 255, to the right, pursues a winding course, with beautiful views, via *Kvikne* (church of 1764) to *Vinstra* (26 km – 16 miles).

# Hallingdal

Norway (Southern).
County: Buskerud fylke.

(i) **Buskerud Reiselivsråd.**
Storgate 2,
N-3500 Hønefoss;
tel. (0 67) 2 36 55.
**Turistkontoret for Geilo og Hol,**
N-3580 Geilo;
tel. (0 67) 8 61 00, ext. 206.

**The Hallingdal is a broad valley extending NW from the northern end of Lake Krøderen and traversed by the Hallingdalselv, here a broad and tranquil stream. The river forms a number of lake-like basins, the largest of which is the Brommavatn. The valley is thickly wooded; the hills are bare, with occasional rocky hummocks worn smooth by ice.**

In the Hallingdal

At *Gulsvik*, lying at the N end of Lake Krøderen, National Highway 7 passes through the "gateway to the Hallingdal", a road tunnel, with the Hallingdalselv to the right. In another 11·5 km (7½ miles) it passes *Flå church* (1858), on the right.

Farther along the road are several camp sites and a variety of overnight accommodation (at Stavn, Kolsrud, on an island in the river, Bromma and Roløkken). 33 km (20 miles): **Nesbyen** (alt. 167 m (548 ft); pop. 1500; hotels: Fagerhøy Fjellstue, 60 b.; Ranten Fjellstue, 70 b., SB, both in Mykingstølen; Smedsgården, 65 b.; Sytøa Hytta, 75 b.; Svenkerud, 102 b.; Thoen, 48 b.; Østenfor, 118 b.; three camp sites, with chalets), situated on a broad detrital cone. To the W is the *Hallingdal Folkemuseum*, with 14 old buildings, a church of 1862 and a new chapel in the style of the stave churches. Large market in the first week in July. Excursions to various beautifully situated summer grazing stations (overnight accommodation; toll roads). – From here it is 21 km (13 miles) to the important road junction of **Gol** (alt. 207 m (679 ft); pop. 1800; hotels: Eidsgaard Turisthotel, 60 b.; Hallingen Høyfjellshotell, 256 b., SB; Kamben, 70 b., SB; Oset Høyfjellshotell, 200 b., SB; Pers Hotel, 550 b., SB, SP; Storefjell Høyfjellshotell, 20 km (12 miles) away, 350 b., SB; four camp sites, with chalets). Chair-lift (length 1600 m (5250 ft), height difference 450 m (1475 ft); fine views from top). – 1·5 km (1 mile) beyond Gol Road 49 goes off on the right to *Fagernes* (52 km – 32 miles). 25 km (15 miles): Sanderstølen Høyfjellshotell (170 b., SB). At *Leira* Road 49 joins E68 (Oslo–Hønefoss–Fagernes).

2 km (1¼ miles) beyond Gol at the Heslabru, which spans the *Hemsila*, a tributary of the Hallingdalselv (beautiful waterfall), Road 52 branches off on the right and runs NW up the **Hemsedal**. After passing the new church of Gol it crosses the *Robru* (7 km – 4 miles). The valley now becomes somewhat more open. At Granheim (alt. 546 m – 1791 ft), 7 km (4½ miles) farther on, is the 550 m (600 yds) long *Eikre dam* (1959), from which water is conveyed in a tunnel 15 km (10 miles) long to the power station at Gol. On the way to *Ulsåk* (alt 609 m (1998 ft); camp site) the road passes on the left the *Helmens Bru* hydroelectric station, which is supplied with water by a tunnel 14 km (8 miles) long with a fall of 540 m (1770 ft). View of the *Veslehorn* (1300 m – 4265 ft), on the E side of which is a waterfall 140 m (460 ft) high, the *Hydnefoss*, and beyond it the *Storehorn* (1478 m – 4849 ft). From Ulsåk a mountain road (toll) goes off on the right to *Lykkja*, passing the *Skogshorn* (1728 m – 5670 ft), which can be climbed in 2–3 hours; from

Lykkja it is possible either to continue to Røn (48 km – 30 miles) and Fagernes or to turn S to Fjellheim and Gol. – From Ulsåk it is another 3 km (2 miles) on Road 52 to the vacation and winter sports resort of **Hemsedal** (alt. 609 m (1998 ft); hotels: Club Hemsedal, 120 b.; Hemsedal, 144 b.; Skogstad, 170 b.; four camp sites, with chalets). Chair-lift and several ski-lifts. – The road continues to Borlaug, where it joins E68.

From Gol the route through the Hallingdal continues SW of Highway 7, which for much of the way runs close to the tumultuous Hallingdalselv (numerous waterfalls). In 13 km (8 miles) it comes to *Torpo* (alt. 327 m – 1073 ft), with the nave of a 13th c. stave church (fine carving and ceiling paintings). – 8 km (5 miles) farther on, at *Gullhagen*, a road goes off on the right and runs past the new Alpine skiing resort of *Svarteberg* (two ski-lifts) to *Leveld* (chapel). From here it is possible to continue on the *Fanitullvei* to Hemsedal or to the *Bergsjø Høyfjells-hotell* (1084 m (3557 ft); 60 b.), to the NW, or alternatively to return to the main road by way of Hovet. – 3 km (2 miles) beyond Gullhagen is **Ål** (alt. 437 m (1434 ft); pop. 1500; Ål Apartments Hotell, 220 b., SB; Sundre Hotel, 45 b.; three camp sites, with chalets), with a large 18th c. church. Beyond Ål the Hallingdalselv opens out into the *Strandefjord*: the road continues along its N side. At *Kleivi*, at the far end of the fjord, is the Hol 3 power station, and on the other side of the river the Usta station. The road continues to *Hol* (church of 1924), where Road 288 (the *Aurlandsvei*) goes off on the right to the Aurlandsfjord (97 km – 60 miles). This very attractive tourist road, with numerous tunnels, was opened only in 1974.

Beyond Hol, Highway 7 ascends the wooded *Ustadal*, through which the *Ustaelv* flows in a deep gorge to the left of the road, and comes in 11 km (7 miles) to **Geilo** (alt. 795 m (2608 ft); pop. 2000; Highland Hotel, 196 b., SB; Bardøla Høyfjellshotell, 180 b., SP, SB; Geilo Hotell, 145 b., SB; Holms Hotell, 140 b., SB; Vestlia Høyfjellshotell, 148 b., SB; Ustedalen Høyfjellshotell, 150 b., SB; youth hostel; four camp sites, with chalets), a popular holiday resort with excellent Alpine skiing, several ski-lifts and a chair-lift to the *Geilohøyda* (1056 m (3465 ft); restaurant). To the S of the town the Numedal road from Kongsberg joins Highway 7.

3·5 km (2 miles) beyond Geilo, at *Fekjo* (to the left of the road), are 17 burial mounds of the 9th and 10th c., discovered in 1923. The road then climbs steeply for 8 km (5 miles) to *Ustaoset* (alt. 991 m (3251 ft); Høyfjellshotell, 145 b., SB; Fjellstue and Motell, 50 b.; Solheim Fjellstue, 45 b.; camp site, with chalets), on the N side of the *Ustevann*. The dominant feature of the landscape is the *Hallingskarv* (1933 m (6342 ft)): climbed in 6–8 hours), a partly snow-covered mountain to the N. To the S is the *Ustetind* (1376 m (4515 ft): 3–4 hours). Highway 7 continues to the Eidfjord.

# Halmstad

Sweden (Southern).
Province: Hallands län. – Region: Halland.
Altitude: sea level. – Population: 75,000.
Postal code: S-30590. – Telephone code: 0 35.
(i) **Halmstads Turistbyrå,**
　Kajplan;
　　tel. 11 15 81 and 11 75 42.

HOTELS. – *Grand Hotell*, Stationsgatan 44, 187 b.; *Märtenson*, Storgatan 52, 180 b.; *Norre Park Hotel*, Norra Vägen 7, 82 b.; *Scandic Hotel Hallandia*, Rådhusgatan 4, 180 b.; *Kristoffer*, Strandvallen, 224 b. – IN TYLÖSAND to the W: *Tylösand*, 405 b., SB. – Three CAMP SITES.

**Halmstad, main town of the Swedish province of Halland, lies near the outflow of the River Nissan into Laholm Bay. This situation promoted its rapid development into an important trading town and port. The town received its municipal charter in 1307. After a fire in 1619 it was rebuilt, and the old town has preserved much of the appearance of that period.**

Tourism, particularly in the summer months, is now making an increasingly important contribution to the town's economy. The seaside resort of *Tylösand*, 9 km (6 miles) W, is one of the most attractive in Sweden, with long sandy *beaches.

SIGHTS. – The market square (Stora Torg) is dominated by a fountain by Carl Milles (1875–1955), "Europa and the Bull". On the S side of the square stands the **Town Hall** (1938). The interior is decorated with intarsia work (mosaic woodwork) by the Halmstad·Group, an association (established 1929) of six painters, mostly from Halmstad, who became known outside Sweden as the "Swedish surrealists". The carillon plays at 8 a.m., 12 noon and 6 and 9 p.m., and at the same time the four groups of figures below change places. Adjoining the Town Hall is an old half-timbered building, once used as a hospital. Here, too, is *St Nicholas's Church* (14th c.), with a fine exterior. Beyond the Town Hall stands the old *Castle* (early 17th c.), now the governor's residence. On its seaward side is moored "Najaden", a sailing vessel (built 1897) used as a training ship. On the banks of the Nissan is a 14 m (45 ft) high sculpture by Picasso, "Woman's Head", set up in 1971. – From the market square Storgatan runs N to the *Norre Port* (1605), at the S end of the Norre Katt Park. This is the only surviving town gate belonging to the old fortifications, most of which were pulled down in 1734 by order of the town council. To the N of the park in the *Halland Museum* there is an interesting section on ships and the sea. – N of the town is the wooded *Galgenberg*, with a lookout tower and an open-air museum, *Hallands Gården* (old houses, School Museum).

SURROUNDINGS. – 9 km (5 miles) W is the well-known resort of **Tylösand**. The road to it runs past the *Miniland* leisure park, with scale models (1:25) of 30 of Sweden's principal sights, surrounded by beautiful gardens (May–September). St Olof's Chapel (18th c.), originally in Småland, was demolished in 1879 and re-erected in Tylösand in 1949–50. – 16 km (10 miles) N of Halmstad on the coast road is *Haverdalsstrand* nature reserve (area 350 hectares – 800 acres), with a sandy beach 4·5 km (3 miles) long and unusual dune formations. From here the road continues to *Ugglarps* (Motor Car and Aircraft Museum, open June–August) and Falkenberg (24 km – 15 miles).

E6 leads N from Halmstad through partly wooded and gently rolling country. In 13 km (8 miles) it comes to *Kvibille church* (on right), which dates in part from the 13th c. (restored 1670 and 1949–53). – 3·5 km (2 miles) beyond this, to the right of the road, stands the manor-house of *Fröllinge* (main building 1623). Then via *Skrea* (18 km – 11 miles) to **Falkenberg** (pop. 34,000; Grand Hotellet, 80 b.; Strandbadens Fritidshotell, 150 b., SB; Hotel Vista Hästen, 70 b.; youth hostel; three camp sites), located at the outflow of the *Atran*, a river well stocked with salmon (fishing permitted March to August), into the Kattegat. The first mention of the town dates back to medieval times. St Lawrence's Church (partly dating from the 12th c., with fine ceiling and wall paintings from the 17th and 18th c.) is still surrounded by many wooden houses from the 18th and 19th c. The Town House was not completed until 1959; the old toll bridge dates from 1756, the Town Hall from 1830. The Törngrens pottery establishment in Krukmakeregatan has been operating since 1786, and still belongs to the same family. There are only scanty remains of the old castle which was destroyed in 1534 by Engelbrekt and his peasant army. Falkenberg has a sandy beach 8 km (5 miles) long; sea-fishing trips from the harbour.

To the S of Halmstad E6 also follows the coast, but the inland route on Road 117 holds great attraction. 13 km (8 miles) S of Halmstad, at the estate of *St Fladje*, a side road goes off on the left (1 km (¾ mile) E) to the 12th c. Romanesque church of *Eldsberga*, beyond the railway line; old wall paintings were discovered here in 1976. Many Bronze Age tombs, often set on hills commanding good views, can be seen in the surrounding area. – The main road comes in another 10 km (6 miles) to **Laholm** (pop. 20,000; Stadshotellet, 22 b.; camp site), an old town on the River Lagan where life still moves at a rather deliberate pace. It is noted for the numerous works of art in its streets and squares, including a fountain with a sculpture by the Italian Luciano Minguzzi. This commemorates the work for peace of Count Folke Bernadotte (1895–1948), Dag Hammarskjöld (1905–61) and President J. F. Kennedy (1917–63). The Horse Fountain in Hästtorg ("Horse Square") and the Laga Fountain (by John Lundqvist) in the Stora Torg are also notable. On the S gable of the Town Hall (18th c.) mechanical figures perform a jousting scene daily at 12 noon and 6 p.m. – Beside the Castle (17th c.) is a salmon hatchery. 6 km (4 miles) up the Lagan is a 15 m (50 ft) waterfall, the *Karsefors* (power station). 6 km (4 miles) W the seaside resort of *Myllbystrand* (Motell Hallandsgården, 48 b.; camp site) has a sandy beach 12 km (7½ miles) long.

From Laholm the road continues S for 13 km (8 miles) to *Östra Karup* (Hallandsås Motell, 51 b.), where it joins E6. 4 km (2½ miles) E, near *Hasslöv* church, is a Bronze Age burial mound, *Lugnarohögen* (open to the public). We have now left Halland and entered Skåne. From here Road 115 runs 8 km (5 miles) W to the popular resort of **Båstad**, at the S end of Laholm Bay (hotels: Båstad, 150 b.; Enehall, 120 b.; Furuhem, 85 b.; Grand Hotel Skansen, 100 b.; Hemmeslövs Herrgårdpensionaat, 240 b.; Riviera, 100 b.). Located on the northern slopes of the *Hallandsås* hills, it is noted for its mild climate. St Mary's Church dates from the 15th c., but much of it was destroyed in a great fire in 1870. There are numbers of well-preserved old houses in the town. – 4 km (2½ miles) W is *Norrviken*, with beautiful gardens.

From Båstad the route continues on Road 115 via *Hov* to *Torekov* (Hotel Kattegat, 17 b.; camp site), a fishing village which is also a popular seaside resort. Offshore is the little island of *Hallands Väderö*, reached in 30 minutes by boat, which has an abundance of bird life. – The road now turns inland through gentle, fertile country to *Förslövsholm* and continues S to *Skälderviken*, a little resort in the bay of the same name on the Kattegat. 2·5 km (1½ miles) before the town we find *Barkåkra church* (late 12th c.). 5 km (3 miles) farther on is **Ängelholm** (pop. 29,000; Ängelholm Motel, 29 b.; camp site), near the outflow of the Rönneå into the Skäldervik, which has preserved the atmosphere of a small country town (18th c. town hall). It is now primarily a vacation resort, located 3 km (2 miles) from a beautiful sandy beach. From the S side of the bay there is a view of the Kullen range of hills.

# Hämeenlinna (Tavastehus)

Finland (Southern).
Province: Hämeen lääni (Tavastehus län/Häme).
Altitude: 85 m (279 ft). – Population: 41,000.
Postal code: SF-13100. – Telephone code: 9 17.
ⓘ **Kanta-Hämeen Matkailutoimisto,**
Raatihuoneenkatu 13;
tel. 20 23 88.

HOTELS. – *Cumulus*, Raatihuoneenkatu 18. – Two YOUTH HOSTELS.

EVENT. – *Finlandia* cross-country ski race (February).

**Hämeenlinna (in Swedish Tavastehus), main town of the province of Hämeen lääni, is attractively set on a long narrow lake, the Vanajavesi, with the Hattelmala hills bounding it to the S. It was founded in 1639 on a site to the N of the 13th c. Tavastehus Castle by Per Brahe, who also reinforced the castle. The town was moved to its present site in 1777. It was the birthplace of the great Finnish composer Jean Sibelius (1865–1957) and the poet Paavo Cajander (1846–1913), and President Paasikivi went to school here. In recent years there has been a considerable development of industry (woodworking, metalworking, etc.).**

SIGHTS. – In the middle of the town is the market square (*Kauppatori*). On the E side of the square stands the *Lutheran Church* (1789), with a statue of Paavo Cajander in the gardens in front of it, and on the S side the *Town Hall* (1885). – From here the Kirkkokatu runs N to the *Grammar School* (late 19th c.), built on the highest point in the town. Nearby are the *Sibelius Park* and the *Sibelius House* (museum), in which the composer spent his childhood. – At 6 Lukiokatu is the *Municipal Museum*, which contains much material from the Museum of Viborg/Viipuri, now in the Soviet Union. – To the N of the town, on the shores of Vanajavesi, the well-preserved old castle of **Hämeenlinna** (Swedish *Tavastehus Slott*), begun at the end of the 13th c. by the Swedish king Birger Jarl and completed in 1639 by Per Brahe. Farther N lies the Municipal Park, with beautiful views. – To the E of the river, at 2 Viipurintie, is the *Museum of Art*.

Hämeenlinna (Tavastehus) Castle

SURROUNDINGS. – 4·5 km (3 miles) N of the railway station is **Aulanko National Park**, with extensive recreational facilities (riding, golf, rowing, winter sports) and a mock ruined castle (performances of fairy-tale plays in summer). From the lookout tower there are magnificent views. Below, in a cave, is a group of bears by the sculptor R. C. Stignell. – 4 km (2½ miles) S of the station stands the stone-built medieval church of *Vanaja*, with a beautiful altar. – 8 km (5 miles) N, on the Pälkäne road, is the old church of *Hattula*.

**Hämeenlinna to Tampere by the "Silver Line".** – A trip on one of the boats of the "Silver Line", which sail twice daily from Hämeenlinna (one boat taking the western and the other the eastern route), offers a magnificent opportunity to experience the harmony between water and woodland in this part of Finland. – The boat leaves Hämeenlinna and sails along the narrow Vanajavesi; to the right is seen the Rantasipi Aulanko Hotel. The boat then continues into the *Vanajanselkä*, at the W end of which (on right, the old stone church of Sääksmäki) the two routes diverge. – The *eastern route* continues N, and beyond the industrial town of Valkeakoski enters the *Mallasvesi* (locks); ahead, to the right, is the Pälkäne church. In 4½ hours the boat reaches *Vehoniemi*, on the northern shore of *Lake Roine*. From there it is 35 minutes by bus to **Tampere** (p. 262). – The *western route* turns NW through the *Makkaraselkä* to *Toijala*. At *Lempäälä* the boat passes under the road and railway from Hämeenlinna to Tampere and continues to **Tampere**.

**Hämeenlinna to Tampere via Pälkäne and Kangasala.** – This route (83 km – 52 miles) is preferable to the main road (E79) and is only 3 km (2 miles) longer. – From Hämeenlinna the road follows the W side of the Vanajavesi, with Aulanko National Park on the opposite shore. 8 km (5 miles): *Hattula*, with a brick-built church (14th–15th c.) which before the Reformation was a famous place of pilgrimage. It contains many pieces of sculpture, including a figure of St Olav from Lübeck. Fine 15th c. wall paintings. – 2·5 km (1½ miles) farther on is the new church of Hattula. – 12 km (7½ miles): road on left to the industrial town of Valkeakoski (25 km – 15 miles). – 4 km (2½ miles): road on right to *Hauho* (12 km – 7½ miles), the oldest parish in the province of Häme (first mentioned 1329; church, *c.* 1400; museum). – 11 km (7 miles): junction with Road 12. To the right this runs via Hauho (17 km – 10 miles) to Lahti (88 km – 55 miles); to the left it skirts *Lake Pintele* to **Pälkäne** (10 km – 6 miles). The old church (*c.* 1400) is 1·5 km (1 mile) N of the Ihari road. – another 11 km (7 miles) the road reaches *\*Vehoniemenharju*, a beautiful ridge of land between *Lake Roine* and the *Längelmävesi*. It then continues over the *Kaivanto Canal* which links the two lakes and soon afterwards passes *Keisarinharju* (extensive views).

Kangasala (pop. 17,400; camp site) lies at the S end of the *Vesijärvi*. The church has a carved pulpit of 1661 and a picture of the Swedish queen Karin Månsdotter, who died in 1612 on the royal estate of *Liuksiala*, 6 km (4 miles) S. – The main road follows the long straggling lake of *Kaukajärvi*. *Viatala*, to the left, has a modern cemetery chapel. Beyond this is the old church of *Messukylä*. 18 km (11 miles) from Kangasala is **Tampere** (p. 262).

**Hämeenlinna to Tampere on E79.** – The road runs NW through wooded hill country. In 9·5 km (6 miles) a road goes off on the right to *Parola*. Before the level crossing (grade crossing), to the left of the road, is an open-air museum of tanks and anti-tank weapons from 1919 onwards. Then on to *Hattula* (6·5 km – 4 miles). – E79 now runs along the S side of the Lehijärvi at some distance from the lake, and enters in 13·5 km (8 miles) (off the road to the left) the well-known glass-manufacturing town of **Iittala** (conducted tours of glass factories), on the N side of the narrow *Kalvolanjärvi*.

11 km (7 miles) beyond this a road goes off to the left along the S side of the *Makkarselkä* to the railway junction of *Toijala* (Pirkka Hotel, 12 b.), from which E80, coming from Turku, runs N via *Lempäälä* to Tampere.

Continuing N, E79 crosses the Sääksmäen Silta suspension bridge (205 m (225 yds) long) at the W end of the *Vanajanselkä* (restaurant, bathing beach, beautiful view). Soon afterwards the old stone church of *Sääksmäki*, one of the oldest in Finland (*c.* 1550), is visible on the right. – A short distance beyond this a road on the right (3·5 km – 2 miles) leads to the industrial town of **Valkeakoski** (pop. 22,600; hotels: Apia, 48 b., SB; Keski-Häme, 41 b.; youth hostel; camp site). – In another 21 km (13 miles) E79 joins E80, coming from Lempäälä. From here it is 15 km (9 miles) on the highway to **Tampere** (p. 262).

# Hamina
# (Fredrikshamn)

Finland (Southern).
Province: Kymen lääni (Kymmene län/Kymi).
Altitude: sea level. – Population: 11,000.
Postal code: SF-49400. – Telephone code: 952.
ⓘ **Haminan Matkailupalvelu,**
Fredrikinkatu 4,
tel. 4 43 20.
*Flag-Tower* (in summer);
tel. 4 15 81.

HOTELS. – *Seurahuone*, Pikkuympyränkatu 5, 23 b.; *Hamina*, Kaivokatu 4, 30 b. – CAMP SITE.

**Hamina (Swedish Fredrikshamn), located on a peninsula in the bay of Vehkalahti, in the Gulf of Finland, is one of Finland's leading exporting ports (timber products).**

The town, founded in the 14th c., received its municipal charter in 1653. In 1723 it was named Fredrikshavn in honour of King Fredrik I of Sweden; the name

Hamina came later. In 1809 Sweden and Russia signed the treaty of Hamina, under which Sweden ceded the whole of Finland to Russia. In 1812 the Czar returned some territory to Finland. It is 43 km (27 miles) to the Soviet frontier and is the only frontier crossing open to foreign cars (at Vaalimaa). Hamina is 261 km (162 miles) from Leningrad (visa required).

SIGHTS. – The central feature of the town is an *octagonal square* laid out according to a 1723 plan. The square is surrounded by streets on an almost circular layout, with eight streets leading out of the square. In the square stand the *Town Hall* (built 1798; restored, with the addition of a tower, by C. L. Engel in 1840), the *Lutheran Church* (1843; in the gardens a memorial to the 1809 treaty) and the *Orthodox Church* (1837). In the *Market Square*, to the W, is the octagonal *Flag-Tower* (1790: small museum), a remnant of the town's defences. The *Municipal Museum* at 2 Kadettikoulunkatu occupies a house in which the Empress Catherine of Russia and King Gustav III of Sweden negotiated a treaty in 1783. – The old village of *Vehkalahti* has a fine medieval church (restored 1823).

SURROUNDINGS. – Road 7 runs W to Helsinki (150 km – 93 miles). 11 km (7 miles) along this road the road from Kouvola enters on the right. From here there is a first glimpse of the industrial town of **Karhula**, 7 km (4½ miles) ahead (pop. 23,000; Kesti-Karhu Hotel, 40 b.; Kymen Motelli, 302 b., SB). The Sunila cellulose factory in the town was designed by Alvar Aalto. Interesting Glass Museum. – 2 km (1¼ miles) farther on a road goes off on the left (6·5 km – 4 miles) to the important port and industrial town of **Kotka**, on an island in the Gulf of Finland, now linked with the mainland (pop. 34,400; hotels: Koskisoppi, 82 b.; Ruotsinsalmi, 54 b.; Seurahuone, 252 b.; two youth hostels). Lying at the mouth of the largest river in southern Finland, the *Kyminjoki*, the town rapidly developed into a major exporting port. It also has important industries, particularly woodworking. A major naval battle between Sweden and Russia took place off the coast here in 1790. In the market square (large market on the first Thursday of the month) is the handsome Town Hall (by E. Huttunen, 1934). S of the square is the Municipal Park (Kaupunginpuisto), with the Orthodox Church (1795), the only building to survive the British bombardment of the town in 1855. – From the old water-tower (62 m – 203 ft) and the Norska Berg to the SE there are fine views of the offshore islands. Boat trips to the small rocky islands or skerries are run from the harbour; old fortifications can still be seen on some of the islands. – On a nearby island (reached by a side road branching off the road to E3) is the beautifully set "fisherman's hut" of *Langinkoski*, presented to Tsar Alexander II by the Finnish Senate (now a museum; dramatic performances from mid-summer to the end of July). – Road 7 continues W via Loviisa and Porvoo to **Helsinki** (p. 131).

To the E of Hamina the road continues to the frontier post at *Vaalimaa* and, after 100 km (60 miles), reaches **Viborg** (Finnish *Viipuri*). Viborg is the former capital of Finnish Karelia, now in the Soviet Union.

# Hammerfest

Norway (Northern).
County: Finnmark fylke.
Altitude: sea level. – Population: 7600.
Postal code: N-9600. – Telephone code: 0 84.
ⓘ **Hammerfest og Omegns Turistforening,**
Rådhusplassen;
tel. 1 21 85.

HOTELS. – *Brassica*, 37 b.; *Hammerfest*, 52 b.; *Hammerfest Motell*, 192 b.; *Rica Hotel Hammerfest*, 117 b. – YOUTH HOSTEL. – CAMP SITE.

**The busy Norwegian port of Hammerfest, the most northerly town in Europe (lat. 70°39'48" N, long. 23°40' E), lies on the W side of the island of Kvaløy (area 339 sq. km – 130 sq. miles). The sun does not set here between 17 May and 28 July and does not rise from 21 November to 23 January.**

Long an important commercial and fishing port because of its sheltered and ice-free harbour, Hammerfest received its municipal charter in 1789. The town was bombarded by the British fleet in 1809, almost totally destroyed by fire in 1890 and razed to the ground by the Germans in October 1944 after the compulsory evacuation of the population. Only the cemetery chapel was left standing after the Second World War, but the people of Hammerfest soon rebuilt their town on the narrow strip of land between the Salen hills and the sea. Visitors will be struck by

Hammerfest

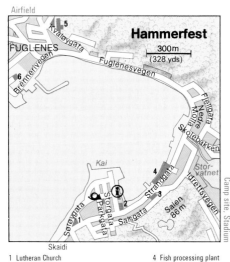

Airfield

**Hammerfest**

300m
(328 yds)

FUGLENES

Kvaløygata

Brennerivegen

Fuglenesvegen

Fjelgata
Nedre Molla
Skolebakken

Kai

Storvatnet

Strandgata

Salen 86 m

Idrettsvegen

Søroygata
Storgata
Parkgata
Salsgata

Skaidi

1 Lutheran Church
2 Town Hall
3 Catholic Church
4 Fish processing plant
5 Hospital
6 Meridianstøtte

Camp site, Stadium

the colourful house-fronts of the reconstructed town.

Hammerfest is the base of Norway's Arctic fishing fleet. It has a large fish-processing industry and a fishery college. The town also caters for increasing numbers of visitors.

SIGHTS. – In the *Market Square* is the **Town Hall** (1957), where visitors can become members of the "Royal and Ancient Society of Polar Bears" upon payment of a single membership fee. This helps finance the building of a museum, and visitors receive a certificate of membership in return for their contribution. – In the square is a bust of the composer Ole Olsen (1850–1927), a native of Hammerfest. From here Storgate runs N to the berths used by the ships of the "Hurtigrute" and by local shipping. – To the W of the market square, in Kirkegata, is the **Lutheran Church** (1961), an impressive example of modern architecture. The church, like most of the new churches in the north, has been built to remind one of a Lapp tent. It has no altar; in the tent-shaped gable a large and very beautiful stained glass window by Jardar Lunde (1962) has been placed as a focus for worship instead. Concerts are given in the church every evening in summer. Close by stands the little wooden chapel which survived the Second World War. – Strandgata runs NE from the market square, passing on the right the small *Catholic Church* (1958), mostly built by German volunteers. The cross was carved

after the war by Georg Wimmer who had been a prisoner of war in Narvik. Farther along, also on the right, is the school (1961). The road continues around the bay to the promontory of *Fuglenes*, with an interesting granite column topped by a bronze globe. This is the *Meridianstøtte*, erected to commemorate the completion of a joint Norwegian-Swedish-Russian survey (1816–52) to determine the size and shape of the earth. Its southern counterpart was set up at Ismail, 2872 km (1785 miles) away at the mouth of one of the arms of the Danube. The concrete slab beside it was erected during a further survey in 1929. From here there is a fine view of the town and the hills rising immediately behind it.

SURROUNDINGS. – From the market square a footpath leads in 20 minutes to the ridge of hills at the S end of the town, **Salen** (the "Saddle": 86 m – 282 ft), which can also be reached on a road running W of the town past the little lake of *Storvatn* (camp site, usually solidly ice-bound until May). From the hill to the W, marked by a stone, there are extensive views of the open sea. – On the southern outskirts of the town is the *Jansvatn*, an open-air swimming pool, and 1 km (¾ mile) beyond this is the most northerly stretch of woodland in the world. The road continues to Skaidi. To the left is a view of *Tyven* (419 m (1375 ft): climbed from Hammerfest in 1½ hours); from the summit there are views to the E of the barren island with its many lakes, to the S and W of the hills with their snowfields and their glaciers, to the N of the infinite expanse of the Arctic Ocean.

EXCURSION TO THE NORTH CAPE. – An attractive alternative to the land route to the **North Cape** (see p. 200) is a trip by sea or by a combination of boat and bus. The fast ships of the "Hurtigrute" leave Hammerfest daily at 5.15 a.m. and reach Honningsvåg at 11.30 a.m. From there a bus leaves for the North Cape (1 hour) at 12.45, returning to Honningsvåg at 2.45 p.m. A bus leaves Honningsvåg for Hammerfest at 5 p.m., arriving at 9.30 p.m. – The return boat does not leave Honningsvåg until the following morning at 5.45, arriving in Hammerfest at midday.

Timetables and fares, and the possibility of special excursions, should be checked with a tourist information office, travel agency or shipping line. – Sturdy footwear and warm clothing are essential, even if the weather on departure from Hammerfest is warm.

There are also charter flights from Hammerfest to the North Cape.

# Hardangerfjord

Norway (SW).
County: Hordaland fylke.
ⓘ Reiselivsrådet for Vest-Norge,
Slottsgaten 1,
N-5000 Bergen;
tel. (05) 31 66 00.
Voss Turistkontor,
Utrågata 9,
N-5700 Voss;
tel. (05) 51 17 16.

The *Hardangerfjord, extending for almost 120 km (75 miles) from Herøysund to Odda on the Sørfjord, with a depth of up to 830 m (2700 ft), is one of the best known Norwegian fjords, made more so by its mild climate. Along its shores are large fruit plantations, primarily cherries and apples, which are especially beautiful when the trees are in blossom in the second half of May.

The main town in the region, situated at the E end of the *Vangsvatn* in the northern part of the fjord system, is **Voss** (alt. 57 m (187 ft); pop. 6000; hotels: Fleischers Hotel, 122 b., SB; Jarl, 100 b., SB; Park Hotell Voss, 96 b.; Rondo Sportell, 50 b.; Voss Motel, 50 b.; Voss Turistheim, 100 b.; Voss Ungdoms hostel, 200 b.; youth hostel; two camp sites with chalets). Voss is an important junction on the Bergen railway, a considerable industrial town and a popular resort in both winter and summer. The church, with a fine interior, dates from about 1270. To the SE of the church is St Olav's Cross, erected in the 11th c. to commemorate the Christianisation of the region. 1 km (¾ mile) W of the station is Finneloftet, a wooden house (c. 1270) which is the oldest secular wooden building in the country (museum). To the N is the Mølster farmhouse and the Voss Folkemuseum. NW of the town is *Bavallen*, Norway's best equipped Alpine skiing resort (cabin cableway 1080 m (3540 ft) long, climbing 550 m (1800 ft); ski-jump, record distance over 100 m − 328 ft.

E68 runs SE from Voss to the Hardangerfjord, reaching its highest point (262 m − 860 ft) in 10 km (6 miles), at the S end of the *Opelandsvatn*. 1 km (¾ mile) beyond this is the beginning of a 3 km (2 mile) stretch of road (built 1863−70) through *Skervet*, a valley enclosed by high rock walls. To the left is the *Skjervefoss*, a

waterfall on the *Granvinelva*. After 10 km (6 miles) of road, with several bends, is *Holven* (alt. 30 m − 98 ft), with the *Granvin church* (1720). One of the church's two bells is believed to be the oldest in Norway. − Here Road 572 leads on the left to the village of **Ulvik**, one of the most popular vacation areas in Hardanger (camp site, with chalets). There is a particularly attractive descent from a height of 350 m (1150 ft) down to the village. Church (1858); State College of Horticulture, where Kristofer Sjursen Hjeltnes planted the first potatoes in Norway in 1765.

Beyond Holven E68 runs along the E side of the *Granvinvatn*; part of the road is blasted out of the rock. In 4 km (2½ miles) E68 comes to *Granvin* (pop. 250; Mælands Turisthotel, 70 b.), at the N end of the *Granvinfjord*. Then along the W side of the fjord to *Kvanndal* (camp site), from which there is a car ferry to *Utne* (15 minutes), at the mouth of the Sørfjord, and *Kinsarvik* (35 minutes). − The road now follows the N side of the *Hardangerfjord*, after 12 km (7½ miles) coming to the little industrial town of *Ålvik* (pop. 1000; jewelry manufacture), with a hydroelectric station using water from the *Bjølsegrøvatn* river (fall 880 m − 2890 ft). − Then through *Ytre Ålvik*, where the Bjølsefoss surged down before the damming of the river. − 12 km (7½ miles) farther on the road crosses the *Fyksesund Bru*, a suspension bridge 344 m (380 yds) long (distance between piers 230 m (250 yds), clearance 27·8 m (91 ft)) built in 1937 over the narrow *Fyksesund* (11 km (7 miles) long) at its junction with the Hardangerfjord. − 9 km (6 miles): *Øystese* (pop. 1500; Hardangerfjord Hotell, 170 b., SB; Øystese Fjord Hotel, 38 b.; youth hostel; camp site, with chalets), beautifully set on the bay of the same name. Opposite the church is a museum devoted to the works of the sculptor Ingebrigt Vik (1867−1927). To the NW is the *Torefjell* (1044 m − 3425 ft). − The road skirts the fjord for another 6 km (4 miles) to **Norheimsund** (pop. 1500; Hardanger Feriesenter Hotel, 50 b.; Norheimsund Fjord Hotel, 78 b.; Sandven Hotel, 72 b.; Solbakken, 10 b.; three camp sites, with chalets). Beautiful view over the fjord to the Folgefonn glacier.

Beyond Norheimsund E68 leaves the fjord and traverses the gentler scenery

The "Troll's Tongue" on the Tyssehøfjell with a view across the Ringedalsvann to the Folgefonn.

of the *Steinsdal*. In 2·5 km (1¼ miles) it comes to the *Steinsdalsfoss* or Øvsthusfoss (on right), a beautiful waterfall on the *Fosselva*. It is possible to walk behind the 30 m (100 ft) wall of water. Then a magnificent stretch of road (3 km – 2 miles) up the wild gorge (many bends, four tunnels, steep rock walls) of *Tokagjelet*. E68 then continues to **Bergen** (85 km (53 miles): see p. 63).

It is not necessary to leave the Hardangerfjord at Norheimsund. Other possibilities are to follow the fjord to Mundheim and from there either continue via Eikelandsosen and Tysse to Bergen (an additional 56 km – 35 miles), or via Eikelandsosen to Fusa, from there to Hattvik by ferry and then by road to Bergen (an additional 20 km – 12½ miles).

From Norheimsund the road runs along the W side of the fjord to the village of *Vikøy* (4 km – 2½ miles), then another 4 km (2½ miles) to the farms of *Ystheim* and *Vangdal* (rock carvings of boats and animals). – 3 km (2 miles): on right, the farm of *Berge*, with a large stand of oaks (a tree rare in Norway). To the right is a view of *Vesoldo* (1046 m – 3432 ft). – 2 km (1¼ miles) farther on lies the village of *Tørvikbygd*, with a car ferry to Jondal (15 minutes). 5 km (3 miles) S is the farm of *Ljones* (at Vikingnes, 1 km (¾ mile) E, large burial mounds. – 8 km (5 miles): *Fosse*, with beautiful views of Vesoldo to the NE, the Folgefonn across the fjord to the E and the Hardangerjøkul to the N. – 2 km (1¼ miles) **Strandebarm**, on the bay of the same name. with beautiful beaches. There was formerly a flourishing boatbuilding industry in this area, but now only a few craftsmen are still making the local type of boat, the "Strandebarmer". The village church dates from 1876. – The road then continues via *Oma* to *Mundheim*, where it joins Road 13 coming from the S.

Road 13 now turns away from the shore of the fjord and runs NW to *Holdhus* (12 km (7½ miles); alt. 130 m – 427 ft), with a chapel (fine interior) which is believed to date from 1726. 6 km (4 miles) beyond this is *Eikelandsosen* (pop. 600; camp site). Just before the village is the *Koldedalsfoss*. Here Road 13 bears right to Tysse, while Road 552 runs along the S side of the *Eikelandsfjord* to *Fusa*, from which there is a ferry (20 minutes) to *Hattvik*. Then via *Osøyra* and *Syfteland* to Bergen.

Many islands lie off the shores of the Hardangerfjord. It is well worth visiting one or two of them.

From *Kvanndal*, at the mouth of the *Granvinfjord*, there is a ferry across the *Utnefjord* to *Utne* (not all boats) and **Kinsarvik** (Kinsarvik Fjord Hotel, 135 b.), at the mouth of the \*Sørfjord, which is given a particular charm by the contrast between the gentle landscape on the shores of the fjord and the wild and rugged mountain scenery which encloses it. The mild climate favours the growing of fruit, and there are abundant cherry and apple trees, particularly in the lower and middle areas of the fjord. – Road 47 runs S for some 40 km (25 miles) along the eastern shore of the fjord. In 10 km (6 miles) it comes to *Lofthus* (Ullensvang Turisthotell, 250 b.; camp site), one of the most beautiful spots in the Hardanger, with a high school and an experimental fruit-growing farm. To the S is the 13th c. parish church of *Ullensvang* (restored 1884 and 1958). – The road continues along the fjord through attractive country, at its most beautiful when the trees are in blossom (end of May). Above the W side of the fjord rises the great **Folgefonn glacier** (34 km (21 miles) long, up to 6 km (10 miles) across, highest point 1654 m (5727 ft). – 26 km (16 miles): *Tyssedal* (pop. 1300; Tyssedal Hotel, 54 b.), at the mouth of the valley of that name (beautiful falls on the *Tysså*), has an aluminium factory and a large hydroelectric station which produces power for the region's industry; chapel (1965). – The road passes through a tunnel 1520 m (1650 yds) long and comes in 6 km (4 miles) to **Odda** (pop. 10,000; Hardanger Hotell, 120 b.; Sørfjordheimen Hotell, 59 b.), a sizeable industrial town at the S end of the Sørfjord. 16 km (10 miles) S, on a road which runs past the Sandvinvatnet, is the *Låtefoss*, a mighty waterfall 164 m (540 ft) high.

From Odda a narrower road (No. 550) leads N between the *Folgefonn* glacier and the W shore of the fjord, coming in 29 km (18 miles) to the little village of *Aga*, with an open-air museum (Agatunet) in the form of a well-preserved peasant settlement of 30–40 buildings clustered around an old courthouse. 16 km (10 miles) farther N is *Utne* (Utne Hotel, 46 b.), with a fine cruciform church of 1858 containing furnishings from an earlier medieval church; and Hardanger Folke-

museum. From Utne there are ferry connections with Kvanndal and Kinsarvik.

From Kinsarvik Road 7 runs NE along the S side of the steep-sided **Eidfjord**, the most easterly branch of the Hardangerfjord. – 18 km (11 miles): *Brimnes*, from which there is a ferry service in summer (recommended when Kinsarvik is busy) over the Eidfjord to Bruravik. 11 km (7 miles) beyond this lies the village of **Eidfjord** (Vøringfoss Hotell, 96 b.), majestically located at the S end of the fjord. Above the northern shore of the fjord rises the snow-covered peak of *Onen* (1621 m – 5319 ft).

# Hardangervidda

Norway (Southern).
Counties: Hordaland fylke, Telemark fylke and Buskerud fylke.
(i) **Telemark Reiselivsråd,**
Nedre Hjellegt 1,
N-3700 Skien;
tel. (0 35) 2 12 79.
**Buskerud Reiselivsråd,**
Storgate 2,
N-3500 Hønefoss;
tel. (0 67) 2 36 55.
**Reiselivsråd for Vest-Norge,**
Slottsgaten 1;
N-5000 Bergen;
tel. (05) 31 66 00.

The \***Hardangervidda, with an area of about 7500 sq. km (2900 sq. miles), is the largest plateau in Scandinavia. It lies at an average height of between 1200 and 1600 m (3950 and 5250 ft). The area is dotted with numerous lakes. The meagre covering of pasture provides grazing for large herds of wild reindeer. There are also about a hundred hill dairy farms in the region. The scenery above the tree-line is barren and desolate but very impressive (popular for skiing). An area of about 3400 sq. km (1300 sq. miles) forms a nature park; other areas are to be made nature reserves.**

This is magnificent walking country, with an extensive system of paths, usually running from one lake (well stocked with fish) to another and linking the numerous mountain huts (usually overcrowded during the height of the season, from 15 July to 15 August). In the interior of the

Hardangervidda there are no motor roads or settlements of any size.

The best means of access is Road 7, from **Geilo** (p. 116) to Eidfjord, which separates the Hardangervidda proper from the **Hardangerjøkul**, a snowfield covering 120 sq. km (46 sq. miles) (highest point 1862 m – 6109 ft) rising to the N of the road and also accessible on the N from the Bergen railway. Road 7 climbs from *Haugastøl* (alt. 990 m – 3248 ft) to reach its highest point at the *Dyranut mountain hut* (1246 m (4088 ft): 40 b.) and then runs down into the valley of the *Bjoreia*. 20 km (12½ miles) beyond Dyranut a narrow road (toll) branches off and runs 1 km (¾ mile) N to the *Fosslihotell* (alt. 729 m – 2392 ft), in a commanding setting above the precipitous Måbødal. From here there is a magnificent view of the **\*\*Vøringfoss**, where the Bjoreia plunges vertically 183 m (600 ft) into a narrow rock basin, always filled with a dense mass of spray (marvellous play of colour, particularly in the afternoon). The Fosslihotell is a good base for mountain walks and climbs. Especially rewarding is the long walk (13–14½ hours) by way of the *Demmevass hut* (1280 m – 4200 ft), on the western edge of the Hardangerjøkul, to *Finse* (1222 m – 4009 ft; mountain hotel) on the Bergen railway (highest station in the country), located on the *Finsevann* in a lonely mountain region.

Beyond the turning for the Fosslihotell the finest and most interesting stretch of Road 7 begins, down the wild *Måbødal*, through tunnels, along almost vertical rock faces, and finally descending in five huge bends to *Måbø* (alt. 250 m – 820 ft), where it reaches the Eidfjord (p. 124).

On the W the Hardangervidda falls steeply to the Sørfjord (p. 124), along the E side of which runs Road 47. The road nearest to it on the S side is the Haukeli Road (p. 266).

# Härjedal

Sweden (Central).
Province: Jämtlands län. – Regions: Jämtland and Härjedalen.
ⓘ **Jämtland-Härjedalens Turistinformation**,
Storgatan 16,
S-83126 Östersund;
tel. (0 63) 12 70 55.

The \* Härjedal, with an area of 11,776 sq. km (4550 sq. miles) and a population of some 13,000, is one of the most sparsely settled parts of Sweden. Its runs from W to E between two large rivers, the Ljunga to the N and the Ljusna to the S, and is bounded on the W by Norway. It is a region of forests and barren upland plateaux. In the past the inhabitants depended almost entirely on the resources of the forest and on farming, but tourism has now developed into a major source of income. Many old upland farms have been transformed into modern hotels and other vacation accommodation. The region offers magnificent walking and excellent facilities for winter sports. The Härjedal is the southern boundary of reindeer herding; bears and wolves are also found here, and there is an abundant and varied plant life.

The Härjedal is reached by way of Road 81, which runs N from Mora on Lake Siljan. From *Sveg* (hotels: Axelssons Hotell, 26 b.; Lilla, 14 b.; Stekhuset Mysoxen, 120 b., SB; camp site). Road 312 runs NW via Glissjöberg and Linsell to *Hedeviken* (67 km – 42 miles), on the N side of the *Vikarsjö* (alt. 413 m – 1335 ft). 12 km (7½ miles) W is *Hede* (Wärdshuset Sanfjället, 32 b. and 4 chalets), some 18 km (11 miles) S of which is the Sånfjäll or Sonfjäll, an isolated hill (1277 m – 4190 ft) rising out of a broad expanse of forest. 2700 hectares (6750 acres) are protected as a National Park, the highest part of which reaches above the tree-line. Sånfjäll is known as Sweden's "Bear Mountain".

From Hede, Road 312 continues up the wooded valley of the *Ljusna*. In 46 km (29 miles) Road 311 goes off on the left and runs S via *Tännäs* for 104 km (65 miles) to **Särna** (alt. 440 m – 1444 ft; Hotel, 60 b.) in a beautiful setting on Lake Särna, with an old wooden church (restored 1766). 3 km (2 miles) S is the mountain of *Mickeltemplet* (624 m – 2047 ft), with a lookout tower. SW of Särna rears up the *Fulufjäll* (1040 m – 3412 ft), on the N face of which is the beautiful *Njupeskärsfall*, the highest waterfall in Sweden (125 m – 410 ft). – From Särna there is a road to Mörkret (24 km – 15 miles); or 28 km (17 miles) to Njupåsen, then (from parking place) 1 hour's walk.

From the turning for Särna, Road 312 continues 15 km (9 miles) NW to **Funäsdalen** (hotels: Baggardens Fritidsby, 320 b. and chalets; Eriksgårdens Fjällhotell, 90 b.). This is the chief town in the western Härjedal, and attracts many visitors. From here a road runs 15 km (10 miles) NW up the valley of the Ljusna to the beautiful village of *Bruksvallarna* (alt. 710 m (2330 ft); hotels: Bruksvallarnas Fjällhotell, 100 b.; Ramundbergets Fjällgard, 140 b., SB; Walles Fjällhotell, 80 b., SB, SP). Another road goes 41 km (25 miles) NE to *Ljungdalen* (alt. 605 m – 1985 ft), from which there is a 19 km (12 mile) walk to *Helagsfjällets Turiststation* (1033 m – 3389 ft), under the NE side of the **Helagsfjäll** (1796 m – 5893 ft). The most southerly glacier in Sweden (climbed in $2\frac{1}{2}$–3 hours) descends from the summit of Helagsfjäll. – 13 km (8 miles) W of Funäsdalen lies the little village of *Tänndalen*, on the *Tänndalsjö* (alt. 725 m (2379 ft); hotels: Siljestroms, 122 b. and chalets; Skarvruets Fjällhotell, 75 b.; Tannedalens Fjällgard, 106 b., SB), with the *Rödfjäll* (1245 m – 4085 ft) to the S and *Skarvarna* (1254 m – 4114 ft) to the N. 12 km ($7\frac{1}{2}$ miles) farther NW **Fjällnäs** (alt. 784 m (2572 ft); Fjällnäs Fjällhotel och Turistgård, 88 b.; Strandgården, 50 b.) has a magnificent setting on the E side of Lake Malmagen, a popular health and winter sports resort (the highest in Sweden), enclosed by hills rising to over 1000 m (3000 ft) (good climbing). – 8 km (5 miles) farther on is the Norwegian frontier (toll road).

# Helsingborg
## (Hälsingborg)

Sweden (Southern).
Province: Malmöhus län. – Region: Skåne.
Altitude: sea level. – Population: 104,000.
Postal code: S-250 . . . – 260 . . .
Telephone code: 0 42.
(i) **Helsingborgs Turistbyrå,**
Rådhuset,
S-25221 Helsingborg;
tel. 12 03 10.

HOTELS. – *Anglais*, Gustaf Adolfs Gata 14–16, 110 b.; *Annexet*, Storgatan 3, 25 b.; *Bristol*, Prästgatan 4, 32 b.; *Brukshotellet*, Bruksgatan 34, 40 b.; *Continental*, Järnvägsgatan 11, 107 b.; *Grand Hotel*, Stortorget 8–12, 210 b.; *Helsingborg*, Stortorget., 100 b.; *Högvakten*, Stortorget 14, 81 b.; *Kronan*, Ängelholmväg 35, 140 b.; *Kärnan i Helsingborg*, Järnvågsgatan 17, 98 b.; *Mollberg*, Stortorget 18,

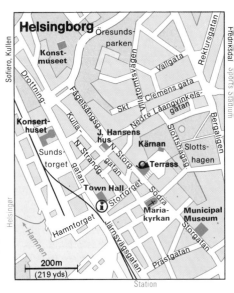

190 b.; *Scandic Hotel*, Florettgatan 41, 369 b., SB; *Stadsmotellet i Helsingborg*, Hantverkaregatan 11, 70 b.; *Viking*, Fägelsängsgatan 1, 51 b.; *Villa Vingård*, Sehistedsgatan 1, 60 b. – Two YOUTH HOSTELS. – CAMP SITE.

**The Swedish town of Helsingborg (Hälsingborg in Swedish), in a strategic position at the narrowest part of the Öresund, was for centuries hotly disputed between Denmark and Sweden. First mentioned in the records in 1085, the town received its municipal charter in 1649. It is now a busy port, commercial and industrial town, and Sweden's main channel of communication with Denmark by sea.**

SIGHTS. – Visitors arriving in Helsingborg from Helsingør, on the Danish side of the Öresund (frequent services), are immediately confronted by the town's principal landmark, a prominent brick tower 35 m (115 ft) high. It is known as **Kärnan** and stands at the upper end of the long market square, *Stortorg*. From here a broad flight of steps flanked by two towers (elevator (lift) in the left-hand tower) leads up to *Konung Oscar II.s Terrass* (terrace restaurant). There stands the old defensive tower, with foundations up to $4\frac{1}{2}$ m thick and a circumference of 60 m (200 ft). It was the central feature of a stronghold built by Valdemar Atterdag (1340–75) on the site of an earlier timber fortress which probably dated from the 10th c. and was destroyed in 1680 with the exception of the tower. From the top of the tower (190 steps) there are magnificent *views of the town, the Sound and Denmark. – At the lower end of the market square is a statue (by J. Börjesson) of the Swedish general *Count Magnus Stenbock* (1664–1717), erected in 1901 to commemorate his victory over the Danes N of Helsingborg in 1710. Opposite it is the Neo-Gothic **Town Hall** (1897; tower 70 m (230 ft) high); stained-glass windows depicting events in the history of the town. In front of the Town Hall are Norwegian and Danish memorial stones commemorating the assistance given by Sweden during the German occupation in the Second World War.

SW of the Stortorg, adjoining the ferry port, is the *Hamntorg* (Harbour Square), with the *Seafarers' Monument*, a column topped by a figure of Mercury (C. Milles). Close by is a modest memorial commemorating the arrival of the French marshal Jean-Baptiste Bernadotte in 1810. He had been chosen by the Swedish Parliament as heir to the throne and adopted by the childless king Karl III; he became king as Karl Johan XIV in 1818.

At the upper end of the Stortorg *Norra Storgatan* bears to the left, and at No. 21 is Helsingborg's oldest private house, *Jakob Hansens Hus* (1641; restored 1931), a handsome half-timbered building. In front of it is a fountain topped by a celestial sphere (1927) commemorating the astronomer Tycho Brahe. – In *Södra Storgatan*, which runs S from the end of the Stortorg, stands the Gothic **St Mary's Church** (*Mariakyrkan*, 13th c., reconstructed in 15th c.), with a beautiful reredos (ornamental altar screen) (*c.* 1450), a splendid pulpit of 1615 and a chart outlining historical records from 900 to modern times. Farther S (No. 31) the *Municipal Museum* contains an extensive collection, including an art gallery; to the rear is an open-air section of the museum.

Järnvägsgatan, which runs SE from the near end of the Stortorg, passes the *Municipal Library* (1965) and the *Station*. Drottningatan leads NW from the Stortorg to *St Jörgens Plats*, where one can see sculpture by A. Wallenberg, "Youth at Play". On the W side of the square we find the *Concert Hall* (Konserthuset: by Sven Markelius, 1932), and behind this the *Municipal Theatre* (1976). To the NE extends the **Öresund Park**, in which

Hamntorg, Helsingborg

there is an old spa, *Hälsan*. On the other side of Hälsovägen, in *Vikingberg Park*, is the *Museum of Art* (Konstmuseet) which houses a collection of both old and modern art (including Frans Hals's portrait of Descartes). – To the rear of Kärnan extends the beautiful park of *Slottshagen*, with a sculpture by C. Eriksson, "The Hunt", and remains of the old castle. To the NE is Stenbocksgatan and beyond this the *Fredriksdal Open-Air Museum*, with a manor-house (1787), various old buildings, a Music Museum, a Botanic Garden and an open-air theatre. In Stenbocksgatan itself is the *Sports Stadium* (Idrottens Hus), with seating for 5000.

SURROUNDINGS. – 4 km (2½ miles) SE is the well-known spa of *Ramlösa Brunn* (established 1707). In Sweden Ramlösa is not merely a brand name but has practically become a synonym for mineral water. – Strandvägen runs NW along the coast past a number of seaside places and the *Palsjö Skog* nature reserve (small 17th c. castle; the Thalassa guest-house). In 5 km (3 miles) the road comes to *Sofiero Castle*, built for Princess Sofie in 1865 by Prince Oscar, later Oscar II. In 1905 it passed to Prince, later King Gustav VI Adolf, grandfather of the present king, as a wedding present, and became the favourite summer residence both of the king and of his second wife, Louise, sister of Earl Mountbatten. The old king was an enthusiastic rhododendron grower, and the castle has a collection of over 500 varieties. After his death in 1973, the castle became the property of the town of Helsingborg.

**Helsingborg to Mölle and Kullen:** an attractive trip of 31 km (20 miles). – Leave on Strandvägen (Road 22), which runs along the coast, passing Palsjö and Sofiero Castle. At the residential suburb of *Laröd* a short detour can be made to the resort of *Hittorp* (to left). – 8 km (5 miles) from Helsingborg, to the left of the road, stands *Kulla Gunnarstorp Castle* (1865–78), in Dutch Renaissance style. Nearby is an old fortified castle, with ramparts and moats. In the park is the largest beech tree in Skåne, 6 m (20 ft) in circumference. – 6 km (4 miles): *Viken*, an old fishing village which is now a holiday resort. – The road continues along the Öresund, and after 6 km reaches the town of **Höganäs** (pop. 22,000), famous for its pottery industry. It then runs past the seaside resorts of *Strandbaden* and Nyhamnsläge. 10 km (6 miles) beyond Höganäs, on the left, is *Krapperup Castle* (1790), with remains of a fortified castle and a large plantation of rhododendrons. Soon after this, the

Kullen promontory appears. 3 km (2 miles): **Mölle** (Grand Hotel, 100 b.; Kullaberg Hotell, 27 b.; Turisthotellet, 27 b.), a small but very popular holiday town at the foot of the Kullen hills (no sandy beach).

* **Kullen** is a 15 km (9 mile) long promontory reaching out into the Kattegat, formed by the sinking of the surrounding land. The round-topped hills, worn smooth by the action of ice, support a variety of vegetation. At many points the hills fall steeply to the sea and have been heavily indented by the waves. The highest point on this peninsula between the Öresund and Skäldervik is *Högkull* (188 m – 617 ft). Many footpaths; golf-course; deer-park. The NW part of the promontory is a nature reserve. From Mölle a road (4 km (2½ miles): toll) climbs past the farm of *Kullagård* to the tip of the promontory. Here is the highest lighthouse in Europe (74 m (243 ft) above sea level), standing since 1561. The present light, installed in 1900, has a range of 43 km (27 miles). Magnificent view of the Kattegat. Along the coasts of the promontory are many caves, among them the "Silver Cave" (Silvergrottan) and the "Stone Huts" (Stenstugorna) on the S side, and the Josefinelust and Djupadal caves on the N. – 7 km (4½ miles) E of Mölle, on the S side of the Skäldervik, is the idyllic fishing village and holiday resort of *Arild* (hotels: Ljunggården, 117 b.; Rusthållargården, 75 b., SP).

To reach Ängelholm from Mölle, return 3 km (2 miles) along Road 22 to *Möllehässle* and turn left into a minor road which leads past *Brunnby* church (dating in part from the 12th c.) to *Tunneberga*; then on Road 112, past *Vegeholm Castle* (16th c.), set in a large and beautiful park on an island in the Vegeå (two square towers), to **Ängelholm** (31 km (19 miles): Hotel Lilton, 24 b.; Angelholm Motel, 29 b.): Old Town Hall (17th c.), local museum.

**Helsingborg to Landskrona.** – The road (with the E6 motorway (highway) running parallel) passes the spa of Ramlösa Brunn and the fishing village and seaside resort of *Råå*. It then cuts through a range of low hills (beautiful view of the Sound, with the island of Ven) to *Glumslöv* (Örenäs Slott Hotel, 254 b., SP) where there is a Carmelite nunnery established in 1961–2 (the first Catholic nunnery in Sweden since the Reformation). – 22 km (14 miles) from Helsingborg is **Landskrona** (pop. 34,000; Ritz Hotel, 25 b.; Öresund Hotel, 250 b.), a busy port and industrial town on the Öresund, with a 16th c. castle (extensive fortifications), a Provincial Museum and an Art Gallery. While working as a teacher here (1885–97), Selma Lagerlöf wrote her novel "Gösta Berling". – Ferry service over the Öresund to Copenhagen (1¼ hours). – There is also a boat service to the Swedish island of **Ven** (area 7·5 sq. km – 3 sq. miles), in the Sound. On the W side of the island is *Bäckviken*, where the boat docks. Near the 13th c. *St Ibb's Church* are the sparse remains of the observatory of *Uranienborg*, built in 1576 by the astronomer Tycho Brahe (1546–1601); small museum.

# Helsingør

Denmark (Zealand).
County: Frederiksborg amt.
Altitude: sea level. – Population: 57,000.
Postal code: DK-3000.
Telephone code: 02.
ⓘ **Helsingør Turistbyrå**,
　　Havnepladsen 3;
　　tel. 21 13 33.

HOTELS. – *Marienlyst*, Nordre Strandvej 2, 420 b., SB; *Hamlet*, Bramstræde 5, 70 b.; *Skandia*, Bramstræde 1, 80 b.; *Pension Brinkly*, in Snekkersten, Strandvejen 258, 18 b. – YOUTH HOSTEL. – Nordre Strandvej 24, 200 b. – CAMP SITE. – *Grønnehavn Camping*, Sundtoldvej 9.

EVENTS. – *Performances of "Hamlet"* in Kronborg Castle (August–September).

**The old Danish port and trading town of Helsingør (more familiar in English as Hamlet's Elsinore), which received its charter in 1426, lies on the NE coast of the island of Zealand, only 4·5 km (3 miles) from the Swedish town of Helsingborg on the other side of the Øresund. Tolls paid since the 15th c. by all vessels passing through the Sound from the N were abolished in 1857. The town has a productive shipyard and engineering works as well as brewing and textile industries.**

SIGHTS. – Opposite the pier used by the DSB (Danish Railways) ferries is the *Station*. In the square, to the N, is the 12 m (40 ft) high *Svea Column* (Sveasøjlen), erected in 1947 to commemorate the help given by Sweden to refugees from Denmark at the beginning of the Second World War. The next street to the SW is

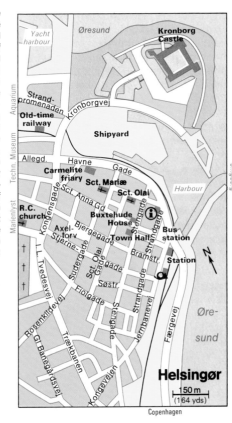

Helsingør

150 m
(164 yds)

Copenhagen

Kronborg Castle, Helsingør

*Stengade*, the main street of Helsingør. Many handsome old half-timbered houses and the **Town Hall** (1855); stained glass in Council Chamber depicting scenes from the history of the town (by Poul and Fanny Sæbye, 1936–9). To the NW stands *St Olaf's Church* (begun *c.* 1200, completed 1480–1559), raised to cathedral status in 1961. 150 m (164 yds) W, just off Skt. Annagade, is the late medieval *St Mary's Church* (fine interior), where the composer Dietrich Buxtehude was organist from 1660 to 1668; he lived at 6 Skt. Annagade. Until 1851, the service in St Mary's was conducted in German. The church is the S wing of a well-preserved *Carmelite friary* built in 1430 (arcaded cloister). The W wing houses the arts and crafts section of the *Municipal Museum*. – To the W, in Axeltorv, a fountain by E. Utzon-Frank (1926) commemorates King *Eric of Pomerania*, who gave the town its charter.

Nygade and Marienlyst Allé run NW, passing *St Vincent's Church* (R.C.), to the late 18th c. mansion of *Marienlyst*, with a park laid out as the pleasure grounds of Kronborg. The original decoration and furnishings (Louis XIV) have been preserved on the 3rd floor; art exhibitions organised by the Municipal Museum. – To the S, parallel to Stengade, is *Strandgade*, which has many fine old houses, including Nos. 77–9, the *Old Pharmacy* (1577 and 1642), and Nos. 72–4, the *Courthouse* (*c.* 1520). – At 23 Nordre Strandvej is the **Danish Museum of Technology** (*Danmarks Tekniske Museum*), with comprehensive collections in the fields of science and technology. The transport section (motor vehicle, 1866, aircraft, 1905) is in Ole Rømersvej. – From *Grønnehave*, on the North Harbour, an old-time railway (all locomotives and rolling-stock (railcars) dating from 1885 to 1920) operates on Sundays in summer, carrying passengers to Gilleleje (24 km – 15 miles).

To the NE of the town, prominently situated on a peninsula in the Øresund, is the handsome *Kronborg Castle. The site was originally occupied by a fortified castle built by Eric of Pomerania in about 1400. The new castle was built by King Frederick II between 1574 and 1585 to the specifications of two Dutch architects, Hans van Paescheng and Anthonis van Opbergen. It was rebuilt by Christian IV in 1635–40 after a catastrophic fire in 1629; the cost was met by increasing the Sound tolls. From 1785 to 1922 the castle was occupied by the military, but was restored in 1924. The S wing contains the *Chapel*, which survived the 1629 fire (magnificent Renaissance interior, wood-carving by German masters), and, in the N wing is the *Knights' Hall*, 63 m (200 ft) long. The Castle also houses the *Commercial and Maritime*

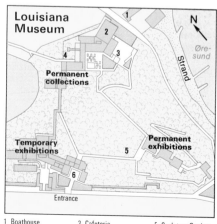

Louisiana Museum

N

Øresund

Strand

Permanent collections

Temporary exhibitions

Permanent exhibitions

Entrance

1 Boathouse
2 Concert Hall
3 Cafeteria
4 Water Garden
5 Sculpture Garden
6 Old Villa

*Museum*. In the fortified walls (*case-mates*) is a statue (by H. P. Pedersen-Dan) of *Holger Danske*, the national hero who, it is said, will come to life again in the country's hour of need. – From the SW tower (Telegraftårnet: 145 steps) there is a magnificent* view. – The *Flag Battery* is the "platform before the castle" on which the ghost appears to Hamlet in Shakespeare's play. – There is a pleasant walk around the outer bastions. – To the W of the castle, on the seafront promenade, is the *Øresund Aquarium*, displaying the marine life of the Sound.

SURROUNDINGS. – 10 km (6 miles) S of Helsingør, on the coast road, is the village of *Humlebæk*. The *Louisiana Museum, founded by the merchant Knud W. Jensen in 1958, stands in a park overlooking the Øresund. It has a good international collection of modern art from about 1950, and in the beautiful old park is an outstanding display of contemporary sculpture, including works by Hans Arp, Alexander Calder, Max Ernst, Alberto Giacometti, Henry Moore and Jean Tinguely. Regular special exhibitions as well as concerts and poetry festivals take place.

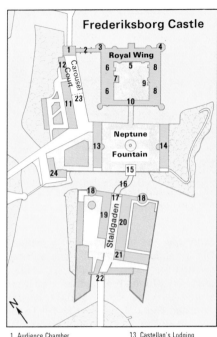

**Frederiksborg Castle**

| | |
|---|---|
| 1 Audience Chamber | 13 Castellan's Lodging |
| 2 Long Corridor | 14 Chancery |
| 3 Mint Tower | 15 Gatehouse Tower |
| 4 Jægerberg Tower | 16 South Bridge |
| 5 Great Gallery | 17 Christian VI's Gateway |
| 6 Chapel Wing | 18 Frederick II's Round Towers |
| 7 Chapel Tower | 19 Royal Stables |
| 8 Princesses' Wing | 20 Hussars' Stables |
| 9 Kitchen Well | 21 Herluf Trolle's Tower |
| 10 Terrace Wing | 22 Town Gate |
| 11 Storeroom Wing | 23 Former Carousel Gate |
| 12 Tearooms | 24 Restaurant |

Frederiksborg Castle

**Helsingør to Gilleleje** (24 km (15 miles); on Sundays, June–September, trips on old-time railway). – The road runs past many seaside resorts to the northern tip of Zealand. Leave Helsingør on Strandvejen, passing the mansion of Marielyst in 1·5 km (1 mile) and *Julebæk* (beautiful beach) in another 2·5 km (1½ miles); then *Hellebæk* (Hellebæk Kyst Hotel, 90 b.), various fishing villages, and through a stretch of woodland along the coast to the popular resort of **Hornbæk** (Søbakkehus, 35 b.; Trouville Hotel, 99 b., SB; Bretagne, 75 b.; camp site), with a beautiful beach only 50 m (55 yds) from the town.

The road continues through the resorts of *Villingebæk* and *Dronningmølle* (Hulerød Kysthotel, 50 b.; camp site). – 2 km (1¼ miles) S, on a hill on the Villingerød–Esrum road, are a park and museum containing works by the painter and sculptor Rudolph

Tegner (1873–1950: some 200 pictures and 200 sculptures). – Shortly before Gilleleje, on a high cliff to the right of the road, is the *Nakkehoved* lighthouse (54 m – 177 ft), with extensive views (camp site). From here it is 4 km (2½ miles) to **Gilleleje** (Strand Hotel, 43 b.; Pension Gilleleje, 36 b.; camp site), an old fishing village (fish auction daily) which is also a popular holiday resort. From the breakwater there are good views of the Kattegat, extending to the Swedish coast. – 1 km (¾ mile) W is *Gilbjerg Hoved*, the most northerly point on Zealand.

**Helsingør to Hillerød.** – Road 6 runs SW (14·5 km – 9 miles) to *Fredensborg* (Country House, 40 b.; Hotelpension Bondehuset, 24 b.), with Fredensborg Castle (1720–4; fine domed hall). Fredensborg is the spring and autumn residence of the royal family. The *park extending NW to Lake Esrum, with its fine avenues and sculptures, is one of the most impressive in Denmark.

Road 6 continues through the southern part of the *Gribskov*, an area of forest bounded on the E by *Lake Esrum* (area 14 sq. km – 5½ sq. miles). 8 km (5 miles) farther on is the main town of northern Zealand, **Hillerød** (pop. 25,000; KFUM Missionshotel, 40 b.). Features of interest are the Museum of Northern Zealand in the Jægerbakken park, the Money Museum in Frederiksborg Bank (Slotsgade 16) and the Æbelholt Monastery Museum (6 km (4 miles) from the town of the Frederiksværk road).

Hillerød's principal attraction, however, is **Frederiksborg Castle**, built on three islands in a small lake. The most splendid achievement of the Danish Renaissance, it was erected between 1602 and 1620 by Christian IV on the site of an earlier castle of Frederick II's time and restored in the original style after a fire in 1859. In the outer courtyard is a copy (1888) of a Neptune Fountain by Adrian de Vries (1623) which was carried off to Sweden in 1658. On the third island stands the main castle building, with three four-storey wings. Since 1877, thanks to financial assistance from the Carlsberg Foundation, the castle has housed the *Museum of National History* (pictures, portraits and other works of art illustrating the development of Danish history and culture). In the W wing is the *Chapel*, which survived the 1859 fire; it has a fine interior with inlaid stalls, an elaborately decorated pulpit, an oratory and a fine organ).

# Helsinki/ Helsingfors

Finland (Southern).
Province: Uudenmaan lääni (Nylands Län/Uusimaa).
Altitude: sea level. – Population: 500,000.
Postal code: SF-0010 . . . – Telephone code: 90.

(i) **Suomen Matkailun Edistämiskeskus**
(*Finnish Tourist Board*),
Kluuvikatu 8, 3rd floor,
SF-00101 Helsinki 10;
tel. 65 01 55.

**Helsingin Kaupungin Matkailutoimisto**
(*Helsinki Tourist Information Office*),
Pohjoisesplanadi 19,
SF-00100 Helsinki;
tel. 17 40 88 and 1 69 37 57.

**Autoliitto**
(*Finnish Automobile and Touring Club*),
Kansakoulukatu 10,
SF-00100 Helsinki;
tel. 65 00 22.

EMBASSIES. – *United Kingdom*: Uudenmaankatu 16–20, Helsinki 12 (tel. 64 79 22). – *USA*: Itainen Puistotie 14A, Helsinki (tel. 17 19 31). – *Canada*: Pohjoisesplanadi 25B, Helsinki 10 (tel. 17 11 41).

LARGE BOOKSHOPS. – *Academic Bookshop*, corner of Pohjoisesplanadi and Keskuskatu; *Suomalainen Kirjakauppa*, Aleksanterinkatu (opposite Stockmann's department store).

CITY TOURS. – Departure from Simonkatu 1 (near Central Station). The 3T tram (trolley), starting from the station, runs past some of the principal sights of Helsinki, giving information by loudspeaker in Swedish, English and German. A day ticket (24 hours) gives unrestricted use of all bus and tram (trolley) services displaying a yellow board with two black arrows.

HOTELS (advance booking advisable). – *Hesperia*, Mannerheimintie 50, 560 b., SB; *Inter-Continental*, Mannerheimintie 46, 1100 b., roof SB; *Kalastajatorppa*, Kalastajatorpanti 1, 493 b., SB, 2·8 km (1¾ miles) from the centre on the lake, own beach; *Marski*, Mannerheimintie 10, 297 b.; *Palace*, Etelaranta 10, 93 b.; *Ramada Presidentti*, Etelainen Rautatiekatu 4, 1000 b., SB; *Rivoli Jardin* (no rest.), Kasarmikatu 40, 122 b.; *Anna*, Annankatu 1, 99 b.; *Aurora*, Helsinginkatu 50, 139 b., SB; *Finn*, Kalevankatu 3B, 63 b.; *Helka*, P. Rautakiekatu 23, 230 b.; *Helsinki*, Hallituskatu 12, at the station, 231 b.; *Hospiz*, Vuorikatu 17B, 374 b.; *Klaus Kurki*, Bulevardi 2, 208 b.; *Marttahotelli*, Uudenmaankatu 24, 79 b.; *Merihotelli*, Hakaniemenranta 4, 153 b., SB; *Metrocity*, Kaisaniemenkatu 7, 118 b.; *Olympia*, Lantinen Brahenkatu 2, 170 b.; *Park*, Pohjolankatu 38, 80 b., SB; *Pasila*, Maistraatinportti 3, 516 b.; *Seurahuone*, Kaivokatu 12, at the station, 221 b.; *Torni*, Yrjönkatu 26, 280 b. noted for its cuisine; *Ursula*, Paasivuorenkaati 1, 78 b.; *Vaakuna*, Asemaaukio 2, at the station, 481 b. – SUBURB OF ESPOO: *Dipoli*, Otaranta, 426 b., SB; *Espoo*, Nihtisillantie 1, 268 b., SB; *Tapiola Garden*, Tapiontori, 170 b., SB; – SUBURB OF HAAGA: *Haaga*, Nuijamiestentie 10, 218 b., SB; – NEAR VANTA AIRPORT: *Rantasipi Airport*, 354 b., SB; – SUMMER HOTELS (1 June–31 Aug.) *Academia*, Hietaniemenkatu 14,

Finlandia Hall, Helsinki

308 b., SB; *Mercur*, Ruusulankatu 5, 98 b. – *Kaukokiito-Motelli*, Metsäläntie 2, 153 b.

YOUTH HOSTELS – *Retkeilymaja Academica*, Hietaniemenkatu 14, 190 b. (1 June–1 Sept.); *Stadionin Maja*, Pohj. Stadiontie 3B, 261 b.; etc.

CAMP SITE. *Camping Rastila*, 16 km (10 miles) E of the city centre.

RESTAURANTS. – In most of the hotels listed; particularly recommended are those on the top floors of the *Vaakuna*, *Palace* and *Torni* hotels, with fine views of the town. Also recommended are the following: \*Motti, Töölöntorinkatu 2; \*Havis Amanda, Unioninkatu 23 (fish specialties in cellar); \*Karl König, Mikonkatu 4 (first-class cuisine); *Adlon*, Fabianinkatu 14 (excellent smörgåsbord); *Bellevue*, Rahapanjankatu 3 (Russian specialties); *Kulosaaren Casino*, Hopeasalmenpolku 49 (attractive setting on the water); *Troikka*, Caloniuksenkatu 3 (Russian specialties); restaurant in *Stockmann*'s department store, Keskuskatu 2; *Esplanaadinkappeli*, Esplanadinpuisto (on market square); *Frazer*, Kluuvikatu 3 and City Center (pleasant cafés); *Walhalla* (summer restaurant), on island of Suomenlinna; etc. – Many reasonably priced self-service restaurants (*baari*).

EVENTS. *Helsinki Summer Concerts* (international orchestras and soloists), mid-June to mid-August; *Helsinki Festival* (concerts, exhibitions, opera and ballet of international standard), end of August and beginning of September.

\*Helsinki (Swedish Helsingfors), capital of Finland and main town of the province of Uusimaa (Nyland), lies mainly on a rugged granite peninsula on the northern shores of the Gulf of Finland, with numerous offshore islands. With a university, a college of technology, two business colleges and other scientific and cultural institutions, it is the intellectual hub of Finland. It is also the country's largest industrial town (shipbuilding, engineering, porcelain, textiles) and a port with a large import trade. Here are the headquarters of most of the major Finnish firms (international technological trade fair, held annually). – The central city, in neo-classical style, was built in the first half of the 19th c. by the Berlin architect Carl Ludwig Engel (1778–1840) in accordance with a plan drawn up by Johan Albrekt Ehrenström. With its handsome streets and boulevards, the city creates an air of spaciousness, and the white façades of its buildings have earned it the name of the "white city of the North". The new residential areas on the outskirts of the town, including the garden city of Tapiola, are admirably planned. –

The first section of the Helsinki underground railway system (from the city centre eastwards) is in operation.

HISTORY. – Helsinki was founded by Gustav I Vasa in 1550 on a site to the N of the present central city at the outflow of the Vantaanjoki (Swedish Vanda) into the Gulf of Finland, as a rival to the trading town of Reval (now Tallinn). In 1639, however, Queen Christina ordered the transfer of the town to a more favourable site on the peninsula of Vironniemi. The construction of a fortress on the offshore island of Suomenlinna began in 1748. In 1808 the town, still a place of little consequence, was unable to withstand an attack by Russian forces, and was incorporated into the Russian Grand Duchy of Finland. Tsar Alexander made it the capital of Finland in 1812. In 1816 C. L. Engel was commissioned to rebuild the town, a third of which had been burned down in 1808.

After the collapse of the Russian Empire, a republic was proclaimed in Helsinki on 6 December 1917. In 1918, with the help of German troops, the town was cleared of Bolshevist forces and became capital of the independent Republic of Finland. During the Second World War Helsinki was one of the few European capitals not occupied by foreign forces. The Summer Olympic Games were held here in 1952, and the Conference on Security and Cooperation in Europe in 1975.

## Museums, Galleries, etc.

In general, the opening times for Sundays apply also to public holidays.

Almost all institutions are closed on Mondays and 1 January, Good Friday, Easter Day, 1 May, 1st Friday after 22 June, Independence Day (6 December) and Christmas Eve and Christmas Day.

**Amos Anderson Museum of Art,**
Yrjönkatu 27;
2 May to 14 October, Mon.–Fri. 10 a.m. to 4 p.m.; 15 October to 31 December, Mon.–Fri. 11 a.m. to 5 p.m., Sat., Sun. 12 noon to 5 p.m.

**Museum of Applied Art,**
Korkeavuorenkatu 23;
Tues.–Fri. 11 a.m. to 5 p.m., Sat., Sun. 11 a.m. to 4 p.m.

**Arabia-Museum** (ceramics),
Hämeentie 135;
Mon. 10 a.m. to 12 noon, Tues.–Fri. 10 a.m. to 5 p.m., Sat. 9 a.m. to 2 p.m., Sun. 10 a.m. to 4 p.m.

**Museum of Architecture,**
Kasarmikatu 24;
Mon.–Sun. 10 a.m. to 4 p.m.

**Art Gallery** (*Taidehalli*),
Nervanderinkatu 3;
Tues.–Sat. 11 a.m. to 6 p.m., Sun. 12 noon to 5 p.m., in summer, Mon.–Fri. 11 a.m. to 5 p.m., Sun. 12 noon to 4 p.m.

**Athenaeum (Ateneum) Museum of Art,**
(at present Kansakoulukatu 3),
1 September to 31 May, Mon.–Sat. 9 a.m. to 5 p.m., Sun. 11 a.m. to 5 p.m.
1 June to 31 August, Mon.–Fri. 9 a.m. to 5 p.m., Sat., Sun. 11 a.m. to 5 p.m.

**Museum of Aviation,**
Helsinki-Vantaa Airport;
daily 12 noon to 6 p.m.

**Botanic Garden of University,**
Unioninkatu 44;
1 October to 30 April, Tues., Fri., Sun. 12 noon to
3 p.m.; 1 May to 30 September, Mon.–Fri. 12 noon to
3 p.m., Sun. 12 noon to 3 p.m.; group tours by
appointment (tel. 63 11 50) throughout the year.

**Cathedral,**
Senaattitori (Senate Square);
daily 9 a.m. to 7 p.m.; crypt by appointment (tel.
62 99 54).

**Coastal Defence Museum,**
Kustanmiekka works, island of Suomenlinna;
12 May to 31 August, daily 11 a.m. to 5 p.m.; 1–30
September, Sat., Sun. 11 a.m. to 5 p.m.

**Coins and Banknotes,**
**Exhibition of** (*KOP Bank*),
Pohjoisesplanadi 29;
Mon.–Fri. 9.15 a.m. to 4.15 p.m.

**Didrichsen Museum of Art,**
Kuusilahdenkuja 3 (buses from Bus Station, platform
50);
Wed. and Sun. 2 to 4 p.m.; also by appointment (tel.
48 90 55).

**Espoo Car Museum,**
Gutshof Pakankyia Espoo;
1 May to 31 May, Sat., Sun. 10 a.m. to 6 p.m.; 1 June
to 31 August, daily 10 a.m. to 6 p.m.; 1 September to
30 September, Sat., Sun. 10 a.m. to 6 p.m.

**Finnish Maritime Museum,**
Hylkysaari (water bus from the market or the bridge);
1 September to 30 April, Sat., Sun. 10 a.m. to 3 p.m.;
2 May to 31 August, daily 10 a.m. to 3 p.m.

**Gallén-Kallela Museum,**
Gallén-Kallelantie 27;
16 September to 14 May, Tues.–Sat. 10 a.m. to 4 p.m.,
Sun. 10 a.m. to 5 p.m.; 15 May to 15 September,
Tues.–Thurs. 10 a.m. to 8 p.m. Fri.–Sun. 10 a.m. to
5 p.m.

**Herttoniemi Museum** (manor-house and farm),
Linnanrakentajantie 14;
Sun. 12 noon to 3 p.m. also by appointment.

**Kluuvi Gallery,**
Unioninkatu 28B, 3rd floor;
Tues.–Sat. 11 a.m. to 6 p.m., Sun. 12 noon to 4 p.m.

**Linnanmäki Amusement Park,**
Tivolintie;
28 April to 14 May, Sun. and public holidays 1 to 10
p.m.; 15 May to 2 September, Tues.–Fri. 5 to 10 p.m.,
Sat. 2 to 10 p.m., Sun. 1 to 10 p.m.

**Mannerheim Museum,**
Kalliolinnantie 14;
Fri. and Sat. 11 a.m. to 3 p.m., Sun. 11 a.m. to 4 p.m.

**Market Square** (*Kauppatori*);
market Mon.–Sat. 7 a.m. to 2 p.m.

**Military Museum** (*Sotamuseo*),
Maurinkatu 1;
Sun.–Fri. 11 a.m. to 3 p.m.

**Mineralogical Museum,**
Kivimiehentie 1, Espoo (buses from Bus Station);
Sun. 12 noon to 3 p.m.; also by appointment (tel.
4 69 32 43).

**Municipal Art Collection,**
Meilahti, Tamminiementie 6;
Wed.–Sun. 11 a.m. to 6.30 p.m.

**Municipal Museum,**
Karamzininkatu 2;
Sun.–Fri. 12 noon to 4 p.m., Thurs. also 4 to 8 p.m.

**National Museum** (*Kansallismuseo*),
Mannerheimintie 34;
1 October to 30 April, Mon.–Sat. 11 a.m. to 3 or 4 p.m.;
2 May to 30 September, daily 11 a.m. to 4 p.m., Tues.
also 6 to 9 p.m.

**Nordic Art Centre,**
Island of Suomenlinna, Beach Barracks;
October to April, daily 10 a.m. to 6 p.m.; May to
September, Mon.–Fri. 12 noon to 8 p.m., Sat., Sun.
10 a.m. to 8 p.m.

**Observatory,**
Kaivopuisto Park, Ullanlinnanmäki;
15 February to 30 April and 1 October to 30
November, on clear nights.

**Paper Museum,**
Tekniikantie, Espoo (from the Bus Station);
Mon.–Fri. 8 a.m. to 4 p.m.

**Parliament Building,**
Mannerheimintie 30;
conducted tours Mon.–Fri. 2 p.m., Sat. 11 a.m., Sun.
12 noon and 1 p.m., also by appointment (tel.
44 00 51).

**Photographic Museum,**
Vattuniemenkuja 4;
Sun.–Fri. 11 a.m. to 3 or 4 p.m.

**Pijlajasaari**
(island with swimming and recreation area);
motorboats from Laivurinkatu (tel. 63 00 65) end of
May to August.

**Postal and Telegraph Museum,**
Tehtaankatu 21B;
Tues.–Fri. 12 noon to 3 p.m., Wed. 12 noon to 6 p.m.

**Senate Square** (Senaatintori),
Empire Centre of Carl Ludwig Engel (1778–1840).

**Seurasaari** *Open-Air Museum,*
island of Seurasaari (terminus of No. 24 bus);
May to September.

**Sinebrychoff Museum of Art,**
Bulevard 40;
1 September to 31 May, Mon.–Sat. 9 a.m. to 5 p.m.,
Sun. 11 a.m. to 5 p.m.; 1 June to 31 August, Mon.–Fri.
9 a.m. to 5 p.m., Sat., Sun. 11 a.m. to 5 p.m.

**Sport Museum of Finland,**
Olympic Stadium;
Tues.–Fri. 11 a.m. to 5 p.m., Sat., Sun. 12 noon to
4 p.m.

**Stadium Tower,**
Olympic Stadium;
daily 9 a.m. to 5 p.m.

**Submarine "Vesikkö",**
island of Suomenlinna, Tykistölahti Bay;
mid-May to end-September.

**Museum of Technology,**
Viikintie 1;
1 October to 30 April, Wed.–Sun. noon to 4 p.m.,
1 May to 30 September, Tues.–Sun. 11 a.m. to 6 p.m.

**Temppeliaukio Church,**
Lutherinkatu 3;
Mon.–Sat. 10 a.m. to 9 p.m., Sun. 4.30 to 9 p.m.

**Theatre Museum,**
Aleksanterinkatu 12;
Tues.–Sun. 12 noon to 4 p.m. Wed. also 4 to 6 p.m.

**Uspensky Cathedral** (Orthodox),
Kanavakatu 1;
by appointment (tel. 63 42 67).

**Viapori-Sveaborg** (old marine fortress),
island of Suomenlinna (ferry from the market).

**Workers' Museum,**
Kotkankatu 9;
Tues.–Fri., noon to 3 or 4 p.m.

**Zoo,**
island of Korkeasaari (ferry from North Harbour from beginning of May to around end of September; rest of year, footbridge from Mustasaari);
October to February, daily 10 a.m. to 4 p.m.; March, daily 10 a.m. to 5 p.m.; April, daily 10 a.m. to 6 p.m.; 1 May to 30 September, daily 10 a.m. to 8 p.m.

**Zoological Museum,**
Pohjoinen Rautatiekatu 13;
1 September to 31 May, Mon.–Fri. 9 a.m. to 3 p.m., Sun. 12 noon to 4 p.m.; 1 June to 31 August, Mon.–Fri. 9 a.m. to 2 p.m.

# Sightseeing in Helsinki

The heart of Helsinki is the **Market Square** (*Kauppatori*), which is the scene of lively activity on market mornings (Monday to Saturday, 7 a.m. to 2 p.m.) and preserves its own particular charm even in the cold winter months. It lies on the N side of the South Harbour, and has an obelisk commemorating the Empress Alexandra's visit to Helsinki in 1833. From here there are boat services to Suomenlinna and the rocky islets called skerries, and the ferries from Sweden come in to the quays on either side of the harbour. On the N side of the square is the *Town House* (Kaupungintalo; by Engel, 1833), with a light blue façade. To the NE is

the *President's Palace*, and beyond it the *Guard-House*. On the W side of the square, between the two lanes of the *Esplanade*, is the *Havis Amanda*, a beautiful decorative fountain by V. Vallgren (1908) round which students dance after Graduation, and beyond this the popular Esplanadikappeli Restaurant, with a stage where concerts are given in summer. A little way S, on the seaward side of the Eteläranta, stands the picturesque *Market Hall* (Kauppahalli, 1891). – From the Market Square a bridge leads E to the island of *Katajanokka*. Here the gilded domes of the Orthodox *Uspensky Cathedral* (1868) stand out on a hill to the left (icons and paintings in interior).

Parallel to the Esplanade on the N is *Aleksanterinkatu*, Helsinki's principal shopping and commercial street. Halfway down the street, in the imposing *Senate Square* (*Senaatintori*), stands a bronze statue of Tsar Alexander II (by W. Runeberg, 1894). On the N side of the square a broad flight of steps leads up to the very white Lutheran **Cathedral** (*Tumiokirkko*) of St Nicholas (frequently called "the Wedding Cake"), standing 10 m (35 ft) above the square on a granite crag (begun in 1830 to the specifications of Engel and completed in a different style in 1852). (Statues of Luther, Melanchthon and the Finnish reformer M. Agricola; a fine organ.) On the W side of the square is the **University** (*Yliopisto*), built by Engel in 1828–32 and extended in 1936 to Fabianinkatu. To the N of the University is the *University Library* (Yliopiston Kirjasto), also designed by Engel (1836–45), containing 1,500,000 volumes and 2000 manuscripts, including the largest collection of Slav works in the West. The Library is generally regarded as the finest building by Engel in Helsinki. Opposite the University stands the *Government Palace* (Valtionenvoston Linna), which from 1809 to 1918 housed the Senate of the Grand Duchy of Finland. It is now occupied by the Foreign Ministry and other government offices. The Russian Governor-General, Nikolay Bobrikov, was assassinated on the steps of the Senate by Eugen Schauman in 1904. – On the other side of Aleksanterinkatu can be seen the two-storey *Sederholm House*, the oldest stone building in the city. Beyond the Government Palace is the *Knights' House* (Ritarihuone, 1858–61), once the meeting-place of the knights and

South Harbour, Helsinki, with the Market Square and Cathedral

nobility, now little used and partly rented out for a variety of purposes. On the first floor are the coats of arms of the Finnish nobility. Opposite the Knights' House, on the other side of Hallituskatu, are the headquarters of the *Finnish Literary Society* (Suomen Kirjallisuuden Seura), founded in 1831.

From Senate Square Snellmaninkatu runs N, passing on the right, on the far side of Kirkkokatu, the former *House of Estates* (1891), now occupied by various learned societies. Above the entrance is a bronze group (by Wikström, 1903) depicting Tsar Alexander I at the Diet of Borgå in 1809. Opposite, in front of the *Bank of Finland* stands a bronze statue of the Finnish statesman and philosopher J. V. Snellman (1806–81), who secured the recognition of Finnish as an official language on an equal basis with Swedish. Opposite the Bank to the N, at the corner of Rauhankatu, are the *National Archives*. A little way NE, at 1 Maurinkatu, is the *Finnish Military Museum*.

From Senate Square Aleksanterinkatu runs W; this section of the street is busier and livelier than the lower part. In the middle of the street, at its intersection with the broad Mannerheimintie, is a sculpture by F. Nyland, the "Three Smiths" (1932), scarred by Soviet bombing. To the left is **Stockmann's department store**, established by a Lübeck man, G. F. Stockmann, who started with a small general store at the corner of Aleksanterinkatu and Unioninkatu in 1862. The present store extends to the left along Mannerheimintie almost to the Esplanade.

In the gardens between the two lanes of the *Esplanade* stands the semicircular building of the *Swedish Theatre* (Ruotsalainen Teatteri), originally built to Engel's plans in 1863–6 and replaced by the present structure (by Jarl Eklund and Eero Saarinen) in 1936. To the E of this are a sculptural group by G. Finne (1932) commemorating the Swedish-Finnish poet Zachris Topelius and a bronze figure of the Finnish writer *Eino Leino* (1878–1926) by Lauri Leppänen (1953). Half-way along the Esplanade is a bronze statue of the poet *J. L. Runeberg* by his son W. Runeberg (1885); on the base is the first verse of the Finnish national anthem, "Our Country", which was written by the elder Runeberg. – In the northern part of the Esplanade (Pohjoisesplanadi), at the corner of Kluuvikatu, is a building which was removed stone by stone in the early 1960s so that the unstable foundations could be renewed and then was rebuilt, leaving the façade unchanged. In this building, formerly a hotel, Finland announced its surrender at the end of the Winter War in 1940. Earlier, in 1918, it had been a German headquarters. – Almost opposite, at the corner of Etelä Esplanaadikatu and Fabianinkatu, is a small *palace* (by Engel, 1824) which was the residence of the

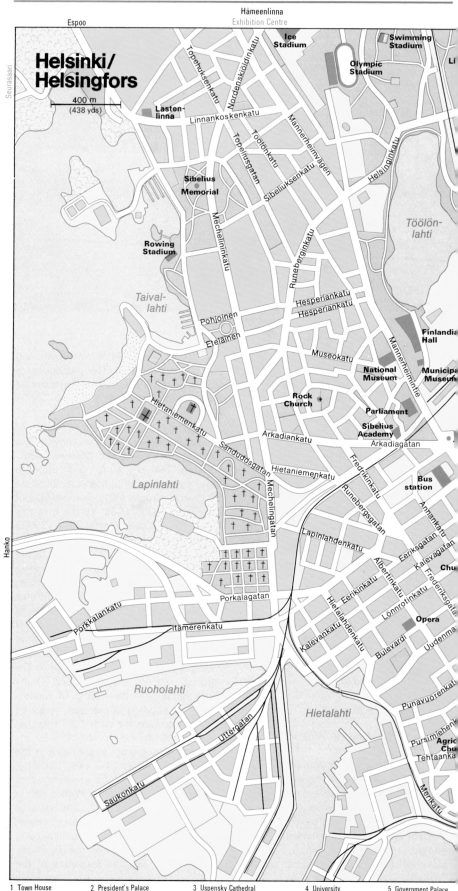

# Helsinki/
# Helsingfors

400 m
(438 yds)

Espoo

Hämeenlinna
Exhibition Centre

Ice
Stadium

Swimming
Stadium

Olympic
Stadium

Li

Seurasaari

Lasten-
linna

Topehuksenkatu

Nordenskiöldinkatu

Linnankoskenkatu

Mannerheimvägen

Helsinginkatu

Töölön-
lahti

Sibelius
Memorial

Topelius gatan

Töölönkatu

Sibeliuksenkatu

Rowing
Stadium

Mechelininkatu

Runeberginkatu

Taival-
lahti

Pohjoinen

Eteläinen

Hesperiankatu

Hesperiankatu

Finlandia
Hall

Museokatu

National
Museum

Municipal
Museum

Mannerheimintie

Rock
Church

Hietaniemenkatu

Parliament

Sibelius
Academy

Arkadiankatu

Arkadiagatan

Sanduddsgatan

Hietaniemenkatu

Lapinlahti

Bus
station

Fredrikinkatu

Runebergsgatan

Annankatu

Mechelingatan

Lapinlahdenkatu

Eriksgatan

Kalevagatan

Albertinkatu

Eerikinkatu

Frederiksgatan

Chu

Hietalahdenkatu

Lönnrotinkatu

Porkalagatan

Opera

Porkkalankatu

Itämerenkatu

Kalevankatu

Bulevardi

Uudenma

Ruoholahti

Punavuorenka

Hietalahti

Pursimiehen

Agric
Chu

Uttergatan

Tehtaanka

Saukonkatu

Merikatu

Hanko

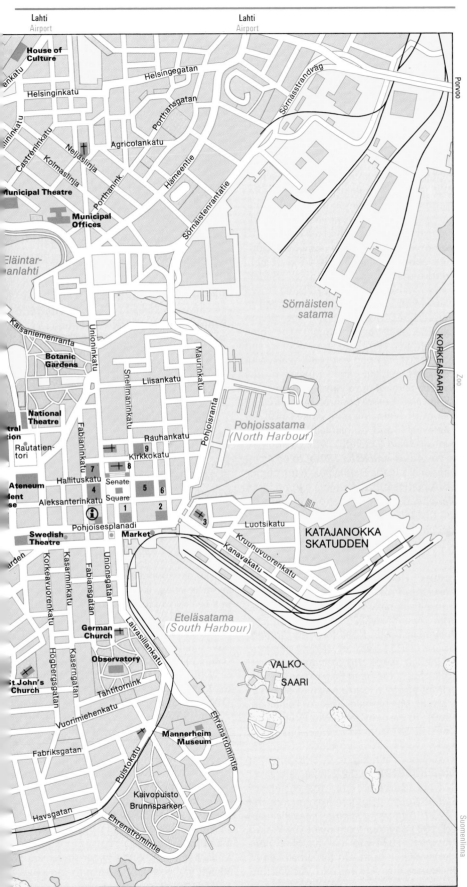

Russian Governor-General from 1832 to 1917. Now used as a state guest-house, it is popularly known as Smolna, having been the temporary headquarters of the revolutionary government in 1918, as was the Smolny Institute in Petrograd.

The Esplanade is continued SW by the *Boulevard* (Bulevardi). On the right of this street, beyond Yrjönkatu, are a cemetery (used until 1829), the wooden *Old Church*, built by Engel for use pending the completion of the Cathedral, and two monuments commemorating the Finnish and the German dead of the 1918 war of liberation. At the corner of Yrjönkatu and Lönnrotinkatu is a *mausoleum* containing the remains of J. Sederholm, architect of the Helsinki town plan. Many plague victims are buried in the cemetery here. Opposite the church can be seen a monument (by Emil Wickström, 1902) to the doctor and philologist *Elias Lönnrot* (1802–84), who collected, edited and published the various parts of the Finnish national epic "Kalevala". Beside Lönnrot, on the monument, is Väinämöinen, the smith in "Kalevala", and at his feet is Suomen Neito ("Maid Finland"). At 27 Yrjönkatu is the *Amos Anderson Museum of Art*. – Farther along the Boulevard, at the corner of Albertinkatu (on right), stands the *National Opera House*, and at the far end, on the left, the *Sinebrychoff Art Collection* contains 17th and 18th c. pictures; furniture and other works of art.

Farther along *Mannerheimintie* from Aleksanterinkatu is the *Old Student House* (originally 1870), with two figures from the "Kalevala", Väinämöinen and Ilmarinen. Beyond it is the *New Student House* (1911). After crossing Kaikovatu, on the left, is the *Bus Station* and to the right, ahead, the *Head Post Office* (1940), in front of which is an equestrian statue of Marshal Mannerheim (by A. Tukiainen, 1960). To the right of the Post Office is the **Central Station** (*Rautatieasema*) with its 48 m (160 ft) high clock-tower, the most important building by E. Saarinen in Finland (1919). In the E wing is a small Railway Museum. – On the N side of *Station Square* (Rautatientori) stands the *Finnish National Theatre* (Kansallisteatteri, 1901), with a monument (by Wäinö Aaltonen, 1934) to the national poet Aleksis Kivi in front. On the other side of the square the *Ateneum or Athenaeum

(by Theodor Höijer, 1884–7) houses a college of art and an art gallery, with the finest collection in Finland. The picture gallery contains works by Finnish artists, including A. Edelfelt (1854–1905), E. Järnefelt (1863–1937), P. Halonen (1865–1933), and A. Gallén-Kallela (1865–1935), and by foreign masters (Rembrandt's "Monk Reading", Watteau's "Swing", pictures by Frans Hals, etc.) as well as modern European art. The sculpture hall displays work by such Finnish sculptors as V. Vallgren, W. Aaltonen, W. Runeberg and S. Hildén. In front of the entrance is a bronze figure of Albert Edelfelt by V. Vallgren (1929). – Behind the National Theatre is the *Botanic Garden*.

NW of the Post Office, in Mannerheimintie, stands the **Parliament Building** (*Eduskuntatalo*), a monumental structure by J. S. Sirén (1930). In front, to the right, are statues of former Presidents P. E. Svinhufvud (1861–1944), K. J. Ståhlberg (1865–1952) and, in the gardens a bit apart, K. Kallio (1873–1940). – Farther along Mannerheimintie, on the left, we come to the *National Museum* (*Kansallismuseo*, 1912), with a tall spire. It contains an interesting collection of material which provides a comprehensive history of the culture and ethnography of Finland. Particularly notable is the Finno-Ugric collection, presenting numerous traditional costumes and objects of everyday use.

Diagonally opposite the National Museum, in a park, is the *Municipal Museum*, and to the N of this, on the S shore of the Töölönlahti, the **Finlandia Hall** (by Alvar Aalto, 1971), a concert and convention hall. – Rather more than a kilometre (less than $\frac{3}{4}$ mile) farther N, at the intersection of Mannerheimintie and Helsinginkatu, is the *Old Exhibition Hall*. Beyond this is the **Olympic Stadium** (1938), with a tower 72 m (235 ft) high (elevator) and a magnificent view of the city. In the Stadium is the *Finnish Sport Museum*, and outside the entrance is a bronze figure (by Aaltonen, 1952) of the famous runner Paavo Nurmi (1897–1973). Beyond the Stadium, to the E, is the *Swimming Stadium*, and to the W the *Ice Stadium*. – To the E of these sports facilities, beyond the railway line, extends the *Linnanmäki* amusement park, with a water-tower; and adjoining this is the *House of Culture* (by

Alvar Aalto). 1 km (¾ mile) S stands the *Municipal Theatre* (1968), and to the SE of this the *Municipal Offices*. – Near the Olympic Stadium Linnankoskenkatu branches off Mannerheimvägen (the continuation of Mannerheimintie) and runs W to *Lastenlinna* (the "Children's Castle", a home and training institution for badly handicapped children; Mannerheim Children's Hospital).

From here Merkannontie runs S past the *Sibelius Park*, in which can be seen the

**Sibelius Memorial** by Eila Hiltunen (1967). This at first aroused violent criticism for its radical departure from the conventional type of memorial and, to compromise, Hiltunen added a bust of the composer. – Continuing along the sea-front, we pass the *Rowing Stadium* and soon come to the beautiful sandy beach of *Hietaniemi*. Adjoining the beach is *Hietaniemi Cemetery*, topped by a cross which commemorates the fallen. (This is a military cemetery as well as a civil one.) Marshal Mannerheim (1867–1951) is

## Finnish National Museum, Helsinki
## Suomen Kansallismuseo

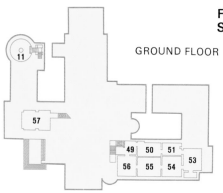

GROUND FLOOR

GROUND FLOOR

11      Medieval church textiles
57      Silver (coins, medals)

Finno-Ugric collection
49–51   Lapps (Samians)
53      Ostyaks, Voguls, Hungarians
54      Votyaks, Cheremisses (Mari), Mordvins
55      Estonians, Votians, Livonians
56      Karelians, Veps

FIRST FLOOR

Prehistoric section
1       Stone Age and Bronze Age
2       Iron Age

Historical sculpture
5       Medieval sculpture
6       The medieval church
7       Tomb monuments
8       Lutheran church art (17th–18th c.)
9       Icons
15      Weapons
16–17   Medieval implements and utensils

Ethnographic section
40      Hunting (seals, etc.)
41      Fishing
43      Domestic equipment
44      Early 19th c. hut and old furniture
45–46   Furniture

FIRST FLOOR

SECOND FLOOR

Historical section
18      Renaissance room
19      Guild equipment; pewter, copper
20      Burgher Baroque
21      Baroque
22      Late Baroque
24      Glass
25      Rococo room from Jakkarila manor-house
26      Rococo press from Jakkarila; clothes
28      Gustavian room
29      Empire, Biedermeier and neo-Rococo
30      Throne-room (pictures, etc.)
32      Art Nouveau

Ethnographic section
33      West Finnish costumes
34      Karelian costumes, ornaments, bridal trousseaux, etc.
35      Textiles
36      Carpets
37      Tools and equipment used in textile manufacture
39      Village life; folk traditions

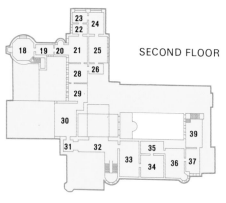

SECOND FLOOR

Sibelius Memorial, Helsinki

buried here. It is the Finnish custom to place a lighted candle on each grave at Christmas. Near the entrance are the graves of the politicians Risto Ryti, Väinö Tanner, T. M. Kivimäki and E. Linkomies, who – as a condition of the 1944 armistice – were tried by a special court and given prison sentences for their political activities during the war.

From the cemetery, Hietaniemenkatu returns towards the middle of the city. To the left, set back from the road, is the *Crematorium* (by B. Liljeqvist, 1927), with a grove for ash-urns behind it. Hietaniemenkatu runs into Mechelinenkatu: turn left along this street and soon afterwards right into Arkadiankatu. At the next intersection are the *Finnish* (on left) and *Swedish* (on right) *Commercial Colleges*. In front of the Finnish college is a fountain, "Profit", by A. Tukiainen (1954). Beyond this Fredrikinkatu, on left, leads to the **Rock Church** (*Temppeliaukio* or *Taivalahdenkirkko*), an underground church hewn from rock, dome 13 m (43 ft) high, by T. and T. Suomalainen, 1968–9). – At the intersection of Arkadiankatu with Pohjoinen Rautatiekatu is the *Sibelius Academy* (Conservatoire), and opposite this, to the W, the *Zoological Museum*.

To the S of the Market Square, at the end of Unioninkatu, is the *German Church*, and beyond this Observatory Hill (38 m – 125 ft) on which stands the *Observatory* (Engel, 1833). On a terrace (extensive views) on the E side of the hill is a sculpture by Robert Stigell (1897), "The Shipwrecked Mariners". – To the W of Observatory Hill, at 19 Kasarmikatu, is the *Design Center*, and farther W again *St John's Church* (1893), with twin spires 74 m (243 ft) high. To the SW of St

John's stands the *Agricola Church* (1934), identified by its tall, slender spire. – Following the coast road (Ehrenströmintie) to the S, we come to Kalliolinnantie, where, at No. 14, is Marshal Mannerheim's house, now the *Mannerheim Museum*. Beyond this lies the beautifully situated "Park of the Spring", *Kaivopuisto*.

To the NE of the city, 15 minutes from the middle of Hämeentie (the road to Lahti), is the large *Arabia Porcelain Manufactory* (museum). A little way NE, at the mouth of the Vantaanjoki, is VANHAKAUPUNKI (the Old Town), the site on which Helsinki was founded in 1550. In Vanhakaupunkintie a stone on the left marks the position of the first church and churchyard. Farther along, on the right, is a wall of black granite with a *portrait of Gustavus Vasa*. On the ground is a slab inscribed with a plan of the original town, and on the highest point a triangular pillar topped by a sphere (B. Brunila, 1932).

SURROUNDINGS. – *To the SE of the city* (motorboats from Market Square) is the **Suomenlinna** (Swedish *Sveaborg*) group of islands, with the remains of the 18th c. fortress. The barracks house the "Nordic Art Centre" which is financed jointly by the four Scandinavian states and Iceland. – To the S (boats from Merisatamaranta, to the W of Kaivopuisto) lies the island of **Pihlajasaari** (Swedish *Rönnskär*; sandy beach).

*To the E* (by Itäväylä, the Porvoo road) is the suburb of **Herttoniemie** (7·5 km – 4½ miles), with the *Topelius Museum*, commemorating the poet Zachris Topelius (1818–98). – On the island of **Korkeasaari** (Swedish *Högholmen*: motorboats from North Harbour in 10 minutes, footbridge from Mustikkamaa recreation area) are the *Zoo* and a summer restaurant.

*To the W of the city*, linked to it by a footbridge, lies the island of **Seurasaari** (Swedish *Fölisö*), where can be seen an open-air museum with old peasant houses, the church of Karuna (1686) and other timber buildings. It can be reached by way of Mannerheimintie, then left along Linnankoskenkatu, right along Paciuksenkatu for a short distance, then left into Seurasaarentie, which leads to the bridge. Nearby, at 7 Meilahti, is an old timber house now occupied by the *Friends of Finnish Handicrafts*, with an exhibition of Rya carpets and other textiles and where visitors can watch weaving and knotting. – At 6 Tamminiementie (the continuation of Seurasaarentie) is the *Municipal Art Collection*. – On the other side of the bay, 6 km (4 miles) from the middle of the city on the road to Hanko (Länsiväylä), is the garden city of **Tapiola** (Swedish *Hagalund*; pop. 30,000), part of Espoo. Although dating from the 1950s, this is still an exemplary piece of modern town planning. To the NE, on the *Otaniemi* peninsula, stands the Helsinki College of Technology, with the striking Students' House, Dipoli (by A. Ruusuvuori and R. Paatelainen, 1966).

**Helsinki to Hanko** (135 km – 84 miles). – Leave Helsinki on the western Länsiväylä, in a SW direction, and in 3 km (2 miles) cross a 500 m (550 yd) long bridge to the island of *Lauttasaari* (camp site); then in another 3 km (2 miles) return to the mainland on a further bridge and continue past the garden city of Tapiola to *Stensvik* (14 km – 9 miles). – 5 km (3 miles) beyond this, Road 50 bears right to **Espoo** (8 km – 5 miles; old church), now the midpoint of an urban region with a population of about 150,000 (car museum with over 100 vehicles). – 7 km (4½ miles): *Kyrkslätt* (1 km (¾ mile) on right) has a stone church dating from the 14th c. (restored 1958–9) and the attractively situated *Hvitträsk*, a complex of buildings of architectural interest, including the studio of the architect Eliel Saarinen (museum; restaurant). To the S of the main road we come to the *Porkkala* peninsula, part of which was a Soviet base until 1956. – 9 km (5½ miles): road on right to *Siuntio* (Swedish *Sjundeå* 11 km – 7 miles), with a church (1460, old coats of arms). – Continue on Road 51: 38 km (24 miles) to *Karjaa* (Swedish *Karis*: Seurahuone Hotel, 18 b.), with a 14th c. stone church renovated by C. L. Engel in 1828–31. – Continue SW on Road 53, skirting the *Salpausselkä* ridge of hills. In 4 km (2½ miles) a road goes off on the left to *Snappertuna* (7 km – 4½ miles); 1 km (¾ mile) S of the church are the remains of *Raseborg Castle* (14th c.). – Road 53 continues past *Raasepori* station and another road to Snappertuna branches off on the left. Just before Ekenäs, on the left, are the barracks of the Dragsvik Brigade, the only Swedish-speaking brigade in the Finnish army (commands are given in Finnish). – 14 km (9 miles): **Ekenäs** (Finnish *Tammisaari* pop. 7500; Kaupungin-hotelli, 40 b., SB; Motel Marine, 70 b.; camp site), an attractive old town situated on a promontory, with a population which is 80% Swedish-speaking. It is a popular vacation resort in summer, as it has a beautiful beach. 17th c. stone church. – 1·5 km (1 mile) beyond Ekenäs, Road 52 goes off on the right to Turku: Road 53 continues SW. On the remaining 35 km (22 miles) to Hanko remains of various fortifications can be seen; they date from the period after the Winter War of 1939–40, when Finland was obliged to lease the Hanko area to the Soviet Union.

**Hanko** (Swedish *Hangö*: pop. 10,000; Regatta Hotel, 79 b.; Motel Silversand, 36 b.; camp site), located at the tip of a peninsula, is Finland's most southerly town – a commercial, industrial and tourist area and the only Finnish free port (rail ferry terminal). International sailing regatta and tennis tournament in July; open-air concerts and theatrical performances in summer; bathing beach 5 km (3 miles) long. – On the Vådberg are a church (1892) and a water-tower 50 m (165 ft) high (panoramic views of the city and sea). – Soviet war memorial (1960), with the graves of over 400 soldiers. On the offshore islands are old fortifications built by the Swedes in the 18th c. and destroyed by the Russians in 1854. In the East Harbour is a museum. – Approximately half the population of the town is Swedish-speaking.

**Helsinki to Turku via Lohja and Ekenäs** (219 km (136 miles); about 50 km (31 miles) longer than the direct road to Turku). – Leave Helsinki by way of Mannerheimintie and take the Turku motorway (highway). In 44 km (27 miles), at the end of the motorway, take Road 53, which runs SW, skirting a lake, and in 14 km (9 miles) reaches **Lohja** (Swedish *Lojo*: pop. 13,700; Laurinporti Inn, 31 b.; Hotel Lohjan Kievari, 22 b.; camp site), beautifully set in wooded country on the shores of the *Lohjanjärvi* (alt. 31 m (102 ft); area 110 sq. km (42 sq. miles); maximum depth 58 m – 190 ft); water-tower, with café (good view as far as Tallinn). The 14th c. church (restored 1886–9), built of undressed stone, contains fine

16th c. wall paintings. – 19 km (12 miles) NW is *Sammatti*. In the churchyard is the grave of E. Lönnrot (born on Paikkari farm, 4 km (2½ miles) N), collector and editor of the Finnish national epic "Kalevala". – Road 53 continues SW and is joined in 10 km (6 miles) by the road from Siuntio. – 23 km (14 miles): *Karjaa*. – 18 km (11 miles): *Ekenäs* (Finnish *Tammisaari*). Rewarding detour to Hanko. – Continue on Road 52 through flat country, thickly wooded. – 14 km (9 miles): *Tenala*, with a church first mentioned in the 14th c. 19 km (12 miles) SW, on a charming road which crosses an island and then runs around a bay, is *Bromarv*. Near here, in *Rilaks Bay*, Peter the Great defeated the Swedish fleet in 1714. – Continues on Road 52, via *Pernio* (21 km (13 miles): 14th–15th c. church); then another 22 km (14 miles) to **Salo** (Kaupunginhotelli, 55 b.; Salo, 42 b.), where Road 52 joins E3, coming from Helsinki: follow this road W to reach **Turku** (53 km (33 miles): see p. 273).

During the summer there are excursions from Helsinki to *Leningrad* by sea and bus (4 days).

# Hønefoss

Norway (Southern).
County: Buskerud fylke.
Altitude: 97 m (318 ft). – Population: 12,000.
Postal code: N-3500. – Telephone code: 0 67.
(i) **Ringerike Reiselivsforening,**
P.O. Box No. 289,
tel. 2 21 42.

HOTELS. – *Bergland*, 102 b., SB; *Grand Hotel*, 80 b.; *Klækken*, 130 b., SB, SP. – YOUTH HOSTEL. – CAMP SITE.

**The Norwegian town of Hønefoss, at the junction of the Begna (Ådal-selv) and the Randselv, is the industrial and administrative capital of the district of Ringerike. It is an important traffic junction. The Begna divides the town into a northern and a southern half, forming the double falls, the Hønefoss, from which it takes its name. The falls (hydroelectric power station) are impressive only when the water level is high.**

The falls have provided the basis for the town's industrial development; in 1668 there were 23 sawmills here. In addition to woodworking, the local industries include clothing factories and the manufacture of skis and tools.

SIGHTS IN SURROUNDING AREA. – An attractive trip from Hønefoss is via Klækken to the *Ringkollen* (701 m (2300 ft): 15 km (9 miles) E on a toll road; magnificent views, weather station). – 4 km (2½ miles) S of Hønefoss, on E68, is *Norderhov*, with a medieval church containing the tombs of the pastor, Jonas Ramus, and his wife, Anna Kolbjørnsdatter. The local legend has it that the lady enticed a hostile

Swedish force into an ambush in which the Swedish colonel, Löwen, was taken prisoner (1716). Souvenirs of the event are on display in the Ringerike Museum in the old presbytery. – In 10 km (6 miles) begins a beautiful stretch of road (3 km – 2 miles) along the **Steinsfjord** (on left). After this the road crosses the *Kroksund*, which links the Steinsfjord with the **Tyrifjord** (alt. 62 m – 203 ft); at the end of the bridge, on the right, is the Sundøya Restaurant. Then comes *Sundvollen*, 15 km (9 miles) from Hønefoss, a popular resort at the NE end of the Tyrifjord (alt. 76 m (250 ft); Sundvollen Hotel, 240 b.). To the S rises *Krokkleiva (443 m – 1453 ft), reached either by a 4 km (2½ mile) side road (toll) or by a "barrel lift" (*tønneheis*) 1266 m (4150 ft) long. Below the hill is the Kleivstua (restaurant; 24 b.), with the beautiful "Queen's View" (Dronningens Utsikt). There is an even finer view from the projecting spur of rock called the *King's View (Kongens Utsikt, 379 m – 1243 ft), 25 minutes' walk away.

3·5 km (2 miles) farther along E68, on the right, is the Tyrifjord Restaurant. There are a number of fine views of the fjord. 9·5 km (6 miles): *Skaret* (alt. 252 m – 827 ft), with a magnificent prospect of the Tyrifjord and Steinsfjord. Here Road 285 from Drammen (20·5 km – 13 miles) enters on the S. E68 now leaves the shores of the fjord and climbs 3 km (2 miles) E, with many bends, to *Sollihøgda* (341 m (1119 ft); inn). Magnificent view of the Tyrifjord below. – From here it is 28 km (17 miles) to Oslo via Sandvika (E18).

Road 7 runs NW from Hønefoss, passing (on the right) the large stone bridge carrying the Bergen railway. It then climbs gradually up the *Soknadal* and through *Sokna* (24 km (15 miles): alt. 143 m – 469 ft) to *Hamremoen* (14 km (9 miles): 135 m – 443 ft), with an old storehouse raised on posts. – 5 km (3 miles): *Noresund*, where a road goes off on the left (9·5 km (6 miles): toll) to the *Norefjell* (Fjellhvil Hotel, 96 b.), a popular skiing area, with facilities from the 1952 Olympics (two ski-lifts; chair-lift from 750 m (2450 ft) to 1000 m – 3300 ft). – The main road follows the E side of the beautiful *Lake Krø*deren (area 43 sq. km (17 sq. miles), length 41 km (25 miles), depth 119 m – 390 ft). – 22 km (14 miles): *Ørgenvika*. Higher up, to the right, is the end of the Haversting Tunnel (2312 m – 2500 yds) on the Bergen railway. – From here it is 13 km (8 miles) to Gulsvik, the gateway to the Hallingdal (see p. 115).

Road 68 runs N from Hønefoss on its way to the Valdres district (p. 282). An alternative route to Bjørgo is by Road 35, running along the E side of the Randsfjord, an additional distance of 37 km (23 miles).

Road 35 goes off on the right at *Hov*, 2 km (1¼ miles) from Hønefoss. E68 follows the valley of the *Begna* (*Ådalselv*), running through forest for part of the way, and after 29 k (18 miles), at Finsand (alt. 155 m – 509 ft), to *Lake Sperillen (alt. 148 m (486 ft); 23 km (15 miles) long, up to 2 km (1¼ miles) wide, up to 108 m (350 ft) deep). It then runs along the E shore of the lake for 26 km (16 miles). Shortly after the *Buttingsrud* camp site there is a view of the church at *Viker* on the other side of the lake. Before the road reaches Nes, it offers a glimpse of the church with its slender spire (1860).

*Nes i Ådal* (alt. 150 m (492 ft); pop. 250) lies on the right bank of the Begna above its outflow into Lake Sperillen. Road 243 goes off on the left (25 km – 15 miles) to *Hedal*, with a 13th c. stave church. The church was converted into a cruciform church in 1738

(restored 1901; fine furnishings). – From Hedal it is possible either to continue to Nesbyen (47 km – 30 miles) on an unmade road or to return to E68 at Begndal (6·5 km – 4 miles).

From Nes, E68 runs through wooded country along the left bank of the Begna. A few miles on it passes from Buskerud county into Oppland and enters the Valdres district.

The alternative route into Valdres, along the Randsfjord (Road 35), leaves E68 on the right at Hov, 2 km (1¼ miles) N of Hønefoss. As far as *Jevnaker* (13 km – 8 miles) there is an attractive alternative (beautiful scenery, large farms, fine views) from Hønefoss to Klaekken (5 km – 3 miles), then turning left into Road 241 (9 km – 5 miles).

*Jevnaker* (alt. 141 m (463 ft); pop. 3000) lies at the S end of the **Randsfjord**, the fourth largest lake in Norway (area 136 sq. km (53 sq. miles), length 73 km (45 miles), depth up to 108 m – 350 ft). The little town has two glass factories – *Hadelands Glassverk (1765: conducted tour) and Randsfjords Glassverk (1949) – as well as clothing manufacture and engineering works. – Road 35 continues along the E side of the lake. The road on the W side (87 km (55 miles) to Dokka) is of poorer quality but offers a wider variety of scenery. – 25 km (15 miles): *Tingelstad*, from which a side road runs a short distance E to *Halvdanshaugen*. In Halvdanshaugen are a Romanesque church (unsued) and the Hadeland Folkemuseum. – 4 km (2½ miles): *Brandbu* (alt. 178 m (584 ft); pop. 2000), which also lies on Road 4 (74 km (46 miles) to Oslo, 55 km (34 miles) to Gjøvik). – 5·5 km (3½ miles) S of Brandbu (3·5 km (2 miles) on Road 4, then a side road to the right) is *Gran*, with two old churches (c. 1100). Road 35 continues to *Røykenvik (4 km – 2½ miles); to the right is a hill with far-ranging views (*Brandbukampen*, 522 m – 1713 ft). Then on via *Hov i Land* (37 km (23 miles): alt. 134 m – 440 ft), with a church (1781), and *Fluberg* (11 km (7 miles): 155 m – 509 ft) which has a church (1703; altarpiece, 1752, a copy of one by Rubens), to *Singvoll* (2 km – 1¼ miles), where Road 33 goes off on the right to Gjøvik (28 km – 17 miles). Finally, via *Odnes* (ski-jump: record 108 m – 354 ft) to **Dokka** (14 km (9 miles): alt. 148 m (486 ft); pop. 2000; Centrum Hotel, 21 b.), main town of the district of Nordre Land. Local museum with 15 old houses. The Dokkaelv flows into the *Etna* here. The road from Jevnaker, along the W side of the Randsfjord (No. 245), joins Road 35, which follows the valley of the Etna. – 5 km (3 miles): *Nordsinni* church (built at Haugnar in 1758, moved to Nordsinni in 1898, restored 1961; beautiful interior). – 8 km (5 miles): *Møllerstugufossen*, with 12 rock carvings about 4000 years old. – 16 km (10 miles): *Tonsåsen* (alt. 624 m – 2047 ft), where a road enters on the left from Bagn. – Soon afterward Road 33 reaches its pinnacle (726 m – 2382 ft), and then drops down to 510 m (1673 ft) at *Bjørgo* (12 km – 7½ miles), in the wooded Valdres district, where it meets E68, on the way from Hønefoss.

# Lake Inari
## (Inarijärvi/Enareträsk)

Finland (Northern).
Province: Lapin lääni (Lapplands län/Lapland).

*Lake Inari is the third largest lake in Finland (area 1100 sq. km (425 sq. miles), length 80 km (50 miles), width 41 km – 25 miles) – although because of its many indentations and ramifications it is not possible to determine its exact size. The number of islands in the lake is usually given as 3000. This bizarre area straddling the 69th parallel is one of Finland's most fascinating regions.

The shores of the lake are rocky. The trees found here are spruce, pine and birch, in dwarf Arctic forms; on the NW shores of the lake, NE of *Partakko* (on the Kaamanen–Sevettijärvi road), the line above which the spruce will not grow reaches down to the lake. Here the climate is of Arctic severity until well into spring, since the Scandinavian mountains block the moderating influence of the Gulf Stream which washes the Norwegian coasts. The ice on the lake frequently does not disappear until June. In this region the final phase of winter merges almost imperceptibly into the beginning of summer, with at most one or two weeks which can be regarded as spring.

Visitors heading for Norway on Road 4 will get some impression of this strange area on the stretch of road between Ivalo and Inari. Those spending at least one night in the region should include in their itinerary a boat trip on the lake, perhaps to the island of *Ukkokivi*. In pagan times the island was regarded by the Lapps as the most sacred of the many islands of Inarijärvi.

The lake, which extends from NE to SW, is served by only three roads. Road 4, coming from the S (Sodankylä), runs along the SW shore; beyond Inari it runs N. Beyond *Kaamanen* the road forks: No. 4 turns W in the direction of *Karigasniemi* and the Norwegian frontier, while Road 970 continues N to *Utsjoki* and then follows the River *Tenojoki* to *Nuorgam*. From Kaamanen, a little country road runs NE to Partakko and the Skolt village of *Sevettijärvi* and, after about 130 km (81 miles), reaches the Norwegian frontier 10 km (6 miles) before Neiden. From *Ivalo*, Road 9681 runs NE to *Nellimö* and the Soviet frontier (no entry). Visitors cannot approach the frontier itself either by car or on foot, since a strip of territory on the Finnish side 1 km (¾ mile) wide is closed

On Lake Inari (Finnish Lapland)

except to permit-holders. It is patrolled by frontier guards. (Under a frontier agreement between Finland and the Soviet Union, both countries are required to protect the frontier.)

There are no motor roads on the much-indented NE side of the lake, and even walkers find this difficult country, since much of it is boggy and impassable. There are no villages here, just isolated cottages and huts.

There is good fishing on the shores of the lake, around the islands and on the open lake. Information about fishing permits can be obtained in the villages and hotels. Although in this thinly populated region the enforcement of the regulations may be difficult, visitors who fish without permission will be unpopular with the local people.

The commune of Inari is the largest in Finland, with an area of 17,000 sq. km (6560 sq. miles). Of its population of 7000 people, a fifth are Lapps (Samer). In the village of Inari, there are separate schools for Lapps and Finns.

The great attraction of this region is its unspoiled natural scenery. Large areas show no trace of the hand of man. There is no need, therefore, to head for any particular spot: the whole region is beautiful.

**Ivalo** (Ivalo Hotel, 189 b.; camp site, with chalets, to the S of the village), on the *Ivalojoki*, spanned by a large bridge, has the most northerly airport in Finland. Halfway between Ivalo and Inari is the *Karhunpesäkivi* ("Bear's Den Rock"), with a café, picnic area and telephone; fishing.

**Inari** (Inari Touristhotel, 46 b.; Sommerhotel Muotkan Ruoktu, 14 b. outside the town), at the outflow of the *Joenjoki* (good fishing) into the lake, has a high school for Lapps. Next to the forestry office is a *Lapp Open-Air Museum* (Lapp village). A walk of 7·5 km (4½ miles) to the NE leads to the old Lapp church of *Pielppajärvi* (originally 17th c., rebuilt 1762). In earlier times, the Lapps had to bury their dead on islands in the lake, since the bears (still numerous here in the 19th c.) used to dig up the graves.

A boat trip on the rivers *Ivalojoki* and *Lemmenjoki* offers unspoiled natural scenery.

# Jämtland

Sweden (Central).
Province: Jämtlands län.

(i) **Jämtland-Härjedalens Turistförening,**
Storgatan 16,
S-83126 Ostersund;
tel. (0 63) 14 40 01.
**Härjedalsfjells Turistbyrå,**
Rörosvägen 17,
S-82095 Funäsdalen;
tel. (06 84) 2 14 20.

EVENTS. – Every summer geological, botanical, musical and dancing weeks are organised in Jämtland. Information about dates can be obtained from tourist information offices.

**Jämtland, a mountainous province of central Sweden bordering on Norway, is one of the last unspoiled natural regions in Europe. Only 1·4% of the area of this well-wooded territory is under cultivation. With its great expanses of lush green pastureland, its crystal-clear rivers and its snow-capped peaks, Jämtland is equally attractive in both summer and winter. Here animals threatened with extinction (including the bear, the glutton – similar to the wolverine – and rare species of**

marten) **live undisturbed, and Jämtland's 3000 lakes and streams contain many species of fish to attract the angler. The best months for fishing the mountain streams are July and August; in the forest regions June is preferable.**

The capital of the province of Jämtland is **Östersund** (p. 219), on the Storsjö, from which Road 14 runs W to the Norwegian frontier.

**Järpen** (alt. 324 m (1063 ft); hotels: Hållandsgården, 90 b.; Sundets Fjällgard, 45 b.) is a busy little industrial town on the Indalsälv (power station), which drains the *Kallsjö* (N of the town). The area is well wooded. To the W, beyond the Indalsälv, the *Rista Falls* (14 m (45 ft) high) tumble into the Åreälv. The calcareous soil favours the growth of mosses and other simple plant forms.

**Åre** (alt. 378 m (1240 ft): hotels: Åregården, 400 b., SB; Årevidden, 200 b., SB; Björnen, 125 b., SB; Diplomat, 100 b.; Fjällgarden, 75 b.; Sunwing, 820 b., SB.) a popular mountaineering and winter sports resort, has an old stone church probably dating from the 13th c. with a well-known representation of St Olof. A cableway goes up to about 1300 m (4267 ft); there are several chair-lifts and ski-tows. A funicular runs up to the *Östrå Platå* (Eastern Plateau, 557 m – 1828 ft), from which two double chair-lifts go up to the *Mörvikshummel* (887 m – 2911 ft; inn). To the N rears **Åreskutan** (1420 m – 4659 ft) from which there is a magnificent view. 8 km (5 miles) W of Åre lies the winter sports resort of **Duved** (384 m – 1260 ft; Hotel Duved Gården, 47 b.) lifts to the *Mullfjåll* (1031 m – 3384 ft).

To the W of Duved, Road 322 goes off on the right and runs NW to the * * **Tännfors**, a waterfall in a nature reserve. The Indalsälv pours into the *Nornsjö* from a

The Tännfors falls (Jämtland)

height of 32 m (105 ft), with a width of 60 m (200 ft) to make this one of the finest waterfalls in the N.

**Storlien** (alt. 592 m (1942 ft); hotels: Storlien, 31 b.; Storliens Högfjällshotell, 509 b., SB; Storvallens Stughotell, 141 b. in chalets, SB), with Sweden's highest railway station, lies in a popular winter sports area (numerous lifts). In summer there is pleasant canoeing. The Norwegian frontier is 4 km (2½ miles) W of Storlien.

**Strömsund** (alt. 288 m (945 ft); Grand Hotell, 60 b.) is reached from Östersund on Road 88, running NE. It is a trim little place set in fertile country. To the S lies the *Russfjärd*. 2·5 km (1½ miles) NE, on the *Grelsgård*, stands a lookout tower with a view extending to the mountains on the Norwegian frontier. – To the NW the string of lakes known as *Ströms Vattudal* extends to the Norwegian frontier. This lake system, through which the *Faxälv* flows, is a paradise for anglers. Near the frontier is a nature reserve, with the *Hällingsafall* (waterfall, 55 m high, 10 m wide). – To the N, via a minor road from Gäddede, is *Ankarede*, a traditional meeting-place of the Lapps, with a chapel (1896). The annual Lapp fair held here in the middle of summer attracts many visitors.

E of Östersund, in the Ragunda valley (Road 87), is **Hammarstrand** (Lergodset Hotell, 36 b.; camp-site), at the foot of the *Kullstaberg*. From the lookout terrace on the hill there is a view of the *Indalsälv*, which, until 1796, was a lake 15 m (50 ft) deep. The lake disappeared within four hours on the night of 6–7 June 1796, when a channel for rafts was opened.

# Joensuu

Finland (Eastern).
Province: Pohjois-Karjalan lääni (Norra Karelens län/ Northern Karelia).
Altitude: 79 m (260 ft). – Population: 44,000.
Postal code: SF-80100. – Telephone code: 973.
(i) **Pohjois-Karjalan Matkallutoimisto**,
  Koskikatu 1;
  tel. 2 51 14.

HOTELS. – *Karelia*, Kauppakatu 25, 68 b.; *Kimmel*, Itarante 1, 300 b., SB; *Pohjois-Karjala*, Torikatu 20, 100 b.; *Viehka*, Kauppakatu 32, 68 b.; *Wanha-Jokela*, Torikatu 26, 21 b.; *Wiiri*, Suvilkatu 19, 113 b. (1 May to 31 August). – CAMP SITE.

EVENTS. – *Sirmakka*, festival of Karelian music (June); *Orthodox Festival* in Ilomantsi-Hattuvaara (28 and 29 June and 19 and 20 July in the church, in August at Ilomantsi-Mustalahti); *Huttujuhlat*, traditional local festival with open-air dramatic performances (September).

**Joensuu, situated at the outflow of the Pielisjoki into the Pyhäselkä, on the NE fringe of the Finnish Lake Plateau, was founded in 1848. It is**

Joensuu – a bird's-eye view

**now the cultural, administrative and commercial capital of Northern Karelia, and has one of the most recent universities in Finland.**

SIGHTS. – The **Town Hall** (by E. Saarinen, 1914), with a massive tower, also houses the *Municipal Theatre*. Between the Town Hall and the Market Square lies the *Freedom Park*. Near the Town Hall, on the river, is the quay used by the boats for Savonlinna and Koli and by cruise boats. From this part of the town Saarikatu crosses a bridge on to the island of Niskasaari, from which another bridge leads to Ilosaari. On this island are a bathing beach and the **Karelian House**, founded in 1954 to promote Karelian culture (interesting museum). – A short distance upstream, on the site of the original town, is the *Library* (art gallery). Also in this area we find the Eastern Orthodox **St Nicholas's Church**, and at the mouth of the river the *Hasanniemi open-air theatre* (revolving stage), with a camp site and walkers' hostel close by. Immediately adjoining the camp site is a beach, and there is an indoor swimming pool beside the sports ground across from the hostel.

SURROUNDINGS. – 17 km (10 miles) W, on the shores of the Orivesi, near Liperi, is *Harila holiday village*. – 71 km (45 miles) E on Road 74 is **Ilomantsi** (Hotel Ilomantsi, 80 b.; camp site), with an Eastern Orthodox church. SE of the town is the *Petkeljärvi Nature Park*. – 72 km (45 miles) W, between Joensuu and Varkaus, are the Orthodox monastery of *Uusi Valamo* and nunnery of *Lintula* (see p. 92). – **Koli Hills**: see p. 162.

# Jönköping

Sweden (Southern).
Province: Jönköping län. – Region: Småland.
Altitude: 91 m (300 ft). – Population: 107,000.
Postal code: S-55 . . . – Telephone code: 0 36.
(i) **Jönköpings Turistbyrå,**
Västra Storgatan 9;
tel. 16 90 50.

HOTELS. – *City Hotel*, Västra Storgatan 23–25, 100 b.; *Grand Hotel*, Hovrättstorget, 100 b.; *Klosterkungen*, Klostergatan 26, 199 b., SB; *Portalen*, Västra Storgatan 9, 286 b.; *Ramada*, Huskvarna, Strandväg, 1, 226 b., SB; *Scandic Hotel*, Rosenlund, 369 b.; *Stora Hotellet*, Hotellsplan, 185 b.

EVENTS. – "*Green World*" (garden show, all year); *Scandinavian Game Fair* (May); International Trade Fair on Forestry and Sawmilling Technology (June).

**Jönköping, beautifully set at the southern tip of Lake Vättern, was granted its municipal charter by Magnus Ladulås in 1284. It is now a focus point for agriculture and forestry, a commune which has grown to considerable size with the incorporation of Huskvarna and Gränna; it is also the head-quarters of the governor of Jönköping province. Destroyed several times by fire, the town was largely rebuilt, beginning in 1835.**

SIGHTS. – In the original heart of the town between Lake Vättern and the two small lakes of Munksjö and Rocksjö a number of older buildings have been preserved. In *Hovrättstorget* are the *Provincial Court* (Göta Hovrätt; 1639–55) and the former *Town Hall* (late 17th c.). To the NE is the *Kristina Church* (1649–73), and to the SE the *Provincial Museum* (Länsmuseet), with a collection which includes Småland pottery and ironware and primitive art.

The match factory, to the W of the station, was founded in 1844 by J. E. Lundström and achieved world renown for the production of safety matches (1852 onward; *Match Museum*). Farther W lies the large *Municipal Park*, in which are an *Ornithological Museum* (some 1400 species, rich collection of eggs), an *Open-Air Museum* with interesting old wooden houses from Småland (15th–18th c.), *Bäckaby church* and an 18th c. *belfry* from Solberga.

SURROUNDINGS. – 14 km (9 miles) S is the **Taberg** (343 m – 1125 ft), a hill of iron ore (no longer worked) which is now a nature reserve and attracts many

visitors. From the summit there are extensive views as far as 80 km (50 miles) in good weather. – 15 km (10 miles) NW of Jönköping is *Habo church*, a large red timber building (16th c.). The interior walls of the church are covered with vividly coloured paintings on Biblical themes in Peasant Baroque style.

# Jostedalsbre

Norway (Western).
County: Sogn og Fjordane fylke.
Altitude: 2038 m (6687 ft).

**The *Jostedalsbre, between the Sognefjord to the S and the Nord-fjord to the N, is the largest ice sheet in continental Europe (almost 100 km (60 miles) long), comparable to the great icefields of Greenland.**

Together with the adjoining icefields the Jostedalsbre covers an area of over 1000 sq. km (380 sq. miles). Only a few low rocky hummocks emerge from the ice, the depth of which is estimated to be some 500 m (1650 ft). Twenty-six major glaciers reach down into the surrounding valleys, including the Tundbergdalsbre, the largest glacier in Europe after the Aletsch glacier in Switzerland. Since the ice of these glaciers, like the ice almost everywhere in Norway, has been retreating for many years, the ascent to the ice sheet has become steadily steeper and more strenuous.

At *Røneid*, on the *Lusterfjord* (on the S shore stands the Urnes stave church), Road 604 branches off Road 55, which runs along the N shore of the fjord, and makes its way up the *Jostedal*, a rift

Bøydal glacier, Jostedalsbre

running from N to S through the massive mountain plateau and bounded on the W by the Jostedalsbre. The road follows the course of the tumultuous Jostedalselv.

25 km (15 miles) from Røneid is **Jostedal** (alt. 201 m – 659 ft), with a wooden church (1660). The road continues over the *Høgebru*. At *Gjerde*, a narrow road goes off on the left into the *Krundal* and continues to Bergset, with *Høgenipa* (1535 m – 5036 ft) rearing above the valley on the S.

From *Bergset* there is a magnificent but strenuous climb (3 hours, with guide) past the *Bjørnestegbre* to the *Jostedalsbre*, continuing over the icefield to the *Høgste Breakullen* (1953 m – 6408 ft); from there an hour's walk NW, when an impressive view of the mountains along the Nordfjord appears; then a descent (sometimes difficult) through the *Kvanndal* to *Nesdal*, near the S end of the *Loenvatn*.

From Gjerde, Road 604 continues N. At *Elvekrok* (alt. 340 m – 1116 ft) a private road bears off on the left to the *Nigardsbre.

To the NW of the Jostedalsbre, Road 60 runs along the **Innvikfjord**. Near the E end of the fjord, at *Olden* (church, 1746–49, restored 1971), a road branches off and runs S into the beautiful *Olderdal*. After passing the *Oldenvatn* (11 km (7 miles) long) and numerous waterfalls, it comes to *Briksdal* (alt. 150 m – 492 ft). From Briksdal a footpath leads, in one hour, to the **Birksdalsbre*, an arm of the Jostedalsbre rearing its blue masses of ice above the scrub forest.

# Jotunheim

Norway (Western).
Counties: Oppland fylke, Sogn og Fjordane fylke.
Altitude: 2468 m (8098 ft).

The *Jotunheim, the largest of the few Alpine-type regions on the Norwegian high plateau, extends from the Sognefjord in the W to the Gudbrandsdal in the NE. Its name ("Home of Giants") was coined by Norwegian students, referring to the "frost and ice giants" of the Edda. Most of the mountains in the Jotunheim rise to heights of no more than 1800–2000 m (6000–6500 ft), but the region also includes the

highest peaks in Scandinavia, *Galdøpig (2469 m – 8098 ft) and *Glittertind (2452 m – 8045 ft). The valleys mostly lie above the tree-line and are notably barren. Magnificent views of rocky crags and fields of ice add up to a memorable experience of natural beauty.

The Jotunheim is best reached from the Lillehammer–Trondheim road (E6), branching off at *Otta* into Road 15, which runs W to the Nordfjord (see p. 197). Following this road up the Ottadal, we come to **Vågåmo**, with the church of *Vågå* (first mentioned in 1270; font, 1050), and continue along the S side of the *Vågåvatn* via *Randen* to **Lom** (stave church), where we take Road 55, which runs through the *Bøverdal* in the direction of the Sognefjord (p. 239). To the SE extends the **Jotunheim**, which can be explored on foot from a number of bases in the valley.

At *Galdesand* a road branches off to the left and climbs steeply (21 bends, with extensive views) to the *Juvvashytta* (14 km – 9 miles). This mountain hut, in a rugged and treeless region, is the highest point in Norway reachable by car (1817 m – 5963 ft).

From the Juvvashytta, *Galdhøpig, the highest mountain in Scandinavia (2469 m – 8098 ft), can be climbed in 4 hours (guide required). From the summit there are superb views: to the E, beyond the *Visdal*, towers *Glittertind (2452 m – 8045 ft), with its massive crown of snow.

Sognefjell (Jotunheim)

Beyond Galdesand, Road 55 continues along the *Leirdal*, passing the splendidly situated hotel *Jotunheimen Fjellstue* (125 b.). It then ascends the *Breiseterdal*, through magnificent mountain scenery, to the **Sognefjell**, a pass used since time immemorial (1440 m – 4725 ft). To the left is an impressive glacier, the *Smørstabbre*. Beyond the pass, the road descends past a number of mountain lakes and a magnificent viewpoint at *Oscarshaug to the *Turtagrø* hotel. This is a good base for walks and climbs in the *Hurrungane (*Horunger*), the finest mountain group in the Jotunheim.

A particularly rewarding climb in the Hurrungane is to the **Skagastølsbotn**, with the *Skagastølsbre* glacier and the *Skagastølstinder* behind it. This ascent takes about 3 hours; if a climb of the *Store Skagatølstind* (2404 m (7888 ft): strenuous) is included, an additional 4 hours should be allowed. – To the E of Turtagrø is *Fanaråk (2075 m – 6808 ft), which can be climbed in 4–5 hours, and to the NW *Klypenåsi (1145 m (3757 ft: 2½ hours). For all these climbs a guide is required.

Gjendesheim climbers' hostel (Jotunheim)

From Turtagrø the road winds its way downhill to Hauge, on the Lusterfjord (see p. 239).

In the southern part of the Jotunheim there are many beautiful lakes. From *Randen*, on the S side of the Vagavatn, Road 51 passes the *Lemonsjø* and below *Rindehøvda* (155 m – 509 ft), a fine view. It continues up the *Sjodal*, passing a series of small lakes, to *Maurvängen*. A little way W is *Lake Gjende. Bygdin*, beyond the *Valdresflya* plateau, much of which is covered with bog, is situated between Lake Bygdin (on the right) and the *Vinstervatn* (on the left).

On **Lake Bygdin**, motorboats ply between Bygdin and the *Eidsbugaren Høyfjellshotel* (Høyfjell Museum). From there a road (3·5 km – 2 miles) which affords panoramic views leads up to the *Tyinholmen Hotel*, on the N side of *Lake Tyin* (area 35 sq. km (13½ sq. miles); motorboat trips), the shores of which are uninhabited. In a commanding setting on the S side of the lake stands the *Tyin Høyfjellshotel*.

# Jutland (Jylland)

Denmark.
Counties: Sønderjyllands amt, Ribe amt, Vejle amt, Ringkøbing amt, Århus amt, Viborg amt and Nordjyllands amt.

**The peninsula of Jutland (Jylland), the largest geographical unit in Denmark, extends N from the mainland of Germany (Schleswig-Holstein), bounded by the North Sea, the Skagerrak and the Kattegat. Its southern border with Germany is Denmark's only land frontier. Jutland offers a wide variety of attractions, including beautiful bathing beaches, wide expanses of heath and woodland and interesting towns.**

Formerly devoted exclusively to farming and fishing, Jutland now has well-developed industries, though agriculture still plays an important part in its economy (export of pork and bacon). Its land, half of which was still covered by heath as recently as the 19th c., has been settled and made fertile. The drift of population from Jutland to Copenhagen has been halted, and indeed to some extent reversed: the attractions of life in the country's smaller towns are now increasingly appreciated.

The line of the Danish-German frontier, long disputed and fought over, was finally established in 1920 after a referendum and reinforced after the German occupation of 1940–5. In recent years the Danish minority S of the frontier and the German minority in Jutland have established reasonably good-neighbourly relations.

The beauty and interest of Jutland can be discovered in the two itineraries suggested here, with a variety of attractive excursions. One route goes along the W side of the peninsula at some distance from the coast; the other traverses eastern Jutland, ending at Frederikshavn, from which there is a ferry service to Gothenburg in Sweden; there are also services to Larvik, Oslo and Frederikstad in Norway.

**Tønder to Holstebro** (Road 11). – Starting from the frontier village of *Sæd*, the road comes to **Tønder** (pop. 7500; Hostrups Hotel, 46 b.; youth hostel; camp site), referred to as a "good harbour" by the Arab geographer Idrisi as early as 1130. In the 16th c. a series of dikes was built to protect the town from frequent flooding; as a consequence this former port town is now more than 10 km (6 miles) from the coast. Tønder has an old established lace-making industry, the products of which are still much in demand. The town has preserved many old buildings, including the Digegrevens Gård in Vestergade and the Old Pharmacy in Østergade. The Kristkirke (richly decorated interior) has a tower belonging to an earlier church. The Museum contains interesting collections of Dutch tiles and pillow-lace. The town is now the nesting place of many of the storks which used to make their homes in Ribe and other Jutland towns.

To the W of the town is the district of *Møgeltønder*, probably older than Tønder itself, with a church whose earliest parts date from about 1200. The organ is one of the oldest in the country. Slotsgade, lined with old houses, leads N to *Schackenborg Castle*. The park was laid out in the 17th c.; the present building is 19th c.

From *Brede* it is well worth making a detour to **Løgumkloster** (pop. 2000; Løgumkloster Hotel, 32 b.; youth hostel), with a Cistercian abbey founded in 1144. This now serves as a religious folk high school and for other ecclesiastical purposes. Of the old monastic buildings only part of the E wing remains. The church (1173–1300), in a mingling of Romanesque and Gothic styles, has no tower; it contains an altarpiece (*c.* 1500) and a painted reliquary (1300). – Opposite the main buildings stands a 25 m (80 ft) high tower, with a carillon (plays at 8 and 11 a.m. and 3 and 9 p.m.).

Along the W coast of Jutland are massive dikes designed to protect the land from the devastating storm tides which used to wreak havoc; in 1634, for example, 6000 people and 50,000 head of cattle were drowned in a single night. A side road at *Skærbæk* goes down to the coast.

A causeway 5 km (3 miles) long leads on to the island of **Rømø** (area 99·7 sq. km – 38 sq. miles), a popular seaside resort, separated from the German island of Sylt by the Listerdyb. The sandy beach on the W coast is one of the finest in Denmark; the E side of the island is covered with heather. In the *Kommandørgard* at **Toftum**, at the N end of the island, is a local museum. At the S end stands the "Seamen's Church", with a Renaissance pulpit, a Baroque altar and five votive models of ships; in the churchyard are the graves of 17th and 18th c. whaler captains. From *Havneby* a ferry service serves Sylt. Several rare species of birds breed on the mud-flats.

The main road runs N from Skærbæk to *Brøns*, which has a massive church built of stone from the Rhineland (interesting frescoes). – From **Ribe** (see p, 223) an attractive country road goes off on the right to *Gram*, where the castle is set in a beautiful park on the shores of a small lake. A narrow road continues to *Fole* (13th c. church).

Beyond Ribe a road runs NE to **Vejen**. In the *Billingland* is an interesting collection of remote-controlled model aircraft and ships. – At *Gredstedbro* a road goes off on the left to **Esbjerg** (p. 88) but A11 continues N to Varde crossing A1 (Esbjerg–Copenhagen) near the small airport of Skast.

**Varde** (pop. 10,000; Hotel Hojskoleh-jemmet, 22 b.; leisure park), a busy little industrial town, has a number of old houses and an interesting local museum (furniture and decorative art from the Renaissance to the present day).

The coastal region, which begins to the W of Varde and extends northward for a considerable distance, is particularly attractive. At *Blåvand* is *Blåvands Huk*, the most westerly point in Denmark. The road to Blåvand passes through *Oksbøl*, which has a Romanesque church with 13th c. frescoes. Inland from the coast are a series of plantations designed to protect against drifting sand. In the Blåbjerg plantation is the *Blåbjerg*, a 64 m (210 ft) high dune (fine views of the

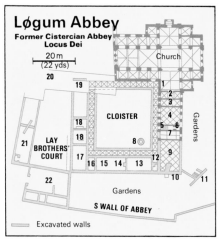

**Løgum Abbey**
Former Cistercian Abbey
Locus Dei

20 m
(22 yds)

Church

Gardens

CLOISTER

LAY BROTHERS' COURT

Gardens

S WALL OF ABBEY

Excavated walls

1 Former stair to dormitory
2 Sacristy (treasury above)
3 Library
4 Chapterhouse
5 Stair to dormitory (archive room below)
6 Lockup
7 Passage
8 Well
9 Room for study and work
10 Heating furnace
11 Monks' reredorter (toilet)
12 Stair to upper floor
13 Monks' refectory
14 Kitchen
15 Warming room/pantry?
16 Cellarer's parlour
17 Lay brothers' refectory (dormitory above)
18 Store-rooms
19 Presumed site of the Cloister Gate
20 "Palace" (abbot's lodging?) now courthouse
21 Workshop and stable?
22 Infirmary and lay brothers' reredorter (toilet); workshops; store-room

surrounding area). The coast road now runs along the spit of land (*Holmsland*) between the *Ringkøbing Fjord* and the sea. Half-way along is **Hvide Sande** (hotels: Skodbjerge, 65 b.; Sømandshjemmet, 32 b.; camp site), a fishing port and tourist resort. The whole of this area forms an interesting bird sanctuary.

At *Skjern* a road branches off on the left to **Ringkøbing** (pop. 6300; Fjordgården Hotel, 111 b.; youth hostel; two camp sites), which has a squat brick church of the late medieval period. The Museum contains a large collection of coins and a collection of material from Greenland assembled by the explorer Mylius Erichsen. – On the coast, 9 km (6 miles) NW, surrounded by dunes, is the resort of *Søndervig* (Hotel Søndervig, 44 b.; Strandkroen, 28 b.; two camp sites). – Road 16 runs N from Ringkøbing to *Hee*, with a granite church (restored in the 19th c.); leisure park "Sommerland West", wildlife park and bird sanctuary. NW of Hee, on a minor road, lies *Stadil*, at the N end of the *Stadil Fjord*. The church has a famous "Golden Altar" (Renaissance, *c.* 1625). A gilded bronze relief of about 1200 is set in the central panel of the altar. – Road 16 continues to *Ulfborg*, where there is an interesting church and *Nørre Vosborg Castle*, protected against either enemy attack or flooding by ramparts measuring up to 6 m (20 ft) high.

From Ringkøbing, Road 15 runs E to join Road 11 and continues to **Herning** (pop. 33,000; Eyde Hotel, 163 b.; Missionshotel, 77 b.; Østergårds Hotel, 160 b.; youth hostel; camp site). The town had but 21 inhabitants in 1840; it now figures importantly in commerce and industry (textiles). The Angligård, originally a factory, now houses a technical college and a museum of art. Around the inner courtyard of the building, which is in a circular layout, runs a ceramic frieze (200 m (650 ft) long, by C. H. Pedersen). – From Herning, Road 18 runs NW to Holstebro, where it joins Road 11.

**Holstebro** (pop. 25,000; Schaumburg Hotel, 65 b.; Krabbes Hotel, 27 b.; Bel Air, 114 b.; youth hostel; camp site), located on the *Storå*, is first mentioned in the records in 1274. In addition to several museums, the most interesting of which is the Museum of Art (Danish painting and sculpture, etc.), it has the unusual Nørreland Church (1969), built around an inner courtyard (carillon). – From Holstebro a road to the W crosses the heath to the coast.

Road 11 runs through *Vejrum* (old church) and *Struer* via the narrow causeway which separates *Nissum Bredning* (Broads) from Venø Bugt (Bight) to the long peninsula of Thy with its miles of natural beauty-spots and the N shore of **Limfjord** (see p. 177).

From Holstebro, a minor road leads NE to *Vinderup* (Vinderup Hotel, 32 b.), to the E of which we find *Sahl* church, with a beautiful "golden" altar and extensive views from the top of the tower. Nearby is the **Hjerl Hede** nature park (1000 hectares – 2500 acres), on the Flyndersø, with an open-air museum, *Den gamle Landsby* (30 old buildings).

NE of Vinderup is *Håsum*, from where a road runs W to the churches of *Lem* and *Lihme* (the oldest church of dressed granite in northern Jutland). – NW of Håsum is **Spøttrup Castle**, the oldest part of which (the S wing) was built about 1450. Some of the rooms were remodelled in late Baroque style, and the building was restored in 1937. The castle is surrounded by a double moat; park, with a collection of medicinal herbs.

**Skive** (pop. 17,000; Hilltop Hotel, 125 b.; Gammel Skivehus, 120 b.; camp site) lies on the Skive Fjord, on the E side of the Salling peninsula. The Old Church (12th c.) has 16th c. frescoes.

## Kruså to Frederikshavn (E3).

– The route starts from the frontier village of *Kruså*. To the NE, on the *Nybøl Nor*, an offshoot of the Flensborg Fjord, is **Gråsten** (pop. 3000; Hotel Axelhus, 10 b.; camp site), the Queen's summer residence. The castle, built in 1709 and rebuilt after a fire in 1759, has a richly decorated Baroque chapel.

Gråsten is surrounded by a wide expanse of forest and lakes, with many Stone Age tombs. On a peninsula 8 km (5 miles) SE is *Broager*; church with two imposing towers (good views), decorated with frescoes of the 13th–16th c.

At *Dybbøl* are old entrenchments which Prussian forces took by storm in 1864 during the Danish-German war and the later Schleswig-Holstein wars, opening the way to Alsen (p. 58). The Dybbøl windmill, rebuilt four times, has become a symbol of Danish resistance to German expansion.

**Åbenrå** (pop. 20,000; Grand Hotel, 75 b.; Hvide Hus, 100 b.; youth hostel; camp site), attractively situated on the Åbenrå Fjord, is an old fishing town with the largest harbour in southern Jutland. The older parts of the town have preserved all the charm of the past. The Museum has a section devoted to ships and the sea, including a collection of ships in bottles.

The beautiful N coast of the fjord can be reached on minor roads. In the hilly *Løjtland* area is *Løjt church*, with a late Gothic altar (four panels) and perfectly preserved frescoes (*c.* 1530). – To the N of Løjt is the *Knivsbjerg*, with extensive views over the bay.

Between Åbenrå and Haderslev, E3 runs at some distance from the coast. Along the coast are some of the most popular beaches in Jutland. The inland area is heavily wooded. The climate of the Baltic is much milder than that of the North Sea.

**Haderslev** (pop. 21,000; Haderslev Motel, 60 b.; Norden, 64 b.; youth hostel; camp site), on the narrow Haderslev Fjord, was a busy trading town as early as the 12th c. The present town is dominated by the Cathedral, dating in part from the 13th c., with rich furnishings including a bronze font and a Baroque pulpit; the altar has a modern altar screen with 15th c. figures of Apostles; 13th c. crucifix. To the W of the old town stands St Severin's Church; to the E is an open-air museum with prehistoric exhibits and old houses.

3 km E of the town, on the Årøsund road, is *Starup church*. The oldest parts of the church date from the 11th or 12th c. From Årøsund a ferry crosses to the island of **Årø**.

E3 continues to *Christiansfeld*, founded in 1773 by the Moravian Brethren; the old part has preserved its original unity. The church (1776), plain and undecorated, has neither altar nor pulpit, only a liturgical table. – NE of Christiansfeld rises the hill of *Skamlingsbanken*, a memorial site which attracts many visitors (good views, extending as far as Funen).

Runic stones, Jelling

**Kolding** (pop. 42,000; hotels: Kolding, 80 b.; Saxildhus, 148 b.; Tre Roser, 220 b.; youth hostel; camp site.), on the Kolding Fjord, is an old trading town and hub of communications. Koldinghus Castle built as a frontier fortress in the early 13th c., is surrounded by a lake which was formerly part of the fjord. Destroyed by fire in 1808, it was not completely restored until after 1900. It contains a collection of art, handicrafts and militaria. A romantic path, the "Lovers' Walk", runs along the shores of the castle lake. In the middle of the town are a number of well-preserved 16th and 17th c. houses. – To the SE of the town is the "Geographical Garden", with plants from all over the world (largest bamboo grove in Europe, gigantic trees from California).

Just N of Kolding E66 (highway) branches off on the right and runs E over the Little Belt to Funen (p. 95). Shortly before the bridge over the Little Belt a road branches off on the left to Fredericia.

**Fredericia** (pop. 36,000; hotels: Hyby-Lund, 24 b.; Landsoldaten, 122 b.; Postgården, 115 b.; youth hostel; camp site), was founded in the mid-17th c. to protect communications with the islands and was laid out on a regular plan. The town began to expand only after the demolition of the fortifications in 1909. A bronze figure of the "Valiant Soldier" commemorates the Danish victory over Schleswig-Holstein in 1849.

NE of Fredericia, on *Trelde Næs*, extends a region of dunes. On the coast is the resort of *Hvidbjerg* (Hotel Faegekroen, 6 b.), with a broad sandy beach and white dunes up to 27 m (90 ft) high.

From Kolding E3 runs N to **Vejle** (pop. 50,000; Missionshotellet Caleb, 50 b.; Park Hotel, 80 b.), an industrial town beautifully set in a valley. St Nicholas's Church (carillon) dates from the 13th c. – W of the town is *Skibet church*, with a Romanesque tympanum on the W front and late Romanesque paintings on the E wall of the choir. – 6 km (4 miles) E, on the Vejle Fjord, is the hilly and wooded *Munkebjerg* region (93 m (305 ft); Munkebjerg Hotel, 280 b., SP), which attracts many visitors.

NW of Vejle, best reached on the beautiful road through the *Grejsdal* (wooded slopes, many view-points), is **Jelling**, with two royal burial mounds in which the remains of King Gorm the Old (d. about 935) and his wife Thyra Danebod were found in 1978. Between the two mounds stands a little church, begun in the 11th c., which contains the oldest frescoes in Denmark. Beside the church are two runic stones; the smaller of the two was set up by Gorm for his wife, the other by their son Harald Bluetooth, for his parents. Beneath the choir of the present church

Legoland, Billund

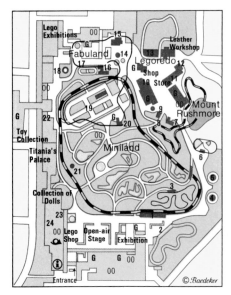

## Legoland

1 Lego-train
2 Mini boats
3 Lego Safari
4 Lego-copter
5 Caterpillar (merry-go-round)
6 Timber ride (slide)
7 Gold-mine
8 Mine Train
9 Indian Camp
10 Sheriff's office
11 Legoredo News (press)
12 Photo studio
13 Pony rides
14 Fabuland merry-go-round

15 Lego-games tables
16 Gondola
17 Fabuland cars
18 Legoland planes
19 Traffic school
20 Monorail
21 Lego-top (observation tower)
22 Educational exhibition
23 Puppet theatre
24 Laquerwork pictures
    collection

G  Refreshments
00  Toilets

are remains of the wooden church erected by Harald, who introduced Christianity to Denmark. – N of Jelling lies the *Givskud Safari Park*, with lions, elephants, buffaloes, monkeys, etc.

28 km (17 miles) W of Vejle is *Billund* (Billund Kro, 20 b.), with \***Legoland**, a miniature town built of the famous Lego plastic bricks, with reproductions of well-known buildings, a Wild West town, a collection of dolls and much more besides.

Beyond Vejle the road forks. Road 13 runs N to Silkeborg, while E3 bears NE for **Horsens** (pop. 44,000; hotels: Bygholm Parkhotel, 130 b.; Jørgensens Hotel, 48 b.; Postgården, 70 b.; Motel Thorsvang, 16 b.; youth hostel; two camp sites), at the head of Horsens Fjord; the town originally developed around an early medieval stronghold. In the 18th c. Horsens was a large commercial town, as the many old patrician houses testify. In the middle of the old town is the early 13th c. Church of Our Saviour (Vor Frelser), with a carved Baroque pulpit. The nearby Klosterkirke is all that remains of an old Franciscan friary (15th c. choir-

stalls and altarpiece). To the W of the town, in the grounds of the old manor-house of Bygholm (now a hotel), are the ruins of a royal castle built by Erik Menved in 1313. – SE of the town is the *Glud* open-air museum, the oldest in Denmark.

**Skanderborg** (pop. 11,000; Skander-borghus Hotel, 100 b.; Slotskroen, 30 b.; youth hostel; two camp sites), attractively set on Skanderborg Sø, grew up around its castle, which was frequently a royal residence during the Middle Ages. Only the chapel and the adjoining round tower remain; the rest was demolished from 1767 on. The parish church dates from the 12th c.

W of Skanderborg, on the *Mossø*, is *Emborg*, with the sparse remains of the Cistercian abbey of *Øm*, founded in 1172 (demolished 1560). Nearby is a small museum displaying excavated material.

Between Skanderborg and Silkeborg, rising steeply from the shores of the Julsø in a setting of notable beauty, is the \***Himmelbjerg** (Heaven Mountain; 147 m – 482 ft), with many viewpoints linked by woodland footpaths. On the summit is a 25 m (80 ft) high lookout tower. During the 19th c. various political and church assemblies met here (commemorative monuments). An old paddle-steamer on the *Julsø*, "Hjejlen", carries passengers to Silkeborg.

**Silkeborg** (pop. 30,000; Dania Hotel, 80 b.; Impala, 104 b.; Scandinavia, 62 b.; youth hostel; several camp sites), on the Silkeborg Langsø, rose to importance as a paper-making town in the 19th c. The Museum of Art contains an important collection of modern painting and graphic art (by Asger Jorn, etc.). The old manor-house of Silkeborg (Hovedgården; *c.* 1770) is now a museum. The most notable exhibit in the museum is Tollund Man, a well-preserved 2000-year-old head found in a bog near the village of Tollund, a short distance away. – S of the town, at *Bryrup*, is an antique railway.

From Skanderborg, E3 runs NE to **Århus** (p. 60). An attractive excursion can be made to the Djursland peninsula, to the NE.

Road 15 follows the shore of *Kalø Bay* and then cuts across the Djursland peninsula to the ferry port and popular seaside resort of **Grenå**, on the Kattegat (pop. 12,000; Hôtel du Nord, 240 b.; camp sites). Old church; Djursland Museum, in a half-timbered house (1750). Nearby the leisure park "Djurs Sommerland". – Pleasant boat trip to the island of *Anholt* (nature reserve).

Road 16 runs inland from Grenå to Randers, passing **Gammel Estrup**, an imposing old manor-house which dates in its present form from the 16th and 17th c. and now houses the *Jutland Manor-House Museum*.

**Randers** (pop. 60,000; Kongens Ege Hotel, 172 b.; Randers, 145 b.; youth hostel; camp site) lies deep inland at the outflow of the *Gudenå* into the *Randers Fjord*. In medieval times an important religious settlement with three monastic houses, the town enjoyed another period of prosperity in the 18th c. and later developed into an important industrial town. The central area of the town contains many old houses dating from the 15th and 16th c.; the oldest stone house is the Paskesønnernes Gård in Rådhustorvet (Town Hall Square). St Morten's Church dates from the 15th c. The Helligåndshus (House of the Holy Ghost; *c.* 1435) is a remnant of a religious house which was dissolved *c.* 1550. The House of Culture contains an interesting museum and library.

Randers is a popular port of call for canoeists on the *Gudenå*, Denmark's longest river (170 km – 106 miles), which rises near Tørring. There are many boat-rental agencies along the river.

The direct route from Randers to Hobro is on E3. It passes through *Råsted*, where an early 12th c. church contains a splendidly preserved series of frescoes (*c.* 1130; restored 1939–42).

A more attractive route is on minor roads via **Mariager** (Landganger Hotel, 12 b.), set picturesquely on the Mariager Fjord, which runs inland to Hobro. It is Denmark's smallest town (pop. 1600). Only certain parts of the old monastery and Gothic church have been preserved. In the church is "Christ's Coffin", a carved chest with a figure inside. – To the S of the town is the *Hohøj* burial mound. – On Sundays in summer an antique railway runs from Mariager to the village of *Handest*, situated SW of the town on Road 10.

**Hobro** (pop. 10,000; Motel Hobro, 26 b.; youth hostel; camp site) lies at the W end of the Mariager Fjord. The Museum contains a collection of Viking material. The neo-Gothic church was designed by M. G. B. Bindesbøll (also responsible for the Thorvaldsen Museum in Copenhagen). 3 km (2 miles) SW of the town is the reconstructed Viking stronghold of *Fyrkat*, which dates from about A.D. 1000. Material recovered during excavation is in the Hobro Museum.

E3 now traverses the large forest of Rold Skov (see p. 57) to **Ålborg** (p. 55) and continues to **Frederikshavn** (p. 94). Road 14 runs N through Vendsyssel via Bronderslev to Hjørring.

**Hjørring** (pop. 20,000; hotels: Kirkedal, 33 b.; Marinella, 211 b.; Phønix, 120 b.; youth hostel; two

camp sites) is an old market town. In the churchyard of St Catherine's Church (Romanesque) are eight 2000-year-old stone tombs. The Vendsyssel Museum is housed in the old deanery and other old buildings. On the SW side of the town is an open-air museum. Road A14 then continues to Hirtshals.

**Hirtshals** (Hirtshals Kro, 45 b.) is a popular resort on the Skagerrak (the North Sea Museum is worth a visit) and an important port for traffic with Norway. The battle of Jutland was fought in the Skagerrak on 31 May and 1 June 1916.

# Jyväskylä

Finland (Southern).
Province: Keski-Suomen lääni (Mellersta Finlands län/Central Finland).
Altitude: 85 m (279 ft). – Population: 65,000.
Postal code: SF-40100. – Telephone code: 941.

ⓘ **Kaupungin Matkailutoimisto**
(*Municipal Tourist Information Office*),
Vapaudenkatu 38;
tel. 29 40 83.
*Branch office in Vesilinna lookout tower,*
Harju Park;
tel. 29 40 87.

HOTELS. – *Alexandra*, Hannikaisenkatu 35, 220 b., SB; *Areena*, Asemakatu 2, 160 b., SB; *Cumulus*, Vainönkatu 3–5, 392 b., SB; *Jyväshovi*, Kauppakatu 35, 225 b., SB; *Milton*, Asema-aukio, 75 b.

VACATION and SUMMER HOTELS. – *Amis*, Sepänkatu 3, 370 b. (1 June to 7 August); *Rantasipi*, Laajavuori leisure complex, 450 b., SB, beach; *Rentukka*, Taitoniekantie 9, 272 b. (1 June to 31 August).

EVENTS. – *Jyväskylä Winter Festival* (January or February) and *Jyväskylä Summer Festival* (end of June/beginning of July), with programmes of cultural and artistic events and debates on social and political themes in various languages; *Finlandia Marathon Race* (May); *Finn Cycling Tour* (July); *Rally of the Thousand Lakes* (July or August).

SPORTS and RECREATION. – Swimming, riding, fishing, canoeing, parachute jumping.

**The Finnish town of Jyväskylä, founded in 1837, is set attractively on the northern shore of the little lake of Jyväsjärvi. The Jyväsjärvi is linked with Lake Päijänne (Finland's second largest lake), to the S, by the narrow strait of Aijälänsalmi.**

Jyväskylä is an important traffic junction, the administrative and cultural capital of the province of Central Finland (Keski-Suomen lääni) and an industrial town with several factories (woodworking, metal industries). It has a University (founded in 1934, previously a teachers' training college) and other educational

Jyväskylä

establishments; the first Finnish-language secondary school was established here in 1858. The town is characterised by a mingling of old wooden houses and modern stone buildings; it has an unusually large number of buildings designed by the famous Finnish architect Alvar Aalto.

SIGHTS. – NW of the small harbour, in *Kirkkopuisto* (Church Park), stands the neo-Gothic *parish church* (1880); monument to the Finnish woman writer Minna Canth (1844–97). On the way to the harbour and the Jyväsjärvi are two buildings by Alvar Aalto, the *Police Headquarters* (1970) and *Local Government Offices* (1978). In Kauppakatu, toward Kalevankatu, is Aalto's *Municipal Theatre* (1925). In Rajakatu is the *Orthodox Church* (1954).

In Cygnaenskatu, 1 km (¾ mile) W of the parish church, another building by Alvar Aalto, the *Museum of Central Finland* (Keski-Suomen Museo, 1961), houses material on the history of the town, an

ethnological collection and decorative arts. To the SE is the *University* (new buildings by Alvar Aalto), with the University Museum (Yliopiston Museo: collection illustrating the history of education). At Seminaarinkatu 7 is an *Alvar Aalto Museum* (mementoes of the architect), in a building which Aalto himself designed.

From the *Water Tower* (tourist information office; café) in the Harjupuisto park and from the park on the hill of *Syrjänharju*, to the NE of the town, there are attractive views. Both of these hills are eskers (long gravel ridges) deposited by glacier action during the Ice Age.

SURROUNDINGS. – 70 km (43 miles) W on the road to Virrat, at the N end of the lake of Keuruunselkä, lies the village of *Keuruu* (old wooden church, 1756–8). – From the harbour (near the station) there are trips by fast hydrofoil to Lahti over the lakes of Jyväsjärvi and Päijänne (3 hours).

**Lake Päijänne** (alt. 78 m – 256 ft) is Finland's second largest lake (area 1111 sq. km (429 sq. miles); 140 km (87 miles) long, up to 28 km (17 miles) wide, up to 93 m (305 ft) deep). It is exceeded in size only by Lake Saimaa (p. 231). The shoreline of the lake, much of it rocky, is irregularly patterned, with many inlets and peninsulas. At the N end the lake is enclosed by wooded hills; toward the S the slopes along the lake fall away more steeply.

# Kajaani (Kajana)

Finland (Central).
Province: Oulun lääni (Uleåborgs län/Oulu).
Altitude: 127 m (417 ft). – Population: 33,000.
Postal code: SF-87100. – Telephone code: 9 86.
ⓘ **Kainuun Matkapalvelu**,
    Kirkokatu 21;
    tel. 2 50 79.

HOTELS. – *Seurahuone*, Kauppakatu 11, 65 b.; *Valjus*, Kauppakatu 20, 82 b., SB; *Vanha Kulkuri*, Syväojankatu 1, 24 b.; *Vanha Välskäri*, Kauppakatu 21, 24 b.

**The Finnish town of Kajaani, in the middle of the Kainuu district (roughly half-way between the Gulf of Bothnia and the Soviet frontier), lies on the S bank of the Kajaaninjoki (here harnessed by a hydroelectric power station), which flows into the lake of Oulujärvi (alt. 124 m (407 ft); area 1002 sq. km – 387 sq. miles) just to the NW of the town.**

The town owes its development to the trade in tar, which was bought by

## Jyväskylä

500 m
(547 yds)

Oulu

Kuopio, Mikkeli

Tampere, Helsinki

Kortesuonkatu
Harju-
puisto
Oikokatu
Pirkkatu
University
Hannikaisenkatu
Halrakatu
Harjukatu
Yliopistonkatu
Kilpisenkatu
Asemakatu
Väinönkatu
Kauppakatu
Vapaudenkatu
Bus station
Station
Lutakontie
Dock
Jyväsjärvi

1 Grammar School
2 Water Tower
3 Municipal Theatre
4 Parish Church
5 Police Headquarters
6 Town Hall
7 Government Offices
8 Municipal Library
9 Museum of Central Finland
10 Alvar Aalto Museum

merchants in eastern Kainuu and conveyed by water to the ports on the Gulf of Bothnia, shipped to Sweden and later to Britain and used for the caulking of boats. The area now has a considerable woodworking industry; several thousand of its inhabitants also work in Soviet industrial establishments across the frontier.

The doctor and poet Elias Lönnrot (1802–84) lived in Kajaani from 1833 on as district medical officer. He travelled about the countryside collecting fragments of the Finnish national epic "Kalevala", which he then edited and published.

SIGHTS. – On the bank of the Koivukoski is the market square, with the new *Town Hall* (1906); the old Town Hall, a wooden building designed by Carl Ludwig Engel, is to be found in Vanhatori. To the NE, on the little island of Linnasaari, are the ruins (restored 1937) of the fortress of *Kajaneborg* (built 1607–66, taken by the Russians and destroyed in 1716), in which the Swedish historian and poet Johannes Messenius (1579–1636) lived as a prisoner from 1620 to 1635 and wrote a rhyming chronicle of Finland. – Orthodox church. There are extensive views from the water-tower.

SURROUNDINGS. – 12 km (7½ miles) NW, in *Paltaniemi*, on the S side of the Paltaselkä (a wide inlet at the E end of the Oulojärvi), is the wooden church of *Paltamo* (1726), with wall and ceiling paintings by Mikael Toppelius (d. 1821). Nearby is the so-called "Emperor's Stable", recalling Tsar Alexander I's visit to Finland. Paltamo was the birthplace of the great Finnish lyric poet Eino Leino (1878–1926).

# Kalmar

Sweden (Southern).
Province: Kalmar län. – Region: Småland.
Altitude: sea level. – Population: 80,000.
Postal code: S-39 . . . – Telephone code: 0480.
ⓘ **Kalmar Läns Turistnämnd,**
    Box 86,
    S-39121 Kalmar;
    tel. 2 82 70.

HOTELS. – *Continental*, Larmgatan 10, 70 b.; *Kalmarsund*, Fiskaregatan 5, 168 b.; *Ritz*, Larmgatan 6, 80 b.; *Scandic Hotel*, Dragonväg 7, 313 b., SB; *Slotshotellet*, Slottsvägan 7, 60 b.; *Stadshotellet*, Stortorget 14, 280 b., SB.

**Kalmar, capital of the province of that name in SE Sweden, lies on the Kalmar Sound, which separates the island of Öland from the mainland. It** is one of the oldest towns in Sweden: in Viking times it was a trading station and entrepôt, due to its favourable location on the sound, and in the early medieval period it was the main city of the North. Fortified in the 11th c. as a coastal stronghold against Denmark, the town became a member of the Hanseatic League. In 1389, Queen Margaretha of Denmark-Norway was appealed to by the Swedish nobles to help overthrow the German Albrekt of Mechlenburg. She defeated him in battle and was proclaimed ruler of the three countries and their dependencies. In 1396 she named Eric of Pomerania as her successor and negotiated the Treaty of Kalmar (1397) which made him nominally king of a United Scandinavia though he did not, in fact, actually rule until after her death. In 1412 Eric tried to increase his powers and, once more, the nobles revolted. After struggles between Sweden and Denmark and a short period under Danish rule, a revolt under the leadership of Gustav Eriksson Vasa finally broke the Union and Gustav I Vasa was elected to the throne of Sweden, so founding the Vasa dynasty. The town lost its role as a fortress at the beginning of the 18th c., and its population became mainly occupied in trade, seafaring and craft production. Its modern industries include foodstuffs, shipbuilding, engineering, motor vehicles (Volvo branch factory) and building.

SIGHTS. – In the oldest part of the town (largely rebuilt after a great fire in 1647), on the island of **Kvarnholmen**, is the *Stortorg* (Market Square), with the *Cathedral* and *Town Hall*, two Baroque buildings erected in the second half of the 17th c. according to the plans of Nicodemus Tessin the Elder. To the S of the Stortog, at the entrance to the harbour, is the *Kavaljer* (1697), a gate in the old circuit of town walls (fragments). SW of the gate in the *Lille Torg* are the old *Bishop's Lodging* (Domprostgården), *Burgomaster's House* (Borgmästaregården) and *Governor's Residence* (Länsresidenset, 1676). Storgatan, on the S side of the market square, runs SW to the *Larmtorg*, with a *fountain* (1928) in honour of Gustavus Vasa, who landed at

Kalmar Castle

Stensö, SW of Kalmar, on 31 May 1520. On the W side of the square stands the *Theatre* (1863). To the N is the 65 m (215 ft) high *Old Water Tower* (late 19th c.). From the Theatre you can head for one of the bridges linking Kvarnholmen with the mainland.

You now come to the *Municipal Park*, with a summer restaurant. In Slottsvägen, on the NW side of the park, is the *Museum of Art* and, near the Castle, the *Krusenstiern House* (Krusenstiernska Gården), an 18th c. burgher's mansion. *Kalmar Castle*, lying on the waterside and surrounded by walls and moats, is a massive five-towered structure, the earliest parts of which were built at the beginning of the 11th c. It was enlarged in the 16th c. and restored at the end of the 19th. Between 1307 and the beginning of the Kalmar War (1611), the castle withstood 24 sieges. In the courtyard is a Renaissance fountain. The chapel, in the S wing, was completed in 1592. In the N tower is the old *King's Chamber of Eric IV, with rich intarsia panelling and 16th c. hunting scenes. Other rooms worth seeing are the Lozenge Room and the Golden Room (Gyllene Salen), dating from the time of Johan III. Many of the rooms in the castle are occupied by the *Kalmar Provincial Museum* (Länsmuseet).

To the N of the town the *Öland Bridge* (Ölandsbro), opened in 1972, links Kalmar with the island of **Öland** (p. 203). It is the longest bridge in Europe (6070 m – 6600 yds). Further N stands the *New Water Tower* (fine views from the top).

# Karlskrona

Sweden (Southern).
Province: Blekinge län. – Region: Blekinge.
Altitude: sea level – Population: 60,300.
Postal code: S-37 . . . – Telephone code: 04 55.
ⓘ **Turistbyrå**,
S. Smedjegsatan 6,
S-37131 Karlskrona;
tel. 8 34 90.

HOTELS. – *Savoy*, Borgmästaregatan 13, 70 b.; *Siesta*, Borgmästaregatan 5, 29 b.; *Stadshotellet*, Ronnebygatan 37–39, 145 b., SB. – YOUTH HOSTEL in Karlshamn. – Two CAMP SITES.

**Karlskrona, capital of the province of Blekinge, lies on the Baltic near the entrance to the Kalmar Sound. The town is built on a number of islands linked to each other by bridges. This old seafaring town dates from Sweden's days as a great power. The town was founded in 1680, when the headquarters of the Swedish fleet were established on the island of Trossö. In the 18th c. Karlskrona was Sweden's second largest town, but then it declined in importance. It is now a large industrial town (manufacture of telephones, shipbuilding, plastics, construction of atomic reactors, manufacture of electric bulbs), and also has Sweden's largest cold-store plants and much of its fish-processing industry.**

SIGHTS. – In the central square, the *Stortorg*, are the neo-classical *Town Hall*, the Baroque *Frederikskyrka* (1744) and the round *Trinity Church* (1709), which was built for the German community in the town. Both of the churches were designed by Nicodemus Tissen the Younger. – In the square, which has a *statue of Charles XI* by Börjesson (1897), a colourful Flower Market is held four days before Midsummer Eve (June), at which garlands and flowers from the hillsides and meadows of Blekinge are sold. – Farther S, in Admiralitätstorg, the *Blekinge Museum* houses a collection illustrating the history of the town and province (Baroque garden on terrace). Here, too, is a timber *belfry*, built in 1700 and restored in 1856. Also to the S of the town is the *Shipping Museum*, with a collection of famous figureheads of the late 17th c. and much more. – Near the shipyards stands the *Admiralty Church* (1685), the largest timber-built church in Sweden. In front of it is an appealing wooden figure of "Old Rosenbom", a character in Selma Lagerlöf's book "The Wonderful Journey of Nils Holgersson with the Flying Geese". – In the Björkholmen district, to the E, are picturesque little 17th c. *seamen's houses*. – In Vänö Park is an *open-air museum*.

SURROUNDINGS. – 28 km (17 miles) E we come to **Ronneby** (pop. 12,000), a spa with chalybeate (iron-bearing) springs. Holy Cross Church (Heliga Kors kyrka, 11th c., 14th–15th c. frescoes, brought to light during restoration work). A door bearing the marks of burning and axe strokes is preserved in the church; it is believed to date from 1564, when the troops of Eric XIV ravaged the town. Near the church, in the district of Bergslagen, is a local museum, Möllebackagården. In Silverforsen, an old Blekinge farmhouse serves coffee. The Björketorpssten is an interesting runic stone (*c.* 700). There are other burials at *Hjörtaham-mar*.

61 km (38 miles) E of Karlskrona is **Karlshamn** (pop. 18,000; Scandic Hotel, 220 b., SB), a port town of some importance. The old town has 17th and 18th c. timber houses, including the Asschiersska Hus, built in 1682 as the Town Hall, and the Skottsberskagården, an excellently preserved merchant's house (*c.* 1760). One old house, Smith-skagården, is now a museum. In the Hamnpark a monument by Axel Olsson, "The Emigrants Kristina and Karl Oskar", recalls Karlshamn's role as the port from which many Swedes emigrated to America in the 18th c. – On the island of *Kastelholm*, outside the harbour entrance, are fortifications built in 1675. – To the E of the town lies the *Väggapark*, a pleasant recreation area. The *Mörrumså*, the best salmon-fishing river in Sweden is near here. – To the W of the town can be seen the Karlshamn nuclear power station.

# Karlstad

Sweden (Central).
Province: Örebro län. – Region: Värmland.
Altitude: 45 m (148 ft). – Population: 72,000.
Postal code: S-65 . . . – Telephone code: 0 54.
ⓘ **Karlstads Turistbyra,**
Tingvallagatan 10,
S-65224 Karlstad;
tel. 19 59 01.

HOTELS. – *Carlton*, Järnvägsgatan 8, 58 b.; *Drott*, Järnvägsgatan 1, 140 b.; *Grand Hotel*, Västra Torggatan 8, 111 b.; *Gustaf Fröding*, Hojdgatan 3, 330 b.; *Gösta Berling*, Drottninggatan 1, 130 b. SB; *Savoy*, Västra Torggatan 1A, 128 b.; *Scandic Hotel*, Sandbäcksgatan 6, 345 b., SB; *Stadshotellet*, Kungsgatan 22, 206 b., SB; *Winn*, Norra Strandgatan 9–11, 340 b. – YOUTH HOSTEL.

**Karlstad, the cultural and commercial hub of Värmland, capital of its province and the see of a bishop, lies in the delta of the Klarälv, at the point where the river flows into Lake Vänern after its course of 500 km (300 miles). The town is named after Charles IX, who, in 1584, granted a municipal charter to the settlement on the island of Tingvalla. It had existed since the early Middle Ages as a trading station and place of assembly. The negotiations on the dissolution of the union between Sweden and Norway took place here in 1905. Karlstad is an important industrial town (mainly woodworking) as well as an administrative capital.**

"Old Rosenbom", Karlskrona

Picasso sculpture, Kristinehamn

SIGHTS. – Älvgatan, a street of old burghers' houses, is a remnant of the older town which survived a great fire in 1865. The *Cathedral* (1723–30) and *Bishop's House* (1780) date from the same period. – In the *Stora Torg* is a "Peace Monument" by Ivar Johnsson. It commemorates the dissolution of the Swedish-Norwegian union in 1905. On the W side of the square is the *Town Hall* (1869). A little way E, in *Kungsgatan*, stands the *Old Grammar School*, in its day one of the handsomest school buildings in Sweden; it now houses the Diocesan Library. In *Residenstorg*, to the W of the Stora Torg, is the Governor's residence, and in front of it a *bronze statue of Charles IX* (1926). Farther SW is the *Town House* (1963). Also to the SW of the town in *Marienbergsskogen*, a layout which includes a wildlife park, an open-air museum, a theatre and an amusement park.

To the N of the town extends Sandgrund Park in which is situated the *Värmland Museum* (art, local history; special exhibitions on topical themes). – To the NE the Klarälv is spanned by the *Östra Bro*, the longest stone bridge in Sweden, with 12 arches (1761–70). One of the sights of Karlstad, especially in the spring, is to see the rafts containing thousands of logs travelling down the Klarälv.

SURROUNDINGS. – 8 km (5 miles) SW, on a peninsula projecting into Lake Vänern, is **Skoghall**, with timber stores, sawmills and cellulose and other factories. 5 km (3 miles) E of Skoghall is the old wooden church of *Hammarö* (medieval paintings, tabernacle and shrine).

At *Alster*, 6 km (4 miles) N of Karlstad, the manor-house (Alster Herregård) was the place where the well-known lyric poet Gustav Fröding (1860–1911) lived as a child. In a grove on the estate can be seen the *Fröding Stone*.

45 km (28 miles) E of Karlstad, on Lake Vänern, is the little port of **Kristinehamn** (see p. 285), with a 15 m (50 ft) high sculpture by Picasso.

**To the Fryken Lakes**. – Leave Karlstad on Road 61, which runs along the right bank of the Klarälv through mostly wooded country. In 13 km (8 miles) the road passes a small lake (on left) and then ·comes to a junction at which Road 61 bears left, while Road 62, to the right, continues up the Klarälv valley. 7·5 km (5 miles) farther along Road 61 a side road goes off on the left and runs SW (3 km – 2 miles) to *Kil*, an important railway junction (line N to Torsby).

Road 61 now comes to the S end of the chain of three * **Fryken Lakes** (alt. 62 m (203 ft); total length 71 km (45 miles); boat trips), in a region familiar to readers of Selma Lagerlöf's novel, "Gösta Berling". It passes the church of St Kil (on right), then, 6·5 km (4 miles) from the turning for Kil station, crosses the *Norsälv*, the river which drains the Fryken Lakes, and comes to another fork. Here, we turn right into Road 234, which runs up the pleasant *Fryksdal*, passing several farms and small lakes. – Off the road to the W is Frykerud church (1799; modern stained glass).

In another 25 km (15 miles) the road reaches *Västra Ämtervik*, a village above the *Mellan Fryken* (Middle Lake Fryken: 27 km (17 miles) long). Opposite the village, on the E side of the lake, stands the church of Östra Ämtervik. – 1 km (about a ½ mile) beyond the Västra Ämtervik church, a country road (SP Arvika) goes off on the left and climbs towards the *Kringerås* (272 m – 892 ft), with magnificent views over the Fryksdal (rewarding detour, about 5 km – 3 miles).

The main road continues at some distance from the shore of the lake, and in another 6·5 km (4 miles) crosses the *Rottnaälv*, which links Mellan Fryken with the beautiful *Lake Rottnen* (Finnfallet skiing area). Soon after this, the road comes to **Rottneros** and, beyond this (on right), the manor-house of the same name, the Ekeby of "Gösta Berling", set in a beautiful park (large collection of sculpture; main block rebuilt after a fire in 1929). 5·5 km (3½ miles) beyond this is **Sunne** (Länsmansgården Hotel, 65 b.; Gästis, 70 b.), the Broby of "Gösta Berling", a pleasant industrial town which attracts many summer visitors; it is set on the channel between the Middle and Upper Lakes Fryken; church of 1888 above the village. 9 km (5 miles) SE is the manor-house of *Mårbacka* (now owned by a foundation and open to the public), the former home of Selma Lagerlöf (1858–1940), who is buried in the Östra Ämtervik churchyard, 6 km (4 miles) SW.

From Sunne there are two possible routes to Torsby – either on Road 234 along the E side of the forest-fringed *Övra Fryken* (Upper Lake Fryken), via Lysvik (distance 41 km – 25 miles) or (preferably) on a country road along the W side of the lake, passing the manor-house of *Stöpfors* (14 km – 19 miles) and the hill of *Tåssebergsklätten* (342 m (1122 ft): views).

# Kemi

Finland (Northern).
Province: Lapin lääni (Lapplands län/Lapland).
Altitude: sea level. – Population: 28,000.
Postal code: SF-94100. – Telephone code: 9 80.
ⓘ **Information Office,**
Town Hall,
Valtakatu 26;
tel. 29 94 50.

HOTELS. – *Cumulus*, Hahtisaarenkatu 3, 230 b., SB; *Kemi*, Meripuistokatu 9, 47 b.; *Merihovi*, Keskuspuistokatu 6–8, 103 b.; *Palomies*, Valtakatu 12, 70 b.; *Motel Reissumies*, Eteläntie 4, 40 b.

**The Finnish town of Kemi lies at the N end of the Gulf of Bothnia, near the mouth of the River Kemijoki. It received its municipal charter in 1869, and with the development of industry also became an important port. Woodworking factories play a major economic role.**

The Kemijoki was once heavily stocked with fish; there were large numbers of salmon at spawning time (hence the salmon which features in the town's coat of arms). In recent years, however, the development of industry and the construction of hydroelectric power stations have restricted their freedom of movement and reduced their numbers.

SIGHTS. – The town is well laid out, with broad streets. In the *Town Hall* (1939) is a "panoramic café" (views). The modern brick *church* in the Church Park was built in 1902. The *Art Gallery* contains works by Finnish artists. The Museum occupies an old peasant house, complete with a fish-smoking hut.

SURROUNDINGS. – To the N of the town, on the Kemijoki, is the large *Isohaara power station*. – 9 km (5 miles) N of the middle of the town stands the 16th c. *Kemi parish church*, built of undressed stone. The vaulted wooden ceiling has paintings of the Passion; under the choir is the mummified body of a 17th c. parish priest, Nikolaus Rungius (d. 1629). – There is a very attractive road up the Kemijoki to Rovaniemi (p. 229).

# Kirkenes

Norway (Northern).
County: Finnmark fylke.
Altitude: sea level. – Population: 5000.
Postal code: N-9900. – Telephone code: 085.
ⓘ **Turistkontor,**
Parkvejen 1;
tel. 9 14 91.

HOTELS. – *Rica Gjestehus*, 31 b.; *Rica Hotell Kirkenes*, 115 b. – CAMP SITE.

**The Norwegian port and industrial town of Kirkenes lies on the S side of the Varangerfjord, on a promontory between the Langfjord and the broad estuary of the Pasvikelv. A major source of income is the working and processing of iron ore. The midnight sun provides a memorable experience here; it lasts for two months, beginning 20 May.**

SIGHTS. – In the middle of the town there are several modern office buildings. To the N of the town, on the *Holmengrå* peninsula and the little island of *Kjøøya*, are two stone *mazes*, probably medieval but possibly dating from the Iron Age.

SURROUNDINGS. – To the N of the town the **Varangerfjord** drives deep inland from the E and combines with the *Tanafjord* to separate the **Varanger peninsula** from the mainland. From Kirkenes boats ply to *Vadsø* on the N side of the Varangerfjord.

**Vadsø** (pop. 6000; Vadsø Hotell, 67 b.), on the S coast of the Varanger peninsula, is the administrative capital of Finnmark county and a busy port, shipping fish and fish products. There are boat services ("Hurtigrute") several times weekly to Hammerfest and S to Bergen. On the offshore island of *Vadsøya* is an airship anchoring mast which was used by Amundsen in 1926 and Nobile in 1928.

Kirkenes

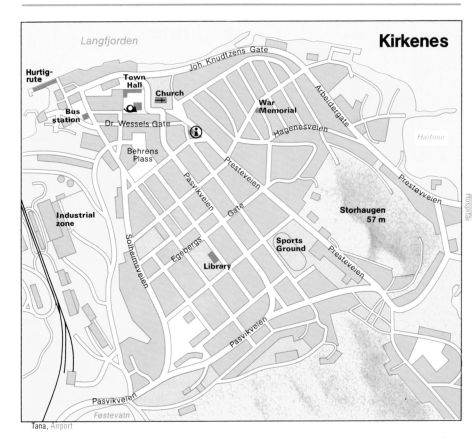

There are boat services from Kirkenes and Vadsø to *Vardø*, the most easterly town in Norway.

**Vardø** (pop. 3500; Lailas Gjestehus, 12 b.) received its municipal charter in 1788. The North Harbour, sheltered by two breakwaters, is the base of a substantial fishing fleet. The fleet is responsible for most of the town's income. Note the large racks for drying stockfish. – To the W of the town is the fortress of *Vardøhus* (1737). From the *Vardefjell*, a rocky crag 59 m (195 ft) high, there are fine views of the town and island, and also of the rugged and barren interior of the Varanger peninsula.

# Kiruna

Sweden (Northern).
Province: Norrbottens län. – Region: Norra Lappland.
Altitude: 506 m (1660 ft). – Population: 30,000.
Postal code: S-981 . . . – Telephone code: 09 80.
ⓘ **Kiruna Turistbyrå,**
    Hj. Lundbomsvåg 42;
    S-98131 Kiruna;
    tel. 1 88 80.

HOTELS. – *Ferrum*, Köpmangatan 1, 320 b.; *Kebne*, Mangigatan 4, 80 b. – YOUTH HOSTEL.

**Kiruna, the most northerly town in Sweden, lies in the same latitude as central Greenland. It is the middle of a commune which borders on both** Norway and Finland and, with an area of 20,000 sq. km (7700 sq. miles), is the largest in the country. The midnight sun is visible here from mid-May to mid-July. Originally a small Lapp settlement, the town began to develop about 1900, when the local iron ore began to be mined. By the time Kiruna received its municipal charter in 1948, the population had risen to 11,000.

SIGHTS. – SE of the station is the *Town Hall* (1963; carillon and an art collection). The wooden *church* (Gustav Wickman, 1912) is shaped, as many of the churches in the N are, to represent a Lapp tent. It contains an altarpiece painted by Prince

Kebnekaise, seen from Nikkaluokta.

Kiruna by night

Eugen of Sweden and an altar group of carved wood by Christian Eriksson and Ossian Elgström. The underground *iron mines at Kirunavaara are open to visitors daily. Geophysical observatory (research into Northern Lights).

SURROUNDINGS. – Within the commune, though some 90 km (56 miles) W of Kiruna itself, is Sweden's highest mountain, *Kebnekaise (2117 m – 6946 ft). The ascent of the S peak takes about 8–9 hours and should be undertaken only by experienced and properly equipped climbers. In a high valley on the slopes of *Keipack* (789 m – 2589 ft) is the *Kebnekaise climbing base.* – 45 km (28 miles) N of Kiruna a *rocket station* was established in 1965 by the European Space Research Organisation for the launching of research rockets. Other scientific establishments are the *Glaciological Research Station* in the Tarfala valley and the *Scientific Research Station* at Abisko. Also at Abisko (p. 54), 95 km (60 miles) from Kiruna, is the **Abisko National Park**, a large nature reserve on the shores of Lake Torneträsk. – Kiruna to Narvik (Norway) on the Lapland railway: see p. 54.

# Kokkola (Gamlakarleby)

Finland (Western).
Province: Vaasan lääni (Vasa län/Vaasa).
Altitude: sea level. – Population: 33,000.
Postal code: SF-67100. – Telephone code: 9 68.
(i) **Keski Pohjanmaan Matkailutoimisto,**
Pitkänsillankatu 39;
tel. 1 19 02.

HOTELS. – *Chydenius*, Rautatienkatu, 70 b.; *Grand Hotel*, Pitkänsillankatu 20B, 150 b.; *Seurahuone*, Torikatu 24, 143 b.; *Rantataku* 16, 180 b., SB. – YOUTH HOSTEL. – CAMP SITE.

EVENTS. – *Folk Music Festival* at Kaustinen, 40 km (25 miles) SE (July); *Venetian Weekend*, with theatre performances, concerts, exhibitions, etc. (August).

**Kokkola, one of the oldest towns in Finland (founded 1620), was almost entirely Swedish-speaking until the 20th c. It was known then as Gamlakarleby. With the development of industry, however, the language boundary was obliterated and Finnish came increasingly into use. Originally located on the sea, the town is now 5 km (3 miles) inland, as a result of the rise in the level of the coast. The harbour is the deepest on the W coast of Finland.**

HISTORY. – The town was founded by Per Brahe in 1620 at the behest of King Gustav II Adolf (Gustavus Adolphus). Its favourable location for communications made it a prime focus of commerce and shipping between 1750 and 1860. Kokkola lost much of its merchant shipping fleet during the *Crimean War* (1854–6).

SIGHTS. – In *Mannerheim Square* (Mannerheiminaukio) is the *Town Hall* (Engel,

Kiruna
300 m
(328 yds)

Tivägen
Bangårdsvägen
Stinsgatan
Förare-gatan
Adolf
Steinholtsgatan
Hjalmar
Hermelinsgatan
Hedinsvägen
Konduktörsgatan
Mangi Föreningsgatan
Geologgatan
Stations
Järnvägsgatan
Lundbohmsgatan
Bergmästare-gatan
Villagatan
Villastigen
Gruvvägen

**Swimming Pool**
**Station**
(i)
**Sports Hall**
**Indoor Swimming Pool**
**Town Hall**
**Church**

LKAB

1845). The *church* was built in 1960. The *Renlund Historical Museum*, in a wooden house (1696), contains material on the history of the town and a collection of ship models. The *Renlund Art Gallery* has works by Finnish artists. On the banks of the Kaupunginsalmi, the *English Park* (Englantilainen Puisto) commemorates an unsuccessful attack by British forces in 1854, during the Crimean War. A captured British longboat is displayed in the park. – The old town has preserved much of its original character.

SURROUNDINGS. – The area S of Kokkola abounds in historical memories, not only for Finland, but for the entire kingdom of Sweden and Finland, torn apart by Tsar Alexander I's victorious campaign in 1808–9.

The best route S is the road via *Öja* and *Risöhäll*. The road, which runs over islands and around inlets of the sea, has beautiful views of the Gulf of Bothnia. In 40 km (25 miles) it comes to **Jakobstad** (Pool Hotel, 110 b., SB; Kaupunginhotelli, 250 b.; youth hostel; camp site), a town of 20,000 inhabitants. Jakobstad was founded in 1653 by Ebba Brahe, widow of the military leader Count Jacob de la Gardie. The area around the commune of Pedersöre, on which the town now stands, was a fief of the de la Gardie family; Queen Christina of Sweden took back the fief but granted Marshal de la Gardie the right to found a town. After his death, Ebba Brahe, whose youngest brother, Per Brahe, had founded Gamlakarleby and Nykarleby, carried the project through and named the new town after her late husband. – Jakobstad is overwhelmingly Swedish-speaking. Its Finnish name is *Pietarsaari*, which is derived from the original name of the commune, Pedersöre. – In Jakobstad is the oldest tobacco factory in Scandinavia, Strengberg Oy, with a *Tobacco Museum. J. L. Runeberg* (1804–74), one of the leading Swedish-language poets of the 19th c., was born in the town. His best known work is the "Songs of Ensign Stål", a glorification of the Swedish-Finnish resistance to the Russian invasion of 1808–9. Since the war was waged under Swedish command – Finland providing the soldiers and NCOs, Sweden the officers – the work is also a reflection of Swedish attitudes.

The church in *Pedersöre* was probably founded in the 14th c. and was built in stone on a rectangular plan. It became the model for the wooden churches with pointed spires erected in northern and eastern Finland during the 17th c. In 1787–95, however, it was rebuilt on a cruciform plan by Jacob Rijf. – The School Park in Jakobstad occupies the site on which, 200 years ago, the Strengberg family tried to grow tobacco in greenhouses. A similar readiness to try something new can be seen in the fact that the park today contains more than 1000 different species of plants. – 10 km (6 miles) from the middle of the town is the sandy beach of *Fäboda*.

20 km (12 miles) S of Jakobstad is **Nykarleby**, founded in 1620, where Per Brahe established the first secondary school in Österbotten (1640). The little town is still overwhelmingly Swedish-speaking; its Finnish name, *Uusikaarlepy*, is a translation of its Swedish one. It was the birthplace (1818) of Zachris Topelius, who, after Runeberg, was the most important 19th c. Finnish poet writing in the Swedish

language. – General von Döbeln defeated the Russian army near Nykarleby during the Swedish-Russian war of 1808–9.

# Koli Hills

Finland (Eastern).
Province: Pohjois-Karjalan lääni (Norra Karelens län/Northern Karelia).

The *Koli Hills, one of the most attractive areas in Finland, lie on the SW shore of Lake Pielinen, on the NE fringe of the Finnish Lake Plateau.

At *Ahmovaara*, on Road 18, which runs N from Joensuu, a side road goes off on the right and runs through rocky and partly wooded country to a parking place at the *Koli Hotel* (84 b.; Finnish sauna, SP). From the S side of the hotel a stepped footpath ascends the rocky **Ukko-Koli** (347 m – 1139 ft). From the top of Ukko-Koli there is a magnificent view of *Lake Pielinen* 253 m (830 ft) below, with its numerous wooded islands. To the S are two other peaks in the Koli Hills, *Akka-Koli* (339 m – 1112 ft) and *Paha-Koli* (334 m – 1096 ft). To the N is *Ipatti* (316 m – 1037 ft).

There are more than 20 km (12 miles) of footpaths and some facilities for winter sports in the area around the hotel. 10 km (6 miles) N is the *Loma-Koli* vacation area, with a hotel, chalets and a camp site. – *Lieksa*: see p. 94.

# Kongsberg

Norway (Southern).
County: Buskerud fylke.
Altitude: 170 m (558 ft). – Population: 20,000.
Postal code: N-3600. – Telephone code: 03.
ⓘ **Turistkontor,**
Storgate 36;
tel. 73 15 26.

HOTELS. – *Grand*, 166 b.; *Gyldenløve*, 90 b.,
YOUTH HOSTEL. – Two CAMP SITES.

Kongsberg owes its foundation and early prosperity to the nearby silver-mines, which began to be worked in 1624, during the reign of Christian IV, and remained open until 1957. The town – the third oldest in Norway after Trondheim and Bergen – lies astride the River Lågen,

Kongsberg from the Funkelia chair-lift

# Kristianstad

Norway (Southern).
County; Vest-Agder fylke.
Altitude: sea level. – Population: 60,000.
Postal code: N–4600. – Telephone code: 0 42.

ⓘ **Reiselivslaget for Kristiansand**
H. Wergelandgate 17;
tel. 2 60 65.

HOTELS. – *Bondeheimen*, 47 b.; *Christian Quart*, 230 b.; *Evenbye's Ernest*, 120 b.; *Norge*, 130 b.; *Rica Fregatten*, 100 b.

YOUTH HOSTEL: Roligheden, 3 km (2 miles) SE. – Two CAMP SITES.

**which here flows over a series of rapids, in the southern Numedal.**

SIGHTS. – On the right bank of the river is the *Market Square*, with a large wooden **church** (1741–61: fine organ, church plate). To the N of the church stands a monument to Christian IV. In Hyttegate, to the E of the church, is a small *Silver-Mine Museum*. On the other bank of the river, here spanned by the *Nybro*, is the *Lågdal Museum*, with antiquities from the surrounding area. – 7 km (4½ miles) S of the town are the old **Silver-Mines** (conducted tours). The *Kongensgrube* (King's Mine) at *Saggrenda* penetrates into the hillside for a distance of 2300 m – 1½ miles (mine railway).

SURROUNDINGS. – Going past the old silver-mines and continuing W on E76, we reach the **Heddal**; then via *Notodden* (pop. 9000) to the Heddal *stave church (38 km (24 miles): see p. 266).

There is a very attractive trip along the **Numedal** to Geilo. The valley, which offers particularly fine scenery in its upper reaches, is traversed by the *Lågen*, coming down from the central Hardangervidda (see p. 124). – Leave Kongsberg on Road 8, going N. Beyond *Flesberg* (31 km – 20 miles) the valley narrows. At *Djupdal* station (46 km – 29 miles) the road crosses the Lågen, here flowing through a deep gorge, and continues past the old church of *Rollag* and beyond this the *Mykstufoss power station*.

At **Rødberg** are the Nore I and II power stations, supplied by two lakes in a side valley, the *Pålsbufjord* and the *Tunnhovdfjord*. Shortly before *Vasstulen* the road reaches its highest point (1100 m – 3610 ft). To the left is the *Sigridfjell* (1231 m – 4039 ft). After going over two further heights the road comes to **Geilo**, in the *Ustadal* (Bardøla Høyfjellshotell, 180 b.; Highland Hotel, 174 b.; Geilo Hotell, 145 b.; Holms, "120 b.; Geilo Høyfjellspensjonat, 32 b.; youth hostel; camp site), a popular vacation and winter sports resort (several ski-lifts). A chair-lift serves the *Geilohøyda* (1056 m (3465 ft): restaurant at upper station). To the NW is the *Prestholtskarv* (1857 m (6093 ft): road to 1350 m – 4430 ft).

The port of **Kristiansand is on a level and almost square peninsula in the Skagerrak at the mouth of the Tor-ridalselv (the lower course of the Otra). The town was founded by Christian IV in 1641, burned down on several occasions (most recently in 1892) and then rebuilt on a regular grid plan. It is the administrative capital of the county of Vest-Agder and the see of a bishop; its main sources of employment are industry and shipping.**

SIGHTS. – In the middle of the town is the *Market Square* (Torget) in which stands the neo-Gothic **Cathedral** (1882–5): fine interior (open only 9 a.m. to 2 p.m.; beautiful altar). In the adjoining gardens is a *monument* by Vigeland to the poet *H. Wergeland* (1808–45), a native of the town, and on the E side of the square a bronze *statue of King Håkon VII* (1872–1957).

On the SW side of the town is the *West Harbour*, bounded on the S by the little peninsula of *Langmannsholm*. On the peninsula, in a former powder store, is the **Vigeland Collection**, with some 130 pieces of sculpture by Gustaf Vigeland (1869–1943). To the E, between Lang-mannsholm and the island of *Odderøy*, is the *fishing harbour*. There are remains of old fortifications on Odderøy.

On the SE side of the peninsula lies the *East Harbour*, with the small 17th c. fort, *Christiansholm*.

Outside the town, to the NE, is the **Vest-Agder Fylkesmuseum** (County Museum).

This open-air museum, the largest in the country, has old *farmhouses* from Vest-Agder and the Setesdal, a town street and several rooms displaying furniture, textiles, glass, stoneware and old liturgical utensils.

To the NW of the town, beyond the park-like *Baneheia* (several lakes with facilities for bathing), is the **Ravnedal Nature Park**. There are fine views from the top of the crags which rear above the park.

SURROUNDINGS. – 45 km (28 miles) W on E18 is the most southerly town in Norway, **Mandal**, straddling the *Mandalselv* (pop. 6500; Solborg Turisthotell, 120 b.; Bondeheimen, 70 b.; youth hostel, 48 b.). The town has a number of handsome old burghers' houses and a large wooden church (1821). From the rocky hill of *Uranienborg*, to the N, there are very fine views. – 28 km (17 miles) SW of Mandal is **Lindesnes** (alt. 38 m – 125 ft), the most southerly point on the Norwegian mainland (lat. 57°58'42" N), on which the first lighthouse in Norway was built in 1655.

Railway enthusiasts will be tempted, if it is Sunday, to visit **Grovane** (N of Kristiansand via *Vennesla*), from which a train drawn by a steam locomotive (1894) runs along a 5 km (3 mile) stretch of the old Setesdal railway (Sundays only).

It is well worth while taking a trip from Kristiansand to the coastal towns of Grimstad and Arendal, to the NE (E18: 72 km (45 miles) to Arendal).

The road crosses the much indented *Topdalsfjord* on a 608 m (660 yds) long * suspension bridge (opened 1956) and in 11 km (7 miles) passes a *wildlife park* (dyrepark). It has an almost complete collection of the species of animals found in Scandinavia and is also a noted camel-breeding establishment.

The road continues via *Lillesand* (pop. 1500; Norge Hotel, 40 b.) and the manor-house of *Norholmen*, once the home of Knut Hamsun (museum), to the little town of **Grimstad** (pop. 2500; Helmershus Turisthotel, 78 b.), in a fertile agricultural region. In Østregate, near the dock, is the old pharmacy (now a museum) in which Ibsen worked as a pharmacist (1847–50) and wrote his first work, "Catilina".

**Arendal** (pop. 12,000; hotels: Bondeheimen, 20 b.; Central, 50 b.; Phønix, 150 b.; Ritz Pensjonat, 27 b.), administrative capital of the county of Aust-Agder, is located on the slopes of a hill (important harbour and shipyards). In the S of the town stands the fine Town Hall, after the Stiftsgård in Trondheim (p. 272), the largest timber building in Norway. – Offshore are the islands of *Hisøy* and *Tromøy* (bridge). Tromøy has a 13th c. church and a fine view of Vardåsen from the hill.

**Setesdal**: see p. 233.

# Kristianstad

Sweden (Southern).
Province: Kristianstads län. – Region: Skåne.
Altitude: 5 m (16 ft). – Population: 45,000.
Postal code: S-291 . . . – Telephone code: 0 44.
ⓘ **Kristianstads Turistbyra,**
   Vastra Boulevard 15,
   S-29132 Kristianstad;
   tel. 12 19 88.

HOTELS. – *Aston*, Ö. Vallgatan 35, 34 b.; *Grand Hotel*, V. Storgatan 15, 275 b.; *Stadshotellet*, Stora Torg, 50 b.; *Turisten*, V. Storgatan 17, 70 b.

**Kristianstad, on the Helgeå in SE Sweden, was founded by King Christian IV of Denmark in 1614 when Skåne was still part of the kingdom of Denmark. The town, protected by ramparts and bastions, was also a powerful fortress designed to ward off Swedish attacks on Skåne. The layout – the earliest example of Renaissance town-planning in northern Europe – is unusual, with the rectangular street grid adjusted to the line of the fortifications.**

SIGHTS. – The *Town Hall* (1891) stands in the Stora Torg. In a niche opposite is a *statue of Christian IV*, inscribed with his greeting to the townspeople, "Frid med Eder" ("Peace be with you"). Also in the square are the Freemasons' Lodge, opened by Oskar II in 1884; the *Burgomaster's House*, built in 1640 (given its present form about 1800); the *Stora Kronohus* (1840–1), a handsome white building in Empire style, originally occupied by a courthouse and a regiment of artillery and still used by the military; and the *Trinity Church (1617–28), the largest and finest Renaissance church in northern Europe (magnificent organ and carved choir-stalls, most excellently preserved).

To the E of the church, housed in the old Armoury, is the *Municipal Museum* (local history, art). In Tivoligatan are a *dyer's workshop* (1660) and a number of 17th c. houses. – The *Norreport*, a town gate built in 1760, leads to barracks of the same period, later occupied by a regiment taking part in the campaigns against Napoleon (memorial stone commemorating the battle of Leipzig, 1813). In Östra Storgatan is a *Film Museum*, occupying the studios in which the first Swedish films were made (1909–11). At 40 Västra Storgatan is the *Cardell House* (1760), with a beautifully carved doorway. This was the home of General Cardell, who is said to have had the street closed so that his afternoon nap should not be disturbed.

The house at 39 Storgatan was occupied about 1700 by Charles XII and from 1711 to 1714 by the exiled king of Poland,

Stanislas Leszczynski. – Other features of interest are the large **Tivoli Park** (theatre, restaurant) and the *Water-Tower* (1966, magnificent view).

SURROUNDINGS. – 3 km (2 miles) SW are the ruins of *Lillhöhusborg*, birthplace of Herluf Trolle, a well-known Danish nobleman. – 6 km (4 miles) S *Norra Åsum church* was built in 1200 by Bishop Absalon of Roskilde. – There are interesting medieval churches at *Färlöv*, *Kiaby*, *Vittskövle* and *Fjälkinge*. – To the S, in a beautiful wooded setting, is the 10 m (35 ft) high *Forsaker waterfall*. Swimming pool; 25 vacation chalets. – 17 km (10 miles) NE of Kristianstad stands the *Kongsgård*, a castle which was a monastery in medieval times (hotel and restaurant). There are other castles at *Ovesholm* (10 km – 6 miles), with a beautiful English-style park; *Maltesholm* (20 km – 12½ miles), on the Linderödså; *Trolle Ljungby* (13 km – 8 miles), built about 1600; *Vittskövle* (20 km – 12 miles), dating from the same period; and *Råbelöv* (9 km (5½ miles): also *c.* 1600), on a lake of the same name. – In the Ivösjö is the island of *Ivö* (china clay deposits, porcelain manufacture).

# Kuopio

Finland (Central).
Province: Kuopion lääni (Kuopios län/Kuopio).
Altitude: 80 m (262 ft). – Population: 77,000.
Postal code: SF-70100. – Telephone code: 971.
(i) **Kaupungin Matkailutoimisto**
(*Municipal Tourist Information Office*),
Haapaniemenkatu 17;
tel. 18 21 11.

HOTELS. – *Atlas*, Haapaniemenkatu 22, 110 b., *Cumulus*, Asemakatu 32, 253 b.; *Kapunginhotelli*, Maaherrankatu 5–7, 40 b.; *Kuopio*, Haapaniemenkatu 20, 51 b.; *Martina*, Tulliportinkatu 19, 70 b.; *Puijonsarvi*, Minna Canthin Katu 18, 141 b.; *Rauhalahti*, Katiskaniemientie 6, 302 b., SB; *Savonia*, Sammakkolmmentie 2, 200 b.

SUMMER HOTELS. – *Rivoli*, Satamakatu 1, 351 b., SB; *Savonia Summer Hotel*, Sammakkolammentie 2 (1 June to 15 August) 52 b. – Several CAMP SITES.

EVENTS. – *Puijo International Winter Games* (March); *Kuopio Dance and Music Festival* (June); *Cross-Country Motorcycle Race* (July); *International Athletic Games* (summer).

SPORTS and RECREATION. – Tennis, squash, bowling, riding, archery, gliding, walking, swimming, water-skiing, sailing, rowing, canoeing; in winter skiing (downhill and cross-country).

**Kuopio is beautifully situated on a peninsula in the Kallavesi, with Puijomäki rearing up on the N. It is the economic and cultural hub of the province of the same name and the see of a Lutheran bishop as well as of the archbishop of the Orthodox Church in Finland. It has Finland's most recent university, founded in 1972. The town is an important focus of communications, for traffic both by water and on land, in a flat but richly diversified region intermingling woodland and water.**

Kuopio received its municipal charter from Per Brahe in 1652, was deprived of its privileges for a period but was granted a new charter by Gustav III in 1782.

Kuopio – general view from Puijomäki

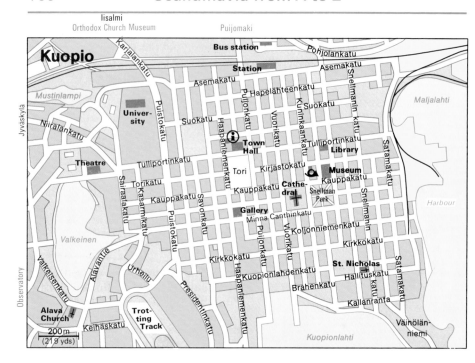

During the 1808–9 war the town surrendered to the Russians without a fight. It was later recaptured in a surprise attack by a Finnish unit under Colonel Sandels.

One of the outstanding Finnish figures of the 19th c., the philosopher, politician and statesmen J. V. Snellman, was rector of the grammar school from 1843 to 1849. He persuaded Alexander II of Russia in 1863 to agree that Finnish should be one of the official languages, together with Swedish and Russian (little used in practice), of the Grand Duchy of Finland.

SIGHTS. – The central feature of the town is the *Market Square* (Kauppatori), in which the local specialty, *kalakukko* (a fish and pork pie), can be bought. Around the square are the *Town Hall* (by F. A. Sjöström, 1884), opposite it the *Market Hall*, and beyond this, on the far side of Kauppakatu, the *Grammar School* (1825). Kauppakatu runs E to the **Cathedral**, situated on a low hill (designed by Jacob Rijf; completed in 1815 by Pehr Granstedt). Immediately beyond it is *Snellman Park*, with a bronze statue of Snellman. To the N of the park, in Kauppakatu, are the *Municipal Museum* (history, folk traditions) and the Municipal Library. Along the E side of the Snellman Park runs Maaherrankatu, at the N end of which, in a small garden to the left, is a monument to the important Finnish writer *Minna Canth* (1844–97).

To the SW of the town, adjoining a large sports field, is a modern children's home and hospital, *Savon Lastenlinna*. It is the counterpart of the similarly named institution in Helsinki. – To the SE is the Orthodox **St Nicholas's Church** (1903), seat of the Archbishop, who is responsible for two dioceses, each with 30,000 members – Karelia (14 parishes) and Helsinki (11 parishes). – To the S of the church is the narrow peninsula of *Väinölänniemi*, with a park, sports grounds, a bathing beach and (at the southern tip) a summer restaurant, the Peränniemen Kasino. At the near end of the peninsula is a statue of *Hannes Kolehmainen*, winner of the marathon in the 1920 Olympics.

To the W of the town, near Lake Valkeinen (sports facilities, fishing), is the modern *Municipal Theatre*. A little way N, on a smaller lake (Mustilahti), are an indoor swimming pool and a bowling alley. Karjalankatu, to the E, runs N to the *Orthodox Church Museum** (1969), part of a complex which also includes the Archbishop's residence, a seminary for priests and the offices of the Finnish Orthodox Church, the second largest religious community in Finland. – To the NW, in Vuorikatu, Kirkkokatu and Savonkatu, are timber houses in the 18th c. Finnish style.

SURROUNDINGS. – Immediately N of the town, on the wooded hill of **Puijomäki**, is a *lookout tower*

75 m (245 ft) high (1963) which stands 225 m (740 ft) above the Kallavesi. It has two viewing platforms and a restaurant (65 m – 213 ft) with a revolving floor (360° per hour). – There are "water-buses" to the resort of *Ritoniemi*, on the island of *Soisalo*.

# Kuusamo

Finland (NE).
Province: Lapin lääni (Lapplands län/Lapland).
Altitude: 255 m (837 ft). – Population: 18,000.
Postal code: SF-93600. – Telephone code: 9 89.
ⓘ **Kuusamon Lomat Oy**
   (*Tourist Information Office*),
   Kitkantie 20;
   tel. 1 19 11.

HOTELS. – *Iivaaran Lomakeskus*, 90 b.; *Kuusamo*, Kirkkotie 23, 223 b., SB; *Otsola*, Ouluntie 3, 75 b.; *Ukkoherra* (motel), 20 b. – IN KITKA: *Kitkapirtti* (motel), 15 b. – ON RUKATUNTURI (25 km/15 miles N): *Rantasipi Rukahovi*, 280 b., SB.

**Kuusamo lies at the NW end of the Kuusamojärvi, a lake surrounded by wooded hills. The extensive area included within the commune of Kuusamo attracts many anglers in summer with its numerous lakes and rivers, and in winter it offers excellent skiing (ski-jump and ski-lift on Rukatunturi).**

Roughly a third of the population lives by farming and forestry (including reindeer herding). The local industries (wood-working, foodstuffs) are primarily small-scale. About half the population of the commune live in the town of Kuusamo. The town is a good base from which to explore the natural beauties of the area, either by car or on foot.

SURROUNDINGS. – The contrast between the extensive areas of water and bogland and the tracts of rocky country give the scenery of this region its parti-cular stamp. The lakes are frequently edged by sheer granite cliffs; in many places the rivers are hemmed in by the rocks, flowing through deep gorges and over rapids.

For an attractive excursion in the country round Kuusamo, leave on the Kemijärvi road (No. 5), which runs 25 km (15 miles) N to **Rukatunturi** (482 m (1581 ft); chair-lift, ski-jump; extensive views from top; strongly recommended). From there continue on Road 5 for another 10 km (6 miles) and then turn right into Road 950.

In 5 km (3 miles) a side road runs E past Säkkilänvaara to *Juuma* and the *Jyrävä* rapids (good fishing). From here return to Road 950 and in 9 km (5 miles), at *Käylä*, turn right into the road to Kiikasenvaara, which comes in 15 km (10 miles) to the **Kiutaköngäs** rapids, where the *Oulankajoki*, flowing between sheer rock walls, drops 14 m (45 ft) over a distance of 600 m (650 yds).

Here the road cuts across the *Bear Trail* (Karhunkierros), a marked footpath some 70 km (45 miles) long, with shelter huts, etc. The trail ends at Rukatunturi. Experienced walkers can begin the walk there; others should start from the Suorajärvi bus stop on Road 950, from which the going is easier. Since the trail is never too far from civilisation it is possible to take a break at any time.

Kuusamojärvi (Lake Kuusamo)

# Lahti

Finland (Southern).
Province: Hämeen lääni (Tavastehus län/Häme).
Altitude: 90 m. – Population: 94,000.
Postal code: SF-15100. – Telephone code: 918.
ⓘ **Lahden Kaupungin Matkailutoimisto**
   (*Municipal Tourist Information Office*),
   Torikatu 3 B;
   tel. 18 25 80.

HOTELS. – *Ascot*, Raukankatu 14, 268 b.; *Kauppa-hotelli*, Rautatienkatu 12, 47 b.; *Lahti*, Hämeenkatu 4, 171 b.; *Musta Kissa*, Rautatienkatu 21, 165 b.; *Seurahuone*, Aleksanterinkatu, 14, 210 b., SB. – OUTSIDE THE TOWN: *Messila*, Messila, 114 b., SB; *Mukkulan Kartano*, Mukkula, 240 b.; *Mukkula Summer Hotel*, Ritaniemenkatu 10, 210 b. (2 May to 31 August); *Tallukka*, Tallukantie 1, Vääksy, 324 b., SB.

EVENTS. – *Finlandia Cross-Country Ski Race* (February); *Salpausselkä Winter Games* (March); *Skating Marathon* (March); *International Organ Festival* (August).

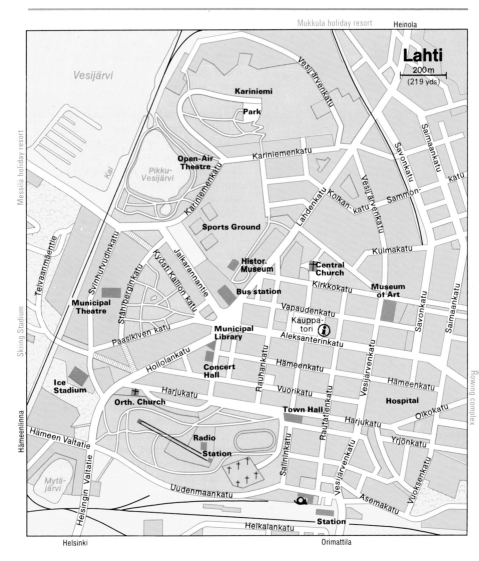

Lahti

200m
(219 yds)

Water tower, Lahti

Lahti lies in wooded hills 100 km (60 miles) NE of Helsinki, on the NW fringe of the Salpausselkä ridge, near the S end of the 24 km (15 miles) long Vesijärvi (alt. 82 m (269 ft); area 113 sq. km – 44 sq. miles). Finland's fifth largest town, Lahti owes its rapid rise in prosperity to its excellent geographical situation and good communications. It is now an important industrial town (several large furniture factories; glass, textiles, metal-working, electrical goods), and also a popular winter sports resort. It has a powerful radio transmitter and an Academy of Music.

SIGHTS. – The central feature of the town is the large *Market Square* (Kauppatori), surrounded by commercial buildings. There is a wooden church (1890) on the N side. At 4 Kirkkokatu stands the new *Central Church* (Alvar Aalto, 1978). In an old manor-house at the W end of Kirkkokatu is housed the **Historical Museum**, which includes pictures, prehistoric material, etc. from the museum of Viipuri (now Vyborg, in the Soviet Union). – To the S of the Market Square is the *Town Hall* (E. Saarinen, 1912), and nearby the Freedom Monument commemorates the liberation of the town from Communist commandos. NW of the Town Hall is the *Concert Hall* (1954).

A short distance SE of the Town Hall, at the station, is a monument to Marshal Mannerheim (by Veikko Leppanen, 1959).

SW of the Market Square, at 5 Harjukatu, is the *Orthodox Church* (1954), a copy of the church of the Prophet Elijah in Viipuri. – To the NE, at 1 Ilmarisentie in the Metsäpelto district, is the *Joutjärvi Church* (by Unto Ojonen, 1962). – Other features of interest are the *Museum of Art* (Vesijärvenkatu 11), the *Radio Museum* and the *Skiing Museum*.

SURROUNDINGS. – In the Kiverio district stands the 50 m (165 ft) high *Water-Tower* (Mustankallioumäki; café at 40 m – 130 ft). – To the W of the town is the *Skiing Stadium*, with a 90 m (295 ft) high ski-jump (viewing platform) and three smaller jumps (70, 35 and 25 m – 230, 115 and 80 ft), cross-country ski runs and a floodlit sawdust run 1000 m (1100 yds) long. – 11 km (7 miles) NW of Lahti we come to the hill of **Tiirismaa** (223 m (732 ft): radio transmitter), a skiing resort with two ski-lifts and a slalom run. This is a foothill of the *Salpausselkä* ridge, which runs along the S side of the lake district of central Finland and extends 550 km (340 miles) NE into Karelia. – 5 km (3 miles) N, on the E side of Vesijärvi, is the *Mukkula* recreation and holiday resort, 6·5 km (4 miles) NE on the road to Heinola the *Takkula* recreation area, and 8 km (5 miles) NW, on the W side of Vesijärvi, the *Messilä* holiday resort.

8·5 km (5 miles) farther NW is *Hollola*, with a 14th c. church (medieval wood-carving). Near the church is a local museum.

There is a hydrofoil service from Lahti to **Jyväskylä** (see p. 153); the trip takes about three hours. – A shorter trip (25 minutes) is to the *Vääksy* lock. In summer there are also steamer excursions. There is a boat service from Lahti to Heinola (see p. 92).

# Lapland

Norway (Lapland), Sweden (Lappland), Finland (Lappi) and the Soviet Union (Laplandiya).

**Lapland is the northern part of Scandinavia, extending over Norway, Sweden, Finland and the Soviet Union. It has a total area of about 260,000 sq. km (100,000 sq. miles). It slopes down toward the E from the Norwegian and Swedish mountains in the W, consists of treeless tundra and bog in the N, and is mostly forest-covered in the S.**

**Of the population (about 380,000) only 30,000–32,000 are true Lapps (Samer).**

The climate is continental, except in the coastal regions, with short summers (mosquitoes) and long, cold winters. Since most of Lapland lies N of the Arctic Circle, the *midnight sun* shines in summer; in winter the *Arctic night* prevails. – In the fauna of Lapland the reindeer occupies a special place. Brown bears are now rare, and with the advance of modern civilisation the lynx has practically disappeared. During the winter, wolves will venture near human settlements. – Those who want to do any walking in Lapland should be equipped with sturdy footwear (rubber boots will be useful), good maps, a compass and sufficient food: Lapland is beautiful, but it has a character of its own which visitors must respect. Under no circumstances should anyone go walking alone.

There are 30,000–32,000 **Lapps** or *Samer* in Lapland as a whole, including some 20,000 in northern Norway and 8500 in Sweden. The old collective Nordic term for Lapps was "Finns" – hence the geographical name *Finnmark* while the Finns were called "Kväner". Then, in the Middle Ages the Swedes started calling them *Lapps* probably from the Finnish word *Lappi* meaning the far-off north lands and this word was adopted by most of the north except by the Finns who, while still using the word *Lappi* for Lapland, call the individual *Lappalainen*. The Lapps themselves dislike being called by that name and have worked for decades to get the word *Samer* (singular *Same*) used. In their own language which is vaguely related to Finnish, but differs considerably from it, they call themselves *Sameh* with a singular form of Sapme, Same or Sämi according to the different dialects, so different in fact that a Lapp living only a hundred miles from another will frequently be unable to understand the other even though they are speaking the same language. Their origin is obscure. They are short, round-headed and broad-faced, with yellowish skin and dark hair. Although Christian missions began to work among them in the 17th c., they have preserved certain pagan practices. Three broad groups of Lapps are distinguished – the nomadic mountain Lapps, now steadily declining in numbers, who move between the forest and mountain regions with their herds of reindeer in regular migrations; the forest Lapps, who live a settled life with their herds in particular areas; and the poorer lake Lapps, who live by fishing. The characteristic Lapp costume, which distinguishes little between men and women, consists of a knee-length skirt of blue or brown material with red and yellow trimming and tightly fitting trousers. The man's cap is of the same material; in Norway it has four stiffened points (the cap of the four winds), in Sweden and Finland the cap is finished with huge red balls of wool, while the women Lapps wear variations of a bonnet, usually red, but decorated according to their tribe. The shoes are of soft reindeer-skin, with turned-up toes (*gabmagak; skalkomager*, skin boots). The winter garment is of reindeer skin. Lapp costumes and ornaments of carved

The ecological balance of Lapland is extremely delicate, and visitors should be very careful not to disturb it. It may take many years for a tin can to rust away, since it is subject to corrosion only in the few frost-free months of the year. During the dry summer months great caution is required with open fires: during this period there are certain stages of alert restricting the lighting of fires, and all visitors to Lapland must be informed of the current alert situation, since ignorance is no defence against substantial fines. Whatever the weather, care should be taken to completely extinguish any fire before leaving.

One possible hazard for motorists in Lapland is collision with elk or reindeer. Animals tend to prefer main roads, where there is likely to be a breeze to keep away the mosquitoes. If an animal is critically injured in an accident, it should be put out of its misery. If the motorist is unable or unwilling to do so, a local inhabitant should be informed and driven to the spot in order to do what is necessary. The nearest police or frontier post should then be informed.

*Elks* belong to no one; however, a motorist who kills one has no right to it, since holders of an elk-shooting permit are the only ones entitled to dispose of a dead elk, following the veterinary regulations.

*Reindeer* always belong to someone, and any motorist who takes the meat of a reindeer is guilty of theft. In accidents of this kind the facts are recorded by the authorities and that ends the matter. The question of responsibility for the accident is not pursued. The motorist is not liable for compensation, since the owner of the animal can claim this from the state. Since he is not exposed to any legal action, either criminal or civil, the driver need not hesitate in reporting the matter and giving all the information required. Failure to do so will usually have unpleasant consequences, since the local people will know what caused the bump on your car and the "bush telegraph" will associate it with an accident which may have occurred hours or days before and many miles away.

Lapps with reindeer (Northern Finland)

The Lapps' main form of property is the **reindeer** (*ren*; Finnish *poro*), a species of deer, accustomed to cold conditions, in which both sexes have antlers. There are estimated to be about half a million reindeer in Lapland. A Lapp requires a minimum of 100–200 head for subsistence, but rarely possesses more than 500. With 800 reindeer he is a rich man; herds of several thousand are sometimes found, but these belong to nomadic families travelling together. The hooves of a herd of reindeer make a characteristic clicking sound as they move about on the hard ground. Reindeer meat is a delicacy; every visitor should make a point of sampling it. Since the vegetation takes many years to grow again after being cropped by reindeer, the herds require very large areas for grazing. – In addition to reindeer, many Lapps have other kinds of stock and may cultivate certain crops.

### NORWEGIAN LAPLAND.

– Norwegian Lapland includes the counties of Troms and Finnmark, the coasts of which are much indented by fjords and inlets. In Troms there is still arable land and rich pastureland, but the country to the NE becomes increasingly bare and inhospitable. From the high ranges of mountains in the W, the land falls to low plateaux in the E, with occasional bare rounded hills. The chief towns of the two countries are Tromsø (see p. 268) and Vadsø (p. 159).

reindeer horn are now made for the tourist trade. – The normal Lapp dwelling is a timber or earth hut (*gammen*; Lapp *darfe goattek*). The nomadic Lapps have canvas tents, with an opening at the top to let the smoke out. – In the remoter regions the normal means of transport in winter, apart from snowshoes, is the *pulka* or *akja*, a boat-shaped sledge hauled on a single rope by a reindeer.

On the *Altafjord* in western Finnmark is the important commercial town of **Alta** (Alta Hotell, 105 b.; Altafjord Turisthotell, 118 b.), formerly known as *Bossekop in Alta* ("Whale Bay", from the Lapp word *bosso*, whale). Alta is the administrative capital of Finnmark and home of the famous "Alta Bataljon" which covered the retreat of the British and French forces from Narvik and district in 1940, suffering tremendous casualties in the process. The population lives by salmon-fishing and working the local slate. The area around the fjord, which can be surprisingly warm in summer, has a remarkably rich growth of vegetation.

Lapp huts at Arvidsjaur (Northern Sweden)

On Road 93 driving S from Alta lies *Masi*, a very typical Lapp settlement and school where one can see reindeer skins pegged on the walls to dry out and 130 km (80 miles) S of Alta (Road 93), in the *Finnmarksvidda*, is **Kautokeino** (pop. 1600, mainly Lapps; hotels: Alfreds Kro, 40 b.; Kautokeino Turisthotell, 96 b.; youth hostel; camp site), with a new church (1958; the old church, dating from 1703, was destroyed in 1944) and a school.

NE of Alta, on Road 6, is *Kistrand*, with a pretty little wooden church, on the **Porsangerfjord**, which extends S for 120 km (75 miles) from Honningsvåg on the island of Magerøy (see p. 200). The road runs around the end of the fjord and continues to **Kirkenes** (p. 159).

wild mountainous area, largely untouched by man, which reaches its highest point in *Kebnekaise (2117 m (6946 ft): see p. 161). A number of rivers, heavily stocked with fish, rise here (Umeälv, Skellefteälv, Piteälv, Luleälv, Kalixälv, Torneälv, etc.) and flow SE toward the Gulf of Bothnia. Most of the area is covered with bog and forest; toward the E and N the forest gradually opens and finally ends in a scrub of stunted birch-trees. – The inhabitants live primarily by timber-working, with some agriculture and stock-farming. In addition, there are the iron mines of Gällivare and Kiruna. The area is traversed by a number of roads and by the mineral railway from Luleå to Narvik. A great part of it is, however, very difficult terrain and virtually unmapped.

**Jokkmokk** (Gästis Hotel, 50 b.; Jokkmokk, 108 b.), an old Lapp village, is now the chief place in the commune of the same name (pop. 3200). Roughly half the area lies above the tree-line. The village was established by Charles IX as a meeting-place for the Lapps. A Lapp assembly, church festival and fair was held here every February. Some traditions, including the fair, have been preserved. The church (1753) was burned down in 1972 and rebuilt in 1974–5. The Museum contains an interesting collection of material on the culture of the Lapps and Swedish settlers. There are displays of Lapp handicrafts on sale. There is a Lapp secondary school, established in 1942, as well as a school for nomad children.

SURROUNDINGS of Jokkmokk. – There are a motor road and a footpath up the *Storknabben*, the "hill of the midnight sun". 1 km (¾ mile) N are the *Kaitum Falls*. – The **Arctic Circle** (Swedish *Polcirkeln*) runs 7 km (4½ miles) S of the town. – 12 km (7½ miles) S is *Kåivovallen*, an old summer settlement for the Lapps and their reindeer. The hills around Jokkmokk are suitable for both beginners and experienced climbers.

A young Lapp of Kautokeino (Northern Norway)

**SWEDISH LAPLAND** (Swedish **Lappland**). – This is the most northerly region in Sweden, the largest, with an area of 120,000 sq. km (46,000 sq. miles), and the most sparsely populated. It extends for 600 km (370 miles) from N to S, with a width of 250 km (150 miles). The land rises from E to W in a series of plateau-like steps. Towards the Norwegian frontier is a

**Riksgränsen** (alt. 552 m (1811 ft); Hotel Riksgränsen, 400 b.), the last Swedish station on the Lapland railway (p. 54), is a tourist area and Sweden's leading summer skiing resort (chair-lift). It frequently has temperatures of 15–20 °C (60–70 °F) while the snow is at freezing point. – Nearby is *Björkliden*, on Lake *Torneträsk*, with good skiing and a chair-lift to 750 m (2460 ft) on *Njulla* (1199 m – 3934 ft). Torneträsk, at the head of the Torneälv, is surrounded by high crags.

On the Royal Trail

Lapp settlements are scattered on the N side of the lake.

The *Royal Trail (Kungsleden), a 393 km (244 miles) long footpath (time required 22–25 days; experienced walkers only; maps, compass, rubber boots, etc.), runs through the mountain region of Lapland, with overnight accommodation in mountain huts and tourist facilities. It extends from Abisko (p. 54) in the N by way of the Kebnekaise range (p. 161) and southern Lapland to *Tärnaby*. There is a tourist base at Abisko. Visitors should not fail to see *Abisko National Park*, with its unusual vegetation, and the *Njulla gorge* (reached by chair-lift).

The *National Park* of **Stora Sjöfallet**, with a waterfall on the *Stora Luleälv*, is Sweden's third largest nature reserve. The Stora Luleälv rises in this hilly region, slashed by numerous valleys, and reaches its highest point in *Akka* (2015 m – 6611 ft). The National Park, established in 1909, extends from the coniferous forests in the E over a mountain region of varying height and a variety of animal and plant life. The nature reserve originally covered an area of 1500 sq. km (580 sq. miles), but after ten years 120 sq. km (45 sq. miles) around the lake were released to permit the construction of a dam for the *Porjus hydroelectric station*. The waterfall giving its name to the park is formed by the water of the mountain lake *Kårtjejaure* pouring into *Lake Langas*. The falls are at their best · when the water level is high.

The Royal Trail (see above) runs through the National Park. Hunting and fishing are prohibited.

*Sarek is another typical mountain region containing a *National Park* (1950 sq. km – 750 sq. miles), between the *Stora* and the *Lilla Luleälv*. It has about a

hundred glaciers, 87 peaks over 1800 m (5900 ft) and 8 others over 2000 m (6500 ft), with plateaux and valleys between the hills. The best known valley is the *Rapadal*, on *Lake Laidaure*. Hunting and fishing are prohibited; sleigh-dogs may be used from January to April, but otherwise dogs are banned. The *Rapaälv* flows down the Rapadal, receiving melted water from 30 glaciers and depositing its sediment in the Laidaure delta. There is a remarkable contrast between the barren world of the mountains and the rich plant and animal life in the valley. To the W is *Alkavare*, where silver was mined into the late 17th c.; remains of silver-mines, *chapel* of 1788. – The Sarek nature reserve was established in 1909 to preserve this striking mountain region. A mountain walk through the National Park takes a full week, and should be undertaken only by experienced hill walkers, with proper equipment, tents and adequate supplies of food.

Lapp church, Saltoluokta (Northern Sweden)

**Tärnaby** (Laisalidens Fjällhotell, 46 b.; Tärnaby Fjallhotell, 238 b.) lies in a magnificent mountain setting on the southern slopes of the *Luxfjäll* (824 m – 2704 ft), 38 km (24 miles) from the Norwegian frontier. Equipped to cater for · skiers, the little town has a Lapp Museum and a school for nomad children. – 12 km (7½ miles) W, on a marked footpath or a motor road, are the *Västensjö* and the hill of *Gieravardo* (fine views). – The neighbouring village of *Hemavan*, which also offers good skiing, has developed into a tourist resort. From here there are panoramic views extending to the hills of Jofjället and Okstindern, on the Norwegian side of the frontier. Canoes and gliders can be rented in summer. Fishing is permitted in the lakes above the village. – 60 km (38 miles) NE of Tärnaby (road from Sorsele) is the little village of *Ammarnäs* (Ammarnäsgården, 60 b. and 25 chalets; Fjallhotellet i Ammarnäs,

66 b.), with an old Lapp church; fishing, cross-country skiing, downhill skiing.

**Vilhelmina** (Wilhelmina Hotell, 128 b.; Vilhelmina Kyrkstad, 138 b.), in the middle of southern Lapland, is the head-quarters of the body officially represent-ing the Lapp community and has an interesting Lapp Museum. 95 km (60 miles) NW, by way of *Laxbäcken* (school of agriculture), is the village of **Saxnäs** (Hotel Saxnäsgården with summer chalets). It is in a magnificent mountain setting (hills over 1500 m – 5000 ft) on the S side of the *Kultsjö* (alt. 540 m – 1772 ft), and has fishing, walking and skiing (Pension Saxnäsgården, with vacation chalets).

**FINNISH LAPLAND** (Finnish **Lappi**), a forest-covered area of hills and bog (about 94,000 sq. km – 36,000 sq. miles), is similar in many respects to Swedish Lapland, but its elevations are lower. Only in the extreme NW, where a finger of territory reaches into the Scandinavian mountain region, is there a mountain of greater height – *Haltiatunturi* (1324 m – 4344 ft), the highest peak in Finland. Most of Finnish Lapland is covered with forest; in the S spruce predominates, but beyond **Lake Inari** (p. 143) there are only pines and birches. At higher altitudes, there are areas of treeless, lichen-covered tundra. The area has been made more easily accessible to visitors by the development of good roads and the provision of hotels and other accom-modation. The administrative capital of Finnish Lapland is **Rovaniemi** (p. 229), a bit S of the Arctic Circle.

The main traffic route from S to N is the **Arctic Highway** (Road 4 as far as Ivalo). The highway runs from Kempi (p. 159) via *Rovaniemi* (p. 229) and *Sodankylä* (hotels: Kantakievari, 103 b., SB; Kan-takievari Luosto, 26 b.); wooden church, 1689), to *Ivalo*, at the S end of Lake Inari (p. 143). From Ivalo the highway con-tinues NE and ends in another 54 km (34 miles) at the Soviet frontier. (It formerly extended to the port of Petsamo on the Arctic Ocean, now the Soviet town of Pechenga.) – Road 4 continues to Kaama-nen and then runs NW to the Norwegian frontier at Karigasniemi. Another road runs N via Utsjoki and then along the frontier river, the Tenojoki, and over the frontier to the Norwegian port of Berlevåg on the Arctic Ocean.

# Lappeenranta (Villmanstrand)

Finland (SE).
Province: Kymen lääni (Kymmene län/Kymi).
Altitude: 76 m (249 ft). – Population: 54,000.
Postal code: SF-53100. – Telephone code: 953.

ⓘ **Kaupungin Matkailutoimisto**
*(Municipal Tourist Information Office)*,
Bus station;
tel. 1 88 50.

HOTELS. – *Cumulus*, Valtakatu 31, 180 b., SB; *Karelia-Park*, Korpraalinkuja, 204 b. (1 June to 31 August); *Lappee*, Brahenkatu 1, 300 b.; *Lappenranta Spa*, Ainonkatu 17, 81 b., SB; *Patria*, Kauppakatu 21, 130 b.; *Viikinkihovi*, Valtakatu 41, 67 b., SB. – YOUTH HOSTEL. – CAMP SITE.

RESTAURANTS. – *Sirmakka*, Valtakatu 36; *Prinsessa Armaada*, in an old Lake Saimaa cargo boat in the harbour.

EVENTS. – *Folk music and dancing* (June); *Humppa* dance marathon (July); *open-air concerts* three times a week and occasional *open-air theatre performances* during the months of June, July and August.

SPORTS and RECREATION. – Tennis, golf, bowling.

**The Finnish town of Lappeenranta (Villmanstrand), on the S side of the Lappvesi, was founded by Queen Christina in 1649. It is the most southerly port of call of the boats on Lake Saimaa. In view of its exposed situation on the frontier facing the Russian Empire, it became a garrison town in the 17th c. – the only town in Finland on whose history, develop-ment and layout the Finnish cavalry exerted such a large influence. Lap-peenranta has the reputation of being one of the most cosmopolitan towns in Finland and is one of the most popular with visitors.**

HISTORY. – The town originated as a medieval trading station. In 1741 it was the scene of a decisive battle in which a Swedish-Finnish army was defeated by the Russians. Under the treaty of Åbo (Turku) Lappeenranta passed to Russia in 1743; it remained Russian until 1811. There are remains of fortifications dating from the 17th–18th c., as well as the Russian period. – After the discovery of a radioactive mineral spring (1824), the town developed as a spa, particularly favoured by Russian nobility. Since 1974, the spa has operated throughout the year; it specialises in the treatment of cardiac and circulatory conditions and rheumatism.

Lappeenranta lies at the N end of the *Saimaa Canal*. Construction of the canal was planned by several Swedish kings but actually undertaken only during the reign of Tsar Alexander II; it was completed in 1856. Until 1944 it ran through Finnish

Lake Saimaa boats, Lappeenranta

all towns in Finland and Sweden usually have high water-towers, attractively designed, and from which can be seen panoramic views.

SURROUNDINGS. – Lappeenranta is the base for attractive trips on Lake Saimaa (see p. 231). There are services to Mikkeli (p. 190) and Savonlinna (p. 231), as well as a variety of cruises ranging in length from a few hours to several days. In summer there are excursions to the Saimaa Canal and the Soviet frontier, along the Saimaa Canal to Vyborg (formerly Viipuri) and Helsinki (p. 131), and to Leningrad (to which there are also coach (bus) excursions; Soviet visa required).

territory, but, since almost its entire length, including its terminal port at Viipuri on the Gulf of Finland, lay within the territory which Finland was compelled to cede to the Soviet Union, it was closed. In the 1960s, however, the Soviet Union leased the canal zone back to Finland, and the Finns then built a new canal on the old line, with modern locks.

SIGHTS. – The main street is *Kauppakatu*, running from N to S. A little bit E of its intersection with Valtakatu, in the *Keskuspuisto* park (which lies roughly in the middle of the town near the market square), stands the *church* (1749) of the old commune of Lappee (separate *tower*, 1864). Nearby is a military cemetery for Karelians killed in the war with the Soviet Union (1941–4), with a monument (Väinö Aaltonen, 1951). To the NW of the church, at the intersection of Kauppakatu and Raastuvankatu, is the wooden **Town Hall** (by C. L. Engel, 1829). – Going N along Kauppakatu, on a hill on the left (alt. 130 m (427 ft); 60 m (200 ft) above Lake Saimaa) is the *Town Church* (1924). Still farther N, at the head of a promontory projecting into the lake (on left), is the *Old Park*, with a *monument* commemorating the 1741 battle in which the Russians decisively defeated a Swedish-Finnish army. To the NW, beyond the monument, are the remains of old fortifications (*Museum of Southern Karelia*). NE of the monument, on the other side of the street, we come to the *Orthodox Church* (1785). – A little way E, in an inlet on the lake, is Lappeenranta harbour. On the S side of the inlet is the *Spa Establishment*. At the N end of Ainonkatu an old Lake Saimaa boat, the "Prinsessa Armaada", now houses a restaurant. At the E end of the inlet lies Kimpinen Park (bathing beach). – To the E of the town, on the right of the Imatra road, is the *Water-Tower* (café), from which there are good views. Nearly

40 km (25 miles) E of Lappeenranta is **Imatra** (pop. 40,000; Valtionhotelli, 200 b.; Niskahovi, 100 b.), famous in the 19th c. for its waterfalls. The waterfalls attracted many visitors, including the composer Richard Wagner. Here the River Vuoksen, which flows from Lake Saimaa into the Gulf of Finland, falls 18 m (60 ft) within a very short distance, and the force of the water has gouged a channel 20 m (65 ft) wide out of the granite. The water has been diverted to provide hydroelectric power, and it is only on Sunday afternoons that the sluices into the old bed are opened. The Valtionhotelli was built at the falls during the Tsarist period and established Imatra's position as a vacation resort. On the W bank of the river is a large *tourist resort*, with a camp site, chalets, walkers' hostels, a riding school, a boat harbour, running tracks and bathing beaches.

# Larvik

Norway (Southern).
County: Vestfold fylke.
Altitude: sea level. – Population: 9000.
Postal code: N-3251. – Telephone code: 0 34.
ⓘ **Turistkontor**;
   tel. 8 26 23.

HOTELS. – *Grand Hotel*, 214 b.; *Holms Motel*, 126 b.; *Seierstad Gjestergård*, 24 b.

**The former county town of Larvik is set attractively on the Norwegian S coast. To the S of the town the Larvikfjord runs inland; to the N is a 20 km (12½ mile) long lake, the Farrisvatn.**

Larvik has two mineral springs – King Håkon's Well, a spring of sulphurous saline water marketed under the brand name Farris, and a chalybeate spring. The town does not, however, operate as a spa. Larvik was the birthplace of the anthropologist Thor Heyerdahl (b. 1914), best known for his voyages in the balsa-wood raft, "Kon-Tiki" from Peru to Polynesia, and also in the papyrus boat, "Ra" (1969–70) and the reed boat, "Tigris" (1978).

SIGHTS. – The central feature of the town is the *Market Square* (Torget). To the NW, on the outskirts, is a magnificent beech forest, *Bøkeskogen* (extensive views from hill; 1500-year-old cemetery). NE of the forest is the district of *Farris Bad* (beautiful park).

On *Herregårdsbakken*, to the SE of the town, is the **Herregård**, a large wooden manor-house which was the residence of the Counts of Larvik from 1670 to 1680. It now houses the *Municipal Museum*. To the S, beyond the railway, is the **church** (1674–7), which contains a portrait of Martin Luther by Lucas Cranach the Elder (to the left of altar). From the church there is a fine view over the fjord.

NW of the church, in the old Custom House on the harbour, is a small *Seafaring Museum*. – Storgata, parallel to the railway line, runs W to the *Bødkerfjell*, a hill with far-ranging views. Here there is a private *museum* with material on the ironworking industry of Larvik, which was of some consequence between 1640 and 1868 (oven plates, casting moulds, etc.).

SURROUNDINGS. 7·5 km (5 miles) S is the seaside resort of **Stavern** (Wassilioff Hotel, 83 b.), with a fine church (1756). In the churchyard is the grave of the writer Jonas Lie (1833–1908) and his wife.

7 km (4½ miles) E of Larvik is *Tjølling*, where there is another interesting church (Romanesque, with a Renaissance pulpit and a Rococo baptistery; font, *c.* 1700).

# Lillehammer

Norway (SE).
County: Oppland fylke.
Altitude: 180 m (590 ft). – Population: 22,000.
Postal code: N-2600. – Telephone code: 0 62.
ⓘ **Turistkontor**,
Storgata 56;
tel. 5 10 98.

HOTELS. – *Breiseth*, 80 b.; *Ersgård*, 50 b.; *Langseth*, 70 b.; *Lillehammer*, 320 b., SB, SP; *Oppland Turisthotell*, 140 b., SB; *Rica Victoria*, 200 b., SB; *Smestad Touristheim*, – IN SJUSJØEN (22 km/14 miles E): *Sjusjøen Fjellstue*, 127 b.; *Sjusjøen Hoyfjellshotell*, 120 b., SB, SP; *Sjusjøen Panorama Hotel*, 110 b. – IN NORDSETER (14 km/9 miles NE): *Nevra Hoyfjellshotell*, 80 b. SB; *Nordseter Hoyfjellshotell*, 83 b. – IN HUNDER (24 km/15 miles N): *Fossegården*, 50 b.; *Nermo Fjellstue*, 54 b. – Several CAMP SITES in surrounding area.

RECREATION and SPORTS. – Riding, swimming, discothèque.

WINTER SPORTS. – Ice rink, curling rink, sleigh rides, excellent cross-country skiing (220 km (140 miles) of trails); chair-lift up Kanten (500 m – 1 640 ft) and ski-lift on Bergebakken (to N: 520 m – 1 700 ft); several good runs. Skiing school. IN NORDSETER (850 m – 2790 ft): 200 km (125 miles) of ski trails, two ski-lifts and one ski-cable, skiing school. IN SJUSJØEN (850 m – 2790 ft): largest group of huts in Norway, 120 km (75 miles) of ski trails, ski-lift.

**Lillehammer, main town in the county of Oppland, is located on Lake Mjøsa, at the S end of the Gudbrandsdal, and is divided by the River Mesna. It is one of the best known vacation resorts in Norway, attracting large numbers of visitors not only in summer but in winter, too (excellent skiing; lifts, illuminated ski trails).**

View of Lillehammer

SIGHTS. – The principal sight of Lillehammer is the **Maihaugen Open-Air Museum** on the SE outskirts of the town, which contains the \*Sandvig Collection of more than 100 old buildings. The museum was founded in 1887 by a local dentist, Anders Sandvig (1862–1950). All the buildings have been re-erected in their original form and furnished with old domestic equipment and implements. The collection illustrates the development of dwelling-houses and also includes entire farmhouses from the heyday of peasant culture (18th c.). In addition, various craft workshops are housed in a large separate building. The oldest building in the collection is the stave church from Garmo. Another notable item is the Peer Gynt Hut (Peer Gynts Stue), a dwelling of about 1700, said to have been the home of the prototype of Ibsen's hero. – In the market square of Lillehammer (Stortorget) is the *Municipal Art Gallery* (Malerisamling), with pictures by Norwegian artists; on the Nordseterweg the house of the writer Sigrid Undset.

SURROUNDINGS. – From the N bank of the Mesna there is a chair-lift up *Kanten* (restaurant).

THE HILLS TO THE E. – From Maihaugen Park a road ascends to the SE past the Langseth Hotel (alt. 350 m – 1150 ft) and the little *Bädshaugtjern Lake* (585 m –

1920 ft) and soon afterwards crosses the *Bustokelv*, which flows out of the *Søndre Mesnasjø* (512 m – 1680 ft), on the right, into the slightly lower *Nordra Mesnasjø* on the left. Beyond Mesnalien (520 m – 1705 ft), the road turns N and continues climbing,

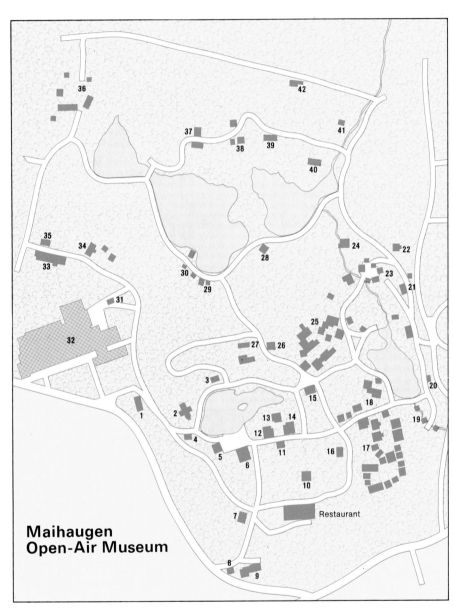

# Maihaugen Open-Air Museum

1 Main entrance, tickets, souvenirs
2 Church (c. 1200) from Garmo, Gudbrandsdal
3 Smoke house (c. 1700) from Hesta, Romsdal
4 Tolstad House (15th c.), from Tolstadløkken, Vågå
5 Headman's house or dower house (mid-17th c.) from Mytting, Ringebu
6 Presbytery (mid-17th c.) from Vågå
7 "Guest-house."
8 Workshop
9 Constable's house
10 Armoury (mid-18th c.) from Toftemoen, Dovre
11 Store-room from Dagsgård
12 Lykre House (mid-18th c.), the first house in the Museum
13 Vigenstad House (early 18th c.)

14 Hjeltar House (c. 1600)
15 Schoolhouse (mid-19th c.) from Skjåk
16 Village office with prison cells
17 Bjørnstad farm (c. 1700), from Bjørnstad, Vågå
18 Chapel and presbytery from Isum, Sør-Fron
19 Mills
20 Blacksmith
21 Brassworker's workshop
22 Skrefsrud hut
23 Knutslykkja farm (c. 1800)
24 Dyer's workshop
25 Øygården farm (18th c.), from Øygården, Skjåk
26 Peer Gynt Hut
27 Meviken
28 Knuvel hut from Fåberg
29 Fishermen's huts

30 Fishermen's chapel (mid-15th c.) from Fåberg
31 Toilets
32 Old workshops and concert hall
33 Kirkestuen/summer restaurant
34 Changing station
35 Potter's workshop
36 Valbjor shieling (shelter on summer grazing ground), from Vågå
37 Barhus shieling (c. 1800), from Gausdal
38 Øygård shieling (c. 1700), from Skjåk
39 Korpberg shieling (c. 1700), from Nord-Fron
40 Kleiv shieling (c. 1600), from Vågå
41 Shieling huts from Lesja and Ringebu
42 Lunde shieling (mid-19th c.) from Ringebu

passing the *Sjusjø* (795 m – 2610 ft) on the right and coming soon afterwards to the holiday village complex of **Sjusjøen** (830 m – 2725 ft), with hotels and numerous huts and summer chalets. Beyond this point, the road is narrow but still easily negotiable. Then in another 6 km (4 miles) take a road on the left which runs along the S side of the *Mellsjø* (893 m – 2930 ft) and joins a road coming from Lillehammer. Along this road, to the left, is **Nordsetter** (786 m – 2580 ft), another holiday complex, from which it is a 1¼ hours' climb to the summit of the *Neverfjell* (1086 m (3563 ft): fine views). From Nordsetter, the road runs down through wooded country to Lillehammer.

**Up the Gausdal.** – Leave Lillehammer on a road which runs SW and crosses the narrow N end of *Lake Mjøsa* on a long bridge; then turn right into Road 253 along the W side of the lake, passing *Jørstadmoent* and the airport on the left. At the church (1724) in *Fåberg* turn left into Road 255, which runs up the *Gausdal*, the valley of the *Gausa*; there is another attractive road running parallel on the hillside to the E. At **Follebu** (alt. 310 m – 1015 ft) a road goes off on the right (2 km – 1¼ miles) to an old stone church on the hillside (422 m – 1385 ft). – 1 km (¾ mile) beyond Follebu, on the right, is *Aulestad*, a handsome house once occupied by the dramatist Bjørnstjerne Bjørnson (1832–1910), with souvenirs of the writer. From *Segalstad Bru* Road 255 bears left up the valley, which grows steadily narrower, to **Vestre Gausdal** where we find a church of 1784. From here Road 254, to the right, continues up the Østre Gausdal. – On to *Svingvoll* (alt. 480 m – 1575 ft), from which it is possible either to bear left for the "Peer Gynt Road" (p. 115) or to turn right via Tretten into the Gudbrandsdal.

# Limfjord

Denmark (Jutland).
Counties: Viborg amt, Nordjyllands amt.
(i) **Lemvig Turistkontor**,
    Toldbodgade 4,
    DK-7620 Lemvig;
    tel. (07) 82 03 72.
    **Nykøbing Turistkontor Mors**,
    Havnen 4,
    DK-7900 Nykøbing;
    tel. (07) 72 04 88.
    **Thisted Turistkontor**,
    Store Torv
    DK-7700 Thisted ;
    tel (07) 92 19 00.

**The Limfjord is a strip of water 180 km (110 miles) long, extending from the North Sea to the Kattegat. It separates the Nørrejyske Ø, the island of North Jutland, from the rest of Jutland. With its beautiful scenery and calm water it offers ideal sailing conditions; its many little ports and anchorages provide every facility for those who enjoy a vacation on the water or merely "messing about in boats".**

A fishing boat in the Limfjord

A brochure listing all ports and anchorages is available from local tourist information offices. – Motorists should bear in mind that the Limfjord can be crossed only at certain places. There are bridges over the Oddesund, Vilsund and Sallingsund (island of Mors) and the Aggersund, and a bridge and tunnel at Ålborg. In addition there are a number of ferries which make the crossing in a few minutes, including one at each end of the fjord.

The western entrance to the Limfjord from the North Sea is the *Thyborøn Channel* (ferry), on the N side of which is the popular vacation and bathing area around *Agger* and Vestervig. *Vestervig*, in the 11th c. the seat of the bishop of Vendsyssel (the most northerly part of Jutland), is now a small village with less than 1000 inhabitants. The church, a three-aisled basilica, still recalls the great days of the past. After heavy alteration and restoration through the centuries, it was restored to nearly its original form in the 1920s. It contains a number of Romanesque tombstones, including the oldest dated stones in Denmark (1210).

Vestervig suffered a rapid decline after its harbour silted up; many other ports on the Limfjord met the same fate. The process of silting up alternated with storm tides which wrought havoc with the land, and much fertile land as well as a number of towns disappeared under the sea. The tiny church and beacon tower of *Lodbjerg*, standing solitary among the dunes, bear mute witness to this destruction. The *Agger Tange*, a spit of land on the N side of the Thyborøn Channel, is now protected by dikes and groynes, following the example of Holland.

On the S side of the *Nissum Bredning*, at the W end of the Limford, is **Lemvig** (pop. 6500; Industriehotellet, 30 b.; Hotel

Nørre Vinkel, 52 b.; Scandinavian Holiday Center, 148 apartments; camp site), an attractive town in a hilly setting (Gothic church, interesting museum). The surrounding area is a paradise for nature-lovers with its expanses of woodland, bog and heath, the sand dunes on the W coast (such as the *Bovbjerg Klint*, 43 m (141 ft) high, 12 km (7½ miles) W of Lemvig) and a distinctive fauna which includes many rare species of waterfowl.

From Lemvig a good road (No. 11) skirts the fjord and crosses a bridge over the *Oddesund* on to the *Thyholm* peninsula. It then continues along the NW side of the Limfjord to **Thisted**, the chief place on Thyholm (pop. 11,000; Hotel Ålborg, 48 b.; Missionshotel Merci, 50 b.; camp site), which has a library with paintings by Jens Skovgaard and a museum with an interesting historical collection.

22 km (14 miles) N of Thisted lies the little port and fishing village of *Hanstholm*, at the NW tip of Thyholm. To the S is the resort of *Klitmøller*, named after the old water-mills which once stood here (very good beach). – Beyond Thisted, Road 11 continues E to *Fjerritselv*, *Brovst* and *Åbybro*, where it turns N. From here Road 17 runs SE along the Limfjord to **Ålborg** (p. 55), through a region of forests and small fjords; it is less than half an hour's drive to the North Sea from this road. An interesting feature at the W end of the *Jammerbugt* is the *Skarreklit*, an isolated rock 15 m (50 ft) high which once was part of the coast but now stands 100 m (110 yds) offshore.

In the Limfjord itself there are several islands of varying size; the largest, **Mors**, can be reached by bridges over the Sallingsund to the S and the Vilsund to the N or by ferries over the Neessund and the Feggesund. The charm of Mors lies in its magnificent scenery. A particularly notable feature is the *Hanklit*, a 65 m (200 ft) high crag which falls almost vertically to the sea and contains animal and plant fossils of the Tertiary period. The rock has been carved into fantastic forms by Ice Age glaciers. At the northern tip of Mors is the *Feggeklit*, on which, according to legend, Hamlet killed his stepfather, Fegge.

The chief town on Mors is **Nykøbing** (pop. 10,000; Bendix Hotel, 80 b.), noted for the culture of oysters and as a herring-fishing port. The Mors Historical Museum is in *Dueholm Abbey*; only one building of the original abbey, founded by the Knights of St John in 1370, is still preserved.

To the E of Mors on the little island of *Fur* is a museum containing a large collection of fossils. An overall view of the island's beautiful natural scenery is possible from the *Stendalshøj*.

Beyond Ålborg, the Limfjord runs E in a narrow channel, the *Langerak*, into Ålborg Bugt on the Kattegat. There is a ferry across the mouth of the Langerak from *Hals*, a resort with remains of its old fortifications (Powder Tower, Armoury).

# Linköping

Sweden (Southern).
Province: Östergötland län.
Region: Östergötland.
Altitude: 40 m (130 ft). – Population: 115,000.
Postal code: S-58 . . . – Telephone code: 0 13.
ⓘ Linköpings Turistbyrå,
  Agatan 39,
  S-58101 Linköping;
  tel. 20 68 35.

HOTELS. – *Baltic*, Hantverkaregatan 1, 107 b.; *Ekoxen*, Klostergatan 68, 235 b., SB; *Hotel du Nord*, Repslagaregatan 5, 30 b.; *Frimurarehotellet*, St Larsgatan 14, 360 b.; *Park Hotell*, Järnvägsgatan 6, 75 b.; *Rally*, Storgatan 70–76, 200 b.; *Scandic Hotel*, Rydsvägen, 260 b., SB; *Stångå City Hotel*, Tullgränd 4, 80 b.; *Stora Hotellet*, Stora Torget 9, 150 b.

**Linköping, capital of the province of Östergötland, the see of a bishop and a university town, lies on the W bank of the Stångå, which flows into Lake Roxen a little way N of the town, on the road from Stockholm to Gothenburg. The name of the town first appears in the records in 1120, in connection with the founding of Vreta Abbey. At a church council held in Linköping in 1152, Sweden was declared a province of the Church of Rome. Here, on the banks of the Stångå, Duke Charles of Södermanland (Charles IX, the defender of the Reformation) defeated King Sigismund of Poland, John III's Catholic son, in 1598. Sigismund's supporters were executed in the main square of Linköping in 1600, in**

what became known as the "Bloodbath of Linköping".

SIGHTS. – The main square of Linköping is the *Stora Torg*, with the *Folkung Fountain* (Folkungabrunn, 1927), one of Carl Milles's best-known works; it depicts Folke Filbyter, legendary ancestor of the royal family of the Folkungs. To the E stands *St Lars' Church* which has a 12th c. tower; the church contains pictures by one of the leading Swedish painters of the Romantic school, Pehr Hörberg (1746–1816), noted for his primitive style and fine use of colour. The *Cathedral, to the NW of the Stora Torg, was begun about 1150 in Romanesque style (N doorway) and later altered and enlarged in Gothic style; the tower, 105 m (345 ft) high, was added in 1886. The late Gothic choir was the work of Master Gerlach of Cologne. To the right of the altar is the marble sarcophagus of the Lutheran Bishop Terserus (d. 1678); in the S transept is an altarpiece by the Dutch master van Heemskerck (d. 1574), which John III bought in 1581 for 1200 tons of wheat. To the N of the Cathedral are the *Bishop's Palace* (1733) and the *Diocesan Library* (old manuscripts, rare books). SW of the Cathedral, in the *King's Garden* (Kungsträdgården), stands the *Castle* (built before 1500, restored 1931–2), now the governor's residence.

In the *Vasatorg* to the N, reached from the Cathedral by way of Gråbrödragatan, are the *Municipal Museum* and the *Östergötland Museum* (ethnographical collections; good picture gallery, with works by Cranach). – On the banks of the Stångå, to the E, is the *Stångebro Monument*, commemorating the battle of 1598. The bridge itself, linking the two halves of the town, was built in 1655. The old part of the town, **Gamla Linköping**, is noted for its assemblage of old buildings, mostly timber houses, which were transferred here from the middle of the town, beginning in 1950. A number of historic old buildings from the province of Östergötland were also brought here. Many craft workers have now established themselves in this part of the town.

SURROUNDINGS. – One attractive excursion is a trip on the **Kinda Canal**, which links Lake Roxen with a number of other lakes to the S and through which the Stångå flows. The canal, 80 km (50 miles) long, has 15 locks. The boat passes old manor-houses (among them the handsome Sturefors manor-house (1704) on *Lake Erlang*), and the trip ends at *Horn*, at the S end of *Lake Åsund*.

8 km (5 miles) E of Linköping is the 12th c. round church (restored 1940) of **Vårdsberg**, with 16th c. paintings in the vaulting. – 6 km (4 miles) E is *Askeby* church (remains of a 12th c. nunnery). – 7 km ($4\frac{1}{2}$ miles) NW stands *Karga* church, built by King Sverker (d. 1156) on the old pagan cult site of *Allguvi* (the shrine of all the gods). The church has numerous paintings; those in the nave are by Master Amund, those in the choir by his pupil the Master of Risinge. – 11 km (7 miles) NW on the road to Motala we come to **Vreta abbey church**, a 13th c. building (restored 1915–22), which belonged to a house of Cistercian nuns. Immediately N of the church, which contains several monuments, are the foundations of the old abbey buildings.

# Lofoten Islands

Norway (Northern).
County: Nordland fylke.
Area: 1308 sq. km (505 sq. miles).
Population: 27,000.
Telephone code: 0 88.
(i) **Lofoten Reiselivslag**,
    Storgate 47,
    N-8300 Svolvær;
    tel. 7 10 53.

RECREATION and SPORTS. – Fishing from the pier and from rowboats, deep sea-fishing, climbing, shooting.

ACCESS. – By boat from Bodø (6 hours), Skutvik (2 hours) or Narvik (9 hours) to Svolvær. The coastal steamers also dock at the Lofotens. Air services from Bodø and Evenes (Narvik) to Svolvær and other places.

The **Lofotens are a chain of hilly islands some 150 km (90 miles) long strung NE to SW and separated from the mainland by the Vestfjord, which is some 80 km (50 miles) wide at its broad southern end. The four large islands of Austvågøy, Vestvågøy, Moskenesøy and Flakstadøy, together with a number of medium-sized islands, lie so close together that from the distance they appear to be a single long jagged range of hills. The main islands are surrounded by smaller islets, and have numerous inlets and fjords with rock walls up to 1000 m (3280 ft) high. The mountains are of Alpine type with characteristic steep-sided summits (highest point 1266 m – 4154 ft), bare and sometimes snow-capped. In many places there are cliffs where sea birds nest.**

The first Commando raid on enemy-occupied territory was made on four fishing villages of the Lofotens in March 1941 and the reprisals taken by the Gestapo virtually created the great Norwegian Resistance movement. A second landing was made at Reine in the outer Lofotens in December 1941, the intention being to remain throughout the winter and harass the German iron-ore boats sailing from Narvik and so aid the resistance on the Finnish front. However, the bombing of Pearl Harbor made it necessary for the force to withdraw, taking with it as many civilians as possible to Scotland to save them from German reprisals – which is why many of the people in the Lofotens today speak with a Glaswegian accent.

There are few trees. Near the coasts of the islands are bogs, lakes, pastureland and some areas of arable land. The climate is wet, but mild in winter. The main sources of income are fishing and its associated industries; there is also a certain amount of sheep-farming; mink-farming has been introduced recently. The summer vacation trade also makes a contribution to the economy of the islands, and fishermen's huts (*rorbuer*), either old-style (with very few amenities) or modernised, can be rented at astonishingly low rates.

The chief town in the Lofotens and the administrative headquarters of the islands is **Svolvær**, on the S coast of the island of **Austvagøy** (Hotel Havly, 90 b.; Lofoten Nordic Hotell, 92 b.; youth hostel), with a normal population of 4000, which greatly multiplies during the fishing season. It is the main fishing port in the islands, the hub of communications and the principal commercial area. – On *Svinøy* is the

The season for the Lofoten **fisheries**, for which thousands of fishermen gather with their boats, is from mid-January to mid-April. The main catch is cod (Norwegian *torsk*). From the beginning of January the cod, predatory fish which normally live deep in the Atlantic, head for the coast in long shoals several yards deep to spawn. The depth at which they swim varies according to the temperature of the water, ranging between 100 m (328 ft) and 300 m (985 ft). – Once landed, the cod are cut open (*rundfisk*) or cut up completely (*klippet*) and the head and entrails removed. They are then either hung on timber racks (*hjeller*) to dry, remaining on the racks until June (*tørrfisk*, stockfish); or they are salted and laid out on the rocks (*klippfisk*), and then piled in heaps, which are covered to protect them from moisture. Some of the fish are not dried but are salted in barrels (*laberdan*). The heads are processed in guano factories to produce fertilisers, the roe tinned, and the livers used in the manufacture of cod liver oil. – After the winter fishing season, most of the fishermen head N to Finnmark and the summer fisheries in coastal waters.

Kunstnernes Hus (Artists' House), which displays works by the many painters who have found inspiration in the Lofotens. Opposite the wharf on the little island of *Gunnarholm* (road bridge from Svolvær) is the grave of the Nordland painter Gunnar Berg (b. Svolvær 1864, d. in Berlin 1894). – From the steep-sided hill to the N, *Blåtind* (597 m (1959 ft): 5 hours round trip for fit walkers), there are magnificent views; midnight sun from the end of May to mid-July. – An attractive trip is by motorboat (2 hours) to the S end of the island of *Hinnøy*, in the Vesterål group (see p. 291), where *Digermulkollen* offers a rewarding climb (1¼ hours). The boat also sails through the southern part of the *Raftsund* (8 km (5 miles) long), between the Lofotens and the Vesterål islands. On the W side of the Raftsund a narrow rocky opening gives access to the **\*\*Trollfjord**. Behind the Trollfjord the snow-covered *Higravtinder* (1161 m – 3908 ft) and the jagged *Trolltinder* (1045 m – 3429 ft) rise above the \**Trollfjordvatn*, a mountain lake 3 km (2 miles) long (almost always frozen). The most popular day trip to the Trollfjord is by bus from Svolvær via Fiskebøl to Stokmarknes and back by the "Hurtigrute" boat, which sails via the Trollfjord. – 10 km (6 miles) SW of Svolvær (bus) is the village of **Kabelvåg** (many holiday houses called "Rorbu" or "Sjøhus"; several camp sites), with a Fisheries Museum, the Lofoten Aquarium (fish and other marine fauna from the Vestfjord) and Vågan church, the largest wooden church N of Trondheim.

The Nusfjord on the island of Flakstadøy (Lofotens)

At the SW tip of Austvågøy, under *Vågekalle* (942 m (3091 ft); 3½ hours' climb), is *Festvåg*. A ferry crosses in 12 minutes to the typical little fishing settlement of *Henningsvær*, on a group of small islands; a large fishing fleet gathers there in winter.

On the SE coast of the large island of **Vestvågøy** is **Stamsund** (Stamsund Lofoten Hotels Rorbuer and other summer houses; youth hostel), one of the largest of the little fishing towns in the archipelago and the hub of communications in the western Lofotens. – At the SW end of Vestvågøy is the fishing village of *Ballstad*, at the foot of Ballstadaksla (466 m – 1529 ft).

On the NW coast of the island of **Flakstadøy** lies Ramberg (Summer houses in Nusfjord), administrative headquarters of the island. To the E of the village stands the church (1780), originally built of driftwood.

The chief place on the island of **Moskenesøy** is the fishing village of *Reine* (Havly Hospits, 11 b.) on the Kirkefjord, a resort popular with painters and climbers. 10 km (6 miles) SW is the little settlement of *Å*, at the end of the Lofoten road. From the higher ground above the village, there is a view of the *Moskenesstraum*, a whirlpool between the cape of Lofotodde and the island of Moskenesøy. It was described by Jules Verne and Edgar Allan Poe as the Maelstrom.

From Reine there are boat trips to the little island of **Værøy**, to the SW. At the S end of this island is the *Mostadfjell, rearing steeply above the abandoned village of Mostad. These heights are a paradise for birds; more than a million birds – primarily puffins, but also guillemots, cormorants and white-tailed eagles – breed between May and August. The nesting sites can be reached by renting a boat from the village of Værøy (20 minutes). – On Værøy are the last specimens of a curious breed of dog with six toes, known as a puffin hound since it is used for catching these birds.

There are also boat trips from Reine (5 hours), as well as from Bodø (5 hours) and Værøy (2¼ hours), to the remarkable **Røst** islands (Roald Olsens Sjøhus), almost 100 km (65 miles) from the mainland, with a series of high *crags

(Vedøy, Storfjell, Stavøy, the Nykan rocks) inhabited by one of the largest assemblages of seabirds in the world, including some 3 million puffins, as well as rare species like storm petrels and fulmars. The crags can be reached by boat from Røstland; during the season there are also helicopter flights from Bodø.

# Lolland

Denmark.
County: Storstrøms amt.
Area: 1214 sq. km (470 sq. miles).
Population: 80,000.

ⓘ **Maribo Tourist Information Office,**
Jernbanegade 8,
DK-4930 Maribo;
tel. (03) 88 04 96.
**Nakskov Tourist Information Office,**
Axeltorv 6,
DK-4800 Nakskov;
tel. (03) 92 21 72.
**Nysted Tourist Information Office,**
Adelgade 65,
DK-4880 Nysted;
tel (03) 87 19 85.
**Rødby Tourist Information Office,**
Havnegade 19,
DK-4970 Rødby;
tel. (03) 90 50 43.
**Sakskøbing Tourist Information Office,**
Torvegade 4,
DK-4990 Sakskøbing;
tel. (03) 89 58 30.

**Lolland, lying W of Falster, is the third-largest Danish island (if Greenland is not counted), coming after Zealand and Funen. It has relatively little industry; the largest enterprises are in the area round Nakskov. The main economic activity is the growing of sugar-beet, with sugar refineries at Nakskov and Sakskøbing. Fishing, formerly of importance, has declined considerably. Thanks to the ferry services Lolland now attracts tourist and vacation traffic. – The islands of Lolland, Falster and Møn, with the adjoining smaller islands, are known in Denmark as the "South Sea islands".**

Lolland lies on the direct route from Germany to Copenhagen, known as the Fugleflugtsline ("As the crow flies" line), linking with a ferry service from Puttgarden in Germany to Rødby Havn (reservations necessary in summer). Lolland is connected with Falster by two bridges over the Guldborgsund, and with Langeland and Funen by a ferry from Tårs, near Nakskov.

**Tour of Lolland**. – The ferry from Puttgarden docks at *Rødby Havn*, from which E4 runs to Copenhagen (highway (motorway) to Sakskøbing, then a good main road, and from Rønnede on Zealand motorway again). Observing the Danish speed limits a motorist can cross Zealand in just over half an hour. Those who are less pressed for time will find it worthwhile to pause in **Rødby** (pop. 5000; Danhotel, 80 b.; Euro Motel, Sadinge, 128 b.). The town was once a port (and visitors can still see a half-timbered warehouse beside which boats were moored); but it was subject to frequent flooding and was cut off from the sea by a system of dikes. A column in Nørregade shows the high-water mark of the great flood of 1872. – 6 km (4 miles) NW of Rødby is *Tirsted* church, a brick Romanesque church (notable tower and 15th c. frescoes).

17 km (10 miles) from Rødbyhavn is Maribo. Just before reaching the town, turn left into A9 (signposted Nakskov). A short distance along this road, on the left, is *Østofte* church, another brick Romanesque church, with a Gothic tower and porch, 15th c. vaulting in the nave and a transept (1656). The choir has well-preserved frescoes of Old Testament scenes (*c.* 1400). – Farther on is *Stokkemarke*, which has a church with a massive tower.

**Nakskov**, on the Nakskov Fjord (pop. 16,000; Harmonien Hotel, 54 b.), is an industrial town with Denmark's largest sugar refinery and a shipyard. St Nicholas's Church is Gothic, with a three-tier Baroque altar. Narrow medieval lanes in the middle of the town; old houses between the harbour and Axeltorv, the main square, in which are an old pharmacy and a half-timbered house, Theisens Gård. – From Tårs, 13 km (8 miles) NW of Nakskov, there is a ferry (45 minutes) to Spodsbjerg on Langeland.

Along the S coast of Lolland are the finest beaches on the island, from Maglehøj Strand in the W to Drummeholm to the E. They are primarily sandy beaches.

To the N of Nakskov is *Løjtofte* church, a small Romanesque church without a tower, containing a magnificent font and a sandstone sculpture (1100) by the Gotland artist known as the Master of the Christ in Majesty. The road continues to *Kong Svends Høj*, a Neolithic passage grave, and *Kragenæs*. There are car ferries from Kragenæs to the islands of *Fejø* and *Femø* (good sailing).

Instead of continuing to Kragenæs you can bear right along the main road, which runs past the ruined castle of *Ravnsborg* (attractive view of the Smålandsfarvand). 13 km (8 miles) farther on is *Bandholm* (car ferry to Askø), the port of Maribo. An old steam train runs between Maribo and Bandholm on summer weekends. – To the S of Vandholm stretches **Knuthenborg Safari Park**, the largest manor-house park in Scandinavia (600 hectares – 1500 acres), laid out in the English style in the 19th c. and converted to its present use in 1970. The park, which is surrounded by a wall 8 km (5 miles) long with four gates, contains a unique collection of about 500 species of deciduous and coniferous trees from all over the world, seven miniature castles and Denmark's largest collection of antelopes, giraffes, zebras, camels, rhinoceroses, elephants, ostriches and

Maribo Cathedral (Lolland)

monkeys. A motor road runs through the park and through an enclosure containing Bengal tigers. There is also a children's zoo, with pony rides.

Beyond Knuthenborg the road runs into A7, which soon reaches Maribo.

**Maribo** (pop. 5000; Ebsenshotel, 34 b.; Hvide Hus Hotel, 128 b., SP; youth hostel; camp site) lies in a beautiful setting on the Søndersø, in the heart of Lolland. The town grew up around Maribo Abbey in the 15th c. Only ruins remain of the abbey, in a garden immediately N of the church (beautiful view of the lake). Maribo Cathedral was built between 1413 and 1470 as the church of a Brigittine abbey and has two choirs, one for monks and the other for nuns. The plan of the church is roughly similar to that of the church designed by St Bridget for the mother-house (principal church) of her order at Vadstena in Sweden: Maribo was the first daughter-house of Vadstena Abbey. Maribo Cathedral, however, departs from the prescribed form by having a broad central aisle of greater height than the lateral aisles. In the S aisle are a late 15th c. triumphal crucifix and a High Renaissance painted pulpit. – Maribo also has an interesting museum (historical section; art collection) and an open-air museum of farmhouses and other buildings reflecting the old peasant culture of Lolland and Falster. – There are pleasant walks around the Maribo *lakes* (on the N side Engestofte manor-house, opposite it Søholt, with a French-style garden). Particularly beautiful is the *Røgbøllesø*, with old oak-trees along its shores.

From Maribo E4 continues to *Sakskøbing* (pop. 4400; Sakskøbing Hotel, 39 b.). 4 km (2½ miles) NE is the little Renaissance manor-house of *Berritsgård*, which has an octagonal tower with a copper roof. In a beautiful setting on the Sakskøbing Fjord lies *Orebygård*. 4 km (2½ miles) NW of the town stands a 16th c. manor-house, remodelled in late Renaissance style in 1872–4. The motorway (highway) ends just beyond Sakskøbing, and E4 continues NE to *Guldborg* and over the bridge to the island of Falster. A9 branches off on the right and runs SE towards Nykøbing (Falster), coming almost immediately to *Radsted*, with a Neolithic dolmen and, close by, the fine manor-house of *Kren-kerup*, first referred to in the time of Queen Margaret. Just before Nykøbing a road goes off to the right and runs SW to Nysted (17 km – 11 miles), passing *Frejlev Forest* (Bronze Age remains; sanctuary).

**Nysted**, an attractive little place, is the most southerly town in Denmark and one of the smallest (pop. 1230; Den Gamle Gård, 52 b., SP). The town, which received its charter in 1409, grew up around Ålholm Castle, a massive 12th c. structure resembling a pirates' stronghold. The oldest part is the NE tower. In the Stubberupgård, near the Castle, is the *Automobile Museum*, Denmark's largest collection of cars, ranging from the 1890s to 1939. All the cars are in good condition and in running order. There is also a model railway layout 600 sq. m (700 sq. yds) in size, with scenery reproducing that of Switzerland, Italy and Germany. A steam engine draws a train down to the bathing beach. – In the town itself, which has preserved its original layout, there is a 15th c. Gothic church, with a massive tower of a later date topped by a tall copper steeple.

An alternative route back to the main traffic arteries from Nysted is on a road running W; it rejoins the motorway (highway) in 21 km (13 miles), passing through *Holeby*, one of the smallest townships in Denmark but so widely scattered that it can claim to have the country's longest main street.

# Luleå

Sweden (Northern).
Province: Norrbottens län. – Region: Norrbotten.
Altitude: sea level. – Population: 68,000.
Postal code: S-95 . . . – Telephone code: 09 20.
ⓘ **Turistbyrå,**
Storgatan 35,
S-951 31 Luleå;
tel. 9 30 00.

HOTELS. – *Luleå Stads Hotel*, Storgaten 15, 175 b.; *Max*, Storgatan 59, 182 b.; *SAS Luleå Hotel*, Storgatan 17, 330 b., SB; *Scandic Hotel*, Mjölkudden, 337 b., SB.

**The Swedish port of Luleå, at the N end of the Gulf of Bothnia, is the largest town in Norrbotten, the see of a bishop and the seat of the regional governor. It is also the gateway to the mountains of Lapland and the tundras of its northern**

regions. **The offshore islets and skerries, more than 300 in number, are noted for their animal and plant life. Although Luleå is only 110 km (70 miles) from the Arctic Circle the climate is mild: the average annual temperature is only 2 °C (3·5 °F) lower than at Malmö in southern Sweden, and in July Luleå has the highest number of sunshine hours in Sweden (300–310). During the summer, Luleå ranks with Narvik as one of the two principal ports for the shipment of the iron ore transported from Gällivare and Kiruna on the Lapland railway. Luleå harbour is usually frozen over until May.**

Old warehouses on the quay, Luleå

Luleå was founded by Gustavus Adolphus in 1621 and moved in 1649 to its present site on a promontory in the Luleälv. Most of the town's old houses have been destroyed by fire. Luleå was slow to develop, and by 1940 had a population of only 14,000. A state-owned ironworks (Norrbottens Järnverk AS) was built on the island of Svartö and, within ten years, the population had doubled. It continues to grow.

SIGHTS. – In the middle of the old town stand the new **Cathedral** (1887–93) and the ten-storey *Town Hall* (1957). To the E, in Storgatan, the main business street of the town, is a modern shopping complex. At the W end of Storgatan lies *Hermelinspark*. On the southern outskirts of the town is the *Norrbotten Museum* (interesting collection illustrating Lapp customs and traditions) and to the W of the Museum are the *Provincial Government Offices* (Länsresidens). To the NW is the promontory of *Gültzauudde*, with a good bathing beach, tennis courts and other sports facilities, and restaurants. Open-air performances are given here on Thursdays during the summer.

SURROUNDINGS. – 10 km (6 miles) W, on the original site of the town, is **Kyrkstaden**, the "church town" – a settlement of little wooden houses designed to provide overnight accommodation for a congregation which had to travel long distances to attend church. With almost 500 "church huts" (*kyrkstugor*) this is the largest church town in Sweden. The church itself dates from the early 14th c.; it is richly decorated and has an altar (1520) from Antwerp. – 40 km (25 miles) NW of Luleå in the valley of the Luleälv is **Boden** (pop. 28,000; Bodensia Hotel, 195 b.), a garrison town and railway junction where the Luleå–Gällivare mineral railway meets the N–S line. The rather military atmosphere of the town has a long tradition. The fortress built here in 1901 was almost entirely blasted out of the rock. There is also an Army Museum.

80 km (50 miles) NE of Luleå, at the mouth of the *Kalixälv*, is **Kalix** (Valhall Hotel, 95 b.), which reflects a combination of old peasant traditions with the early development of industry. The church (1472) has a late medieval reredos, a fine font and a modern altar window (Pär Andersson). On the road to Lappträsk, to the N, is the Englundsgård (typical 19th c. peasant interior). The Kalix Museum is in the offices of the commune. A view of the way of life of the wealthier classes at the end of the 19th c. is provided by the manor-houses of *Björknäs*, *Filipsborg* and *Grytnäs*, at the mouth of the Kalixälv. Some 10 km (6 miles) beyond Kalix a restricted area extends to the Arctic Circle: there are limitations on traffic through the area, and camping is prohibited.

58 km (36 miles) SW of Luleå is **Piteå** (pop. 10,000; Cristofer Hotel, 68 b.; Stadshotellet, 255 b.), a port and industrial town at the mouth of the Piteälv. The town was originally founded by Gustavus Adolphus in 1621 on the site now occupied by *Öjebyn*, but in 1666 it was moved 6 km (4 miles) to the mouth of the river. The 15th c. church at Öjebyn is surrounded by 17th c. *kyrkstugor* (see above). The wooden church in Piteå dates from 1648 (restored 1950–1); its pulpit (1702) is similar to those of the Gammelstad and Öjebyn churches. Most of the town's old timber houses are to be found in the vicinity of the market square (mid-19th c. Town Hall). 6 km (4 miles) SE, on Pitholmen, is *Havsbaden*, a beach 10 km (6 miles) long.

# Lund

Sweden (Southern).
Province: Malmöhus län. – Region: Skåne.
Altitude: 92 m (300 ft).   Population: 78,000.
Postal code: S-22 . . . – Telephone code: 0 45.
ⓘ **Lunds Turistbyrå,**
   St Petrikyrkogatan 4,
   S-22221 Lund;
   tel. 12 45 90.

HOTELS. *Grand Hotel*, Bantorget 1, 130 b.; *Sparta*, Tunavägen 39, 280 b.

**Lund, located about 20 km (12 miles) NE of the large port of Malmö in the southern Swedish region of Skåne, is a university town (University founded 1666, college of technology) and the see of a bishop.**

Lund Cathedral

**From the 12th to the 15th c. it was the largest town in Scandinavia and the see of a Danish archbishop, known as the "Metropolis Daniae".**

SIGHTS. – In the middle of the town is the *Stortorg*, with the modern *Town Hall*. To the N stands the *Cathedral, the oldest and finest Romanesque church in Sweden, founded about 1080 by the Danish king Knut den Helige (St Canute). The present building dates from the 12th c.; the twin towers, popularly known as the "lads of Lund" (Lunna påga), were once a prominent landmark. The Cathedral now stands in the heart of the town – a reminder of the fact that Lund was once the oldest archiepiscopal see in Scandinavia, with 27 churches and 8 religious houses.

INTERIOR of the Cathedral. – The magnificently carved reredos was the work of a 14th c. North German master. The completely preserved choir-stalls, also finely carved, date from the 15th c. and were originally made for the monks of the monastery to which the church belonged. Mosaic figure of Christ (by Joakim Skovgaard, 1925) in the apse. In the *crypt are the tombs of Archbishop Birger (d. 1519) and Archbishop Herman. The fountain, with satirical inscriptions in Low German, was the work of a Westphalian master named van Düren who lived in Lund from 1512 to 1527. The roof of the crypt rests on stone piers. The carved figures on the piers are said to represent the giant Finn who, according to legend, built the Cathedral for St Lawrence. In the aisle is the famous 14th c. *Astronomical Clock*, with figures which emerge and perform twice daily (at 12 noon and 3 p.m. on weekdays, 1 and 3 p.m. on Sundays).

To the N of the Cathedral lies the *Lundagård,* a park which features prominently in the life of the University. At the SE corner is the *Historical Museum** (prehistoric and ecclesiastical antiquities). The *Lundagårdshus* or *Kungshus* in the park, now occupied by the University, was built in the second half of the 16th c. as a residence for the Danish king Frederik II. King Charles XII of Sweden is said to have ridden up the oak spiral staircase when he took up his quarters in Lund on returning from his campaigns on the Continent. At the end of Sandgatan, to the N, are the *Bishop's Palace* and beyond it the *University Library*, which contains old 12th c. manu-scripts and some 2,500,000 volumes in all fields of knowledge. Adjoining the Library is the largest hospital complex in Sweden, to the E of it the *College of Technology* and to the NE the *Zoological Museum*. To the SE, along Sölvegatan, is the *Archive of Decorative Art*, where visitors can follow the development of a work of art from the first sketch to the finished article.

To the SE we find the *Botanic Garden*, with 7000 plants from all over the world. W of this the *Museum of Cul-tural History** (*Kulturhistoriska Museet*,

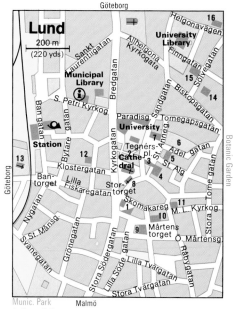

1  Town Hall
2  Lundagård
3  Historical Museum
4  Chapterhouse
5, 6  Museum of Cultural History
7  Students' Union
8  Krognos House
9  St Lawrence's Chapel
10  Art Gallery
11  Folkets Hus/Municipal Theatre
12  Tegnér House
13  St Peter's Church
14  Museum of Antiquities
15  Archive of Decorative Art
16  Zoological Museum

commonly known as "Kulturen"), one of the largest and finest of Sweden's open-air museums, has farms, presbyteries and town houses from all over southern Sweden; particularly notable is an old church from Bosebo in Småland. There are also collections of pottery, porcelain, textiles and folk art. Nearby is Tegnérs Plats, with a monument to the poet *Essaia Tegnér*, author of "Frithjof's Saga"; his house in Gråbrödersgatan is now a museum. To the S, in *Mårtenstorget* (fruit, vegetable and flower market), are the medieval *Krognos House* and the *Art Gallery* (Konsthallen, 1957), with a collection of modern Swedish art; major international exhibitions are also held here from time to time.

SURROUNDINGS. – 13 km (8 miles) SE is *Dalby*, with one of the oldest stone churches in the northern countries (12th c. crypt).

# Lyngenfjord

Norway (Northern).
County: Troms fylke.

**The ** **Lyngenfjord is perhaps the most magnificent fjord in the Nordland. It runs S for about 80 km (50 miles) from the Lyngstuva promontory (alt. 395 m – 1296 ft) at the northern tip of the Lyngen peninsula, a snow-and-glacier-covered granite ridge which rises directly out of the sea between the Lyngenfjord and the Ullsfjord to the W.**

The Lyngenfjord is reached from Tromsø by taking E78, which runs SE to *Nordkjosbotn* and then turns E up the valley of the *Nordkjoselv*, through birch forest and between high hills, to *Øvergård*. It then descends, with a view of the fjord ahead, to *Oteren*, at the S end of the *Storfjord*, the southern arm of the Lyngenfjord; to the SE is the jagged *Mannfjell* ridge (1533 m – 5030 ft). At Oteren the road divides. One can continue up the main Road 6 along the W coast of Storfjord and by the W coast of Lyngenfjord to Lyngen and from Lyngseidet take

the ferry (45 minutes) across to Kåfjord. Alternatively one can take Road 78 from Oteren by the E coast of Storfjord and Lyngenfjord to *Skibotn* from which there is a very fine view of the W shores of the fjord with Pollfjell and beyond it the Jiekkevarre with its glaciers. At *Odden*, from which there is a good view of the glaciers at the N end of the far side of the fjord, the road turns SE and runs along the W side of the 20 km (12 mile) long *Kåfjord*, enclosed between precipitous hills, to *Kåfjordbotn*, at the head of the fjord.

The road now runs NW along the E side of the fjord to the village of Kåfjord and then to **Olderdal** (Kåfjord Verthus, 42 b.). Kåfjord was once the home of the very successful Kåfjord mines which were founded and run by a British company, but known also for two other things: one, the very beautiful "English" church, quite unlike anything else erected in Norway and built by the company, but most especially for the fact that Kåfjord is for Norwegians generally and most Scandinavians an almost sacred place. It was here, only just round the corner from the English church that the German ship "Tirpitz", badly damaged, was spotted by three young Norwegian Resistance fighters who, at great danger to their lives, managed to get a radio message sent via Sweden to the British High Command. British aircraft made an unsuccessful attempt to attack her, but she was too well hidden. Midget submarines then made another heroic attack disabling her slightly, but she was able to limp to Tromsø for proper repairs, where the R.A.F. made an all-out attack as a result of which she now lies bottom-up. Naturally, the Germans made reprisals. The three young men were found and taken to Tromsø H.Q. by the Gestapo. One died there, the other two escaped during another attack; the older to Britain where had joined the allied forces; the younger, only 17, was hidden by the Resistance and now lives within a short distance of the spot where the "Tirpitz" lay hidden. The English church miraculously survived the bombings and is well worth a visit. From Olderfal there are two alternatives – either continuing along the E side of the fjord, with magnificent views, in the direction of Rotsund, or by ferry (45 minutes) to **Lyngseidet** (Gjestgiveri, 22 b.) on the W side of the fjord. From Lyngseidet there are two good climbs, each taking 4 hours – *Goalsevarre* (1289 m – 4229 ft) and *Rørnestind* (1250 m – 4101 ft). The road runs S to **Furuflaten**, under the *Pollfjell* (1280 m – 4200 ft). From here it is a 4–5 hours' climb up the *Njallasvarre* (1530 m – 5020 ft). Here is a magnificent view to the W of the glaciers on *Jiekkevarre* (1833 m – 6014 ft), one of the highest mountains in northern Norway, first climbed by Geoffrey Hastings in 1898. – From here the main road to Tromsø returns to Oteren.

SURROUNDINGS. – **Excursion into Finland** (*Kilpisjärvi* and Saanatunturi). – From the Olderbakken road junction, E78 runs SE to Kilpisjärvi. The first section of the road bears SW up the broad wooded valley of the Skibotnelv (good fishing), with the little *Øvrevann* to right. It then comes to the winter customs post at *Helligskogen*, followed by the *summer customs post*, and soon afterward crosses the **Norwegian-Finnish frontier**. E78 now continues as the Finnish Road 21, with many ups and downs; ahead, to the right, is a view of Kilpisjärvi. In another 5 km (3 miles) the *Finnish frontier post* (customs) is reached.

˙Saanatunturi, on the shores of Kilpisjärvi

The road continues close to the shores of **Kilpisjärvi** (alt. 476 m (1560 m), area 39 sq. km – 15 sq. miles), which lies along the Swedish frontier (good fishing). At the NW tip of the lake (motorboat from hotel) is a round boundary stone marking the "meeting-place of the three countries" (Sweden, Norway and Finland); to the left is the characteristic outline of Saanatunturi. 3 km (2 miles) beyond the frontier post, on the left, is a climbers' hostel, from which it is a 2–2½ hours' climb (sturdy footwear essential) to the summit of the distinctively shaped *Saanatuntur (1024 m – 3360 ft), the "sacred mountain of the Lapps", from which there are panoramic views: to the N, the Malla National Park and, behind it, to the N and NW, the Norwegian mountains; to the W, Sweden and to the S, Kilpisjärvi; to the E, the rolling forest-covered landscape of Finland and to the N, Finland's highest mountain, Haltiatunturi (1324 m – 4344 ft), a remote and inaccessible peak (a walk of 120 km (75 miles) from Kilpisjärvi: organised climbing parties, with guide).

5 km (3 miles) beyond the climbers' hostel, to the right of the road, is *Kilpisjärvi Turisthotel* (70 b.), with a number of chalets. – Road 21 continues SE alongside the Swedish frontier to Muonio and Tornio (p. 267); side road from Muonio to Rovaniemi (p. 229).

# Lake Mälar

Sweden (Eastern).
Provinces: Stockholms län, Södermanlands län, Västmanlands län.
Regions: Södermanland, Uppland, Västmanland.

*Lake Mälar, Sweden's third largest lake (after Lakes Vänern and Vättern), lies immediately W of Stockholm. 117 km (73 miles) long, it extends through the provinces of Västmanland, Södermanland, Uppsala and Stockholm to the Baltic, with a total area of 1140 sq. km (440 sq. miles) and a greatest depth of 64 m (210 ft). It is irregularly shaped, with many ramifications and inlets. Its principal tributary rivers are the Eskilstunaå, Arbogaå, Hedström, Kolbäckså, Svartå, Örsundaå and Fyriså.**

At one time Lake Mälar was an arm of the Baltic, but since the 12th c., because of a fall in the water level, it has been an inland lake. Since 1943, the lake has been regulated to prevent flooding, and to avoid unduly low water levels hindering shipping. Vessels with a draught of up to 5·5 m (18 ft) can now sail from the Baltic to Stockholm on the Södertälje Canal and Hammarbyleden. On the shores of Lake Mälar are many castles and manorhouses.

**Strängnäs** (O'Henry's Hotel, 166 b.; Hotel Rogge, 60 b.) is a small 13th c. town in which Gustavus Vasa was chosen as king in 1523. The Cathedral was begun in the 13th c. and completed in the 15th by Bishop Rogge. The vault paintings in the nave date from the 14th c., the paintings in the choir from the second half of the 15th c. The reredos (1490) on the high altar, with a profusion of figures, came from Brussels. In front of the altar, to the left, is the splendid gilded armour of Charles IX, whose tomb is in the Cathedral. Other monuments are those of Isabella, daughter of John III, and. Bishops Thomas and Rogge. – The 17th c. printing press once belonging to the Cathedral is now in Strängnäs Museum. Near the Cathedral are the medieval Consistory House and the Paulinska Hus, built for Laurentius Paulinus Gothus, bishop of Strängnäs from 1609 to 1637.

It is also worth stopping at the craft workshop of Grassagården (open to

visitors in summer). – Although Strängnäs is now a garrison town as well as the
administrative and cultural hub of the
surrounding area, it has preserved an
attractive old-world charm, with narrow
lanes and red-painted timber houses.

**Eskilstuna** (pop. 70,000; hotels: City,
100 b.; Eskilstuna, 405 b., SB; Smeden,
138 b.) lies on the Eskilstunaå, which links
Lake Mälar with Lake Hjälmar. The little
trading settlements of Tuna and Fors grew
up here at an early stage. Legend has it
that St Eskil, the apostle of Södermanland, is buried at Tuna.

The beginnings of the ironworking industry in this
region date to the 16th c. In 1654, a large iron foundry
was established here by a Livonian, Reinhold
Rademacher, at the behest of Charles X; this was the
nucleus out of which the later steel industry
developed. The foundry was designed by Jean de la
Vallée, the architect responsible for the planning of
the town.

In the middle of the town is the *Fristad-
storg*, with the Town Hall (1897), a
fountain ("The Honour and Joy of
Labour") by Ivan Johnson and a sculpture ("The Smiths") by Allan Ebeling. The
church on the other side of the square was
designed by Otar Hökerberg (1929).
Nearby is Fors Church, which dates from
the 12th c., with later alterations and
restorations; notable features of the
interior are the unusual wood-carving and
the coats of arms. – The six best preserved
of Reinhold Rademacher's forges, at 50
Rademachergatan, form part of the
town's Open-Air Museum, which also
includes the Folkets Park (People's Park)
and a zoo. There are also displays
illustrating the town's modern industries,
particularly cutlery, for which Eskilstuna is
renowned. Dramatic performances are
given daily in the park during the month
of July. – Eskilstuna also has a Museum
of Technology and a Museum of Art
(primarily works by Scandinavian artists).

Björkö, *Gripsholm Castle, Mariefred: see under
Stockholm. – **Västerås**: see p. 287.

# Malmö

Sweden (Southern).
Province: Malmöhus län. – Region: Skåne.
Altitude: sea level. – Population: 229,000.
Postal code: S-21 . . . – Telephone code: 0 40.
(i) **Malmö Turistbyrå,**
   Hamngatan 1,
   S-21122 Malmö;
   tel. 34 12 70.

HOTELS. – *Anglais*, Stortorget 15, 130 b.; *Garden
Hotel*, Baltzarsgatan 20, 260 b.; *Savoy*, Norra Vall-
gatan 62, 150 b.; *Scandic Hotel Segevångt*,
Segesvången, 348 b., SB; *Skyline Hotel*, Bisittare-
gatan 2, 535 b.; *St Jörgen*, Stora Nygatan 35, 467 b.;
*Winn*, Jorgen Kocksgatan 3, 202 b. – YOUTH
HOSTEL. – CAMP SITE.

**Malmö, located on the Öresund in
southern Skåne, opposite the Danish
capital of Copenhagen, is the capital
town of its province and Sweden's
third largest city. It is a major port
and an important industrial town
(engineering, shipbuilding, textiles,
cement).**

HISTORY. – Malmö grew up in the second half of the 13th c., helped largely by its sheltered anchorages in the shallow Lomma Bay, where the boats of the Hanseatic towns fished for herring. The town's first fortifications were built during the reign of the Danish king Eric of Pomerania; he also granted Malmö its coat of arms in 1473. The town passed to Sweden under the treaty of Roskilde (1658). The construction of the harbour and the energy of a merchant named Franz Suell (statue in Norra Vallgatan) brought great prosperity to Malmö in the 18th c., and it developed further after the building of the railway between Malmö and Stockholm in the following century.

SIGHTS. – In the middle of the city, to the S of the harbour, is the OLD TOWN, bounded by canals; it has preserved much of its original character, particularly around the *Stortorg*. In the square is an *equestrian statue* (1896) of *Charles X*, who united Skåne with Sweden in 1658. On the E side is the **Town Hall** (Dutch Renaissance style, 1546; altered 1864–9). On the first floor are St Knut's or St Canute's Hall (Knutsalen), in which the influential St Knut's Guild used to meet, and the Council Chamber (Landstingssalen), with portraits of Danish and Swedish kings. At the NE corner of the square stands the *Governor's Residence* (1730; restored in the 19th c.). The street between the Town Hall and the

Residence leads to **St Peter's Church** (*St Petri*), a handsome 14th c. brick building undoubtedly modelled after St Mary's Church in Lübeck (pulpit, 1500; Baroque altar, 1611). To the left of the entrance is the Krämer Chapel, with late Gothic wall paintings and a font (1601). – SW of the Stortorg is the attractive *Lilla Torg*, with 16th–18th c. houses. – Malmö has many fine old burghers' houses, notably the *Flensburgska Hus* (1595), 9 Södergatan; *Jörgen Kocks Hus* (1525), 2 Västergatan now a restaurant; *Rosenvingeska Hus* (1534), 5 Västergatan; *Tunnelns Hus* or Ulfeldtska Hus (1519), 4 Adelgatan; *Diedenska Hus* (1620), 6 Östergatan; and *Thottska Hus* (1558), 8 Östergatan. The *Kompanihus* in the Stortorg, built at the beginning of the 16th c. by a firm of merchants, is now used for meetings and various functions.

Statue of Charles X, Stortorg, Malmö

To the W of the town is the beautiful *Kungspark*, with a summer restaurant. From the Kungspark a bridge leads directly into the park of **Malmöhus Castle**, a moated fortress built in 1537–42 (restored 1870, after a fire); it now houses the *Municipal Museum* (archaeology, history and art). – Nearby is the *Museum of Technology* (industrial technology and all forms of transport). To the SE of the Castle Park stands the *Municipal Library* and to the S of this the **Municipal Theatre** (1942–4), the largest theatre in Scandinavia, with seating for 1700 (visits permitted). Still farther S is **Pildammspark**, with an *open-air theatre*, the *Stadium* (1958) and the *Exhibition Halls*. – In Drottningtorg, to the E of the middle of the city, is the *Carriage Museum*, in the old Town Hall.

To the SE of the town, on Admiralsgatan, lies the *Folkets Park* (People's Park), an amusement park with several restaurants. – To the SW, on the Öresund, are the *Ribersborg* bathing beach and *Limhamn* (camp site; ferry to the Danish fishing village of Dragør).

During the summer there are daily tours of the city, starting from Gustav Adolfs Torg; also cruises around the harbour and canal boat trips.

SURROUNDINGS. – 14 km (9 miles) E, in a beautiful park, is the well-preserved **Torup Castle** (16th c.); it belongs to the city of Malmö (conducted tours during the summer).

# Mikkeli (Sankt Michel)

Finland (Southern).
Province: Mikkelin Lääni (Sankt Michels län/Mikkeli).
Altitude: 80 m (260 ft). – Population: 29,000.
Postal code: SF-50100. – Telephone code: 9 55.
ⓘ **Mikkelin Matkailu Oy,**
Hallituskatu 3A;
tel. 1 39 38 and 1 19 51.

HOTELS. – *Cumulus*, Mikonkatu 9, 197 b., SB; *Kaleva*, Hallituskatu 5, 55 b.; *Niujamies*, Porrassalmenkatu 21, 75 b.; *Rantasipi Varsavuori*, Kirkonvarkaus, 250 b., SB; *Tekuila*, Raviradantie 1, 138 b. (15 May to 30 August); holiday centre *Visulahti*, 178 b. – YOUTH HOSTEL. – CAMP SITE.

EVENTS. – *Open-air theatre* performances at Naisvuori (in summer); *Crayfish and Vendace Festival* (first weekend in August).

RECREATION and SPORTS. – Eight sandy beaches; sailing, water-skiing, canoeing; tennis, bowling, golf, gliding; in winter, slalom running.

**The Finnish town of Mikkeli, capital of the province of the same name, lies on one of the western arms of Lake Saimaa. As its Swedish name, Sankt Michel, indicates, it is named after the Archangel Michael. Life in this area can be traced back for more than a thousand years, and the first Christian community in the Savo region was established here, as the little stone sacristy of the wooden church of Savilahti still bears witness.**

HISTORY. – The village of Sankt Michel was granted the right to hold a market in 1745 and received its municipal charter in 1838. In 1843 it became the capital of the province and in 1945 the see of a bishop. A garrison town as early as the 17th c., it was the headquarters of Marshal Mannerheim during the three campaigns of the Second World War – the Winter War of 1939–40, the war of 1941–4 against Soviet forces and the Lapland War against German forces in 1944–5. Its role in the Second World War is commemorated by the Freedom Cross (a Finnish order) and the marshal's batons in the town's coat of arms.

A secondary school was established in Mikkeli in 1872. The town's economy made great strides with the development of industry in the second half of the 19th c. Its principal industries are woodworking, textiles, metalworking and foodstuffs.

SIGHTS. – The brick *church* dates from 1897, the *Provincial Government Offices* from 1843, the *Town Hall* from 1912 and the *rural parish church*, built in wood, from 1816. From the hill of *Naisvuori*, in the middle of the town, there are fine panoramic views (lookout tower; enclosed swimming pool cut from rock). To the NE, at the N end of Porrassalmenkatu, is the sacristy (*kivisakasti*) of the Savilahti church, built in 1320, which now houses a small *Church Museum*. To the SW, at 11 Otavankatu, is the *Savo Regional Museum* (historical and ethnological collections). Also of interest are the Provincial Archives (documents from the 15th c. on) and the *Headquarters Museum*. On the SE outskirts of the town is an interesting geological feature, a "*glacier mill*". To the N beyond the town boundary can be found the tourist centre Visulahti with a waxworks exhibition and "Miniland" (models of Finnish buildings).

SURROUNDINGS. – There are boat services from Mikkeli to the nearby resort (chalet village) of *Pistohiekka*, and also to Lappeenranta and Savonlinna. – 5 km (3 miles) N of the town is the esker (a gravel ridge deposited by glaciers) of *Pikku-Punkaharju*, surrounded by water on both sides. – 6 km (4 miles) S on Road 13 is the narrow sound of *Porrassalmi*, and 18 km (11 miles) beyond this, at *Ristiina*, are the remains of *Brahelinna Castle*, begun by Per Brahe but never completed.

# Lake Mjøsa

Norway (SE).
Counties: Oppland fylke, Hedmark fylke, Akershus fylke.
Altitude: 124 m (407 ft).
ⓘ **Hedmark Reiselivsråd,**
   St, Olavsgate 61,
   N-2300 Hamar;
   tel. (065) 2 70 00.
   **Vestoppland Reiselivslag,**
   Kauffeldtgården,
   N-2800 Gjøvik;
   tel. (0 61) 7 16 88.

**Lake Mjøsa, Norway's largest lake, extends for 100 km (60 miles) through a fertile region from Eidsvoll in the S to Lillehammer in the N. Reaching a maximum width of 15 km (9 miles), it has an area of 362 sq. km (140 sq. miles), slightly less than Lake Garda in Northern Italy. Its greatest depth is 443 m (1450 ft). The lake is heavily stocked with trout.**

ROUND THE LAKE. – Lake Mjøsa is reached from Oslo on E6. From the little town of **Eidsvoll**, on the right bank of the broad, clear River *Vorma*, there is a boat service up Lak Mjøsa to Lillehammer (about 6 hours) between mid-June and mid-August. – E6 continues N and beyond *Minnesund* crosses a bridge over the Vorma at its outflow from the lake (beautiful view); it then runs along the E side of Lake Mjøsa, through attractive scenery, climbing slightly. Soon after *Espa*, a little place on the picturesque *Korsødegårdsbugt*, E6 leaves the lake and does not return to its shore until Hamar. Those who want to keep close to the lake should take Road 222, which runs parallel to E6 to the W. This road runs through *Stange*. 3 km (2 miles) W of Stange is the village church (Stange Kirke), one of the two most beautiful churches in Hedmark (the other is Ringsaker), founded about 1250 and remodelled in the 17th c. Between the road and the lake, sometimes directly on the lakeside, are several prosperous farmhouses (*storgårder*), many dating from the 18th c. They bear witness to the wealth of this fertile region.

The next place of any size is **Hamar** (pop. 16,000; hotels: Astoria, 120 b.; Bellevue, 20 b.; Rica Olrund, 350 b., SP, SB; Victoria, 225 b.), country town of Hedmark. Hamar is located on the N side of the Akersvik and at the mouth of the *Furnesfjord*, which runs N for some 15 km (10 miles). To the W of the town, on the peninsula of *Storhamarodde* (Domkirkeodde), are the ruins of the 12th c. Cathedral and the Hedmark Museum, with a number of old wooden buildings (the oldest from 1583), an open-air theatre and a restaurant; nearby is a camp site. A little way N is Norway's only Railway Museum (Jernbanemuseet).

28 km (17½ miles) E of Hamar, on the Glomma, is **Elverum** (alt. 188 m (615 ft);

pop. 7500), once a fortified town, with the interesting Glomdal Museum (80 old peasants' houses from the prosperous Østerdal, with period furnishings) and the Norwegian Forest Museum (forestry management, fishing, shooting).

Beyond *Brumunddal*, E6 reaches the N end of the Furnesfjord and turns W. At the village of *Ringsaker* (old church with a carved and painted Flemish altar) it returns to Lake Mjøsa, and continues via *Moelv* along the long narrow N arm of the lake to Lillehammer.

It is also possible to take a ferry across the lake from Hamar, passing between the large peninsula of *Nes* on the right and *Helgøy* (the "island of saints") on the left, to **Gjøvik** (pop. 16,000; hotels: Gjøvik, 150 b.; Hovdetun, 154 b., SB; Rica, 150 b., SP, SB; youth hostel), capital of the district of Toten on the W side of Lake Mjøsa. From Gjøvik, Road 4 goes N to Lillehammer, while Road 33 runs S down the W side of the lake. To the W of *Kapp* (pop. 1100) is the Toten Museum, a farmhouse (1790). On a promontory N of *Skreia* (pop. 900) is *Balke* church (*c.* 1200; restored 1967). The road now keeps close to the shore, with the *Skreia* ridge of hills to the W (*Skreikamp*, 708 m −2323 ft). At the farm of Bjørnstad, a road leads N to the *Feiring ironworks* (Feiring jernverk), established in 1797, with 24 buildings (stamping mill, blast furnace, etc.) which give visitors an idea of the state of technology at this early stage of the industry. − At Minnesund we return to the starting-point of the tour.

# Mo i Rana

Norway (Northern).
County: Nordland fylke.
Altitude: sea level. − Population: 12,000.
Postal code: N-8600. − Telephone code: 0 78.
ⓘ **Turistkontor,**
Strandgate;
tel. 5 04 21.

HOTELS. − *Holmen*, 75 b.; *Meyergården*, 240 b.; *Ranafjord*, 36 b.; *Revelen Motell*, 68 b. − YOUTH HOSTEL. − CAMP SITE.

SPORTS and RECREATION. − Fishing.

**Mo i Rana is a busy industrial and commercial town at the E end of the Nordranafjord. The town is dominated by the steelworks and rolling mills of the Norsk Jernverk Company, which primarily uses iron ore from the Dunderlandsdal.**

SIGHTS. − The *steelworks* to the NE of the town are open to visitors during the holiday season. − The *church*, in the middle of the town, dates from 1832 (altarpiece, 1786). − Near the station, on the W side of the town, stands the *Municipal Museum* (history of the town, crafts, mining, geology). Nearby is the *Stenneset* open-air museum. − Above the town, to the S, rises the **Mofjell** (410 m − 1345 ft), with a cabin cableway to the top; there are magnificent views (particularly toward sunset) of the town and the Svartisen glacier.

SURROUNDINGS. − E6 runs NE from the town, through beautiful scenery and in 2·5 km (1½ miles) crosses the *Rana*. There is a salmon-ladder in the river at *Reinforshei*.

**Røssvoll** (13 km − 8 miles) has a small circular wooden church. Here a road goes off on the left, passes the Mo airport and, in 10 km (6 miles), comes to *Grønli*. A footpath (800 m − a ½ mile) leads to Grønli farmhouse; nearby is a cave.

The **Grønli cave** (1200 m (1300 yds) long) is the most famous of the 120 caves discovered in this area. There are conducted tours of the cave (visitors should walk with great care, since the path is not always good).

The road ends in 32 km (20 miles) at the *Svartisvatn*, above which rear the great snowfields and glaciers of Svartisen. The lake is crossed by motorboat; it is then 45 minutes' walk to the foot of the glacier.

* **Svartisen** ("Black Ice") is the second largest glacier area in Norway (about 460 sq. km − 180 sq. miles). The plateau lies at an average height of 1200−1400 m − 3900−4600 ft), with individual peaks rising above this level, including *Snetind* (1599 m − 5246 ft), *Sniptind* (1591 m − 5220 ft) and *Istind* (1577 m − 5174 ft).

91 km (57 miles) SW of Mo i Rana on E6, at the outflow of the Vefsnelv into the *Vefsnfjord*, is the pleasant little town of **Mosjøen** (pop. 10,000; hotels: Fru Haugans Hotel, 120 b.; Lyngengården, 42 b.; Sandvik Folkehøgskule, 70 b., SB; Stenhaugs Verthus. 50 b.), with weaving mills and an aluminium plant. The church in the Dolstad district is the oldest octagonal church in Norway (1734). Nearby is an open-air museum with ten old houses. There are fine views of the town and the fjord from the hill of *Haravoll*.

# Molde

Norway (Western).
County: Møre og Romsdal fylke.
Altitude: see level. – Population: 20,000.
Postal code: N-6400. – Telephone code 0 72.
ⓘ **Informasjonskiosk,**
   Rådhustaket;
   tel. 5 20 60.

HOTELS. – *Alexandra*, 215 b., SB; *Knausen Molde*,
175 b.; *Nobel Hotel*, 76 b.; *Norrøna Kafe og Pensjonat*,
18 b. – YOUTH HOSTEL. – CAMP SITE.·

SPORT and RECREATION. – Fishing; boat rentals.

EVENT. – International Jazz Festival (August).

**The county town of Molde, in western Norway, lies on the N side of the Moldefjord, sheltered on the N and W by a range of hills.** The surrounding area is noted for its surprisingly rich vegetation (large numbers of roses). During the summer, the town attracts lively vacation and tourist traffic.

The town was founded in the 15th c. and received its municipal charter in 1742. It was largely destroyed during the Second World War, but was rebuilt in modern style. The main industries are textiles and ship fittings.

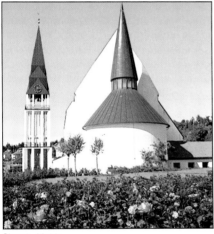

Church, Molde

SIGHTS. – In the middle of the town are the *Town Hall* (1966) and, immediately E of it, the new *church* (1957), with an altarpiece by Axel Ender (19th c.). To the W of the town is the hilly and wooded park of *Rekneshaug (monument to writer Alexander Kjelland, 1840–1906); at the far end of the park is the *Romsdal*

*Museum*, with many old Romsdal houses. To the NE of the park is the *Stadium* (indoor swimming pool).

SURROUNDINGS. – In the fjord, to the S of the town, is the little island of **Hjertøya** (motorboat from harbour), with a small *Fisheries Museum.*

There are pleasant walks along the shores of the fjord, particularly to the E, past the *Fannestrand* beach. – Fine views are possible from two hills near the town, *Tusten* (696 m 2284 ft): 3 hours' climb) and **Varden** ("heap of stones": 407 m – 1335 ft), which can be reached by road (4 km – 2½ miles).

28 km (17½ miles) N of the town, on Road 67, is the "**Trolls' Church**", a cave 70 m (75 yds) long and up to 7 m (23 ft) high, with a waterfall, in a bed of limestone in the *Tverfjelle* (a mountain). Sturdy footwear and a flashlight are essential for visiting the cave.

# Møn

Denmark.
County: Storstrøms amt.
Area: 216 sq. km (85 sq. miles). – Population: 13,000.
ⓘ **Tourist Information Office,**
   Storegade 5,
   DK-4780 Stege;
   tel. (03) 81 44 11.

**The Danish island of Møn lies at the E end of Storstrømmen, the channel between the islands of Zealand and Falster. The white chalk cliffs at the E end of the island are one of Denmark's great tourist attractions; but Møn has far more to offer – old churches, strikingly beautiful scenery and good bathing beaches. It is connected with Zealand by a bridge from Kalvehave, and can be reached from Falster by taking the ferry from Stubbekøbing to the island of Bogø; from Bogø there is a causeway to Møn.**

There are many prehistoric remains on Møn; especially interesting are a number of the Neolithic chambered tombs known as "Huns' graves". Popular legend associated these tombs with two giants – the Green Huntsman, who ruled over western Møn, and the giant Upsal, king of the cliffs, to whom the E end of the island belonged. Upsal was long regarded as the protector of the island, since it was he who caused enemy ships to be shattered on the island's rocky coast.

**Tour of Møn.** – The bridge from Zealand crosses the *Ulvsund* to Møn. 2 km (1¼ miles) from the bridge, a side road goes off on the right and runs through beautiful scenery (a fine view of the sound from Borren) to the Neolithic tombs known as *Kong Askers Høj* and the *Klekkende Høj* (the best preserved passage grave, 9 m (30 ft) long and 1·25 m (4 ft) high). – 11 km (7 miles) from the bridge, the main road comes to the chief town on the island, **Stege** (pop. 4000; Stege Bugt, 54 b.; camp site). The town rose around a castle built by Valdemar I (*c.* 1175). In the 15th c., it was surrounded by walls and a moat; one of the three town gates, Mølleporten, has been preserved – the only surviving medieval town gate in Denmark besides one at Fåborg. St Hans' Church was built about 1250 and enlarged by the addition of a three-aisled choir about 1460; the interior has rich fresco decoration.

From Stege, the main road continues towards the E end of the island. A minor road leads N into the *Ulvshale* peninsula, the first large nature reserve established in Denmark (rare birds, unspoiled natural forest). This seldom-visited part of Møn has some of the island's finest beaches.

The road E from Stege runs through *Keldby*, which has a church richly decorated with frescoes, the oldest of which, in the choir, date from the 13th c. On the walls are vividly imagined scenes from the Bible, and the vaulting has paintings by the Master of Elmelunde, whose work is frequently found in the churches of Møn. His primitive paintings, full of humour, contain many details taken from everyday life, such as the Nativity scene depicting Joseph making gruel for the newborn infant Jesus. – S of Keldby is *Keldbylille*, with a museum.

The road continues to *Elmelunde,* 8 km (5 miles) from Stege. The church, a prominent landmark for sailors, is in the style typical of eastern Denmark and contains frescoes by the Master of Elmelunde (Childhood of Jesus, Last Judgment, Entry into Jerusalem, as well as ploughing and harvest scenes). 10 km (6 miles) farther on, the road reaches the main attraction of the trip, the chalk cliff known as *\*Møns Klint, the highest point of which is 128 m (420 ft) above the sea. The brilliant white of the chalk standing out against the deep blue of the sea is particularly striking when the sun is

Møns Klint

shining. A toll is due on the last section of the road (Hundsøgård Hotel, 57 b.; Store Klint summer hotel, 30 b.; camp site). There are footpaths along the cliffs (about 1 hour), and two steep flights of steps lead from *Storeklint* and *Jydeleje* to the sea. Fossils of marine animals and plants can be found on the shore. Along the top of the cliffs an expanse of open woodland (beeches) contains rare species of plants in the undergrowth. The best view is from *Sommerspiret* (102 m – 335 ft); at *Taleren* one can hear a remarkable echo. There is an archaeological and geological museum in the car park.

A short distance N of Møns Klint is the romantic little country house of *Liselund*, built about 1795 by the governor of the island, Antoine de la Calmette, for his wife and named after her. In the course of his wide travels, he had acquired a taste for French architecture and the "back to nature" movement of the Romantic period; the house was therefore designed in the style of a simple peasant house. There are many other romantic features in the park, including artificial lakes and waterways, a "Swiss cottage" and a "Chinese" tea pavilion. Hans Christian Andersen wrote his story, "The Tinder-Box" while staying in the Swiss cottage. Other buildings in the park were destroyed in a landslip in 1905.

The return journey from Møns Klint is via the same road as far as Stege. From there a detour of 7 km (4½ miles) S can be made to Æbelnaes, where there is another Stone Age passage grave.

At the S end of the island is the *Grøn Jægers Høj*, the "Hill of the Green Huntsman", another burial mound. Also here is *Fanefjord*, with a church containing the richest series of paintings (*c.* 1500) by the Master of Elmelunde. The paintings form a kind of "Biblia pauperum" (Bible of the poor"), but do not hold rigorously to the Biblical accounts; scenes from the Old and New Testaments mingle with non-scriptural and legendary scenes. There are also frescoes of the High Gothic period (*c.* 1350) on the choir arch (St Christopher, St Martin, knights and emblems of the Apostles).

Instead of returning to Zealand, it is possible to continue on the main road over a causeway on to the island of *Bogø* (pop. 925), once known as the "island of mills"; there is now only one survivor (*Bogø Mølle*), a windmill of Dutch origin. From *Nyby*, there is a small ferry to Falster (12 minutes).

# Narvik

Norway (Northern).
County: Nordland fylke.
Altitude: sea level. – Population: 15,000.
Postal code: N-8500. – Telephone code: 0 82.
ⓘ **Turistkontor,**
Kongensgate 66;
tel. 4 33 09.

HOTELS. – *Bjerkvik*, 110 b.; *Royal*, 220 b.; *Malm*, 50 b.; *Nordstjernen*, 50 b.; *Victoria Royal*, 76 b. – YOUTH HOSTEL. – CAMP SITE.

SPORTS and RECREATION. – Fishing; cruises in the fjords.

BOAT SERVICES to the Lofoten Islands (p. 179).

**The northern Norwegian port of Narvik is situated at the W end of a peninsular between the Rombaksfjord to the N and the Beisfjord to the S. These fjords are branches of the Ofotfjord, which gives Narvik its access to the Atlantic. In the 1880s a British company obtained a concession to develop the iron-ore mines in Kiruna (Sweden) and permission to build a railway from Kiruna to a small village on the ice-free shores of Ofotfjord. Its offices were built by the first Manager, William Spear, who called the place Speargården. He was very autocratic and caused a great deal of trouble. After his departure the English called the harbour Victoriahaven, after the Queen, but after the English had gone the Norwegian Storting renamed the port Narvik after the name of an old manor-house which had previously stood on the site.**

**The town, which received its municipal charter in 1902, is of great economic importance as the terminus of the Ofot railway (Lapland railway) from the Kiruna iron-mines in Sweden and as an ice-free harbour. The occupation of Norway during the Second World War assured**

Narvik – a panoramic view

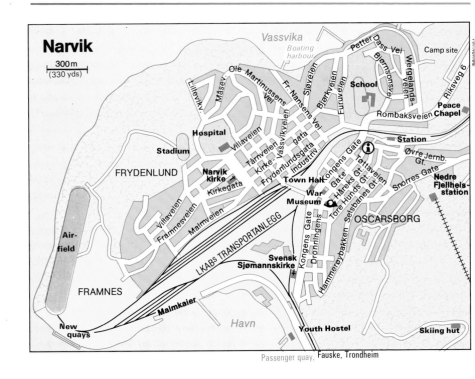

Narvik

300m
(330 yds)

Vassvika
*Boating harbour*

Petter Dass Vei    Camp site

Bjørnsonsvei    Wergelands veien    Riksveg 6

School

Peace
Rombaksveien Chapel

Hospital

Stadium

FRYDENLUND

Narvik
kirke

Kirkegata

Villaveien

Framnesveien

Malmveien

Air-
field

FRAMNES

Malmkaier

New
quays

LKABS TRANSPORTANLEGG

Havn

Station

Øvre Jernb.
Gt.

Nedre
Fjellheis-
station

Town Hall

War
Museum

Svensk
Sjømannskirke

OSCARSBORG

Youth Hostel

Skiing hut

Passenger quay, Fauske, Trondheim

supplies of Swedish iron ore for the Germans. Great Britain sought to prevent this and there were fierce battles in which the town suffered severe damage. When it was rebuilt after the war, the old wooden houses were replaced by new stone buildings.

SIGHTS. – The town is divided in half by the extensive installations of the *ore port, modernised and enlarged in 1977. The ore brought by rail from Sweden is carried by long conveyors to various depots and to the *Malmkai* (Ore Quay). The port can now handle ore-carriers of up to 350,000 tons, and has a total handling capacity of some 30 million tons

a year. On the S side of the loading installations in a small park there is an attractive sculpture of a group of children. Along the E side of the port installations runs the town's main street, *Kongensgate*. In the *Torg* (market square) is the *Town Hall* (1961), and, in front of this, a signpost with 23 signs giving the distances to the North Pole and many cities throughout the world. Nearby is a *War Museum*. At the S end of the Kongensgate stands the *Swedish Seamen's Church* (Svensk Sjømannskirke) (library). Diagonally opposite is a monument to the Norwegian warships "Norge" and "Eidsvold", which were sunk during the 1940 fighting. To the N, beyond the

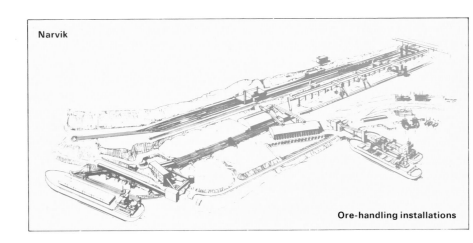

Narvik

Ore-handling installations

railway, is the *Gulbransonspark*, and to the W of this are 4000-year-old *rock carvings*. – Some distance E of the town is the *cemetery*, with the graves of allied and German soldiers.

20 minutes W of the town is a fine lookout, *Frammeåsen* (102 m – 335 ft), with a view embracing the Ofotfjord and the hill of Kongsbaktind.

SURROUNDINGS. – SE of the town is the **Fagernesfjell** (1250 m – 4101 ft), with a cableway up to 700 m (2300 ft) (restaurant at upper station). The hill offers magnificent views; midnight sun from the end of May to mid-July.

**Narvik to Abisko by rail** (there is also a new road). – The section of the line within Norwegian territory is known as the Ofot Railway, the Swedish section as the Lapland Railway. The line, completed in 1903, serves primarily for the transport of iron ore from the Kiruna and Gällivare mines (both in Sweden) to Narvik. In good weather a trip on the railway into Swedish Lapland is very attractive, taking the visitor in barely two hours from the fjord to the desolate Arctic uplands. The best view is on the left-hand side. In addition to the many ore trains using the line, there are also passenger trains.

From Narvik, the line runs along the S side of the *Rombaksfjord*, already beginning to climb (beautiful views). Beyond Rombak there is a further climb, with an impressive view, looking backwards, of the *Rombaksbotn* and the end of the fjord. The line runs through many tunnels and over viaducts, and the landscape becomes increasingly bare of trees and shrubs. – Beyond *Bjørnfjell*, the last Norwegian station, the watershed between the Baltic and the Arctic Ocean is crossed at an altitude of 525 m (1720 ft), and soon afterwards the **Norwegian-Swedish frontier** is reached. 2 km (1¼ miles) farther on is the Swedish town of **Riksgränsen**, in a magnificent mountain setting, (Hotel Riksgränsen, 400 b.; very popular skiing area). From here to Abisko, see p. 54.

\*\***Lofoten Islands:** p. 179 – **Vesterålen:** p. 291.

# Nordfjord

Norway (Western).
County: Sogn og Fjordane fylke.
Telephone code: 0 57.
ⓘ **Stryn Turistkontor,**
N-6880 Stryn;
tel. 7 15 26.

RECREATION and SPORTS. – Sailing, fishing, climbing.

The \*Nordfjord, lying almost exactly on the 62nd degree of northern latitude extends – parallel with the Sognefjord to the S – for a distance of over 90 km (55 miles) from Maløy to Olden, with a depth of up to 565 m (1850 ft). The various parts of the fjord have different names; in the past the name of Nordfjord was applied to the entire district. The juxtaposition of wide expanses of water, mighty mountains and glaciers give the inner branches of the fjord a particular charm.

The Nordfjord is reached from the S on E6, which runs via Lillehammer to Otta. From Otta Road 15 runs W via Lom to *Stryn* on the N side of the **Innvikfjord**, the most easterly ramification of the Nordfjord.

Strynsvatn

Across the *Strynselv* and along Road 60 on the steep N shore of the fjord, to **Loen** (hotels: Alexandria, 400 b., SB; Gjestehuset, 20 b.; Pensjonat, 48 b.; Richards Hotell, 45 b.), at the mouth of the beautiful *Loendal* (small octagonal wooden church, 1937). From here Skåla (1937 m – 6355 ft) can be climbed (6 hours, with guide). – From Loen a narrow road runs 14 km (9 miles) along the E side of the picturesque \*Loenvatn (alt. 43 m (140 ft), area 10·2 sq. km (4 sq. miles), greatest depth 193 m – 635 ft) by way of the *Bødal tourist resort* to *Kjenndal*, under the N side of the *Nonsnibba* (1823 m – 5981 ft). Above the W shore of the Loenvatn rises the snow-capped peak of the *Ramnefjell* or *Ravnefjell* (2003 m – 6570 ft), a northern outlier of the extensive snowfields of the Jostedalsbre (see p. 146). To the E of Kjenndal rises the *Lodalskappa*.

The Innvikfjord, S of Stryn

Road 60 continues along the shores of the fjord from Leon to **Olden** (Yris Hotel, 78 b.), at the S end of the fjord, with a church (1746–9, restored 1971). – From here a road runs 4·5 km (3 miles) S through the beautiful Olderdal to *Eide*, on the northern shore of the *Oldenvann (alt. 37 m (120 ft); area 8·4 sq. km (3 sq. miles); 11 km (7 miles) long, up to 90 m – 295 ft deep), and continues along the lake (motorboat services), past several waterfalls (views of snow-covered hills to right and left), to *Rustøy* (13 km – 8 miles), at the S end of the lake. From here it is another 5·5 km (3½ miles) (narrow road places for passing) to *Briksdal* (alt. 150 m (490 ft); inn), from where an hour's walk brings one to where the **Briksdalsbre**, an offshoot of the Jostedalsbre snowfields, rears its bluish ice masses above the scrub forest.

From Olden, Road 60 runs along the S side of the fjord and comes in 17 km (10 miles) to *Innvik*, with a view to the S of the snow-covered *Storlaugpik* (1556 m – 5105 ft) and the *Ceciliekruna* (1775 m – 5824 ft).

Beyond *Utvik*, an attractive, widely scattered settlement (church), the road leaves the shore of the fjord and winds its way (magnificent views of the fjord), up to the *Utvikfjell* (640 m – 2100 ft). From Utvikfjell there is a splendid panorama, with the Jostedalsbre to the S. Road 14 then descends to *Byrkjelo*. To the left is the Sognefjord (see p. 239): to the right is **Sandane**, attractively situated at the E end of the **Gloppenfjord**, another arm of the Nordfjord (pop. 2000; Sivertsen's Hotel, 48 b.; Toben Vertshuset, 36 b.). The Nordfjord Folk Museum is in Sandane (16

old buildings). On the W side of the fjord are the Gjemmestad church and several Iron Age burial mounds; on the E side is one of the largest burial mounds in Vestland, the Tinghogjen (50 m (165 ft) across, 7 m – 23 ft high), which captures the last evening sunlight on Midsummer Day.

The E shore of the Gloppenfjord leads to its junction with the **Utfjord**, another part of the Nordfjord. To the right lies the little airfield of Sandane. From *Anda*, on the point between the two fjords, there is a car ferry (10 minutes) to *Lote*, on the N side of the Utfjord.

From Lote, Road 14 runs NW to **Nordfjordeid** (pop. 1700; Hoddeviks Hotell, 75 b.; Nordfjord Turisthotell, 94 b.) across the strip of land between the **Hundviksfjord** and the **Eidsfjord**, and from there continues W along the N side of the Eidsfjord. Beyond *Stårheim*, birthplace of the popular poet Mathias Orheim (1884–1958: hut with souvenirs of the poet), it reaches the main arm of the fjord system, the **Nordfjord** proper. After passing through Bryggja, it comes to *Almenningen*, from which there is a view of Europe's highest cliff, *Hornelen*, rising vertically from the lake to a height of 860 m (2820 ft); in popular legend this was the place where witches and trolls held their revels. Soon afterward, a bridge 1224 m (1300 yds) long crosses the Ulvesund to **Måløy** (Hagens Hotel, 80 b.), on the island of Vagsøy. Of interest here are the Kannesten, a rock eroded into hourglass shape (11 km (7 miles) from Måløy on the shore of the fjord), and an old trading station on the *Vagsberg*, with seven historic buildings. A boat can be taken from Hagens Hotel to Vingen (opposite Hornelen), with the largest group of *stone carvings* in the north, the Helleristningsfelt (2000 figures, mostly stags).

# Norrköping

Sweden (Eastern).
Province: Östergötlands län.
Region: Östergötland.
Altitude: sea level. – Population: 118,000.
Postal code: S-60 . . . – Telephone code: 0 11.
ⓘ **Norrköpings Turistbyrå,**
Drottninggatan 18,
S-60181 Norrköping;
tel. 12 47 15.

HOTELS. – *Centric*, Gamla Rådstugugatan 18–20, 52 b.; *Grand Hotel*, Tyska Torget 2, 391 b., SB; *Lilla Hotellet*, Eneby Centrum, 31 b.; *Majgarden*, Kneippgatan 7, 24 b.; *Princess*, Skomakaregatan 8, 225 b.; *Scandic Hotel*, Järngatan 4, 315 b., SB; *Standard*, Slottsgatan 99, 238 b.; *Södra Hotellet*, Södra Promenaden 142, 29 b. – YOUTH HOSTEL. – CAMP SITE.

**The port of Norrköping lies at the outflow of the River Motala into the Bråvik, an inlet on the Baltic which stretches inland for 50 km (30 miles). The Bråvik forms a natural boundary between the wooded region of Kolmård to the N and the fertile arable land of Vikboland to the S. Norrköping is a busy commercial port (important harbour) and industrial area (metalworking, textiles).**

SIGHTS. – To the E of the station are the remains of the *Johannisborg*. Although nothing is left standing but the gate and the adjoining walls, there is enough to give some impression of what this 17th c. castle was like in its heyday. The gate tower was restored in 1934. – S of the station is *Karl Johans Park*, with an interesting collection of cacti; every year a new species is added to the 25,000 plants already there. In the park is a monument to King Karl XIV Johan (by Schwanthaler, 1846). Facing the park is the *Town House*. – On higher ground, SW of the station, stands the neo-Gothic *St Matthew's Church* (1892).

On the S bank of the River Motala is the *Tyska Torg* (German Market), with *St Hedvig's Church*, built in 1673 for the town's German community (altered in the 18th c.; altarpiece painted by Pehr Hörberg). – The **Town Hall** (1907–10) on the S side of the square has a tower 68 m (225 ft) high (carillon, daily at 12 noon and 5 p.m.). In Drottninggatan, the town's main street, is the *Clock-Tower* (1750), the great symbol and landmark of Norrköping; the watchman used to call the hours from the tower. One of the oldest churches in the town, the **Östra Eneby church** (12th c.), contains medieval ceiling paintings, valuable tapestries and a beautiful font (basin of Kolmård marble).

The *Gamla Torg*, where the Town Hall and the Burghers' Guildhall once stood, is now surrounded by handsome early 19th c. houses. In the square can be seen a *monument to Louis de Geers*, the Dutchman who brought industry to the town in the 17th c. by Carl Milles. The monument faces the Holmen works, which de Geers founded (tower painted in the colour known as Norrköping yellow). – In the Södra Promenade is the *New Municipal Library*; in Kristinaplats the *Norrköping Museum*, with departments of older and of modern art; in St Persgatan a *Dyeing Museum* (Färgagården); and in Lidaleden a *Museum of Crafts*. Gammalt Hantverk displays tools and implements of 40 different crafts. – To the W of the town are the *People's Park* and *Himmelstalund Park*, with the former spa establishment and a 200-year-old theatre.

SURROUNDINGS. – 5 km (3 miles) NW on the road to Svärtinge we find the manor-house of *Ringstad*. Near here are old graves and the remains of a 7th c. Viking stronghold, identified as the one mentioned in the Helgi lays of the Edda. – 29 km (18 miles) NW of Norrköping is **Finspång**, in an old mining area, with modern industry and a castle (1668). 10 km (6 miles) NE of Finspång is *Rejmyra*, with a glassworks (products of the factory are for sale). – 10 km (6 miles) SW of Norrköping is *Lövstad Castle*.

**Kolmård Forest** lies on the boundary between Södermanland and Östergötland, to the N of the long inlet of Bråvik – a wooded upland region extending for 100 km (60 miles) from W to E. The rocks are primarily reddish gneiss, but there is also red and black granite. Stone from this area was used in the construction of the Parliament Building in Stockholm in the 19th c. There is also a certain amount of iron and copper in Kolmård. The famous green marble found in the eastern part of the region was worked at intervals over a period of 300 years (1673–1960). Farther E is a *Wildlife Park*, which is steadily increasing in size. Nearby can be found the Stone Age occupation site of *Fagervik*. – *Eriksgatan*, the old main road between Götland and Svealand, cut through the Kolmård area from the Krokek Inn to Utterberg Castle. A forerunner of today's inns was the *Monastery of Our Lady* (Vårfrueklostret) in Kolmård, which provided accommodation for travellers. Beside the monastery a chapel was built – using stone from its ruins – and in 1747 the old church of *Krokek*, now also ruined.

15 km (10 miles) SE of Norrköping is **Söderköping** (pop. 6000; Söderköpings Brunn, 205 b., SB), founded in the 13th c. as a trading station for Lübeck merchants, who built a large church here (as well as at Sänninge). The church (St Lawrence's) was not completed until 200 years later at the end of the 15th c. – Excavations, particularly in Storgatan and Vintervadsgatan, have uncovered merchants' and craftsmen's houses and equipment which show that during the Middle Ages Söderköping was one of Sweden's principal commercial areas. In 1567, the town was partly destroyed by Danish forces; it was rebuilt in stone. John III made Norrköping the administrative headquarters of the region and promoted the development of mining. Trade declined and the German merchants left Söderköping; the town turned to fishing in the skerries for survival. On the islands of Björkeskär and Viskär, a trading settlement enjoyed a monopoly of fishing on the Östergötland coast for 80 years, until 1731. Later, the mineral water of St Ragnhild's Spring acquired some reputation and was marketed commercially. – Features of interest in the town include the *Drothem*

*quarter* (church) and a number of old-world buildings around St Lawrence's (St Lars') Church, including the belfry (1582) and the old schoolhouse. On Gilleskullen is an open-air museum, with old houses from the surrounding area. There are fine views from the *Ramunderberg* (castle).

# North Cape

Norway (Northern).
County: Finnmark fylke.

ACCESS. – *By car*, leaving Tromsø, Road 6 at first runs close to the coast for most of the time, passes through Alta and comes to *Olderfjord*; from there, Road 95 runs up the Porsanger peninsula to *Kåfjord*, from which there is a car ferry (¾ hour; 6–11 times daily, according to season) to *Honningsvåg*. – From *Lakselv* airfield there are buses to Kåfjord. – *By sea*, the trip from Hammerfest is recommended; the only boats available, however, are the "Hurtigrute" ships from Bergen to Kirkenes. These have limited accommodation; the trip takes about 6 hours. From Honningsvåg buses or taxis go to the North Cape. – *By air*, there is a service from Hammerfest to Honningsvåg. Cruise liners land either at Honnigsvåg or at Skarsvåg in Risfjorden, from where they take the shorter route to the cape.

The **North Cape (alt. 307 m (975 ft); lat. 71°10'21" N, 25°47'40" E), is a precipitous crag of slate, furrowed by deep clefts, on the N coast of the island of Magerøy. It is regarded as the northernmost point of Europe, although the cape of Knivskjellodden reaches a little farther N (lat. 71°11'8" N). The most northerly point on the mainland is the promontory**

The North Cape

**of Nordkinn (or Nordkyn or Kinnarodden, alt. 234 m – 768 ft), between the Laksefjord and the Tanafjord (lat. 71°8'1" N, long. 27°40'9" E – 68 km (42 miles) E of the North Cape).**

The island of **Magerøy** is considered to be the most northerly outpost of Europe. Between fjords cutting deep into the land, its promontories jut out into the Arctic Ocean – massive and much fissured ridges of rock between 300 and 400 m (1000 and 1300 ft) high, flat-topped and, for the most part, falling steeply to the sea. Only an occasional patch of vegetation can be seen in this desolate landscape. – The boats dock at Skarsvåg (no hotel) or at the little fishing town of **Honningsvåg** on the SE coast of the island (Nordkapp Hotell, 332 b.), from which there are buses and taxis to the **North Cape**. On the farthest point is a restaurant (North Cape certificates, special stamps and cancellations). An arrow marks the direction of due north; there is a granite pillar commemorating King Oskar II's visit to the North Cape in 1873. In good weather the view extends over the open Arctic Ocean to the W, N and E. To the SW are the islands of Hjelmsøy and Rolvsøy; to the E, in the distance, the Nordkinn promontory; to the S the Magerøy plateau with its snowfields, lakes and scanty vegetation. Since 1929 the North Cape has been protected as a nature reserve, and the removal of plants is prohibited. – The midnight sun is visible here from 14 May to 30 July, reaching its lowest point at 11.35 p.m. (Central European Time).

North Cape

Knivskjellodden
Nordkapp
Tuffjorden
Skarsvåg
Gjesvær
Kamøyfjorden
Magerøya
417 m
Kamøyvær
Vannfjorden
Honningsvåg
Magerøysundet
Kobbfjorden
Kåfjord
493 m
Porsangen
Skuottanjargga
Sværholt
Halvøya
Rèpvåg
10 km
(6 miles)
Olderfjord

# Nyköping

Sweden (Eastern).
Province: Södermanlands län.
Region: Södermanland.
Altitude: sea level. – Population: 35,000.
Postal code: S-61100. – Telephone code: 01 55.

ⓘ **Turistbyrå,**
Stora Torget;
tel. 8 12 74.

HOTELS. – *Ekeby*, Bergshamar, 20 b.; *Nya Hotellet*, V. Storgate 15A, 137 b.; *Piccolo Hotel*, Fruängsgatan 21, 35 b.; *Scandic Hotel*, Gumsbacken, 205 b., SB; *Tuna Motell*, 36 b. – YOUTH HOSTEL.

**Nyköping, chief town of Söderman-
land, lies on the Nyköpingså just
above the point where it flows into
the Baltic. In the Middle Ages it was
one of the most important towns in
Sweden, and between the 13th and
16th c. it was the meeting-place of
the Riksdag (Parliament) on 15 occasions. It is now a busy industrial
town manufacturing furniture, electric bulbs, motor vehicles, and other
goods.**

SIGHTS. – In the main square, the *Stora Torg*, are the *Town Hall* (1720), the *Governor's Residence* (1803) and the old church of *St Nicholas* (rebuilt, 18th c.). A short distance S, by way of Slottsgatan (signposted), on the right bank of the Nyköpingså, stands the massive castle of **Nyköpingshus**, which probably dates from the time of the Folkung kings (burned down in 1665 and later partly restored). King Birger Jarl imprisoned his two brothers in the castle and starved them to death in 1318. There survive the main gate, *Vasaporten*, and *Duke Charles's Tower* or Kungstornet on the W side, in which a model of the castle is displayed (Sörmland Museum). To the NW of the castle is the *Museum of Art. All Saints Church* (Allhelgona Kyrka), in the SE part of the town was rebuilt in the 17th c.

SURROUNDINGS. – Pleasant excursions to the lakes N of the town (*Yngaren, Långhalsen, Båven*).

13 km (8 miles) SE (highway) is the port of **Oxelösund** (pop. 15,000; Ankaret Hotel, 188 b.; Stiftsgården Stärnholm, 75 b.), with a large steel-works and an interesting modern church (1975). – 28 km (18 miles) W, on the coast, is the Swedish atomic research plant of *Studsvik*.

7 km (4½ miles) along the Stockholm highway (motorway) is an exit (Road 223) leading to the large burial mound of *Uppsa-Kulle* (10 m (33 ft) high), 15 km (10 miles) N. 11 km (7 miles) farther N stands

*Ludgo* church, which has an altar by B. Precht and two 15th c. sculptures from Western Europe (French or Flemish). – Another 20 km (12 miles) to the end of the motorway and 1·5 km (1 mile) along the ordinary road, turn right on to Road 218 to the Baltic seaside resort of *Trosa*, 6 km (4 miles) S (Strömsborg Hotel, 60 b.; large fish-smoking plant). – Another 3·5 km (2 miles) along the main road, a minor road goes off on the right (2 km (1¼ miles); signpost) to the manor-house of *Tullgarn* (1719–28), a royal summer residence (beautiful park).

# Odense

Denmark (Funen).
County: Fyns amt.
Altitude: 25 m (80 ft). – Population: 171,000.
Postal code: DK-5000. – Telephone code: 09.

ⓘ **Odense Turistforening,**
Rådhuset;
tel. 12 75 20.

HOTELS. – *Missionshotellet* Ansgar, Østra Stations-vej 32, 70 b.; *Frederik VI's Kro*, Rugårdsvej 590, 92 b.; *Golf Plaza*, Østra Stationsvej 24, 105 b.; *Grand Hotel*, Jernbanegade 18, 218 b.; *H. C. Andersen*, Claus Bergsgade 7, 290 b.; *Kahema*, Dronningensgade 5, 19 b.; *Windsor*, Vindegade 45, 107 b.; *Ydes Hotel*, Hans Tausengade 11, 39 b.

YOUTH HOSTEL. – *Kragsbjerggården*, Kragsbjergvej 121.

CAMP SITES. – *DCU-Camping*, Odensevej 102; *Blommenslyst*, Middelfartvej 494.

RESTAURANTS. – *Den gamle Kro*, Overgade 23; *Næsbylund Kro*, Bogensevej 105; *Næsbyhoved Skov*, Kanalvej 52; *Skoven*, Hunderup Skov; *Rode*, Ø. Stationsvej 34; *Under Lindetræet*, Ramsherred 2; *Franck-A*, Jernbanegade 4.

Hans Christian Andersen Monument, Odense

*Odense, Hans Christian Andersen's home town, lies on the island of Funen, on the important main road (E66, A1) from Copenhagen to Jutland. Denmark's third largest town (after Copenhagen and Århus), it is located on the little Odenseå, which flows into the Odensefjord a bit N of the town. It is one of the oldest towns in Denmark and a considerable commercial and industrial city. It has a University (founded in 1966).

HISTORY. – The name of Odense first appears in the documents in 988, when the bishop of the town received a letter of safe-conduct from the German Emperor, Otto. No doubt it was originally a cult-site devoted to the worship of Odin (Wotan): hence its name. In 1086, the Danish king Knud (Canute) was murdered in St Alban's church here; 15 years later he was canonised by the Pope. An ecclesiastical headquarters and place of pilgrimage in the Middle Ages, Odense survived secularisation during the Reformation and remained an important commercial town. At the beginning of the 19th c., *Kerteminde*, 15 km (10 miles) away, became the port of Odense. The old town was gradually occupied by shops and businesses, so that although it has preserved its original layout it has few old buildings. Odense's most celebrated son is the fairytale writer, Hans Christian Andersen (the initials H.C. are pronounced *ho-tsay* in Danish; the *d* in Andersen is not pronounced). He was born here on 2 April 1805, but he moved to Copenhagen, where he became famous, because he felt unappreciated in his native town. This feeling is reflected in the story, "The Ugly Duckling".

SIGHTS. – Hans Christian Andersen is believed to have been born in a house on Hans Jensens Stræde, **H. C. Andersens Hus**, which has been restored and is now a museum. It is a single-storey half-timbered house which contains furniture, pictures, manuscripts, documents and books belonging to the writer. Between the ages of 3 and 15 he lived in a house in Munkemøllestræde, *H. C. Andersens Barndomshjem*, now also a museum, which gives a good idea of the living conditions of a modest family in the early 19th c.

From Hans Christian Andersen's childhood home it is only a few steps (through the H. C. Andersen Park, with a statue of the writer) to Odense's Cathedral, **St Knud's Church**, named after the Danish saint who founded it. The original building was burned down in the 12th c., and, after another fire, Bishop Giscio (13th c.) began the construction of a new church. It took almost 200 years to complete it. A notable feature of this Gothic church is the crypt, with the tombs of King Knud and his brother Benedikt. Behind the high

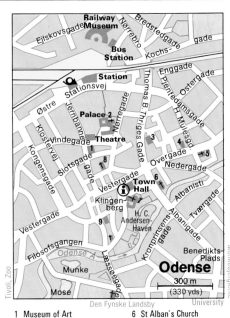

1  Museum of Art
2  St Hans' Church
3  Hans Christian Andersen's
   House (Museum)
4  Møntegården (Museum)
5  Vor Frue Kirke
6  St Alban's Church
7  St Knud's Church
8  Franciscan Friary
9  Hans Christian Andersen's
   Childhood Home

altar is a huge reredos with magnificent carvings by Claus Berg (bronze font, 1620; pulpit, 1750; carillon).

Opposite the Cathedral is the **Town Hall** (Tourist Information Office), a late 19th c. building modelled on Italian town halls in Gothic style, with an extension (1939–55) in concrete and red tiles. It contains many works of art, including an interesting sculpture, "Spring on Funen". In front of the Town Hall can be seen a statue of Knud by Utzon Franck. – To the E, at the end of Albanitorv, is *St Alban's Church* (R.C.) Farther E, by way of Overgade, is the *Old Mint* (Møntergården), now a *Museum of Cultural History* – part of a complex which includes other 16th and 17th c. houses and a Baroque warehouse (collections of stoneware and silver and material on the history of Odense). Just beyond the Old Mint is **Vor Frue Kirke** (Church of Our Lady), a late Romanesque aisleless brick church with a partly preserved group of Romanesque windows in the E wall (tower, 15th c.; pulpit, 1639).

Adjoining the *Kongens Have* (King's Park) is **St Hans' Church** (oldest parts, 13th c.; choir, 15th c.), originally belonging to a monastery of the Order of St John. On the N wall hangs a large 15th c. crucifix; the font is late Romanesque. On the SW wall is an external pulpit accessible from inside the church (the only external pulpit in Denmark). The monastic buildings, in the park, were converted by Frederick IV into a Baroque *palace*, which was remodelled in neo-classical style by Frederick VII (1841).

In Jernbanegade, which runs from the station towards the middle of the town, we find the **Museum of Art** (works by Funen painters; prehistoric section). Beyond the station is a *Railway Museum*.

Two of Odense's more modern churches are particularly interesting, the Fredenskirke and the Munkebjerg church. The *Fredenskirke* (Peace Church), in Skibshusvej, was built in 1916–20; the design (by Jensen Klint) was originally intended for a church in Århus which was never built; an adaptation of the brick churches of the Gothic period, it was a preliminary study for Klint's famous Grundtvig Church in Copenhagen. The *Munkebjerg church*, in Østerbæksvej, was the result of an architectural competition in 1942. The winning design was for an unusual polygonal structure, but local resistance prevented the construction of the church until 1962, when another team of architects took over and produced a building similar to the original plan, the unconventional style having, in the meantime, become generally accepted. The church is hexagonal, with the air of a huge tent, and has a free-standing tower.

SURROUNDINGS. – 4 km (2½ miles) S of the middle of the town, in *Hunderup Skov*, is **Den fynske Landsby**, an open-air museum containing 20 old Funen buildings (farms, houses, a blacksmith's workshop (forge), a mill, an inn, a brickworks). The museum represents a village of about 1750. Agriculture is practised according to traditional methods. Various cultural activities. – Boating on the Odenseå.

To the SW of the town are a *Zoo* and the *Tivoli Amusement Park*. On the southern outskirts is **Dalum**, with a church which originally belonged to a Benedictine house, moved here from Odense about 1200 (interesting wall paintings). Farther E is *Fraugde*, with the half-timbered 16th c. manor-house of *Fraugdegård*; in the late 17th c. it belonged to Denmark's most famous ecclesiastical poet, Thomas Kingo (later a bishop).

# Öland

Sweden.
Province: Kalmar län.
Area: 1346 sq. km (525 sq. miles).
Population: 21,000.
Postal code: S-380 . . . – Telephone code: 0485.
(i) **Ölands Turistförening**, Hamnen,
    S-38700 Borgholm.

CAMP SITES. There are a very large number on the island. At Böda and Löttorp in the north, at Borgholm, Köpingsvik and Färjestaden in the centre of the island and at Mörbylånga, Stenåsa and Degerhamn in the south.

**Öland, lying off the S coast of Sweden, is the second largest island of that country. A boldly arched bridge spans the Kalmar Sound which separates the island from the mainland. It has two rural communes and one town, Borgholm. The scenery and vegetation of the island are very different from those of the adjoining mainland. Since the island is no more than 16 km (10 miles) across at its widest point, there is always a light sea-breeze blowing. The strangest part of Öland is the desolate Alvar steppe country, where the limestone rock is exposed or covered only by a thin layer of earth.**

The *Stora Alvar* extends from Vickleby to Ottenby, covering an area 40 km (25 miles) long by 10 km (6 miles) wide – a treeless limestone steppe made up of bare rock, karstic formations, grassy heathland and expanses of flat bog. This southern part of Öland, however, also contains the most fertile arable land on the island (e.g. around Mörbylånga). The landscape pattern of central Öland, between Borgholm and Färjestaden, is different, with deciduous and coniferous forest predominating along the Kalmarsund and a broad swath of hazel scrub and flower-spangled wooded meadowland in the interior. Northern Öland has a rocky W coast, a series of alternating promontories and low-lying inlets on the E coast; between are meadowland and some steppe country, with clumps of junipers; and on the higher ground in the Böda area, coniferous forest extends from coast to coast. – Öland has a long history of human habitation. Among its most striking remains of the past are the cemeteries, most dating from the Iron Age, and the refuge forts constructed for the defence of the settled areas during the period of the great migrations. In the 12th and 13th c., the churches were fortified by the construction of defensive towers – sometimes one at each end of the church. Although most of the present churches were built in the 19th c. there are still some surviving medieval churches. Other remnants of earlier days are the stone walls, the fishermen's huts, the windmills and the villages with their houses dotting the main street. The windmills of Öland, numbering almost 400, have become the very symbol of the island. They are primarily small mills, built to serve the needs of each individual farm. All the windmills are now recorded historical monuments. The island's main source of income is agriculture (stock-farming); it provides employment for 40% of the population.

Windmills, Öland

SIGHTS. – In the N of the island, 2 km (1¼ miles) from the little fishing village of Byxelrok, are *Neptuni Åkrar* ("Neptune's Fields"), a curious beach formation of loose stones; they are covered with flowers at the height of summer. From here there is a view of the huge granite dome known as the *Blue Maiden* (Blå Jungfrun). Above the beach is a cemetery of 35 graves, with a ship-setting of the Viking period. – To the N, E and S extends the *Krono Park*, an area of some 6000 hectares (15,000 acres) with more than 50 species of trees. Within the park is *Trollskogen*, a wood of pine-trees twisted into bizarre shapes by the wind. To the S, on the W coast, is the *Källa Ödekyrka*, a 13th c. fortified church which has preserved its defensive aspect; dedicated to St Olof, it provided lodging for travellers and others coming from the nearby port of Källahamn. In the interior of the island to the W, S of the new church of Källa, lies the *Vi Alvar* cemetery, with Iron Age

"judgment rings" and sacrificial stones. At *Jordhamn*, on the W coast, can be seen a *skurverk*, a wind-powered device for grinding limestone. Limestone is also worked at *Sandvik*, farther S, which has the largest Dutch windmill in Sweden. To the S is the *Knisa Mosse* nature reserve, with a rich variety of bird-life. At a road junction (SW to Borgholm, SE to Egby) stands *Föra church*, with a 12th c. defensive tower; outside the church is the 15th c. St Martin's Cross. The road continues down the W coast via the resorts of *Bruddestad* and *Äleklinta* (cliffs) to *Köpingsvik*, with the overhanging limestone cliffs of Köpings Klint, on which there are burials and judgment rings. 300 m (300 yds) from the church is a runic stone 3 m (10 ft) high. – 4 km (2½ miles) W is Borgholm.

**Borgholm** (pop. 6500; hotels: Borgholm, 55 b.; Halltorps Gästgiveri, 18 b.; Strand 360 b.), the only town on the island and a popular holiday resort. 1 km (¾ mile) SW of the town, on higher ground, are the imposing ruins of *\*Borgholm Castle*, begun in 1572, subsequently rebuilt and destroyed by fire in 1806. There are fine views of the island and the Kalmarsund from the ramparts. – At 22 Tullgatan is the Forngård Historical Museum of Öland. In Strandgatan, by the harbour, the Archaeological Museum (Kronomagasinet) occupies a building dating from 1819.

3 km (2 miles) S is *Solliden*, a mansion built in 1903–6 for Queen Victoria, now a royal summer residence. In the beautiful park much of the original vegetation has been preserved, but there is also a Dutch rose-garden, as well as many deciduous trees not usually found in this area. The park is open to the public in summer from 12 noon to 2 p.m. daily. – 12 km (7½ miles) E of Borgholm stands *Egby church*, the smallest on the island. In spite of restoration and rebuilding in 1818, when the tower was added, it has preserved its original Romanesque character. Notable features of the interior are the font and stone altar (12th c.); the Baroque pulpit and reredos date from about 1750. – 15 km (10 miles) SE of Borgholm is Öland's best preserved medieval church, *Gärdslösa Kyrka* (Romanesque. 12th c.; late 13th c. Gothic choir). It has wall paintings of Old Testament scenes and fragments of 14th c. frescoes. The pulpit (1666) and

The Öland Bridge over the Kalmarsund

the beautiful Rococo altar (1764) are also richly painted.

**Himmelsberga**, 23 km (15 miles) SE of Borgholm, is worth visiting for its open-air museum (typical Öland farmhouses with old furnishings and equipment). These are handsome old half-timbered buildings, mostly of oak. *Norrgården* (1842) has almost the character of a manor-house, while *Karls-Olsgården* is a late 18th c. turf-roofed cottage with wall paintings in the parlour. – 27 km (17 miles) SE of Borgholm is *Ismanstorpborg*, the most striking of the refuge forts on Öland, probably dating from the time of the great migrations. 125 m (400 ft) in diameter, it has well-preserved ramparts, within which are 88 hut bases. Since it has nine entrances – very unusual – it is thought to have been primarily a cult site. – 17 km (10 miles) S of Borgholm is *Karums Alvar*, a large Iron Age cemetery with a ship-setting 30 m (100 ft) long known as "Noah's Ark". Nearby are two limestone hills to which Odin is said to have tethered his horse, Sleipnir. – *Lerkaka*, 25 km (15 miles) S of Borgholm, has a handsome row of five well-preserved windmills. There is also a large runic stone here.

On the W coast of the island, opposite Kalmar, lies the little port of *Färjestaden*. From Möllstorp, to the N of the town, the *Öland Bridge (6070 m (6600 yds) long, with 153 piers) crosses the sound to Svinö (Kalmar). – 500 m (500 yds) from the end of the bridge is the fine *Öland Zoo* (Ölands Djurpark). – 8 km (5 miles) N of Färjestaden we find the **Gråborg**, the largest refuge fort on the island, probably constructed during the great migrations, and which continued in use into the Middle Ages. The ramparts, up to 6 m (20 ft) high, enclose an elliptical area 220 m (240 yds) long by 165 m (180 yds) wide. There are remains of an impressive vaulted gateway. Nearby is the ruined 13th c. St Knut's Chapel.

4 km (2½ miles) S of Färjestaden (signposted "Runsten") is the *Karlevisten*, the oldest runic stone on Öland, with a long inscription explaining that it was set up at the end of the year 1000 by Sibbe the Wise, a Danish sea-king (probably without lands). – 6 km (4 miles) NE of the little port of *Mörbylånga* is the Romanesque church of *Resmo* (c. 1150), with frescoes of the same period in the choir. The upper part of the E tower was demolished in 1826, but part of the staircase and the S wall have been preserved. – 5 km (3 miles) E of Mörbylånga is *Mysinge Hög*, a Bronze Age burial mound. There is a magnificent view of the Stora Alvar from here. In this area there are also Neolithic chambered tombs, the only ones of their kind in eastern Sweden. The remains of 30 people were found in these 4000-year-old tombs, which were built from nine large blocks of granite.

Near the S end of the W coast is the little port of *Degerhamn*, 3 km (2 miles) N of which is the *Gettlinge Gravfält*, a large Iron Age cemetery with two limestone mounds marking the graves of chieftains. Nearby are a ship-setting, a judgment ring and a number of burial places of different types. – 9 km (5 miles) E of Degerhamn we find another Iron Age cemetery, the *Seby Gravfält*, with the remains of limestone mounds still rising prominently. 1 km ($\frac{3}{4}$ mile) away, by the roadside, a large runic stone has an inscription recording that Ingjald, Näf and Sven set it up in honour of their father, Rodmar. – 16 km (10 miles) SE of Degershamn is *Eketorps Borg*, a refuge fort with ramparts enclosing an almost perfectly circular area. The original fort, dating from the 4th c., was enlarged in the period of the great invasions. It developed into a sort of small fortified town, and habitation continued for several hundred years. Its population lived by farming and stock-rearing. In the western part of the fort, hut foundations have been exposed by excavation. At the end of the Viking period, the inhabitants built wooden houses; these remained in occupation well into the medieval period. Finds of material dating from this period show that the people who lived here had by then taken to trading and seafaring.

The S end of the island is occupied by the **Stora Alvar**, a great expanse of steppe-land which is aglow with colour when the heather and thyme are in bloom; in certain favoured spots, too, thousands of orchids flower in spring. A very common flower is the trailing tormentil; rare species such as the large sand-lily and the little blue globularia are also found. Many plants are protected by law (including the yellow pheasant's-eye which grows on coastal grassland). – Near the southernmost tip of the island is *Ottenby*, which in the 13th c. belonged to a monastery. It was taken over by Gustavus Vasa and remained Crown property thereafter. The manor-house of Kungsgård dates from 1804. To the N, visible from the road, is an Iron Age cemetery. 2 km ($1\frac{1}{4}$ miles) W are two high limestone mounds, the *King's Stones*. The Kungsgård estate is bounded on the N by a wall running from coast to coast, built in 1653 to protect the peasants' fields to the N from the royal deer. – On the promontory stands Sweden's tallest lighthouse, *Lange Jan* (42 m (140 ft) high), built in 1785. Nearby are a *bird-watching station* and *ornithological museum*.

# Örebro

Sweden (Central).
Province: Örebro län. – Region: Nârke.
Altitude: 24 m (80 ft). – Population: 115,000.
Postal code: S-700 . . . – Telephone code: 0 19.

ⓘ **Örebro Turistbyrå,**
Drottningatan 7,
S–70210 Örebro;
tel. 13 07 60.

HOTELS. – *Anglé*, Klostergatan 17, 40 b.; *Ansgar*, Järnvägsgatan 10, 70 b.; *Bergsmannen*, Drottninggatan 42, 102 b.; *Continental*, Järnvägsgatan 2, 64 b.; *Grand Hotel*, Fabriksgatan 21–25, 600 b.; *Grev Rosen*, Södra Grev Rosengatan 2, 139 b.; *Ritz och Royal*, Drottninggatan 24, 53 b.; *Scandic Hotel*, Västhagagatan 1, 497 b. – YOUTH HOSTEL. – CAMP SITE.

**Örebro, capital of the Närke region, lies in the plain on both sides of the Svartå, near the W end of Lake Hjälmar. It has a long tradition as a commercial area, having served for centuries as a link between the mining region and the farming country of central Sweden. It developed around a ford on the Svartå, which from the end of the 13th c. was protected by a tower 25 m (80 ft) high, built by Birger Jarl to watch over and defend the river crossing. On the foundations**

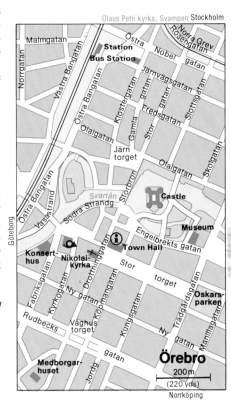

Örebro
200 m
(220 yds)

Örebro Castle

with a number of old wooden houses, including the *Kungsstuga* (King's House, 15th or 16th c.) and the *Borgarstuga* (17th c.).

To the N of the town, in Storgatan, is the *Olaus Petri Church* (1912), in front of which stands a bronze monument (by Nils Sjörgren) to the brothers Laurentius and Olaus Petri, leading figures of the Reformation in Sweden during the reign of Gustavus Vasa. Farther NE a 60 m (200 ft) high water-tower, called *Svampen* (the "mushroom"), has a restaurant from which there are extensive views over the surrounding countryside.

**of this tower the castle was built. It played an important role, on many occasions, as the meeting place of the Riksdag (Swedish parliament).**

SIGHTS. – The central feature of the town is the *Stortorg*. At the W end of this stands **St Nicholas's Church** (*Nikolaikyrka*, 18th c.), in which the French marshal Bernadotte was chosen as heir to the throne in 1810. The church also contains the tomb of Sweden's legendary national hero, Engelbrekt Engelbrektsson. Opposite the church, in front of the neo-Gothic **Town Hall** (1856–62), is a bronze statue of Engelbrekt (Qvarnström, 1865). To the W of St Nicholas's, on the banks of the Svartå, are the *Concert Hall* (Konserthus) and, in the same building, the *Municipal Library*. – From the W end of the Stortorg Drottninggatan runs S to the *Medborgarhus* (Citizens' House, 1964), with a youth club and the Hjalmar Bergman Theatre, named after the great Swedish novelist and dramatist, a native of the town.

A little way N of the Stortorg, by way of Kungsgatan, we come to the venerable old **Castle**, on an island in the river. It is a 16th c. Renaissance structure with four corner towers (restored 1897–1900), which now houses the provincial government offices. To the SE of the Castle is the *Castle Park*, with the *Strömparterren* restaurant, and on the E side of the park are the *Art Gallery* (temporary exhibitions) and the *Provincial Museum* (local history and culture). – From the Castle, the Kanalväg runs along the S side of the river to the attractive *Municipal Park*, to the E of which, on the banks of the river, is the *Wadköping* open-air museum,

SURROUNDINGS. – SW of the town, on the Karlstad road, is the *Gustavsvik* open-air swimming pool. – A few miles E of Örebro lies the *Oset bird sanctuary* (land area 45 hectares (110 acres), water area 85 hectares (210 acres)), frequented by many species of birds. – 10 km (6 miles) NE on the old Fellingsbrovägstands the *Nastasten*, a runic stone with the inscription "Tored had this stone set up for Lydbjörn, his good son". – 15 km (10 miles) from Örebro in the same direction is the manor-house of *Ekebergs Herregård*, from which Gustavus Vasa's second wife, Margareta Leijonhufvud, came. The famous Ekberg marble, used in the Town House and Dramatic Theatre in Stockholm, came from the nearby village of **Glanshammar**, which has a church dating from the middle of the 12th c. One of the richest churches in the province, it has magnificent Renaissance paintings and a fine processional crucifix. 200 m (220 yds) W of the church are the old *silver-mines* which gave the place its name. (Silver-mining ceased in 1530.) NE of the church is a ship burial, part of a cemetery which extends along the road to Fellingsbro.

3 km (2 miles) W of the middle of the town stands the old 16th c. manor-house of *Karlslundsgård*, now owned by the town. Some rooms of the house are used for occasional special exhibitions. Here too is one of the oldest power stations in Sweden.

17 km (10 miles) S of Örebro is the **Mosjö church**, a medieval building which has survived almost unaltered. It contains a copy of the 12th c. Mosjö Madonna (75 cm (30 in.) high), now in the State Historical Museum in Stockholm. This carved wooden figure, in the costume of a Nordic goddess, is one of the oldest Madonna figures in Scandinavia. – To the E of the church are tombs and a judgment ring.

40 km (25 miles) E of Örebro, on the Arbogaå, is **Arboga**, founded after the river was made navigable in the 12th c. Arboga rapidly developed into a busy trading town with a Franciscan friary and a Hospice of the Holy Ghost. Until the early 17th c. it was one of the best-known towns in Sweden, but declined steadily in importance as a commercial area after the foundation of the mining settlements of Nora and Lindesberg (1643) and the construction of the Hjälmar Canal. The town has preserved much of its original charm, with many old merchants' and craftsmen's houses. St Nicholas's Church, in which provincial assemblies were held, is a medieval church (restored 1921) with a fine reredos (German, 16th c.) and old wall paintings. In front of the church is a

statue (1935) of the national hero, Engelbrekt Engelbrektsson, who was elected Governor of the Realm (Rikshövitsman) or Regent at a meeting of the Riksdag held here in 1435. To the W of the church stands the 18th c. Town Hall.

**Lake Hjälmar** (area 483 sq. km (190 sq. miles), greatest depth 28 m – 90 ft) extends eastward into Södermanland and is linked with Lake Mälar by the *Hjälmar Canal* and the Arbogaå. Between 1877 and 1888, the water level was lowered by 1·8 m (6 ft), making 27,000 hectares (67,500 acres) of land available for cultivation. The lake is heavily stocked with fish and is frequented by many species of birds; there is a bird-watching tower at *Segersjöviken*.

# Oslo

Norway (Southern).
County: Oslo fylke.
Altitude: sea level. – Population: 447,000.
Postal code: N-Oslo. – Telephone code: 02.
(i) **Nortra**
(*Norwegian National Tourist Office*).
Langkai 1,
N-Oslo 1;
tel. 42 70 44.
**Reisetrafikkforeningen for Oslo og Omegn**
(*Oslo and District Tourist Organisation*),
Rådmannsgården, Rådhusgate 19,
N-Oslo 1;
tel. 42 71 70.
*Turistinformasjonskontoret,*
Town Hall,
tel. 41 48 63.
Accommodation Register (Innkvarterins-sentralen),
Central Station, Oslo Østbane;
**Norges Automobil-Forbund** (*NAF:*
*Norwegian Automobile Association*),
Storgate 2–6,
N-Oslo 1;
tel. 33 70 80.
**Kongelig Norsk Automobilklub** (KNA:
Royal Norwegian Automobile Club),
Parkveien 68,
N-Oslo 2;
tel. 56 26 90.

EMBASSIES. – *United Kingdom*: Thomas Heftyes-gate 8, N-Oslo 2 (tel. 56 38 90–97). – *USA*: Drammensveien 18, N-Oslo 1 (tel. 56 68 80). – *Canada*: Oscarsgate 20, N-Oslo 3 (tel. 46 69 55).

CITY TOURS: departure from Town Hall.
HARBOUR TOURS: departure from Town Hall Quay.

HOTELS – *Bristol*, Kristian IV's gate 7, 220 b., *Continental*, Stortingsgata 24–26, 300 b.; *Grand Hotel*, Karl Johansgate 31, 525 b., SB; *Scandinavia*, Holbergsgate 30, 960 b., SB, restaurants, shopping arcade; *Ambassadeur*, Camilla Coletts vei 15, 51 b.,. SB; *Ansgar*, Møllergate 26, 80 b; *Bondeheimen*, Rosenkrantzgate 8, 108 b.; *City*, Skippergatan 19, 105 b., *Europa*, St Olavs gate 31, 290 b.; *Fønix*, Dronningens gate 19, 96 b.; *Gabelshus*, Gabelsgate

16, 95 b.; *IMI Hotell*, Staffeldtsgate 4, 238 b.; *KNA-hotellet*, Parkveien 68, 277 b.; *Linne Hotel*, Statsråd Mathiesens vei 12, 176 b.; *Müllerhotell Astoria*, Akersgate 21, 162 b.; *Munch*, Muchsgate 5, 225 b.; *Nobel Hotel*, Karl Johansgate 33, 115 b.; *Norge*, Ankerveien 6, 130 b.; *Norrøna*, Grensen 19, 60 b.; *Norum*, Bygdoy Alle 53, 90 b.; *Rica Carlton*, Parkveien 78, 92 b.; *Ritz*, Frederik Stangs gate 3, 75 b.; *Saga*, Eilert Sundtsgate 39, 67 b.; *Sara Hotel Oslo*, Biskop Gunnerusgate 3, 464 b.; *Savoy* Universitetsgate 11, 90 b.; *Standard Hotell*, Pilestredet 27, 72 b.; *Stefan-hotellet*, Rosenkrantzgate 1, 210 b.; *White House*, Pr. Harbitz gate 18, 45 b.

IN THE SURROUNDING AREA: *Holmenkollen Park Hotel*, Kongeveien 26, 9 km (5 miles) NW on Holmenkollen, 340 b., SB; *Park Royal Hotel*, Fornebuparken, at the airport, 7 km (4 miles) SW of the city centre, 503 b.; *Sheraton Oslo Fjord*, in Sandvika, 23 km (14 miles) W of the city and 11 km (7 miles) from the airport, 486 b.; *Helsfyr Nye Hotel*, Strømsveien 108, 3 km (2 miles) SW of the city centre, 225 b.; *Müllerhotell Mastemyr*, Lienga 1, in Kolbotn, 300 b.; *Scandic Hotel*, Ram-stadsletta 12–14, in Høvik, 11 km (7 miles) SW of the city centre, 103 b.; *Smestad*, Sorkedalsveien 93, 5·5 km (3 miles) NW, 45 b.; *Volksenåsen*, Ullveien 4, about 12 km (7 miles) NW of the city centre towards Tryvannsbøgda, 115 b.

SUMMER HOTELS: *Anker Hotel*, Storgate 55, 500 b.; *Fjellhaug Sommerhotell*, Sinsenveien 15, 270 b.; *Holtekillen Sommerhotell*, Michelets vei 55, in Sta-bekk, 137 b.; *Panorama Sommerhotell*, Songsveien 218, 800 b.; *Blinderen Studenthjem*, Blindernveien 41, 300 b. (1 June–31 August).

YOUTH HOSTELS: *Haraldsheim*, Haraldsheimveien 4, Grefsen, 5 km (3 miles) NE, 270 b.; *Bjerke*, Trondheimsveien 271, Grefsen, 159 b.

CAMP SITES. – *Bogstad*, on Bogstad Lake (10 km (6 miles) NW), with chalets; *Ekeberg*, Ekebergsletta 4 km (2½ miles) SE of the middle of the city).

RESTAURANTS. – *Blom* (an artists' restaurant with a striking interior), Karl Johansgate 41; *Frascati* (French), Stortingsgate 20; *La P'tite Cuisine chez Ben Joseph* (French), Solligate 2; *Cossack* (Russian), Kongensgate 6; *Coq d'Or*, Skovveien 15; *King George Steakhouse*, Torggate 11; *Theatercaféen*, Stor-tingsgate 24–26; *Cheese Inn* (cheese specialties), Vikaterrassen, Ruseløkkveien 3; *Najaden*, at Ship-ping Museum, Bygdøy. – RESTAURANTS WITH VIEW: *Frognerseteren* (popular); *Holmenkollen*.

WINTER SPORTS. – The Oslo region (Oslomarka) with Nordmarka, Krogskogen, Vestmarka, Østmarka, etc., offers excellent skiing, with a reasonable assurance of good snow conditions from January to March. The Nordmarka is most easily reached on the Holmenkollen railway. There are 2200 km (1400 miles) of marked cross-country ski trails; there are 153 km (95 miles) with floodlighting. There are *downhill pistes*, with lifts, at Tryvannskleiva, Rød-kleiva, Wyllerløypa, Kirkerudbakken, Ingierkollen, Grefsenkleiva, Fjellstadbakken, Trollvannskleiva, Var-dåsen and Varingskollen. The most accessible Alpine skiing area is on the *Norefjell* (2½ hours' drive NW via Hønefoss and Noresund), with four lifts up to 1800 m (5700 ft). – Ski schools; 130 ice-rinks (3 with artificial ice) within the city; curling at Bygdøy.

Oslo (known from 1624 to 1877 as Christiania and from 1877 to 1924 as Kristiania), capital of Norway and chief town of the counties of Oslo and Akershus, lies in a magnificent setting, surrounded by wooded hills, at the head of the long Oslofjord (the little Akerselv flows into the Oslo-fjord at this point). It is the head-quarters of government, the see of a Lutheran and, since 1953, a Roman Catholic bishop, and has a university and several other institutions of higher education. – The port is one of the largest in Norway, the base of a large merchant shipping fleet and several shipping lines. The city's principal industries are metalwork-ing, foodstuffs, clothing manufac-ture and shipbuilding.

HISTORY. – Oslo, was probably founded in 1050 by Harald Hårdråde, but it is likely that there was already a small settlement and dock on the site. Harald's son, Olav Kyrre, made the town the see of a bishop and built a cathedral, and thereafter Oslo remained for centuries one of the religious hubs of the country, even though the kings resided in first Trondheim then Bergen. Håkon V made the move from Bergen to Oslo about 1300 and began to build the stronghold of Akershus. About the same time, the Hanseatic League established a trading station in Oslo. After a great fire in 1624, Christian IV of Denmark rebuilt the town on the N side of Akershus Castle and called it Kristiania. It was only after the separation of Norway from Denmark in 1814 that Kristiania again became a capital and a royal residence; during the reign of King Johan it enjoyed a new rise to prosperity. On 1 January 1925 it resumed its old name of Oslo.

# Museums, Art Galleries and Other Sights

## CITY

**Akershus Castle**
(entrance in Rådhusgate);
2 May to 15 September, Mon.–Sat. 10 a.m. to 4 p.m., Sun 12.30 to 4 p.m.; 16 September to 31 October, Sun. 12.30 to 4 p.m.; 15 April to 1 May, Sun. 12.30 to 2.45 p.m.
Conducted tours: 15 April to 1 May, Sun. at 1.30 p.m.; 2 May to 15 September, weekdays at 11 a.m., 1 p.m. and 3 p.m., Sun. at 1 p.m. and 3 p.m.; 16 September to 31 October, Sun. at 1 p.m. and 3 p.m.

**Art Union** (*Kunstnerforbundet*),
Kjeld Stubsgate 3;
1 September to 30 June, Mon.–Fri. 10 a.m. to 5 p.m., Sat. 10 a.m. to 3 p.m., Sun. 12 noon to 3 p.m.; 1 July to 30 August, Mon.–Fri. 10 a.m. to 4 p.m., Sat. 10 a.m. to 2 p.m.

**Bogstad Hovedgård** (manor-house of 1756), Sørkedalen (10 km (6 miles) from the middle of the city);
May to September, Wed. 6 to 7 p.m., Sun. 12 noon to 5 p.m. (conducted tours every hour).

**Customs Museum** (*Norsk Tollmuseum*),
Tullbugate 1a;
15 May to 15 September, Tues. and Thurs. 12 noon to 3 p.m.; 16 September to 14 May, Thurs. 12 noon to 3 p.m.

**Defence Museum** (*Forsvarsmuseet*),
Akershus Castle;
Tues. and Thurs. 10 a.m. to 8 p.m., Wed. 10 a.m. to 3 p.m., Sat. and Sun. 11 a.m. to 4 p.m.; 1 October to 1 April, Tues.–Fri. 10 a.m. to 3 p.m., Sat. and Sun. 11 a.m. to 3 p.m.; closed on public holidays.

**Ethnographical Museum** (*Etnografisk Museum*),
Frederiksgate 2;
15 May to 14 September, Tues.–Sun. 11 a.m. to 3 p.m.; 15 September to 14 May, daily 12 noon to 3 p.m.

**Folk Museum** (*Norsk Folkemuseum*),
Museumsveien 10, Bygdøy;
1 September to 14 May, Mon.–Sat. 11 a.m. to 4 p.m., Sun. 11 a.m. to 4 p.m. or 12 noon to 3 p.m.; 15 May to 31 August, daily 10 a.m. to 6 p.m.

**Fram Museum,**
Bygdøynes;
15 April to 30 April, daily 11 a.m. to 3 p.m.; 2 to 16 May, daily 11 a.m. to 5 p.m.; 17 May to 31 August, daily 10 a.m. to 6 p.m.; September, daily 11 a.m. to 5 p.m.; October, daily 11 a.m. to 3 p.m.

**Gamle Akers Kirke,**
Akersbakken 26;
15 May to 1 September: guided tours 12.30 to 2 p.m., Sun. service at 11 a.m.

**Historical Museum** (*Historisk Museum*),
Frederiksgate 2;
15 May to 14 September, Tues.–Sun. 11 a.m. to 3 p.m.; 15 September to 14 May, Tues.–Sun. 12 noon to 3 p.m.

**Kon Tiki Museum,**
1 April to 16 May, daily 10.30 a.m. to 5 p.m.; 18 May to 31 August, daily 10 a.m. to 6 p.m.; 1 September to 31 October, daily 10.30 a.m. to 5 p.m.; 1 November to 31 March, daily 10.30 a.m. to 4 p.m.

**Munch Museum,**
Tøyengate 53;
throughout the year, Tues.–Sat. 10 a.m. to 8 p.m., Sun. 12 noon to 8 p.m.

**Museum of Applied Art,**
(*Kunstindustrimuseet*),
St Olavsgate 1;
throughout the year Tues.–Sun. 11 a.m. to 3 p.m.; also 7 to 9 p.m. on Tues.

**Museum of Technology,** (*Norsk Teknisk Museum*),
Kjelsasveien 141;
throughout the year, Tues.–Sun. 10 a.m. to 8 p.m.

**National Gallery** (*Nasjonalgalleriet*),
Universitetsgate 13;
throughout the year, Mon.–Fri. 10 a.m. to 4 p.m., Sat. 10 a.m. to 3 p.m., Sun. 12 noon to 3 p.m., also 6 to 8 p.m. on Wed. and Thurs.

Harbour and Town Hall, Oslo

**Natural History Museums** (*Universitets Natur-historiske Museer*).
Sarsgate 1, Tøyen;
*Botanic Garden:* 1 May to 15 August, Mon.–Fri. 7 a.m. to 8 p.m., Sat. and Sun. 10 a.m. to 8 p.m.; 16 August to 30 September, Mon.–Fri. 7 a.m. to 7 p.m., Sat. and Sun. 10 a.m. to 7 p.m.; April, Mon.–Fri. 7 a.m. to 6 p.m., Sat. and Sun. 10 a.m. to 6 p.m.
*Hothouses:* throughout the year, Tues.–Sun. 12 noon to 3 p.m.
*Mineralogical, Geological, Palaeontological and Zoological Museum:* throughout the year, Tues.–Sun. 12 noon to 3 p.m.

**Oscarshall,**
Oscarshallveien, Bygdøy;
3 June to 30 September, Sun. 11 a.m. to 4 p.m.

**Oslo Art Union** (*Oslo Kunstforening*),
Rådhusgate 19 (a building dating from 1626);
September to June, Tues.–Fri. 11 a.m. to 5 p.m., Sat. 11 a.m. to 3 p.m., Sun. 12 noon to 4 p.m.

**Oslo Ladegård,**
(models of the town, etc.)
Oslogate 13;
1 May to 30 September, Wed. 6 to 7 p.m., Sun. 1 to 2 p.m.

**Parliament Building** (*Stortingsbygningen*),
Karl Johansgate;
conducted tours from beginning of June to middle of September, Mon.–Sat. at 11 a.m., 12 noon and 1 p.m.

**Postal Museum** (*Postmuseet*),
Dronningensgate 15;
throughout the year, Mon.–Fri. 10 a.m. to 3 p.m., Sat. 10 a.m. to 1 p.m.

**Resistance Museum** (*Norges Hjemmefront-museum*),
Akershus Castle;
1 October to 30 April, Mon.–Sat. 10 a.m. to 3 p.m., Sun. 11 a.m. to 4 p.m.; 1 May to 30 September, Mon.–Sat. 10 a.m. to 4 p.m.,

**Royal Palace** (*Det Kongelige Slott*),
Drammensveien 1;
admission to grounds only.

**Shipping Museum** (*Norsk Sjøfartsmuseum*),
Bygdoynesveien 37;
May to September, daily 10 a.m. to 8 p.m.; October to April, Mon., Wed. and Fri. 10.30 a.m. to 4 p.m., Tues. and Thurs. 10.30 a.m. to 7 or 8 p.m., Sun. 10.30 a.m. to 5 p.m.

**Skiing Museum** (*Skimuseet*),
Holmekollbakken;
Kongeveien 5;
1 May to 30 June, daily 10 a.m. to 7 p.m.; July, daily 9 a.m. to 9 p.m.; 1 August to 30 September, daily 10 a.m. to 7 p.m.; 1 October to 30 April, daily 10 a.m. to 4 p.m.

**Town Hall** (*Rådhuset*),
Rådhusplassen;
1 October to 31 March, Mon.–Sat. 11 a.m. to 2 p.m., Sun. 12 noon to 3 p.m.; 1 April to 30 September, Mon.–Sat. 10 a.m. to 3 p.m.

**University Great Hall**
(murals by Edvard Munch),
Karl Johansgate 47;
1 July to 30 July; at other times by appointment (tel. 42 90 10, ext. 756).

**Emanual Vigeland Museum,**
Grimelundsveien 8, Slemdal;
throughout the year, Sun. 12 noon to 3 p.m.

**Gustav Vigeland Museum,**
Nobelsgate 32;
throughout the year, Tues.–Sun. 12 noon or 1 to 7 p.m.

**Vigeland Park,**
Frogner;
throughout the year, day and night.

**Viking Ships Museum** (*Vikingskiphuset*),
Huk Aveny 35, Bygdøy;
1 November to 31 March, daily 11 a.m. to 3 p.m.; April, daily 11 a.m. to 4 p.m.; 2 May to 31 August, daily 10 a.m. to 6 p.m.; September, daily 11 a.m. to 5 p.m.; October, daily 11 a.m. to 4 p.m.

**Young Artists' Union** (*Unge Kunstneres Samfund*),
Rådhusgate 19;
Tues.–Fri. 11 a.m. to 5 p.m., Sat. and Sun. 12 noon to 4 p.m.; closed 25 June to 20 August.
Temporary exhibitions.

## SURROUNDINGS

**Amundsen's House,**
Uranienborg, Bålerud;
15 May to 15 September, daily 11 a.m. to 5 p.m.; conducted tours every hour.

**Eidsvollsminnet**
(Memorial to 1814 Constitution),
Eidsvoll;
1 October to 30 April, daily 12 noon to 2 p.m.; 2 May to 14 June, daily 10 a.m. to 3 p.m.; 15 June to 14 August, daily 10 a.m. to 5 p.m.; 15 August to 30 September, daily 10 a.m. to 3 p.m.

**Henie-Onstad Art Center,**
Høvikodden;
throughout the year, Mon.–Fri. 9 a.m. to 10 p.m., Sat. and Sun. 11 a.m. to 10 p.m.

**Haslum Church,**
Gamle Ringeriksveien 84;
1 June to 19 August, Mon.–Sat. 2 to 8 p.m., Sun. 1 to 5 p.m.

**Tanum Church,**
Tanumveien;
23 June to 20 August, Mon.–Fri. 12 noon to 6 p.m., Sat. 10 a.m. to 1 p.m., Sun. 1 to 4 p.m.

# Sightseeing in Oslo

Oslo's main shopping and business street is the *Karl Johansgate*, which runs NW from the *East Station* (Østbanestasjonen) to the Royal Palace. Half-way between the station and Eidsvollplass in the *Stortorg*, usually known simply as *Torget*, stands a statue of Christian IV (by C. L. Jacobsen, 1874). The **Cathedral** (*Domkirke*), on the SE side of the square was consecrated in 1697, restored by the Hamburg architect A. de Chateauneuf in 1849–50 and internally renovated in 1948–50. The main entrance has bronze doors (1938); notable features of the interior are the ceiling paintings by H. L. Mohr (1936–50), the pulpit and altar (1699), the organ-case (1727) and the stained glass by E. Vigeland (1910–16). In the *Chapel of Our Saviour*, built 1949–50, is a fine silver sculpture by Arrigo Minerbi, "The Last Supper".

Beyond two side streets leading to the Stortorg lies the busiest part of Karl Johansgate (many shops). On the far side of the intersection with Akersgate is the **Parliament Building** (*Storting*); in the Chamber hangs a large picture by O. Wergeland of the constitutional assembly at Eidsvoll in 1814. On the S side of the Parliament Building is a monument to the poet *J. H. Wessel* (1742–85), and opposite this the *Freemasons' Lodge*. – In the tree-lined Eidsvollplass adjoining the Parliament Building can be seen a statue of the poet, *Henrik Wergeland*, of Bergslien (1808–45). In No. 10, Rosenkrantzgate, which crosses Karl Johansgate here, is the *Oslo Nye Teater* (plays, revues, etc) and to the NW of Eidsvollplass the **National Theatre** (*Nasjonalteatret*) (H. Bull, 1895–9). In front of the latter are bronze statues of *Ibsen* and *Bjørnson* (by S. Sinding); behind it are a statue of the actor *J. Brun* and the entrance to an underground (subway) station (several lines, including the one to Holmenkollen). Diagonally across from the National Theatre is the *Norske Teater* (classical, modern and foreign plays). To the NE of the National Theatre, in the gardens on Karl Johansgate, stands a statue of the playwright *Ludvig Holberg*, a native of Bergen, who created the Danish-Norwegian comedy.

Just S of the National Theatre, in Fridtjof Nansens Plass, we come to the monumental * **Town Hall** (*Rådhus*: by Arnstein Arneberg and Magnus Poulson, 1931–50), one of the city's great landmarks. (Fine interior, richly decorated with modern frescoes; 38-bell carillon in E tower.) Beyond the Town Hall is the quay from which motorboats leave for *Bygdøy* and other destinations in the Oslofjord. – To the NE of the National Theatre, on the other side of Karl Johansgate, is the **University** (founded by Frederik VI of Denmark in 1811; present buildings, 1839–54). In front of the central building are statues of. the legal scholar, *A. M. Schweigaard* (1808–70: on left) and the historian *P. A. Munch* (1810–63: on right). The Great Hall in the rear building, which was added in 1911, boasts fine * murals by Edvard Munch (1926). – Most of the students from outside Oslo live in the University City in Sognsvei, on the N side of the town, a series of uniformly designed buildings used as hotels during the summer vacation. Distributed within these buildings is an extensive collection of works of art (Edvard Munch, Per Krohg, etc.). To the W of Sognsvei, in the Blindern district, are several new University buildings.

In No. 13 Universitetsgate, which skirts the E side of the University, is the * **National Gallery** (*Nasjonalgalleriet*:

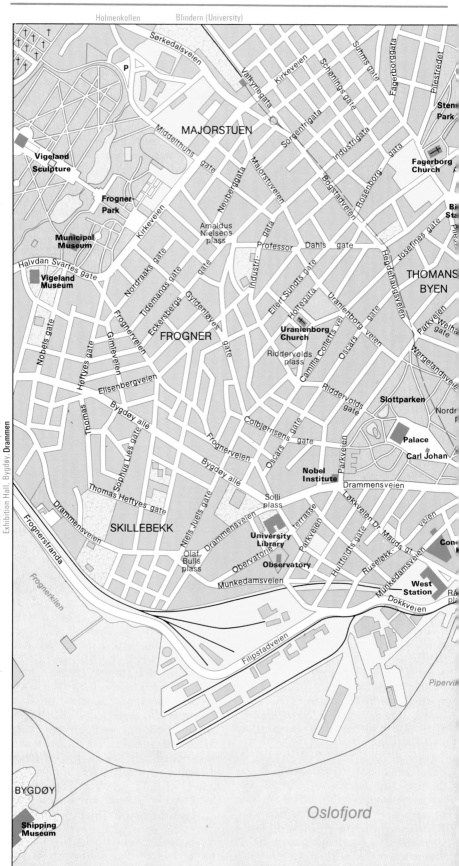

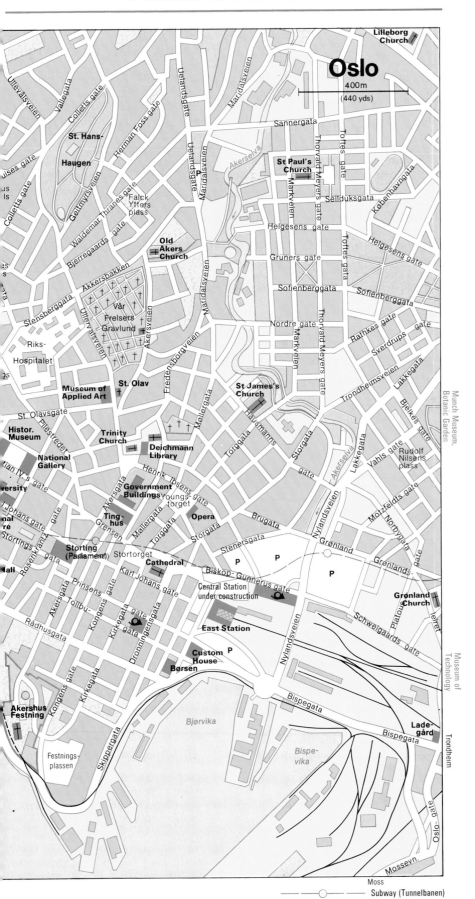

Oslo

400m
(440 yds)

Lilleborg Church

St Paul's Church

Ulevålsveien · Valle gata · Colletts gate · Uetlandsgate · Herman Foss gate · Maridalsveien · Akerselva · Sannergata · Thorvald Meyers gate · Toftes gate · Københavngata

St. Hans-Haugen

Geitmyrsveien · Waldemar Thranes gate · Collette gate · Louises gate · us gata · ls

Falck Ytters plass

Seilduksgata · Markveien · Helgesens gate · Helgesens gate

Old Akers Church

Bjerregaards gate · Stensberggata

Gruners gate · Sofienberggata · Toftes gate · Rathkes gate · Sverdrups gate · Lakkegata

Akersbakken · Vår Frelsers Gravlund · Ullevålsveien · Akersveien · Maridalsveien

Nordre gate · Markveien · Thorvald Meyers gate · Sofienberggata · Trondheimsveien

Riks-Hospitalet · Stensberggata

Fredensborgveien · Møllergata

St James's Church

Museum of Applied Art · St. Olav · St. Olavsgate · Histor. Museum · Pilestredet

Trinity Church · Deichmann Library

Torggata · Hausmanns · Storgata · gate · Akerselva · Lakkegata · Vahls gate · Bjelkes gate · Rudolf Nilsens plass · Moltfeldts gate · Norbygata

National Gallery · tian IV's gate · versity · Johans gate · nal · re · Stortings · gata

Henrik Ibsens gate · Akersgata · Youngs torget · Møllergata · Torggata · Storgata · Government Buildings · Opera · Brugata · Stenersgata · Grønland · Grønlands

Ting-hus · Grensen

Storting (Parliament) · Stortorget · Cathedral · Karl Johans gate · Prinsens gate · Rosenkrantz gata

Biskop Gunnerus gate · Central Station under construction · East Station · Nylandsveien · Grønland Church · P

Mall · Akersgata · Tollbu- · Kongens gate · Kirkegata · gate · Dronningensgata

Rådhusgata · Schweigaards gate

Custom House · Børsen · P

Akershus Festning · Kongens gate · Kirkegata · Skippergata

Festnings-plassen

Bjørvika

Bispegata

Lade-gård · Bispegata

Bispe-vika

Mossevn. · Moss

Munch Museum, Botanic Garden · Museum of Technology · Trondheim · Oslo gate

Moss
Subway (Tunnelbanen)

built 1879–81; extensions, 1907 and 1924), which offers an excellent survey of Norwegian painting from the 19th c. to the present. It is particularly rich in works by J. C. Dahl (1788–1857), T. Fearnley (1802–42), H. F. Gude (1825–1903), H. O. Heyerdahl (1857–1913), C. Krohg (1852–1925), G. P. Munthe (1849–1929), E. Petersson (1852–1928) and A. Tidemand (1814–76). A special room is devoted to *Edvard Munch*. There are also works by Danish and Swedish artists, pictures by Rubens, Rembrandt, Lucas Cranach, El Greco and other European masters, and a good collection of works by modern French artists (Cézanne, Degas, Gauguin, Manet, Matisse, Picasso, etc.). – NW of the National Gallery in the *Historical Museum (Historisk Museum*: entrance at No. 2 Frederiksgate), are the University's historical and ethnographic collections. Among the Nordic antiquities, the rich collection of material from the Viking age (*c.* 800–1050) is particularly noteworthy. There is also a good collection of material on the Eskimo and Siberian peoples and also a collection of *coins and medals*.

At the NW end of Karl Johansgate, standing on higher ground, in a large park, can be seen the **Royal Palace** (*Det Kongelige Slott*). It is a long, sober building erected between 1825 and 1848 (closed to the public). In front of the palace is an equestrian statue of Karl XIV Johan (B. Bergslien, 1875). Nearer Karl Johansgate is a striking monument to the mathematician, *N. H. Abel* (G. Vigeland) and beyond the palace, on the right, a bronze statue of the woman writer, *Camilla Collet* (1813–95), also by Vigeland. – Along the S side of the palace grounds runs Drammensvei, and, at its intersection with Parkvei, on the right, is the *Nobel Institute*. The Nobel Peace Prize is presented annually, to a person selected by the Norwegian Storting (Parliament), in the Great Hall of the University. – To the W, at the intersection of Drammensvei with Observatoriegate, the *University Library* (1913, with extensions of 1933 and 1945) houses 3 million volumes. From here Frognervei leads NW to the Frognerpark.

From the Parliament Building, Akersgate runs NE past the *Oslo Tinghus* (Council House, 1903) and the modern *Government Buildings* (1957–9; at Nos. 42–44)

to the *Trinity Church* (Trefoldighedskirke, 1853–58), which contains beautiful stained glass by F. Haavardsholm and one of the oldest organs in the country. Beyond this, to the E, are the *Deichman Municipal Library* (founded 1780; present building 1929), with about 850,000 volumes, and the Swedish *Margaretakirke* (1926). To the SE, in Youngstorg or Nytorg, is the *Norske Opera* (Folketeatret, 1958), the city's largest theatre (opera, ballet). – At the N end of Akersgate stands *St Olav's Church* (1853: R.C.), and, opposite, at No. 1 St Olavsgate the **Museum of Applied Art** (*Kunstindustrimuseet*), which gives an excellent survey of the development of the applied and decorative arts in Norway (tapestries, including the fine *Baldishol tapestry, c.* 1180, from Baldishol church in Hedemark; metal articles, glass, furniture, etc.). Associated with the Museum is a School of Arts and Crafts. – To the N of the Museum, between Ullevålsvei and Akersvei, is the **Cemetery of Our Saviour** (*Vår Frelsers Gravlund*). Near the middle can be seen the tomb of Bjørnson, below is the grave of *Ibsen*, above, to the right those of the painter *H. F. Gude* and the poet *Wergeland*. – At the N end of Akervei, on the right, is the *Gamle Akers Kirke* (Old Akers Church), an Anglo-Norman or basilican church which first appears in the records before 1150 and may have been founded by Olav Kyrre (restored 1861). – To the N of the cemetery, by way of Ullevalsvei, is the beautiful park on *St Hanshaugen*.

In the old part of the town to the S of the Parliament Building and Karl Johansgate are the head offices of several large banks and business houses. To the SW of the East Station stands the *Exchange* (Børsen; built 1827, enlarged 1910). Farther W, in Bankplass, rises the massive granite building of *Norges Bank* (1904). – To the W of this part of the town, rising above the Oslofjord, is *Akershus Castle** (building begun by Håkon V in the late 13th c.). The entrance, in Festningsplass, leads to the castle proper; visitors are shown a number of casemates (chambers built in the walls), various rooms and the chapel (tomb of King Håkon VII, 1872–1957, in crypt). In the *Resistance Museum* (Hjemmefrontmuseum or Home Front Museum) are relics and souvenirs of the war years (1940–5). In the old Arsenal, below, is the new *Norwegian Defence Museum*, opened in 1978, which traces the history of the defence of Norway, with emphasis on the Second World War.

To the NW of the town, reached by way of Drammensvei and Frognervei, is the beautiful **Frognerpark** (main entrance in Kirkevei; several restaurants; popular open-air swimming pool), with the *Municipal Museum* (Oslo Bymuseum) in an old manor-house. SW of the Museum, beyond Halvdan Svartesgate, is the workshop (now a museum) of the great Norwegian sculptor *Gustav Vigeland* (1869–1943); he created the principal feature of the *Vigeland Sculpture Park**. This is an extraordinary collection of sculpture, some 600 m (650 yds) long,

Sculpture by Vigeland in Frognerpark, Oslo

which Vigeland, financed by the city of Oslo, worked on for 40 years. The Vigeland Bridge alone is flanked by 58 bronze groups. The oldest part of the complex is the fountain, depicting the cycle of human life. Beyond this is a *pillar 17 m (55 ft) high, carved rom a single piece of stone, with 121 intertwined human bodies; at the far end is a circular group, the "Wheel of Life" (1933–4). – To the W, in front of the Colosseum cinema (F. Nansenveien 6), is a bronze statue of *Charlie Chaplin* (by Nils Aas, 1976).

On the E side of the town extends the *Botanic Garden* (Botanisk Have: entrance in Trondheimsveien), and on the hill above the garden are the *Zoological Museum* and the *Museum of Mineralogy and Geology*, with the *Palaeontological Museum*. On the S side of the Botanic Garden, at No. 53 Tøyengate, is the *Munch Museum*, with pictures, sketches and drawings (23,864 items)

by Edvard Munch (1863–1944), Norway's leading painter. – Farther SE, at No. 1 Fyrstikkallé, is the *Museum of Technology*. – SE of the station, at No. 13 Oslogate, stands *Oslo Ladegården*, a Baroque mansion restored in 1957–68 (models of the old town, etc.).

SURROUNDINGS. – 3 km (2 miles) S of the East Station is the **Ekeberg**, with the popular *Ekeberg Park* (riding school; restaurant) and the *School of Seamanship* (frescoes by Per Krohg inside). From here there is a beautiful view (particularly in the morning) over Oslo harbour. Between the School of Seamanship and Kongsveien is an area containing 5000-year-old *stone carvings* (helleristninger).

To the W of Oslo (6 km (4 miles) by road; motorboats from Rådhusplass) is the **Bygdøy** peninsula, which offers a variety of attractions, particularly the Folk Museum and the Viking ships. – The ***Norwegian Folk Museum** (*Norsk Folkemuseum*) consists of a number of museum buildings containing collections of everyday objects, furniture (including Ibsen's study), religious art and material from Lapland, together with the *Old Town* (Gamle Byen: old town houses) and an extensive *open-air museum* of old wooden buildings arranged under regions (particularly noteworthy items are the 12th c. *stave church from Gol, brought here in 1885, and the Raulandstue from the Numedal, dating from about 1300).

To the S of the Folk Museum is a large hall (*Vikingskiphuset*) specially built to house the *Viking ships**, three seaworthy 9th c. vessels, used by the Vikings on their long-distance voyages and also for the burial of their chieftains. The *Oseberg Ship* (21·50 m (70 ft) long and rather more than 5 m (16 ft) wide), the finest and richest pre-Christian find in the northern countries, was discovered N of Tønsberg in 1903. Built about 800 and used for a burial in the 9th c., it was a luxury vessel belonging to a chieftain's wife, probably intended for short voyages. It is famous for the rich grave goods, known as the *Oseberg collection*, which were found in the ship. The *Gokstad Ship* (23·20 m (76 ft) long, 5·24 m (17 ft) wide), a seagoing vessel and therefore less richly decorated than the Oseberg Ship, was found at Gokstad in 1880; it had also been used for a burial. It was designed for use either under sail or with oars; the warriors' shields would be hung along the thwarts. An exact replica of this ship sailed to America in six weeks (1893). The *Tune Ship*, found 10 km (6 miles) from Frederikstad in 1867, is the most poorly preserved of the three (remains only of the ship's bottom); it shows the same type of construction as the others.

On the SE side of the peninsula (motorboat dock) are the *Fram Museum**, containing the famous vessel in which Fridtjof Nansen sailed to the Arctic in 1893–6, and the *Shipping Museum*. In front of the Shipping Museum is the "*Gjøa*", in which Amundsen sailed through the North-West Passage in 1903–6. – In an adjoining building is the balsa-wood raft *"'Kon-Tiki"* in which the Norwegian anthropologist, Thor Heyerdahl, and five companions sailed from the Peruvian port of Callao to Eastern Polynesia (28 April to 7 August 1947). Here, too, are a 9·5 m (30 ft) high figure from Easter Island, prehistoric boats, an underwater exhibition-and a reproduction of an Easter Island family cave, as well as the 14 m (46 ft) long papyrus boat "*Ra II*" in which Thor Heyerdahl and representatives of eight nations crossed the Atlantic in 1970.

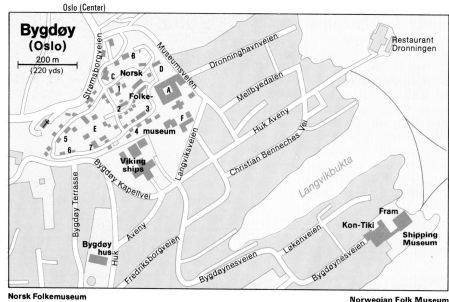

**Norsk Folkemuseum**

| | | |
|---|---|---|
| A | Main building (furniture, etc.) | D | Theatre |
| B | Gol stave church | E | Square |
| C | Restaurant | F | Gamle Byen |

PEASANT HOUSES
1　Østerdal
2　Numedal
3　Telemark

**Norwegian Folk Museum**
4　Hallingdal
5　Vestland
6　Jaeren
7　Østland

On Høvikodden, 12 km (7½ miles) SW of the middle of the city, on E18, is the **Sonja Henie–Niels Onstad Art Center** (1966–8; 20th c. painting; restaurant).

An attractive excursion from Oslo to* **Holmenkollen** (529 m – 1736 ft), the wooded range of hills NW of the town, attracts many visitors for the beautiful view and, in winter, it is the great skiing area of the people of Oslo (good road to Frognerseteren, 13 km (8 miles); electric train from National Theatre, 35 minutes). – Motorists should leave Oslo on Drammensveien, turn right into Frognerveien, then alongside the Frognerpark on Kirkeveien, and left at the junction with Bogstadveien; after running parallel with the Holmenkollen for some time, the road bears right and winds its way up through the forest, passing many villas. – 11 km (7 miles) from the middle of the city, on the left, is the towering *Holmenkollen Ski-Jump*; a footpath leads up to it in 7 minutes (also accessible by road). There is an elevator to the top of the tower; on the platform are a restaurant (cafeteria) and a *Skiing Museum* (Skimuseet), with a large collection of skis of all kinds and pieces of equipment used by Nansen and Amundsen in the Arctic. – The road continues uphill, passing a small chapel. 1 km (¾ mile) from the ski-jump, Voksenkollveien goes off on the left, and another 1 km (¾ mile) along this road is a * viewpoint (469 m – 1540 ft), with a bronze statue of Hans Krag, the engineer in charge of the construction of the road. It is a 10 minutes' walk from Voksenkollen to the Tryvannshøgda. – 1 km (¾ mile) beyond the turning for Voksenkollen, the main road comes to the popular *Frognerseteren* restaurant (486 m – 1595 ft), from which there is a superb view of Oslo and where diners can also see aircraft, flying below them, coming in to land at Fornebu. Opposite the restaurant are a number of old buildings from Telemark and the Hallingdal. From here it is a 20–25 minutes' walk NW to the *Tryvannshøgda* (529 m – 1736 ft), the highest point in the Holmenkollen range, with a lookout tower (Tryvannstårnet) 118·5 m (389 ft) high (1962; lift; panoramic views).

Another pleasant excursion (9 km – 6 miles), is to **Grefsenkollen** (*Grefsenås*, 364 m (1194 ft)), to the NE of Oslo (magnificent views of the city and the fjord).

# Oslofjord

Norway (Southern).

Counties: Oslo fylke, Buskerud fylke, Vestfold fylke, Akershus fylke, Ostfold fylke.

ⓘ **Reisetrafikkforeningen for Oslo og Omegn,**
Rådhuset,
N-Oslo 1;
tel. (02) 42 71 70.
**Drammen Turistinformasjon,**
P.O. Box 301,
N-3000 Drammen;
tel. (03) 83 40 94.
**Tønsberg Informasjon,**
Honnørbryggen,
Hotell Klubben,
N-3100 Tønsberg;
tel. (0 33) 1 62 39.
**Larvik Turistkontor,**
P.B. 200,
N-3251 Larvik;
tel. (0 34) 8 26 23.
**Moss Turistinformasjon,**
Chrystiesgate 3,
N-1500 Moss;
tel. (0 32) 5 54 51.
**Fredrikstad Turistkontor,**
Turistsenteret,
N-1600 Fredrikstad;
tel. (0 32) 2 03 30.
**Halden Turistkontor,**
Tollboden,
N-1751 Halden;
tel. (0 31) 8 24 87.

The Oslofjord, extending for more than 100 km (60 miles) northward from the Skagerrak to the Norwegian capital, is composed of wide basins, dotted with islands, and of narrow straits. Its rocky shores, of moderate height, are broken up by many little towns and settlements. The W side of the fjord was an area of early settlement (Viking ships); the trim towns on the E side can also look back on a long tradition. The beaches, with fine sand on the eastern shores, and the skerries are popular with the people of Oslo for vacations and at weekends. In addition to agriculture and timber-working, the Oslofjord has some busy industries, and the coastal towns are considerable commercial ports.

A road runs down the W side of the fjord, known as the **Vestfold**, to *Sandvika*, at the mouth of the Sandvikelv, *Tanum* (old church), *Skaugum* (residence of the Crown Prince) and **Drammen** (pop. 51,000; Müllerhotell, 154 b.; Park Hotel, 190 b.), main town of Buskerud, picturesquely set on the Dramsfjord, at the mouth of the Dramselv. The town has considerable industry and is an important port, shipping Norwegian timber, cellulose and paper. It is also the country's principal port for the import of cars. In the market square, Bragernes Torg, is the attractive modern St Hallvard's Fountain. – In the *Bragernes* district is a conspicuous church (1871). From here a toll road runs up in a spiral tunnel 1700 m (1850 yds) long (six turns, radius 35 m (115 ft), gradient 10%) on to *Bragernesås* (293 m (960 ft); Åspaviljongen summer restaurant; extensive views). A short distance NE is the lonely woodland lake of *Klopptjern* (alt. 218 m – 715 ft). – In the *Stromsø* district, on the S bank of the Dramselv, are the Drammen Museum (history of the town; Buskerud county; Marienlyst, an 18th c. farmhouse) and a church of 1667 (altered in 1840).

Beyond Drammen there are two routes – either down the W side of the Dramsfjord via *Svelvik*, or direct by the island road – to *Sande*, on the Sandebukt; then along the S side of this inlet to *Holmestrand* (pop. 9000; aluminium works; church, 1674; and limestone quarry).

The first town on the Oslofjord itself is the port of **Horten** (pop. 15,000; Grand Hotel, 62 b.; Ocean Hotel, 130 b.), with *Karl Johansvern* (Naval Museum), the main base of the Norwegian navy until the end of the Second World War. From here there is a car ferry (45 minutes) to Moss, on the E side of the fjord.

Near here are the medieval church of *Borre*, with a magnificent Baroque interior, and, in the Borre hills, a small national park containing the largest group of *royal graves* in northern Europe (Ynglingeætten; 6 large and 21 smaller burial mounds). On the fjord to the SE is the

The Oslofjord – a paradise for sailing and boating enthusiasts

Bridge over the Svinesund between Norway and Sweden at Halden

well-known seaside resort of *Asgård-strand* where the painter Edvard Munch lived for several years (memorial museum).

To the S, at the N end of the narrow Tønsbergfjord, is **Tønsberg** (pop. 13,000; Grand Hotel, 80 b.; Klubben Hotel, 175 b.; Maritim, 45 b.), which first appears in the records in the 11th c. and is now the main town of Vestfold, with a considerable merchant fleet and a nautical college. The whaling ships sailed from here until whaling was stopped for conservation reasons in 1951. At the near end of the town, on left, is a monument to the Polar explorer Roald Amundsen (1872–1928), who reached the South Pole in 1911, flew over the North Pole in 1926 and was lost on a flight to Spitzbergen in 1928. On the W side of the town is the rocky Slottsfjell (Castle Hill, 63 m – 206 ft), with a lookout tower and the foundations of the old castle of Tunsberghus (fine view of the harbour). Other features of interest are the Vestfold County Museum (on the Larvik road), with an Arctic section (whaling); the Cathedral (1858); and St Olav's Church, the largest round church in the northern countries. – A minor road runs S to the long straggling islands of *Nøtterøy* and *Tjøme* (beautiful beaches), linked by a bridge; they lie between the Tønsbergfjord and the Oslofjord.

To the SE, off the main road, is **Sandefjord**, on the fjord of the same name. A former whaling port, it is now a seaside resort (pop. 7000; Kong Carl, 49 b.; Park Hotel, 273 b.). Whaling Museum; Seafaring Museum. The town has a modern merchant fleet. There are good facilities for swimming and sailing.

To the SW is **Larvik**, at the N end of the Larvikfjord (see p. 174). – To the S we come to the resort of *Stavern* (p. 175), with the old coastal fortress of Frederiksvern, and the smaller resort of *Helgeroa* and *Nevlunghamn*.

The road from Oslo down the E side of the Oslofjord, **Østfold**, passes the attractive little resort of *Drøbak* (fine wooden church, 1736) and reaches the town of **Moss** (pop. 26,000; Refsnes Gods Hotel, 81 b.), located on the *Mossesund*, which runs between the offshore island of Jeløy and the mainland (bridge). The treaty of union between Norway and Sweden was signed at Moss (1814). Car ferry (45 minutes) to Horten on the W side of the fjord. – To the S, on the shores of the fjord, is the resort of *Larkollen*.

The main road then comes to **Sarpsborg** (pop. 14,000; hotels: Saga, 120 b.; St Olav 131 b.; Victoria, 30 b.), originally founded by St Olav in the 11th c.; it is now a busy industrial town (paper, cellulose, electrical engineering), with the Borgarsyssel Museum (old houses, ruined 12th c. church) and the beautiful Kulås Park. To the SW (Road 109) is the commercial and industrial town of **Frederiksstad** (pop. 30,000; City Hotell, 200 b.; Victoria, 82 b; arts center). – On the left bank of the river, reached by a bridge 824 m ($\frac{1}{2}$ mile) long, is the Old Town (*Gamlebyen*), formerly fortified, with interesting old military buildings, some of them now occupied by craftsmen's workshops. (Church of 1778; monument to King Frederik II, who founded the town in 1567.) To the W of Vikene there is a ferry to the island of *Hankø* (beautiful coniferous forest), now a popular holiday resort (sailing school).

From Sarpsborg the main road continues past *Tune* (church, 1060, later altered) to **Halden** (pop. 27,000; Grand Hotel, 61 b.; Park Hotel, 85 b.), on the Swedish frontier. Known from 1665 to 1927 as Frederikshald, the town withstood several attacks by the Swedes, and, after suffering severe damage in a fire, was rebuilt on a regular plan in 1826. It has a variety of industries, including woodworking and the manufacture of boots and shoes, and is the principal area for the timber trade in eastern Norway. On higher ground, to the SE of the town, is the fortress of Fredrik-*sten* (alt. 113 m (370 ft); fine views), built in 1661–71. An iron pyramid erected 1860 commemorates King Charles XII of Sweden, who was killed during the siege of the town in 1718. Here, too, is the Municipal Museum ("Haldens Minner"). Halden has a Theatre (1830, Baroque stage). On the E side of the town is the Atomic Energy Institute, with a reactor which came into service in 1959.

# Östersund

Sweden (Central).
Province: Jämtlands län. – Region: Jämtland.
Altitude: 292 m (960 ft). – Population: 40,000.
Postal code: S-831 . . . – Telephone code: 0 63.

ⓘ **Turistbyrå,**
Rådhusgatan 29,
S-83182 Östersund;
tel. 14 40 01

HOTELS. – *Britannia*, Prästgatan 26, 40 b.; *Jämteborg*, Storgatan 54, 35 b.; *Linden*, Storgatan 64, 55 b.; *Mitt-Inn*, Korfaltets Centre, 134 b.; *Scandic Hotel*, Krondikesväg 97, 281 b.; *Winn*, Prästgatan 16, 382 b., SB. – CAMP SITE.

EVENTS. – *Music Week* (July); **Expo Norr** (trade fair: July).

SPORTS and RECREATION. – Tennis, golf, fishing.

**Östersund,** the only town in Jämtland and the administrative, economic and cultural hub of the province, is on elevated land above the E shore of the Storsjö. The town was founded by Gustav III in 1786, and has preserved its original rectangular street plan. In the lake opposite the town is the hilly island of Frösö.

SIGHTS. – In the main street, Rådhusgata, stands the *Town Hall* (F. B. Wallberg, 1912). Diagonally across from it are the *Municipal Museum* and the *Old Church* (1846). The *New Church* (L. I. Wahlman, 1940) has frescoes by H. Linnqvist in the choir. – Parallel with Rådhusgata, to the W, is *Storgata*, lined with 19th c. houses.

To the N of the town, in a building designed by F. B. Wallberg (1928–30), is the *Jämtland Provincial Museum* (history and culture of the province), with a small art gallery. To the NW is the **Fornbyn Jamtli** open-air museum, with old wooden houses from Jämtland and the Härjedal.

SURROUNDINGS. – In the *Storsjö (area 448 sq. km (175 sq. miles), greatest depth 74 m – 240 ft), is the fertile island of **Frösö**, linked with Östersund by two bridges. At the old Frösöbru is an 11th c. *runic stone*. From the *Öseberg* (468 m – 1536 ft) there are fine views of the lake and the large forests on the island. – 6·5 km (4 miles) W of the bridge is a *church*; its earliest parts date from the 12th c. (rebuilt 1898; free-standing tower). In the churchyard is the grave of the composer W. Petersen-Berger, whose country house, Sommarhagen, is nearby. Also nearby is a wildlife park. – 1 km ($\frac{3}{4}$ mile) W of the church is the farm of *Stocke*, with the *Stocketitt* lookout tower (view reaching to the mountains on the Norwegian frontier).

There is a car ferry from Frösö to the island of *Anderso*, which (like Skansholm and Isö) is a nature reserve; remains of 17th c. fortifications. – On the shores of the lake to the S is *Sunne* church, with the remains of a castle built by King Sverre in 1178 after the defeat of the Jämts on the frozen lake.

# Oulu (Uleåborg)

Finland (Northern).
Province: Oulun lääni (Uleåborgs län/Oulu).
Altitude: sea level. – Population: 96,000.
Postal code: SF-90100. – Telephone code: 9 81.

ⓘ **Kaupungin Matkailutoimisto**
(*Municipal Tourist Information Office*),
Kirkkokatu 2
tel. 1 53 30 and 1 51 21.

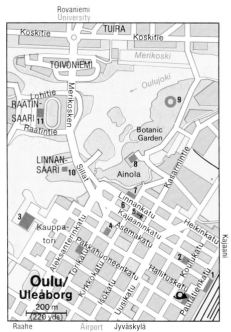

Oulu / Uleåborg
200 m
(220 yds)

1 Station
2 Museum of Art
3 Theatre
4 Town House
5 Cathedral
6 Franzén Gardens
7 Provincial Government Offices
8 Municipal Library,
  Provincial Museum
9 Summer Theatre
10 Ruins of Castle
11 Indoor swimming pool

HOTELS. – *Arina*, Pakkahuoneenkatu 16, 115 b.; *Cumulus*, Kajaaninkatu 17, 350 b., SB; *Hospiz*, Asemakatu 31, 58 b.; *Oulun Kauppehotelli*, Asemakatu 7, 139 b.; *Otokylä*, Haapanatie 2C, 176 b. (1 May to 31 August); *Vaakuna*, Hallituskatu 1, 450 b., SB; *Välkkylä*, Kajaanintie 36, 104 b. (1 June to 31 August). – YOUTH HOSTEL. – CAMP SITES.

EVENTS. – *Ski race* (March); *Winter Games* (March); *Oulu Races* (May); *Oulu Regatta* (July); *Rock Festival* (July); *Northern Finland Car Rally* (November).

RECREATION and SPORTS. – Golf, riding, tennis, skiing.

**The industrial town of Oulu (Swedish Uleåborg), capital of its province and the see of a bishop, lies on the Gulf of Bothnia at the mouth of the Oulujoki. It has a University founded in 1959.**

HISTORY. – Toward the end of the 16th c., King John III of Sweden built a castle (Finnish *linna*) on an island at the mouth of the river, now known as Linnansaari, and the town grew up around this island, receiving its municipal charter in 1610. It was almost completely destroyed by fire in 1822, and was rebuilt on a plan prepared by C. L. Engel.

SIGHTS. – At the N end of the busy *Kirkkokatu* stands the **Cathedral** (Engel, 1830–2; interior renovated and decorated with paintings in 1932). To the left of the entrance a monument by Wäinö Aaltonen commemorates those who fell in the fight for liberation in 1918. In the gardens in front of the church is a bronze bust (by E. Stenberg) of the Finnish-Swedish poet and bishop, F. M. Franzén (1772–1847), a native of Oulu. On the N side of the gardens, at No. 3 Linnankatu, are the *Provincial Government Offices* (Lääninhallitus, 1888). – From the N end of Kirkkokatu, a small bridge leads into the beautiful **Ainola Park**, on an island. In the W half of the island is a handsome building (1930) which houses the *Municipal Library* (Kirjasto) and the *Provincial Museum*, with historical and ethnographic collections. A stone in front of the building commemorates the woman writer, *Saara Wacklin* (1790–1846), who was born in Oulu. To the N are the *Botanic Garden* and a *summer theatre*.

SW of the Cathedral, in Hallituskatu, is the **Town House** (*Kaupungintalo*, 1894), and beyond it, in Torikatu, the old Town House, now the police headquarters. – To the W, on the banks of the Oulujoki, lies the spacious *Market Square* (Kauppatori), with the *Theatre* (1974) which is also used as a convention hall. To the N is the Bus Station. – Just E of the Market square, two bridges lead on to Linnansaari (Castle Island), where there are the sparse remains of the castle (built 1590, destroyed by an explosion in 1793); summer restaurant. The road continues over another arm of the river to the island of *Raatinsaari* (park, a stadium, an indoor swimming pool). Another bridge runs N, on to the island of *Toivoneimi*, which has a modern residential district designed by Alvar Aalto; on the E side of this district is a hydroelectric power station which uses the water of the *Merikoski*, the rapidly flowing lowest reach of the Oulujoki. A fourth bridge leads to the suburb of *Tuira*, on the N bank of the river, with a number of schools. – In the N part

Modern apartment houses, Oulu

of the town (Puolivälinkangas) is the *Water-Tower* (lookout platform).

SURROUNDINGS. – 20 km (12½ miles) N, near the coast, is *Haukipudas* (Samantta Hotel, 47 b.), with a wooden church (1762) containing wall paintings by the well-known Finnish church painter, Mikael Toppelius. – 13 km (8 miles) SE of Oulu, on the left bank of the Oulujoki, is the **Turkansaari Open-Air Museum** (also accessible by boat from Oulu), with more than 20 old buildings, including a church (1694). The road continues to *Muhos*, with the oldest wooden church in Finland (1634); 6 km (4 miles) upstream is the Pyhäkoski power station.

75 km (47 miles) SW of Oulu, on the coast, lies **Raahe** (Swedish Brahestad: pop. 14,000; Tiiranlinna Hotel, 160 b.), founded by Per Brahe in 1649. In the Pekkatori is a statue of Per Brahe, a copy of the original in Turku. The town was rebuilt in 1810 after a fire, and has houses dating from that period. The interesting Museum (founded 1862) has a collection of material concerning ships and seafaring, as well as objects brought back by seamen from their voyages. The church (J. Stenbeck, 1912) has an altarpiece by the painter, E. Järnefelt (1863–1937)

# Pallastunturi Hills

Finland (Northern).
Province: Lapin lääni (Lapplands län/Lapland).
ⓘ **Sodankylä Tourist Information Office,**
Kantakievarintalo,
SF-99600 Sodankylâ;
tel. (93 93) 1 34 74.

**The Pallastunturi Hills, with their treeless slopes, one of Finland's most popular skiing areas, lie in the NW of the country, near the Swedish frontier, in the middle of a mountain chain extending from Yllästunturi (740 m – 2428 ft) in the S, to Ounastunturi (738 m – 2421 ft) in the N. The highest point is Taivaskero (821 m – 2694 ft); to the NW is Laukukero (777 m – 2549 ft), to the E Palkaskero.**

From **Muonio** (Äkäskero Hotel, 114 b.; Olostunturi, 115 b.), a trim village at the junction of the *Jerisjoki* with the *Muonionjoki*, the Rovaniemi road (No. 79) runs to the E. – 7 km (4½ miles): on the right, *Olostunturi* (524 m – 1719 ft), a hill commanding extensive views (footpath to top). – 5 km (3 miles): Särkijärvi, where we turn left and climb up through beautiful hill scenery. – 15 km (9 miles): crossroads. The narrow road on the right goes to Pallasjärvi (4 km – 2½ miles): the left-hand road ascends (7 km – 4½ miles) to the magnificently situated *Pallastunturi-Turisthotel* (78 b.; natural

The Pallastunturi Hills

history museum), at the foot of Taivaskero (good skiing country; lift). The midnight sun shines here from 27 May to 16 July. – From here a marked trail runs 60 km (40 miles) NW (5 huts providing overnight accommodation) to *Enontekiö* or Hetta (Hetta Hotel, 20 b.), with a modern church and a silversmith's workshop. The trail runs through the *Pallastunturi-Ounastunturi National Park* (area 500 sq. km – 200 sq. miles), typical of the barren upland country of Lapland.

# Pori (Björneborg)

Finland (SW).
Province: Turun ja Porin lääni (Åbo och Björneborgs län/Turku-Pori).
Altitude: 15 m (49 ft). – Population 79,000.
Postal code: SF-28100. – Telephone code: 9 39.
ⓘ **Kaupungin Matkailutoimisto**
(*Municipal Tourist Information Office*),
Antinkatu 5;
tel. 1 57 80.

HOTELS. – *Cumulus*, Itsenäisyydenkatu 37, 117 b., SB; *Juhana Herttua*, Itapuisto 1, 118 b.; *Karhun Kruunu*, Rautatienpuistokatu 2, 115 b.; *Satakunta*, Gallen-Kallelankatu 7, 300 b. – AT YYTERI BEACH: *Rantasipi Yyteri*, 226 b., SB. – SOUTH OF TOWN: *Raumantien Motelli*, Raumantie, 30 b.

SUMMER ACCOMMODATION. – *Tekunkorpi Motelli*, Korventie 52, 110 b. (5 May to 28 August).

EVENTS. – *Pori Jazz Festival* (July); *Whitefish Festival* (end of August); *Pori Days* (end of September).

SPORTS and RECREATION. – Tennis, bowling, squash, riding, fishing, swimming, rowing, sailing, skiing.

**The old commercial and industrial town of Pori is on the S bank of the Kokemäenjoki, some 20 km (12 miles) above the mouth of the river in the Gulf of Bothnia. The town was originally farther upstream, but was moved in 1365 and**

again in 1558, because the mouth of the river was moving steadily farther W due to the rise in the level of the land and the continuing deposit of sand. The town received its municipal charter in 1558 from Duke John, Gustavus Vasa's son. The last of a series of fires, in 1852, made it necessary to replan the town, and the new Pori was laid out around two broad avenues intersecting at right angles. In addition to a fishing harbour and two commercial harbours, it has woodworking and metal-working industries.

Market Square, Pori

SIGHTS. – The main features of interest are situated near the N end of Pohjois-puisto Avenue, on the banks of the Kokemäenjoki. On the W side is the **Museum** of the Satakunta District (founded 1888), with a collection of 35,000 items. Nearby stands the **Munici-pal Theatre** (1884; 20th c. restoration) and the Museum of Art (modern painting and sculpture). Facing the avenue is the Venetian-style **Town Hall** (August Krook, 1895), originally the mansion of the Junnelius family. To the E, in a small park, is the neo-Gothic *church* of central Pori (G. T. Chiewitz, 1863), with a tower 75 m (246 ft) high; altarpiece (the Resur-rection) by R. W. Ekman. – In Paanake-donkatu, which leads from the church to the Tampere road, is an *indoor swimming pool.*

To the W of mid-town is the Old Cemetery, and beyond this the New Cemetery, with the *Juselius Mausoleum* (Josef Stenbäck, 1902), commissioned by the industrialist, F. A. Juselius, for his

daughter, who died at the age of eleven. The frescoes in the mausoleum were originally by the well-known painter of the Finnish "national Romantic" school, Akseli Gallén-Kallela, but when the origi-nals deteriorated they were replaced by new paintings by the artist's son, Jorma, following his father's original designs. – On a peninsula on the N bank of the river, at the outflow of the Luotsimäenhaara, is the *Kirjurinluoto Park*, the scene of the Jazz Festival, with the Summer Theatre.

SURROUNDINGS. – A very attractive excursion from Pori is on Road 265 to the sandy beach of **Yteri**, continuing to *Mäntyluoto* and over a causeway to the island of *Reposaari*, passing on the way the Kaana water-tower (café; view). At Yteri are a hotel, a camp site and vacation chalets. On Reposaari can be seen a church in Norwegian style and, by the harbour, a monument to the torpedo-boat *S2* which sank in a storm in 1927. – Road 2 runs SE from Pori to Helsinki. Some 7 km (4 miles) from Pori a side road goes N to *Ulvila*, the site of Pori from 1365 to 1558 (church, 1429).

S of Pori, on Road 8, is **Rauma**, a town with distinctive traditions of its own; many of its 30,000 inhabitants speak a special dialect which is not understood in the rest of Finland. The town was founded in the 13th c. and received its charter from King Kristoffer in 1442. About 1550 it was temporarily evacuated when its inhabitants were ordered to move to the newly founded town of Helsinki, but after some years they were allowed to return. In the 17th c., Rauma developed into a busy seafaring town. In foreign countries, its seamen learned the art of making pillow lace, still practised in the town.

The layout of the old town dates from the 16th c., but the present timber buildings are mainly 18th and 19th c. In this area are the Holy Cross Church, originally belonging to a 15th c. Franciscan friary, and the ruins of the 14th c. Trinity Church. In the middle of the old town (many specialised shops) is the Museum, housed in the former Town Hall (C. H. R. Schröder, 1776). To the S of the old town are an indoor swimming pool and a water-tower and a restaurant, from which there is a panoramic view, and adjoining the tower a sculpture by Aila Salo, "Through Difficulties to Victory" (1976). To the NW, beyond the railway line, is the recreation area of *Otanlahti*, with sports facilities, a swimming pool, baths and a sauna. Next to Otanlahti is the Poroholma camp site, with the dock used by the motorboats which, in summer, run regular cruises among the offshore islands.

# Porvoo/Borgå

Finland (Southern).
Province: Uudenmaan lääni (Nylands län/Uusimaa).
Altitude: sea level. – Population: 20,000.
Postal code: SF-06100. – Telephone code: 915.
ⓘ **Kaupungin Matkailutoimisto**
   (*Municipal Tourist Information Office*),
   Rauhankatu 20;
   tel. 14 01 45.

HOTELS. – *Grand Hotel*, Raatihuoneenkatu 8, 25 b.; *Herlevi*, Runeberginkatu 33, 46 b.; *Seurahovi*, Rauhankatu 27, 147 b.; *Haikon Kartano* manor-house hotel, SW of town, 314 b., SB. – YOUTH HOSTEL. – CAMP SITE.

EVENTS. – *Cycle race* (June); *Porvoo Day* (June); *Postmäki Festival*, with theatre performances, folk music and folk dancing (July).

SPORTS and RECREATION. – Tennis, squash, riding.

**Porvoo (Swedish Borgå) is located 50 km (30 miles) NE of Helsinki, on the left bank of the Porvoonjoki (Swedish Borgåå), near the mouth of the river, which flows into an inlet in the Gulf of Finland. The town was founded in 1346 by King Magnus Eriksson of Sweden, and the population is still 45% Swedish-speaking. In 1508, Porvoo was burned down by the Danes. It 1723 it became the see of a bishop. In 1809, Tsar Alexander I, who had become Grand Duke of Finland under the treaty of Frederikshamn, received the homage of the country here. Porvoo was the birthplace of the sculptors, W. Runeberg and V. Vallgren, and the home of a number of other artists. A major portion of the town's economy is contributed by the oil port of Sköldvik, around which several industrial enterprises have been established.**

SIGHTS. – The old town, with its narrow winding streets, is built on the slopes of a hill rising above the river on the N side of Porvoo. Here too stands the small Gothic **Cathedral** (1414–18; restored 1978), with its decorated red brick gable looking on to the river. In the Rococo interior is a bronze statue of Tsar Alexander I (by W. Runeberg, 1909), commemorating the meeting of the Diet of Porvoo in 1809 (at which Alexander received the homage of the country and guaranteed the inviolability of the Finnish constitution and religion). Adjoining the Cathedral, to the SE, are the belfry and a small Finnish wooden church (1740); to the S is the *"Poets' House"* (1765). To the E of the cathedral can be found the Janttis Art Collection (Finnish painting, graphic art, drawings and carvings).

In a square below the Cathedral is the **Municipal Museum**, housed in the former Town Hall (1764). The corner house to the E of the Museum contains a collection of sculpture by Ville Vallgren (1855–1940) and pictures by Albert Edelfelt (1854–1905). – Some 500 m (550 yds) S, in Runeberginkatu, can be seen a bronze statue of J. L. Runeberg, a small-scale copy of the statue in Helsinki. Farther S, at the corner of Runeberginkatu and Aleksanterinkatu, we come to the *Runeberg House*, home of the national poet J. L. Runeberg (1804–77), who taught in the grammar school from 1837 to 1857 and from 1863 until his death was crippled by paralysis; the house is furnished as it was in Runeberg's lifetime. In a nearby house is the sculpture collection of Walter Runeberg, the son of the poet. In the *cemetery* on the W bank of the Porvoonjoki, on the Helsinki road, are the graves of J. L. Runeberg and the young patriot, Eugen Schauman, who shot the Russian General Bobrikov in Helsinki in 1904 and then took his own life.

SURROUNDINGS. – To the S of the town is a charming scatter of little islands or skerries. – 10 km (6 miles) NE is the manor-house of *Sannäs* (1836–7), now recorded as an ancient monument and used as a conference hall.

40 km (25 miles) E of Porvoo is **Loviisa** (Swedish *Lovisa:* pop. 9000; Zilton Hotel, 22 b.), picturesquely set at the N end of the Lovisavik, a long inlet on the Gulf of Finland. Still predominantly Swedish-speaking, the town was founded in 1745 under the name of Degerby; it was renamed Lovisa in 1752 in honour of Queen Luise Ulrike of Sweden, sister of Frederick the Great. In the middle of the town, now a well-known health resort, are the large neo-Gothic church (1862–5) and the Town Hall (1856). To the N of the town are the trotting track and near this the Municipal Museum in the old Commandant's House. On the outskirts of the town are remains of the old fortifications. – 12 km (7½ miles) SE, on the island of *Hästholm*, stands a nuclear power station.

# Ribe

Denmark (Jutland).
County: Ribe amt.
Altitude: 10 m (33 ft). – Population: 8000.
Postal code: DK-6760. – Telephone code: 0 5.
ⓘ **Ribe Turistbureau,**
Torvet 3–5;
tel. 42 15 00.

Porvoo

HOTELS. – *Dagmar*, Torvet 1, 78 b.; *Kalvslund Kro*, Koldingveg 105, 10 b.; *Sønderjylland*, Sønderports-gade 22, 23 b.; *Weis Stue*, Torvet 2, 9 b. – YOUTH HOSTEL: *Hovedengen*. – CAMP SITES: *Ribe, Farup-vej* and *Villebøl*.

RESTAURANTS. – *Backhaus*, Grydergade; *Klubbens Kro*, Skolegade; *Stenbohus*, Torvet.

\*Ribe is Denmark's oldest town (though Viborg might dispute this claim), preserving many reminders of its heyday in the Middle Ages, when it was the most important town in western Jutland. It is a charming little place, with its old half-timbered houses and narrow winding lanes.

An old half-timbered house in Ribe

HISTORY. – By around 850, when its name first appears in the records, Ribe was already a prosperous trading town. The first church in what is now Denmark was built here – a wooden church erected in 862 by the Frankish monk, St Ansgar. He had been sent by the Emperor Louis the Pious to evangelise the northern countries and gained the favour of King Horich the Younger. In 948, Ribe became the see of a bishop. King Niels built a castle outside the town in 1115, but Ribe was of more importance as an ecclesiastical than as a secular area: by the late medieval period it had four religious houses and six churches. With the Reformation, however, came a period of decline; Ribe was reduced to the status of an impoverished little country town. It began to recover only after the First World War, when northern Slesvig (southern Jutland) returned to Denmark.

SIGHTS. – The development of industry has not destroyed the pattern of the old town since the new buildings have been erected in the outskirts. A walk around the middle of Ribe is an exploration of the past, disturbed only by the cars which now invade its narrow streets. – In the market square stands the Romanesque and Gothic **Cathedral**, built partly in grey stone from the Rhineland and partly of Danish brick (begun before 1134, probably completed in 1225).

The 50 m (164 ft) high **tower**, square and without a spire, was built for defensive purposes in the 13th c., and offers a magnificent panoramic view of the flat surrounding country. The great weight of the tower endangered the safety of the whole structure, which was built on unstable alluvial land, and only thorough restoration work at the turn of the 19th c. saved the church.

The nave originally had a flat roof; it was replaced by vaulting in the 13th c. The INTERIOR is noteworthy for its simple and massive forms, which create an effect of lightness and space. The nave is flanked by double lateral aisles; over the choir is the only Romanesque masonry dome in Denmark. Three doorways (W, S and N) are well preserved or restored. The S doorway is popularly known as the "Cat's Head Door" because of the Gothic lion's head on the bronze door; it is framed by two granite columns on each side, the outer column resting on the figure of a lion devouring a man. In the tympanum of the S doorway is a Romanesque relief of the Descent from the Cross (probably 1150); in the triangular relief above the doorway is a representation of the Heavenly Jerusalem.

The *carillon* plays a psalm, "Den yndigste Rose" ("The Fairest Rose"), at 8 a.m. and 6 p.m. daily and the popular tune "Queen Dagmar" at 12 noon and 3 p.m.

The \*OLD TOWN of Ribe contains a unique assemblage of old half-timbered houses, the most notable of which is the *Puggård*, the oldest surviving secular building in the town. At the corner of Sønderportsgade and Puggårdsgade, the last relic of the old street lighting system can be seen – a small scroll under the gas-lamp below the roof overhang from which an oil-lamp was suspended. – In Skolegade, which opens off Sønderportsgade, is *Hans Tausens Hus*, once part of Bishop Tausen's house, now occupied by an archaeological museum. In Puggårdgade is the aristocratic mansion of *Tårnborg*, a turreted stone house (1550). The Gothic **Town Hall** (1528) houses a small Municipal Museum. The *Museum of Art* contains works by Danish painters from the 18th c. to the present.

One of the attractions of Ribe is the storks' nests to be seen on old chimneystacks. SW Jutland is one of the last stork refuges, but since they are becoming steadily rarer Ribe is in danger of losing its claim to being the "city of the storks".

At the Dagmar Bridge are **St Catherine's Church** and the adjoining **monastery**, a

Dominican house founded in 1228, with some of the finest monastic buildings in Denmark. The cloister, with its open arcades, breathes an atmosphere of peace and contemplation. St Catherine's Church underwent thorough renovation in 1928–32 to restore it to its 15th c. form. In the course of 500 years, one side of the church had sunk 60 cm (2 ft), but during the restoration work it was brought back to a horizontal position within six days. – On a hill, NW of the town, are the excavated remains of the 12th c. castle of *Riberhus* (tombs, fragments of wall, statue of Queen Dagmar). From the hill there is a fine view of the town.

Ribe lies on the little *Ribeå*, which flows into the sea a short distance from the town. When storm winds blow from the W, the sea is driven inland, and Ribe is still occasionally exposed to severe flooding, in spite of the dikes and sea walls that have been built. On the harbour quay, Skibbroen, is the *Stormflodssøjle*, a column showing the height reached by flood-water in various years from 1634 to 1911. On Nedermannen is the *Ydermølle*, a water-mill driven by the Ribeå. In summer there are boat trips on the river (rich bird-life).

SURROUNDINGS. – 10 km (6 miles) away lies the little island of **Mandø**, the smallest inhabited island in the *Vadehav* (North Sea Flats), with a church, a local museum, an ornithological collection and an inn. Most of the island (area 6 sq. km (2½ sq. miles), pop. 109) consists of marshland, surrounded by dikes. To the W are dunes up to 12 m (40 ft) high. At low tide it is possible to wade out to the island. There is a road from Vester Vedsted to the island which is covered by water when the tide comes in. Visitors should not attempt to use this road in their own car, but should take the mail bus, which carries passengers and goods; the driver of the bus knows when and which way it is safe to go.

6 km (4 miles) from Ribe is **Hviding**, a prosperous port and commercial town until it was displaced by Ribe in the 13th c. The church (12th c.) was enlarged in the 16th c.; it has a fine late Gothic altarpiece with side panels, with a rare representation of the Crucifixion surrounded by a rosary.

# Romsdal

Norway (Western).
County: Møre og Romsdal fylke.

**The *Romsdal, the valley of the Rauma, is one of the most beautiful valleys in Norway, extending for a distance of some 60 km (40 miles) in**

View of the Romsdalshorn

**a SW direction from Åndalsnes, on the magnificent *Romsdalsfjord.**

The valley can be reached either from Åndalsnes or from the SE by way of the Gudbrandsdal (see p. 112), from the head of which E69 runs over the watershed between the Skagerrak and the Atlantic and down into the upper Romsdal. Beyond the inn at *Stugaflåten*, the last place in the Gudbrandsdal, the road passes from the county of Oppland (to the SE) into Møre og Romsdal (to the NW). The Romsdal, which the road now descends, gets steadily narrower. From the road, as it winds its way down the valley, there are striking views of the *Rauma* flowing tumultuously below. At the ***Slettafoss**, the river has carved a wild gorge out of the rock masses.

At **Verma** (alt. 273 m – 895 ft) there is a stone commemorating the opening of the railway in 1924. Here the railway line crosses the river on the *Kyllingbru* (76 m (240 ft) long, 59 m (195 ft) high). Nearby is the Vermafoss hydroelectric power station.

A short distance farther on the road reaches the valley bottom, with steep hills on either side. At *Flatmark* (alt. 127 m – 417 ft) the 1676 m (6000 ft) peak of *Døntind* is seen on the left.

At *Kors* is a church built in 1919 with parts of the old church of Flatmark. It has a fine altar screen by Jacob Klukstad, the "Master of the Acanthus".

In a wider part of the valley, under the massive bulk of the *Kalskråtind* (1799 m –

5903 ft), is **Marstein**. To the N, dominating the scene, rises the *Romsdalshorn* (1550 m – 5086 ft); to the W are the *Trolltinder* (1794 m – 5886 ft), with almost vertical rock faces, never climbed until 1966. The height of the mountains means that, for almost five months of the year, the sun is not visible in the valley.

At the *Sogge* bridge the *Trollstigvei* bears off on the left and runs through the *Isterdal* to Valldal. It crosses the *Stigfoss* and continues up to the *Trollstig-heimen Fjellstue*, on the pass, after which it descends to *Valldal* on the magnificent *Tafjord*.

At the *Grøtør* bridge a side road leads to *Grytten* church. E69 continues to Åndalsnes.

**Åndalsnes** (pop. 3000; Grand Hotel Bellevue, 92 b.; Gjerset Pensjonat, in Istfjorden, 13 b.; youth hostel 70 b.; camp site), on the beautiful *Romsdalsfjord*, is a lively vacation resort with an important harbour and shipyards for (among other things) oil-rigs.

# Røros

Norway (Eastern).
County: Sør-Trøndelag fylke.
Altitude: 628 m (2060 ft). – Population: 3300.
Postal code: N-7460. – Telephone code: 0 74.
ⓘ **Turistkontor**,
    Bergmannsplassen;
    tel. 1 11 65.

HOTELS. – *Bergstadens Turisthotell*, 140 b., SP; *Bergstadtunet Vertshus*, 24 b.; *Fjellheimen Turist-stasjon*, 36 b.; *Røros Turisthotell*, 226 b., SP.; *Rørosheimen Turistsenter*, 50 b. – YOUTH HOSTEL.

**The mining town of Røros was founded in 1644, after the discovery of large deposits of copper in the region.**

SIGHTS. – There are several old *miners houses* in the town, some of them 250 years old, particularly in *Bergmannsgata* the main street. At the N end of the street is a small museum (*Kobberverks Samlinger*) illustrating the mining and processing of copper.

To the NW of and parallel to Berg-mannsgata, in Kjerkgata, is the **church** (1784), once the only stone building in the town. It is the symbol of Røros and can be seen for miles around. It has

particularly good music especially at Christmas and Ascension Day (mid-May).

To the W of the town is the little *Doktortjønna Lake*. On its N side is the **Røros Museum**, which gives an excellent picture of the life of the local miners and peasants.

SURROUNDINGS. – The *Christianus Quintus (Christian V) Mine* 8 km (5 miles) E of the town, an old copper mine, is open to visitors in summer. The Røros tourist information office arranges bus trips and conducted tours.

# Roskilde

Denmark (Zealand).
County: Roskilde amt.
Altitude: sea level. – Population: 49,000.
Postal code: DK-4000. – Telephone code: 03.
ⓘ **Tourist Information Office**,
    Fondens Bro (near Cathedral);
    tel. 35 27 00.

HOTELS. – *Lindenberg Kro*, Lindenborgvej 90, in Gevninge, 30 b.; *Prindsen*, Algade 13, 72 b.; *Risø*, Frederiksborgvej, 39 b.; *Roskilde Motorhotel*, Hoved-vej A1/E66; *Svogerslev Kro*, Hovedgaden 45, in Svogerslev, 25 b.

YOUTH HOSTEL. – *Hørgården*, Horhusvej.

CAMP SITE. – *Vigen Strandpark Camping*, 4 km (2½ miles) N of Roskilde on A6.

RESTAURANTS. – *Byparken*, Frederiksborgvej; *Palæ*, Stændertovet 8; *Toppen*, Bymarken 37; *Club 42*, Skomagergade 42.

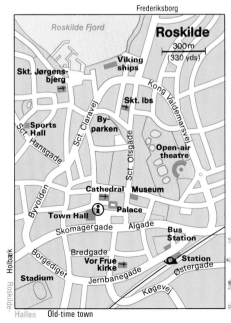

Roskilde

EVENTS. – *Roskilde Festival*, the largest festival of pop, jazz and folk music in N (last weekend in June); *flea-market* in Stændertorv on Saturdays.

SPORTS and RECREATION. – Canoe trips in Roskildefjord and Isefjord (scope for a variety of long trips); sailing club, many moorings for yachts in Roskildefjord.

**The Danish town of Roskilde lies 30 km (20 miles) from Copenhagen on the Roskildefjord, which cuts deep into the island of Zealand. During the Middle Ages it was a royal residence, and the Cathedral contains the remains of 38 Danish kings. It is now the largest county town on Zealand and has a University.**

Roskilde can be reached from Copenhagen either by road or rail in under half an hour. Every visitor should see this fine old town.

HISTORY. – Roskilde is one of the oldest towns in Denmark. As early as 960 there was a wooden church here, on the northern edge of the terrace from which the land slopes down to the fjord. The church was founded, it is believed, by Harald Bluetooth, who converted the Danes to Christianity. About 1030, the wooden church was rebuilt in stone. In the 11th c., Roskilde was a royal and episcopal residence, and in the following century it enjoyed its period of greatest prosperity. It was principally an ecclesiastical area, possessing great power and wealth, particularly after King Valdemar brought about the appointment as bishop of a young, Paris-educated priest – the great Bishop Absalon. In 1168, Valdemar presented his favourite with the town and harbour of Havn, and Absalon thus became the real founder of Copenhagen, then a fishing village of no consequence. Thereafter the focus of power was in Roskilde. The situation changed, however, at the Reformation. Eleven parish churches and all the town's religious houses were closed, and the economic and intellectual life of Roskilde declined. The town later recovered some importance, and in 1658, the peace treaty between Denmark and Sweden was signed in Roskilde Cathedral. By this treaty Denmark lost all its possessions beyond the Kattegat and the Öresund. Much of the old town was destroyed in a series of fires during the 18th c. The economic revival of Roskilde began only in the mid 19th c., after the construction of a railway line from Copenhagen. Roskilde is now one of the major industrial, educational and scientific areas of Denmark, with the Roskilde University Complex (RUC: social sciences) and an atomic research station at Risø.

SIGHTS. – Roskilde has one of Denmark's great national monuments, the *Cathedral of St Luke. This imposing structure, standing on higher ground above the fjord, dates from the time of Bishop Absalon and was begun about 1170. It occupies the site of three earlier churches, including the wooden church built by King Harald Bluetooth. The building of Bishop Absalon's cathedral began at the E

Roskilde Cathedral

end on the plan of a Romanesque basilica with transepts, but this plan was modified about 1200 under the influence of North French Gothic. The church, in red brick, thus shows a mingling of Romanesque and Gothic architecture, and the exterior

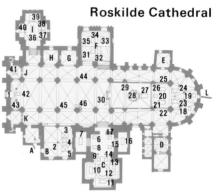

**Roskilde Cathedral**

| | |
|---|---|
| A | Entrance |
| B | Christian I's Chapel (Three Kings Chapel) |
| C | Frederik V's Chapel |
| D | Chapterhouse |
| E | Oluf Mortensen's Porch |
| F | Christian IV's Chapel |
| G | St Andrew's Chapel |
| H | St Birgitte's Chapel |
| I | Christian IX's Chapel |
| J | N Tower Chapel |
| K | S Tower Chapel |
| L | Absalon's Arch |

1  Main entrance
2  Royal Column
3  Monument of Christian III and Queen Dorothea
4  Tombs of Christian I and Queen Dorothea
5  Monument of Frederik II and Queen Sophie
6  Tomb of Caroline Amalie
7  Tomb of Sophie Magdalene
8  Tomb of Christian VIII
9  Tomb of Marie Sophie Frederike
10  Tomb of Queen Louise
11  Tomb of Frederick V
12  Tomb of Juliane Marie
13  Tomb of Christian VII
14  Tomb of Frederik VI
15  Tomb of Louise Charlotte
16  Tomb of Christian VI
17  Tomb of Frederik VII
18  Helhestens Sten
19  Gravestone of Bishop Peder Jensen Lodehal
20  Monument of Duke Christopher
21  Tomb of Frederik IV
22  Pillar with remains of Svend Estridsen
23  Tomb of Christian V
24  Tomb of Charlotte Amalie
25  Pillar with remains of Estrid, Knud the Great's sister
26  Tomb of Queen Louise
27  Tomb of Queen Margaret
28  High altar
29  Choir-stalls (1420)
30  Font
31  Tomb of Frederik III
32  Tomb of Sophie Amalie
33  Tomb of Anne Catherine
34  Tomb of Christian IV
35  Tomb of Prince Christian
36  Tomb of Frederik IX
37  Tomb of Queen Alexandrine
38  Tomb of Christian X
39  Double tomb of Christian IX and Queen Louise
40  Double tomb of Frederik VIII and Queen Louise
41  Tomb of Anne Sophie Reventlow
42  Kirsten Kimer, Per Døver and St Jørgen
43  Vincentz Hahn's armour
44  Royal Gallery
45  Organ
46  Pulpit

is further altered by the addition of several funerary chapels. For the last 400 years, the Cathedral has been the burial-place of Danish kings and queens. The two W towers were added in the 14th c., and their slender spires, sheathed in copper, date from 1635–6. The "Royal Doorway" between the towers is opened only for royal funerals; visitors enter by the S doorway.

The *INTERIOR, with lateral aisles flanking the nave, is particularly notable for the magnificent mid-15th c. carved *choir-stalls, above which are reliefs of scenes from the Old Testament (S side) and New Testament (N side). An interesting feature of the New Testament series is the representation of the Ascension: the footprints left by Christ can be seen on the ground, and his legs are still visible at the top of the scene. – The large carved and gilded altar screen on the high altar, made in Antwerp in the 16th c., was originally intended for the chapel in Frederiksborg Castle, but was presented to Roskilde by Christian IV. The altar has been excellently restored after a fire in 1968. In the central chapel of the three, in the N aisle, is an early 16th c. figure of St John. Also in the N aisle is the gallery with the royal throne, with rich 17th c. decoration. Other noteworthy items are the pulpit (of sandstone, alabaster, marble and black limestone) and the font (1602).

In the funerary chapels built on to the Cathedral and entered from the aisles are the tombs of 38 Danish monarchs, from Margaret I (d. 1412), who united the crowns of the three northern kingdoms, to Frederik IX, who was buried here in 1972. These royal tombs provide a unique history of funerary monumental art from the early 15th to the 20th c. The finest of the monuments is the recumbent alabaster figure (Gothic) of Queen Margaret, behind the high altar. Christian IV's chapel, on the N side, with a massive vaulted roof, has wall paintings by Wilhelm Marstrand and a bronze statue of the king by Thorvaldsen. Also on the N side are the chapels of Christian IX, St Birgitte and St Andrew. In the Chapel of the Three Kings, on the S side, is a granite column supporting the vaulting, marked with the height of various kings; the tallest is Christian I, in whose reign the chapel was built – a height of 2·10 m (6 ft 10½ in.), although the king's skeleton measures only 1·88 m (6 ft 2 in.). Also on the S side are Frederik V's neo-classical chapel, modelled after the Pantheon in Rome, with a dome and high windows, and the chapterhouse.

Only small parts of the Cathedral's medieval frescoes have survived.

The Cathedral is linked by Absalon's Arch (built 1210–20, after Bishop Absalon's death) with the Palace, formerly the meeting-place of the Estates and now the Bishop's Palace: an 18th c. building with a handsome courtyard and staircase.

In addition to the Cathedral Roskilde also has some of the oldest churches in Denmark, including Vor Frue Kirke (Church of Our Lady) to the S of the old town, with remains of walls belonging to an 11th c. church. According to the Danish historian, Saxo (d. 1220), it was built about 1080 by Bishop Sven Normand; the character of the church has been much altered by later restorations. The church of Skt Jørgensbjerg, outside the old town on a hill near the fjord, has a choir and nave dating from the end of the 11th c.; the N doorway, now walled up, belongs to an even earlier building, dated by coin finds to 1040. From the hill there is a magnificent view of the sea.

In Skt Olsgade is the Roskilde Museum (traditional costumes, folk art, medieval material). In Frederiksborgvej, the continuation of Skt Olsgade, stands the beautiful St Lawrence's Church (R.C.).

On the shores of the fjord, to the N of the town, is Roskilde's second great tourist attraction, the *Viking Ships Museum, opened in 1969. It is a "working museum", since the ships on display have not been completely restored; the public can observe work in progress.

The wrecks of five Viking ships were discovered at a narrow passage in Roskildefjord in 1957. They were brought to the surface in 1962, and since then have been meticulously pieced together and restored. They had been sunk and covered with stones at some time between 1000 and 1050, to block the fjord and protect the trading town of Roskilde from hostile attack – probably by Norwegian Vikings, who were then prowling the coasts of Denmark. The local fishermen had long known of this underground barrier but had believed it to be of much later date: the tradition was that the accumulation of stones covered a ship of the time of Queen Margatet I. It was only when the Danish National Museum carried out underwater excavations that the barrier was found to date from the Viking age and to consist of more than one ship. In 1962 a cofferdam was built to enclose the site and the five ships were excavated. They were found to comprise – broken up into a thousand fragments – a deep-sea trading ship (the only one of its kind yet discovered, designed for trade with Britain, Iceland and Greenland); a smaller merchant ship (for sailing on the Baltic, the North Sea and on rivers, with a crew of not more than six men, the cargo being stowed under skins amidships); a warship (long and narrow, powered by sail or by 24 oarsmen); a ferry or fishing boat; and a longship (so long – 28m (92 ft) – that it was originally thought to be two boats), the dreaded Viking man-of-war, seaworthy yet easy to beach, fast and manoeuvrable in battle. Of this last vessel, only about a fifth was preserved. Although the Viking ships of Roskilde are of little significance to the art historian, they are of great interest from a historical point of view.

SURROUNDINGS. – There are cruises in the Roskildefjord on weekends in the coal-fired museum ship "Skjelskør"; departure from the harbour. – On the E side of the fjord is the Vigen beach park (camp site, 4 km (2½ miles) from Roskilde). To the SE of the town lies Vindinge Nature Park, with large enclosures where animals live in semi-freedom. – 10 km (6 miles) SW of Roskilde (just outside Lejre) we come to **Ledreborg**, a grand 18th c. country house with a sumptuously decorated chapel and a large park in the English and French styles.

4 km (2 miles) NW of Lejre visitors can return to the Iron Age. In the **Historico-Archaeological Lejre Research Centre** (signposted "Oldtidsbyen") the past is brought to life. The object of the complex is to re-create the social and material culture of early times. The main attraction is the "Iron Age village", with potters', weavers', dyers', brickmakers', smiths' and woodworkers' workshops, houses and domestic animals, all in the style of the period. During the holidays volunteer "Iron Age" families attempt to adapt to the earlier way of life, doing without modern conveniences. In the "Valley of Fire", visitors can cook meat and bake bread on prehistoric hearths.

# Rovaniemi

Finland (Northern).
Province: Lapin lääni (Lapplands län/Lapland).
Altitude: 95 m (310 ft). – Population: 30,000.
Postal code: SF-96200. – Telephone code: 9 91.
ⓘ **Kaupungin Matkailutoimisto**
(*Municipal Tourist Information Office*),
Aallonkatu 2;
tel. 1 62 70

HOTELS. – *City*, Pekankatu 9, 224 b.; *Lapinportti*, Kairatie 2, 42 b., SB; *Polar*, Vaitakatu 23, 120 b., SB; *Rantasipi Pohjanhovi*, Pohjanpuistikko 2, 450 b., SB.

– OUTSIDE THE TOWN: *Ounasvaara*, 167 b.; *Rova-Motelli*, Kemintie, 84 b.

HOLIDAY and SUMMER HOTELS. – *Oppipoika*, Korkalonkatu 33, 80 b., SB (February to August); *Rovaniemi Ammattikoulun, Kesahotelli*, Kairatie 75, 108 b. (15 June to 5 August).

EVENTS. – *Ounasvaara Winter Games* (24–25 March); *Midnight Sun Festival* on Mt Ounasvaara (23 June); *Arctic Yacht Race* for light boats on Iso Vietonen Lake, 50 km (30 miles) NW of the town (June); *Ars Arctica* art exhibition (end June to end July).

SPORTS and RECREATION. – Tennis, golf, riding, shooting, fishing, swimming, rowing, sailing; skiing in winter (downhill and cross-country), reindeer sledge-rides.

**Rovaniemi is the administrative capital of the Finnish province of Lapland, by far the largest of the country's provinces, with an area of over 90,000 sq. km (35,000 sq. miles). The only town in Lapland and the province's economic and cultural hub, it stands at the junction of the Kemijoki, Finland's longest river (510 km – 320 miles) with the Ounasjoki (320 km – 200 miles).**

There was a settlement here in the 16th c., when the tax-collectors of the region's

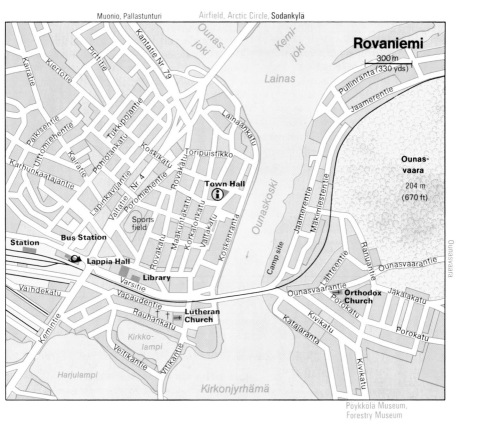

Rovaniemi – a bird's-eye view

Swedish and Russian rulers first began to appear in these northern territories. With the increase in the demand for timber following the development of industry, Rovaniemi increased considerably in importance, lying as it did at the junction of two of the principal rivers down which rafts could be floated from the interior of Lapland and into the Baltic. The present town was carved out of the rural commune in 1929 and, in 1938, it became the capital of the province of Finnish Lapland. It received its municipal charter in 1960, and plans to increase its development potential by the incorporation of the rural commune are being considered.

Until quite recently, Rovaniemi, like other places in the northern territories, consisted almost entirely of timber houses. In the winter of 1944–5, however, more than four-fifths of the town was burned down during the fighting between Finnish and German forces. Alvar Aalto was commissioned to rebuild the town and based the layout of the main streets on the pattern of a reindeer's antlers. The buildings erected since the war are almost all of stone, and

some of the public buildings have provided a model for the whole of Lapland by their functional conception and their adaptation to the landscape.

Rovaniemi attracts about 400,000 visitors each year, and accordingly the service trades are of major importance to the economy of the town.

SIGHTS. – In the SE of the town, near the large two-level road and railway bridge, are the *Provincial Government Offices*. To the S, beyond the railway line, stands the *Lutheran Church* (Bertil Liljequist, 1950), with an altarpiece, "The Source of Life", by Lennart Segerstrah. To the left of the entrance a stone marks the site of the earlier church (1817–1944). Behind the church is the churchyard, with a large war memorial to the dead of 1939–45. Opposite the church is a monument to the Finnish freedom fighters of 1918. – At No. 11 Hallituskatu is the **Lappia Hall** (Alvar Aalto, 1975), with a threatre and conference hall and the *Lapland Provincial Museum* (material illustrating the traditions of the Lapps and gipsies; ornithology). Adjoining, at No. 9 Hallituskatu, the *Municipal Library* (Alvar Aalto, 1965) houses a collection of minerals and an exhibition room. – On the E bank of the Ounakoski is the *Orthodox Church* (Toivo Paatela and Ilmari Ahonen, 1957), with valuable icons from Valamo monastery.

To the NW of the town, on the banks of the Kemijoki, is the Pohjanhovi Hotel. To the N, in the gardens by the river, stands a bronze statue of a bark-stripper (Kallervo Kallio, 1939–52). – 4 km (2½ miles) S of the middle of the town, also on the Kemijoki, are the *Pöykkölä Ethnographic Museum* (old houses; 19th c. peasant culture) and the *Lapland Forestry Museum*, which illustrates the work of the timber-workers immortalised in the sculpture of Kallervo Kallio.

SURROUNDINGS. – SE of Rovaniemi, on the left bank of the Kemijoki, is the hill of **Ounasvaara** (204 m (670 ft), with a café (view), a ski hut and a large ski-jump. From the top of the hill, the midnight sun is visible from 18 to 28 June. – 8 km (5 miles) N the road to Kemijärvi crosses the **Arctic Circle** (Finnish *Napapiiri*: see p. 49). Here there is a log cabin with a café and a post office (special postmark), and visitors can get a certificate to show that they have crossed the Arctic Circle. Nearby is the *"Lappland" children's village*, opened in October 1979. – 30 km (19 miles) from Rovaniemi, on the Aavasaksa road, is the *Pohtimolampi* tourist and sports resort (hotel, 150 b.; restaurant), with a ski-lift and reindeer-driving for visitors.

NAPAPIIRI
POLCIRKELN
POLARKREIS
ARCTIC CIRCLE
CERCLE POLAIRE
ПОЛЯРНЫЙ КРУГ

Arctic Circle, Rovaniemi

Lake Saimaa – a typical stretch of Finnish lake scenery

# Lake Saimaa

Finland (SE).
Provinces: Kymen lääni (Kymmene län/Kymi), Mikkelin lääni (Sankt Michels län/Mikkeli).

*Lake Saimaa, the "lake of a thousand islands", is the most southerly part of an intricate system of lakes, linked by numerous rivers and narrow channels, extending over the whole of the eastern part of the Finnish Lake Plateau. It is abundantly stocked with fish.

Lake Saimaa itself, lying at an altitude of 76 m (250 ft), has an area (excluding its countless islands) of some 1300 sq. km (500 sq. miles), with a maximum depth of 90 m (295 ft); the lake plateau of which it forms part has an area of some 7000 sq. km (2700 sq. miles). The low southern rim of the lake is formed by the Salpausselkä ridge.

Passenger boat on Lake Saimaa

The whole system of lakes – the dark colour of which, taking on a yellowish hue in the shallower places, comes from the numerous bogs in the region – is drained by the River Vuoksi, which flows out of Lake Saimaa to the N of the town of Imatra and flows into Lake Ladoga after 150 km (95 miles). The hilly shores of the lake and most of its islands are almost entirely covered with coniferous forest, with some birch forests farther to the N.

A number of agencies, mostly in Lappeenranta (see p. 173), run cruises on Lake Saimaa (either day cruises or cruises lasting several days).

# Savonlinna (Nyslott)

Finland (SE).
Province: Mikkelin lääni (Sankt Michels län/Mikkeli).
Altitude: 76 m (250 ft). – Population: 29,000.
Postal code: SF-57130. – Telephone code: 9 57.
ⓘ Kaupungin Matkailutoimisto
(Municipal Tourist Information Office),
Olavinkatu 35;
tel. 1 34 93.

HOTELS. – Casino, Kasinonsaari, 213 b., SB; Kyronsalmi, Olavinkatu 5, 98 b.; Malakias, Pihlajavedenkatu 6, 460 b. (1 June to 31 August); Rauhalinna, Lehtiniemi 18 b. (1 June to 19 August); Tott, Satamakatu 1, 93 b.; Kasinosaari, 326 b., SB (1 June to 30 August). – YOUTH HOSTEL. – CAMP SITE.

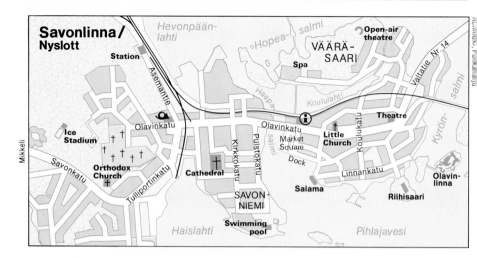

EVENTS. – *Opera Festival, Music Days and Summer Music Seminar* (July); *Savonlinna Rowing Regatta, Lake Saimaa Sailing Regatta* (July).

SPORTS and RECREATION. – Fishing (salmon, trout), shooting, riding, boating and sailing; skiing.

**Savonlinna (Swedish Nyslott), a very popular spa and vacation resort, lies in the middle of the Saimaa lake system, between Haapavesi to the N and Pihlajavesi to the S. The town grew up around the castle of Olavinlinna or Olofsborg and received its municipal charter in 1639. The oldest part of the town is on an island, between two swiftly flowing channels; the newer districts are on the mainland to the W. Savonlinna is one of the principal bases for the boats on Lake Saimaa.**

SIGHTS. – The town's main traffic artery is *Olavinkatu*, a long street running E to W. At the W end of the old town, on the Haapasalmi channel, is the *Market Square*, with the dock used by the Lake Saimaa boats. From here a bridge leads N over the Koululahti inlet to the VÄÄRÄ-SAARI peninsula, with the *Spa* (modern treatment facilities; casino; summer restaurant), a summer theatre and an attractive park. – Olavinkatu runs E from the Market Square into another spacious square, *Olavintori*, with the *Little Church* (L. T. K. Visconti, 1845; originally Orthodox, Lutheran since 1940) and the old *Grammar School* (L. Gripenberg, 1890). On the S side of the island stands the **Riihisaari Museum**, in an old granary (E. B. Lohrman, 1851) in which exhibitions are organised during the Opera Festival. To the W, on the *Haapasalmi* strait, is the *museum ship "Salama"*, a steam-powered schooner, launched in Viipuri in 1874, which carried passengers and cargo between Savonlinna, St Petersburg and Lübeck. The ship sank in Lake Saimaa in 1898 and lay in more than 30 m (95 ft) of water until 1971, when it was raised, restored and opened to the public as a museum ship in 1978.

On the SAVONNIEMI peninsula, between the Haapasalmi channel and the inlet of Kirkkolahti, is the **Lutheran Cathedral**, a neo-Gothic brick church (A. H. Dahlström, 1879) which was destroyed by wartime bombing and reconsecrated in 1949. To the W, in Savonkatu, is the *Orthodox Church*, opposite the district of Heikinpohja.

Savonlinna Castle

Every visitor should see the castle, *Savonlinna (Swedish *Olofsborg*), SE of the old town on an islet in the Kyrönsalmi channel (reached by a bridge). The castle was built by Erik Axelsson Tott, governor of Viipuri Castle, in 1475. After the Nordic War (1743), it was ceded to the Russians, who strengthened it several times. The castle is entered by a vaulted gateway on the W side which leads into a small courtyard, the oldest part of the structure. The castle, which has been excellently restored, contains a number of handsome rooms which are used for receptions and conferences, among them the King's Hall or Knights' Hall, the Congress Hall and the Great Hall. There are three massive circular towers; on the third floor of the Church Tower is a small chapel, still used for worship and for weddings. In the Great Bastion is a summer café. From the loopholes and small windows in the towers, there are attractive glimpses of the surrounding country. Conducted tours; small historical museum. Theatrical performances are given in the castle courtyard in summer.

SURROUNDINGS. – *Boat trips* to other towns on Lake Saimaa. – Other places which can be reached by boat are *Punkaharju (p. 93), the monasteries of *Heinävesi* and *Lintula* and, nearer Savonlinna, the old hunting lodge of the Tsars (now the *Rauhalinna Hotel*).

15 km (10 miles) E of Savonlinna by Road 71 and Lake Puruvesi is *Kerimäki*, with the largest wooden church in the world (see p. 93).

# Setesdal

Norway (Southern).
Counties: Aust-Agder fylke, Vest-Agder fylke.

**The Setesdal (or Sæterdal), the valley of the Otterå (Otra), extends almost due N for a distance of 230 km (140 miles) from Kristiansand, on the S coast of Norway, forming an important traffic route to Bergen and the Hardangerfjord. It has much to offer the visitor, with its beautiful scenery and a population still bound by old customs and traditions.**

Road 12 runs NW from **Kristiansand** (see p. 163), turning away from the River Otra and passing the cemetery and the road leading to the Ravnedal Park. At *Mosby*, a road leads off on the right to *Vennesla* and *Grovane* (old-time railway: see p. 164). – Road 12 then passes the *Langevann* and *Eigelandsvann*, goes through *Hægeland* (octagonal church, 1830), and crosses a wooded heathland region and the Otra, on the *Birkeland bridge*.

**Evje** (alt. 185 m (607 ft); pop. 1500;

Dolen Hotel, 36 b.; Grenaderen Motell – Kafetaria, 58 b.) has boatyards, woodworking industry and felspar quarries. At *Evjemoen*, to the S, was a nickel works (closed 1946) using ore from Flåt. The minerals of the region (amazonite, beryl, aquamarine, etc.) will be of interest to geologists.

*Byglandsfjord* (alt. 207 m (680 ft); Revsnes Turisthotell, 84 b.), on the southern shore of the lake of the same name, through which the River Otra flows, is today a winter sports resort (chair-lift, ski trails). It was formerly the terminus of the Setesdal railway (closed 1962). – Road 12 follows the E side of the *Byglandsfjord*, with the *Årdalsfjell* (760 m – 2494 ft) rising above the fjord on the right. Sections of the road have been blasted from the rock.

**Årdal** has an interesting church (1827), with a runic stone in the churchyard. 300 m (300 yds) S of the church is a 900-year-old oak-tree. On a hill to the NE is the Landeskogen home for the mentally handicapped.

**Bygland** (Longerak Turistsenter, 80 b.), at the foot of *Lysheia* (845 m – 2772 ft), has a church (1838); in the churchyard are prehistoric cult stones. There are several old burial mounds in the surrounding area. Good fishing in the fjord.

The road crosses the fjord on the *Storestraum bridge* and runs along its western shore. To the left is the *Reiarsfoss*. At the N end of the fjord are old store-rooms built on piles (*stabbur*). Following the course of the Otra, the road runs past the *Rustfjell* (1070 m – 3511 ft) on the left.

The road continues through magnificent scenery to **Helle**, an old-established silversmithing town.

At **Nomeland**, a road branches off on the left to the *Brokke* power station (beautiful view of the valley). Nearby is *Sylvartun*, an old wooden house which contains a collection of silversmiths' work.

Soon afterward, the *Hallandsfoss, a 15 m (50 ft) high waterfall with several deep "glacier mills" (cavities gouged out by swirling melt-water), is passed on the left. Beyond this, in a wider part of the valley, is the main town in the Setesdal, **Valle** (alt. 307 m (1007 ft); Valle Motell, 32 b.; Valle Sommer Motell, 72 b.; camp site, old houses, church of 1844).

9 km (6 miles) beyond Valle is the farm of *Flateland*, where a side road (2 km – 1¼ miles) leads to the **Setesdal Museum** (old wooden houses).

Road 12 continues high above the Otra, running through a gorge to Bykle, a short distance E of the *Bossvatn*.

**Bykle** (alt. 549 m (1801 ft); Bykle Hotell, 55 b.) is an old village steeped in the peasant traditions of the valley. The 13th c. church has a fine 16th c. interior. N of the church is the Huldreheim Museum (16th c. wooden houses). A little E of the village is the *Sarvsfoss*, the highest waterfall in the Setesdal (30 m – 100 ft). A number of marked footpaths lead from Bykle into the hilly surrounding country.

N of Bykle, the valley becomes flatter and the landscape more mountainous in character. The road crosses the Otra again on the *Berdal bridge* and then skirts the E side of the *Hartevatn*.

**Hovden** (alt. 740 m (2428 ft); Hotel Hovdenhytta, 75 b.), beautifully set above the outflow of the Otra into the Hartevatn, is the primary winter sports and climbing resort of the Setesdal (lift).

Beyond Hovden, the road runs past the *Lislevatn*, *Breivatn* and *Sessvatn*, and reaches its highest point (917 m – 3009 ft); it then descends through **Haukeligrend** and from there on the Haukeli Road (p. 266) to Haugesund.

# Lake Siljan

Sweden (Central).
Province: Värmlands län. – Region: Dalarna.
(i) **Mora Turistbyrå,**
Ångbåtskajen,
S-79200 Mora;
tel. (02 50) 2 65 50.
**Rättviks Turistbyrå,**
Torget,
S-79500 Rättvik;
tel. (02 48) 1 09 10.
**Leksands Turistbyrå,**
Norsgate,
S-79301 Leksand;
tel. (02 47) 1 04 11.

*Lake Siljan, enclosed by gently rising hills with large areas of forest, lies in the heart of Dalarna (Dalecarlia), with the Österdalälv flowing in one end and out the other. 36 km (22 miles) long and 25 km (15 miles)

Mora girls in traditional costume

wide, it has an area of 290 sq. km (110 sq. miles) and a greatest depth of 120 m (390 ft). In the NW part of the lake is the island of Sollerön. The maximum depth of 120 m (390 ft) is reached in a curious channel which runs from Mora to Leksand; the rest of the lake has an average depth of only 60 m (195 ft). Lake Siljan, which has been artificially regulated since 1926, is renowned for its scenic beauty, which attracts large numbers of visitors (excursions, cruises and excellent boating on the lake).

**Mora** (Mora Hotell, 206 b.; Siljan, 110 b.), where the Österdalälv flows into the NW end of the lake, is a small market town which attracts visitors in both summer and winter. The 13th c. church has a separate tower (1672); it is the distinguishing landmark of Mora. The town has associations with two very different characters – Gustavus Vasa and the artist, Anders Zorn. Gustavus Vasa, founder of the Swedish state, sought refuge in the town in 1520 and called upon the men of Dalarna to rise against Danish rule. He is commemorated by the *Vasa Run*, the longest cross-country ski race in the world, which is held on the first Sunday in March every year and ends at Mora. On the hill of *Klocksgropsbacken* is a statue of Gustavus Vasa by Anders Zorn (1860–1920), Mora's most famous son. The *Zorn Collections*, presented to the town by Anders and Emma Zorn, comprise the Zorn Museum, Zorngården, Zorns Gammelgård and Gopsmor, the painter's studio (open July and August). The Zorn Museum contains a selection of Zorn's own work (watercolours, oils, sculpture, graphic art). In the same grounds is Zorn's own house, Zorngården, furnished in the style of the turn of the 19th c. Zorns Gammelgård, on the outskirts of the town, gives a comprehensive view of the old popular culture of Mora and the surrounding district: it is an open-air museum of 40 old farmhouses and cottages through which the development of the local style of timber architecture can be seen.

An attractive trip, within easy reach of Mora, is to the top of the *Gesunda Berg* (501 m (1644 ft); cableway, superb panoramic views). While in the hills, it is well worthwhile to visit some of the old summer farmsteads (though many of these are no longer used as such but have become vacation homes). – An unusual museum is the *Siljanfors Forest Museum*, on the road to *Malung* (17 km – 10 miles). Other places of interest are *Våmhus*, where the old craft of basketwork is demonstrated; *Oxberg*, with a picturesque wooden chapel; an old *water-mill* on the Axi; and *Nusnäs*, where visitors can see the traditional little orange-red wooden horses (the symbol of Dalarna) being made. – To the N of Mora is *Lake Orsa* (alt. 161 m (528 ft), greatest depth 97 m – 320 ft), with the village of *Orsa* at the N end. – 35 km (22 miles) NE of Orsa, on *Lake Skattung*, is the little tourist resort of **Furudal** (Hotel Oreborg, 120 b.), frequented in summer by anglers and in winter by skiers (ski-tow). The church (*c.* 1870) contains medieval wood-carving. – At *Norboda*, 15 km (10 miles) SE of Furudal, are more than 30 old log houses.

**Rättvik** (hotels: Gärdebygården, 90 b.; Persborg, 120 b.; Stiftsgården, 70 b.; Utby Värdhus, 60 b.), on the NE shore of the lake between Leksand and Mora, is the chief town in a commune to which Vikarbyn, Boda, Furudal and Bingsbö also belong. A tourist resort, it offers year-round attractions. On a promontory, reaching out into the lake, is the 13th c. church (rebuilt in 18th c.). Around the church are some 90 huts, some of them dating from the 17th c. (they provided overnight accommodation for members of the congregation, and for their horses, coming from far away. On the S side of the church is the Vasa Stone, erected in 1893 to commemorate Gustavus Vasa's first address to the men of Dalarna in 1520 on the precinct wall of the church. – Located in a park (which also includes a vacation village and a heated swimming pool), is Rättviks Gammelgård, with a display of old tools and implements, household goods and costumes. – In Gudmunds Slöjd visitors can see the little horses of Dalarna being made, particularly the grey horses which are a specialty of Rättvik.

The making of pottery can be watched in the Nittsjö factory. – In the church school is a natural history museum (local geology, plant and animal life). From the *Tolvåsberg* and the *Vidablick lookout tower* (325 m – 1066 ft), there are magnificent views of Lake Siljan.

**Leksand** (Hotel and Restaurang Furuliden, 62 b.; Motell och Restaurang Moskogen, 200 b.), on the Österdalälv, is the main town of the commune of that name, to which more than 90 small villages and hamlets belong. The church dates from the early 13th c.; its onion-domed tower was added in the 18th c. The interior is predominantly Baroque (fine 14th c. crucifix). The Hembygsgård is a local museum, with a varied collection. The Tinghus contains a collection of pictures by local artists. Every year, during the first week in July, groups of fiddlers in traditional costume can be seen all over Leksand, and indeed, throughout the commune, during the Lake Siljan musical festival, "Musik vid Siljan"

*Sammilsdal* is the hub of the local midsummer celebrations, and in the second half of July a mystery play similar to "Everyman", the *Himlaspel*, is performed here. In winter, large numbers of winter sports enthusiasts come to Leksand, which has an *ice-rink* and a cableway up the *Åsledsberg* (437 m – 1390 ft).

Matsgården, in *Östbjörga*, and Skräddargården, in *Stumsnäs*, are well-preserved wooden farmhouses with collections of the folk paintings for which the area is famous (*Dalmålingar*). – The main event in the summer is the Lake Siljan musical festival, "Musik vid Siljan" (July), which proves the old saying that "when two Rättvik men meet, three of them play the fiddle". – Another sight worth seeing is the "church boats", in which the local people, often wearing

Lake Siljan, near Rättvik

traditional costume, row to church for high mass between midsummer and August.

SE of Lake Siljan is the hilly mining and smelting region of **Bergslagen**. The local mines yield iron ore and some copper (Falun), the largest output of the Grängesberg Exportfält. In the vicinity of the Bergslagen mines are a series of ironworks – at Borlänge, Fagersta, Domnarvet, Avesta, Uddeholm, Degerfors, etc.

# Skåne

Sweden (Southern).
Provinces: Kristianstads län, Malmöhus län.
(i) **Skånes Turistråd**,
Stora Södergatan 8c,
S-22223 Lund;
tel. (0 46) 12 43 50.

**Skåne (Scania) is Sweden's southernmost region, lying between the Kattegat, the Öresund and the Baltic. Its 500 km (300 mile) long coastline is fringed with sandy beaches and wooded dunes, with stretches of rocky coast in the NW. Northern Skåne is a region of granite and gneiss, forests and gently rolling countryside. The fertile plain of Skåne is the granary of Sweden.**

The farmhouses of Skåne, built on an elongated rectangular plan, are designed to provide protection from the strong winds that blow over the plain. The grass-covered field walls (another characteristic feature of the region) have frequently had to give way to the requirements of modern traffic. Another traditional feature of the landscape, Dutch windmills, once so common, have now all but disappeared.

The large Iron Age chambered tombs in Skåne are a reminder that this area was settled at an early period in human development. During the Bronze Age, there were roads across the mud flats to Denmark; this, combined with the mild climate, led to an increase in the number of settlements. The population continued to grow during the Iron age, and many Vikings set out from Skåne on their long sea voyages to Britain and France.

Since Skåne was under Danish rule until the middle of the 17th c., many Danish bishops, kings, nobles and merchants left their mark on its architecture. This Danish influence can be seen, for example, in Glimmingehus Castle and Kristianstad. Under the treaty of Roskilde (1658) Skåne became part of Sweden.

Toward the end of the Middle Ages, Skåne had established a stable and healthy economy, based on agriculture, the herring fisheries, coal-mining and the supplies of clay which gave rise to its brickmaking industry.

The traditional costumes of Skåne , with their rich adornment of silver, recall the prosperity of the region in the 16th c., when its inhabitants began to wear finer clothing and jewelry. The style of that period has largely survived in the various local costumes and in furniture decoration.

Glimmingehus Castle

**Glimmingehus**, SW of Simrishamn, is one of the best preserved castles in Sweden. It was built in 1499 for the Danish admiral and privy councillor, Jens Holgersen Ulfstad. The architect was Adam van Düren, whose name is also associated with the building of Cologne and Lund cathedrals. The castle, which has remained unchanged since it was built, was both a residence and a stronghold and is surrounded by a moat. It is referred to in Selma Lagerlöf's "Wonderful Journey of Little Nils Holgersson". Acquired by the state in 1924, it is now open to the public.

**Trelleborg** (pop. 25,000; Standard, 22 b.), founded in the 12th c. owed its prosperity in the Middle Ages to the abundant supplies of herring in the Baltic. In 1619, it lost its municipal charter to Malmö, but recovered it in 1865, following a revival of its trade. Development progressed with the construction of the town's harbour and the coming of the railway. In 1875, Trelleborg was linked to the Swedish railway system by the construction of a line from Lund; in 1897, it was connected to the mainland of Europe by the establishment of a ferry service to Sassnitz on the island of Rügen. A ferry connection was later established with Travemünde, near Lübeck.

In the oldest part of the town, the medieval street plan has been partly preserved. The *church*, originally dating from around 1250, was almost completely rebuilt at the end of the 19th c. Near the church, and in *Gamla Torget*, some of the old houses, each containing a single dwelling, have been preserved. Foundations of the 13th c. church of the *Franciscan friary* which stood in Gamla Torget were excavated in 1932. – The *Municipal Museum* is housed in *Skyttsgården*. The *Ebbe Hall* (1935) is in the Municipal Park. The Hall houses a collection of works by the sculptor, Axel Ebbe (1868–1941). In Stortorget is the *Sea Serpent Fountain*, by Ebbe. Nearby stands the 58 m (190 ft) high *Water-tower* (by Tengbom, 1912).

# Skellefteå

Sweden (Eastern).
Province: Västerbottens län.
Region: Västerbotten.
Altitude: sea level. – Population: 73,000.
Postal code: S-931 . . . – Telephone code: 09 10.

(i)  **Skellefteå Turistbyrå,**
     Storgatan 46,
     S-9331 Skellefteå;
     tel. 7 72 60.

HOTELS. – *Dahlström*, Stationsgatan 9, 9b.; *Hof*, Tjärnhovsgatan 14, 118 b.; *Malmia*, Torget 2, 250 b.; *Statt*, Stationsgatan 8–10, 162 b.; *Stensborg*, Vinkelgränd 4, 23 b.; *Stiftsgården*, Brännavägen 25, 60 b.; *Victoria*, Trädgårdsgatan 8, 40 b.

**Skellefteå, on the estuary of the Skellefteå in the Gulf of Bothnia, is mentioned as a trading town in 1621, but did not receive its municipal charter until 1845. In 1912, the railway reached the town, and this, combined with the explosive expansion of the Boliden mines, led to the rapid development of Skellefteå. Since the incorporation of neighbouring settlements, some of them as far as 20 km (12 miles) away, it has increased its population to 73,000.**

SIGHTS. – The middle of the town is well preserved, with the original rectangular street plan and wooden houses in typical Norrland style. The late 18th c. **Church of the Provincial Assembly** incorporates some medieval work. It contains a collection of medieval sculpture in wood and

a fine reredos (altar screen). Adjoining the church is **Bondstan**, with 150 huts for the overnight accommodation of churchgoers. In the *Nordanå Park*, alongside the river in the old part of the town, is an *open-air museum*. Here, too, we find the *Provincial Museum* (bronze ornaments of A.D. 300–400).

The **Town House** (1955), adjoining the *Municipal Park* (1873), contains a mosaic by Evert Lundquist. The Baroque-style *Town Church* (1927) has a striking black granite doorway; the interior decoration is by Carl Fagerberg and Gunnar Torhamn.

SURROUNDINGS. – 16 km (10 miles) SE of the middle of town is the port of **Skelleftehamn**, with St Örjan's Church (1935), which has a roof and bells made of copper from Boliden and contains an altarpiece of the Spanish school, perhaps by Velázquez. – At *Rönnskär*, 3 km (2 miles) beyond this, are a large foundry belonging to the Boliden company and a sulphuric acid plant.

35 km (22 miles) NW of Skellefteå is the mining town of **Boliden**, where large deposits of copper were discovered in 1925–6. Today ore containing gold, silver, lead and arsenic is mined here, and there are also deposits of selenium and sulphur. From Boliden, there is a 96 km (60 mile) long cable railway via Rakkejaur to *Kristineberg*, where ore containing copper, sulphur and zinc is mined.

# Småland

Sweden (Southern).
Provinces: Jönköpings län, Kronobergs län, Kalmar län, Hallands län.

**Småland is notable among the regions of Sweden for its many lakes. The uplands in the northern part of the region slope down toward the S and SW and give way to a plain. Here begins the "endless forest" celebrated in so many Swedish songs. The countless rocky hills, smoothed and rounded by the glaciers of the Ice Age, with lakes and flat expanses of peat-bog between them, are characteristic of Småland. The barren ground is covered with mosses and lichens.**

Until the 18th c., the population of Småland depended almost exclusively on agriculture for their subsistence, but the stony morainic terrain yielded poor returns. Many peasants sought employment in factories to eke out a meagre income. Many were unable to make a living, and there was a great emigration of young people from Småland between 1750 and 1850.

The mining of iron ore in Småland began in the 15th c., with Taberg the principal mining area. There was a great surge of activity in ironworking when foreign smiths came to Småland and passed their skills to the local people. In the middle of the 19th c., however, the woodworking and glass industries moved into first place. The Swedish glass industry was established when Gustavus Vasa brought skilled glass-blowers from Venice in 1556. In time over 200 glassworks were established, more than half of them in the SE corner of the Småland forest region: hence the name of *Glasriket* ("Glass Kingdom"), given to the stretch of forest between Nybro and Växjö. Most of the glassworks were originally established as iron foundries, in the days when bog ore (impure iron ore) was still being used.

Orrefors glass

A relic of these early days can be seen in the *old hammer-mill* in **Orrefors** (Sandgrens Pensionat, 12 b.), 17 km (10 miles) from Nybro. In this village of about 900 inhabitants, an iron foundry using bog ore was still working in the latter part of the 19th c. The glassworks here were established in 1898 and now belong to the **Orrefors Glass Company**, founded in 1937. Originally producers of window-glass and glass for industrial use, the company later switched to lamps and decorative glassware. With the Sandvik Glass Company in Hovmantorp, it also produces domestic glass for everyday use. The Orrefors works can claim to have pioneered the manufacture of the famous Swedish glassware, having employed the first designers in this field in 1915. This

marked the beginning of what is known in Sweden as the "Gate-Hald period", making Swedish glass famous around the world. Gate and Hald were two of the designers who, along with others like Lindstrand, Landberg, Palmqvist, Öhrström and Lundin, gave Orrefors glass its artistic form. The Orrefors works has a *museum* (display of glass from the Gate-Hald period).

**Oskarshamn** (pop. 28,000; hotels: Corallen, 50 b.; Post, 94 b.), founded only 100 years ago, is a port and industrial town on the Döderhultsvik, an inlet on the Baltic coast between Kalmar and Västervik. It was the birthplace of the Swedish doctor and author, Axel Munthe (1857–1949), whose "Story of San Michele" was a best-seller in many languages. – It is a town of many ups and downs, reflecting its hilly topography. At Nos. 18–20 Hantverksgatan is the House of Culture, containing the Seafaring Museum, the Municipal Library and an art gallery displaying Småland woodcarving and works by the sculptor, Axel Pettersson (1868–1925), born in Döderhult, near Oskarshamn. On a hill in the Municipal Park is a neo-Gothic church (1874–6). – Opposite the harbour is the well-preserved *Fnyket* quarter of little wooden houses. – On the way to *Döderhultsdalen*, it is worth visiting the local museum in *Frederiksberg Herregård*, with its beautiful 18th c. great hall and the municipal reception rooms. – From Långa Soffan (the "Long Bench"), in the old *seamen's quarter* around the harbour, there is a fine view. 20 km (12 miles offshore), half-way between the mainland and the island of Öland, lies the rocky island of *Blå Jungfrun*, the "Blue Maiden" (alt. 85 m (280 ft): National Park). – In summer there are daily ferry services to Byxelkrok on Öland and Visby and Klintehamn on Gotland.

**Värnamo** (hotels: Turisten, 18 b.; Varnamo, 180 b.), on the banks of the Lagå, is the capital of southern Småland. Although known as a meeting-place of the *ting* (assembly) in 1236, and as a trading station in 1620, the town failed to develop. In 1859, it had still no more than 300 inhabitants. Since then, the development of industry and the incorporation of neighbouring places has brought its population to 30,000. Some 60% of the population are engaged in crafts and industry, especially the furniture industry, notable in the annual "Swed-Expo" trade fair. – In the middle of the town is the *Apladal* nature park, with the Folk Museum (local way of life and traditions). – On Sundays and public holidays, in summer, an *old-time railway* operates over the 15 km (10 mile) stretch of line between Bor and Osbruk. – 25 km (15 miles) S of Värnamo is an *Automobile Museum*, with motorcycles, tractors and an aircraft, as well as cars. – 25 km (15 miles) NE of Värnamo is a nature reserve around the ruins of the 12th c. *Nydala Abbey*, near *Kävsjömyren*.

# Sognefjord

Norway (Western).
County: Sogn og Fjordane fylke.

(i) **Turistkontor Balestrand,**
N-5850 Balestrand;
tel. (0 56) 9 12 55.

**The *Sognefjord, the largest of the Norwegian fjords, surpasses the gentler scenery of the Hardangerfjord with the austerity of its mountain setting. From Sygnefest, at its western end, it extends inland for 180 km (110 miles) to Skjolden, at the eastern end of the Lusterfjord, with an average width of no more than 5 km (3 miles). Its greatest depth is 1245 m (4085 ft).**

At its eastern end the fjord is split into a number of narrow arms, enclosed by steep rock walls rising to over 1700 m (5500 ft). Dotted along the narrow strip of land on the shores of the fjord one finds cornfields, orchards and trim residential houses. The eastern part of the fjord has a continental climate, with warm summers and long, cold winters.

Since there are no roads running along the whole length of the fjord it is best explored by boat. From Bergen (see p. 63) a number of ships (some carrying cars) run trips to the Sognefjord.

BOAT SERVICES. – Ships of the **Hurtigrute** (Express Route) sail from Bergen to Årdalstangen, at the E end of the Årdalsfjord, twice daily from June to August (afternoons only from 15 to 31 May and from 1 to 20 August). The boats leaving Bergen in the morning stop at Lavik, Balestrand, Leikanger, Midfjord and Flåm (transfer from there to Gudvangen and to Revsnes and Årdalstangen); the afternoon boats at

Rysjedalsvika, Lavik, Nordeide, Balestrand, Vangsnes, Leikanger, Revsnes and Årdalstangen. These boats carry passengers only; no cars, bicycles or animals. The luggage allowance is 15 kg (33 lb). Passengers are not allowed on deck during the journey. It is advisable to book at least a day in advance.

*Within the Sognefjord* there are various local services (some of them carrying cars) which offer attractive excursions.

From Balestrand, there is a service via Leikanger to the Aurlandsfjord (Aurland and Flåm), which from 15 to 31 May and from 1 to 20 September supplements the Hurtigrute services (above).

There are also car ferries from Balestrand to Hella and Fjærland in the Fjærlandsfjord, from Balestrand to Hella and Vangsnes, from Flåm to Aurland and Gudvangen, from Årdalstangen to Ornes and Solvorn in the Lusterfjord, from Kaupanger to Revsnes and from Flåm to Gudvangen, Revsnes, Kaupanger and Årdalstangen.

There are also mini cruises from Bergen which call at places on the Nordfjord (see entry), lying to the north of the Sognefjord. They operate on weekdays and at weekends and last two or three days. The ships have lounges and small but comfortable cabins. These cruises give tourists an opportunity of seeing the majestic scenery of the fjords; the Norwegians use them to transport vital supplies to remote communities.

Information: *Fylkesbaatane i Sogn og Fjordane,*
Strandgata 197,
N-5000 Bergen;
tel. (05) 32 40 15.

*Rysjedalsvika* lies at the extreme western end of the Sognefjord, which at this point is enclosed between low hills worn smooth by glacier action, and with scant vegetation.

**Lavik** is the chief place in the western Sognefjord and an important junction of land and water-borne traffic (ferry to Brekke on the S side of the fjord). The church dates from 1865.

*Vadheim* (pop. 600), on the Vadheimsfjord, has an electrochemical factory.

*Nordeide,* at the entrance to the Høyangerfjord, is connected by ferry with Kongsnes, also on the N side of the Sognefjord, and with *Svortemyr,* on the S side. It is a small vacation resort.

**Høyanger** (pop. 2200; hotels: Eides, 40 b.; Øren, 64 b.), at the end of the Høyangerfjord, has a power station and an aluminium plant. Good hill walking in the surrounding area; fishing.

**Balestrand** (pop. 700; hotels: Balestrand Pensjonat, 25 b.; Dragsvik Fjordhotell, 80 b.; Kringsjå, 90 b.; Kvikne's Hotel, 365 b.; youth hostel), the principal tourist resort in the Sognefjord, is surrounded by high hills. See the little English church built in the last century. To the NW lies the little *Esefjord.

To the N of Balestrand the* **Fjærlandsfjord** extends almost to the Jostedalsbre (p. 147). There is a boat service from Balestrand along this fjord (26 km (16 miles) long) to *Fjærland* (Fjærland Fjordhotell, 45 b.; Mundal, 72 b.), a popular starting-point for walks and climbs in the glacier area.

There is a ferry from Balestrand to *Hella*, on the E side of the Fjærlandsfjord.

*Vik* (Hopstock Hotell, 70 b.; youth hostel; camp site), on the S side of the Sognefjord opposite Balestrand (ferry), has a power station and aluminium and woodworking plants. Nearby are *Hopperstad* stave church (12th c.) and a Romanesque stone church. – From here it is possible to drive via Voss to Bergen.

**Vangsnes** (Vangsnes Pensjonat; youth hostel; camp site) lies on the S side of a promontory opposite Hella (ferry). It has a *statue of Fridtjov* 12 m (40 ft) high, presented by Kaiser Wilhelm II (commemorating the story of two lovers of the Viking times, written in the 13th c., the Frithjof Saga is an Icelandic heroic tale of the 13th c.). Nearby are three fine burial mounds.

**Leikanger** (Leikanger Fjord Hotell, 85 b.; camp site) and **Hermansverk** (Sognefjord Turisthotell, 40 b., SB) combine to form the chief place of Sogn og Fjordane county. They are located in a fertile region and have a large fruit harvest. Leikanger has a 13th c. stone church. To the S, there is a magnificent view up the Aurlandsfjord.

The *Aurlandsfjord** is a southern off-shoot of the Sognefjord, a cleft in the mountains 1·5 km (1 mile) wide, flanked by rock walls rising to 900–1200 m (2900–3900 ft). **Aurlandsvangen** (hotels: Aurland Fjordstue, 25 b.; Ryggatun, 78 b.), administrative hub of the commune of Aurland, has the oldest stone church in the region (*c.* 1200). Nearby is *Undredal church* (only 3·7 m (12 ft) wide, with seating for 40), a stave church (altered about 1700). – To the S of

Aurlandsvangen, surrounded by high mountains at the S end of the fjord, lies the tourist resort of *Flåm* (Fretheim Hotel, 140 b.; Heimly Lodge, 67 b.; camp site), at the mouth of the Flåm valley. This is the terminus of the *Flåm railway*, a branch line of the Bergen railway. – The western branch of the Aurlandsfjord is the **Nærøyfjord**, hemmed in by almost vertical rock faces, so that during the winter months the sun never reaches the bottom of the fjord. At its SW tip is **Gudvangen** (Gudvangen Hotell, 75 b.; camp site). Near here is the *Kjelsfoss* waterfall. From here, E68, joined at *Vinje* by Road 13 from Vik, runs via Voss to Bergen.

**Kaupanger** (Husum Motell, 32 b.), on the N shore of the *Amlabugt*, is connected by ferry with Revsnes, Gudvangen and Årdalstangen. It has a fine 13th c. stave church (restored 1862) and an open-air museum, the Heibergske Samlinger (old houses).

E of Kaupanger, the Sognefjord splits up into the Lusterfjord, which runs N towards the Jotunheim (p. 147), the Årdalsfjord to the E and the Lærdalsfjord to the SE.

The *Lusterfjord, 45 km (30 miles) long, owes the milky colouring of its water to the glacier-fed streams which flow into it. – At *Urnes*, on the E side of the fjord, is one of the oldest stave churches in the country, originally dating from before 1100. – From *Skjolden*, at the northern tip of the fjord, to the Jotunheim, see p. 147.

The **Årdalsfjord** is the most easterly branch of the Sognefjord. At its head, on an old raised beach, is **Årdalstangen** or *Årdal* (pop. 2300; Klingenberg Fjordhotell, 66 b.; camp site), with a beautiful church and a large aluminium plant. To the S is the highest peak of the Slettefjell, *Sauenosi* (1352 m – 4436 ft). – To the N, on the *Årdalsvatn*, is the industrial township of *Øvre Årdal*. From there a road runs N to *Hjelle*, from which it is a 3–4 hours' climb up the *Vettisgjel gorge* to the *Vettisfoss*, a waterfall 260 m (850 ft) high which has been protected as a nature reserve since 1924.

The **Lærdalsfjord** extends SE from Kaupanger. At the head of the fjord, at the mouth of the Lærdal, is **Lærdalsøyri**

Kaupanger ferry station on the Sognefjord

(Lindstrøm Turisthotell, 152 b.; Offerdal Pensjonat, 80 b.), with a number of old houses, including the Hanseatic House.

**Road from the Lærdal to Florø.** – The only roads of any consequence in the Sognefjord are the E68 from Valdres (see p. 282) and its continuation, No. 5.

From the fork in the road beyond *Øye* (p. 283), E68 runs past the *Otrøvatn* and through the *Smeddal*, via *Borlaug*, to the **Lærdal**.

**Borgund** (alt. 345 m – 1130 ft) has a small *stave church*, black with pitch, the best preserved in the country. It was probably built around 1150, and first appears in the records in 1360. Apart from one newer window, it has been carefully restored to its original form. Both of its doorways are richly decorated, and the W doorway has a runic inscription which gave valuable help in dating the church. The belfry, between the old and the new church, was restored about 1660 in its original form. (Photograph, p. 39). – The road now runs through the picturesque *Svartegjel gorge*, carved by the Lædalselv (good salmon-fishing), through the rock barrier of the *Vindhella*. Beyond *Husum* (alt. 316 m (1037 ft)) it passes through another magnificent *gorge.

**Lærdalsøyri:** see above.

The road continues along the S side of the Lærdalsfjord. Between *Revsnes* and *Kaupanger*, the Sognefjord is crossed by ferry.

**Sogndal** (hotels: Hofslund Fjord, 86 b.; Loftesnes Fjord Pensjonat, 25 b.; Sogndal, 190 b.; youth hostel) lies at the N end of the Sogndalsfjord. It has an interesting runic stone (*c.* 1100) and a number of burial mounds. – The road now follows the N side of the Sognefjord to *Hermansverk*, *Leikanger* and *Hella*, from which there is a ferry to *Balestrand* (above). It then turns N, following the W side of the *Vetlefjord*, to **Førde**, primary town in the Sunnfjord area, located at the end of the *Førdefjord* (hotels: Førde, 120 b.; Sunnfjord, 330 b., SB, SP; camp site), and **Florø** (pop. 5000; Victoria Hotell, 150 b.), a port and industrial town, in a charming setting on the island of *Brandsøy* (bridge).

# Spitzbergen (Svalbard)

Norway (administrative district of Svalbard).
Area of archipelago: 61,723 sq. km (23,830 sq. miles).

TRAVEL. – Flights between Tromsø and Longyearbyen three times weekly throughout the year. By sea

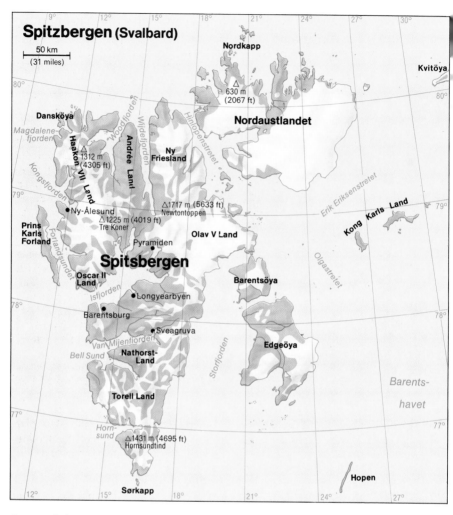

there are "adventure cruises" from Oslo or from Tromsø but no regular service.

**Accommodation.** – Since there are no tourist hotels on Spitzbergen visitors must stay at one of the two camp sites, the amenities of which are rather spartan. If unable to get private accommodation visitors must be equipped to look after themselves (tent, sleeping bag, etc.) and must also bring sufficient food. Visitors arriving inadequately equipped will be required to leave. Small quantities of alcoholic beverages for personal consumption may be imported. A visitor who is in possession of a firearms licence may bring a gun and ammunition from a Norwegian airport or port. Equipment control on arrival. The import of living animals is prohibited.

**Conservation.** – In recent years, about 27,000 sq. km (10,500 sq. miles), 44% of the total area, have been given legal protection. There are three National Parks (S Spitzbergen, Forland, NW Spitzbergen), two nature reserves, two plant reserves and fifteen bird reserves.

As a result of the extreme climatic conditions, it takes many years for refuse to decay. In order to avoid disturbing the delicate ecological balance, visitors should dispose of their rubbish (garbage) properly.

The *Spitzbergen (Spitsbergen in Norwegian) archipelago, since 1925 part of the Norwegian adminis-

**Warning.** – There is always the possibility, even during the summer, of encountering **polar bears.** Since they are usually of an aggressive nature and liable to attack without warning, extreme caution should be observed.

trative district of Svalbard (which includes the islands lying between long. 10° and 35° E and lat. 74° and 81° N), lies between lat. 76°28′ and 80°48′ N, some 700 km (450 miles) from Hammerfest and 1000 km (625 miles) from the North Pole. It has a total area of 61,723 sq. km (23,830 sq. miles).

The main island, West Spitzbergen (Vest-spitsbergen) is broken up by deeply indented fjords. Off the W coast is the small island of Prins Karls Forland (Prince Charles Foreland). To the NE, separated from the main island by the Hinlopen Strait, is Nordaustlandet (North-East Land), almost completely covered with ice. To the SE are Barentsøya (Barents Island) and Edgeøya (Edge Island), and beyond these, the narrow little island of Hopen.

Spitzbergen has rich **coal** deposits from the Tertiary era, occasionally used in the past by visiting ships to supplement their supplies and now mined both by Norwegians (about 1000, at Longyearbyen) and Russians (about 2000, at Barentsburg and Pyramiden). The mines are on West Spitzbergen, mainly on the S side of the Isfjord (Longyearbyen, Barentsburg, Pyramiden, etc.). The coal can be shipped only during the few ice-free summer months. – Since 1960, there have been test drillings for oil at various places in Spitzbergen.

Warm rainproof and washable clothing, and sturdy footwear are essential for a visit to Spitzbergen. Great caution should be exercised in venturing on to glaciers.

HISTORY. – Spitzbergen is believed to have been discovered as early as 1194 by Norwegians, who named it Svalbard (the "cold land"). In 1596 it was again discovered by the Dutch navigator Willem Barents, during his quest for the North-East Passage to China. Under the Treaty of Sèvres (1920), Norway was granted sovereignty over Spitzbergen, and Russia was given the right to work three coal-mines. In 1925, the territory was incorporated into Norway under the old name of Svalbard. The islands are ruled by a governor (*sysselmann*). – Many of the islands and their natural features are named after seamen, fishermen, hunters, scientists and statesmen of different nationalities, recalling the history of their discovery and exploration. – Apart from a few mining settlements on the W coast, the islands are uninhabited.

Geologically, Spitzbergen belongs to the European continental shelf and shows a history of development from the Pre-Cambrian rocks to the Tertiary era. The huge glaciers reaching down to the sea and the pointed summits of the mountains create an impression of an Alpine world which has sunk under the ocean. The highest peak is Newtontoppen (1717 m – 5633 ft), NE of Isfjord. About four-fifths of the land surface is covered by perpetual ice. As a result of the warm Gulf Stream which washes the W coast, the drift ice retreats farther here in summer than anywhere else in the Arctic regions at the same latitude. – Seals, polar bears, reindeer, Arctic foxes and some 30 species of birds inhabit the region. – Plant life, which grows during the brief summer, consists of small blossoming plants, ferns, mosses and lichens. – The climate varies,

with frequent mist, and the temperature rises above freezing point only during the short summer months. The midnight sun is visible from about 19 April to 24 August, while from 27 October to 15 February, the sun remains continually below the horizon.

The tourist ships dock only on the W side of the archipelago. – After passing the South Cape ((Sørkapp) of **West Spitzbergen** (lat. 76°26' N) the ships sail past the 15 km (9 mile) wide **Hornsund**, the southernmost inlet on the W coast, with the towering *Hornsundstind* (1431 m – 4695 ft), and then past the Torell glacier and the Bell Sund. It then comes to the *Isfjord, the largest fjord on the W coast, cutting 100 km (60 miles) into the land with a width of up to 25 km (15 miles) and with a number of arms branching off. The landscape on the N side is of Alpine type, while on the S side, with the mining settlements, the fjord is edged with steep-sided tabular hills. In the *Adventfjord* is **Longyearbyen** (named after the 19th c. American mining engineer, J. M. Longyear), the largest settlement on the island. It is a very serious offence (punishable by imprisonment) to pick any of the tiny flowers that grow here in the summer.

The scenery is even finer and grander farther up the coast. The ship sails along the W side of the long island of **Prins Karl Forland** with its jagged glaciated peaks (Mt Monaco, 1084 m – 3557 ft) and after rounding the northern tip of the island, comes into sight of the wide **Kongsfjord** (King's Fjord), with the pyramidal peaks of the *Tre Kroner* (Three Crowns, 1225 m – 4020 ft) rising above the 14 km (9 mile) wide *King's Glacier*, the largest glacier on the W coast. On the S side of the fjord is the former mining settlement of **Ny Ålesund** (mining abandoned after an accident in 1962). Here is the most northerly "post office" in the world (special postmark) and a radar and satellite tracking station (pop. about 30: scientific research on ionosphere). Near here is a monument commemorating Amundsen's flight in the airship "Norge" (1926). The Kongsfjord was the starting-point of a number of Polar flights. Amundsen's attempt to reach the Pole with two aircraft in 1925 was unsuccessful, but in the following year he flew over the Pole in the "Norge", two days after the Americans Byrd and Bennett, and landed

Spitzbergen – cruise ship in the Kongsfjord.

at Teller in Alaska. In 1928, the Italian, Nobile, set out from here in his airship, but was lost on the return flight.

To the N of the Kongsfjord are the *Krossfjord and the *Møllerfjord, with Møllerhavn ("Lloyd Hotel" hut, with visitors' book). – 30 km (20 miles) N of the Kongsfjord is a 30 km (20 mile) wide expanse of glaciers, with seven huge rivers of ice reaching down to the sea between steep and jagged peaks. Still farther N is the 9 km (5 mile) long *Magdalenefjord, at the head of which is the Waggonway glacier (named for the deep rifts in the ice like cart-ruts), 2 km (1¼ miles) wide, with a cliff-like front up to 100 m (330 ft) high; to the left is the Miethe glacier. On the S side of the fjord are the Adams and Gully glaciers, in the NE corner the pyramidal Rotgesberg (802 m – 2631 ft). To the N is the island of Danskøya, from which a Swede named André set out to fly to the Pole in a balloon but perished, along with his companions, in the attempt. – Beyond this island is Amsterdamøya (also known as Smeerenburg, from smeer, "blubber"), the base of the 17th and 18th c. Dutch whalers. In earlier days, whaling was such a source of wealth that the little summer settlement of Smeerenburg for a time ranked equal with Batavia on Java. The cauldrons in which the whale oil was melted down used to stand on the low flat hills above the shore.

# Stavanger

Norway (SW).
County: Rogaland fylke.
Altitude: sea level. – Population: 89,000.
Postal code: N-4000. – Telephone code: 0 45.

(i) **Turistinformasjon,**
Turistpaviljongen,
at railway station;
tel. 52 84 37.

HOTELS. – *Atlantic, 582 b.; *KNA-Hotellet, 155 b.; *Scandic Hotel Stavanger, 270 b., SB; Alstor, 156 b.; Bergeland Gjestgiveri, 100 b.; Commandør, 71 b.; Fjelltun Gjesteheim, 106 b.; Hafrsfjord, 50 b.; St Svithun, 100 b. – YOUTH HOSTEL. – CAMP SITE.

Event. – Angling Festival (August).

SPORTS and RECREATION. – Angling trips.

**Stavanger, county town of Rogaland, lies on the Byfjord or Boknafjord, an arm of the Stavangerfjord, near the S end of the Norwegian W coast. It is the commercial hub of the surrounding area, and has an excellent harbour sheltered by offshore islands. Major elements in the town's economy are an oil refinery, fish-canning factories and, most importantly, its shipyards (construction of oil-rigs). Some 320 km (200 miles) SW of Stavanger are the Norwegian offshore oilfields Tor, Ekofisk and Eldfisk.**

HISTORY. – Stavanger is one of the oldest towns in Norway. From the 12th to the 17th c. it was the see of a bishop, but lost this status to Kristiansand in 1682. Toward the end of the 18th c., the town had its own merchant shipping fleet. A great economic upswing began in the second half of the 19th c., with the growth of the herring and sprat fisheries and the fish-canning industry. In recent years, Stavanger has gained increased importance with the development of the North Sea oil industry.

SIGHTS. – In the middle of the town, at the N end of Kongsgate, stands the *Cathedral, a three-aisled Romanesque pillared basilica built at the end of the 11th c. by Bishop Reinald, also known as Reginald of Winchester (d. 1135). It is the largest cathedral in Norway (after Trondheim). The choir was rebuilt in Gothic style after a fire in 1272, and the entire church was restored in 1867–72. It has a richly carved pulpit (1658) and a stone font of the Gothic period. – S of the Cathedral, on the N shore of the *Breivatn*, is the *Kongsgård*, formerly the Bishop's Palace and now a grammar school (Kongsgård Skole), with the bishop's private chapel (Bispekapellet). To the NW, extending to the inlet of *Vågen*, which contains the harbour, is the *Market Square* (Torget), the scene of lively activity on weekdays, with a bronze statue (Vigrestad) of the Stavanger-born novelist and playwright Alexander Kielland (1849–1906). To the N of the square, between Vågen and the East

Stavanger in winter

Harbour (Østre Havn), lies the *Holmen* peninsula, the oldest part of the town. To the W of the busy Kirkegate, which runs N from the Cathedral, rises the *Valberg Tower* (Valbergtårnet), an old watch-tower which now houses an exhibition of handicrafts (fine view). NE of the Cathedral, in Nytorv, is *St Peter's Church* (Petri Kirke). On the S side of the Breivatn we come to the *railway station*, and beyond this the *Theatre*. Farther beyond, in Muségata, is the **Municipal Museum** (antiquities, natural history, ethnography, ships and the sea). To the SW, in Peder Klows Gata, is the *Vestland School Museum*, and to the W, at No. 33 Madlaveien, the *Art Gallery*.

The finest view of the town, the fjord and the surrounding hills is from the *Valandshaug (85 m (280 ft): reached by way of Hornklovesgate) to the S of the town (park; water-tower).

To the NW of the town, reached by way of Løkkeveien, is the *Bergsted Park*, with a restaurant and a number of fine views.

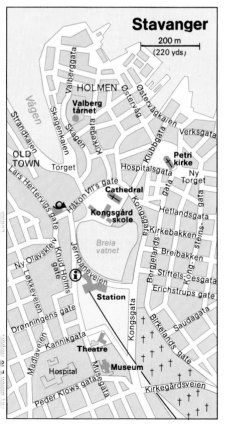

**Stavanger**

200 m
(220 yds)

The "Pulpit", Lysefjord

SURROUNDINGS. – To the W of the town rises the hill of *Byhaugen* (76 m – 250 ft; fine views), extending as far as the Ryfylkefjell to the NE. – 3·5 km (2 miles) SW of the town is the *Ullandhaug* (131 m – 417 ft) with a telecommunications tower (lookout platform) and a plaque commemorating Harald the Fair-Haired's naval victory in 872, which gave him control of the whole country. – 10 km (6 miles) NW of the town, at *Viste*, are the remains of Stone Age troglodytic dwellings.

In the fjord to the N of the town are several islands of varying size. On the little island of **Klosterøy**, which is connected with the larger *Mosterøy* by a bridge, is the Augustinian abbey of *Utstein* (first mentioned in the records in the 13th c.), the best preserved monastic house in Norway. Klosterøy can be reached from Stavanger by motorboat.

To the E of Stavanger, on the far side of the *Høgsford* (pleasant trip by motorboat from the Strandkai), is the *Lysefjord*, a cleft in the mountains 37 km (23 miles) long, 0·5–2 km (550–2200 yds) wide and up to 457 m (1500 ft) deep. The fjord is enclosed on both sides by sheer walls of rock, almost entirely bare of vegetation, rising to 1000 m (3000 ft) or more. The most striking feature is the *"Pulpit"* (*Prekestolen*), 597 m (1960 ft) high, which can be reached from Stavanger by Road 13. 24 km (15 miles) from Stavanger, the road comes to *Lauvvik* on the *Høgsfjord* (ferry to Oanes), and continues on the far side of the fjord to *Jøssang*, where a minor road bears off on the right to the *Prekestol hut*; then, after a climb of about 2 hours, to the Prekestol.

# Stave Churches

**The wooden \*\*stave churches of Norway are the most famous and characteristic achievements of medieval Norwegian architecture. The distinguishing feature of their construction – in contrast to the "log-cabin" technique in which the timber is laid horizontally – is the use of vertical planks or "staves" which are either anchored in the ground or connected to a horizontal base.**

There is evidence of the building of stave churches (Norwegian *stavkirker*) in the 9th c., but their period of greatest popularity was in the 12th and 13th c. – at a time when, together with the advance of Christianity, the technique of building in

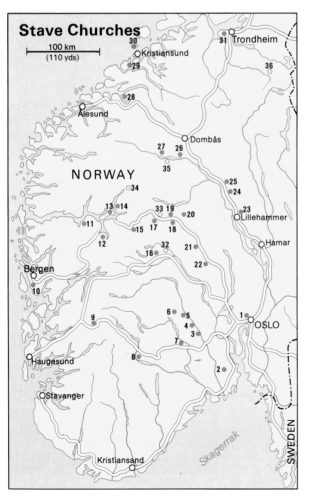

Of the 31 stave churches in Norway which still survive, 27 are on their original site. Four have been taken down and re-erected elsewhere. In addition, one church has been re-erected in Germany.

STAVE CHURCHES
surviving complete or in part

1 Gol (c. 1250: Norwegian Folk Museum, Oslo)
2 Høyjord (?)
3 Flesberg (altered 1731)
4 Rollag (?)
5 Nore (c. 1250)
6 Uvdal (c. 1250)
7 Heddal (c. 1300)
8 Eidsborg (c. 1300)
9 Roldal (c. 1300?)
10 Fortun (early 13th c.: Fantoft, Bergen)
11 Hopperstad (early 13th c.)
12 Undredal (?)
13 Kaupanger (c. 1200)
14 Urnes (c. 1200)
15 Borgund (c. 1250)
16 Torpo (c. 1250)
17 Øye (12th c.; rebuilt in modern times)
18 Lomen (c. 1250)
19 Hurum (c. 1250)
20 Hegge (c. 1250)
21 Reinli (c. 1300)
22 Hedal (c. 1200)
23 Garmo (Maihaugen, Lillehammer)
24 Fåvang (?)
25 Ringebu (?)
26 Vågå (17th c.)
27 Lom (early 13th c.)
28 Rødven (c. 1300?)
29 Kvernes (c. 1300?)
30 Grip (?)
31 Holtålen (c. 1300: Sverresborg, Trondheim)

ORIGINAL SITES

32 Gol (removed 1884: see No. 1)
33 Vang (removed 1840: now at Brückenberg in Silesia)
34 Fortun (removed 1833: see No. 10)
35 Garmo (removed 1885: see No. 23)
36 Holtålen (removed: see No. 31)

stone came to Scandinavia. Romanesque forms now became assimilated into the ancient tradition of timber building, though at first the ornament remained wholly in the Viking tradition, which remained vigorously alive into the 12th c. The fantastic animal and interlace decorative carving which is so striking dates from this period.

This figural decoration began to be regarded as "pagan", however, and it was replaced in the Norman period by the more restrained ornament which had its prototypes in the stone buildings of the period. At the same time, the basilican type of church with a higher nave separated from the lateral aisles by mast-like timber columns appeared alongside the old aisleless plan. The basilican-type church became predominant at a time when the first regular bishops' sees were being established in Norway: before, there had been only itinerant evangelist bishops. The figural decoration grew richer again, and there was a renaissance of the Viking tradition; the pagan ornament of earlier times, however, was replaced by Christian themes showing European influence. This gave rise to the "dragon style". In the 13th c., the St Andrew's cross began to appear in some cases inserted into older churches. Arcading, apses and roof turrets appeared for the first time. Finally, at the Reformation, pews and pulpits began to be provided in churches.

About the year 1300, there are believed to have been more than a thousand stave churches in Norway. When the country was depopulated by plague, most of them fell into disrepair. Between the 17th and 19th c., many churches were demolished because they were too small for growing congregations. As a result, there are only about thirty surviving stave churches, some much altered from their original form. Not until the middle of the 19th c. was there a revival of interest in these old churches, and a movement for their restoration began. Unfortunately the restoration work frequently distorted the original effect: new windows were often inserted, although the old churches had been only dimly lit by small openings high up on the walls.

The surviving stave churches are all in southern Norway, extending N to Trondheim.

# Stockholm

Sweden (Eastern).
Province: Stockholm län.
Regions: Södermanland and Uppland.
Altitude: sea level. – Population: 660,000 (with suburbs 1,300,000).
Postal code: S-11 . . . – Telephone code: 08.

ⓘ **Sveriges Turistråd**
(*Swedish Tourist Board*),
Hamngatan 27, Box 7473,
S-10392 Stockholm;
tel. 7 89 20 00.

**Stockholm Information Service**
Sverigehuset,
Kungsträdgården,
S-10393 Stockholm;
tel. 7 89 20 00.

*Hotellcentralen*, Central Station,
Vasagatan,
S-11120 Stockholm;
tel. 24 08 80.

*Turistbyrån Stadshuset*
(May–September);
tel. 51 21 12.

*Turistbyrån Värtahamnen*,
Silja Lines Terminal
(June–August);
tel. 24 86 10.

*"Miss Tourist"*
(recorded information service in English);
tel. 22 18 40.

**Motormännens Riksförbund**
(*M: National Motorists' Association*),
Sturegatan 32,
S-11436 Stockholm;
tel. 7 82 38 00.

**Kungl. Automobil Klubben**
(*KAK: Royal Automobil Club*),
Sturegaton 32,
S-11436 Stockholm;
tel. 67 05 80.

EMBASSIES. – *United Kingdom*: Skarpögatan 6–8, S-11527 Stockholm (tel. 67 01 40). – *USA*: Strandvägen 101 (tel. 63 05 20). – *Canada*: Tegelbacken 4, 7th floor, S-10323 Stockholm (tel. 23 79 20).

HOTELS (reservations suggested). – AT BRUNKEBERG-STORG: No. 9 *Sergel Plaza*, 795 b., SB. – ON BLASIEHOLMEN: *Grand Hotel*, Södre Blasieholmshamnen 8, 535 b.; *Strand Hotell*, Nybrokajen 9, 199 b. – IN CITY CENTRE: *Lord Nelson*, Västerlånggattan 22, 40 b.; *Reisen*, Skeppsbron 12–14, 197 b., SB, fine view. – IN RIDDARHOLMEN: *Mälardrottningen Hotell*, ship with 65 cabins and 130 berths. – IN NORRMALM: *Sheraton-Stockholm*, Tegelbakken 6, at main station, 920 b.; *Anglais*, Humlegårdsgatan 23, 360 b.; *Continental*, Klara Vattugrånd 4, 430 b.; *Stockholm*, Norrmalmstorg 1, 180 b. – DROTTNINGGATAN: *Frälsningsarméns Hotell Gamla Stan*, Lilla Nygatan 25, 110 b. – VASAGATAN: No. 38 *Central*, 110 b.; No 20 *Terminus*, 230 b.; No. 40 *Vasa Park*, 30 b. IN KUNGSHOLMEN: *Amarantan*, Kungsholmsgatan 31, 702 b., SB; *Kristineberg*, Hjalmar Söderbergsväg 10, 220 b.; *Palace*, St Eriksgatan 115, 400 b. – IN ÖSRERMALM: *Diplomat*, Strandvägen 7C, 207 b.; *Stockholm Plaza*, Birgir Jarlsgatan 29, 233 b.; *Eden*, Sturegatan 10, 80 b.; *Esplanade*, Strandvägen 7A, 44 b.; *Karelia*, Birgir Jarlsgatan 35, 193 b.; *Kung Carl*, Birgir Jarlsgatan 23, 180 b.; *Mornington*, Nybrogatan 53, 223 b.; *Wellington*, Storgatan 6, 73 b. – IN VASASTADEN: *Birgir Jarl*,

Riddarholmen – the old town of Stockholm

Tulegatan 8, 435 b., SB; *Oden*, Karlbergsvägen 24, 270 b. – IN SÖDERMALM: *Aston*, Mariatorget 3, 139 b.; *Malmen*, Götgatan 49–51, 500 b.; *Sjofartshotellet*, Katarinavagen 26, 365 b. – IN SOLNA: *Flamingo*, Hotellgatan 11, 267 b. – IN SUNDBYBERG: *Park-Hotel*, Karlavägen 43, 400 b.

IN BROMMA, (9 km (5 miles) W of the city centre): *Bromma*, Brommaplan 1, 227 b.; *Flyghotellet*, Brommaplan, 136 b. – TO THE S IN ALVSIO: *Royal Starhotel*, Mässvägen, 157 b. – TO THE N IN SOLLENTUNA: *Starhotel Sollentuna*, Aniaraplatsen 8, 820 b., (only suites), SB. – AT ARLANDIA AIRPORT: *SAS Arlandia*, 600 b., SB. – IN THE NE: *Jerum*, Studentbacken 21, 240 b.

YOUTH HOSTELS – in the former sail training ship *af Chapman*, Skeppsholmen, 130 b.; *Hantverkshuset*, Skeppsholmen, 140 b.; *Zinken*, Pipmarkargränd 2, 200 b.

Several CAMP SITES. – Summer chalets can be rented on the small islands or skerries.

RESTAURANTS. – *Berns Salonger*, Näckströmsgatan 8; *Cattelin* (fish specialties), Stora Gråmunkegränd 8; *Cosmopolite*, Sverigehuset, Hamngatan 27; *Den Gyldene Freden*, Österlånggatan 51; *Fem Små Hus*, Nygränd 10; *Maxim*, Drottninggatan 81 B; *Operakällaren* (smörgåsbord), in the Opera House; *Riche*, Birger Jarlsgatan 4; *Stallmästaregården*, in Haga Park; *Stortorgskällaren*, Stortorget 7; *Teatercaféet*, Kulturhuset, Sergels Torg; *Zum Franziskaner* (German specialties), Skeppsbron 44. – DJURGÅRDEN AND SKANSEN: *Alhambra*, *Djurfårdsbrunns Värdshus*, *Hasselbacken*, *Kaknäs Tower* (Balloptikon), *Solliden*. – *Flygrestaurangen & Stekhuset New Orleans*, Bromma Airport.

EVENTS. – *State Opening of Parliament* (11 January); *Walpurgis Night* (30 April); *National Day* (various celebrations: 6 June); *Midsummer celebrations* (21 June); *Bellman Week* (July); *St Eric's International Trade Fair* (August–September); *Nobel Festivities* (December); *St Lucia's Day procession* (13 December).

SPORTS and RECREATION. – Tennis, golf, winter sports, sailing, fishing.

**\*Stockholm, Sweden's capital, lies at the outflow of Lake Mälar into the Baltic, forming a deep inlet dotted with skerries and contributing – along with the omnipresent rocks and water channels encompassing the city – to the beauty of the setting for which Stockholm is famous. The surrounding area, with its abundance of woodland and water, is equally beautiful. Stockholm is the see of a bishop, a university town with several other higher educational establishments and scientific institutes as well as the Nobel Foundation. It is also an important industrial city, particularly in the areas of metal-working, engineering, textiles and the foodstuffs industries. An underground railway system (Tunnelbana or T-bana), begun in 1930 but not intensively developed until the Second World War, links the city with its various suburbs.**

HISTORY. – Stockholm originally grew up on the islands of Staden, Helgeandsholmen and Ryddarholmen, which were fortified by Birger Jarl in 1252 to protect the citizens against the attacks to which they were routinely exposed, especially from the sea. These islands now form the Old Town of Stockholm. Later, the town gradually expanded to the mainland to the N and S. The great days of Stockholm came in the 17th c., when it was the capital of Sweden's Baltic empire. In the 18th and 19th c., several fires destroyed Stockholm's old wooden houses; as a result, the town now consists almost exclusively of substantial stone buildings. The architecture effectively combines old Nordic traditions with modern styles. The new central city around the Hötorg and Sergels Torg, developed since 1950, is a showpiece of contemporary Swedish architecture.

# Museums, Galleries and Other Sights

### Times of Opening

Most museums, etc., are closed on the following public holidays: 1 and 6 January, Good Friday, Easter (two days), 1 May, Ascension (fortieth day after Easter – Holy Thursday), Whitsun (seventh Sunday and Monday after Easter), Midsummer (the Saturday nearest 21 June), All Saints Day (1 November) and Christmas (two days).

For information about special events and changes in opening times, consult the *Museinyckeln* ("Key to Museums") column in the Saturday editions of the newspapers "Dagens Nyheter" and "Svenska Dagbladet"

## CITY

### Army Museum
(*Armémuseum*),
Riddargatan 13;
11 a.m. to 4 p.m. daily; film shows on Sat. and Sun. at 12 noon and 2.30 p.m.

### Berzelius Museum
(*Berzeliusmuseet*),
Roslagsvägen;
only by appointment (tel. 15 04 30).

### Biological Museum
(*Biologiska Museet*),
Djurgården;
April to September, 10 a.m. to 4 p.m. daily; October to March, 10 a.m. to 3 p.m. daily.

### Botanic Garden
(*Bergianska Trädgården*),
Frescati (opposite Natural History Museum);
gardens open all day; hothouses March to October, 1 to 4 p.m., November to February, 1 to 3 p.m., closed on public holidays.

### Brewery Museum (Pripporama)
(*Bryggerimuseet*),
Voltavägen 29, Bromma;
by appointment only (tel. 98 15 00).

### East Asian Museum
(*Östasiatiska Museet*),
Skeppsholmen;
Wed.–Sun. 12 noon to 4 p.m., Tues. 12 noon to 9 p.m.

### Carl Eldh's Studio
(*Eldhs Ateljé Museum*),
Lögebodavägen 10,
Bellevuepark;
May to September, Tues.–Sun. 12 noon to 4 p.m.

### Ethnographic Museum
(*Etnografiska Museet*),
Djurgårdsbrunnsvägen 34.
Tues. – Fri. 11 a.m. to 4 p.m., Sat. and Sun. 12 noon to 4 p.m.

### Gröna Lund
(*Amusement park*)
Djursgården;
June–August weekdays 2 p.m. to midnight, Sun. 12 noon to midnight; September to May, Tues.–Fri.

7 p.m. to midnight, Sat. 2 p.m. to midnight, Sun. 12 noon to midnight.

### Gustav III's Pavilion
(*Gustav IIIs Paviljong*),
Haga;
May to August, Tues.–Sun. conducted tours at 12 noon to 3 p.m. September, Sat. and Sun. 1 to 3 p.m.

### Gustavsberg Museum (Ceramics)
(*Gustavsbergs Museum, Keramiskt Centrum*);
May to September, Mon.–Fri. 10 a.m. to 3 p.m., Sat. 11 a.m. to 2 p.m.; otherwise by appointment (tel. 0766/3 91 00).

### Hallwyl Museum
(*Hallwylska Museet*),
Hamngatan 4 (near Norrmalmstorg) –
Tues.–Sun. 12 noon to 2 or 3 p.m.

### Historical Museum
(*Historiska Museet*),
Narvavägen;
Tues.–Sun. 11 a.m. to 4 p.m.

### House of Culture
(*Kulturhuset*),
Sergels Torg 3;
daily 10 a.m. to 6 p.m.; for information about exhibitions and concerts tel. 14 11 20.

### Kaknäs Tower
(*Kaknästornet*),
N. Djurgården;
May to August, daily 9 a.m. to midnight; April and September, daily 9 a.m. to 10 p.m.; October to March, daily 9 a.m. to 6 p.m.

### Liljevalch Art Gallery
(*Liljevalchs Konsthall*),
Djurgårdsvägen 60;
Tues.–Sun. 11 a.m. to 5 p.m., Tues and Thurs. until 9 p.m.

### Mediterranean Museum
(*Medelhavsmuseet*),
Fredsgatan 2;
Wed.–Sun. 10 a.m. to 5 p.m., Tues. 11 a.m. to 9 p.m.

### Millesgården,
Lidingö;
May to 15 October, daily 10 a.m. to 5 p.m.; June and July, Tues. and Thurs. 7 to 9 p.m. also.

### Modern Museum
(*Moderna Museet*),
Fredsgatan 2,
Skeppsholmen;
Tues.–Fri. 11 a.m. to 9 p.m., Sat. and Sun. 11 a.m. to 5 p.m.

### Municipal Museum
(*Stadsmuseum*),
Slussen, in Old Town Hall;
June to August, Fri.–Mon. 11 a.m. to 5 p.m., Tues.–Thurs. 11 a.m. to 7 p.m.; September to May, Fri.–Mon. 11 a.m. to 5 p.m., Tues.–Thurs. 11 a.m. to 9 p.m.

### Museum of Architecture
(*Sveriges Arkitekturmuseum*),
Skeppsholmen;
Mon.–Fri. 9 a.m. to 5 p.m., closed July and August.

### Museum of Maritime History
(*Sjöhistoriska Museet*),
Djurgårdsbrunnsvägen;
10 a.m. to 5 p.m. daily; in winter, Tues. 6 to 8.30 p.m. also.

**Museum of Photography**
(*Fotografiska Museet*),
Skeppsholmen (W wing of Modern Museum);
Tues.–Fri. 11 a.m. to 9 p.m., Sat. and Sun. 11 a.m. to
5 p.m.

**Museum of Technology and Telemuseum**
(*Tekniska Museet med Telemuseum*),
N. Djurgården, Museivägen 7;
weekdays 10 a.m. to 4 p.m. Sat. and Sun. 12 noon to
4 p.m.

**Museum of the Dance**
(*Dansmuseet*),
Laboratoriegatan 10
(near Strandvägen 76);
Tues.–Sun. 12 noon to 4 p.m.

**Music Museum,**
(*Musikmuseet*),
Sibyllegatan 2;
Tues.–Sun. 11 a.m. to 4 p.m.

**National Museum,**
Södra Blasieholmshamnen;
Wed.–Sun. 10 a.m. to 4 p.m., Tues. 10 a.m. to 9 p.m.

**Natural History Museum**
(*Naturhistoriska Riksmuseet*),
Frescati;
weekdays 10 a.m. to 4 p.m., Sundays and public
holidays 11 a.m. to 5 p.m.

**Nordic Museum**
(*Nordiska Museet*),
Djurgården;
Mon.–Fri. 10 a.m. to 4 p.m., Sat. and Sun. 12 noon to
5 p.m.; September to May, Tues., Wed., Fri. 10 a.m. to
4 p.m., Thurs. 10 a.m. to 8 p.m., Sat. and Sun. 12 noon
to 5 p.m.

**Postal Museum,**
Lille Nygatan 6;
Mon.–Sat. 12 noon to 3 p.m., Sun. 12 noon to 4 p.m.,
Thurs. also 7 to 9 p.m.

**Riddarholm Church**
(*Riddarholmskyrkan*);
May to August, weekdays 10 a.m. to 3 p.m., Sun. 1 to
3 p.m.

**Riddarhuset,**
Riddarhustorget;
conducted tours daily 11.30 a.m. to 12.30 p.m.

**Rosendal House**
(*Rosendalsslott*),
Djurgården;
June to August, conducted tours Tues.–Sat. at 12
noon, 1, 2 and 3 p.m., Sun. at 1, 2 and 3 p.m.;
September, Sat. and Sun. at 1, 2 and 3 p.m.

**Royal Armoury**
(*Kungl. Livrustkammaren*),
Royal Palace;
10 a.m. to 4 p.m. daily, September to April, closed on
Mon.

**Royal Coin Cabinet**
(*Kungl. Myntkabinettet*),
Narvavägen 13–17
(in Historical Museum);
Tues.–Sun. 11 a.m. to 4 p.m. daily.

**Royal Library**
(*Kungl. Biblioteket*),
Humlegården;
Mon.–Thurs. 8.45 a.m. to 10 p.m., Fri. and Sat. 8.45
a.m. to 6 p.m., Sun. 11 a.m. to 5 p.m.; Midsummer (21
June) to 20 August, Mon.–Thurs. 8.45 a.m. to 8 p.m.,
Fri. 8.45 a.m. to 6 p.m., Sat. 8.45 a.m. to 2 p.m.

**Royal Palace**
(*Stockholms Slott*):
*State Apartments, Bernadotte Rooms and Guest
Rooms,* when not in use: May to August, Tues.–Sat.
10 a.m. to 3 p.m., Sun. 12 noon to 3 p.m.; September
to April, Tues.–Sun. 12 noon to 3 p.m.
*Treasury:* 2 May to 15 September, weekdays 10 a.m.
to 4 p.m., Sun. 12 noon to 4 p.m.; 16 September to 30
April, weekdays 11 a.m. to 3 p.m., Sun. and public
holidays 12 noon to 4 p.m.
*Hall of Estates and Chapel:* 2 May to 30 September,
daily 12 noon to 3 p.m.; 1 October to 1 November,
Sat. and Sun. 12 noon to 3 p.m.
*Palace Museum:* 1 June to 31 August, daily 12 noon
to 3 p.m.
*Gustav III's Museum of Antiquities:* 1 June to 31
August, daily 12 noon to 3 p.m.
See also *Royal Stables.*

**Royal Stables**
(*Kungl. Hovstallet*),
Väpnargatan 1;
Sun. 1 to 3 p.m.; closed July to August.

**Skansen Open-Air Museum,**
Djurgården;
park (including elephant house, aquarium, fun-fair
and glassworks) May to August daily 8 a.m. to 11.30
p.m.; April and September daily 8 a.m. to 8 p.m.;
October to March daily 8 a.m. to 6 p.m.; interesting
historical buildings (craftsmen and women at work) in
summer 11 a.m. to 5 p.m.

**Strindberg Museum (Blå Tornet),**
Drottninggatan 85;
Tues.–Sat. 10 a.m. to 4 p.m., Tues. also 7 to 9 p.m.,
Sun. 12 noon to 5 p.m.

**Thiel Gallery**
(*Thielska Galleriet*),
Djurgården;
weekdays 12 noon to 4 p.m., Sun. 1 to 4 p.m.

**Tobacco Museum**
(*Tobaksmuseet*),
Gubbhyllan, Skansen;
1 June to 31 August, daily 11 a.m. to 5 p.m.;
1 September to 31 May, daily 11 a.m. to 3 p.m.

Detail from the Swedish coat of arms on the "Wasa"

**Town Hall**
(*Stadshuset*),
Hantverkargatan 1;
conducted tours (English-speaking guides) week-
days at 10 a.m., Sundays 10 a.m. and 12 noon.
*Tower:* 1 May to 30 September, 11 a.m. to 3 p.m. daily.

**Tramway Museum**
(*Spårvägsmuseet*),
Odenplan Underground station;
May to September, Mon.–Fri. 10 a.m. to 5 p.m.,
October to April, Mon.–Sat. 10 a.m. to 5 p.m.

**Waldemarsudde**,
Djurgården;
Tues.–Sun. 11 a.m. to 4 p.m., in summer 11 a.m. to 5
p.m., June to August also Tues. and Thurs. 7 to 9 p.m.

**Wasa Museum**,
Djurgården;
"*Wasa*" (Royal flagship): in summer, 9.30 a.m. to 7
p.m. daily; in winter, 10 a.m. to 5 p.m. daily.
*Lightship "Finngrundet":* throughout the year, Sun.
12 noon to 5 p.m.

**Wine and Spirits Museum**
(*Vin- och Sprithistoriska Museet*),
AB Vin- & Spritcentralen,
St Eriksgatan 119;
Tues.–Fri. 10 a.m. to 3 p.m., in winter conducted tours
on Sun. at 1 and 2.30 p.m.

### SURROUNDINGS

**Chinese Pavilion**
(*Kina Slott*),
Park, Drottningholm;
May to August, weekdays 11 a.m. to 4.30 p.m., Sun.
and public holidays 12 noon to 4.30 p.m.; April,
September and October, 1 to 3.30 p.m. daily.

**Drottningholm Palace**
(*Drottningholms Slott*),
May to August, weekdays 11 a.m. to 4.30 p.m., Sun.
and public holidays 12 noon to 4.30 p.m.; September,
1 to 3.30 p.m. daily.

**Drottningholm Palace Theatre and Palace
Museum**
(*Drottningholms Slottsteater och Teatermuseum*);
May to August, weekdays 11 a.m. to 4.30 p.m., Sun.
12 noon to 4.30 p.m.; September, 12.30 to 3 p.m.
daily. Conducted tours (in English and other languages) half hourly during the season.

**Gripsholm Castle**
(*Gripsholms Slott*),
Mariefred;
15 May to 31 August, 10 a.m. to 4 p.m. daily.

**Rosersberg Castle**
(*Rosersbergs Slott*);
15 May to 15 September, Wed. and Thurs. 11 a.m. to 3
p.m., Sun. 12 noon to 3 p.m.; closed in July.

**Sturehov Manor-House**,
Botkyrka, Lake Mälar;
Sun. 1 to 4 p.m.

**Svindersvik Manor-House**,
Nacka;
15 May to 15 September, Sun. 1 to 4 p.m., conducted
tours on the hour.

**Tullgarn Castle**
(*Tullgarns Slott*),
Vagnhärad;
15 May to 15 September, conducted tours on
weekdays 11 a.m. to 4 p.m., on the hour; half-hourly
on Sun. and public holidays.

**Vaxholm Castle Museum**
(*Vaxholms Fästnings Museum*);
15 May to 31 August, 12 noon to 4 p.m.

# Sightseeing in Stockholm

HELGEANDSHOLMEN, one of the three
islands on which the first settlement
developed, is reached by way of the
*Norrbro*. The E end of the island is
occupied by a small park, *Strömparterren*,
with a summer café. To the W is the old
*Parliament Building* (1898–1904), in
High Renaissance style, with the *Riksbank* (Swedish National Bank) beyond it.

The Norrbro leads on to the island of
STADEN; the main part of the old town
(Gamla Staden) is here. Straight ahead is
the *Royal Palace, a Renaissance-style
building designed by Tessin the Younger
(d. 1728) and completed by his son, K. G.
Tessin. The palace occupies the site of an
earlier Vasa castle (destroyed by fire in
1697).

The INTERIOR is decorated in Baroque and Rococo
style. On the first floor are the apartments occupied by
King Oskar II (d. 1907), the "Bernadotte Rooms"; on
the second floor the State Apartments and the Guest-
Rooms; in the S wing the Chapel and the great Hall of
Estates. The *Museum of Antiquities* and the *Treasury*,
with the royal regalia, are open to the public.

Beyond the Palace, to the SW, stands the
**Cathedral** (*Storkyrka*), as old as Staden
itself. Consecrated in 1306, its construction took almost another 200 years,
and between 1736 and 1743 it was
remodelled in Baroque style. Here the
kings and queens of Sweden are married
and crowned. Near the altar (reredos of
silver and ivory, *c.* 1640) is a large Gothic
**sculpture in polychrome wood of St
George and the dragon by the Lübeck
sculptor Bernt Notke (d. 1509). It was
presented by Sten Sture, Regent of
Sweden, after the victory over the Danes
in the battle of Brunkeberg (1471). The
massive organ is 18th c.

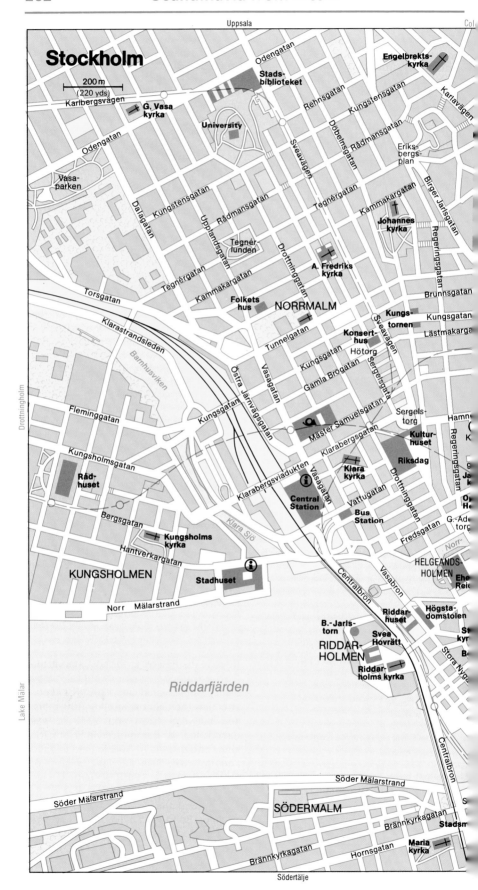

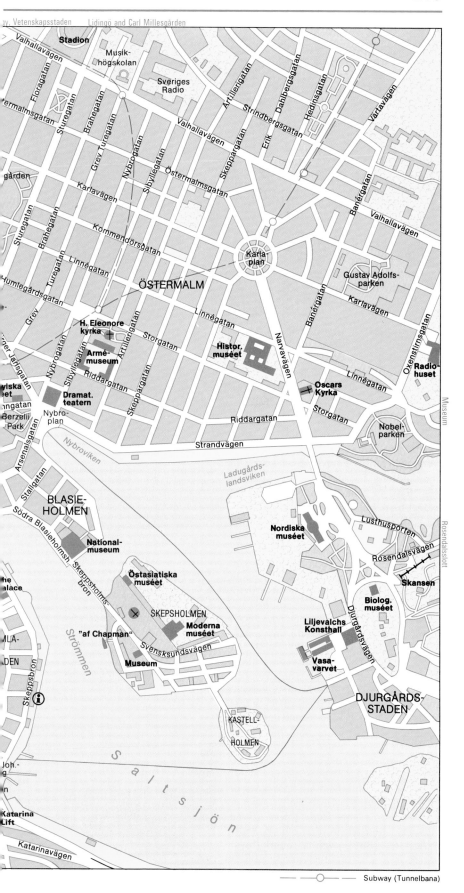

ıy. Vetenskapsstaden     Lidingö and Carl Millesgården

Valhallavägen

Stadion

Musík-
högskolan

Sveriges
Radio

Floragatan

Sturegatan

Braheg atan

rmalmsgatan

Grev Turegatan

Nybrogatan

Valhallavägen

Skeppargatan

Artillerigatan

Strindbergsgatan

Erik

Dahlbergsgatan

Hedinsgatan

Värtavägen

gården

Karlavägen

Sibyllegatan

Östermalmsgatan

Barférgatan

Valhallavägen

Sturegatan

Braheg atan

Turegatan

Linnégatan

Kommendörsgatan

ÖSTERMALM

Karla-
plan

Gustav Adolfs-
parken

Karlavägen

Banérgatan

Humlegårdsgatan

Grev

Linnégatan

Linnégatan

Nybrogatan

Sibyllegatan

Artillerigatan

Storgatan

Narvavägen

Oxenstlrnsgatan

Radio-
huset

Linnégatan

ner Jahsgatan

H. Eleonore
kyrka

Armé-
museum

Riddargatan

Skeppargatan

Histor,
muséet

Oscars
Kyrka

Storgatan

yiska
eet

nngatan

Berzelii
Park

Dramat.
teatern

Nybro-
plan

Riddargatan

Nobel-
parken

Arsenalsgatan

Nybroviken

Strandvägen

Ladugårds-
landsviken

Museum

Stallgatan

BLASIE-
HOLMEN

Lusthusporten

Rosendalsslott

Södra Blasieholmsh.

Skeppsholms-

Nordiska
muséet

Rosendalsvägen

National-
museum

Skansen

he
alace

Östasiatiska
muséet

Biolog.
muséet

MLA-

Strömmen

Skeppsbron

"af Chapman"

×

SKEPSHOLMEN

Moderna
muséet

Svensksundsvägen

Museum

Liljevalchs
Konsthall

Djurgårdsvägen

Vasa-
varvet

DJURGÅRDS-
STADEN

DEN

Joh.-
g

ⓘ

KASTELL-

HOLMEN

Katarina
Lift

S  a  l  t  s  j  ö  n

Katarinavägen

———  ———O———  —  Subway (Tunnelbana)

To the S of the church is the *Stortorg*, a square surrounded by 17th and 18th c. buildings. One of the finest of these is the *Exchange* (Börsen: by Erik Palmstedt, 1778), now occupied by the Swedish Academy and the Nobel Library. In 1520, the Stortorg was the scene of the "Stockholm Bloodbath", when Christian II of Denmark executed 82 leading Swedes in order to strengthen his hold on the country. SE of the Stortorg is the *German Church (Tyska Kyrkan*: St Gertrude's), which, more than any other church in the city, preserves the character and style of the 17th c. It has a richly gilded altar, an outstanding ebony and alabaster pulpit by Tessin the Elder, a royal pew and an organ presented to the church in 1971 by the German community (the oldest German congregation outside of Germany). To the E of the church, in Österlånggatan, is an interesting old restaurant established in 1721, *Den Gyldene Freden* ("Golden Peace"). It has associations with the Stockholm poet of the Baroque period, Carl Michael Bellman, among whose best known songs is "Fredmans Epistel".

To the W of the German Church, Västerlånggatan runs S, lined by small shops, to the Järntorg. The old *Riksbank* building (*c.* 1670) is believed to be one of the oldest bank buildings in the world. – At the NW corner of Staden is the *Riddarhustorg*, with a *monument to Gustavus Vasa*. On the N side of the square, in the *Old Town Hall* (Bondeska Palatset, 17th c.), is the *Supreme Court* (Högsta Domstolen). Here, too, is the *Knights' House (Riddarhuset)*, in a Baroque style which shows Dutch influence (by Justus Vingboons and Simon de la Vallée, 1641–74). The Knights' Hall, with the coats of arms of all the Swedish noble families, was, until 1866, the meeting-place of the Estate of the Nobility. – From the W side of Riddarhustorg, a bridge leads on to the little island of RIDDARHOLMEN. In Birger Jarlstorg stands a column bearing a *statue of Birger Jarl*, the founder of Stockholm, and also the 15th c. *Birger Jarl's Tower* (Birger Jarlstorn), from which there are fine views of Lake Mälar and the Town Hall. – Also in the square is the *High Court* (Svea Hovrätt), housed in the old *Wrangel Palace* (*c.* 1650), with a round tower which is a relic of Stockholm's earliest fortifications. On the S side of the square

stands the *Riddarholm Church (Riddarholmskyrkan*), originally belonging to a Franciscan friary but extensively altered in later centuries. The cast-iron steeple (1841), 90 m (295 ft) high, is a prominent landmark. Since 1807, the church has been used for funerals and memorial services only; it is the burial-place of Swedish monarchs.

## Riddarholm Church     Stockholm

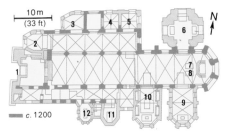

| | |
|---|---|
| 1   W entrance | 8   Tomb of Karl Knutsson (d. |
| 2   Torstensson Chapel (1651) |     1470) |
| 3   Wachtmeister Chapel (1654) | 9   Gustav II Adolf's Chapel |
| 4, 5 Lewenhaupt Chapels (1654) |     (1633–4) |
| 6   Caroline Chapel | 10 Bernadotte Chapel |
|     (1671–1743) |     (1858–60) |
| 7   Tomb of Magnus Ladulås | 11 Vasaborg Chapel (1647) |
|     (d. 1290) | 12 Baner Chapel (1636) |

INTERIOR. – The walls are covered with the coats of arms of knights of the Order of the Seraphim, founded in 1336. The floor is covered with gravestones. – In the choir, in front of the high altar (1679), are the tombs of Kings *Magnus Ladulås* (d. 1290) and *Karl Knutsson* (d. 1470). To the right is the funerary chapel of *Gustavus Adolphus* (Gustavianska Gravkoret) with a green marble sarcophagus. He was killed in the battle of Lützen in 1632. Opposite, the Caroline Chapel (Karolinska Gravkoret, 1671–1743) contains the tombs of *Charles XII* (d. 1718) and *Frederik I* (d. 1751). Adjoining Gustavus Adolphus's chapel is the Bernadotte Chapel (Bernadotteska Gravkoret), with the massive red porphyry sarcophagus (middle, rear) of *Karl XIV Johan* (d. 1844) and in front of it, the sarcophagus of his wife, *Desideria* (d. 1860); other tombs in this chapel include that of *Gustav V* (1858–1950). – In the S aisle are the chapels of the *Counts of Vasaborg* and the Swedish field marshal, *Johan Banér* (d. 1641). – In the N aisle to the left of the entrance, are the chapel of the *Counts of Torstensson*,

Opera House, Stockholm

the chapel of General *Wachtmeister* (d. 1652) and the two chapels of the *Counts Lewenhaupt.*

To the N of Staden lies the large district of NORRMALM, reached via the Noorbro. Immediately over the bridge is Gustav Adolfstorg (equestrian statue of Gustavus Adolphus, 1796). The *Crown Prince's Palace* (1783) on the left has been occupied since 1906 by the Foreign Ministry. On the right, with a view of Strömmen, is the **Opera House**, and, beyond this, *St James's Church* (Jakobskyrka, 1643; tower 1735). To the N extends a series of public gardens, with *Kungsträdgården* and *statues of Charles XII* and, pointing to the E, Charles XIII.

SE of Gustav Adolfstorg, at the southern tip of the peninsula of BLASIEHOLMEN, is the *National Museum*, with Sweden's finest art collection, including not only pictures and sculpture but graphic and applied art.

The *picture gallery contains works by Dutch masters, including major works by **Rembrandt ("Conspiracy of Claudius Civilis", his largest picture after the "Night Watch", and "The Painter's Cook"), *Rubens ("Bacchanale" and "Sacrifice to Venus") and *Frans Hals the Elder ("Fiddler"). Also included are many works by 18th c. French painters, a collection equalled only in Paris and London (including *Boucher's "Triumph of Venus"); and modern Swedish painting, including fine works by D. K. Ehrenstrahl, Alexander Roslin, Carl Larsson, Bruno Liljefors, Anders Zorn and Prince Eugen.

In the gardens, NW of the museum, is a bronze group, *"The Wrestlers"* ("Bältespännare", 1867), depicting an old Nordic form of wrestling in which the contestants were bound together at the waist.

To the S of the National Museum a bridge leads to the attractive island of SKEPPSHOLMEN, formerly occupied by the Swedish navy, where are to be found the *Skeppsholm Church* (1842), the *East Asian Museum* (Far Eastern art) and the *Modern Museum* (20th c. art), with a Museum of Photography. Moored on the W side of the island is the *sail training ship* "Chapman", now a youth hostel (closed in winter).

Along the N end of Kungsträdgården runs *Hamngatan*, now regarded as Stockholm's main street. There are magnificent views of the city from the rooftop restaurant of the *NK (Nordiska Kompaniet) department store*. At No. 4 Hamngatan is the *Hallwyl Palace*,

Klarakyrka and tower blocks in the Hötorg

with a façade showing Spanish inspiration and an interior in *fin de siècle* style; it is now a museum, and is also used for theatrical performances. In *Berzelius Park*, named after the famous chemist, J. Berzelius, is a popular restaurant, *Berns Salonger* famous for its food and its musical performances. In Nybroplan stands the **Royal Dramatic Theatre** (*Kungl. Dramatiska Teatern*), opened in 1907.

At the W end of Hamngatan is Stockholm's new central feature, *Sergels Torg*, with a tall modern *fountain* and the **House of Culture** (*Kulturhuset:* by P. Celsing, 1974), containing a congress centre; a library, reading rooms and a theatre. *Sergelsgatan*, a pedestrians-only street with numerous shops and an underground market hall, runs to the *Hötorg*; a market is held here each summer. On the W side of the square is the *Concert Hall* (Konserthus, 1962), home of the Stockholm Philharmonic Orchestra, in which the presentation of the Nobel Prizes takes place. In front of it stands the *Orpheus Fountain* by Carl Milles (1936). – Kungsgatan, to the N, one of Stockholm's principal shopping streets, has the *PUB department store* and the *Kungstornen* ("King's Towers"), two 17-storey buildings. The broad Sveaväg runs NW from the Concert Hall, passing on the left the *Adolf Frederikskyrka* (1774), which contains sculpture by J. T. Sergel (d. 1814) and a monument to the French philosopher Descartes, who died in Stockholm in 1650 (his remains were taken to Paris in 1666). Toward the far end of the street are the *Commercial College* and the *Municipal Library* (Stadsbiblioteket), and, at the end, the *Wenner-Gren Research Centre* (1961). From the Library Karlbergsvägen runs E to *Karlberg Castle* (17th c.), now a military academy, on the lake of the same name.

Stockholm Town Hall

Parallel to Sveavägen is Drottninggatan, another busy shopping street. At No. 85, once the home of the dramatist August Strindberg (1849–1912), is the *Strindberg Museum*. At the N end of the street are the main buildings of the **University**, founded in 1878. To the W stands the **Klarakyrka**, with a spire 104 m (340 ft) high; in the churchyard is the grave of the 18th c. poet, *C. M. Bellman*. Beyond this is the **Central Station** (with a Model Railway Museum).

On KUNGSHOLMEN (King's Island), separated from the rest of the town by a narrow channel, is the *Town Hall (Stadshuset)*, the great landmark and emblem of Stockholm. At the SE corner of the building (Ragnar Östberg, 1911–23) is a square tower crowned by a lantern, on the tip of which (106 m – 350 ft) are the three golden crowns of the Swedish coat of arms. From the platform under the bell-cote (elevator three-quarters of the way up), there is a superb *view. On the N wall is a mobile sculpture of St George and the dragon. The carillon in the tower plays twice daily in summer, at noon and 6 p.m. Under a pillared canopy at the foot of the S side of the tower is a recumbent figure (G. Sandberg) of Birger Jarl, founder of Stockholm. The Town Hall contains offices and reception rooms, including the Blue Hall, a covered inner courtyard with a colonnade, the large Council Chamber and the Golden Hall, with magnificent mosaics.

A little W of the Town Hall, in Hantverkargatan, is the 17th c. *Kungsholm Church*. NW of the church, in Scheelegatan, is the **Rådhus** (Law Courts; C. Westmann, 1911–15), and beyond it the *Police Headquarters*.

The ÖSTERMALM district, to the E, is bounded on the W by Birger Jarlsgatan

and on the S by the inlet of *Nybrovik*. Along the waterfront runs one of Stockholm's finest streets, *Strandvägen*, with a number of embassies. The *Army Museum* in Riddargatan contains a large collection of uniforms and weapons. Nearby, in the park of *Humlegården*, is the **Royal Library** (built 1870–7, with later extensions), Sweden's National Library. Among other rarities, it possesses the *Codex Aureus*, an 8th c. Latin translation of the four Gospels. – On the E side of the park, at No. 14 Sturegatan, is the *Nobel Foundation*, established by the Swedish chemist Alfred Nobel, in 1900, which annually awards five prizes for outstanding achievement in physics, chemistry, medicine, literature and the cause of peace. – In Karlavägen is the *Engelbrektskyrka*, a granite and red-brick building (Lars Israel Wahlman, 1914). To the E, in Valhallavägen, we find the *Stadium*, a wooden structure built for the 1912 Olympic Games. To the N is the **College of Technology**.

In the southern part of Östermalm the *National Historical Museum (Historiska Museet)* occupies a building which also houses the *Royal Coin Cabinet*. Nearby are the headquarters of Swedish radio and television (*Radiohuset*), and a short distance away, in Borgvägen, is the *Swedish Film Institute*. – In Djurgårdsbrunnsvägen, the continuation of Strandvägen to the E, are the *Museum of Maritime History*, the *Museum of Technology* and the *National Ethnographic Museum*. To the NE rises the **Kaknäs Tower**, 155 m (510 ft) high, with a restaurant and lookout platform.

Very characteristic of Stockholm is the southern district of SÖDERMALM with its picturesque setting and street layout adapted to the rocky terrain. It is reached from the old town (Staden) by a double bridge over the *Söderström*. At this point there is a sluice (Slussen) separating the fresh water of Lake Mälar from the salt water of the Baltic. In Södermalmstorg (on left) is the *Katarinahiss*, an elevator leading up to a restaurant (alt. 36 m – 120 ft) from which there are beautiful *views of the old town and the northern districts of the city. From the viewing platform an iron gangway leads to Mosebacketorget.

The *Old Town Hall* (17th c.), on the S side of Södermalmstorg, now houses the **Municipal Museum** (*Stadsmuseet*). To the S, in Medborgarplatsen, is the *Medborgarhus* (Community House, 1939), used for a variety of purposes. In Hornsgatan stands *St Mary's Church* (Mariakyrka), a 16th–17th c. building (steeple added in 1825). A little W the tree-shaded Adolf Frederikstorg has a fountain sculpture by Wissler, "Thor with the Midgard Snake".

DJURGÅRDEN. – On an island, reached from Strandvägen over the *Djurgårdsbro*, is *Djurgården, a park laid out on the site of an earlier deer-park. This was a royal hunting preserve from the 16th to the 18th c. – At the far end of the bridge, on the right, is the *Nordic Museum (*Nordiska Museet*), illustrating the life of Sweden over the centuries. The *Royal Armoury* on the ground floor displays the way of life of the privileged classes; there are other sections devoted to peasant life, arranged according to the various Swedish provinces, and to the culture of the Lapps. – To the S of the Nordic Museum, in a wooden building styled after the Norwegian stave churches, is the *Biological Museum* (birds and mammals of Scandinavia). – A short distance away is *Liljevalchs Konsthall*, an art gallery which from time to time mounts special exhibitions.

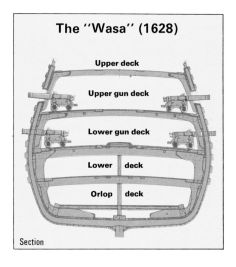

**The "Wasa" (1628)**

Upper deck

Upper gun deck

Lower gun deck

Lower    deck

Orlop    deck

Section

At the W end of the island (also accessible from the city by boat) is the **Wasa Museum** (*Vasavarvet*), which houses the "Wasa", the royal flagship which sank on its maiden voyage in 1628 and was brought to the surface in 1961.

The "Wasa" was located on the seabed in 1956, lying at a depth of 32 m (105 ft), and the process of recovering and preserving it began three years later.

This was a large-scale operation for which entirely new techniques had to be devised, and a special dry dock had to be built to house the vessel, which is 62 m (200 ft) long. Reconstruction work is now almost complete. Numerous finds from the ship – furniture, everyday objects, coins, carved ornaments, etc. – are displayed in a special exhibition.

The *Skansen Open-Air Museum* (established 1891), extends over a large area to the E. The founder and initiator of Skansen was Artur Hazelius, who wished to save something of the older Sweden before the development of industry had irreversibly changed the country. The old buildings brought together here include a church and a manor-house, Lapp dwellings and an upland shieling (summer dairy farm), smallholders' cottages and peasant farmhouses, and a whole quarter of a town with craftsmen's workshops. Over the years, 150 old buildings have been assembled at Skansen, which is now ten times larger than it was when it was first established. In the various houses and workshops, visitors can see butter and cheese making, baking, weaving, basketwork, printing, wood-turning and glass-blowing.

But Skansen is a **Zoological Garden** as well as a museum of cultural history. Its spacious grounds contain specimens of the various animals that live in Sweden, with goats, hill cattle, etc., in their appropriate setting, with separate enclosures for brown and polar bears, bison, elks and reindeer. There are also non-Scandinavian animals, including monkeys, elephants, sealions and penguins, and many smaller animals and birds live wild. The zoo is open throughout the year. – To the N of the park is the *Bredablick lookout tower*, to the S the *Solliden restaurant* (fine view). Here concerts, displays of folk dancing and theatrical performances are given daily in summer.

To the E of Skansen is *Rosendal Castle*, built by King Karl XIV in 1823–7 and since 1913 a Karl Johan Museum, furnished in the style of the period. – On the opposite side of the island the promontory of *Waldemarsudde* was formerly the residence of the royal painter, Prince Eugen (1865–1947) and has a fine collection of pictures. – At the E end of Djurgården is the *Thiel Gallery* (mainly 19th and 20th c. Swedish pictures). – Nearby stands a monument of industrial archaeology, an old *oil-mill* (1785).

On the N side of Stockholm is the district of VETENSKAPSSTADEN ("City of Learning"), in which are the Royal Academy of Sciences and the *National

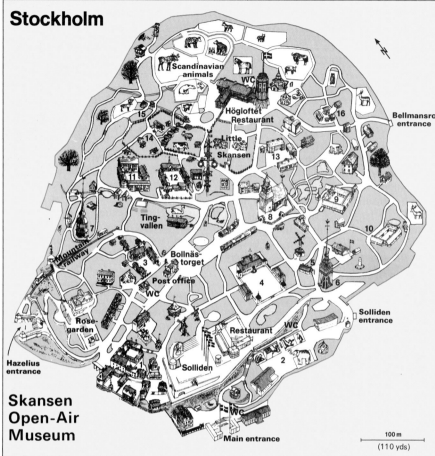

# Stockholm

Scandinavian animals

WC

Högloftet Restaurant

Little Skansen

Bellmansro entrance

Mountain railway

Ting-vallen

Bollnäs-torget

Post office

WC

Rose-garden

Restaurant          WC

Solliden entrance

Hazelius entrance

Solliden

Main entrance

WC

# Skansen Open-Air Museum

100 m
(110 yds)

1  Town buildings (17th–19th c.)
2  Non-Scandinavian animals
3  Älvrosgården (farmhouse from Mora, 16th–17th c.)
4  Skogaholms Herrgård (manor-house from Närke, c. 1680, reconstructed 1793–94)
5  Agricultural worker's (1920)
6  Belfry from Östergötland (1732)
7  Belfry from Eastern Jämtland (1778–9)
8  Seglora church, from Västergötland (1729–30; tower 1780)
9  Oktorpsgården (farmhouse from Halland, 18th c.)

10  Skånegården (farmhouse from Skåne)
11  Delsbogården (farmhouse from Hälsingland, 18th–19th c.)
12  Moragården (farmhouse from Dalarna, 16th–17th c.)
13  Miner's house from Västmanland (17th c.)
14  Peasants' houses from upland Dalarna (17th–18th c.)
15  Lapp camp
16  Finngården (peasants' houses from Lekvattnet, Värmland, 16th–17th c.)

---

*History Museum* (Naturhistoriska Riksmuseet), with an outstanding collection. – To the NE, in the villa suburb of **Lidingö** on the island of the same name, is *Millesgården, the former home and studio of the Swedish sculptor Carl Milles (1875–1955), with an open-air museum of works by Milles and others by foreign sculptors.

SURROUNDINGS. – 11 km (7 miles) W of the middle of the city (45 minutes by boat), on the island of Lovö, stands **Drottningholm Palace**, now the residence of the royal family. The palace, based on French and Dutch models, was built for Queen Eleonora in 1662 by Nicodemus Tessin the Elder. It contains pictures by David Klöker Ehrenstrahl and Johan Philip

Lempke and sculpture by Nicolaes Millich and Burchardt Precht. In the beautiful park, laid out with terraces and avenues of lime-trees, are bronze sculptures brought from Denmark and Bohemia as

Drottningholm Palace

war trophies. In 1744, Queen Luise Ulrike, a sister of Frederick the Great, was given Drottningholm as a wedding present, and new wings were added by Carl Hårleman and Carl Fredrik Adelcrantz, with rooms decorated in French Rococo style; one of the finest of these is the Library. Adelcrantz was also responsible for the *Theatre* (added in 1766), now frequently used for performances, with stage machinery from the time of Gustav III; 18th c. scenery and costumes are displayed in the theatre museum. The *Chinese Pavilion* (1766) in the park was also built for Queen Luise Ulrike as a summer residence; the interior is a mingling of French Rococo and Chinese elements. Nearby is the little settlement of "Canton" (1750–60), built to house the craftsmen making furniture and carpets for the Chinese Pavilion.

28 km (18 miles) W of Stockholm, in Lake Mälar, lies the little island of *Björkö (Birch Island). During the Viking period Björkö was a trading station with a population in the 10th c. of several thousand – merchants, craftsmen, peasants and slaves. Here, too, about 830, St Ansgar preached the Gospel. Excavation has revealed much about the life of the period (remains of houses, implements and domestic equipment, hearths, etc.). Outside the area of the settlement is a *cemetery* with about 2500 graves, the largest in Sweden. Björkö's extensive trading connections were indicated by finds of silver coins from Arabia, silk from China, pottery from Friesland and glass from France. The whole site is now protected as a national monument. Nearby is *St Ansgar's Chapel*, consecrated in 1930. – During the summer there are regular boat services from Stockholm and Södertälje to Björkö.

**Södertälje** (pop. 60,000; Scandic Hotel, 289 b., SP; Hotel Skogshöld, 370 b., SP.), now an industrial town, developed from a Viking trading station set between Lake Mälar and the Baltic. Originally named simply Tälje, it became Södertälje when the adjoining settlement of Norrtälje was established. The industrial development of the town was fostered by the construction of the Södertälje Canal in 1807–19 and the building of the Stockholm–Gothenburg railway line, which passed through the town. In Stortorget are *St Ragnhild's Church* (13th c., much altered, but with some remains of the original structure), the *Town Hall* (1965) and other modern buildings. The old Town Hall was moved to a site on the Canal. On the *Torekällberg* is an *open-air museum* (Östra Sörmlands Museet), with old houses and workshops (reconstructed). Among the group of town houses is the *Strömstedt House*, with a collection of historical material. There is also a working bakery which produces a local speciality, Södertälje *kringlor*. – 2 km (1½ miles) S of the town is a beach, *Södertälje Havsbad*.

An attractive excursion from Stockholm is a boat trip on Lake Mälar (about 3 hours) to **Mariefred** (pop. 2600; Gripsholms Värdshus, 11 b.), an idyllic little town in a lush setting. Mariefred owes its origin and name to the Carthusian monastery of Pax Mariae, founded in 1493, which ceased to exist at the beginning of the Reformation. The town is dominated by the church (17th c.) on the hill. Below this, in the older part of the little town, wooden houses line narrow lanes, most of which run down to the lake. To the N of the church, in the market square, is the Town Hall (1784), also built of wood (tourist information office). On the S side of the hill, below the church, is a local museum. To the W, on the far side of Stallarholmsvägen, are the ruins of Kärnbo church. – W of the middle of town lies an attractive villa suburb.

Gripsholm Castle in Lake Mälar

The most notable building in Mariefred is *Gripsholm Castle*, on an island close to the shores of the lake. It takes its name from a stronghold built in 1380 by Bo Jonsson, known as Grip. The present castle was built by Henrik von Göllen in the reign of Gustavus Vasa (1537–44). Its last occupant (1864) was King Karl XV. In the past it was a prison as well as a residence; Gustavus Vasa's sons and the deposed King Gustav IV were confined here.

With its massive walls, towers and defensive structures, Gripsholm has preserved its medieval character in spite of extensive alteration and new building. The large bronze cannon in the cobbled courtyard are trophies of the Russian wars in the time of Johan III. One of the *runic stones* beside the drawbridge has an inscription recording a journey to Russia by Ingvar Vitfarne.

INTERIOR. – Visitors can view 60 of the castle's 102 rooms (among which are the *Round Saloon* and the pretty little *Theatre* in the Knights' Wing, built for Gustav III in the second half of the 18th c.). The collection of 2800 portraits of royal personages and other leading figures is one of the largest in Europe. Portraits of private citizens from 1809 to the present day are housed in an annexe to the Folk High School in Mariefred.

There are regular boat services between Stockholm and Mariefred. – Another attractive possibility for railway enthusiasts is a trip on the *old railway* (Östra Södermanlands Järnväg) running between Mariefred and Läggesta (40 minutes).

**Vaxholm** lies on the island of *Vaxö*, NE of Stockholm, on the channel leading into the capital from the Baltic. On a rocky island between Vaxö and Rindö is a *defensive tower*, built by Gustavus Vasa to protect this

Old railway, Mariefred

entrance channel. During the 17th c., it was developed into a fortress. In the following century, Rindö was also fortified. The fortress of Vaxholm was rebuilt in 1838, but lost its importance immediately after this rebuilding, since its wall could not withstand modern artillery. It is now a museum, with a collection of material from its days as a fortress. Until 1912, the building of stone houses in Vaxholm was prohibited. During the 19th c., Vaxholm was a favourite summer resort of the people of Stockholm, and the little summer houses with carved decoration and enclosed verandas, in which the residents drank their evening punch, are relics of that era.

20 km (12 miles) SE of Stockholm (25 minutes on the suburban railway), in a bay in the *Baggensfjärd*, is the fashionable bathing resort of **Saltsjöbaden** (Grand Hotel, 150 b.), with a yacht harbour, golf-course and tennis courts. The Stockholm Observatory is also here.

60 km (40 miles) S of Stockholm, on the *Södertörn* peninsula, is the industrial town of **Nynäshamn** (Hotel Trehörningen, 31 b.); there is a boat service to Visby on the island of **Gotland** (p. 107).

There are also very attractive boat trips, in good weather, to the **skerries**.

Lake Mäler: see p. 187.

# Sundsvall

Sweden (Eastern).
Province: Gävleborgs län. – Region: Medelpad.
Altitude: sea level. – Population: 93,000.
Postal code: S-850 . . . – 855 . . .
Telephone code: 0 60.
(i) **Sundsvall Turistbyrå**,
    Torget,
    S-85230 Sundsvall;
    tel. 11 42 35.

HOTELS. – *Bore*, Trädgårdsgatan 31–33, 262 b., SB; *Continental*, Rådhusgatan 13, 25 b.; *Grand Hotel*, Nybrog 13, 80 b.; *Neptun*, Sjögatan 11, 70 b.; *Scandic Hotel*, Värdshusbacken 6, 355 b., SB; *Strand*, Strandgatan 10, 291 b., SB.

**Sundsvall is one of the most important ports and commercial towns in the northern countries. It lies between two hills, the Norra Stadsberg and the Södra Stadsberg, at the mouth of the Selångerå, halfway up the Gulf of Bothnia. It is an oil port and known for its wood-working and papermaking industries.**

Due to its excellent location and the trade routes to the W which passed through this area, Sundsvall was an important trading post as early as the 6th c. It received its charter from Gustavus Adolphus in 1624. A period of prosperity began in the 19th c., when numerous sawmills were established here: for a time there were no fewer than 40 operating on the offshore island of Alnö alone. The layout of the old town was the work of Tessin the Elder, but whole districts of the town were destroyed by a devastating fire in 1888 and only Norrmalm remained unscathed. To avoid any further disasters of this kind, the new town was built of stone, with wide streets; it is now known as Stenstaden, the "stone town".

SIGHTS. – Around the Stora Torg a great variety of architectural styles are represented. In the middle of the square is a bronze *statue of Gustavus Adolphus*; on its S side stands the *Town Hall*. At Storgatan 29 is the *Municipal Museum*; beyond this the neo-Gothic *Gustav Adolfskyrka* (1894), which contains wood-carvings by Ivar Lindekrantz. In the Esplanade, the town's other main street, it is worth visiting the *Hirsch House*. – In a small park in the middle of the town is a lake, the *Bünsowska Tjärn*. – From the town's two hills, *Södra Stadsberget* (240 m – 790 ft) and *Norra Stadsberget*, there are fine views. On Norra Stadsberget is an open-air museum, *Medelpads Fornhem*, with wooden houses from the Medelpad region (restaurant).

SURROUNDINGS. – On the island of **Alnö**, reached by a road bridge 1024 m (1100 yds) long and 40 m (130 ft) high, is a fine 13th c. stone church (2 km (1¼ miles) N of Alvik), with vivid wall paintings and sculpture; the church is one of the major sights of the Sundsvall area. – The new church (1896) has one of Sweden's great treasures of religious art, a carved wooden font (12th–13th c.). – At the SE tip of the island lies the attractive little fishing village of *Spikarna*, with the popular Vindheim summer restaurant.

**Härnösand** (Stadshotellet, 137 b.; Scandic Hotel, 115 b.), a port at the mouth of the Ångermanälv, was formerly an important trading and market town, chartered in 1585. In the 17th and 18th c. it was the administrative and cultural hub of Upper Norrland. It has been the see of a bishop since 1772.

The old town on the island of Härnö is reached from the mainland by the Nybrogata. The *Town Hall* (1791), with a circular portico by Olof Tempelmann, is one of the town's finest buildings. The neo-classical *Cathedral* (Ludwig Hawerman, 1846; restored 1935) has a fine Baroque organ-case and 17th c. chandeliers. – In the *Municipal Park* is a statue by Carl Milles of Mikael Franzén, who was bishop of Härnösand from 1831 to 1847 and a poet of some reputation. W of the Cathedral is the Market Square, with the old 18th c. *Governor's Residence* (Lansresidens). To the N of the Nybro, on the *Murberg*, an *open-air museum*, the largest in Sweden after Stockholm's Skansen, contains farmhouses and cottages reflecting the old peasant culture of Norrland. – From the *Vårdkasberg* (175 m – 575 ft;

restaurant) there are extensive views of the surrounding countryside and the coast. – 6 km (4 miles) SE of the old town is the bathing beach of *Smitingsviken*.

**Hudiksvall** (pop. 15,000; Hotel Hudik, 100 b.; Stadshotellet, 276 b., SP.), a port and woodworking town on the Hudiksvallfjärd, is the oldest town in Norrland after Gävle (chartered in 1582) and the oldest foundation built by the Vasa kings. In the past, the town was frequently ravaged by fire.

*Fiskarstaden*, an old-world quarter of wooden houses around the harbour, was rebuilt after a fire in 1792; it is the best-preserved part of the town. The *church* is 17th–18th c. Also of interest is the 19th c. *Hantverksgårdens Hus*, with a richly decorated façade on Storgata – an early example of a specially designed store front. Nearby is the *Hälsingemuseum*, with a rich collection of material on local history and traditions and a picture gallery of works by Swedish artists. – The *Theatre* (1881, restored 1972) is in a beautiful park by the Lillfjärd. – To the E of the town is the *Köpmanberg*, with a park and restaurant. – 3·5 km (2 miles) NW of Hudiksvall is the medieval church of *Hälsingtuna*, with an old grave chamber.

# Sunndal

Norway (Central).
Counties: Sør-Trøndelag fylke, Møre og Romsdal fylke.

ⓘ Turistkontor,
   N-7400 Oppdal;
   tel. (0 74) 2 17 60.

The *Sunndal is crossed by the lower course of the River Driva, which is joined at Oppdal by the Ålma. The valley extends W from Oppdal, roughly half-way between Dombås and Trondheim, and reaches the Sunndalsfjord at Sunndalsøra.

**Oppdal** (alt. 545 m (1790 ft); pop 3500; hotels: Fagerhaug Inn Motell, 59 b.; Hovd-Inn Sportell, 94 b.; Kongsvold Fjeldstue, 65 b.; Mullerhotell Oppdal, 108 b.; Oppdal Turisthotell, 160 b.; youth hostel) lies in a wide part of the valley, at an important road junction where Road 16 branches off from E6 (Dombås–Trondheim) and runs W. The Ålma, coming from the E, flows into the Driva here. Oppdal is a tourist and winter sports resort, with a chair-lift, several ski-tows and with altogether more than 70 km (45 miles) of cross-country ski trails. The town's main sources of revenue are stone quarries and the manufacture of furniture, sporting goods and glass. There is an interesting district museum (old houses, store-rooms (*'stabbur'*), etc.). – Road 16 runs down the valley of the Driva, passing

a *Viking cemetery* and, 2·5 (1½ miles) from the town, *Oppdal church*, at the foot of Ørsnipen (1378 m – 4520 ft). The wooden church dates from the 17th c. and has a prominent steeple; the interior furnishings (pulpit, altar) are 17th–18th c.

At *Vognill* a road branches off (22 km (14 miles) NW) to the *Gjevilvass hut* (700 m – 2300 ft), set commandingly on the N shore of the *Gjevilvatn* (663 m – 2175 ft). From there, an 8–9 hours' walk NW leads to the *Trollheim hut* (531 m – 1740 ft), base for the ascent to the commanding peaks of the **Trollheimen** range, including the *Trollhetta* (1614 m (5295 ft); round trip 7–8 hours, with guilde) and *Snota*, the highest peak in the area (1668 m (5473 ft); round trip 8–9 hours, with guide).

The old manor-house of *Gravaune* has an interesting collection of historical weapons and everyday objects. – The road continues past the *Ålbu* power station to *Lønset* (521 m – 1710 ft) (church). Here a road turns off on the right up the *Storlidal*, past the *Storfall*, to the *Storli hut* (652 m – 2140 ft), another good base for climbs in the Trollheimen area.

After crossing the county boundary the road descends more steeply, with many curves and attractive views, to *Gjøra* (camp site). A rewarding detour (to the left) through the *Jenstadjuvet gorge* (waterfall) into the *Gruvedal* (fine walking country) can be made from here.

The road continues down the Sunndal alongside the river, now known as the *Sunndalselv*.

**Romfo** (138 m – 453 ft) has a church (1824); a short distance W is the *Driva power station* (140 MW).

*Fale* is a good fishing area (salmon). Beyond this is **Grøa** (100 m (330 ft); camp site); ahead, to the right, is *Hovsnebba* (1609 m – 5280 ft).

The river is crossed on the *Elverhøy* bridge. On the far side are the **Sunndal Bygdemuseum** and an Iron Age cemetery.

**Sunndalsøra** (pop. 5000; Müllerhotell 99 b.; youth hostel; camp site) lies at the head of the *Sunndalsfjord, which is enclosed by snow-covered mountains. It has a large power station (290 MW) and an aluminium plant. Visitors can tour the fishery research station. – There is a charming road along the SW shore of the

Kristiansund

fjord to *Eidsvåg* (40 km – 25 miles) and Molde (95 km (60 miles): see p. 193). – 39 km (25 miles) S of Sunndalsøra (2 km (1¼ miles) on the Molde road, then turn left) is the *Aursjø* (hut, 860 m – 2920 ft), with one of the largest dams in Norway. Water is channelled under pressure from here to the Sunndalsøra power station.

The road to Kristiansund continues along the steep E shore of the fjord for another 8·5 km (5 miles; several tunnels), then runs through the wooded *Øpdalseid* area. – In another 11·5 km (7 miles), on the left, is the octagonal church of *Alvundeid*. – At the *Ålvundfoss* (85 m (280 ft) high; power station) the road divides. Road 16, to the left, now runs along the SW shore of the *Ålvundfjord*.

**Tingvoll** (pop. 1000; Sortdal Gjestgård, 20 b.; camp site), on the Tingvollfjord, has an interesting 13th c. stone church containing a runic stone and remains of frescoes. – The road continues along the NE shore of the fjord.

From *Kvisvik* there is a ferry to *Kvalvåg*, on the island of *Frei*. Road 16 continues from Kvalvåg to Kristiansund.

**Kristiansund** (pop. 19,000; hotels: Fosna, 75 b.; Grand Hotel, 220 b.; Verthuset, 18 b.; youth hostel; camp site), the county town of Møre og Romsdal, was founded in 1742. Built on three islands which enclose the harbour, it is the base of a large fishing fleet and does a large trade in the shipment of fish products. It was destroyed during the Second World War and was rebuilt in modern style. It has a fine church by Odd Østbye (1964). From the Varden lookout tower, to the NW of the town, there is a good view of the islands of *Nordland*, *Gomaland*, *Kirkeland*, with the main part of the town, and *Innland*, connected to each other by bridges.

In the open sea 15 km (10 miles) NW of Kristiansund (boat service) is the island of **Grip** (youth hostel), the largest of a group of 82 islands and islets, with a lighthouse and a 15th c. wooden church.

# Tampere (Tammerfors)

Finland (Southern).
Province: Hämeen lääni (Tavastehus län/Häme).
Altitude: 85 m (280 ft). – Population: 167,000.
Postal code: SF-33210. – Telephone code: 9 31.
ⓘ **Municipal Tourist Information and Congress Office**,
Aleksis Kivenkatu 14B;
tel. 12 66 52 and 12 67 75.
*Tourist Information Office* at station.
**Tampere Provincial Tourist Organisation**,
Aleksis Kivenkatu 14B;
tel. 2 44 88 and 2 32 07.

HOTELS. – *Cumulus*, Koskikatu 5, 400 b., SB; *Grand Hotel Tammer*, Salakunnankatu 13, 181 b., SB; *Jäähovi*, Sammonvaltatie 2, 175 b., SP; *Kaupunginhotelli*, Hämeenkatu 11, 122 b.; *Otavala* Rautatienkatu 22, 46 b.; *Rosendahl*, Pyynikintie 13, 453 b., SB; *Tampere*, Hämeenkatu 1, 520 b., SB; *Victoria*, Itsenäisyydenkatu 1, 160 b., SB.

VACATION and SUMMER HOTELS. – *Domus*, Pellervonkatu 9, 365 b., SB (1 June to 31 August); *Ilves*, Sovantokatu 5, 667 b., SB; *Rasti*, Itsenäisyydenkatu 1, 218 b. (1 March to 31 August); *Motel Harmala*, Nuolialantie 50, 180 b. (11 May to 31 August).

Two YOUTH HOSTELS. – Several CAMP SITES.

RESTAURANTS. – *Hämeensilta*, Hämeenkatu 13; *Aleksi*, Aleksanterinkatu 20; *Kustaankellari* and *Kustaa III*, Hämeenkatu 26; *Sorsapuiston Grilli*, Sorsapuisto 1; *Näsinneula* (lookout tower), Särkänniemi; *Tiiliholvi*, Kauppakatu 14B.

EVENTS. – *International Short Film Festival* (February); *Holiday Equipment Exhibition* (April); *International Festival of Folk Music and Dancing* (beginning of June); *Tampere in Chorus* (international choir festival; alternate years – 1983, etc. – end of May to beginning of June); *Tampere Theatre Summer* (second half of August); also, throughout the summer, open-air concerts, folk dancing displays, performances in Pyynikki summer theatre and cruises on the lakes.

Old Church and Theatre, Tampere

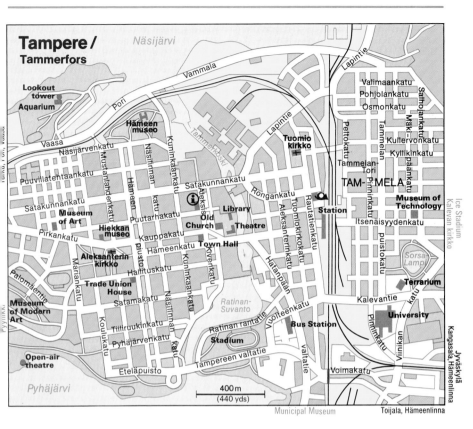

Municipal Museum                    Toijala, Hämeenlinna

SPORTS and RECREATION. – Bowling, squash, archery, tennis, golf, riding, swimming, rowing, water-skiing, fishing.

Tampere (Swedish Tammerfors), Finland's second largest city and leading industrial town, was founded in 1779. It lies on both sides of the Tammerkoski, a stretch of rapids 945 m (1000 yds) long, with a fall of 18 m (590 ft), between the Näsijärvi to the N and the Pyhäjärvi to the S. The development of industry in the town (mainly footwear and leather-working, textiles, metal-working and papermaking) followed its exemption from customs duties between 1821 and 1906. It is now a lively modern town with large new buildings, beautiful parks and gardens, a university, a college of technology, numerous schools and first-rate social amenities.

SIGHTS. – Tampere's main street is the broad *Hämeenkatu*, lined with large office buildings. On this street, on the W side of the Tammerkoski, is the *Keskustori* (Central Square), with the **Town Hall** (*Kaupungintalo*, 1890), the *Theatre* (1912) and the *Old Church* (1824). – Immediately N of the Theatre is the *Library*

(*Kirjastotalo*); in front of the library is a monument to the poet Aleksis Kivi (Wäinö Aaltonen, 1929).

At the W end of Hämeenkatu, beyond its intersection with the broad Hämeen-puisto (Park Avenue), are the gardens surrounding the *Alexander Church* (Aleksanterinkirkko, 1881). Nearby, at No. 2 Pirkankatu, is the *Natural History Museum*, and at No. 5 Pirkankatu the *Hiekka Museum* (art collection, including works by Wäinö Aaltonen). To the W, in Puutarhakatu, is the *Museum of Art* (Taidemuseo). – Hämeenpuisto Avenue runs N to the *Municipal Park* on the shore of the Näsijärvi, in which is the *Häme Museum* (local history and traditions). On a peninsula to the W of the park can be found the **Särkänniemi** tourist office, with an *Aquarium* and *Planetarium*, the Näsinneula lookout tower (173 m (570 ft) high; revolving restaurant at 124 m – 400 ft), an amusement park and a children's zoo. – To the S of the Alexander Church, at the intersection of Hämeenpuisto Avenue with Hallituskatu, is the large *Trade Union House*, with the Workers' Theatre and a Lenin Museum. – 1 km (¾ mile) SW of the Alexander Church rises the wooded hill of

Näsinneula Lookout Tower, Tampere

**Pyynikki** (152 m – 500 ft), laid out as a park, with a lookout tower. On the NE side of the hill is the *Museum of Modern Art*. On its southern slopes, on the shore of the Pyhäjärvi, is an open-air theatre.

To the E of the Keskustori, Hämeenkatu crosses the Tammerkoski on the Hämeensilta, a bridge decorated with four pieces of sculpture by W. Aaltonen. On the banks of the river are several water-powered factories On a peninsula, to the S, is the *Ratina Stadium*. – At the E end of Hämeenkatu is the **Station** (1936), with a tall clock-tower. – On a low hill N of the station, reached via Rautatienkatu, stands the **Cathedral** (*Tuomiokirkko*, 1907), a handsome building of bluish-grey granite with a red roof.

To the E of the railway lies the district of TAMMELA, with numerous factories, the *University*, *Sorsa Park* (lake, terrarium), the *Museum of Technology*, many tall apartment buildings and the *Kaleva Church* (1966). On the southern edge of the district is *Kalvankangas Cemetery*, with a beautiful military cemetery for those who died in the Second World War. – On the NE outskirts of Tampere, in the district of KISSANMAA, rises the modern *Central Hospital* (14 storeys, 1000 beds). – To the E of the town, at Kehätie 2, is the *Ice Stadium* (1964–5) and to the S, on the Hatanpää peninsula, the **Municipal Museum**.

SURROUNDINGS. – An attractive trip, 14 km (9 miles) to the E of Tampere, is through the beautiful village of *Kangasala* to the *Vehoniemenharju*, a narrow ridge of hills between *Lake Roine* to the W and the *Längelmävesi* to the E. – 35 km (22 miles) N of Tampere, on the Näsijärvi, is the large vacation and recreation area of *Maisansalo* (Maisa Hotel, 164 b.; vacation houses, youth hostel).

*Tampere to Virrat by boat** (8 hours; by road, via Teisko, 120 km – 75 miles). – This route, renowned for its scenic beauty, is known as the "Poets' Highway"; it runs through a stretch of very typical Finnish scenery. – From Tampere (departure from Mustalahti, to the N of the town) the boat sails N up *Näsijärvi* (alt. 95 m – 310 ft), with its many bays and inlets, passing the village of *Teisko* on the E shore of the lake. In 2½ hours it reaches the *Murole Canal* (lock). While the boat is passing through the lock, there is time to visit the Murole Falls, a bit to the right. The canal leads into the next lake, *Palovesi*, the boat then continues through narrow channels and the open *Jäminselkä* into the *Kautu Canal* (swing bridge), and into *Ruovesi*. On a crag, to the left, is the former home of the well-known Finnish painter, Akseli Gallén-Kallela (1865–1931). Beyond, on the W side of the lake, is the picturesquely set village of **Ruovesi** (4¾ hours from Tampere), which attracts many summer visitors. The poet J. L. Runeberg was a tutor in a private household here (commemorative plaque). – The boat continues N into *Tarjannevesi*, a lake dotted with many islands, and passes through the *Visuvesi Canal* into *Vaskivesi* (alt. 98 m – 320 ft), at the N end of which is the village of **Virrat**. The trip ends here.

Another very attractive excursion from Tampere is on a motor-launch operated by the "*Silver Line*" to **Hämeenlinna** (see p. 118).

# Telemark

Norway (Southern).
County: Telemark fylke.
ⓘ **Turistkontor,**
Rådhusgata 2,
N-3700 Skien;
tel. (0 36) 2 12 79.
**Turistkontor,**
Kverndalen 8,
N-3700 Skien;
tel. (0 35) 2 82 27

**The Norwegian county of Telemark extends N from the Skagerrak to the southern Norwegian uplands and the outliers of the Hardangervidda. Along the rocky coast are many bathing resorts; the interior is hilly and well forested, while the Hardanger is a desolate high plateau. Telemark played a part in the development of skiing techniques – the Telemark turn was quite popular between the First and Second World Wars.**

**Skien** (pop. 30,000; hotels: Dag Bondeheim. 80 b.; Hoyers Hotel, 120 b.; Ibsens

**Heddal stave church, Telemar**

Hotel, 236 b.; Norrøna Gjesteheim, 30 b.; two camp sites), on the N bank of the *Skienselv*, is a busy industrial town and the administrative capital of Telemark county. The church (1894), with two tall spires, stands on elevated ground. A little way S is a monument to the great Norwegian dramatist, Henrik Ibsen (1828–1906), a native of Skien. To the E of the town, on the hill of *Brekke* (55 m – 180 ft), is the Brekke Park (restaurant, summer theatre), with the **Telemark County Museum** (*Fylkemuseum*), which has a small Ibsen collection and a number of old Telemark houses. 2 km (1¼ miles) NE of the town is the 13th c. church of *Gjerpen* (restored 1921). 6 km (4 miles) beyond, a narrow road on the left (signpost) runs up 750 m (½ mile) to the *Kikuthytta* (325 m – 1065 ft; refreshments), from which there are magnificent views.

From Skien, the *Telemark Canal* goes NW through the *Norsø* and the *Bandaksvatn*, a picturesque lake enclosed by mountains, to *Dalen* (105 km (65 miles) from Skien). From the beginning of June to the middle of August, motor-ships sail from Skien to Dalen daily, taking about 10 hours.

50 km (30 miles) N of Skien as the crow flies, at the outflow of the *Tinnelv* into the *Heddalsvann*, is the town of **Notodden** (alt. 31 m (100 ft); pop. 9000; Telemark Hotel, 150 b.; youth hostel; camp site), which lies on E76 from Kongsberg (p. 163). W along E 76, Heddal stave church appears.

*Heddal stave church**, which dates from the mid-13th c. (restored in 1849–51 and again in 1952–4), is the largest of the old wooden churches of Norway. Notable features of the interior are the 14th c. *wall paintings* and the carved *bishop's throne*. The windows were inserted during the 19th c. restoration. Across the road stands the separate belfry. – Near the church is the *Heddal District Museum*.

*Sauland* (alt. 90 m (295 ft); Løvheim Turisthotel, 70 b.), at the junction of the Tuddal with the Heddal, has a church (1857), erected on the site of an earlier stave church, and a storehouse (*stabbur*) of 1718.

An attractive detour can be made on a narrow road which runs up the *Tuddal* (to the right). In 22 km (14 miles), it comes to the late 18th c. church of *Tuddal* (468 m – 1535 ft). 6 km (4 miles) beyond this is the commanding *Tuddal Høyfjellshotell* (50 b.), base for

Gausta, Telemark

the climb of **Gausta** (1883 m (6178 ft); skiing; view), the highest peak S of the Bergen railway.

E76 continues to *Seljord* (alt. 120 m (395 ft); Gjestgivergården, 40 b.). To the E is the **Lifjell**, the highest peak of which is *Gyrannaten* (1550 m – 5085 ft). On 25 November 1870, two Frenchmen who had escaped from the besieged city of Paris by balloon landed on the SW slopes of the Lifjell.

At *Høydalsmo*, Road 45 branches off on the left to Dalen, at the end of the Telemark Canal from Skien. Just before Dalen is the village of *Eidsborg*, with a stave church (1354, with later alteration), and also an open-air museum. **Dalen** (Bandak Hotel, 21 b.; camp site) is in a fine location at the W end of the 26 km (16 mile) long *Bandaksvatn*.

From Dalen, Road 38 runs N past the steep rock face of the *Ravnejuv*, and rejoins E76 at Amot.

At **Haukeligrend** is an important road junction where Road 12 goes off on the left to Kristiansand (p. 163). E76 continues straight ahead and is known from here to Haugesund (197 km – 123 miles) as the **Haukeli Road**. Only the first 30 km (20 miles) or so of this road are in Telemark; at Haukeliseter, it enters the county of Hordaland.

The *Haukeli Road (toll), opened in 1886 and later partly re-aligned, is one of the finest routes to the southern part of the Norwegian W coast, passing through scenery typical of the southern Norwegian upland region. There are many unlighted tunnels, especially on the eastern part of the road.

From Haukeligrend, the road climbs up the *Haukelifjell*, passing at *Botn* (915 m – 3000 ft) an old *stabbur* (wooden storehouse). Soon it rises above the tree-line, and the view to the W appears.

**Haukeliseter** (986 m (3235 ft); Haukeli-seter Fjellstue, 88 b.; Vågslid Høgfells-hotell, 100 b.) lies in a lonely mountain setting at the E end of the *Ståvann*, on a long-established route through the mountains. It is now a tourist and winter sports resort (many cross-country ski trails). The road then enters the county of Hordaland. Ahead, to the right, are the sheer rock faces of the *Store Nupsfonn*.

The old road reaches its highest point on *Dyrskar (1145 m – 3757 ft), a pass barely exceeded in magnificence by the great Alpine passes. The modern road runs under a pass on the watershed between the Atlantic and the Skagerrak, in a tunnel 5682 m (3½ miles) long.

The road continues through a desolate wasteland of rocks and snow, with several tunnels. To **Røldal** (390 m (1280 ft); Breifonn Hotell, 35 b.), on the lake of the same name, where there is a stave church (13th c., with later alterations) and an Iron Age cemetery. It then climbs the slopes of the *Røldalsfjell*, with a view ahead of the great *Folgefonn glacier, rising to a height of 1654 m (5427 ft). Beyond the *Seljestad gorge Road 47 goes off on the right to Odda on the Sørfjord (p. 124). E76 now bears SW and follows the S shore of the *Akrafjord*.

**Etne** (Etne Krotell, 36 b.), on the fjord of the same name, has a wooden church (1675, tower 1930). There is good fishing in the *Etneelv*.

**Haugesund** (pop. 28,000; hotels: Haugaland, 36 b.; Maritim, 292 b.; Nep-tun, 96 b.; Park, 210 b.; Saga, 151 b.; youth hostel; camp site), in the county of Rogaland, is a considerable port (con-nections with Stavanger and Bergen) and a busy industrial town, with an airport. The Town Hall also houses the Municipal Museum. An arched concrete bridge links the town with the little island of *Risøy* (fishing harbour; large port installations). – 2 km (1¼ miles) N of the middle of the town is the *Haraldshaug*, said to be the burial-place of Harald the Fair-Haired, whose naval victory at Stavanger in 872 is commemorated by a 17 m (55 ft) high granite obelisk erected in 1872, the 29 blocks of stone representing the tribes which he united into a single nation.

To the S of the town is the *Karmsund Bridge* (690 m (750 yds) long, 50 m (165 ft) high), which leads on to

the island of **Karmøy** (area 176 sq. km – 69 sq. miles). At the E end of the bridge are five standing stones, known as "De fem dårlige Jomfruer" ("The Five Poor Maidens"). In *Avaldsnes* (2·5 km (1½ miles) S) is St Olav's Church (*c.* 1250). 6 km (4 miles) S of Avaldsnes is a large aluminium plant. At the S end of the island (35 km (22 miles) from the middle of Haugesund) lies the port of *Skudeneshavn* (pop. 1500); there is a ferry to Stavanger (p. 244).

# Tornio (Torneå)

Finland (Northern).
Province: Lapin lääni (Lapplands län/Lapland).
Altitude: sea level. – Population: 20,000.
Postal code: SF-95400. – Telephone code: 9 80.

(i) **Kaupungin Matkailutoimisto**
(*Municipal Tourist Information Office*),
Lukiokatu 10;
tel. 4 28 31/2 64,
in summer also
tel. 4 00 48.

HOTEL. – *Kaupunginhotelli*, Itaranta 4, 150 b,, SB; Tornio, Keskikatu 11, 38 b.

EVENTS. – *Rapids shooting contest and White Fish Festival* on Kukkolankoski rapids, 18 km (11 miles) N (last Sunday in July); *Tornio Valley Summer*, with a variety of events (throughout July).

RECREATION and SPORT. – Tennis, riding, fishing, swimming; boat trips to skerries (rocky islets).

**The Finnish frontier town of Tornio (Swedish Torneå), lies on the Gulf of Bothnia, at the mouth of the Tornionjoki (Torneälv), which forms the boundary with Sweden here. It is divided into three parts, the westernmost of which is on the former island of Suensaari, now joined to the mainland on the Swedish W bank of the river.**

The town first appears in the records in the 14th c., when Archbishop Hemming was baptising Finns and Lapps in this area. It received its municipal charter in 1621.

SIGHTS. – The wooden *church* (1864), with a separate tower, has a patterned

Tornio

shingle roof; inside, the ceiling is partly painted; fine 17th c. brass chandelier. In Torikatu, near the crossing into Sweden, is the *Tornio Valley Museum*. – To the N of the church is a sports field, and still farther N is a water-tower with a lookout platform; nearby are tennis courts.

SURROUNDINGS. – 9 km (5 miles) S is the island of Röyttä, the port of Tornio (boat trips to skerries).

A drive up the **Tornio valley** to the N is recommended. In 17 km (10 miles) a detour brings one to the *Kukkolankoski* rapids, which have a fall of 13·8 m (45 ft) over a distance of 3·5 km (2 miles). Fishing; restaurant, with good fish dishes. – 26 km (16 miles) beyond the turning for Kukkolankoski is another side road leading to the *Matkakoski* rapids. – The next place is *Ylitornio*, which has a modern stone church with an old wooden belfry beside it. – 10 km (6 miles) N of the church, Road 930 turns off on the right to Rovaniemi. A short distance along this road, a narrow side road leads to a camp site and car park on the hill of **Aavasaksa** (222 m – 730 ft), with the *Tengeliönjoki* flowing round the foot of the hill. From here, a footpath (350 m – 400 yds) leads to the top, where the midnight sun can be seen on Midsummer Day, although the hill is actually S of the Arctic Circle. Accommodation is available in both summer and winter in comfortable vacation chalets. Ski-lift (length 605 m – 1985 ft).

**Haparanda** (Finnish *Haparanta*), Tornio's Swedish neighbour and counterpart, lies on the W bank of the Torneälv (Finnish Tornionjoki). The town was founded in 1809, after Tornio had passed to Russia together with the rest of Finland. The frontier rampart at the sports field to the N of the town is a reminder of this earlier period of confrontation. The frontier between Sweden and Finland is now regarded by both sides as "the most peaceful frontier in the world". Haparanda is Sweden's easternmost town. It offers the same opportunities for excursions and recreation as Tornio.

During the First World War, Russia and the Central Powers exchanged prisoners unfit for further service through Haparanda. In the churchyard of Nedertorneå church, on the western outskirts of the town, is a stone commemorating the 205 Austrians, 11 Germans and 2 Turks who died on the journey and were buried here.

# Tromsø

Norway (Northern).
County: Troms fylke.
Altitude: sea level. – Population: 43,000.
Postal code: N-9000. – Telephone code: 0 83.
ⓘ **Reisetrafikkforeningen for Tromsø,**
*Tourist Information,*
Kirkegårdsvegen 2;
tel. 8 47 76.

HOTELS. – *SAS Royal Hotel*, Sjogate 7, 333 b.; *Grand Nordic Hotel*, Storgate 44, 169 b.; *Polar Hotell*, Gronnegate 45, 88 b.; *Saga Hotell*, Rich-With-plass 2, 100 b.; *Skipperhuset Pensjonat*, Storgate 112, 34 b.; *Tromsø Hotel*, Gronnegate 50, 70 b.

YOUTH HOSTEL. – *Elverhoy* (only from 20 June to 19 August).

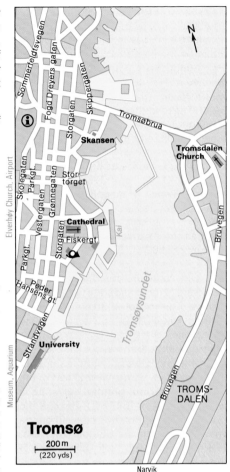

**Tromsø**

200 m
(220 yds)

Narvik

CAMP SITE: *Elvestrand*, on Tromsdalselv (with chalets).

SPORTS and RECREATION. – Fishing; boat rentals; riding; sightseeing flights.

**The Norwegian port and commercial town of Tromsø lies between Narvik and Hammerfest (lat. 69°39′ N), on a small island connected to the mainland by a bridge 1036 m (1100 yds) long and 43 m (140 ft) high. It was built to replace one destroyed in the Second World War. The town developed around a church founded in the 13th c.; it received its municipal charter in 1794. Tromsø is now the largest town in N Norway, the county town of Troms fylke, an important fishing port and the see of the Lutheran bishop of Hålogaland. It has a university (founded in 1972), an observatory for the study of the aurora borealis and the weather station for N Norway. In 1944, the German battleship "Tirpitz" was sunk by British aircraft off the island of Kvaløya.**

Tromsø has been, and still is, a base for expeditions to the Arctic (monument to Amundsen). Ships are outfitted for fishing in the Arctic Ocean here, and many fishing boats use the port as a base. The fast ships of the "Hurtigrute" from Bergen to Kirkenes and from Kirkenes to Bergen stop at Tromsø every day, and in summer the cruises to Spitzbergen leave from here. – Tromsø is notable for its surprisingly rich growth of vegetation. In good weather, the midnight sun is visible from 21 May to 23 July.

SIGHTS. – On the mainland, just before the bridge, is the **Tromsdalen Church**, an interesting modern church (1975) known as the "Cathedral of the Arctic", with a large stained-glass window 23 m (75 ft) high (area 140 sq. m – 1500 sq. ft). – Near the W end of the bridge is the *Skansen Municipal Museum* (local history and traditions; Arctic section). To the W of the dock stands the wooden **Cathedral** (1861), capable of seating a congregation of 750.

From the Cathedral, Storgaten and Strandvegen (on the left, the *University*) lead SW to the *Tromsø Museum, in a park 2 km (1¼ miles) from the middle of the town (excellent natural history and ethnographic collections, including a section on Lapp culture). Near the museum is its *Aquarium*.

To the W of the town is *Elverhøy Church* (1802), the cathedral of Tromsø from

1803 to 1861. It then stood on Prostnes and was moved to its present site in 1975.

SURROUNDINGS. – A cabin cableway (Fjellheisen) ascends to a height of 420 m (1380 ft); superb view; restaurant; good skiing up to mid-May. – Boat trip to the islands and to *Nord-Fugløy*, an island noted for its rich bird life. – Day trip (200 km – 125 miles) to the **Lyngenfjord** (p. 186).

30 km (20 miles) S of Tromsø, on the E coast of the island of *Kvaløy*, is *Hella*; a number of houses from the old town of Tromsø have been re-erected here.

# Trondheim

Norway (Central).
County: Sør-Trøndelag fylke.
Altitude: sea level. – Population: 135,000.
Postal code: N-7000. – Telephone code: 0 75.
(i) **Trondheim Turist og Reiselivslag,**
    Kongensgate 7c;
    tel. 51 14 66.

HOTELS. – *Ambassadeur*, Elvegate 18, 85 b.; *Britannia*, Dronningensgate 5, 180 b.; *Müllerhotel Astoria*, Nordregate 24, 100 b.; *Prinsen*, Kongensgate 30, 120 b.; *Scandic Hotel*, Brøsetveien 186, 250 b.; *Gildevangen*, Søndregate 22, 75 b.; *IMI Hotell*, Kongensgate 26, 110 b.; *Neptun*, Thomas Angells gate 12B, 70 b.; *Norrøna*, Thomas Angells gate 20, 34 b.; *Residence*, Torget, 122 b.; *Royal Garden*, Kjøpmannsgate 73, 600 b.; *Sentrum Nye Hotell*, Cicignons Plass, 76 b.; *Singsaker Sommerhotell*, Rogersgate 1, 200 b. – YOUTH HOSTEL. – two CAMP SITES.

RESTAURANTS. – *Cavalero*, Kongensgata 3; *Galleyen*, Dronningensgata 12 (open 24 hours; discothèque); *Grenaderen*, Kongsgården; *Munken Kro*, Munkegata 25 (Italian); *Naustloftet*, Prinsensgata 42 (fish specialties); *Rotisseriet 1842*, Prinsensgata 38; *Trubadur*, Kongensgata 34; *Vertshuset Tavern*, Sverresborg (building dating from 1739).

SPORTS and RECREATION. – Fishing; golf.

*Trondheim, Norway's third largest city, lies in lat. 63°25' N and long. 10°33' E, in an inlet on the S side of the Trondheimfjord, surrounded by fine hills. The town is on a peninsula formed by the Nidelv which is linked with the mainland only on the W side. Trondheim is the main town in the county of Sør-Trøndelag and the see of both a Lutheran and Roman Catholic bishop, with a number of scientific and educational institutions.**

The favourable temperature conditions (January mean rarely below −3 °C/27 °F) ensure that the fjord is always ice-free and

Tromsø – a panoramic view

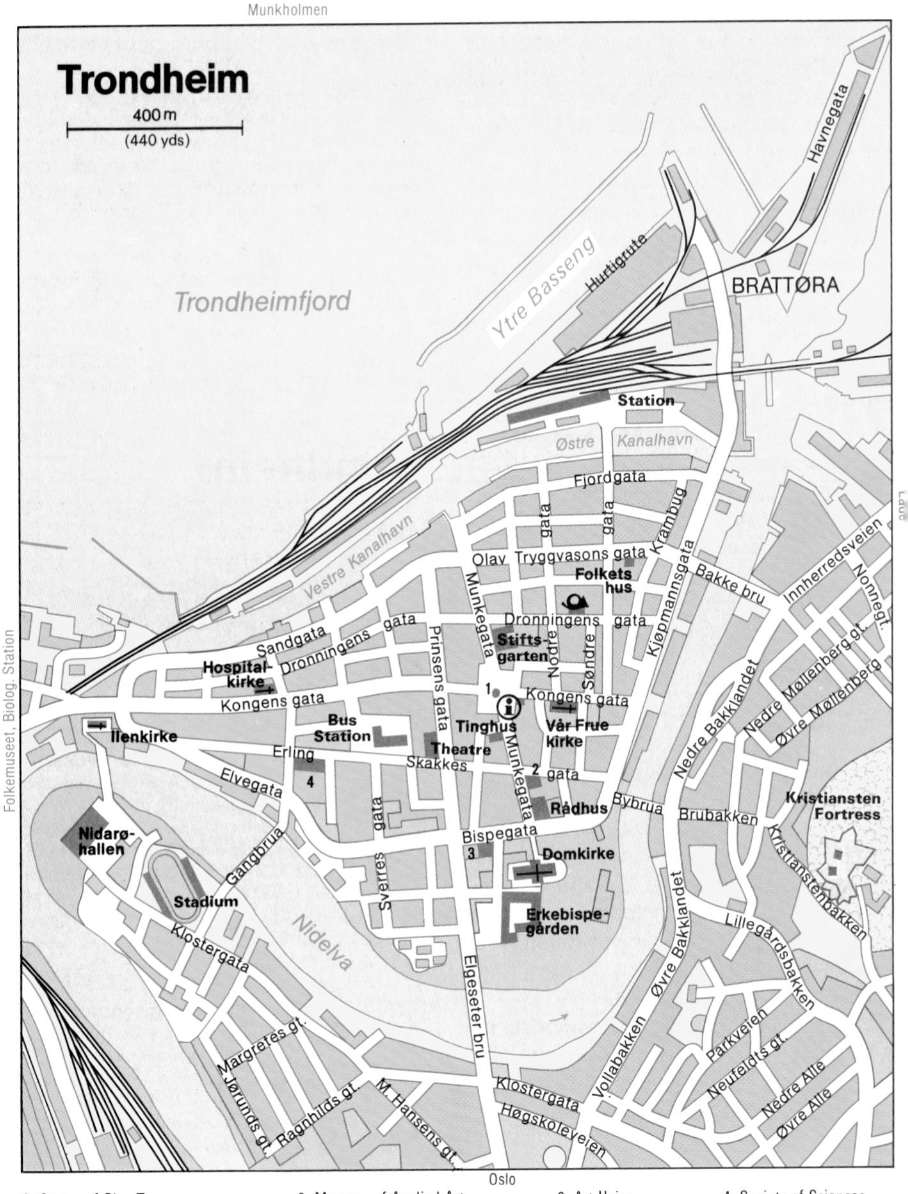

**Trondheim**

400 m
(440 yds)

1 Statue of Olav Tryggvason   2 Museum of Applied Art   3 Art Union   4 Society of Sciences

promote a rich growth of vegetation. The principal industries are foodstuffs, metal-working and engineering. The town's main exports are fish products and canned fish.

HISTORY. – *Trondheim* (formerly spelt Trondhjem) was originally the name of a small settlement at the entrance to Trondheimfjord in the area known as *Tröndelag*. It had, for centuries, been the place of the main "Ting", at which disputes were settled and the local Jarls (princes or earls) were elected. From the time of Harald I (the Fairhair) it achieved greater eminence as the *Øreting* at which the rulers of his line were elected king of Norway, though usually after a good deal of in-fighting.

In 997 Harald's great-grandson, Olav Trygvesson (or Trygvasson), landed there to claim succession to the throne. He was immediately recognised as king by the Trøndelag people, though they subsequently fought against him largely because of the enforced Christianisation he made. Within two years he was acknowledged as king of the then-known Norway. In 997, after having built a fortified residence, he built the Church of St Clement near the outlet of the River Nid (Nidaros). Olav Trygvesson died in battle in 1000 and for sixteen years there was an interregnum with Jarls in all districts proclaiming themselves kings. Olav I's heir, Olav II, fled to England. He sailed from England in 1016 intending to land at Oslo, but, blown from his course by a gale, he landed at Sunnfjord and then after a famous battle at *Nesjar*, sailed all along the west coast, was acclaimed at all the Tings and set the seal of his kingship of Norway at the Øreting in Trondheim. Olav II's was a troubled reign though a very significant one. He established Christianity in Norway on a firm basis and, having a passion for order and security, promulgated a series of laws, still referred to as Olav's

Laws, gained the support of the peasants, but alienated the nobles so that in 1027 there was a general rising; he fled to Russia and the Danish-English King Canute, by the invitation of the nobles, was acclaimed king of Norway at the Øreting in Trondheim. Olav returned in 1030, was decisively beaten at the battle of Stiklestad and his body brought back to the Church of St Clement at Nidaros. Within weeks it was proclaimed that miracles were taking place at Olav's tomb and within a short time Olav II was recognised as "Olav the Saint" and the "Church of Nidaros" at Trondheim as the holiest church in Norway. This began the town's greatest period of wealth and glory when crowds of pilgrims swarmed to the shrine of the king, now declared a saint, and the cult of St Olav made Trondheim the largest and wealthiest town in the country. In addition to the Cathedral, nine other churches and five religious houses were built in the town. In about 1200 Håkon VI removed his court to Bergen, so making that town the capital of Norway. – The Reformation put an end to the pilgrimages; the saint's shrine was removed to Denmark and destroyed; his remains were buried at an unknown spot within the Cathedral. Almost all the churches and convents disappeared. The town was destroyed by fire, either wholly or partially, no fewer than fifteen times; in spite of all this, it was still as large as Oslo at the beginning of the 19th c., with a population of 9500. – The coming of the railway, connecting the town to the rest of the Norwegian railway system (1877) and with the Swedish system (1881), began a period of rapid growth. – The Storting (Parliament) decided that from 1 January 1930, the town should be known by its old name of Nidaros; this decision was reversed in February of the following year due to popular preference for the name of Trondheim (the spelling adopted in place of the previous Trondhjem).

## Trondheim Cathedral

| | |
|---|---|
| ▨ Romanesque | |
| ▢ Gothic | |
| 1 W doorway | 5 Long choir |
| 2 S doorway of choir | 6 High choir (domed octagon) |
| 3 N doorway | 7 St Olav's Spring |
| 4 Transept | 8 Sacristy (chapterhouse) |

20m
(22 yds)

SIGHTS. – The central feature of the town and the hub of its traffic is the Market Square (*Torget*), at the intersection of the two main traffic routes, Kongensgata and Munkegata. In the square, on a high octagonal base, is a prominent *statue of Olav Tryggvason* (1923). At the foot of the monuments are letters marking the cardinal compass points (N – V – S – Ø).

From the Market Square, Munkegata runs S to the Cathedral. On the right (No. 20), is the handsome *Tinghus* (1951), with two bronze doors and coloured ceramic reliefs depicting the town's history. Beyond this, on the right (No. 8), is the *Cathedral School*, in an 18th c. brick building. On the opposite side of the street is the *Nordenfjeldske Kunstindustrimuseum* (Museum of Applied Art). To the S is the *Rådhus* (Town Hall).

The **\*\*Cathedral** (*Domkirke*) was built by King Olav Kyrre (1066–93) over the tomb of St Olav. It was greatly enlarged after the establishment in 1151 of the archbishopric of Nidaros, with authority over the whole of Norway. In conception and execution, the Cathedral is the most

splendid church in the Scandinavian countries. The transept and chapterhouse are in a late Romanesque transitional style influenced by the Norman architecture of England; the early Gothic domed octagon is from the same period. The long choir (beautiful S doorway) was built in the early 13th c.; the massive nave and the tower, also in Gothic style, date from 1230–80. After being ravaged by fire in 1531, 1708 and 1719, the whole western end of the church beyond the transepts was reduced to ruin. The reawakening of national consciousness in the 19th c., however, saved the Cathedral from total destruction. Restoration work began in 1869, and on 28 July 1930, the 900th anniversary of St Olav's death, the church was re-consecrated. The organ (1930, Baroque case) was moved to a new position under the rose window in 1963, and the W front was restored between 1914 and 1968. The Cathedral is built of bluish-grey soapstone (Norwegian *klebersten*) quarried to the S and E of Trondheim. – In the 11th and 12th c., the Cathedral became the burial-place of Norwegian kings; a number of kings were crowned here in the 15th c., and, since 1814, Norwegian monarchs have been required, under the Constitution, to be proclaimed in Trondheim Cathedral.

INTERIOR. – Over the high choir is the fine *\*domed octagon*, in richly decorated Gothic. – *St Olav's Spring*, probably a factor in determining the site of the earliest church here, can be seen from the ambulatory. Adjoining the high choir is the aisled *\*long choir* (26 m – 85 ft long), with a beautiful font based on fragments of an earlier one. – The S lateral chapel in the Romanesque *transept* was dedicated in 1161. The aisled *nave*, almost completely rebuilt, is 42·5 m (140 ft) long and 20 m (65 ft) wide, with 14 pillars supporting the vaulted roof. – The large organ, under the rose window, was made by Steinmeyer of Öttingen in S Germany (1930). – Fine stained glass by Gabriel Kielland (1913–34).

To the E and SE of the Cathedral is the old *churchyard*. – SW of the Cathedral the former *Archbishop's Palace* (Erkebis-pegård), a medieval building now houses a collection of weapons and the *Museum of the Resistance* (1940–5). NW of the Cathedral, in Bispegata, is the art gallery of the *Kunstforening* (Art Union), which from time to time puts on special exhibitions. – Across the *Elgeseter Bridge* over the Nidelv, immediately SW of the Archbishop's Palace, and left along Høgskolevei, is the **College of Technology** (*Teknisk Høgskole*), founded in 1900. – From the *Bybru*, to the NE of the Cathedral, is an attractive view of the old warehouses on the banks of the Nidelv.

N of the Market Square, in Munkegata (on right), stands the *Stiftsgård*, a large yellow wooden mansion (*c.* 1770); the king stayed here when visiting Trondheim. – In Kongensgata, to the E of the Market Square, stands **Vor Frue Kirke**, the Church of Our Lady (13th and 16th–17th c.). In the gardens adjoining the church is a small bronze statue of the Norwegian naval hero Tordenskjold, born in Trondheim in 1691. It is a replica of the original statue by H. W. Bissen in Copenhagen.

SW of the Market Square, at No. 47B Erling Skakesgate, is the headquarters of the **Royal Society of Sciences** (*Det Kongelige Norske Videnskabers Selskab*), with a fine library (old manuscripts) and a variety of excellent collections (bird diorama; botany, mineralogy, zoology; church art; antiquities). To the W, at the end of Kongensgata, we come to the *Ilenkirke*, built of bluish quartz sandstone, and to the S of this, over a bridge, the *Nidarø Hall* (sports, etc.).

Trondheim, with the Nidelv

The oldest **port installations** are those at the mouth of the Nidelv. Along the *Øvre Elvehavn*, which extends N from the

Bybru, are a series of old wooden warehouses, built on piles. The *Kanalhavn* runs between the main part of the town and the station to the N. Beyond the railway is the Ytre Basseng, with the dock used by the ships of the "Hurtigrute". – At No. 6 Fjordgata is a *Seafaring Museum*.

To the E of the town, reached by way of the Bybru and the Bakklandet district, is the small 17th c. fortress of **Kristiansten** (alt. 72 m (236 ft); open to the public from 4 to 6 p.m. in summer); there is a fine *view of the town (seen at its best in the morning). – On a hill to the SW of the town, once occupied by the castle of Sverresborg built by King Sverrir (1177–1202), is the *Folk Museum* (Folkemuseet), an open-air museum with old buildings from the Trondheim area. – To the NW of the town, on the shores of the fjord, is the *Biological Research Station*, with an aquarium – large maritime laboratory.

Prehistoric stone carvings, Bardal

SURROUNDINGS. – 2 km (1¼ miles) N of the town, in the Trondheimfjord, is the fortified island of **Munkholmen** (motorboats from Ravnkloa, at the N end of Munkegata; hourly service, 10-minute trip), with a circular tower belonging to the former Benedictine abbey of Nidarholm, the original site of which is now occupied by the fortifications erected in 1658. – From the near end of Bynesvei (views), to the NW of the town, a footpath on the left ascends steeply to the *Elsterpark*, on the slopes of *Gjeitfjell* (399 m – 1310 ft). – 3·5 km (2 miles) NE of the middle of the town in the district of LADE, is *Ringve Gård*, childhood home of the naval hero, Tordenskjold (museum; collection of musical instruments). – 8 km (5 miles) W of the town, on the Fjellsetervei, running partly through forest, is *Fjellseter* (367 m (1204 ft); good skiing, ski-jump). From here, a footpath leads up in 15 minutes to the summit of **Gråkallen** (556 m – 1824 ft; fine *views of much of the fjord; to the E the mountains along the Swedish frontier; to the S, Snøhetta and the Trollheim mountains; see p. 261). An alternative route is by the Gråkallen electric railway from St Olavsgata, or by bus from Dronningensgata (½ hour), to *Lian* (272 m (892 ft); restaurant), continuing from there on foot via Fjellseter and Skistua to Gråkallen, a pleasant 2–2½ hours' round trip.

E6, the Narvik road, runs E alongside the fjord. At **Værnes** (35 km – 22 miles), shortly before the tunnel under the airfield, is a 13th c. church.

125 km (78 miles) from Trondheim is **Steinkjer**, on the Steinkjerfjord (pop. 10,000; Grand Hotell, 180 b.; camp site), an agricultural market town in the county of Nord-Trøndelag. On the N bank of the Steinkjerelv there is an interesting open-air museum (old peasant houses). At *Bardal*, 10 km (6 miles) W, are rock carvings of the Stone and Bronze Ages. – The road to Namsos, No. 17, branches off at Asphaugen.

205 km (128 miles) from Trondheim lies **Namsos** (pop. 8000; Grand Hotell Namsos, 77 b.; Namsen-Motor Hotell, 107 b.; camp site), on the *Namsen-fjord*, at the mouth of the *Namsenelv* (good fishing). The timber trade provides the town's main source of income. To the E of the town is the Namsdal Museum (old boats, tools and everyday objects). From the 115 m (377 ft) high hill of *Bjørumsklompen*, there is a fine view of the town. – Namsos can also be reached from Trondheim by boat.

# Turku/Åbo

Finland (SW).
Province: Turun ja Porin lääni (Åbo och Björneborgs län/Turku-Pori).
Altitude: sea level. – Population 163,000.
Postal code: SF-20100. – Telephone code: 9 21

ⓘ **Turun Kaupungin Matkailutoimisto**
(*Municipal Tourist Information Office*),
Käsityöläiskatu 3;
tel. 33 63 66.
*Tourist information office* in Market Square;
tel. 1 52 62.
*Tourist information office* in Harbour;
tel. 30 35 63.
**Tourist Association of SW Finland**,
Läntinen Rantakatu 13;
tel. 51 73 33.

HOTELS. – *Hamburger Borsem*, Kauppiaskatu 6, 317 b., SB; *Marine Palace*, Linnankatu 32, 370 b., SB; *Cumulus*, Eerikinkatu 28, 423 b.; SB; *Henrik*, Yliopistonkatu 29a, 165 b.; *Keskushotelli*, Yliopistonkatu 12a, 145 b.; *Rantasipi Ikituuri*, Pispalantie 7, 320 b., SB; *Ritz*, Humalistonkatu 7, 300 b.; SB; *Seurahuone*, Humalistonkatu 2, 124 b.; *Turun Karina*, Itäinen Pitkakatu 30b, 42 b.

HOLIDAY AND SUMMER HOTELS. – *Domus Aboensis*, Piispankatu 10, 160 b. (1 June to 31 August); *Rantasipi Ikituuri Sommer Hotel*, Pispalantie 7, 1152 b., SB (1 June to 31 August).

YOUTH HOSTEL: Linnankatu 39. – CAMP SITES: *Ruissalo* and *Vepsä*.

RESTAURANTS. – *Brahen Kellari*, Puolalankatu 1; *Teatteriravintola Foija*, Aurakatu 10; *Samppalinna*, Itäinen Rantakatu (summer only).

EVENTS. – *Boat Show* (second half of April); *Rock Festival* at Ruissalo (beginning of August); *Turku Music Festival* (beginning of August); *Turku Trade Fair* (mid-August); *Handicraft Days* (first half of September).

**The southern Finnish town of Turku (Swedish Åbo), the country's third largest and oldest city and once its capital, lies on the Gulf of Bothnia, at the mouth of the Aurajoki, sheltered by a number of large islands and by countless skerries. About 5% of the population is Swedish-speaking. It is the administrative hub of the province of Turku and Pori, the see of the Lutheran Archbishop of Finland and the seat (since 1623) of the Provincial Court, with a Finnish and a Swedish university and a commercial college. Together with the neighbouring Naantali, it is a key port for imports, particularly in winter, since the access route through the skerries can be kept open all year. Turku is also an important industrial town (shipbuilding, engineering, foodstuffs, textiles, etc.).**

HISTORY. – The town developed from a settlement on the *Koroinen* peninsula, on the N side of the Aurajoki estuary, and received its charter from Gustavus Vasa in 1525. In 1630, Gustavus Adolphus established a grammar school; the school was raised to university status in 1640 by Queen Christina. The treaty ending the Swedish-Russian war of 1741–3 was signed in Turku. In 1809, the town was passed to Russia, along with the rest of Finland. In 1810, the seat of government was transferred to Helsinki and, after a devastating fire in 1828, the University was also moved there. After the declaration of Finnish independence in 1918, a new Swedish university was established, and in 1920 a Finnish university; Turku thereafter took on a new lease of life. Since the Second World War, there has been a steady development of industry and a rapid increase in the growth of the tourist trade.

SIGHTS. – The hub of the city's traffic is the *Market Square* (Kauppatori: market until 2 p.m. daily), on the N bank of the Aurajoki. At the S corner is the *Swedish Theatre* (1838), on the NW side, the *Orthodox Church* (C. L. Engel, 1846). From here, the busy Aurakatu runs NW to the **Museum of Art** (*Taidemuseo*; by

Flower market, Turku

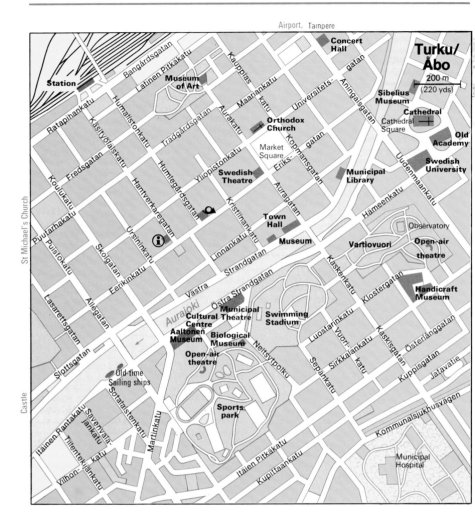

G. Nyström, 1904), a handsome granite building standing on elevated ground, surrounded by gardens (rich collection of pictures and sculpture, primarily by Finnish artists). On the steps leading up to the entrance are figures (W. Aaltonen) of the Finnish painters *R. W. Ekman* (1809–73) and *V. A. Westerholm* (1860–1919). – To the W of the Museum is the*Central Station. – SW of the station, in Puistokatu, stands the neo-Gothic *St Michael's Church* (1905).

Aurakatu runs SE to the *Aura Bridge* (Auransilta). To the right, on the banks of the river, is the *Town House (Kaupungintalo,* 1885), and near this, the oldest surviving wooden house in the town (restored 1957), a *Pharmacy Museum.* – to the left, upstream, is the *Municipal Library* (C. Wrede, 1903), modelled after the Knights' House in Stockholm, with an attractive fountain; beyond this the Cathedral Bridge leads across the river to the Cathedral. In

Aninkaistenkatu, which runs NW from the bridge, are the *Göteborg Commercial College* (No. 9) and the *Concert Hall* (1953), with a sculptured group by W. Aaltonen (1955).

At the SE end of the Cathedral Bridge, from which Uudenmaankatu continues SE, is Cathedral Square, attractively laid out in gardens. On the W side of the square are a statue of the Finnish historian, *H. G. Porthan* (1739–1804), the *Swedish Lyceum* (1724), originally founded in 1630 as the Grammar School, and the *Old Town Hall,* now occupied by the police. – On the E side of the square, on Unikankari Hill, stands the *Cathedral (Tuomikirkko;* formerly St Henrik's), founded about 1230 and consecrated in 1290. This is a massive brick building in late Romanesque style with Gothic and Renaissance additions and a tower 98 m (320 ft) high.

The INTERIOR (restored after a fire in 1827) contains several monuments to notable figures of the past. To the right of the main entrance is the funerary chapel of Torsten Stålhandske (d. 1644), Swedish commander of the Finnish cavalry in the Thirty Years War. To the left of the entrance is the Tavast Chapel, with the tombs of Bishops Magnus Tavast (d. 1452), Olaus Tavast (d. 1460) and Magnus Stjernkors (d. 1500). On the left of the choir is the Kankas Chapel, the finest in the church, built for the Horn and Kurck families; in the middle of this chapel can be seen the granite sarcophagus (1867) of Queen Karin Månsdotter (d. 1612), daughter of a common soldier, who was raised to the throne by Erik XIV. On the right of the choir is the Tott Chapel, built by Per Brahe in 1678, with the tombs of the Swedish general, Åke Tott (d. 1640) and his wife, Sigrid Bjelke.

Immediately SE of the Cathedral, in Hämeenkatu, is the *Old Academy* (1802–15), home of the University until its transfer to Helsinki in 1828, and which now accommodates the provincial government offices, the provincial court of appeal and the Cathedral chapter. Adjoining it to the SW, at the corner of Uudenmaankatu, is the **Swedish University** (*Åbo Akademi*), opened in 1919. In the gardens in front of the building is a bronze statue of *Per Brahe*, governor-general of Finland in 1637–40 and 1648–54 (W. Runeberg, 1888), with an inscription on the base, "Jagh war med landett, och landett med mig wääl till-freds" ("I was well pleased with the country, and the country with me"). – A little way N of the Cathedral, at No. 17 Piispankatu, is the *Sibelius Museum*, with manuscripts and relics of the great Finnish composer. At No. 14 Piispankatu is *"Ett Hem" Museum* (19th c. interior and furnishings). – About 500 m (550 yds) NE of the Cathedral is the **Finnish University** (*Turun Yliopisto*), founded in 1922 (present buildings 1954–60). – From Cathedral Square Uudenmaankatu runs SE to *Kupittaa Park*. In the southern half of the park are a swimming pool and St Henry's Spring, with whose water the first Finnish Christians are said to have been baptised. Christianity came late to Finland when the Swedish King Erik IX led a crusade to Christianise the Finns. An Englishman, Henry, who was Bishop of Uppsala at the time, went with him and was left by Erik to found the first bishopric at Turku. The Finns did not take kindly to this forced Christianisation and Henry was killed. He was later canonised and is now the Patron Saint of Finland.

SW of the Old Town Hall, at the foot of the hill of **Vartiovuori**, we see the headquarters of the *Economic Society*, founded in 1797 to promote the development of agriculture, the arts and industry. Diagonally opposite, in the little Runeberg Park on the banks of the Aurajoki, is a sculpture by Wäinö Aaltonen, "Lilja". – On Vartiovuori itself there are attractive public gardens, the former *Observatory* and a *summer theatre*. – On the S side of the hill, in a number of old houses which survived the 1827 fire, is the **Handicraft Museum** (*Käsityöläismuseo*), with old craft workshops. – Farther W, beyond Kaskenkatu, is the hill of Samppalinna; on the W side of the hill is the *Swimming Stadium*. On the far side of Neitsytpolku the *Biological Museum* offers an excellent representation of the animal life of Finland. To the SW is the *Sports Park*. – NW of the Swimming Stadium, in Itäinen Rantakatu, which runs along the S side of the Aurajoki, is the *Municipal Theatre* (1962), and, in front of it a statue of the writer, *Aleksis Kivi* (W. Aaltonen, 1949). – Farther W, at No. 11 Itäinen Rantakatu, is the *Wäinö Aaltonen Museum* (1967; sculpture, etc.). To the S are an *open-air theatre* and an old windmill.

Moored at St Martin's Bridge (Martin-silta) are two old sailing ships. The "Suomen Joutsen" is now a training ship for sailors; the sailing barque "Sigyn" (built 1887, restored 1971–8) is open to the public in summer. To the SW, in Vilhonkatu, stands *St Martin's Church* (1933). – On the eastern outskirts of the town the new *cemetery* has a fine chapel (1941) by the Finnish architect, E. Bryggman, a native of Turku.

To the W of the town, near the harbour on the right bank of the Aurajoki (reached from Aurakatu by way of Linnankatu), stands *Turku Castle (Turun Linna)*, once the key to Finland. It was probably built about 1300 on what was then an island in the Aurajoki estuary; it was enlarged in the 16th and 17th c. and restored in 1959–61. It now houses the town's *Historical Museum* (portraits, furniture, tapestries, costumes, arms and armour, etc., illustrating the development of Finnish culture). The *castle chapel* displays ecclesiastical antiquities.

SURROUNDINGS. – 2 km (1¼ miles) NE of Cathedral Square, on the outskirts of the town (along Hämeenkatu, then beyond the railway turn left along Kirkkotie), is the little 14th c. *St Karin's Church* (Kaarinan Kirkko). In the churchyard is the tomb of the lawyer, Mathias Calonius (1738–1817), first governor of Finland after its annexation by Russia, who honourably insisted on the observance of the country's old laws which had been guaranteed by the Tsar. – 3 km (2 miles) NE of Turku station on the Tampere road (Tampereentie) stands *St Mary's Church* (Maarian Kirkko), a fine 14th c. church of undressed stone in excellent condition. Nearby are the sparse remains of what is said to have been the first Christian church in the country, built at the village of Räntämäki in 1161.

SW of Turku, off the mouth of the Aurajoki, lies the island of **Ruissalo**, linked with the mainland by a bridge; it has an extensive recreation area (camp site; restaurant; golf, miniature golf, riding, water-skiing). In the middle of the island is a spring with an inscription commemorating the Swedish poet, M. Choräus (1774–1806), who lived on the island for a while. On the S coast is a bathing beach. – On the mainland, to the N of the island, is the oil port of *Pansio*, with storage tanks. – S of Ruissalo in the Ruissalo Sound, the primary shipping channel for Turku, is the little island of *Pikku-Pukki*, a popular excursion from Turku (motorboat services), with the Airisto Yacht Club and a summer restaurant.

On the coast, 17 km (10 miles) W of Turku, we come to the little town of **Naantali** (Swedish *Nådendal*), a popular resort (pop. 8000; Gasthaus Unikeko, 110 b., SB; Naantalin Kylpyla Spa, 196 b.). The town developed around a Brigittine convent founded in 1443. An ancient church on the coast N of the town has a number of old monuments and a 15th c. altar from Danzig. Near the church is a stone commemorating Jöns Budde (d. 1491), the earliest identifiable Finnish writer; he was a monk in Naantali. – Naantali is now Finland's leading port for imports, with the country's first oil refinery. – On the island of *Luonnonmaa*, to the W of Naantali, which is linked with the mainland by the Ukka-Peka Bridge, is *Kultaranta*, summer residence of the President of Finland.

**Turku to Parainen.** – Leave on Road 1, and in 9 km (5 miles), at Kaarina, turn into the beautiful Road 180, which runs S over the *Pohjoissalmi* on to the island of *Kuusisto* (Swedish Kustö). Soon after the bridge a narrow road (6 km – 4 miles) goes off on the left to the meagre remains of *Kuusisto Castle*, at the E end of the island, a stronghold of the bishops of Finland; it was built in 1317 and demolished at the Reformation (1528). – From Kuusisto a suspension bridge 300 m (330 yds) long (1963) crosses the *Rävsund* to the island of *Kirjala*. Here a road branches off on the left to the well-preserved 15th c. *Kvidja Castle*, 7·5 km (5 miles) SE on the N coast of the island of *Lemlahti*, which once belonged to Bishop Magnus Tavast. – 2 km (1¼ miles) beyond this turn, the main road crosses the *Hässund* on a bridge 115 m (125 yds) long and in another 4 km (2½ miles) reaches **Parainen** (Swedish *Pargas*), with limestone quarries, large cement works and an old stone church (fine interior). About 13 km (8 miles) SW of the town, amid a great scatter of skerries, is the island of *Stormälö*, a popular holiday resort. Here is the *Airisto Hotel*, run by the Finnish Tourist Board (71 b.; open from the beginning of June to the end of August). – 16 km (10 miles) SW of Parainen, on the same road as the Airisto Hotel, is the little port of *Lillmälö*. – From Lillmälö it is possible to continue by means of three ferries and a road running SW over the *Nagu Islands* to the island of *Korpo*, lying far from the mainland (35 km = 22 miles) to Korpo church, which contains some old wooden sculpture).

**Turku to Uusikaupunki.** – Road 8 runs via Raisio and Mynämäki to Laitila; 18 km (12 miles) SW on Road 198 is **Uusikaupunki** (Swedish *Nystad*), a port

and commercial town (pop. 12,000) on the Gulf of Bothnia with a large granite-working industry. The town was founded during the reign of Gustavus Adolphus in 1616. The treaty of Nystad which ended the Nordic War and gave Russia possession of Ingermanland, Estonia, Livonia and part of Karelia was signed here in 1721 (monument in market square, erected 1961). In Town Hall Square is the New Church (1863); the Old Church (1629) now houses a small museum of cultural history. – Attractive boat trips to the offshore islands. – 7 km (4½ miles) S of the town is the fine old manor-house of *Sundholm*. – A road runs N via *Pyhäranta* and continues following close to the coast, to Rauma.

**The "Seven Churches Route".** – An attractive round trip taking in seven old churches. – Leave Turku on the Pori road (No. 8). – 7 km (4½ miles) from the middle of town, before the turning for Naantali, the 14th c. stone church of **Raisio** is passed on the left. – 10 km (6 miles) farther on is the little stone church of *Masku*. To the SW is *Kankainen Castle*. – 4·5 km (3 miles) beyond Masku is **Nousiainen**, with an old stone church 3·5 km (2 miles) off the road to the NE. – Turning left into a road signposted to Askainen, after 7·5 km (5 miles) comes *Nyynäinen*. 1·5 km (1 mile) SW is **Lemu** church. – 8 km (5 miles): **Askainen**, with an old stone church. 2 km (1¼ miles) W, on the coast, is the estate of *Luohisaari*, birthplace of Marshal Mannerheim. – The road continues S from Askainen; then a ferry to the much indented island immediately to the S. – 11 km (7 miles): **Merimasku**, at the northern tip of the island, with a wooden church (1726). – 4 km (2½ miles) beyond Merimasku is a road junction; continuing straight ahead (15 km – 10

Interior of Rymättylä church

miles) is **Rymättylä**, with a 15th c. church (wall paintings). – The road to the left at the junction is the return route to Turku. In 1·5 km (1 mile) it crosses a bridge on to the island of *Luonnonmaa* and cuts across the island, passing Kultaranta Castle (1·5 km (1 mile) to left), to the 200 m (220 yd) long Ukku Peka Bridge (1934). – 6 km (4 miles): *Naantali*, from which it is 17·5 km (11 miles) back to Turku via Raisio.

# Umeå

Sweden (Eastern).
Province: Västerbottens län.
Region: Västerbotten.
Altitude: 20 m (66 ft). – Population 84,000.
Postal code: S-90 . . . – Telephone code: 0 90.

(i) **Umeå Turistbyrå**,
Rådhustorget,
S-90247 Umeå;
tel. 16 16 16.

HOTELS. – *Blå Aveny*, Rådhusesplanaden 14, 258 b.; *Blå Dragonen*, Norrlandsgatan 5, 135 b.; *Scandic Hotel*, Yrkesvägan 8, 350 b., SB; *Stora Hotellet*, Storgatan 46, 160 b., SB; *Strandhotell*, Vastra Strandgatan 11, 64 b.; *Wasa* Vasagatan 12, 88 b.; *Winn* Skolgatan 64, 272 b.

**Umeå, main town of the Swedish province of Västerbotten, lies on the left bank of the Umeälv, about 5 km (3 miles) above its outflow into the Gulf of Bothnia. It is a port, an industrial and commercial town and the cultural hub of northern Norrland. It has a variety of industries, principally woodworking. It is the seat of the Provincial Appeal Court and has a university (founded 1963), various schools and other educational institutions, and a library.**

Umeå was granted a municipal charter for the second time in 1622, but its development really began only with the rise of the woodworking industry in the second half of the 19th c. In 1888, a great fire destroyed three-quarters of the town's houses and its three shipyards for wooden vessels, it was then rebuilt with broad streets lined with avenues of birch-trees. The town is particularly attractive when its 5500 trees burst into leaf (about 20 May).

SIGHTS. – In the middle of the town is the *Rådhustorg* (Town Hall Square), with a large bust of Gustavus Adolphus, founder of Umeå. To the S, in Storgata, is the neo-Gothic brick *church* (1892); outside stands an *obelisk* marking the common grave of a Swedish colonel, J. Z. Duncker, and a Cossack colonel, Aerekoff, who died in the fighting at Hörnefors in 1809. In *Döbeln Park*, adjoining the church, is a monument commemorating the Swedish general, G. C. von Döbelm, commander of the last united Swedish-Finnish army; his ashes were scattered here after the war with Russia (1808–9). After the end of the war, in 1809, Finland became an autonomous Duchy of Russia. – On a hill NE of the town is the **Gammlia Open-Air Museum**, with the *Västerbotten Provincial Museum*. Among the buildings here is an 18th c. house, *Sävargården*, headquarters of the Russian general, Kamensky, during the Swedish-Russian war. The *Helena Elisabeth Church*, originally a fishermen's chapel on the island of Holmö, is in part built of wood from wrecked ships. *Lars Fägrares Gård*, now a skiing museum and youth hostel, is a

Umeå

typical old craftsman's house. – SE of the town are the buildings of the *University*.

SURROUNDINGS. – 17 km (10 miles) SE of the town lies its outer harbour, *Holmsund* (large sawmills), from which there is a ferry service to Vaasa in Finland. Holmsund lies on the "Blue Highway", which cuts across E4 and E79 to the W of Umeå and traverses the magnificent scenery of southern Lapland into Norway. The first part of its course follows the *Umeälv* (numerous rapids). – 15 km (9 miles) NW of Umeå, at *Sörfors*, is the large underground power station of *Stornorrfors* (1959), with a fall of 75 m (250 ft) and a turbine hall 24 m (80 ft) high cut from rock (open to visitors June to August). Here, too, is a large *salmon hatchery* which releases 100,000 young salmon annually into the Umeåälv. The salmon can be seen leaping up the small waterfall below the large dam.

120 km (75 miles) S of Umeå, on a skerry-fringed inlet, is **Örnsköldsvik** (hotels: Focus, 106 b., SB; Scandic, 160 b., SB; Statt, 194 b., SB). The town is named after Per Abraham Örnsköld, governor of Västernorrland from 1762 to 1769, who promoted the development of this area. The rise of Örnsköldsvik is primarily due to its sawmills and the development of its shipping trade, aided by a natural deep-water harbour which is ice-free for eleven months of the year and makes regular service to Vaasa possible (see p. 281). With its population of 16,000, Örnsköldsvik is one of the most rapidly expanding towns in Swedish Norrland. It is in a very attractive setting, bounded on the landward side by wooded hills which extend inland, offering good fishing in their streams and good skiing in winter. From the *Varvsberg* (restaurant; motor road) there is a fine view of the sea. In the town itself, there is the Town Hall (1909), and in the Torgpark, the figure of an eagle cut into the local granite (Bruno Liljefors); this has become the emblem of the town. To the E of the town is Fornhemmet (open-air museum).

# Uppsala

Sweden (Central).
Province: Uppsala län. – Region: Uppland.
Altitude: 7 m (23 ft). – Population: 151,000.
Postal code: S-75104... – Telephone code: 018.
ⓘ **Turistinformation,**
Stathuset, Kungsgatan 44,
S-75104 Uppsala;
tel. 11 75 00.

HOTELS. – *Gillet*, Dragarbrunnegatan 23, 278 b.; *Grand Hotel Hörnan*, Bangårdsgatan 1, 70 b.; *Linné*,

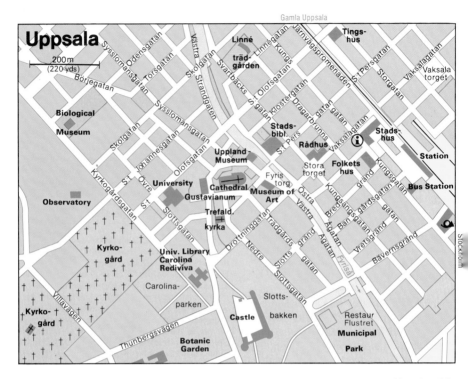

Skolgatan 45, 160 b.; *Scandic Hotel*, Gamla Upp-salagatan 48, 296 b., SB; *Uplandia*, Dragarbrunns-gatan 32, 14 b. – two YOUTH HOSTELS. – CAMP SITE.

SPORTS and RECREATION. – *Linnaean walks* (botanical excursions, in summer); old railway to Lenna (June to August); golf, tennis, riding.

**The famous Swedish university town of *Uppsala lies about 70 km (45 miles) NW of Stockholm in a fertile plain on the banks of the Fyriså. It is the main town of its province and the see of the Lutheran Archbishop of Sweden. There is a variety of industry in the vicinity (primarily engineering, pharmaceu-ticals and printing).**

The province of Uppsala occupies the central part of the region of Uppland, which played a prominent part in the early history of Sweden. The people of Upp-land (Svea) had the right to elect and depose their kings, and the name of Sweden itself (Sverige) is derived from Svea. The term Svea Rike, ''the kingdom of the Swedes'', is still found in the traditional painting of Dalarna (Dalmål-ninger).

HISTORY. – Uppsala can claim to be the historical hub of Sweden. At the time when the Swedish kings resided at *Gamla Uppsala* (Old Uppsala) the present town, then known at *Östra Aros*, was merely the port and trading station of the capital. In 1273 the

archiepiscopal see was transferred to Uppsala, while the royal residence was moved to Stockholm. – The University, which plays a central role in the life of Uppsala, was founded in 1477 by Archbishop Jakob Ulvsson and developed into a major focus of learning, thanks to the patronage of Gustavus Adolphus. The contrast between the two aspects of Uppsala – its ecclesiastical and academic side and its secular and commercial side – can still be felt, although the middle of the town has been largely transformed by the new building of the 1960s and 1970s.

SIGHTS. – The *Cathedral, consecrated in 1435, was originally based on English

In Uppsala Cathedral

models, but later received its High Gothic stamp from a French architect, Etienne de Bonneuil. Total length 118·7 m (390 ft), internal width 45 m (150 ft), height of towers 118·7 m (390 ft). The towers were partly rebuilt after a fire in 1702, and the spires were restored in 1745. Restoration work carried out about 1880 gave rise to much criticism, and in recent years radical changes have been made to restore the original character of the Cathedral.

INTERIOR. – There is a splendid Baroque pulpit by B. Precht (1707). At the E end of the choir is the *Gustavian Chapel*, with the tomb of Gustavus Vasa which was carved in Holland (*c.* 1576). On the N side are the tomb of Katarina Jagellonica (1583) and the marble monument of her husband, Johan III. On the N side is the Oxenstierna Chapel. Also buried in the Cathedral are the scientist, Carl von Linné (Linnaeus), Archbishop Nathan Söderblom and the philosopher, Swedenborg. The *Silver Chamber* contains, among other treasures, the gilded reliquary (1574–9) of King Erik (St Erik), killed by the Danes in 1160. In the N tower is a *museum*, with, among much else, a gold brocade robe (*c.* 1400) which belonged to Queen Margaret, ruler of the united kingdoms of Denmark, Norway and Sweden.

NW of the Cathedral is the *Biological Museum*, with large dioramas illustrating the animal life of Sweden.

Below the Cathedral, on the banks of the Fyriså, is the *Uppland Museum* (regional history and culture). To the W of the Cathedral stands the **Gustavianum** (*c.* 1620), presented to the University by Gustavus Adolphus; it contains the University's *Cultural History Collections*, the *Museum of Nordic Antiquities* and the *Victoria Museum* (Egyptian antiquities). In Fyristorg is the *Art Collection*. – In the University gardens, behind the Gustavianum, are a number of runic stones and a bronze statue of the historian and poet E. G. Geijer. – The new *University* buildings were erected in 1879–86. The University now has about 20,000 students. – To the S of the Gustavianum stands *Trinity Church* (Trefaldighetskyrkan), the oldest parts of which date from the 12th c. (medieval wall paintings).

The **University Library** (*Carolina Rediviva*) is Sweden's largest library, with more than 2 million volumes and 30,000 manuscripts. Its greatest treasure (in the display collection to the right of the entrance) is the famous **Codex Argenteus**, probably written at Ravenna in the reign of Theodoric the Great (6th c.). It contains the translation of the Gospels by the Gothic bishop, Wulfila or Ulfilas (d. 383), in silver and gold letters on 187 pages of purple parchment; the silver binding is 17th c. Other valuable items are the *Codex Uppsalensis* (the oldest manuscript of Snorre Sturlasson's Younger Edda, *c.* 1300), the *Decretum Concilii Uppsaliensis* of 1593, with many signatures, and Olaus Magnus's *Carta Marina* (a map of northern Europe printed in Venice in 1539). The oldest Swedish printed book is dated 1483.

Uppsala University

To the S of the University Library we find the *Botanic Garden*. On elevated ground, to the SE, is the **Castle**, begun by Gustavus Vasa in 1548 but only half completed; it now houses the governor's residence, offices and the provincial archives. Erik IV had Count Sture murdered here, and here also, in the Great Hall, Queen Christina abdicated the throne. From the bastions there are fine views of the town and surrounding countryside. On the NW bastion is a bell, made for Queen Gunilla Bielke, which strikes the hours at 6 a.m. and 7 p.m. daily. Behind the Castle is a *bust of Gustavus Vasa* (by Fogelberg), surrounded by cannon. – To the SE of the Castle extends the *Municipal Park*, with Flustret summer restaurant. – In the *cemetery* to the W is the grave of Dag Hammarskjöld (1905–61), former Secretary General of the United Nations.

From the University Library, Drottninggata runs NE to the Stortorg, in which stands the *Town Hall* (Rådhus, 1883). In the nearby Svartbäcksgata is the *Linnaean Garden* (Linnéträdgården; the great botanist, Linnaeus, was curator here), and the **Linnaean Museum**. Carl von Linné (1707–78), known as Linnaeus, devised the technical language of

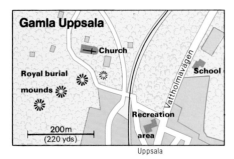

**Gamla Uppsala**

Church

Royal burial mounds

School

Recreation area

200m
(220 yds)

Uppsala

botany and the Linnaean system (published in 1735) of botanical nomenclature, the binomial system which is still in use. – To the E of the Stortorg is the **railway station**, to the W of the station the *Folkets Hus* (People's House), with the Municipal Theatre, and to the N the *Town Hall* (Stadshus).

SURROUNDINGS. – 5 km (3 miles) N is *Gamla Uppsala* (Old Uppsala), once capital of the kingdom of the Svear. The little church of undressed stone is a remnant of the former Cathedral, built about 1125. The old offertory box has been preserved, and the bishop's throne is one of the oldest pieces of furniture in Sweden. Three large *burial mounds*, thought to date from the 6th c., contain the remains of kings Adil, Egil and Aun. From a low hill to the E, the *Tingshög*, the kings addressed their people. In the Odinsborg Inn, visitors can drink mead from silver-mounted drinking horns. To the N is the open-air museum of *Disagården*, with old houses from the surrounding area. – 11 km (7 miles) SE of Uppsala, in a house built

in 1779, are the *Mora Stones* on which kings took an oath after their election; the name of the king was inscribed on the stone. – 3 km (2 miles) away is **Hammarby**, once Linnaeus's summer home and now a museum. – 4 km (2½ miles) NE of the Mora Stones is *Lagga* church, with 15th c. wall paintings.

30 km (20 miles) S of Uppsala, on Lake *Skarven*, is **Sigtuna** (pop. 4000; Stadshotell, 45 b.), one of the oldest towns in Sweden, founded by Olof Skötkonung in the 11th c. The first Swedish coins, with the inscription "Situne Dei", were struck here by coiners brought from England by Olof. The first episcopal see in the land of the Svear and a busy trading town in its early days, Sigtuna declined in importance when the bishop moved his residence to Uppsala in 1130. In 1187, the town was attacked by the Estonians and set on fire. It took Sigtuna five centuries to recover a measure of prosperity. The founding of a Dominican monastery in 1237 marked the beginning of its revival.

The main street, Stora Gatan, follows the same lines it did around 1000, as was shown by the discovery of the old road 3 m (10 ft) below the present ground level. Excavated material, including remains of the earliest buildings on this site, can be seen in the *Museum* in Lilla Torget. The ruins of the churches of *St Lars*, *St Per* and *St Olof* bear witness to the town's past glory. St Olof's church (mid-12th c.) was probably built on the site of an old sacred spring to which offerings were made. Nearby stands the 13th c. *St Mary's Church*, an old monastic church with 13th c. wall paintings and the tomb of Archbishop Jarler (d. 1255), who had been a monk in the monastery. In the choir is a fine 15th c. altar screen. The *Lundströmske Hus*, a handsome old burgher's house, contains period furnishings. To the W of the town is the *Sigtuna Foundation* (1915), with a Lutheran folk high school and a guest-house.

Skokloster Castle

10 km (6 miles) NW of Sigtuna as the crow flies, but accessible only from the Stockholm–Enköping road (E18), is Skokloster Castle, on the *Skofjord*.

*Skokloster Castle* was originally a Cistercian abbey, founded in 1244. The abbey, with the exception of the church, was demolished in 1574. The estate was acquired in 1611 by Field Marshal Herman Wrangel, whose son Karl Gustav, Count of Salamis, was born here in 1613. Karl Gustav Wrangel, later Riksmarskalk and Riksamiral (grand Marshal and Grand Admiral) of Sweden, built the present castle in 1654–7. The architect was first de la Vallée and later Tessin the Elder. The castle, built of brick, is an imposing Baroque pile on a quadrangular plan with an octagonal tower at each corner. The interior, well preserved, is richly decorated, with fine stucco, wall and ceiling paintings and collections of *pictures* and *weapons*. Among items of special interest are the ceremonial shield of the Emperor Charles V, probably made in Augsburg, a sword which belonged to the Hussite leader Jan Žiška and the sword used in the "Bloodbath of Linköping".

The *church* to the N of the castle contains a 13th c. triumphal cross, the *Wrangel burial vault* and a pulpit from Oliva, near Danzig, brought back from the Thirty Years War. Immediately E of the church is a *runic stone* with carved figures of two horsemen which are probably a good deal older than the runic inscription. Nearby is an *Automobile Museum*.

# Vaasa (Vasa)

Finland (Western).
Province: Vaasan lääni (Vasa län/Vaasa).
Altitude: sea level. – Population: 55,000.
Postal code: SF-65100. – Telephone code: 9 61.
(i) **Kaupungin Matkailutoimisto**
   (*Municipal Tourist Information Office*),
   Town Hall;
   tel. 11 38 53.

HOTELS. – *Astor*, Asemakatu 4, 50 b.; *Central*, Hovioikeudenpuistikko 21, 310 b., SB; *Coronet*, Ylatori, 106 b.; *Wasa*, Hovioikeudenpuistikko 18, 320 b., SB; *Waskia*, Lemmenpolku, 400 b. – YOUTH HOSTEL. – CAMP SITE.

EVENTS. – *Vaasa Festival* (June); *Stundars Feast*, with folk singing and dancing (July).

SPORTS and RECREATION. – Bowling, tennis, golf, riding, fishing, sailing.

**The western Finnish town of Vaasa (Swedish Vasa), on the Gulf of Bothnia, is the main town of its province and the seat of the Provincial Appeal Court. A third of the population is Swedish-speaking. The town lies at the narrowest part of the Gulf of Bothnia, sheltered by a girdle of skerries (rocky islets), the archipelago of the Valsöarna and the islands of Vallgrund and Björkö. The shortest route between Finland and Sweden is the Vaasa–Umeå ferry.**

HISTORY. – The town, named after the Swedish royal house of Vasa, was founded in 1606 at Mustasaari, then on the coast but now 6 km (4 miles) inland. It received its municipal charter in 1611. It was twice destroyed in war, in 1714 and 1808, and was devastated by a great fire in 1852. It was rebuilt, beginning in 1862, on the coast, now farther W. The rebuilding was directed by the provincial architect, Carl Axel Setterberg; and, as at Pori, the new town was laid out with broad avenues (*puistikko*) to reduce the fire hazard. Setterberg favoured the neo-Gothic style; other architects went in for a variety of other styles. – In December 1917, after the proclamation of Finnish independence, Vaasa became the temporary capital of the country, when the socialist militia seized control of Helsinki and the Senate was compelled to flee to Vaasa. From here, General C. G. Mannerheim directed operations for the recovery of the capital from the Red Brigades and the Russian troops supporting them. This explains the cross of freedom which features in the town's coat of arms, as it does in the arms of Mikkeli.

SIGHTS. – Between the two wide avenues, Hovioikeudenpuistikko and Vaasanpuistikko, which run SW from the station through the middle of the town, is the *Market Square*, with a monument commemorating the 1918 war of liberation. SW of the square are the neo-Gothic *Trinity Church* (C. A. Setterberg, 1868) with an altarpiece by A. Edelfelt, and the neo-Baroque **Town House** (1881). Opposite the church, to the N, is a bronze *statue* of the writer *Zachris Topelius*. At the W end of Hovioikeudenpuistikko (Appeal Court Avenue), in a square laid out in gardens by the sea, is the *Provincial Court of Appeal* (1859). To the S of the court is a monument commemorating the landing of a Prussian battalion in February 1918. To the N is the Mariepark, with the *Österbotten Regional Museum* (Pohjanmaa Museum). – To the S of the town lies *Hietalahti Park*, with the *Brage open-air museum* and a summer restaurant.

The Vaasanpuistikko runs over a narrow channel (road and railway causeway) on to the island of *Vaskiluoto*. From the causeway, a short side road provides access to the islet of *Hietasaari* (Swedish *Sandö*: park, with bathing facilities).

SURROUNDINGS. – 6 km (4 miles) inland, to the SE, is **Old Vaasa**, the site of the earlier town (destroyed by fire in 1852). Here are the ruins of St Mary's Church, originally on a basilican plan but converted by successive alterations into a cruciform church. Mustasaari church was originally the Court of Appeal, a building in Gustavian style erected in the reign of Gustav III.

The ring of **skerries** in the Gulf of Bothnia offers great variety of beauty and enjoyment. Boats can be rented for fishing trips, or visitors can accompany the local fishermen. There are many huts on the islands, available for rent through the tourist information office. In a particularly hard winter, it is possible to drive across the frozen Gulf of Bothnia from Björköby to Umeå in Sweden.

# Valdres

Norway (Southern).
Counties: Buskerud fylke, Oppland fylke.
ⓘ **Valdres Turistkontor**,
    N-2900 Fagernes;
    tel. (0 61) 5 29 00.

**The fertile region of Valdres, in southern Norway, lies on both sides of the River Begna, which rises in the southern Jotunheim and flows into the Tyrifjord at Hønefoss. It is an attractive valley, with many farms and great expanses of meadowland.**

The base for a trip into Valdres is *Hønefoss* (see p. 141), on the *Begna*, here also known as the *Åndalselv*, which joins the *Randselv* to form the *Storelv*. – 11 km (7

miles) E is the *Ringkollen* (702 m (2303 ft), extensive views). 15 km (10 miles) S, at *Sundvollen* (p. 142), is the panoramic *Kongens Utsikt* (King's View).

From Hønefoss, E68 runs N along the E side of *Lake Sperillen* (23 km (15 miles) long). On the opposite side of the lake, the *Høgfjell* (1010 m – 3314 ft) can be seen.

At the N end of the lake, where the Begna flows in, is the village of *Nes*. Here Road 243 goes off on the left to *Hedal* (13th c. stave church).

E68 now follows the right bank of the Begna to **Begndal** (camp site), in a forest setting. – At *Islandsmoen* is an open-air museum (old houses).

At **Bagn**, a pretty straggling village (radio transmitter), a side road branches off to *Reinli stave church* (12th c.).

**Fagernes** (alt. 360 m (1180 ft); hotels: Fagerlund, 50 b.; Fagernes Hotel, 240 b.,

Valdres – an autumn landscape, Lomen

The Ryfoss, Valdres

# Lake Vänern

Sweden (Southern).
Provinces: Värmlands län, Älvsborgs län, Skaraborgs län.
Regions: Värmland, Dalsland, Västergötland.

(i) **Värmlands Turistråd**,
Box 323,
S-651 05 Karlstad;
tel. (0 54) 10 21 60.

**Lake Vänern, Sweden's largest lake (area 5546 sq. km – 2170 sq. miles), lies in a tectonic basin in the S of the country, to the NW of the road from Göteborg to Örebro. It is divided by the Värmlandsnäs and Kållandshalvö peninsulas, the island of Kållandsö and a number of small islets into two parts, Stora Vänern to the NE and the Dalbosjö to the SW. Its greatest depth is 98 m (320 ft). The hilly nature of the surrounding country leads to a fall in the water level of the lake of about 8 cm (3 in.) per century.**

Plans for regulating the lake were considered in the 16th c., but were not carried through on a large scale until 1938. There is now a heavy shipping traffic on the lake, largely because of the link it provides between the Kattegat and the Baltic, by way of Trollhättan and the Göta Canal.

**Circular Tour of Vänern.** – For motorists coming from Gothenburg, the start of the tour is at Trollhättan. Those coming from Stockholm via Örebro can join the route described below at Kristinehamn, at the NE corner of the lake.

**Trollhättan** (pop. 42,000; Hotell Carliz, 25 b.; Hotell Swania 215 b., SP; Hotell Trollhättan, 70 b.), on the Götaälv, is an industrial town which received its charter only in 1916, although evidence of human occupation here dates back 7000 years. The name first appears in 1413, in the tax records of King Eric of Pomerania; the records state that corn was ground for the castle by the Trollhättan mill. The mills and sawmills of earlier times have now given way to such well-known industrial enterprises as Saab and Nohab, electrochemical plants and engineering works.

The once-renowned **Trollhättan Falls**, where the Götaälv has forced its way through a ridge of gneiss, formerly surged down from a height of 38·5 m (126 ft) to 5·7 m (19 ft) over a distance of 1500 m (1600 yds),

SB, SP; Nythum Høyfjellstue, 40 b.; camp site), set between forest-covered hills at the mouth of the Neselv, which here forms beautiful waterfalls as it flows into the Strandefjord, is a popular tourist resort, a favourite with anglers. *Valdres Folk Museum* (old buildings, domestic equipment, musical instruments, weapons, etc.). – From Fagernes Road 51 runs NW into the Jotunheim (p. 147).

E68 continues in a westerly direction along a number of small fjords and passing through *Lomen* (13th c. wooden church) and *Ryfoss*, to the S shore of *Lake Vangsmjøsa (19 km (12 miles) long), which it follows to *Grindaheim* (alt. 471 m (1545 ft); Grindaheim Turisthotell 120 b.; Mjøsvang Pension og Motell, 90 b.; camp site). The stave church which once stood here was disassembled and reerected at Brückenberg in Silesia in 1841; its place was taken by the white wooden church of *Vang*. Outside the church is a runic stone with the inscription "Gose's sons set up this stone for Gunnar, their brother's son". – A private road runs S from the village to the *Helin National Park* (area 35 sq. km – 14 sq. miles).

At *Øye*, at the W end of Lake Vangsmkjøsa, is a 12th c. stave church, rebuilt from parts found under the floor of a later church.

11 km (7 miles) beyond *Øye*, Road 53 turns off on the right to *Lake Tyin* (p. 148), while E68 continues to the *Sognefjord* (p. 239).

Typical Swedish lake scenery on Lake Vänern

but are now almost dry. In the month of July, when the water level in Lake Vänern usually makes it possible to direct water over the falls, they can be seen in their former magnificence on "Waterfall Day" (mid-July). The huge masses of water which once poured over the falls are now conveyed in underground tunnels to the power station. The Trollhättan Falls have been a problem since the mid-17th c. because they were an obstacle to the creation of a navigable waterway to Norway, and thus to the North Sea, for which the Götaälv provided a basis. To correct this, Christoffer Polhem was commissioned by Charles XII to construct a waterway with eight locks to bypass the falls; but work on the project was halted in 1755, and it was not completed until 1800. Since this canal did not meet the increased demand created by developing industries, it was enlarged in 1844 by the railway engineer, Nils Ericsson. The latest change was in 1916, when a new canal with four locks (height difference 32 m – 105 ft) came into use. About 20,000 vessels now pass through the locks every year. Visitors can see the *locks* and *Oliden power station*. Other features of interest in the town are the *open-air museum*, in a nature park, and the *King's Cave* (Kungsgrottan) at the E end of *Kong Oscars Bro* (King Oscar's Bridge). There is a fine view of the town from *Kopparklinten*.

**Vänersborg** (pop. 20,000; Hotel Gillet, 22 b.; Scandic hotel 286 b., SB; youth hostel), at the northern tip of a promontory reaching out into the lake, is the main town of Älvsborg province. It has an attractive lakeside promenade, Birger Sjöbergsvej, with Skräcklan Park. Here, too, is a statue by Axel Wallenberg,

"Frida" – a figure much celebrated in song. Nearby is the Museum, with material on the history of the town and a collection of exotic birds presented by the explorer, Axel Ericson. In the middle of the town are a number of handsome 18th c. buildings, among them the Governor's Residence (Carl Hårleman, 1754). Nearby is the church (1780).

**Lidköping** (pop. 25,000; hotels: Gyllene Örnen, 45 b.; Sköldmön, 10 b.; Stadshotellet, 115 b.), located on the Kinnevik, at the mouth of the Lidaå, is a port and industrial town with a number of modest industrial establishments, the most famous of which is the Rörstrand porcelain manufactory, established here in 1935. Lidköping received its municipal charter in 1446, when the town lay on the E bank of the Lidaå. When Magnus Gabriel de la Gardie was granted the right to build a town in the county of Läckö in 1670, he laid it out on the W bank, reaching straight down to the river, and the street pattern survives to a large extent in present-day Lidköping. In the Stora Torg Count de la Gardie built a hunting lodge; it later became the Town Hall but burned down in 1960. The new Town Hall was rebuilt on the basis of the original plans. In the square is a statue of de la Gardie. Gamla Staden, the "Old Town" around the Limtorg, has preserved its original buildings and old-world character.

To the N of Lidköping, the peninsula of *Kållandshalvö* reaches out into the lake. Off its northern tip is the rocky island of *Kållandsö*, on the shores of which stands *Läckö Castle, originally built by Bishop Brynolt Algotsson (1298). Investigation has shown that this medieval stronghold, which was much altered in later centuries, had roughly the same ground plan as the present castle. In 1557, after the Reformation, the property passed to the Crown; soon afterward it came into the hands of Svante Sture, and in 1571 was acquired by the Hogenskild Bielke family, who undertook a thorough restoration. In 1615, General Jacob de la Gardie, husband of Ebba Brahe, was granted possession of Läckö Castle along with the title of count. His son, Magnus, did large-scale work on the castle, bringing in two German architects, Elias Holl and Frans Stiemer; they added a fourth floor, new kitchens and an outer work. In 1746, Frederik I had the portrait of Jacob de la Gardie which hung in the Knights' Hall (richly decorated with scenes from the Thirty Years' War) removed to Stockholm; it now hangs in the Military Academy on the Karlsberg. In 1810, Läckö Castle was granted to General Carl Johan Adlercreutz, victor in the battle of Siikajoki, and was renamed Siikajoki in his honour. In 1920, the castle was again thoroughly restored. Since 1965, it has belonged to the Västergötland Tourist Association, which holds exhibitions in the castle during the summer.

SE of Lidköping, away from the lake, lies **Skara** (alt. 113 m (370 ft); pop. 11,000; Tre Hästar Motell, 85 b.; Anglé, 72 b.; Stadshotell, 60 b.; youth hostel; camp site), which developed around an ancient place of assembly (*thing*) and cult site. In the Middle Ages, it became the home of Christian missionaries and the see of a bishop; the seminary for priests established here in the 13th c. was the forerunner of the grammar school founded in 1641. Skara can also claim the first veterinary school in Sweden (1775, now a museum). The Cathedral, originally Gothic (1312–50), was extensively altered in later centuries. The major part of the church (the early 13th c. choir, the early 14th c. nave) is in High Gothic style; the towers date from an early 19th c. rebuilding. The rather unsatisfactory restoration work carried out at the end of the 19th c. was largely corrected after a fire in 1947. In the aisle is the marble sarcophagus of Erik Soop, a cavalry colonel who saved Gustavus Adolphus's life during the Thirty Years' War in 1629. In the Romanesque crypt, below the choir, can be seen the tomb of one of the first bishops, Adalvard. – Opposite the Cathedral is the Diocesan Library. Farther N lies the Municipal Park, with the Västergötland Museum (Fornminnesmuseum) and an open-air museum; together they give a varied and comprehensive picture of life in this region in earlier times. The open-air museum contains a church, as well as old peasants' houses. – In the Stora Torg stands a fine bronze fountain by N. Sjögren (1894).

Varnhem 14 km (9 miles) E of Skara, has a 13th c. church which originally belonged to a Cistercian abbey. It was the burial-place of the kings of Erik's dynasty, and also contains the tomb of Birger Jarl, who died in Västergötland in 1266. After the Reformation and a series of fires, the abbey and its church fell into a dilapidated state. The church was restored by Magnus Gabriel de la Gardie between 1654 and 1673, when it acquired the buttresses which now give the building its characteristic look. De la Gardie and his wife are buried in the church. Conservation work has been carried out on the ruins of the abbey, and some of the finds made during excavations in 1923–7 can be seen in the museum.

***Kinnekulle** (306 m – 1004 ft) is a plateau very characteristic of Västergötland. From the top of the hill (14 km (9 miles) long, 6 km (4 miles) across), covered with coniferous forest (firs), there are fine views of Lake Vänern. The plateaux in this region came into being about 500 million years ago, when the ancient rocks (gneiss) sank into the sea. For millions of years sand, mud and the remains of algae, insects, crustaceans and fish were deposited on the sea floor; in the course of time they turned into stone. Streams of lava later gushed up through clefts in the rock and formed rings around certain areas; then, when the land gradually emerged from the sea again, the more exposed strata were eroded while those protected by the lava remained. The result of this development can be observed on Kinnekulle, with its series of "steps" showing the succession of strata from the ancient rocks upward and throwing important and interesting light on the geological history of the region. Kinnekulle is particularly interesting since it was the last of the plateaux in Västergötland to be formed and has, therefore, the most complete sequence of sediments.

**Mariestad** (pop. 17,000; Sjöstads Hotellet, 68 b.; Hotell Victoria, 30 b.; youth hostel; camp site), located on Lake Vänern, at the mouth of the *Tida*, is an industrial town which was almost completely rebuilt after a fire in 1895. To the N of the town stands the Cathedral (1593–1619; restored 1958–9). On an island in the river is Marieholm Castle, residence of the governor of Skaraborg province (local museum).

The history of **Kristinehamn** (pop. 22,000; Hotel Fröding, 60 b.; Park hotell, 38 b.; Stadshotellet, 70 b.) has been shaped by its location on Lake Vänern. During the Middle Ages it was a market town and port; its importance was enhanced by the development of iron mining in Bergslagen, when Kristinehamn became the port of transhipment of the ore. It received its municipal charter in 1642, during the childhood of Queen Christina, and was named after her. When the railway came to Kristinehamn in the middle of the 19th c., the importance of the town as a port for the shipment of iron and timber was further increased. It retains that important role today. On a promontory extending into the lake is a 15 m (50 ft) high concrete sculpture by Picasso which he presented to the town in 1965 (photograph, p. 158). 4 km (2½ miles) S of the middle of the town is a runic stone dating from the year 500 and 5 km (3 miles) W the *Östervik Chapel* (Georg Adlersparre, 1869), with an attached school.

25 km (15 miles) E of Kristinehamn, at the N end of *Lake Möckeln*, is **Karlskoga** (pop. 38,000; Rex Hotell Skotten, 40 b.; Scandic Hotel 245 b., SP), which obtained its municipal charter as recently as 1940. The surrounding area has been a mining region for centuries. To the E of the town are the Bofors steelworks and rolling mills, established in 1646, which were acquired at the end of the 19th c. by Alfred Nobel, the inventor of dynamite and founder of the Nobel Prizes (housing for staff and employees). To the N of the town is a wooden church (16th c. wall paintings).

At Kristinehamn E18, coming from Stockholm, joins the route around the lake.

**Karlstad:** see p. 157. – Soon afterward, the road begins to turn S and cuts across the root of the Värmlandsnäs peninsula.

**Säffle** (pop. 12,000; Scandic Hotel Royal, 133 b., SB; youth hostel) lies on the Byälv, close to Lake Vänern and the Harefjord. In addition to the large Billerud woodworking and papermaking company, the town has a number of metalworking, engineering and furniture-making plants. Through the town runs the *Säffle Canal*, constructed in 1837 and enlarged in 1866–70; it links the area along the Glavsfjord to the NW with Lake Vänern. In Kungsgården, alongside the town's old water-tower, is Olof Trätäljas Hog, said to be the burial mound of the legendary King Olof Trätälja.

**Åmål** (alt. 49 m (160 ft); pop. 11,000; Stadshotellet, 90 b.) is the only town in Dalsland founded during the reign of Queen Christina (1643). After fires destroyed many of the traditional old wooden houses, the town was largely rebuilt in stone. The old quarter by the Municipal Park, with its wooden houses, is therefore a tourist attraction; this area, with the old market square, is known as Plantaget. The early 18th c. Vagmästare-

gård was long the headquarters of the principal railway official. Before that, it was often the residence of the burgomaster. Nearby is another 18th c. house, the Dalgrensgård (slate roof). In the beautiful Örnäspark is the Hembygdsgård, with a collection of furniture and domestic equipment from the region. Associated with it is a small wildlife park. A short distance away is a lakeside restaurant (beautiful view of the lake).

At the *Köpmannebro* begins the magnificent **Dalsland Canal** (254 km (160 miles) long, with 29 locks), linking a series of lakes: only about 10 km (6 miles) of the total length are recognisable as an artificial canal. This navigable lake system extends from Dalsland into Värmland and Norway. The canal was originally constructed in order to provide a means of transport for the products of the ironworks and sawmills of Värmland and Dalsland; it also formed a convenient link with Norway, and thus with the North Sea. The canal has now outlived its usefulness for the transport of freight, but it is becoming an increasingly popular tourist route, running through beautiful and varied scenery, alternating between fertile farming country, dark forests, rugged hills and barren wastelands. Visitors planning to sail their own boat (or a rented one), through the canal should consult the appropriate tourist information office, since the locks are not always in operation.

The road now leaves the shores of the lake but returns to it at Vänersborg, at its SW corner.

# Värmland

Sweden (Central).
Provinces: Värmlands län, Örebro län.
ⓘ **Värmlands Turistråd**,
   Box 323,
   S-65105 Karlstad;
   tel. (0 54) 10 21 60.

**The beauty of Värmland is in its scenic variety, its alternation between uplands, expanses of plain and many lakes. Although archaeological finds have shown that the region was inhabited by Stone Age people, it was only thinly settled in the medieval period. In those days, there was active border trade with Norway. This was also a route by which Christianity made its way from Norway into Sweden. Given the nature of the soil, agriculture yielded meagre returns. The principal crop grown by the peasants was oats, both for their own subsistence and as fodder for the horses which were used in agriculture but were primarily bred on the landowners' estates.**

In the 16th and 17th c., many Finns settled in Värmland, attracted by the exemption from taxes which was offered as an inducement to settlers. These peasants, known in Sweden as *svedje-bönder*, had their own methods for cultivating the land – they simply burned down the trees. In the course of time, this created difficulties for the mining and ironworking industries, which needed the timber for smelting the iron and for extracting the ore. It was common practice to light fires in the mine shafts to heat the rock, which cracked as it cooled and could be dug out with a pick. This meant that the mines required large quantities of timber, and, since the transport of timber was difficult, the mines were located close to areas of forest. The burning of forests led the mine-owners to complain to the Crown, and this brought the Finnish peasants into conflict with the court. – The development of industry led to increased mining in the middle of the 19th c., and the ore, originally carried by pack-horses and small boats, began to be transported on the canals and by rail.

**Filipstad** (Hennickehammars Herrgård, 104 b.; Scandic Hotel, 105 b., SP), named after Duke Karl Filip, Charles IX's son, is in a beautiful area at the N end of *Lake Daglösen*, surrounded by woodland and lakes. It is within easy reach of hills and attracts many skiing enthusiasts in winter. The town's economy has long depended on the iron mines. Before receiving its municipal charter in 1611, Filipstad was a trading town where iron was exchanged for corn and beef cattle; the agriculture of the region contributed little to its survival. In the last forty years or so, there has been a distinct upsurge of prosperity: old industries have been modernised and new ones begun. Among the town's largest industrial establishments are Wasa Spisbröds Fabrik AB, whose products include a very popular kind of crispbread, and Rosendahls Fabriker, Sweden's largest producer of ink and carbon paper.

The cruciform *church* (1785) was designed by Nicodemus Tessin the Younger. – In the *Eastern Cemetery* (Östra Kyrkogården) is the mausoleum of the engineer and inventor, John Ericsson, whose name is synonymous with the construction of the Swedish railways. In the Market Square (Torget) can be seen an attractive and unusual statue by Bejemark depicting Nils Ferlin, a well-known native of the town, seated on a park bench. (Ferlin was an actor, singer, and the author of popular and satirical songs). Visitors to the town in the first half of September should not miss the traditional Öxhälja market. There are conducted tours of the Wasa crispbread factory. – To the N of Filipstad is the *Storbrohytta*, a 16th c. hammer-mill which remained in operation until 1920.

A popular vacation area in Värmland is the region of the three *Fryken Lakes (p. 158), which, in addition to its beautiful scenery, has many associations with Selma Lagerlöf, and particularly with her famous novel, "Gösta Berling". – At the N end of Upper Lake Fryken is the busy industrial and commercial town of *Torsby* (pop. 3000; Hotell Bjorkarna, 60 b.).

# Västerås

Sweden (Central).
Province: Västmanlands län.
Region: Västmanland.
Altitude: 5 m (16 ft). – Population: 118,000.
Postal code: S-720 . . . – Telephone code: 0 21.
ⓘ **Västerås Turistbyrå,**
  Stora Torget 5,
  S-72215 Västerås;
  tel. 16 18 30.

HOTELS. – *Arkad*, Östermalmsgatan 26, 80 b.; *Astoria Fenix*, Kopparbergsvej 29A, 150 b.; *Park Hotell*, Gunnilbogatan 2, 210 b.; *Scandic Hotel*, Pilgatan, 374 b., SB; *Stadshotellet*, Stora Torget 7, 210 b. – YOUTH HOSTEL.

**Västerås, main town of the very fertile province of Västmanland, lies in an inlet on Lake Mälar, where the Svartå flows in. The town takes its name from its original site on the W side of the river mouth, Västra Aros (aros="river mouth"), which was corrupted into Västerås.**

At the beginning of the 13th c., this was the see of a bishop. Eleven meetings of the Diet were held here. The most important was the one in 1527, during the reign of Gustavus Vasa, at which it was decided to adopt the Reformed faith.

The real development of the town began with the growth of industry in the present century. In 1900, the population was just under 12,000; since then it has increased nearly tenfold. Among the principal industries is the manufacture of electrical appliances (ASEA). It also has an important inland harbour (many pleasure boats).

SIGHTS. – In the middle of the town is the *Stora Torg*. To the S and E run Storagatan

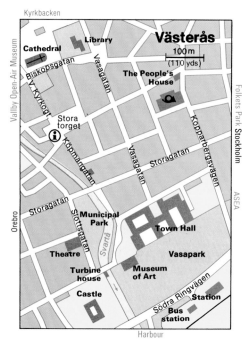

the **Town House** (by Sven Ahlbom, 1959) has a tower 65 m (215 ft) high (carillon). In the old Town Hall is the *Museum of Art* (art from the 17th c. to the present). To the S of the Vasapark, in Södra Ringväg, is the railway station and to the E of the park can be seen the imposing offices of ASEA (electrical appliances). – Storgatan runs E to the *Folkets Park* (People's Park), with recreational and sports facilities and amusements.

SURROUNDINGS. – 2 km (1¼ miles) NW of the middle of the town, on the E18 expressway, is the interesting **Vallby Open-Air Museum**, with old wooden houses and other buildings (including a pharmacy, a silversmith's workshop and a potter's workshop) in which various craftsmen ply their trades. – 6 km (4 miles) NE is the *Anundshög*, with a Viking cemetery (burial mounds, stone-settings). – 2 km (1½ miles) W of the town, in *Lake Märkar*, is the little island of *Elba* (summer restaurant). From Västerås harbour there are regular boat services to this island and to *Östra Holmen* (bathing). – 15 km (10 miles) SW, on the shores of Lake Mälar, is *Tidö Castle* (1640–2), which contains a Toy Museum.

34 km (21 miles) E is **Enköping** (Hotell Park Astoria, 285 b.; Stadshotellet, 115 b., SB), a little town on the Enköpingså whose economy, until the middle of the 19th c., depended upon craft production and the growing of herbs and spices; it became known as the "horse-radish town". From 1880 on, some of the craft workshops developed into small industrial firms and new firms were established, primarily in the engineering field. Today a large proportion of the population is employed in industry. After the last great fire (1799), the town was rebuilt on a rectangular plan, still preserved in the middle of the, town. Most of the buildings are relatively low. The Church of Our Lady (Vårfrukyrkan), built of grey stone, was the seat of a bishop in the 12th c. To the SW of the church are the ruins of the 13th c. St Ilian's Church. On the *Munkssund* are the remains of a Franciscan friary (restored).

**Sala** (Stadshotell, 101 b.; Svea, 20 b.), 49 km (30 miles) NW of Enköping, had its heyday in the 16th c., when the local silver-mines made a major contribution to the country's revenues. The ore worked here is said to have had one of the highest silver contents in the world. Sala obtained its municipal charter in 1624, but mining was already in progress at the end of the 15th c. The mines were controlled by a bailiff who lived in *Väsby Kungsgård*, now a museum. There are conducted tours of the *mining town*, the mines and the museum. The deepest shaft is the Charles XI Shaft (318·8 m – 1046 ft); the Queen Christina Shaft, at the entrance to the mines, is 257 m (843 ft) deep. A large system of water-mills provided power for the mines, which, when they were closed down in 1908, yielded a total of 500 tons of pure silver and 30,000 tons of lead. Although mining continued on a very small scale until about 1950, the yield was insignificant.

In the Stora Torg in the middle of the town are the Town Hall and the Town House. Suckarnas Allé ("Avenue of Sighs"), which runs along Övre Dammen, is named to commemorate the love affair between Gustavus Adolphus and Ebba Brahe. – 1 km

and Vasagatan (both for pedestrians only in this area)..To the N of the Stora Torg stands the *Cathedral (consecrated 1271; altered several times; restored 1959–61), a brick aisled church in Gothic style (tower 103 m (340 ft) high added by Tessin the Younger, 1694). Between the choir and the nave is a 14th c. triumphal cross. The three carved screens in the choir came from Antwerp and Brussels; the one in the middle dates from 1516. Behind the altar is the marble· sarcophagus of King Erik XIV. Other notable features are the Veronica Altar and the marble monument of Grand Marshal Magnus Brahe (1633). In the baptistry are carved woodwork by a North German master and a 15th c. reredos with an inscription in Low German.

In the square in front of the Cathedral is an unusual *bronze statue* (Carl Milles, 1923) of Bishop Johannes Rudbeckius (d. 1646), founder of the grammar school and the Diocesan Library (to the E of the Cathedral), now combined with the *Provincial Library*. – Opposite the Cathedral stands the old *Bishop's Palace*. To the N is the picturesque quarter of *Kyrkbakken*, the oldest part of the town. To the W is the *Djäkneberg Park*, with a monument to famous Swedes. – The **Castle**, on the banks of the Svartå, was originally built in the 13th c.; it now houses the *Provincial Museum* and provincial government offices. – In Fiskartorg

(¾ mile) N of the town is the 14th c. Provincial Assembly Church, with wall paintings (1465) which are the earliest known work of Albertus Pictor; the altar screen (c. 1520) was made in Brussels.

# Västervik

Sweden (Eastern).
Province: Kalmar län. – Region: Småland.
Altitude: sea level. – Population: 21,200.
Postal code: S-593 . . . – Telephone code: 04 90.
ⓘ **Turistbyrån,**
   Strömsholmen,
   S-59300 Västervik;
   tel. 1 36 95.

HOTELS. – *Centralhotellet*, Brunnsgatan 23, 90 b.; *Park Hotell*, Järnvägsgatan 8, 20 b.; *Stadshotellet*, Storgatan 3, 74 b.; *Turist-och Familjehotellet*, Lusärnavägen 2, 22 b. – YOUTH HOSTEL.

**The port of Västervik, on the coast of Småland, is one of the most attractive examples of the old wooden 18th c. towns of Sweden. There are ferry services from here to the island of Gotland.**

SIGHTS. – *St Gertrude's Church* (15th c.) has fine wall paintings and an altar by the Swedish Baroque master, Burchardt Precht (1651–1738). The *Cederflychtska Fattighus* (literally the "poor house"), by Carl Hårleman, 1749–51, is a handsome home for the poor which led a contemporary historian to remark, "In Västervik the poor live better than the rich." – Near here is *Aspagården*, the oldest house in the town, now occupied by three craftsmen. – In Fiskaretorg visitors can sample the local fish specialties, and in the nearby *Batmansgränd* is a row of little red seamen's houses recalling the days when Västervik was a town of seafarers. – Not far away are the ruins of *Stegeholm Castle* (14th c.), which in recent years has been the home of an annual song festival. The Slottsholmen summer restaurant is also here. On the hill of *Kulbacken*, from which there is a fine view of the town, is the *Provincial Museum* (Tjustbygden), with collections of historical material and handicrafts as well as a seafaring section. – 3 km (2 miles) E of the middle of the town is the *Lysingsbad* recreation area. – One of the great attractions of Västervik is its girdle of *skerries*, a scatter of some 5000 small islets.

# Lake Vättern

Sweden (Southern).
Provinces: Skaraborgs län, Östergötlands län, Örebro län, Jönköpings län.
Regions: Västergötland, Östergötland, Närke, Småland
ⓘ **Jönköpings Turistbyrå,**
   Västra Storgatan 9,
   S-55189 Jönköping;
   tel. (0 36) 16 90 50.

*Lake Vättern, Sweden's second largest lake (length 130 km (80 miles), greatest width 30 km – 20 miles), extends through four regions – Östergötland, Västergötland, Närke and Småland. Its water is so clear that the bottom can be seen at depths of up to 10 m (30 ft). The surface appears green as a result of the reflection of light from the sandy bottom.**

The clarity of the water is due to the fact that the lake is fed partly by springs and partly by water from mountain streams, which is purified by passing over gravel. In general, however, the lake is of considerable depth – an average of 40 m (130 ft), reaching as much as 128 m (420 ft) at the deepest spots around Visingsö. This great mass of water stores so much heat that the lake does not freeze until late in the year – rarely before New Year, and in many years not at all. On the other hand, it is slow to warm up in summer. The colder water on the bottom is ideal for many species of fish, including the Vättern salmon (a species of trout).

40 km (25 miles) NE of Jönköping (p. 146) is **Gränna** (pop. 2200; Grännagården, 20 b.; Scandic Hotel, 103 b.), one of

Ruins of Brahehus Castle on Lake Vättern

the few towns with old wooden houses which have not been devastated by fire. With its charming old-world architecture and its beautiful setting on Lake Vättern, at the foot of the Grännaberg, it has become a popular tourist resort.

The town was founded by Per Brahe the Younger, who laid out the main street, Brahegatan, in 1652 in such a way that he could view it from his castle of *Brahehus* (now a ruin). He also built the *Town Hall* with its bell-tower and enlarged the medieval *church* – though at that time there were no more than ten houses in the town. The church, now a handsome Baroque edifice, stands above the town at the foot of the hill. In the cobbled market square is the *Medborgargård*, a community hall. In the *Museigård* is the *Andrée Museum*, commemorating the engineer and Arctic explorer, S. Andrée, a native of the town, who was lost during an attempt to fly in a balloon in 1897 from Spitzbergen to the North Pole.

27 km (17 miles) N of Gränna, at Ödeshög, Road 50 turns off on the left, running at some distance from the lake, and in 8 km (5 miles) reaches *Alvastra* where there are the ruins of a Cistercian abbey (founded in 1143), at the foot of the **Omberg**, a ridge of hills 10 km (6 miles) long which is wooded at the E end and descends steeply to Lake Vättern in the W (*Hjässan*, 263 m (863 ft); footpath 500 m (550 yds) long; lookout). – 6 km (4 miles) farther on, to the right, is *Väversunda*, with a 12th c. church. To the E lies *Lake Tåkern*, the haunt of numerous birds, which features in Selma Lagerlöf's "Adventure of Little Nils Holgersson" and Bengt Berg's animal stories. – 17 km (10 miles) farther N we come to **Vadstena** (pop. 5300; Hotel Solgården, 16 b.; Klosters Gästheim, 60 b.), a town noted for its lace making, which owes its origin to St Birgitta (Bridget). Birgitta was principal lady-in-waiting at the court of King Magnus Eriksson and Queen Blanka, but withdrew from the court after receiving a revelation, and in 1346, was granted the property of Kungsgården for the foundation of an abbey. The abbey was not completed until 1379, after her death. Birgitta was canonised in 1394, and her order spread widely. The little settlement of Vadstena rose to importance as a place of pilgrimage and as a market town and was granted its municipal charter in 1400. After the Reformation, Vadstena declined; in more recent times it has gained importance as a tourist attraction.

Beside the harbour is *Vadstena Castle, a Renaissance structure built by Gustavus Vasa in the 16th c. and later altered and enlarged by his son, Johan III, and his grandson Duke Johan. The high curtain walls along the lake front were razed to supply stone for the construction of the harbour pier.

To the N of the castle is the **Blue Church** (Blåkyrkan), so named because of the colour of the limestone of which it is built. This was the abbey church. Carefully restored in 1898, it has a beautiful interior, with the *reliquary shrine* of St Birgitta and *St Birgitta's Altar*, by a Lübeck master (1459). Most of the nuns' *convent building* has been preserved, together with a more modest building to the S for the monks. – Gustavus Adolphus converted the abbey into a home for old and wounded soldiers and the monks' quarters into the commandant's residence.

Immediately outside the abbey stands *Morten Skinners Hus*, a 16th c. private house. The location of the Town Hall, built in the middle of the 15th c., shows how the middle of the town had moved away from the abbey toward the castle. – In Rådhustorg are a number of well-preserved burghers' houses, notably *Udd Jönssons Hus*; in Storgatan is the *Finspång Hotel*.

**Motala** (pop. 30,000; radio transmitter; Palace Hotell, 90 b.; Stadshotellet, 111 b.), 16 km (10 miles) N of Vadstena, was the meeting-place of the local *thing* (assembly) as early as the 14th c. The church dates from that period. The town became important only after the construction of the *Göta Canal* (p. 100). It is, in fact, the headquarters of the Göta Canal Co. The engineer responsible for the canal, Baltzar von Platen, also prepared the town plan for the district around the *Motalavik*. He is commemorated by a statue by Christian Eriksson in the Stortorg and a mausoleum alongside the canal. – Other features of interest in the town are the nine-arched Storbro (1787) and Borenhults Slusstrappe, a "staircase" of five locks leading into *Lake Boren*.

# Växjö

Sweden (Southern).
Province: Kronobergs län. – Region: Småland.
Altitude: 160 m (525 ft). – Population: 42,000.
Postal code: S-350 . . . – Telephone code: 04 70.
(i) **Växjö Turistbyrå,**
   Kronobergsgatan 8,
   S-35121 Växjö;
   tel. 4 14 10.

HOTELS. – *Cardinal Hotel*, Bäckgatan 10, 77 b.; *Hotell Esplanad*, Esplanaden 21, 56 b.; *Parkhotel*, Sandviksvägen 1, 239 b., SB; *Scandic Hotel*, Hejaregatan 15, 250 b., SB; *Statt*, Kungsgatan 6, 170 b., SB; *Hotell Värend*, Kungsgatan 27, 100 b. – YOUTH HOSTEL.

**Växjö, main town of the province of Kronoberg, lies at the N end of Lake Växjö. There was a trading station here in the Iron Age and in Viking times. In the 12th c. it also became a**

religious focal point when its first church was built by St Sigfrid, a missionary from England, now the town's patron saint. Long predominantly a garrison town and episcopal see, Växjö has developed within recent years into a lively industrial and educational town, with modern buildings and a wide range of recreation facilities.

SIGHTS. – The 12th c. **Cathedral**, after undergoing much alteration in subsequent centuries, was given its present appearance in a restoration carried out in 1959. It has modern stained glass by Jan Brazda, Bo Beskow, Elis Lundquist and Erik Höglund. The organ-case dates from 1779. Under the tower is an interesting exhibition of the church's treasures. – Near the Cathedral is the *Karolinska Gymnasium*, a grammar school at which Linnaeus, Per Henrik Ling and Peter Wieselgren were pupils. The Bishop's Palace, *Östrabo* (1797), was the residence of the poet Bishop Esaias Tegnér until his death in 1846. There is a statue of Tegnér in the gardens by the Cathedral.

On a hill to the S of the station is the **Småland Museum**, with an art collection, coins and medals, and a glass collection illustrating the history of glass-making in Sweden and abroad. *Utvandrarnas Hus*, the Emigrants' House (1968), contains an exhibition on the theme, "The Dream of America", archives and a library devoted to the emigration movement in the second half of the 19th c., when 200,000 Småland people left the country. Here is the source material for Vilhelm Moberg's great novel, "The Emigrants". – 5 km (3 miles) from the middle of the town are the ruins of *Kronoberg Castle*, on the Helgasjö; originally an episcopal residence, it later became the property of the Crown (Kungsgård). Near the castle is *Ryttmästaregården*, an old officer's house which has been transferred to this site.

SURROUNDINGS. – To the N of the town lies a large area of forests and lakes. There are medieval churches at *Drev*, *Dädesjö* and *Sjösås*. – On *Lake Örken* is *Braås Hembygdspark*. From the lookout tower at *Tolg* there are beautiful views of the surrounding countryside.

# Vesterålen

Norway (NW).
Counties: Nordland fylke, Troms fylke.
ⓘ **Vesterålen Reiselivslag,**
  Strandgate 47,
  N-8401 Sortland;
  tel. (088) 2 15 55.

The Vesterålen (Western Islands), lying off the Vestfjord on the NW coast of Norway, are a NE extension of the Lofoten group. The landscape of these islands is less rugged than that of the Lofotens: the slopes are less precipitous, usually grass-covered to a considerable height, and frequently have a growth of forest. – Access to the islands is by a suspension bridge over the Tjeldsund and a number of ferries; the best starting point is Narvik. The midnight sun is visible from the end of May to the end of July.

The much ramified island of **Hinnøy** is the largest Norwegian island after Spitzbergen. Half of it (to the W and S) belongs to Nordland country, the other half to the NE) to Troms. The island's capital, **Harstad** (pop. 20,000; Grand Nordic Hotell, 129 b.; Viking Nordic Hotell, 180 b.; camp site), reached from the mainland by Road 83 over the Tjeldsund bridge, lies in a sheltered area on the *Vågsfjord* to the NE and has large fish-processing industries. A festival (concerts, theatre, exhibitions, jazz) is held here at the end of June, and an angling contest in summer.

On a peninsula 3 km (2 miles) NE is the stone church of *Trondenes* (c. 1250), in medieval times the northernmost church in Christendom. – To the N of the town is the tiny island of *Kjeøy* (Stone Age rock paintings).

From the Tjeldsund bridge, Road 19 runs SW along the coast to a road junction just before Lødingen.

**Lødingen** (Lødingen Hotell, 66 b.), at the S end of the island, is an important traffic junction. From here there is a ferry service to Bognes, to the S.

Road 19 now turns N and cuts across the island and along the *Gullesfjord*; then runs W to the Sortlandsund. Road 82 branches off to the N and, at the northern tip of Hinnøy crosses the *Andøybro* to the island of Andøy.

The peak of Reka on the island of Langøy

**Andøy** is the northernmost of the Vesterålen Islands, with extensive areas of moorland from which a number of hills rise to heights of up to 600 m (1950 ft). On the E side is a seam of coal (not worked) extending into the sea. – At the northernmost tip of the island is the little fishing port of **Andenes** (Andrikken Hotel, 57 b.; Viking Gjestgiveri, 48 b.), with a breakwater 2·5 km (2700 yds) long. With its population of 4000, it has the air of a small town. It has a Polar Museum in an old burgher's house.

Beyond the junction with Road 82, Road 19 crosses the *Sortlandsbru* which links Hinnøy with Langøy.

**Langøy**, with its numerous fjords and peninsulas, is the major island in the western part of the Vesterålen group. On the E coast is the old settlement of **Sortland** (pop. 3000; Sortland Nordic Hotell, 65 b.; camp site), a port of call for the ships of the "Hurtigrute".

From Sortland Road 19 runs S and continues over the *Hadselbru* (1978: toll) to the island of **Hadseløy** and the little town of **Stokmarknes** (pop. 3000; Vesterålen Hotell, 90 b.; camp site), at which the Hurtigrute ships also stop. – From here there are attractive boat trips into the *Eidsfjord*. – On the S side of the island is the little port of *Melbu*, the base of a large trawling fleet. There are magnificent views of the islands from *Husbykollen* (513 m – 1683 ft). Ferry service to the Lofotens (p. 179). – The road back to Stokmarknes, along the W coast, offers delightful views.

# Viborg

Denmark (Jutland).
County: Viborg amt.
Altitude: 30 m (100 ft). – Population: 27,500.
Postal code: DK-8800. – Telephone code: 06.
ⓘ **Viborg Tourist Information Office,**
   Nytorv 5;
   tel. 62 16 17.
   (Bicycle rentals).

HOTELS. – *Kongenshus*, Skivevej 142, in Daugbjerg, 19 b.; *Missionshotellet*, Sct. Mathiasgade 5, 80 b.; *Motel Søndersø*, Randersvej 2, 80 b. (by the lake); *Viborg*, Gravene 20, 23 b. – YOUTH HOSTEL. – CAMP SITES: two at *Tjele* (16 km (10 miles) NE) and one at *Mønsted* (15 km (10 miles) W).

RESTAURANTS. – *Palæ*, Sct Mathiasgade 78, *Salonen*, Ved Borgvold (April to October); *Steakhouse*, Sct Mathiasgade 76.

EVENTS. – *Hærvejsmarchen*, the oldest and the biggest of the "marches" so popular in Denmark, a two-day walk along the old Military Way (30–50 km (20–30 miles) each day).

SPORTS and RECREATION. – Canoe trips on the lakes to Gudenå and Randers (45 km – 28 miles); fishing in many lakes and streams.

**Viborg, one of the oldest towns in Denmark, grew up at the intersection of the old roads from E to W and from N to S, in the heart of Jutland. In addition to its Cathedral, Viborg's attraction is in the beautiful country surrounding it, a region of forests, lakes and expanses of moorland.**

HISTORY. – Archaeological investigation has shown that there was a settlement in the Viborg area about

Viborg Cathedral

the year 700. Although little is known about its size or importance, Viborg vies with Ribe as Denmark's oldest town.

The town was originally known as *Wibjerg* ("sacred hill"), and is thought to have been a pagan cult site, which gave rise to trading activity and so to the growth of a settlement. After the coming of Christianity, Viborg became a religious focal point, and in 1065 the see of a bishop. At this period, it was the capital of Jutland, and the Danish kings were still elected in Viborg until 1340; for another 300 years it remained the place where the Estates paid homage to the newly elected king. Until 1650, it was the largest town in Jutland, and until 1805 the meeting-place of the Landsting (Provincial Assembly). Between 1525 and 1529, the preacher, Hans Tausen, made Viborg a headquarters of the Reformation. Most of the town's old buildings were destroyed by great fires in 1567 and 1726, and of its churches, only the Cathedral (rebuilt in the 19th c.) and the Dominican church survived. Viborg, attractively situated on two lakes, is now primarily a commercial and industrial town.

SIGHTS. – The *Cathedral is a copy, built between 1864 and 1874, of the original 13th c. Romanesque church of granite ashlar, which fell into decay after the Reformation and by 1862, after a number of fires and some clumsy restoration work, was so dilapidated that it had to be closed. Under the direction of Niels Sigfred Nebelong and later Hermann Braagøe, it was torn down to its foundations; only the Romanesque crypt was preserved. The radical restoration which was then carried out gave rise to much controversy, and many people believed – and still believe – that the distinctive character of the original building was lost in the reconstruction. In defence, it must be said that the poor condition of the old building had made a radical renewal of the structure essential.

The new church, built of brick and Swedish granite, was modelled after some of the German cathedrals and the churches of Lund and Ribe. Its most characteristic features are the twin towers with their pyramidal roofs, visible from afar. A few Romanesque sculptured stones have been built into the external walls including the two lions flanking a window in the apse.

The INTERIOR is dominated by the Biblical wall paintings of Joakim Skovgaard (1901–6): in the aisles, Old Testament scenes; in the transepts, scenes from the life of Christ; in the choir, the Resurrection and the Ascension. The ceiling paintings, in oil on mahogany, depict the Nativity, flanked by Moses and David and the Prophets. The altar (19th c.) is in gilt bronze. The aisled Romanesque *crypt* has 12 bays of vaulting borne on 6 columns and 10 semi-columns with granite shafts.

Near the Cathedral stands the *Søndersogn Church*, originally a Dominican church (1227, destroyed by fire in 1726, rebuilt 1728). The original nave and choir survive. The church has a magnificent carved and gilded Flemish altar of about 1520.

The **Regional Museum** (*Stiftsmuseum*) adjoining the Cathedral occupies the Old Town Hall, a Baroque building by Claus Stallknecht of Altona (Hamburg), who was called to Viborg to help with reconstruction after the great fire. The prehistoric collections include Bronze Age material; the modern section displays applied and decorative art of the 16th and 17th c. – The *Skovgaard Museum* contains sketches, paintings and sculpture by Joakim Skovgaard, including his preliminary sketches for the frescoes in the Cathedral.

On the E side of the town is the *Asmild Church* (1100), one of the oldest churches in Denmark (only the walls survive from the original church). This was probably the first Viborg Cathedral, but toward the end of the 12th c. it was given to an Augustinian nunnery of which nothing now survives. Bishop Eskild of Viborg was murdered in front of the high altar in 1132. – From the gardens (Klosterhaven) there is a beautiful view of the Søndersø.

SURROUNDINGS. – 6 km (4 miles) SW, on the NW shore of the **Haldsjø**, is the manor-house of *Hald*, the most recent of the five houses which have occupied the site since the early medieval period. It is a neoclassical mansion (1789). At the entrance are 16 large stones which once marked the boundary of the royal game reserve. The fourth manor-house, built around 1700, lay rather nearer the lake; there are remains of the third in *Hald Park*. The lake, surrounded by hills and valleys, gorges, woodland and heath, offers a wealth of beauty and interest to walkers.

14 km (9 miles) W of Viborg are the *Mønsted limestone quarries*, parts of which are accessible to visitors. The stone of these quarries, which began to be mined around the year 1000, was used in the building of Ribe Cathedral. These underground workings, which were not closed down until 1953, were popularly known as the "King's Quarries" because Frederik VI, after visiting the quarries about 1830, brought reforms which alleviated the previously inhuman working conditions. – 4 km (2½ miles) beyond this are the *Daugbjerg quarries*, which have been first mined about the year 900, in the time of Gorm the Old. – The *Kongehus Mindepark* (area 1200 hectares – 6000 acres) gives some impression of what Jutland must have looked like barely a hundred years ago – great expanses of moorland with only small areas of cultivation. The park, which is a nature reserve, was established to commemorate the peasant farmers who won the land for cultivation. A motor road 10 km (6 miles) long runs through the park.

# Ystad

Sweden (Southern).
Province: Malmöhus län.
Region: Skåne.
Altitude: sea level. – Population: 14,000.
Postal code: S-27100. – Telephone code: 0411.

ⓘ **Ystads Turistbyrå,**
St Knuds Torg;
tel. 7 72 78.

HOTELS. – *Continental du Sud*, Hamngatan 13, 52 b.;
*Prins Carl*, Hamngatan 8, 23 b.; *Ystads Saltsjöbad*,
196 b. – YOUTH HOSTEL.

**Ystad, on the S coast of Skåne, has a history going back to the 13th c. In medieval times, it was one of the principal herring-fishing ports in the Baltic. It enjoyed a great upsurge of prosperity when Napoleon imposed his continental blockade and many of the town's inhabitants carried on a very profitable smuggling trade. From 1664 on, the Ystad mail-boat "Lilla Jägaren" provided Sweden with a regular link with the European mainland. The town now has daily ferry services to the Danish island of Bornholm and to Poland.**

SIGHTS. – The town has preserved many fine medieval half-timbered houses. The *Old Town Hall* in the Stortorg is a building in Empire style (1838–40) erected over a 14th c. cellar with groin vaulting, a relic of the original Town Hall, destroyed by Swedish troops in 1569. The cellar is now a bar, reverting to its original function. – Also in the Stortorg is **St Mary's Church**, a familiar landmark with its copper-sheathed steeple (16th c.). The watchman still looks out over the town from the tower, and his horn sounds four times every hour throughout the night. In the 14th c., a tower was added to the church, but this collapsed during a storm and destroyed part of the nave. With assistance from the Danish King Frederik III, the church was rebuilt and enlarged to twice its previous size. The interior is richly decorated, with fine wood-carving.

Farther N is another 13th c. church, *St Peter's*, adjoining which is a *Franciscan friary* (Gråbrödraklostret), the best-preserved monastic house in Sweden after Vadstena (p. 290). Originally built in 1267, it was used after the Reformation (c. 1530) as a hospital, a brandy distillery and a warehouse. – The old Latin School, founded in the 15th c., is now a grammar school (*gymnasium*). – SE of the Stortorg, at No. 23 Dammgatan, is the *Charlotte Berlin Museum*, a fine town house (19th c. furniture and furnishings). Nearby are the *Museum of Art* and the *Dragoons Museum*, both in the same building. Near here, too, stands the *New Town Hall*, a mansion in Empire style built in 1812 for a prosperous local merchant, C. M. Lundgren.

At the corner of Stora Östergatan and Pilgränd is *Pilgränsgården*, a magnificent half-timbered building (c. 1500), originally a warehouse (restored 1947). *Aspelinska Gården*, at the corner of Östergatan and Gåsegränd, consists of three half-timbered buildings built around a courtyard; it was erected in 1778 for a goldsmith named Jonas Aspelin. – At the corner of Stora Nörregatan and Sladdergatan is the *Brahehus*, a 16th c. mansion built by the Brahe family, who had large possessions in this area and enjoyed great political influence. – The most decorative half-timbered house in Ystad is the *Änglahus*, a 17th c. building which belonged to a civic dignitary named Hans Raffn. The façade is decorated with the carved angels which give the house its name.

SURROUNDINGS. – 5 km (3 miles) NW of the town is the 12th c. church of *Bjäresjö* (wall paintings). – 15 km (10 miles) N is *Örups Stenhus*, one of the oldest fortified castles in Skåne (c. 1490). It strongly resembles Glimmingehus Castle (p. 236). – 17 km (10 miles) E is the 12th c. **Valleberga Kyrka**, the only surviving circular church in Skåne. It has the same ground plan as the circular churches on Bornholm (p. 70), which at one time belonged to the same diocese. The 12th c. font was the work of a Gotland stonemason. A free-standing defensive tower of the late medieval period is now a museum.

A half-timbered house in Ystad

# Zealand

Denmark.
Area: 7517 sq. km (2902 sq. miles).
Counties: Københavns amt, Frederiksborg amt,
Roskilde amt, Vestsjællands amt, Storstrøms amt.

A street in Køge

**Zealand (Danish Sjælland) is
Denmark's largest island, on which
the capital, Copenhagen, and a number of other important industrial
towns are situated. Copenhagen's
airport at Kastrup is the hub of
Scandinavian air traffic. The island
has much to offer the visitor: within
easy reach of Copenhagen are many
splendid castles and churchs (Frederiksborg, Kronborg, Roskilde); the
nearby coast of northern Zealand
has fine beaches.**

There is no land route to Zealand and
the Danish capital. Two bridges, the
Storstrøms Bridge and the Faro Bridge,
connect Zealand with the island of Falster.
There is no immediate prospect of an
overland link: a decision was made to
build a bridge over the Great Belt to
Jutland, but the plan was abandoned on
the grounds of cost.

In northern Zealand there has been a
switch from agriculture to industry, but
agriculture is still predominant in the
southern part of the island. The commut-
ing area of Copenhagen now reaches far
out from the city, for the Danes like to live
in the country and are prepared to put up
with long jorneys to work in order to
achieve this. There is an excellent public
transport system in the Copenhagen area,
and the territory of Greater Copenhagen
now extends as far afield as Køge,
Roskilde, Hillerød and Helsingør.

Motorists who want to cut quickly across
Zealand on their way to Sweden will find
it takes only about an hour to get from the
Storstrøm Bridge or the Faro Bridge to
Copenhagen. For those who want to see
more of Zealand itself, four attractive
routes are suggested below.

**Vordingborg to Copenhagen** (E4). –
From *Rødbyhavn* (p. 182: ferry connections with Puttgarden on the German
island of Fehmarn) the road runs NE
across the islands of Lolland and Falster
and comes to the *Storstrøm Bridge* (3·2
km (2 miles) long), opened in 1937,
which links Falster with Zealand.

**Vordingborg** (pop. 12,000; Kong Valdemar Hotel, 82 b.) is on the S coast of
Zealand. The town grew up around a
castle built by Valdemar the Great, base of
the Danish campaigns against the Wends
in the 12th c. In the "Ruinterræn" are
remains of the castle's walls and the well-
preserved Goose Tower (Gåsetårnet),
with a pointed copper roof topped by the
gilded figure of a goose. It recalls
Valdemar's remark that the Hanseatic
towns were like a flock of gabbling geese.
– In the Gothic Church of Our Lady (Vor
Frue Kirke) are unusual wall paintings.

A bit N of Vordingborg, to the left of the road, is *Udby*,
birthplace of the Danish R :former, Grundtvig. –
Farther W is *Sværdborg*, with a Romanesque church
containing a fresco of the High Gothic period
depicting the end of the world.

At *Bårse*, a road goes off on the right to **Præstø** (Hotel
Frederiksminde, 50 b.), in a beautiful setting, surrounded by woodland, on the Præstø Fjord. The well-
preserved Baroque manor-house of Nysø contains a
collection of sculpture by Thorvaldsen, who spent the
last years of his life here; in the garden is the small
hexagonal building which was his studio.

A road branches off to the left at Bårse and passes
through beautiful wooded country to **Næstved** (pop.
35,000; hotels: Axelhus, 30 b.; Borgmestergården,
60 b.; Menstrup Kro, Menstrup, 140 b.; Vinhuset, 103 b.;
youth hostel; camp site), an industrial town which
was a trading place of some consequence in the
Middle Ages. The great days of its past are recalled by
the numerous attractive old houses in the middle of
the town. St Peter's Church is the largest Gothic
church in Denmark, with a 13th c. crucifix, a richly
decorated pulpit and interesting frescoes. In the
House of the Holy Ghost (Helligåndshuset) is a local
museum. Other fine buildings in the town are the Old
Town Hall, the Kompagnihus and the Apostelgård,
with fine carved woodwork. – On the outskirts of the
town is the old abbey of *Herlufsholm*; for the last 400
years it has been a boarding school. The church
contains a superb funerary monument.

7 k (4½ miles) S of Næstved is the island of **Gavnø**
(linked with Zealand by a causeway), with a
handsome 18th c. mansion on the site of a nunnery
founded by Margaret I in 1402. The house contains a
collection of rare books and fine paintings; the chapel
has a carved altar and pulpit. – NW of Næstved are the
*Holmegård* glass-works.

From Næstved a minor road returns to E4 via *Toksværd*, passing the manor-house of *Sparresholm*, with a large collection of horse-drawn carriages. Just before the beginning of the motorway (highway) a road goes off on the left to **Haslev**, an old town noted for its schools, passing on the way the Renaissance manor-house of *Gisselfeld*, set in a beautiful park.

To the east of E4 extends the *Stevns peninsula*. A good starting-point for a tour of this area is **Fakse** (Faxe Hotel, 14 b.), where there is a well-known limestone quarry, originally a coral reef of the Cretaceous period. 6 km (4 miles) W of Fakse is the Renaissance mansion, *Lystrup*, and S of the town, in a nature reserve, the combined wind- and water-mill of *Blåbæk*. 6 km (4 miles) SE of Fakse is its port, *Fakse Ladeplads* (good bathing beach; Hotel Faxe Ladeplads, 28 b.). – The route continues through country which is at first wooded and later open to reach **Store Heddinge**, the town of the Elf King in the Danish national play "Elverhøj" by Heiberg. The town – lying as it does behind one of the few rocky coasts in Denmark – was regarded in the Middle Ages as invulnerable to pirate raids; it has a church dating from 1200, an octagonal structure with a double choir and spiral staircases concealed in its massive walls.

5 km (3 miles) SE of the town is the chalk cliff of *Stevns Klint* (magnificent views of the sea). Particularly fine is a white crag, rising to 41 m (135 ft) at its highest point, near *Højerup*, where there is a church dating from 1357. The choir of the church was originally a still older chapel, said to have been built by a fisherman saved from peril on the sea. Since the sea is continually washing away the chalk cliff, the story goes that each New Year's night, the church moves a few inches inland to avoid falling into the sea. Apparently this was not enough, for in 1928 the choir – the original chapel – was carried away. the rest of the church has now been protected against collapse.

The road NW from Store Heddinge passes through a number of pretty Zealand villages and in 22 km (14 miles) reaches **Køge** (p. 86), from which it is 30 km (19 miles) to **Copenhagen**, either by the old road (Gammel Køge Landvej) or the highway.

**The beaches of northern Zealand.** – There are two alternative roads N from Copenhagen. The highway, which runs almost to Helsingør, is faster; but the more attractive route is on the *Strandvej*, which traverses Copenhagen's fashionable suburbs and then through stretches of woodland and small coastal villages before joining up with the highway.

35 km (22 miles) from Copenhagen is the *Louisiana Museum at* Humlebæk (p. 130). Beyond Helsingør, along the N coast of Zealand, are the island's finest beaches – sandy beaches fringed by pinewoods and dunes, with water that is clear but decidedly cold. The long run of beaches extends via Hornbeck and *Gilleleje* to *Tisvildeleje* and *Liseleje*, old fishing villages with many summer vacation houses. At *Tisvilde* is the *Tisvilde Hegn*, a large 18th c. plantation (1430 hectares – 3600 acres) designed to prevent the sand from drifting. 3 km (2 miles) S of the little town is *Tibirke church* in the Tibirke Hills (extensive views).

The coast road continues from Liseleje to **Hundested** (Hundested Kro & Hotel, 102 b.), from which there is a ferry to Grenå in Jutland. In Hundested is a house which belonged to Knud Rasmussen, the explorer of Greenland, where can be seen Eskimo costumes and other items from that island. – From here, the return route to Copenhagen is by Roads 16 and 19. The route goes through *Frederiksværk* (Hotel Sandkroen, 13 b.), (interesting local museum), skirts a large lake, the *Arresø*, and comes to the ruined *Æbeltoft Abbey* (12th c.), with a museum containing a large number of skeletons and medical instruments dating from the time when the abbey was used as a hospital. The road continues by way of *Hillerød*, with the magnificent **\*\*Frederiksborg Castle** (p. 130), and past large tracts of forest to Copenhagen.

**Copenhagen to Kalundborg** (Roads 21 and 23). – Road 21 runs W from Copenhagen to **Roskilde** (p. 227), from which Road 23 continues to **Holbæk** (pop. 20,000; Strandparken Hotel, 52 b.), lying to the N of the through road on the *Holbæk Fjord*. Holbæk, which originally developed around a castle built by Valdemar Sejr in the early 13th c., is now a rapidly growing commercial and industrial town. Features of interest are the Museum, a 17th c. half-timbered house and the remains of a Dominican abbey, now occupied by a church community headquarters – 4 km (2½ miles) S of Holbæk is the church of *Tveje-Merløse*, one of the most interesting of Denmark's village churches, with twin towers unique to the architecture of the northern countries. The church contains remains of Romanesque wall paintings.

From Holbæk, an attractive detour can be made to the N, skirting the *Holbæk Fjord* and the *Lammefjord* – both branches of the large *Isefjord* – which rank among Denmark's finest sailing waters. From the *Bavnehøj* (62 m – 203 ft), the highest point in this area, there is a fine panoramic view extending as far as Roskilde. The *Odsherred* peninsula, a popular bathing area with wide dune-fringed sandy beaches, is reached on a road which runs N from *Tuse*, 6 km (4 miles) beyond Holbæk. Tuse church has wall paintings which include some unusual themes (e.g., devils helping peasant women with their butter-making). The major place on the Odsherred peninsula is **Nykøbing S**. (S for Sjælland, to distinguish it from other towns of the same name), which has the largest private collection of ancient glass in northern Europe, the Anneberg Collection. – From Nykøbing, a road runs 24 km (15 miles) W along *Sjællands Odde*, a narrow strip of land from which there is a ferry to Ebeltoft in Jutland (see p. 148). – For the return to the main road from Nykøbing, the best route is the beautiful road which runs down the W coast. From the *Vejrhøj* (121 m – 397 ft), near Fårevejle, there is a splendid view which recompenses a rather strenuous climb. In a glass sarcophagus in *Fårevejle* church is the mummified body of the Earl of Bothwell, third husband of Mary Queen of Scots, who died while confined as a state prisoner in Dragsholm Castle. – *Dragsholm Castle*, now a hotel, is one of Denmark's oldest secular buildings (begun about 1200). About 1690, the castle, whose cellars and keep had been used for the confinement of important prisoners, was converted into a Baroque manor-house (much of the older building was already destroyed during the Swedish wars in 1658–60). – At *Bregninge* (church with interesting wall paintings), Road 23 joins and continues to Kalundborg.

The main road to Kalundborg, for motorists who have not made the detour to the N, continues W, passing the Renaissance mansion of *Løvenborg*, *Mørkøv* (church with wall paintings of 1450) and the *Skarresø*, a lake surrounded by beautiful forests.

**Kalundborg** (pop. 12,000; Ole Lunds Gård, 29 b.; camp site) is notable for its Church of Our Lady (Vor Frue Kirke). This unusual church (on a central plan with five towers), was built between 1170 and 1190 as a castle chapel. The central tower collapsed in 1827 and was rebuilt forty years later. The most notable feature of the interior is the richly carved altar (Lorens Jørgensen of Holbaek). To the W of the church, in the old mansion of Lindegården, is an interesting local museum. A walk around the older part of the town reveals many well-preserved old houses. – To the S of the town stands the Baroque mansion of *Lerchenborg*, now used for a variety of cultural activities, with a Hans Christian Andersen Collection and a large park and rose-garden.

**Copenhagen to Korsør** (Roads 2 and 1). – From Copenhagen, Road 2 leads SW along *Køge Bay* to *Køge* (p. 86), from which a road runs W to Ringsted.

**Ringsted** (pop. 14,000; hotels: Børsen, 8 b.; Casino, 23 b.; youth hostel; camp site) was one of the most important towns in Denmark during the Middle Ages. In the market square are three stones, the *Tingstener*, recalling the time when Ringsted was the meeting-place of Zealand's lawcourt. The finest building in the town is St Bendt's Church, also in the market square. This red-brick Romanesque church, originally belonging to a Benedictine abbey, is one of the oldest brick churches in Denmark (Gothic vaulting and late Gothic tower). It contains 20 royal and princely tombs, the positions of which are recorded in a 13th c. parchment manuscript displayed in the S chapel; and the royalty themselves are depicted in the church's wall paintings. When all the tombs were opened in the 19th c., Queen Dagmar's was found to contain Dagmar's Cross, a replica of which now hangs in the church. Other features of interest in the church are the font (1200), the choir-stalls (1400), with scenes from the Old and New Testaments, and an altar (1699). – From Ringsted Road 1 (E66) continues W.

8 km (5 miles) from Ringsted is *Fjenneslev* church, which has ties with the Hvide family, one of the great noble families of medieval Denmark. The twin brick towers were built about 1170, but the S tower collapsed in 1561 and the church was not restored to its original form until a reconstruction was carried out in 1899. – Beyond Fjenneslev, off the road to the right, is *Bjernede*, with Zealand's only round church. The square-ribbed vault is borne on four round piers and topped by a small octagonal tower.

15 km (10 miles) from Ringsted is **Sorø** (pop. 9000; Postgården Hotel, 44 b.; camp site), which in the time of Bishop Absalon had a mighty Cistercian abbey. The abbey church – the largest in Denmark – contains the tomb of Absalon himself (behind the high altar) as well as several princely tombs and that of the playwright, Ludvig Holberg (in the transept chapel). The church, begun in the 1160s, vies with St Bendt's in Ringsted for the status of the oldest large brick building in Denmark. It contains a triumphal cross of 1527, 8 m (25 ft) high, and an older (13th c.) crucifix in which the cross and Christ's body are carved from a single piece of wood. – Frederik II established a school in the old abbey buildings in 1586, and in 1623 this became an academy for the sons of the nobility. Ludvig Holberg left the Academy his library and other property, but much of

this was destroyed in a fire in the 19th c. In the Academy gardens, which extend to the shores of the Sorø Sø, is a statue of Holberg.

**Slagelse** (pop. 27,000; Hotel E3, Idagårdsvej 1, 148 b.; Hotel Slagelse, Sdr Stationsvej 19, 58 b.; youth hostel; camp site), the third largest of Zealand's county towns, was an important trading town throughout the Middle Ages; it had a mint coining money as early as the 11th c. The central feature of the town is the Gothic St Michael's Church (Skt Mikkels Kirke). To the W of the church is the old church barn, later used as the Latin School; Hans Christian Andersen was a pupil here from 1822 to 1826. The oldest building in Slagelse is the Romanesque St Peter's Church. – In a wood to the SE of the town (Antvorskov) are the ruins of a 12th c. monastery of the order of St John, which later became a royal residence. Here, on the highest flagpole in Denmark (30 m – 100 ft), the Danish flag, originally the banner of the order, is flown every Sunday.

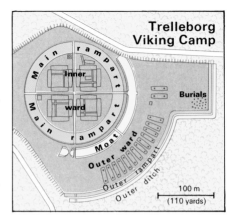

7 km (5 miles) W of Slagelse lies the Viking stronghold of *Trelleborg, dating from the years 1000–1050. It is surrounded by a *circular rampart* with four entrances, giving access to two streets intersecting at right angles and dividing the enclosed area into four quarters. Within the ramparts were 16 houses fashioned in the shape of long ships, each 29·5 m (97 ft) long, with four houses laid out around a square in each quadrant. On the E side of the ramparts was a moat (the other sides of the camp were protected by two small rivers), and between this and an outer rampart was a row of houses similar to those inside the main ramparts. Outside the site is a reconstruction of one of the houses, based on evidence recovered by excavation.

**Korsør** (pop. 15,000; Halsskov Motel, Tårnborgvej 180, 58 b.), a port used by boats sailing across the Great Belt from at least the 11th c., has preserved much of its old-world atmosphere in spite of industrial development. From the defensive tower on the harbour there are fine views of the town and the Belt. – To the N is the ferry port of *Halsskov* (services to Knudshoven on Funen).

15 km (10 miles) S of Korsør is **Skælskør**, a little town in a beautiful and fertile area (fruit orchards) which still preserves the feel of past centuries. St Nicholas's Church (double-aisled) was begun about 1200. – 2 km (1¼ miles) S of Skælskør is the Renaissance manor-house of *Borreby*, with defensive features characteristic of houses built in the unsettled times following the Reformation; houses built later show a trend towards less massive and more graceful forms. – The road continues E to *Ørslev* (church with an interesting frieze depicting a medieval round dance – waltz) and then, through beautiful scenery, to *Holsteinborg*, with a handsome castle dating from the first half of the 17th c. set in a beautiful park (rare trees) on the water's edge.

# Practical Information

The car ferry ''Danmark'' at Rødbyh

# Safety on the Road. Some Reminders for the Vacation Traveller

**Always wear your seat-belt, and make sure that your passengers wear theirs.**
**Note:** Compensation for injury may be reduced by up to 50% if seat-belts are not worn.

**Change the brake fluid in your car at least every two years.**
This vitally important fluid tends to lose its effectiveness in the course of time as a result of condensation of water, dust and chemical decomposition.

**Change your tires when the depth of tread is reduced to 2 mm (0·08 inch).**
Tires must have enough depth of tread to get a good grip on the road and hold the car steady even on a wet surface. In the case of wide sports tires, with their long water channels, a 3-mm (0·12-inch) tread is advisable.

**You will see better, and be more easily seen, if your car lights are functioning properly.**
It is important, therefore, to check your sidelights and headlights regularly. This can be done even without getting out of the car. When you stop at traffic lights in front of a bus or truck you can see whether your rear lights and brake lights are working from the reflection on the front of

the other vehicle, and you can check up on your headlights and front indicators in your own garage or in a shop window.

**When driving at night on wet roads you should stop in a parking place every 50 or 100 km (30 or 60 miles) and clear your headlights and rear lights.**
Even the thinnest coat of dirt on the glass reduces the strength of your headlights by half, and a heavy coating may reduce their output by as much as 90%.

**The best place for fog lights is on the front bumper.**
This gives them the maximum range without dazzling oncoming traffic. If they are mounted below the bumper they will have a range of only 5 or 10 m (16 or 32 feet). Fog lights are most effective when used in conjunction with parking lights only: for safe driving, therefore, they must have an adequate range.

**It is always advisable to carry a first-aid kit. It is compulsory for all drivers, including visitors, to carry a warning triangle. Remember, however, that if these items are kept on the rear shelf they can become dangerous projectiles in the event of an accident.**
The first-aid kit should be kept inside the car, either secured in a holder or under a seat; the warning triangle should be kept ready to hand in the boot (trunk). If there is no more room in the boot any items of equipment or pieces of luggage inside the car should be stowed carefully and securely.

If there is so much luggage in the back of the car that the view through the rear window is obstructed it is a wise precaution, as well as a statutory requirement, to have an outside mirror on the passenger's side. This is useful in any event when driving in heavy traffic on multi-lane highways. It should be of convex type.

**Drivers who keep their left foot on the clutch pedal after changing gear may be letting themselves in for a heavy repair bill.**
This very rapidly wears down the clutch release bearing, giving rise to whining and grating noises.

**As a light bulb grows older its efficiency falls off very markedly. A dark-coloured deposit inside a bulb –**

wolfram from the filament – is an
indication of age.
All bulbs should therefore be checked at
least once a year. It is advisable to change
those which have darkened glass as well
as those which are clearly defective.

**You can save fuel when driving on
highways by keeping the accelerator
pedal at least 2 cm (about ¾ inch)
short of the "foot-down" position).**
The nearer to its maximum speed a car is
travelling the more steeply does fuel
consumption increase. A slightly lighter
touch on the accelerator will make little
difference to your speed but quite a
difference to the amount of fuel you use.

**If you wear glasses you will increase
the safety of night driving by getting special coated lenses; and all
drivers should avoid wearing tinted
glasses after dusk and at night.**
All glass reflects part of the light passing
through it, and even through a clear
windshield only about 90% of the light
outside reaches the driver's eyes inside
the car. If the driver is wearing glasses
there is a further light loss of 10%. With a
tinted windshield and tinted glasses only
about half the light outside reaches the
driver's eyes, and in these conditions
driving at night is not possible.

accident. Ask the other parties for the name of their
insurers and their insurance number.

5. Note down the names and addresses of witnesses;
take photographs and/or make sketches of the scene
of the accident.
After a minor accident the police are usually more
concerned with getting the road clear for traffic than
making a full record of the incident. What you should
try to record in your photographs is not the damage to
the cars involved – that can be established later – but
the general situation at the scene of the accident. It is
particularly important to photograph each of the cars
in the direction of travel from a sufficient distance.

6. If possible fill in the "European Accident State-
ment" (which you will have received along with your
green card if you own the car) and have it signed by
the other party. Do not sign any admission of liability.
If the other party asks you to sign an accident form not
written in English and you are in doubt of its meaning,
add the words "without prejudice to liability" above
your signature.

7. Inform your own insurance company by letter, if
possible, within 24 hours of the accident. If your
car is rented, inform the rental agency by phone
immediately.

8. If the accident involves injury to persons (other than
yourself and your passengers) or damage to property,
inform the bureau named on the back page of your
green card.

9. If you own the car follow the instructions of your
insurance company – which you will normally have
received along with your green card – concerning
repair of damage to your car.

# If you have an
# accident

**However carefully you drive, you
may nevertheless find yourself involved in an accident. If this does
happen do not lose your temper,
however great the provocation: remain polite, keep cool and take the
following action:**

1. Warn other road users: switch on your hazard
warning lights and set out your warning triangle at a
sufficient distance from the scene of the accident.

2. Attend to the injured. Expert assistance should be
summoned immediately. Unless you have a knowledge of first aid you should be extremely cautious
about attending anyone injured in an accident. Call an
ambulance if required.

3. If anyone has been injured, if there has been major
damage to the cars involved or if there is disagreement
between you and the other party, inform the police.

4. Get the names and addresses of other parties
involved; note the registration number and make of
the other vehicles and the time and place of the

# When to go

The best time for travelling in the Scandinavian countries is the summer (June,
July and August), when the weather is at
its warmest and in the far north the sun
never disappears below the horizon, or
sets only for a very brief period. Even in

northern Scandinavia it can be surprisingly warm, and temperatures above 20 °C (68 °F) are not rare. In Lapland the short summer brings out swarms of mosquitoes, and insect repellents should be included in every visitor's equipment.

Peak season varies, of course from country to country:

| | |
|---|---|
| *Denmark* | May to October |
| *Southern Sweden* | May to October |
| *Central Sweden* | June to September |
| *Northern Sweden, Norway* | |
| *and Finland* | July to August |

For winter sports, March and April are the best months, since by then the days are beginning to grow longer.

# Weather

The weather of Scandinavia is mainly determined by two factors. To the W of the ridge of mountains which runs down the Scandinavian peninsula, a maritime climate prevails, with relatively small differences in temperature between summer and winter and relatively high rainfall. In these regions, too, the *Gulf Stream* produces considerably higher average temperatures than would otherwise be expected so far north. To the E of the mountains, continental influences prevail, with lower rainfall, cold winters and sometimes surprisingly warm summers. For a more detailed account of climatic conditions in Scandinavia, see pp. 14 and 15.

# Time

*Denmark, Norway* and *Sweden* are on **Central European Time** (one hour ahead of Greenwich Mean Time – six hours ahead of New York), *Finland* on **Eastern European Time** (two hours ahead of GMT).

In *Denmark, Norway* and *Sweden* **Summer Time** runs from the end of March to the end of September and is one hour ahead of Central European Time, two hours ahead of GMT. *Finland*, during the same period, is one hour ahead of Eastern European Time, three hours ahead of GMT.

# Midnight sun

To the N of the Arctic Circle (lat. 66°33′ N) the sun does not set for a period around midsummer which increases in length 'towards the North Pole. See the entry on the Arctic Circle, p. 59.

# Travel documents

Visitors to the four Scandinavian countries from the United Kingdom, the United States, Canada and many other countries require only a valid passport, without visa, for a stay of up to three months (for all four countries together). A visa is required for a stay of more than three months and by foreigners proposing to take up employment in one of the Scandinavia countries. Within Scandinavia there are no passport controls between the individual countries, which have formed a Nordic Passport and Customs Union.

**Motorists** should carry their national *driver's licence* and *registration*, which are recognised in the Scandinavian countries. It is not now a legal requirement to carry an *international insurance certificate* (*"green card"*) for motorists from EEC countries within other EEC countries and non-EEC countries which have subscribed to the green card agreement (i.e. not only Denmark, a member of the EEC, but Finland, Norway and Sweden, as well): it is, however, very desirable to have the additional protection of a green card. Foreign vehicles must display an *international distinguishing sign* of the approved type and design. Failure to do so may result in a fine. If you are renting a car, of course, all you need is a valid driver's licence.

**Medical care.** – United Kingdom residents are entitled, as citizens of the EEC, to receive free or partly free medical care in *Denmark* on the same basis as Danish nationals. The United Kingdom also has reciprocal arrangements with *Norway* and *Sweden* under which British citizens can get free or partly free care in those countries. You should apply to the Department of Health and Social Security, well before your date of departure, for leaflet SA30 which gives details of reciprocal arrangements for medical treatment and contains an application form for a certificate of entitlement (Form E111). American visitors and others who are not covered by arrangements of this kind should take out short-term, full-cover medical insurance before leaving home.

**Pets.** – There is a four months' quarantine period in Finland, Norway and Sweden. There is no quarantine requirement in Denmark, but animals must have a rabies vaccination certificate.

# Customs regulations

The customs requirements of Norway, Sweden and Finland are about the same, as a result of their membership of the Nordic Passport and Customs Union. Denmark, in addition to being a member of that Union, is also a member of the EEC.

Personal effects and vacation equipment can be temporarily imported without payment of duty. Special regulations apply to the importation of sporting guns, the importation and use of portable radio transmitters and the export of works of art: for information, apply to the national tourist organisation of the country concerned.

## Duty-Free Allowances for visitors from Europe

| Country | Alcohol | Tobacco | Other goods |
|---|---|---|---|
| **Denmark** | 1½ litres spirits or 3 litres sparkling wine, plus 4 litres wine (minimum age 17) | 300 cigarettes or 150 cigarillos or 75 cigars or 400 grammes tobacco (minimum age 17) | maximum value 2300 Dkr. |
| **Norway** | 1 litre wine, 1 litre spirits and 2 litres beer, or 2 litres wine and 2 litres beer (minimum age 20) | 200 cigarettes or 250 grammes of other tobacco goods (minimum age 16) | maximum value 500 Nkr. |
| **Sweden** | 1 litre wine, 1 litre spirits and 2 litres beer, or 2 litres wine and 2 litres beer (minimum age 20) | 200 cigarettes or 100 cigarillos or 50 cigars or 250 grammes tobacco (minimum age 15) | maximum value 600 Skr. |
| **Finland** | 1 litre wine and 2 litres beer (minimum age 18) plus 1 litre spirits (minimum age 20) | 200 cigarettes or 100 cigarillos or 50 cigars or 250 grammes tobacco (minimum age 16) | maximum value 1000 Fmk. |

**Note**: 1 litre = 0·22 gallon or 1¾ pints approx. 450 grammes = 1 lb approx.

# Currency

## Denmark
Monetary unit: **Danish crown** (Dkr.) of 100 øre.
Banknotes: 5, 10, 20, 50, 100, 500 and 1000 kr.
Coins: 5, 10, 25 and 50 øre; 1, 2, 5 and 10 kr.

## Norway
Monetary unit: **Norwegian crown** (Nkr.) of 100 øre.
Banknotes: 10, 50, 100, 500 and 1000 kr.
Coins: 5, 10, 25 and 50 øre; 1 and 5 kr.

## Sweden
Monetary unit: **Swedish crown** (Skr.) of 100 öre.
Banknotes: 5, 10, 50, 100, 1000 and 10,000 kr.
Coins: 5, 10, 25, 50 öre; 1 and 5 kr.

## Finland
Monetary unit: **Finnish mark** (*markka:* Fmk.) of 100 *penniä*.
Banknotes: 1, 5, 10, 50, 100 and 500 mk.
Coins: 1, 5, 10, 20 and 50 penniä; 1, 5, 10, 20, 50, 100 and 200 mk.

It is advisable to take money in the form of travellers' checks and a credit card. Major credit cards are widely accepted.

British visitors who have a current account with the National Girobank can cash "postcheques" at all post offices in Denmark, certain post offices in Norway and Sweden, and branches of the Post Office Savings Bank (Posttipankki) and certain post offices in Finland.

## Currency Regulations

| Country | Import | | Export | |
|---|---|---|---|---|
| | National currency | Foreign currency | National currency | Foreign currency |
| **Denmark** | unrestricted | unrestricted | max. 50,000 Kr. | unrestricted |
| **Norway** | unrestricted | unrestricted | max. 2000 Kr. | unrestricted |
| **Sweden** | unrestricted | unrestricted | max. 6000 kr. | unrestricted |
| **Finland** | unrestricted | unrestricted | max. 10,000 mk. (no notes above 100 Fmk.) | max. 10,000 mk[1]. |

[1] Information from the Tourist Office

# Postal rates

| Country | Letters up to 20 g. Inland/Foreign | Póstcards Inland/Foreign |
|---|---|---|
| **Denmark** | 2.80/3.80 dkr. | 2.80/3.00 dkr. |
| **Norway** | 2.50/3.50 nkr. | 2.50/3.00 nkr. |
| **Sweden** | 2.10/2.90 skr. | 2.10/2.90 skr. |
| **Finland** | 1.60/2.20 Fmk. | 1.60/2.20 Fmk. |

In **Finland** visitors can have their mail addressed to the Main Post Office in Helsinki, where it can be collected between 8 a.m. and 10 p.m. from Monday to Saturday; on Sunday between 11 a.m. and 10 p.m. Letters should be addressed as follows:

(*Name of addressee*),
c/o Main Post Office,
Mannerheimintie 11,
SF-00100 Helsinki,
Suomi/Finland.

Road bridge over the Svendborgsund between the islands of Funen and Tåsinge

# Travelling in Scandinavia

## Travel by road

**The roads.** – Roads play an important part in the transport system of Scandinavia, since the railways are relatively sparse, particularly in Norway, northern Sweden and northern Finland. The network of roads is extended and improved each year; and the condition of the roads is relatively good, permitting reasonable average speeds even in the far north. The main roads and important secondary roads have been further improved in recent years and given dust-free surfaces. Where the surface is still grit or gravel, it is kept as smooth as possible by the use of graders. It is advisable to stay a safe distance behind the car in front, in order to avoid the risk of a shattered windshield. After heavy rain, roads without a hard surface become slippery or even muddy, and extra care is warranted. As a courtesy to other road users, you should fit mudguard flaps. Some roads in the mountains of southern Norway and in northern Norway, Sweden and Finland, where the winter is long, may be open only from about June to October. – The amount of traffic on the roads of Scandinavia has increased considerably in recent years, and in the south is comparable with that on the roads of western Europe.

Although in Denmark, Sweden and Finland no specialised driving skills are generally required, the mountain roads of Norway – sometimes very narrow and frequently with blind corners – call for a high standard of driving and road discipline.

In Denmark the condition of the motorways (*motorvej*), main roads (*hovedvej*: identified by the letter A and a number) and most secondary roads is excellent. All these roads are properly surfaced (mostly asphalt, sometimes concrete). Visitors should avoid the temptation to drive too fast: there is no need to hurry in Denmark. The various Danish islands are connected with one another by bridges and ferries.

In **Sweden** there are the national highways (*riksväg*), numbered from 10 to 99; and provincial or county roads (*länsväg*), with numbers over 100. In addition, there are a number of short stretches of motorway or expressway (*motorväg*), and these are constantly being extended. In the southern part of the country the main roads are all excellent, with firm surfaces; in the far north, however, many roads are still surfaced with grit or gravel. The mountain roads along the Norwegian border are frequently narrow. – Foreign motorists are subject to special regulations in restricted military areas (*skyddsområde*), which are indicated by warning signposts (large areas around Kalix

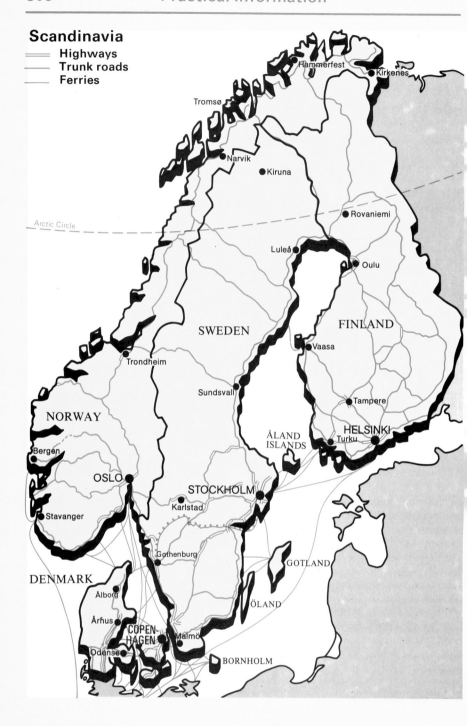

## Scandinavia

— Highways
— Trunk roads
— Ferries

and Boden). In these areas, foreigners may use the roads only for direct transit, and they are not allowed, except with special permission, to stay for more than 24 hours (in some cases 72 hours) in a restricted area. Camping, leaving the road and taking photographs are prohibited.

In **Norway** the most important elements in the road system are the numbered national highways (*riksveg*), the stretches of motorway or expressway (*motorveg*) around some of the larger towns and the numbered county or provincial roads (*fylkesveg*). — In the mountains of southern Norway and on the rocky shores of the fjords, the roads are often narrow, winding and poorly guarded. In these areas, a high standard of driving skill, careful observance of the rules of the road and constant caution are essential. When two vehicles meet, the one going uphill always has priority. Some mountain roads have an alternating one-way system. Visitors with camper vehicles or caravans should obtain information about the feasibility of their route before setting out, either from the Automobile Clubs or from "Vegdirektoratet" in Oslo, Brynildsen, Postboks 8109 DEP. If there has been heavy snow during the winter some sections of mountain roads may not be completely open until June.

In **Finland**, the numbered main roads are divided into first- and second-class roads (*valtatie* and *kantatie*); national highways or trunk roads are indicated by numbers on a red background. Around some of the larger towns are stretches of motorway or expressway (*moottoritie*). Some minor roads and roads north of the Arctic Circle have surfaces of sand, grit or oil-bound gravel. Most roads, however, are wide enough to permit easy passing. In the north of the country, with its long winter, the roads are often not open until the middle of June.

 This sign, frequently seen on the roads of the Scandinavian countries, indicates some sight or feature of particular interest.

**Driving in Scandinavia.** – As in the rest of continental Europe, traffic travels on the right, with passing on the left. At junctions and intersections the car coming from the right has priority. – In *Denmark*, *Sweden* and *Finland* parking is prohibited on all main roads which are marked as having priority. – In *Sweden* and *Finland* all vehicles must drive with dipped headlights (lowbeams), even in daylight. – The use of a *warning triangle* is compulsory in *Norway* and *Denmark*. – In *Norway* and *Sweden* it is recommended that *children* do not occupy the *front seats* of vehicles. – Visiting motorists are required to carry a *spare set of light bulbs* in *Norway*. – It is forbidden to carry *cans of petrol* in your vehicle while driving in *Finland*. – The use of the *horn* should be kept to a minimum in towns. – *Trams* always have priority. – *Rear fog-lights* must not be used. – In all the Scandinavian countries *seat-belts* must be worn and there are severe penalties for *driving under the influence of alcohol*.

The usual international *traffic signs* are in use in all four countries, but there are a number of signs not found elsewhere

(e.g. a white M on a blue background to indicate a passing area on a narrow road; or Al Indkørsel forbudt=No entry). Leaflets illustrating the traffic signs in use can be obtained from the motoring organisations.

| Speed Limits (kilometres per hour) | | | | |
|---|---|---|---|---|
| Country | Motor-way | Other roads | Built-up areas | Cars with trailers braked/ unbraked |
| **Denmark** | 100 | 80 | 50 | 70 |
| **Norway** | 90 | 80 | 50 | 80/60 |
| **Sweden** | 110 | 90 | 50 | 70/40 |
| **Finland** | 120 | 80 | 50 | 80/50 |
| *Equivalents:* | | | | |
| kilometres | 40 | 50 | 60 | 70 | 80 | 90 |
| miles | 25 | 31 | 37 | 43 | 50 | 56 |
| kilometres | 100 | 110 | 120 |
| miles | 62 | 68 | 75 |

**Spiked or studded tires** may be used in Scandinavia during the winter – in *Denmark*, from 1 October to 30 April, in *Norway*, from 15 October to 30 April, in *Sweden*, from 1 October to 30 April and in *Finland*, from 16 October to 15 April in southern and central Finland and 1 October to 30 April in northern Finland.

## Travel by boat

Boat services play a major part in travel between Scandinavia and the rest of Europe and within the Scandinavian countries themselves. In Norway, in particular, several car ferries across the fjords supplement the road system in these areas.

Cruises along the coast and up the fjords are a very popular means of seeing the country. Ships of the "**Hurtigrute**" sail up the west coast of Norway from Bergen to Kirkenes. During the summer, there are daily services in both directions, which take 11 days to cover the total distance of some 2500 sea miles. For many of the ports of call, this is their only connection with the outside world. – For services in the fjords see the descriptions of the various fjords.

Finnjet ferry

# Ferry Services to Scandinavia and within Scandinavia

| SERVICE | FREQUENCY | COMPANY |
|---|---|---|
| **United Kingdom–Denmark** | | |
| Harwich–Esbjerg | daily | DFDS (Danish Seaways) |
| Newcastle–Esbjerg | 4 times weekly | DFDS (Danish Seaways) |
| Harwich–Hirtshals–(Oslo) | weekly | Fred Olsen Lines |
| | | |
| **United Kingdom–Norway** | | |
| Newcastle–Stavanger–Bergen | weekly in summer | Norway Line |
| Newcastle–Oslo | weekly in summer | Fred Olsen Lines |
| Harwich–Kristiansand | weekly in summer | Fred Olsen Lines |
| Harwich–(Hirtshals)–Oslo | weekly | Fred Olsen Lines |
| | | |
| **United Kingdom–Sweden** | | |
| Harwich–Gothenburg | 3–4 times weekly | DFDS |
| Newcastle–Gothenburg | twice weekly in summer | DFDS |
| | | |
| **Inter-Scandinavian services** | | |
| **Denmark–Norway** | | |
| Hanstholm–Egersund | 5 times weekly | ⎫ |
| Hanstholm–Kristiansand | 4 times weekly in summer | |
| Hirtshals–Egersund | weekly in summer | |
| Hirtshals–Stavanger–Bergen | 2–3 times weekly in summer | ⎬ FOL Skagerak-Expressen |
| Hirtshals–Kristiansand | daily | |
| Hirtshals–Oslo | 4 times weekly | ⎭ |
| Frederikshavn–Larvik | daily | Larvik Line |
| Frederikshavn–Frederikstad | daily | Da-No Linjen, Oslo |
| Frederikshavn–Moss | daily | Stena Line |
| Frederikshavn–Oslo | daily | Da-No Linjen, Oslo |
| Frederikshavn–Oslo | daily | Stena Line |
| Copenhagen–Oslo | daily | DFDS |
| Hundested–Sandelfjord | 4 times weekly | Hundested–Sandedfjord–Linie |
| | | |
| **Denmark–Sweden** | | |
| Dragør–Limhamn | daily | DSB/SJ |
| Dragør–Limhamn | daily | Skandinavian Ferry Lines AB, Helsingborg |
| Helsingør–Helsingborg | daily | DSB/SJ |
| Helsingør–Helsingborg | daily | Skandinavian Ferry Lines AB, Helsingborg |
| Helsingør–Helsingborg | daily | Sundbusserne A/S, Helsingør |
| Frederikshavn–Gothenburg | daily | Stena Line |
| Grenå–Helsingborg | daily | Lion Ferry AB, Varberg |
| Grenå–Varberg | daily | Lion Ferry AB, Varberg |
| Rønne (Bornholm)–Ystad | daily | Bornholmstrafikken, Rønne |
| | | |
| **Sweden–Finland** | | |
| Nynäshamn–Helsinki | 4 times weekly | Polish Baltic Shipping Company, Kolobrzeg |
| Stockholm–Helsinki | daily | Silja Line |
| Stockholm–Helsinki | daily | Viking Line |
| Stockholm–Mariehamn (Åland) | daily | Ålands Linjen, Stockholm |
| Stockholm–Mariehamn (Åland) | daily | Silja Line |
| Stockholm–Mariehamn (Åland)–Turku | daily | Viking Line |
| Stockholm–Turku | daily | Silja Line |
| Stockholm–Turku | daily | Viking Line |

| | | |
|---|---|---|
| Kapellskär–Mariehamn (Åland)–Naantali | daily | Viking Line |
| Grisslehamn–Eckerö | daily | Eckerö Linjen, Grisslehamn |
| Sundsvall–Vaasa | daily | Vaasa ferries |
| Umeå–Vaasa | daily | Vaasa ferries |
| Skellefteå–Jakobstad | daily | Jakob Lines, Jakobstad |

## Domestic services

### Denmark

| | | |
|---|---|---|
| Fynshavn–Bødjen | daily | DSB |
| Rudkøbing–Marstal | daily | Marstal Færgen, Marstal |
| Aerøskøbing–Svendborg | daily | Dampskipsselskabet Aero, Aerøskøbing |
| Lohals–Korsør | daily | Sydfenske D., Savenborg |
| Spodsbjærg–Tårs | daily | Sydfenske D., Savenborg |
| Knudshoved–Halsskov | daily | DSB |
| Juelsminde–Kalundborg | daily | Jydisk Færgefart, Kalundborg |
| Kolby Kås–Kalundborg | daily | DSB |
| Århus–Kalundborg | daily | DSB |
| Sjælands Odde–Ebeltoft | daily | Mols-Linjen, Ebeltoft |
| Grenå–Anholt | daily | Grenå-Anholt Faergefart, Grenå |
| Grenå–Hundested | daily | Grenå-Hundested Linien |
| Copenhagen–Rønne (Bornholm) | daily | Bornholmstrafikken, Rønne |

### Norway

| | | |
|---|---|---|
| Horten–Moss | daily | Alpha A/S, Moss |
| Stavanger–Bergen | daily | Stavanger Steamship Co., Stavanger |
| Bergen–Kirkenes | daily | Hurtigruten, Bergen |
| Kinsarvik–Utne–Kvanndal (Hardangerfjord) | daily | |
| Løfallstrand–Gjermundshamn (Hardangerfjord) | daily | Hardamger Sunnhordlandske Dampskipsselskap, Bergen |
| Skånevik–Utåker (Hardangerfjord) | daily | |
| Balestrand–Hella–Fjærland (Sognefjord) | daily | |
| Vangsnes–Dragsvik (Sognefjord) | daily | |
| Vangsnes–Hella (Sognefjord) | daily | Fylkesbaatane i Sogn og |
| Kaupanger–Revsnes (Sognefjord) | daily | Fjordane, Bergen |
| Gudvangen–Kaupanger–Årdalstangen (Sognefjord) | daily | |
| Geiranger–Hellesylt (Geirangerfjord) | daily | More og Romsdal |
| Eidsdal–Linge (Norddalsfjord) | daily | Fylkesbåtar, Molde |
| Bremsnes–Kristiansund | daily | |
| Forvik–Tjøtta | daily | Helgeland Trafikkselskap, Sandnessjøen |
| Bodø–Værøy–Røst (Lofoten) | daily | Vesterålens Dampskipsselskab Stokmarknes |
| Kåfiord–Honningsvåg | daily | Finmark Fylkesrederi og Ruteselskap, Hammerfest |

### Sweden

| | | |
|---|---|---|
| Grankullavik–Visby (Öland–Gotland) | 3 times weekly | Rederi AB Gotland, Visby |
| Oskarshamn–Visby (Gotland) | daily | Rederi AB Gotland, Visby |
| Västervik–Visby (Gotland) | daily | Rederi AB Gotland, Visby |
| Nynäsham–Visby (Gotland) | daily | Rederi AB Gotland, Visby |
| Visby (Gotland)–Stockholm | June 14 to Aug 12 3 times weekly in the season | Rederi AB Gotland, Visby |

### Finland

| | | |
|---|---|---|
| Turku–Mariehamn (Åland) | daily | Silja Line |
| Turku–Mariehamn (Åland) | daily | Viking Line |
| Mariehamn–Naantali (Åland) | daily | Viking Line |

The booking of ferry passages, especially in the high season (July/August), must be made as early as possible. There are also combined tickets for use on several ferries available at reduced rates.

Those with **trailers, motor homes, campers and caravans** should enquire of the shipping line or through a travel agent about the maximum dimensions for vehicles carried on the ferries.

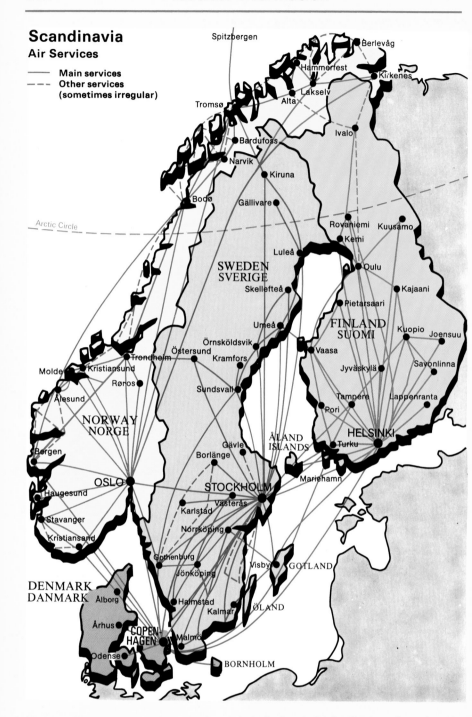

## Scandinavia
### Air Services

——— **Main services**
– – – **Other services
(sometimes irregular)**

Spitzbergen
Berlevåg
Hammerfest
Kirkenes
Lakselv
Alta
Tromsø
Ivalo
Bardufoss
Narvik
Kiruna
Bodø
Gällivare
Arctic Circle
Rovaniemi     Kuusamo
Kemi
Luleå
SWEDEN
SVERIGE
Skellefteå
Oulu
Kajaani
Pietarsaari
Umeå
FINLAND
SUOMI
Kuopio
Joensuu
Örnsköldsvik
Östersund     Kramfors
Vaasa
Savonlinna
Trondheim
Jyväskylä
Molde     Kristiansund
Røros
Tampere     Lappenranta
Ålesund
Sundsvall
Pori
NORWAY
NORGE
HELSINKI
Gävle
ÅLAND
ISLANDS
Turku
Bergen
Borlänge
OSLO
STOCKHOLM
Mariehamn
Haugesund
VÄSTERÅS
Stavanger
Karlstad
Kristiansand
Norrköping
Gothenburg
Visby     GOTLAND
DENMARK
DANMARK     Ålborg
Jönköping
Halmstad
Kalmar     ÖLAND
Århus
COPEN-
HAGEN     Malmö
Odense
BORNHOLM

## Travel by air

Air services within the Scandinavian countries are primarily provided by **SAS** (*Scandinavian Airlines System*) and **Finnair**. A number of domestic services are flown in Norway by *Braathens SAFE* and *Widerøes Flyveselskap*, and in Sweden by *Linjeflyg*. The largest airport for domestic as well as international services is Copenhagen's Kastrup Airport. – There are direct flights (in some cases with calls (stopovers) at intermediate airports) from London to Bergen, Copenhagen, Gothenburg (Göteborg), Helsinki, Kristiansand, Oslo, Stavanger and Stockholm; from Aberdeen to Bergen, Copenhagen and Stavanger; from Dublin to Copenhagen; from Edinburgh to Bergen and Stavanger; from Glasgow to Copenhagen and Stavanger; from Manchester to Copenhagen; from Newcastle to Bergen and Stavanger; and from Norwich to Stavanger. There are also

Signpost at Bodø airfield in northern Norway

numerous services to and from North American airports (to Copenhagen, Helsinki, Oslo and Stockholm).

The inter-Scandinavian network of air services extends throughout the four countries, reaching as far north as Kirkenes, so that all major towns are readily accessible by air. Air fares are particularly reasonable in Finland, which offers Finnair holiday tickets covering an unlimited number of flights within Finland at a cost of 180 US dollars for 15 days.

# Travel by rail Map, p. 314

Except in Denmark and southern Sweden, the Scandinavian railway network is relatively sparse, but it is so well complemented by bus and boat services that all parts of the four countries are easily accessible.

**Denmark** has some 2600 km (1600 miles) of railway lines, some 2000 (1250) of which are run by the Danish State Railways (*Danske Statsbaner, DSB*), which also run 210 km (130 miles) of ferry services. The only electrified line is the Copenhagen S-Bane.

**Norway**'s railway system (4500 km – 2800 miles) is almost exclusively run by the Norwegian State Railways (*Norges Statesbaner, NSB*). The main lines in the south of the country are electrified. Some important main lines have been completed only in recent years, including the Sørland line from Oslo to Stavanger (1943), with the two longest tunnels in the country (8474 m (9270 yds) and 9064 m – 9900 yds), and the Nordland line from Trondheim to Bodø (1960).

The **Bergen line**, through the mountainous country of southern Norway, was built between 1895 and 1909 to provide a link between the two largest towns in Norway, Oslo and Bergen. Of its total length of 492 km (306 miles), about 100 km (60 miles) are above the tree-line. The highest point is at the Taugevann (1301 m – 4270 ft). **Motorail** between Oslo and Bodø.

**Sweden**'s railways have a total length of 12,000 (7500 miles). Almost the whole system, practically all of which is run by the Swedish State Railways (*Svenska Statens Järnvägar, SJ*), is electrified, including the entire north–south line from Narvik to Trelleborg (2200 km – 1375 miles).

**Finland** has about 5900 km (3700 miles) of railway line, including a number of new lines built since 1945, following the changes in the country's frontiers. They belong almost entirely to the Finnish State Railways (*Valtion Rautatiet, VR*). The Finnish railways have the Russian broad gauge of 1·524 m (5 ft), compared with the 1·435 (4 ft 8½ in.) normal in the rest of Europe. The motor express trains are fast and comfortable.

The **Nordic Rail Ticket**, valid for 21 days allows unlimited travel on the railway systems of the four Scandinavian countries and a 50% discount on the scheduled boat services between the countries. The 21-day ticket costs about £87 (approx. $173) second class and £127 (approx. $255) first class. – Similar tickets can be obtained, at lower cost, for each of the four countries separately. – There are also discounts for students and groups.

# Buses

In all four Scandinavian countries, the railway services are complemented by a network of bus services run either by the State Railways, the Post Office or private companies. The buses mainly serve areas without a railway line and are usually timed to connect with main-line train services. Many services operate only from the beginning of June to the end of August. Extra buses are operated if necessary, so that there is usually no difficulty in getting a seat (seats cannot be reserved). On long journeys, there are stops for lunch, etc. – Tickets are issued on the buses themselves, but can also be obtained in advance through travel agencies, particularly for round trips involving a number of different services.

The **Nord-Norge bus** runs between Fauske and Kirkenes (1318 km – 819 miles), with branch services into Finland, from the middle of June to September; in winter, it goes only as far north as Hammerfest. North of Narvik hotel rooms are booked for passengers at the overnight stops. The cost of ferries used by the bus is included in the fare.

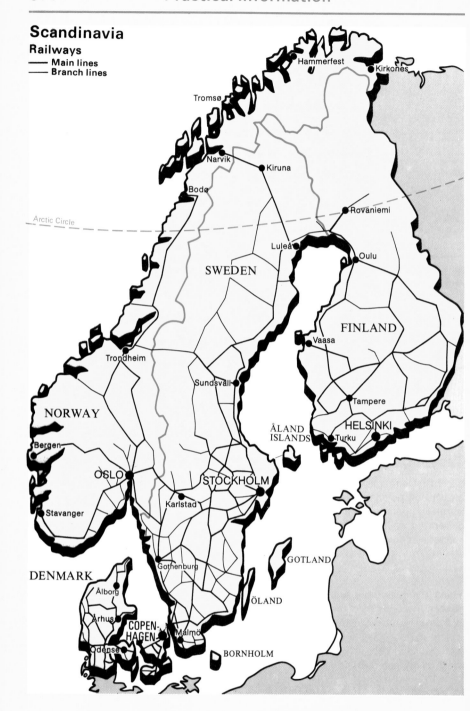

## Scandinavia
**Railways**
—— Main lines
—— Branch lines

Hammerfest
Kirkones
Tromsø
Narvik
Kiruna
Bodø
Rovaniemi
Arctic Circle
Luleå
Oulu
SWEDEN
FINLAND
Vaasa
Trondheim
Sundsvall
Tampere
ÅLAND
ISLANDS
HELSINKI
NORWAY
Turku
Bergen
OSLO
STOCKHOLM
Karlstad
Stavanger
GOTLAND
DENMARK
Gothenburg
Ålborg
ÖLAND
Århus
COPEN-
HAGEN
Malmö
Odense
BORNHOLM

# Suggested Tours

The following suggested tours are intended to help the visitor to get to know the
most interesting parts of the four Scandinavian countries and the most worthwhile sights. However, because of the
extent of the area it is not possible to
include all the scenic and cultural sights of
the four countries. These suggested tours

do not, of course, preclude visitors from
choosing the places they would prefer to
visit, nor the routes they wish to use. The
suggested tours can be followed on the
large general map included with this
guide or on supplementary area maps.

At the beginning of each proposed tour
can be found details of its length and the
time necessary to complete it without a
prolonged stopover at any one place.
Geographical, historical and cultural

notes are also provided and the individual stages of the proposed tour are given.

All the tours described here start from the German-Danish border (either from Flensburg or from Rødbyhavn) but they can equally well be started from any other place on or near the route. Visitors coming from Great Britain by sea may well find it more convenient to start any of the tours from Esbjerg.

# Tour of Denmark

We begin by visiting the elongated peninsula of Jutland where the largest towns (including Århus and Ålborg) and harbours are situated on the eastern side, whereas the west coast facing the North Sea has only smaller towns, of which Esbjerg is Denmark's most important North Sea port. From Jutland the tour crosses the Little Belt to the fertile island of Funen which is an important link between east and west Denmark.

On Funen lies Odense, the birthplace of the celebrated Danish storyteller Hans Christian Andersen. At Nyborg we leave Funen by ferry, crossing the Great Belt to Zealand, the principal island of Denmark, where visits can be paid to several fine castles and impressive old churches. After leaving the old royal town of Roskilde we reach Copenhagen, the splendid lively capital of the country; there is so much to be seen here, that a stay of several days is warranted.

From *Flensburg* we drive along the east side of **Jutland** (E3 or another main road) through *Åbenrå* and *Haderslev* to *Kolding* with its castle, then to *Vejle* and *Skanderborg*, from where a detour to the *Himmelberg* (147 m/482 ft) is recommended, and on to **Århus**, the second largest town in Denmark, where the open-air museum is well worth a visit.

Now along Road 15 to the little resort of *Grenå* continuing on Road 16 to *Randers*; then either west through the old town of **Viborg** with its beautiful cathedral (Road 16) or direct past the *Rebild National Park* (E3) to **Ålborg** on the *Limfjord*; then through the busy port of **Frederikshavn**

to *Skagen*, where we reach the northern-most point of Denmark.

From here we return to Frederikshavn and to *Løkken* on the west coast, from where we can drive for some distance along by the sea. From *Fjerritslev* the visitor should choose the road via Skiva to *Holstebro*, in order to be able to visit *Spøttrup* Castle; then continue to Ringkøbing and across the spit of land called *Holmsland* to the port of **Esbjerg.** From here short excursions to the island of *Fanø* and the old town of *Ribe* can be recommended.

We now leave the west coast and drive to *Kolding*. We take the E66 to *Fredericia* and cross a bridge over the *Little Belt* to the island of **Funen**, in the centre of which stands the town of **Odense**, continuing to *Svendborg* on the south coast and thence along E66, passing several old mansions to *Nyborg*, where the royal castle is one of the oldest castles in the north.

From Nyborg the *Great Belt* is crossed on a ferry which at *Korsør* reaches the large island of **Zealand**, from where we follow E66 through the old royal town of Roskilde to Copenhagen.

From the Danish capital we follow the scenically attractive road along the western shore of the öresund to **Helsingør**, with "Hamlet's" *Kronborg* Castle and then along Road 6 to Castle *Fredensborg* and *Hillerød* with its fine Castle of *Frederiksborg*; from here Road 16 is the return route to Copenhagen.

The last stage of the tour takes us along the E4 from Copenhagen southwards; from *Vordingborg* the visitor has the opportunity of making a short excursion to the island of **Møn** with its chalk cliffs. From the south of Zealand the E4 crosses the *Farø Bridge* to the island of **Falster.** Beyond Nykøbing we cross another bridge over the *Guldborgsund* to the island of **Falster** and on to *Rødbyhavn* on the south-west coast. From here there is a ferry service to *Puttgarden* on the German island of Fehmarn.

# Tour through Denmark and Southern Sweden

The proposed tour (2400–2800 km (1490–1740 miles); 10–14 days) goes through Denmark, which forms a land link with the other Scandinavian countries, and the southern part of Sweden, thus giving the visitor an impression of both countries, their capitals and their most notable sights. Acquaintance is made with the east coast of the Jutland peninsula and parts of the Danish islands of Funen and Zealand with the capital Copenhagen. In Sweden the tour leads the visitor from Gothenburg to Stockholm diagonally across the south of the country, presenting a contrast to the scenery of Denmark. The interior of Sweden consists of a hilly region, interspersed by numerous lakes, with Lake Vättern forming a highlight of the tour. The return journey from the Swedish capital of Stockholm follows the Baltic coast fairly closely, providing excellent opportunities of making excursions by boat to the Swedish island of Gotland and the Danish island of Bornholm, as well as taking in the province of Schonen in the south of Sweden. Schonen is rich farming country and has many fine mansions and old churches, with the Cathedral of Lund the most noteworthy.

From *Flensburg* the tour leads along the eastern side of the Danish peninsula of **Jutland** (E3 or another main road) through the large towns of **Århus** and Ålborg to **Frederikshavn**, from where a detour can be made to *Skagen* in the extreme north of Denmark.
We then cross the *Kattegat* by ferry and arrive in **Gothenburg**, the second largest town in Sweden, where there is a great deal worth seeing.

The tour continues on Road 40 via **Borås** (detour to Castle *Torpa*) to **Jönköping**, well-known for its match factories; from here an attractive excursion to the *Taberg* (343 m (1125 ft)) should not be missed.

Next comes a charming scenic stretch (E4, Road 50 and E3) along beautiful **Lake Vättern**, through *Vadstena*, with an old castle, to *Motala*, where the östergotland section of the Göta canal begins.

Then we go on to **Orebro**, the principal place of the Närke region.

We now continue (E4/E18) to the ancient trading centre of *Arboga* and northwards to **Lake Mälar** with its many islands and bays. Continuing on E18 we traverse the fertile province of Västmanland to its chief place, **Västerås**, with its notable cathedral and *Enköping*. Further on, near the church of *Litslena* we turn left off the main road to Stockholm and arrive at the well-known university town of **Uppsala**; from here, after a detour to *Skokloster* Castle we reach **Stockholm**, where at least 2–3 days should be spent.

We continue along the coastal road (E4 and Road 15) to *Södertäljei* (detour to *Gripsholm* Castle and via **Norrköping** to Oskarshamn, from where we can go by boat in about 4½ hours to the old town of *Visby* on the island of **Gotland**.

From Oskarshamn Road 15 takes us to **Kalmar** (castle; trip to the island of Olland) and to the Swedish military port of Karlskrona. Continuing via *Karlshamn* we reach Kirstianstad, from where those in a hurry can drive across country via *Hässleholm* (Road 21) direct to Helsingborg.

From the important port and commercial centre of **Malmö** the visitor should not fail to make a detour to **Lund**; the cathedral here is one of the most impressive churches in the country.

We bid farewell to Sweden in the important Swedish port of **Helsingborg** and cross the Oresund by ferry to the Danish town of **Helsingør** (Kronborg Castle). From here Roads 6 and 16 take us via *Hillerød* (Frederiksborg Castle) to **Copenhagen** where at least two days should be spent.

There is a choice of routes from Copenhagen; either south to *Rødbyhavn* (E4) from where there is a ferry to *Puttgarden* in Germany, or south-west through the old royal town of **Roskilde** and **Odense** to *Kolding* and *Flensburg* (see "Tour of Denmark").

# Tour through Denmark, Sweden and Norway

This suggested tour of 3100–4600 km (1926–2854 miles), which can be completed in 2–4 weeks, covers Denmark and the southern parts of Sweden and Norway and provides a good impression of the differing landscapes of these three countries. Whereas the countryside of Denmark is similar to that of North Germany, Sweden, with its rocky coasts and hilly woodland of the interior, presents a completely different scenic picture. The sublime beauty of the mountains and fjords of Norway, however, which inspire every visitor, form the climax of the tour.

The return journey from Norway offers two choices.
The most direct route leads back to Oslo and from there by ship across the Skagerrak to Frederikshavn in the north of Jutland and thence south through Ålborg to Flensburg. The alternative route which takes considerably longer is to drive north to the old Norwegian town of Trondheim and then through Sweden, presenting an opportunity of seeing something of Stockholm, the beautifully situated capital of that country.

As described here the tour starts from *Rødbyhavn*, but it may equally well be started from any other point on the route. We first follow the E4 to **Copenhagen**, the capital of Denmark; from here there is a rewarding detour to **Roskilde**; from Copenhagen we drive to the Danish port of *Helsingør* (*Krongborg Castle*), from where we cross the Oresund to **Helsingborg** in Sweden.
From here E6 follows the coast of the *Kattegat* to **Gothenburg**, the second largest city in Sweden. Continuing on the same road we pass through *Kungälv* and *Stenungsund* – a detour to see the fine bridge leading on to the island of Tjörn is highly recommended – and on through *Uddevalla* generally at some distance from the coast of the *Skagerrak*, where there are very many seaside resorts, to the Swedish–Norwegian frontier at the *Svinesund*. From here we go through *Sarpsborg* and *Moss* to the Norwegian capital of Oslo, where about two days should be allowed for sightseeing.

Now on the E18 to Drammen and on to the rocky coast of southern Norway at **Kristiansand**. From here we either continue inland along the E18 (or from Flekkefjord on Road 44 along the coast) to **Stavanger** (interesting cathedral). To reach Bergen we can either travel direct by ship or we can drive and cross sounds and fjords by ferry. Another route is through the beautiful valley of **Setesdal** to *Haukeligrend* (Road 12) and along the *Haukeli Road* through the mountains to the fine Sørfjord and *Odda*; we continue to **Hardangerfjord** and to the old Norwegian town of **Bergen**.

From Bergen we take a ship (limited accommodation for cars) to the magnificent **Sognefjord**, reaching *Balestrand* on the north bank and Lærdalsøry on the southern shore. From here the route continues to *Borgund* (impressive stave church) to the *Tyinsee* descending a fine mountain road to *Årdalstangen* at the eastern end of the Sognefjord, from where a ferry can be taken to *Kaupanger*.

The route now goes north-east on one of the finest mountain roads in Norway, over the *Sognefjell*, passing the mountains of **Jotunheimen** (Galdhøping, 2468 m/8100 ft) to Lom; from here Road 15 leads north-west via *Grotli* to the impressive **Geirangerfjord**.

Next along the "Eagles Road" (north shore of the Geirangerfjord to *Eidsdal* on the Norddalsfjord and by ferry to *Linge*, We continue on Road 63 to *Andalsnes* and then south through the beautiful **Romsdal** (E69) to *Dombås*, where route divides.

The visitor in a hurry should drive through the **Gudbrandsdal** valley to **Lillehammer**, where the open-air museum is worth seeing; then back to Oslo and by ship to **Frederikshavn** in northern Jutland. The last stage is via **Ålborg** and **Århus** to Flensburg.

A more rewarding but considerably longer alternative (at least a week longer) from Dombas is to follow the E6 to **Trondheim**, where the cathedral is the finest ecclesiastical building in the whole of Scandinavia.

From Trondheim the Trondheimfjord is followed through the interior of the country via *Meråker* to the Norwegian–Swedish border, near the winter-sports and health resort of *Storlien* and then on through the mountains and forests of the province of Jämtland (Road 14) passing close to the mighty *Tännfors* waterall and along the Indesälv to the town of **Ostersund**, situated on the *Storsjö*.

We now follow Road 14 as far as *Brunflo*, then Road 18 southwards to **Lake Siljan** in the heart of the province of *Dalarna*. We continue via the old mining town of **Falun** to *Enköping* on the north of **Lake Mälar** with its numerous islands. Passing through **Uppsala** with its notable cathedral we reach **Stockholm** the beautifully situated capital of Sweden.

There are several places of interest which can be visited from Stockholm, including the Palace of *Drottningholm* and the seaside resort of *Saltsjöbaden*. Leaving Stockholm we drive south to *Södertälje* (excursion to Gripsholm Castle) and via *Nyköping* to **Norrköping** (E4), an important industrial and commercial town, then to **Linköping**, well-known for its interesting cathedral and on to *Motala*. From here we skirt **Lake Vättern** and drive in a southerly direction to **Jönköping** and thence via **Borås** westward to **Gothenburg** on the Kattegat.

We now take the ferry to **Frederikshavn** on the eastern shore of Jutland and continue through **Ålborg** and **Århus** back to *Flensburg*.

# Tour of Denmark, Southern Sweden and Finland

This tour covers some 4500 km (2800 miles) and takes about 4–5 weeks to complete.

The quickest way of reaching Finland (apart from by air) is by ship from Travermünde (Germany) or from Stockholm (Sweden).

The following route uses the second of the two sea passages, following the itinerary suggested in "Tour of Denmark" as far as **Helsingør** and crossing to **Helsingborg** in Sweden by ferry.

From here we take the E4 through the hilly northwestern part of the region of Schonen, then through the wooded countryside of Småland to **Jönköping** (detour to the Taberg), at the southern end of beautiful **Lake Vättern**.

We now follow the eastern shore of the lake to *Motala* and on Road 36 through Ostergötland to **Linköping** with its fine cathedral, then by way of the industrial town of Norrköping and via *Nyköping* (E4), the capital of the province of *Södertälje*, from where an excursion can be made to Castle *Gripsholm* before continuing to Stockholm.

From Stockholm, the magnificently situated capital of Sweden, we take a ferry in about 20 hours to the beautiful Finnish capital of **Helsinki**, where a stay of about two days is suggested.

We begin our tour of Finland from Helsinki on the E3 through the southwestern part of the country to the old town of **Turku**, where the cathedral and castle bear witness to its history; then continuing past several old churches and at varying distances from the coast of the *Gulf of Bothnia*, through **Pori** to the town of **Vaasa** in western Finland (Road 8). From here we follow the coast of **Oulu**; if there is time a visit can be made to **Rovaniemi** which is situated not far south of the **Arctic Circle**. From here we first take the E4 and from Kemi Road 4 which runs parallel to the Kemijoki.

The route leads from Oulu on Road 22 south-east past the *Oulujärvi* and on Road 5 to **Kajaani**, then via *Lisalmi* to **Kuopio** on the southeastern slope of the *Puijo-Height*, well known for its fine views.

We now turn south to the **Koli Hills** (247m (1139 ft); view of Lake Pilienen) and on through the eastern part of the **Finnish Lake Plateau** to **Savonlinna**, from where a detour to the *Punkaharju Ridge* (nature reserve; footpaths), which is surrounded by water, should not be missed.

From Savonlinna the route continues westwards to *Juva* (Road 14 and via **Mikkeli** and **Lahti** (Roads 5 and E4)

**Mikkeli** and **Lahti** (Roads 5 and E4) back to Helsinki, from where we return to Stockholm by ferry.

From Stockholm we travel northwards to the celebrated university town of **Upp-sala**, then on the E18 to **Orebro** and on to *Mariestad* on **Lake Vättern**. Passing the wooded *Kinnekulle* we reach **Gothen-burg** in western Sweden, from where we take a ferry to **Frederikshavn** in Jutland in northern Denmark.
The last section of this tour returns to *Flensburg* or *Esbjerg* via **Ålborg** and **Århus**.

# Tour of the Scandinavian Capitals

This tour, covering 2450–2850 km (1525–1770 miles) and taking 2–3 weeks, includes the capitals of the four Scandinavian countries but does not cover a great deal of Norway and Finland. However, by combining this tour with those previously suggested, the itinerary can be extended and can even include the interior of the Scandinavian countries, providing that the visitor has sufficient time available. In view of the size of the area, however, it is wise to make one particular country the focus of the tour.

The visitor who wishes to see something of Finland can leave his vehicle in Stockholm and avoid the expense of conveying it on the ferry, as the section from Helsinki to Turku can be undertaken by bus or rail. In addition, an excursion by Finnair can be made to Lappland, which will give the visitor an excellent general impression of the Finnish countryside.

From *Flensburg* or *Esbjerg* the E3 extends along the east side of Jutland via **Århus** and **Ålborg** to the port of **Frederiks-havn**, from which an extension to *Skagen* is very desirable.
From Frederikshavn we take a ferry over the *Kattegat* to the great port of **Gothen-burg** in western Sweden; it is recommen-ded that at least a day should be spent here.

We continue along the pleasant coastal region of Bohuslän (detour to see the

bridge leading to Tjörn) to the *Svinesund*, the frontier between Sweden and Norway which is spanned by a bridge. On past the Norwegian frontier town of *Halden* (old fortress) via *Sarpsborg* to *Moss* and along the east shore of the **Oslofjord** to Oslo, the capital of Norway, where at least two days should be spent. The visitor who has sufficient time should take an excursion into the mountains (about 4 days) to appreciate to the full the majesty of this part of Norway.

From Oslo the route leads eastwards into Sweden and at **Karlstad** reaches beauti-ful Lake Vänern.

Next we travel along the E18 through *Karlskoga* to Orebro, the chief place of the province of Närke, and on via **Västerås** and the university town of **Uppsala** to **Stockholm**, the Swedish capital, where at least 2–3 days should be spent.

We now take a ship to **Helsinki**, the capital of Finland, (about 20 hours) and from there we follow E3 through the southwestern part of the country to the old town of **Turku** on the Gulf of Bosnia.

From Turku we again embark on a ferry to return to Stockholm by way of the **Åland Islands** and then continue on the E4 to **Norrköping**.

We continue to Helsingborg, either via **Linköping** to **Jönköping** at the southern end of **Lake Vättern**, and thence via *Värnamo*, or from Norrköping on a more rewarding but longer route – the "coastal road" (see "Tour of Denmark and Sweden"), with the possibility of a trip to the island of **Gotland** (return journey 3 days), and thence via **Kalmar**, **Karls-krona** and **Kristianstad** to **Malmö**, from where a worthwhile detour can be made to **Lund** with its notable cathedral. We then continue to **Helsingborg**, where we reach the *Oresund* which separates Denmark from Sweden.

From Helsingborg we cross the Oresund by ferry to the Danish port of **Helsingør**, where *Kronborg* Castle should be visited. Then either along to coast road or via *Hillerød* (Frederiksborg Castle) to **Copen-hagen**, the lively capital of Denmark which requires a stay of about 3 days.

From here the tour along roads 21, 14 and E66 goes obliquely across the island of

**Zealand** through the old royal town of **Roskilde** to *Korsør*, then by ship across the *Great Belt* to the island of **Funen**, the chief town of which, **Odense**, was the birthplace of Hans Christian Andersen. Crossing a bridge over the *Little Belt* to the **Jutland** peninsula, we go on via *Kolding* to *Flensburg* or we return to *Esbjerg* for the ferry to the United Kingdom.

# Grand Tour of Scandinavia

This tour, covering from 6150 to 6650 km (3822–4132 miles) can be completed without difficulty in about 5 to 7 weeks. The tour, which extends as far as the northernmost point of Norway, provides the visitor with a comprehensive impression of all four Scandinavian countries, with their magnificent scenery, old towns and numerous cultural monuments. It covers a part of Europe which is attracting more and more visitors. Although it is mainly low-lying, Denmark, especially in the capital, Copenhagen, and its surroundings has many things worth seeing. The principal attractions of Sweden are its beautiful capital, Stockholm, the very varied scenery of its mountains and forests and the wild nature of Lapland. Finland has the modern capital city of Helsinki, as well as extensive woods and innumerable lakes. The magnificent landscape of Norway, with its mountains and fjords, is unlike any other in central Europe and it has the unique attraction of the "midnight sun".

The suggested tour begins in *Flensburg* in the south of **Jutland**, from where we drive either along the E3 or on roads skirting the eastern coast to **Frederikshavn**.

From here we cross the *Kattegat* to the great port of **Gothenburg** in western Sweden and along the E6 via *Stenungsund* (detour to see the bridge leading to the island of Tjörn) and *Uddevalla* (see "Tour of Denmark, Sweden and Norway") to the Norwegian capital of Oslo, where two days should be allowed for sightseeing.

We now follow E68 northwards to *Hønefoss* and through the valley of the *Begna*, known as *Valdres*, to *Fagernes* before reaching *Kyrkestøjane* we turn off E68 on to Road 53 and drive along beautiful Lake *Tyin* to *Årdalstangen* at the eastern end of the great **Sognefjord**, where a detour can be made to the stave church of *Borgund*.

From Årdalstangen we take a ferry to *Kaupaanger* and from there we drive along a fine panoramic road north-eastwards over the *Sognefjell*, past the **Jotunheimen** mountains, to *Lom*, then via *Otta* to *Dombås*. Continuing on E6 over the *Dovrefjell* we reach the old town of **Trondheim**, with its cathedral, the finest church in Scandinavia.

From Trondheim, still on E6 and passing many fjords, some of which are crossed, we continue to *Mosjøen* and *Mo i Rana*, then across the **Arctic Circle** to the well-known ore-exporting port of **Narvik**. Several excursions can be taken from here; to there **Lofoten Islands** or the **Vesterålen**, lying further north; we can also travel by rail to the Swedish town of **Kiruna**, where iron-ore is mined.

Continuing via *Nordkjosbotn* along the majestic **Lyngenfjord**, where a detour to *Kilpisjärvi* in Finland is highly recommended, to **Hammerfest**, the most northerly town in Europe. From here an interesting excursion can be made to *Honningsvåg*.

The tour continues from Hammerfest on Road 94 and then on E6 to the *Porsangerfjord*, along which we can take a ferry to the island of *Magerøy* and so reach the **North Cape**.

In *Lakselv*, on the southern shore of the Porsangerfjord, we take the E6 south-east to *Karasjook*, beyond which we cross the border between Norway and Finland; then through the woods of **Finnish-Lapland** to the great **Lake Inari** and on to *Ivalo*. We now take the "Road of the Sea of Ice" to the town of **Rovaniemi**, situated just south of the **Arctic Circle**. From here Road 4 takes us to *Kemi*, where the route divides.

The visitor who wishes to see something of *Swedish-Lapland* must drive from **Tornio** (*Haparranda*) to *Töre* and follow Road 98 which leads to **Gällivare**, in the Swedish ore mining area; from here the route turns south through upland forests, with a detour to see the *Stora Sjöfall*. A hydro-electric station has unfortunately somewhat spoiled the former impressiveness of this great waterfall. We continue through *Jokkmokk*, then via *Arvidsjaur* and *Vilhelmina* to **Ostersund**.

From here the tour leads southwards through the thickly forested and thinly populated interior to the popular **Lake Siljan** and by way of **Falun**, once famous for its copper mines, and the university town of **Uppsala**, with its impressive cathedral, to **Stockholm**.

The visitor who wishes to visit the southern part of Finland and its capital, Helsinki, and who is prepared to miss the north of Sweden, should follow E4 from Kemi (see page 159) to **Oulu** and from there drive via **Kajaani, Savonlinna** and **Lahti** through the **Finnish Lake Plateau**, where the *Puijo Heights*, the Koli Hills and *Punkaharju* are the most impressive sights (see "Tour through Denmark, Southern Sweden and Fin-

land") to **Helsinki**, the Finnish capital (two days for sightseeing), from where he can board a ship for the return trip to Stockholm.

A minimum of 2–3 days should be allowed for sightseeing in Stockholm, and then we take E4 via **Norrköping** and **Jönköping** on **Lake Vättern** to **Helsingborg**, from where a ferry crosses the Oresund to the Danish port of **Helsingør**.

We now either continue along the east coast of Zealand or drive via *Hillerød* (see "Tour of Denmark") to **Copenhagen**, the fine capital of Denmark, where at least two days should be spent.

The visitor in a hurry can take the E4 direct to *Rødbyhavn*, but if more of Denmark is to be seen then E66 from Copenhagen leads first south-west and then west, with an opportunity of visiting the towns of **Roskilde** and **Odense**. The grand tour of Scandinavia ends either at *Flensburg*, or, for visitors from the United Kingdom, at *Esbjerg*.

# Languages

English is widely spoken in the four Scandinavian countries, and English-speaking visitors are unlikely to have any language difficulties in the popular tourist areas or in hotels and travel agencies. In the remoter areas, however, particularly in central and northern Scandinavia, it is helpful to know a bit of the language of the country, extending at least to a few common words and phrases. This section can do no more than give minimum information about each language and a brief selection of essential vocabulary. Those who want to know more of a particular language will find no shortage of good grammar books and dictionaries.

A knowledge of either Danish, Norwegian or Swedish will enable a visitor to make himself understood in any of the Scandinavian countries.

*Danish, Swedish* and *Norwegian* belong to the North Germanic or Scandinavian language group. Common to all three is the use of suffixes to form the definite article (Swedish *kyrkan*, "the church"), the plural (*-ar, -er*, etc.) and the passive (Swedish *jag kallas*, "I am called"). The characteristic Scandinavian vowels æ or ä, ø or ö and å appear at the end of the alphabet, after *z*. – *Finnish* is totally different from the other three languages; it belongs to the Finno-Ugrian language group, found in eastern Europe and western Siberia.

**Danish**, which was strongly influenced by Low German and Anglo-Saxon, is closely related to present-day written Norwegian, though Norwegian is more sonorous than Danish, which tends to swallow its words, somewhat like English.

The characteristic feature of the **pronunciation** of Danish is the use of the glottal stop, which occurs frequently, and not solely between vowels as in some local forms of English. The pronunciation of some letters differs from English: *d* after a vowel is softened to the sound of *th* in "the", or may be mute; *g* is hard, as in "go", at the beginning of a syllable, but other times is like the *ch* in "loch" or mute; *j* is like *y* in "yes"; *r* is a soft sound, not trilled; *v* before a consonant or at the end of a word becomes the vowel *u*; the vowel *y* is pronounced like the French *u* in "lune"; *ej* is like the vowel sound in "high", *æ* is like *a* in "take"; *ø* is like *eu* in French "deux"; and *å* has the vowel sound of "awe".

**Norwegian** has two forms – *Bokmål* (formerly Riksmål), the official written language, which is closely related to Danish, and *Landsmål*, a language constructed of various Norwegian dialects; it has also been known since 1929 as *Nyorsk* (New Norwegian). After Norway broke free from Denmark in 1814, the growth of national feeling led to an increased interest in the national language. Nynorsk (Landsmål) is spoken mainly in southern and western Norway, while Bokmål is used in the eastern part of the country and in the towns; both languages have equal status.

The following points of **pronunciation** should be noted: *æ, ø, å* and *y* much as in Danish; *o* is frequently like *oo*; *d* is usually mute before *s* and after *n* and *l*, and also when in final position after *r*; *g* is usually hard as in "go", but before *j* and *y* has the sound of consonantal *y*; in the word *jeg* ("I") the *g* forms a diphthong pronounced somewhere between the diphthongs in English "pay" and "pie"; *j* has the sound of English *y*, either consonantal or, after a vowel, vocalic; *k* before *i*, *j* or *y* is softened to a sound like the German *ch* in "ich", almost like *sh*.

**Swedish** is perhaps the most sonorous of the Scandinavian languages. Like Norwegian, it makes a distinction between the colloquial language, *Talspråk*, and the written or official language, *Riksspråk*. In southern Sweden a certain Danish influence can be detected; in the west and northwest the language shows affinities to Norwegian.

In the **pronunciation** of Swedish, the following points should be noted: *ä* and *ö* are much like Danish *æ* and *ø*, *a* and *y* much the same as in Danish; *o* is sometimes like *oo*; *u* is almost the same as *y*; *c* before *e, i, y, ä* or *ö* is like *s*, otherwise *k*; *ch* before *e, i, y, ä* or *ö* is like *sh*; in *och* ("and") the *ch* is pronounced *k*; *d* before *j* at the beginning of a syllable is mute; *f* at the end of a syllable is pronounced *v*; *g* before *ä, e, i, ö* and *y* and after *l* and *r* is like consonantal *y*, as is *gj* before *o* and *u*; *k* before *ä, e, i, ö* and *y* and in the combination *kj* has a sound almost like English *ch*; *lj* is like consonantal *y*; *sj* is pronounced *sh*; *sk, skj* and *stj* (*sti*) before *ä, e, i, ö* and *y* are like *sh*, and *tj* before these vowels like *ch*.

**Finnish** has no relationship to the other Scandinavian languages, belonging as it does to the Finno-Ugrian group, with affinities in eastern Europe and western Siberia. It has two main dialects, *West Finnish* and *East Finnish*, which are broken up into a number of sub-dialects. Some 6·5% of the population of Finland, particularly on the south and southwest coasts, speak Swedish.

Finnish is a language of many vowels. It has an alphabet of 21 letters; *b, c, d, f, g, w, x* and *z* are found only in foreign words or proper names. – With a few exceptions, the **pronunciation** corresponds to the spelling. The stress is always on the first syllable; in words of more than three syllables the third, fifth and seventh syllables – but never the last syllable – have a lighter stress. Single vowels are short (*y* being pronounced like the French *u*); double vowels are very long. In a sequence of two vowels in which the second one is *i* the first vowel has a slight stress. The letter *h* after a vowel and before a consonant is pronounced like *ch* in "loch". Double consonants do not shorten the preceding vowel as in English, but are themselves given double length or pronounced with particular distinction. – There is no definite article in Finnish.

## Cardinal Numbers

|      | Danish          | Norwegian       | Swedish       | Finnish             |
|------|-----------------|-----------------|---------------|---------------------|
| 0    | nul             | null            | noll          | nolla               |
| 1    | en, et          | en, ett         | en, ett       | yksi                |
| 2    | to              | to              | två           | kaksi               |
| 3    | tre             | tre             | tre           | kolme               |
| 4    | fire            | fire            | fyra          | neljä               |
| 5    | fem             | fem             | fem           | viisi               |
| 6    | seks            | seks            | sex           | kussi               |
| 7    | syv             | syv, sju        | sju           | seitsemän           |
| 8    | otte            | åtte            | åtta          | kahdeksan           |
| 9    | ni              | ni              | nio, nie      | yhdeksän            |
| 10   | ti              | ti              | tio, tie      | kymmenen            |
| 11   | elleve          | eleeve          | elva          | yksitoista          |
| 12   | tolv            | tolv            | tolv          | kaksitoista         |
| 13   | tretten         | tretten         | tretton       | kolmetoista         |
| 14   | fjorten         | fjorten         | fjorton       | neljätoista         |
| 15   | femten          | femten          | femton        | viisitoista         |
| 16   | seksten         | seksten         | sexton        | kuusitoista         |
| 17   | sytten          | sytten          | sjutton       | seitsemäntoista     |
| 18   | atten           | atten           | aderton       | kahdeksantoista     |
| 19   | nitten          | nitten          | nitton        | yhdeksäntoista      |
| 20   | tyve            | tjue, tyve      | tjugo         | kaksikymmentä       |
| 21   | en og tyve      | tjue en         | tjugo en      | kaksikymmentäyski   |
| 22   | to og tyve      | tjue to         | tjugo två     | kaksikymmentäkaksi  |
| 30   | tredive         | tretti          | trettio       | kolmekymmentä       |
| 40   | fyrre           | førti           | fyrtio        | neljäkymmentä       |
| 50   | halvtreds       | femti           | femtio        | viisikymmentä       |
| 60   | tres            | seksti          | sextio        | kuusikymmentä       |
| 70   | halvfjerds      | sytti           | sjuttio       | seitsemänkymmentä   |
| 80   | firs            | åtti            | åttio         | kahdeksankymmentä   |
| 90   | halvfems        | nitti           | nittio        | yhdeksänkymmentä    |
| 100  | hundrede        | hundre          | hundra        | sata                |
| 101  | hundrede og en  | hundre og en    | hundra en     | satayksi            |
| 200  | to hundrede     | to hundre       | två hundra    | kaksisataa          |
| 300  | tre hundrede    | tre hundre      | tre hundra    | kolmesataa          |
| 000  | tusind          | tusen           | tusen         | tuhat               |

## Ordinal Numbers

|      | Danish   | Norwegian | Swedish | Finnish     |
|------|----------|-----------|---------|-------------|
| 1st  | første   | første    | första  | ensimmäinen |
| 2nd  | anden    | annen     | andre   | toinen      |
| 3rd  | tredje   | tredje    | tredje  | kolmas      |

## Fractions

|                 | Danish        | Norwegian     | Swedish       | Finnish   |
|-----------------|---------------|---------------|---------------|-----------|
| $\frac{1}{2}$   | en halv       | en halv       | en halv       | puoli     |
| $\frac{1}{3}$   | en tredjedel  | en tredjedel  | en tredjedel  | kolmasosa |

## Months

| English    | Danish     | Norwegian  | Swedish    | Finnish    |
|------------|------------|------------|------------|------------|
| January    | januar     | januar     | januari    | tammikuu   |
| February   | februar    | februar    | februari   | helmikuu   |
| March      | marts      | mars       | mars       | maaliskuu  |
| April      | april      | april      | april      | huhtikuu   |
| May        | maj        | mai        | maj        | toukokuu   |
| June       | juni       | juni       | juni       | kesäkuu    |
| July       | juli       | juli       | juli       | heinäkuu   |
| August     | august     | august     | augusti    | elokuu     |
| September  | september  | september  | september  | syyskuu    |
| October    | oktober    | oktober    | oktober    | lokakuu    |
| November   | november   | november   | november   | marraskuu  |
| December   | december   | desember   | december   | joulukuu   |

## Days of the Week

| | | | |
|---|---|---|---|
| Sunday | søndag | søndag | söndag | sunnuntai |
| Monday | mandag | mandag | måndag | maanantai |
| Tuesday | tirsdag | tirsdag | tisdag | tiistai |
| Wednesday | onsdag | onsdag | onsdag | keskiviikko |
| Thursday | torsdag | torsdag | torsdag | torstai |
| Friday | fredag | fredag | fredag | perjantai |
| Saturday | lørdàg | lørdag | lördag | lauantai |

## Useful Words and Phrases

| English | Danish | Norwegian | Swedish | Finnish |
|---|---|---|---|---|
| Britain | Storbritannien | Storbritannia | Storbritannien | Iso-Britannia |
| England | England | England | England | Englanti |
| Scotland | Skotland | Skottland | Skottland | Skotlanti |
| Wales | Wales. | Wales | Wales | Wales |
| Ireland | Irland | Irland | Irland | Irlanti |
| USA | De forenede Stater | De Forente Stater | Förenta Staterna | Yhdysvallat |
| Canada | Kanada | Canada | Kanada | Kanada |
| Denmark | Danmark | Danmark | Danmark | Tanska |
| Danish | dansk | dansk | dansk | tanskalainen |
| Finland | Finland | Finland | Finland | Suomi |
| Finnish | finsk | finsk | finsk | suomalainen |
| Norway | Norge | Norge | Norge | Norja |
| Norwegian | norsk | norsk | norsk | norjalainen |
| Sweden | Sverige | Sverige | Sverige | Ruotsi |
| Swedish | svensk | svensk | svensk | ruotsalainen |
| Do you speak . . . | taler De . . . | snakker De . . . | talar ni . . . | puhutteko . . . |
| English | engelsk | engelsk | engelska | englantia |
| I do not understand | jeg forstår ikke | jeg forstår ikke | jag förstår inte | en ymmärrä |
| yes | ja, jo | ja, jo | ja (ha), jo, ju | niin, kyllä |
| no | nej | nei | nej, nej då | en, ei |
| please | værsågod | vær så god | var så god | oikaa hyvä |
| excuse me | undskyld | unnskyld | förlåt | pyydän |
| thank you | tak | takk | tack | kiitos |
| thank you very much | mange tak | mange takk | tack så mycket | kiitoksia paljon |
| good morning | god morgen | god morgen | god morgon | hyvää huomenta |
| good day | god dag | god dag | god dag | hyvää päivää |
| good evening | god aften | god aften | god afton | hyvää iltaa |
| good night | god nat | god natt | god natt | hyvää yöta |
| goodbye | farvel | farvel | adjö | näkemiin |
| man | herre | herre | herre, husbonde | herra |
| woman | dame, kvinde | dame | dam, kvinna | nainen, rouva |
| girl | frøken | frøken | fröken | neiti |
| Where is . . . | hvor er . . . | hvor er . . . | var är . . . | missä on . . . |
| . . . Street | . . . gaden | . . . gaten | . . . gatan | . . . katu |
| . . . Square | . . . pladsen | . . . plassen | . . . platsen, . . . torget | . . . tori |
| the road to . . . | vejen til . . . | veien til . . . | vägen till . . . | tie . . . |
| the church | kirken | kirken | kyrkan | kirkko |
| the museum | museet | museum, museet | museum, museet | museo |
| when? | hvornår? | når? | när? | milloin? |
| open | åbnet | åpent | öppet | auki |
| the Town Hall | rådhuset | rådhuset | rådhuset | kaupungintalo |
| the post office | posthuset | postkontoret | postkontoret | postikonttori |
| a bank | bank | bank | bank | pankki |
| the station | banegården, stationen | jernbane-stasjonen | järnväg-stationen | rautatieasema |
| a hotel | hotel | hotell | hotell | hotelli |
| I should like | jeg vil gerne have | jeg ville gjerne ha | jag skulle gärna ha | haluaisin mielelläni |
| a room | et værelse | et værelse | ett rum | huoneen |
| single | enkelt værelse | med en seng | med en bädd | yhdenhengen huone |
| double | dobbelt værelse | med to senger | med tva bäddar | kahdenhengen huone |
| with bath | med bad | med bad | med bad | kylpyhuoneella |
| without bath | uden bad | uten bad | utan bad | ilman kylpyä |
| the key | nøglen | nøkkelen | nyckeln | avain |
| the lavatory (bathroom) | toilettet | toalettet | toaletten | käymälä |
| a doctor | læge | lege | läkare, doktor | lääkäri |
| to the right | til højre | til høyre | till höger | oikealla |
| to the left | til venstre | til venstre | till vänster | vasemmalla |

| English | Danish | Norwegian | Swedish | Finnish |
|---|---|---|---|---|
| straight ahead | lige ud | rett fram | rakt fram | suoraan eteenpäin |
| up, above | oppe, ovenpå | oppe, ovenpå | uppe, ovanpå | ylhäällä, päällä |
| down, below | nede | nede | nedan, nere | alhaalla, alapuolella |
| old | gammel | gammel | gammal | vanha |
| new | ny | ny | ny | uusi |
| what does it cost? | hvad koster? | hva koster? | vad kostar? | paljonko maksaa? |
| dear | dyr | dyr | dyr | kallis |

Food and drink: see p. 321.

## Road Signs and Warnings

| English | Danish | Norwegian | Swedish | Finnish |
|---|---|---|---|---|
| Stop | Stop | Stopp | Stopp, Halt | Stopp, Seis |
| Customs | Told | Toll | Tull | Tulli |
| Caution | Pas på | Se opp | Se upp, Giv akt | Varokaa |
| Slow | Langsom | Sakte | Sakta | Hitaasti, Hiljaa |
| One-way street | Ensrettet | Envegskjøring | Enkelriktad | Yksisuuntainen liikenne |
| No entry | Ingen indkørsel | Gjennomkjøring forbudt | Infart förbjuden | Läpikulku kielletty |
| Road works | Vejarbejde | Veiarbeide | Vägarbete, Gatuarbete | Tietyö, Katutyö |

## Motoring Terms

| English | Danish | Norwegian | Swedish | Finnish |
|---|---|---|---|---|
| air | luft | luft | luft | ilma |
| battery | batteri | batteri | batteri | paristo, akku |
| brake | bremse | bremse | broms | jarru |
| breakdown | motorskade | motorstopp | motorstopp | konerikko |
| car | bil | bil | bil | auto |
| carburettor | karburator | forgasser | förgasare | kaasutin |
| cylinder | cylinder | sylinder | cylinder | sylinteri |
| driving licence | kørekort | førerkort | körkort | ajokortti |
| fuse | sikring | sikring | säkring | proppu |
| garage (for repairs) | autoværksted, bilværksted | bilverksted | bilverstad | autokorjaamo |
| headlight | lygte | lyskaster | strålkastare | valonheittäjä |
| horn | tudehorn | signalhorn | signalhorn | autotorvi, sireeni |
| ignition | tænding | tenning | tändning | sytytys |
| indicator | blinklys | blinklys | blinkljus | vilkkuri |
| motorcycle | motorcykel | motorsykkel | motorcyckel | moottoripyörä |
| oil | olie | olje | olja | öljy |
| oil change | skifte olie | skifte olje | byt olja | vaihtaa öljy |
| parking place | parkeringsplads | parkeringsplass | parkeringsplats | pysäköinti-paikka |
| petrol (gas) | benzin | bensin | bensin | bensiini |
| petrol (gas) station | benzintank | bensinstasjon | bensinstation | bensiiniasema |
| puncture | punktering | punktering | punktering | |
| radiator | køler | kjøler | kylare | jäähdyttäjä |
| spare part | reservedel | reservedel | reservdel | varaosa |
| sparking plug | tæmdrør | tennplugg | tändstift | tulppa |
| starter | selvstarter | selvstarter | självstart | startti |
| tow away | tag på slæb | ta på slep | taga på släp | hinata |
| tire | dæk | ring | däck | rengas |
| valve | ventil | ventil | ventil | venttiili |
| wash | vaske | vaske | tvätta | pestä |
| wheel | hjul | hjul | hjul | pyörä |
| windscreen (windshield)-wiper | vinduesvisker | vinduspusser | vindrutetorkare | tuulilasin pyyhkijä |

## Geographical Terms

| English | Danish | Norwegian | Swedish | Finnish |
|---|---|---|---|---|
| hill, mountain | bjerg | berg, bjerg | berg | vaara, vuori, tunturi |
| high mountain | fjeld | fjell | fjäll | |
| rocky hill | | skarv | | |
| spur of mountain | | hammer | | |
| high plateau | | vidda | | |
| peak | høj | hø, høi | höjd | huippu |
| sharp peak, pinnacle | | tind, nås(i) | tjåkko | |
| steep-sided peak | | nut | | |
| glacier | jøkel | jøkel, jøkul | glaciär | |
| plateau glacier | | bre, bræ | | |
| snowfield (névé) | | fond, fonn | | |
| rock face | | kliev, klev | klev | kallio |
| slope of hill | | li, lid | lid | |
| hill ridge | ås | ås | ås | selkä, harju |
| low hill | bakke | bakke, koll, kolle | kulle, klätt | mäki |
| valley | dal | dal | dal | laakso |
| gorge | | juv, gjel | | |
| river | elv | elv | älv | joki |
| small river | å | liten elv | å | |
| waterfall | foss | foss | fors | koski |
| arm of sea, channel between two lakes | sund | sund | sund | salmi |
| water, lake | vand | vann, vatn | vatten | vesi |
| beach, flat coast | strand | strand | strand | ranta |
| cliff | klint | klint | klint | |
| island | ø | øy | ö | saari |
| wood, forest | skov | skog | skog | metsä |
| moorland | mose | myr | myr | suo |
| bog, marsh | sump, kær | sump | kärr, träsk | |
| town | by | by | stad | kaupunki |
| church | kirke | kirke | kyrka | kirkko |
| tower | tårn | tårn | torn | torni |
| castle | slot | slott | slott | linna |
| garden, park | have | have | trädgård | puutarha, puisto |
| street | gade | gate | gata | katu |
| road | (lande)vej | (lande) vei | (lands)väg | (maan)tie |
| (market) square | torv, plads | torg, plass | torg, plats, plan | (kauppa)tori |
| bridge | bro | bru | bro | silta |
| railway | jernbane | jernbane | järnväg | rautatie |
| ferry | færge | ferje | färja | lossi, lautta |

# Accommodation

The **hotels** in the Scandinavian countries, noted for their cleanliness, are right up to international standards of comfort and service for the different price categories. The large towns (advance reservation very desirable) have luxury establishments, but many smaller places have excellent hotels combining international standards of comfort with distinctive national features. Even in the far north, there are good hotels and well-equipped **inns** which provide a very adequate standard of comfort. Many establishments have "family rooms" with 3–5 beds which provide reasonably priced accommodation for a family group. Some *mountain hotels* in Sweden, Norway and Finland are open for only part of the year, during the summer and winter seasons. There are also special *summer hotels*.

For a stay of some length, it is more economical to take a room in a *pension* (guest-house). There are also large numbers of *motels* in Scandinavia.

**Youth hostels** admit adults as well as young people, and have family rooms. An international youth hostel card is required.

Information about *vacation houses, vacation villages* and *farmhouse vacations* can be obtained from the national tourist organisations.

In the lists of hotels given in this Guide *b.*=beds, *SP*=swimming pool and *SB*=indoor swimming bath.

In **Denmark** the *kroer* (singular *kro*) – inns, some old and some quite new – offer pleasant and comfortable accommodation, full of character. Also good and reasonably priced are the *mission hotels* (members of the Danish Mission Hotels Federation) to be found in most Danish towns.

| Denmark | | |
|---|---|---|
| | Room charge in Dkr. | |
| | single | double |
| Luxury | 800–1200 | 950–1400 |
| Middle-grade | 230–600 | 280–700 |
| Modest | 120–300 | 220–440 |

In **Norway** there are *luxury hotels* in Oslo and other large towns. In the mountain regions, away from towns, there are comfortable *turisthotels* and *høyfjellshotels*. *Pensjonater* and *hospitser* are smaller hotels with an adequate standard of comfort. Below these are *turiststasjoner* and *fjellstuer* (mountain lodges). The *turisthytter* are mountain huts, often accessible only on foot, which provide simple accommodation, usually in rooms for 4–6 persons. – A *gjestgiveri* is an inn.

| Norway | | |
|---|---|---|
| | Room charge in Nkr. | |
| | single | double |
| Luxury | 450–950 | 500–1200 |
| Middle-grade | 300–600 | 380–800 |
| Modest | 120–300 | 250–450 |

In **Sweden** there are excellent hotels – often called *Stadshotellet* or *Stora Hotel-*

SOK Hotel, Kuusamo (northern Finland)

*let* – even in the smaller towns. There may be a *Järnvägshotell* (Railway Hotel) near the station. A *gästgivaregård* is a country inn, in earlier days a post-house. The *turiststationer*, run by the Swedish Tourist Board, are usually excellent.

In Sweden there is a system of **Hotel Checks** which cover bed, breakfast and reservation of the next night's hotel at a fixed rate. The "budget check" costs 85 Skr. per person per night in any one of the 150 hotels which accept the checks; the "quality check", for hotels of higher standard, costs 200 Skr.

| Sweden | | |
|---|---|---|
| | Room charge in Skr. | |
| | single | double |
| Luxury | 500–800 | 700–1100 |
| Middle-grade | 300–600 | 500–800 |
| Modest | 150–400 | 200–500 |

Finnish sauna

In **Finland** there are *luxury hotels* in Helsinki and other large towns. The Finnish Tourist Board also runs *tourist hotels* offering a high standard of comfort, in the main tourist areas (reservations advisable). In the remoter parts of the country, there are *inns* (*matkustajakoti*), which are of more modest standard but are usually clean. A *majatalo* is a country inn.

Finland also has a hotel check, the **Finncheque**, costing 85 marks per person per night. This is accepted in 145 hotels throughout Finland and covers bed and breakfast (in more modest hotels, a midday meal as well). In category 1 hotels there is an additional charge of 35 marks. The minimum number of checks that can be purchased is four.

| Finland | | |
|---|---|---|
| | Room charge in Fmk. | |
| | single | double |
| Luxury | 350–500 | 450–700 |
| Middle-grade | 200–450 | 230–600 |
| Modest | 100–200 | 180–300 |

Finland is the home of the **sauna**. In the traditional Finnish sauna, a simple wooden hut, stones are heated in a wood fire and water is thrown over them to produce steam and fierce heat. This regular alternation of dry and moist heat distinguishes the Finnish sauna from other types of steam bath. In order to enhance the sweat-producing effect and promote the circulation of blood, the bathers whip themselves with birch twigs.

## Camping and caravanning

Scandinavia is ideal camping country, and in all four countries there are numerous official **camp sites** (Danish *campingplads*, Norwegian *campingplass*, Swedish *campingplats*, Finnish *leirintäälue*). Campers should have an international camping carnet or the membership card of a national camping organisation. Lists of camp sites are issued annually by the national tourist organisations, motoring organisations and camping clubs, giving the location, size, facilities and category (1–3 stars) of the sites. In addition to the usual sanitary and cooking facilities, the larger sites normally have showers and shops selling provisions. On many sites there are also camping huts or chalets (simple wooden huts with sleeping accommodation). – In areas of particular natural beauty, there

Camp site in the Ruovesi (Finland)

are also **vacation villages**, with chalets and log cabins.

Campers who want to camp on their own ("wild" camping – prohibited in nature reserves and military areas, and not generally allowed in Denmark) should always ask the owner's permission before camping on or near private property. In the sparsely populated northern areas, care should be taken to maintain an adequate supply of water (Norwegian *vann*, Swedish *vatten*, Finnish *vesi*). On the coast and on the shore of a fjord, it is advisable to pitch the tent so that the entrance is sheltered from the wind. In Lapland, a mosquito net is essential.

# Food and drink

In addition to the **restaurants** in hotels, there are many other restaurants in the larger Scandinavian towns, ranging from good home cooking to the luxurious. In Denmark, they are often called *kro*, in Sweden, *värdshus*, in Finland, *ravintola*. Many of them are full of character, and in almost all the cuisine is of high quality. For those who want a quick or a cheap meal, there are a variety of *milk bars* or *snack bars* (*bar, matbar, cafeteria*: Finnish *baari* or *ruokabaari*), usually self-service. Although unpretentious, establishments of this kind are clean; the menu, with prices, is usually prominently displayed.

The sale of *alcohol* is regulated in the Scandinavian countries, though some of the severer restrictions imposed in the past have now been relaxed. Visitors frequenting the larger hotels and restaurants are unlikely to be affected by the regulations. The usual drink is *beer* of lager type (*øl* or *öl*, Finnish *olut*), normally

bottled. The Carlsberg and Tuborg breweries in Copenhagen have reputations extending far beyond the boundaries of Denmark. *Wine* is expensive, since it is imported. – A very popular drink in Norway is *milk* (*melk*), which is often served at breakfast or the evening meal without extra charge. Also popular are *cream* (*fløte*) and *sour cream* (*rømme*). – In Sweden *coffee* is a kind of national drink, and Swedish coffee is the best in Scandinavia.

Like other countries, the Scandinavian countries have a variety of **specialties** which the visitor will want to sample. – In *Denmark* there are the famous open sandwiches (*smørrebrød*) in all their variety. In restaurants the waiter will produce the *smørrebrødsseddel*, with a rich assortment of tempting confections on different kinds of bread (*franskbrød*, white bread; *rugbrød*, rye bread; *surbrød*, a kind of "grey" bread also made from rye flour). As appetisers at a main meal or as a second breakfast a variety of tidbits (e.g. eel, salmon, ham, vegetable salads) will

Danish buffet

and *hårtbröd* are types of crispbread, the popularity of which has spread to many other countries. – As in Denmark, a meal is often accompanied by a glass of *snaps*.

In *Norway*, the cold buffet (*koldbord*) is also a national tradition, and the large side table set out with a great variety of appetising dishes is a regular feature of breakfast or dinner in a Norwegian restaurant. The special menu listing various kinds of open sandwiches is less commonly found than in Denmark. There are only a few types of sausage of the European type, and most visitors are likely to prefer ham and cold meat. Particularly popular in Norway are *geitost* (goat's milk cheese) and *mysost*, a sweetish whey-cheese, brownish in colour, which is sliced thin and eaten on bread. A meal often ends with stewed fruit, served with sweet cream. – Norway has excellent *fish* dishes (salmon, trout, cod).

be offered, and this is often followed by a glass of *aquavit*. A meal usually ends with cheese (Danish *ost*).

In some 700 restaurants a typical Danish meal, under the name **"Danmenu"**, is served at a reasonable price.

In *Sweden*, the food is substantial and nourishing. The meal usually begins with cold hors-d'œuvre (*smörgås*), which is either served at the table on a small plate or set out on a side table (*smörgåsbord*). This consists of cold meat, fish, vegetable salads, egg dishes and cheese, and is known, according to the quantity and variety of food offered, as *assietter* or *delikatess assietter*. Particular delicacies are smoked salmon and smoked reindeer meat. The largest *smörgåsbord* is the *gående bord*, a long table with a great range of cold and hot dishes to which each guest helps himself. – Visitors to Sweden at the beginning of August may have the opportunity of participating in one of the *"crayfish feasts"* which take place at this time of the year. – A popular snack, sold at street kiosks, is *korv med mos* (sausage and mash). – *Knäckebröd*

In *Finland* every visitor should try *reindeer meat*, either roasted or smoked. A particular Finnish delicacy is *crayfish*, which are eaten between 20 July and 20 September, boiled in brine with dill seasoning and eaten ice-cold. A speciality of the province of Savo (Kuopio) is *kalakukko* ("fish-chicken"), a kind of fish and pork pie. The Finnish cold buffet, the equivalent of the Swedish *smörgåsbord*, is the voileipäpöytä.

**Cafés** (*kafé*, Finnish *kahvila*) in Scandinavia are usually small establishments serving open sandwiches and other dishes, as well as coffee. Nearer the normal European kind of café is a *konditori* (Finnish also *kahvila*). – **Bars** in the usual European or American sense of the word are found only in the international hotels in the large towns. The Scandinavian *bar* or *matbar* (Finnish *baari*, *ruokabaari*) is a snack bar.

## The Scandinavian menu

| English | Danish | Norwegian | Swedish | Finnish |
|---|---|---|---|---|
| *restaurant* | restaurant | restaurant | restaurang | ravintola |
| snack bar | cafeteria | kafeteria | matbar, bar | ruokabaari, baari |
| breakfast | morgenmad | frokost | frukost | aamiainen |
| lunch | middagsmad | middagsmat | middagsmåltid | päivällinen |
| dinner | aftensmad | koeldsmat, aftensmat | kvällsmat, aftonmåltid | illalinen |
| eat | spise | spise | spisa, äta | syödä |
| drink | drikke | drikke | dricka | juoda |
| a lot, many | meget, mange | mye, mange | mycken, många | paljon, moni |
| a little | lidt | lite | litet | vähän |
| the bill | regning | regning | räkning, nota | lasku |

| English | Danish | Norwegian | Swedish | Finnish |
|---|---|---|---|---|
| pay | betale | betale | betala | maksaa |
| at once | straks | met en gang, straks | strax | heti |
| *menu* | spisekort | spiseseddel | matsedel | ruokalista |
| *soup* | suppe | suppe | soppa | keitto |
| *meat* | kød | kjøtt | kött | liha |
| grilled | stegt på grill | grillet, grilleret | grillad | pariloitu |
| roast | steg | stek | stek | paisti |
| mutton | bede | gjeldvær | gällgumse | lammas |
| roast lamb | fåresteg | fåresteik | fårstek | lampaanreisi (leg) |
| calf (veal) | kalv | kalv | kalv | vasikka |
| lamb | lam | lam | lamm | lammas |
| reindeer | ren | rein | ren | poro |
| ox, bullock | okse | okse | oxe | nauta |
| ham | skinke | skinke | skinka | kinkku |
| pig | svin | svin | svin | sika |
| roast pork | flæskesteg | svinestek | grisstek | sianpaisti |
| sausage | pølse | pølse | korv | makkara |
| *fish* | fisk | fisk | fisk | kala |
| fried | stegt | stekt | stekt | paistettu |
| boiled | kogt | kokt | kokt | keitetty |
| fish balls | fiskeboller | fiskekaker | fiskbullar | |
| cod | torsk | torsk | torsk | turska |
| crayfish | krebs | kreps | kräfta | rapu |
| herring | sild | sild | sill | silli |
| lobster | hummer | hummer | hummer | hummeri |
| salmon | laks | laks | lax | lohi |
| smoked salmon | røget laks | røkelaks | rökt lax | savustettu lohi |
| shrimp | reje | reke | räka | katkarapu |
| trout | ørred | ørret | forell, laxöring | taimen |
| *vegetables* | grøn(t)sager | grønnsaker | grönsaker | vihanneksia |
| beans | bønne | bønne | böna | papu |
| cabbage | kål | kål | kål | kaali |
| cauliflower | blomkål | blomkål | blomkål | kukkakaali |
| cucumber | agurk | agurk | gurka | kurkku |
| green salad | grøn salat | hodesalat | huvudsallat | salaatti |
| peas | ært | ert | ärta | herne |
| potatoes | kartoffel | potet | potatis | peruna |
| red cabbage | rødkål | rødkål | rödkål | punakaali |
| spinach | spinat | spinat | spenat | pinaatti |
| tomato | tomat | tomat | tomat | tomaatti |
| *ice* | is | is | glass | jäätelö |
| *stewed fruit* | kompot | kompott | kompott, sylt | hillo, jälkiruoka |
| fruit jelly | rødgrød | rødgrøt | rödgröt | puuro |
| pudding | budding | pudding | pudding | vanukas |
| whipped cream | flødeskum | krem | vispgrädde | vispikerma, vaahtokerma |
| *fruit* | frugt | frukt | frukt | hedelmät |
| apple | æble | eple | äpple | omena |
| bilberry | blåbær | blåbær | blåbär | mustikka |
| cherry | kirsebær | kirsebær | körsbär | kirsikka |
| cranberry | tyttebær | tyttebær | lingon | puola |
| lemon | citron | sitron | citron | sitruuna |
| orange | appelsin | appelsin | apelsin | appelsiini |
| pear | pære | pære | päron | päärynä |
| plum | blomme | plomme | plommon | luumu |
| raspberry | hindbær | bringebær | hallon | vadelma |
| strawberry | jordbær | jordbær | jordgubbe | mansikka |
| *drinks* | drik | drikk | dryck | juoma |
| beer | øl | øl | öl | olut |
| coffee | kaffe | kaffe | kaffe | kahvi |
| cream | fløde | fløte | grädde | kerma |
| milk | mælk | melk, mjølk | mjölk | maito |
| mineral water | mineralvand | mineralvann | mineralvatten | kivennäisvesi |

| English | Danish | Norweigian | Swedish | Finnish |
|---------|--------|------------|---------|---------|
| tea | te | te | te | tee |
| water | vand | vann | vatten | vesi |
| wine | vin | vin | vin | viini |
| red wine | rødvin | rødvin | rödvin | puunaviini |
| white wine | hvidvin | hvitvin | vitt vin | valkviini |
| *bread* | brød | brød | bröd | leipä |
| white bread | franskbrød | hvetebrød | vetebröd | ranskanleipä |
| roll | rundstykke | rundstykke | franskt bröd | sämpylä |
| cake | kage | kake | kaka | kaakku |

# Manners and customs

The Scandinavians tend to be quiet and unassuming, patient themselves and offended by impatience in others. Their honesty, hospitality and helpfulness are proverbial. Visitors should, of course, try to match the behaviour of their hosts.

Dress in Scandinavia is in line with normal western European standards. In Finland, men are expected to wear a jacket and tie in the better restaurants, particularly in the evening. In view of the changeability of the weather and the wide variation in temperature, particularly in the mountain regions, visitors should take warm clothing, and a raincoat is essential. Sturdy footwear is a "must", and for walking in Lapland, knee-high wellington boots are advisable. For walking and climbing in the mountains, the same clothing and equipment are required as for the Alps – a point inexperienced climbers too often neglect, although their own safety depends on it. *Mountain guides* can usually be engaged through hotels or local tourist information offices.

# National Parks

## NORWAY

1 **Øvre Pasvik**
   (63 sq. km (24 sq. miles); Finnmark)

2 **Stabbursdalen**
   (96 sq. km (37 sq. miles); Finnmark)

3 **Øvre Anarjåkka**
   (1390 sq. km (536 sq. miles); Finnmark)

4 **Ånderdalen**
   (68 sq. km (26 sq. miles); Troms)

5 **Øvre Dividalen**
   (740 sq. km (286 sq. miles); Troms)

6 **Rago**
   (167 sq. km (64 sq. miles); Nordland)

7 **Børgefjell**
   (1087 sq. km (420 sq. miles); Nordland)

8 **Gressåmoen**
   (180 sq. km (70 sq. miles); Nord-Trøndelag)

9 **Femundsmarka**
   (386 sq. km (149 sq. miles); Hedmark)

10 **Gutulia**
   (19 sq. km (7 sq. miles); Hedmark)

11 **Dovrefjell**
   (265 sq. km (102 sq. miles); Oppland)

12 **Rondane**
   (572 sq. km (221 sq. miles); Oppland)

13 **Jotunheimen**
   (1140 sq. km (440 sq. miles); Oppland and Sogn og Fjordane)

14 **Hardangervidda**
   (3430 sq. km (1324 sq. miles); Hordaland, Telemark and Buskerud)

15 **Ormtjernkampen**
   (9 sq. km (3½ sq. miles); Oppland)

## SWEDEN

16 **Vadvetjåkko**
   (25 sq. km (10 sq. miles); Lapland)

17 **Abisko**
   (75 sq. km (29 sq. miles); Lapland)

18 **Stora Sjöfallet**
   (1380 sq. km (533 sq. miles); Lapland)

19 **Sarek**
   (1940 sq. km (749 sq. miles); Lapland)

20 **Padjelanta**
   (2010 sq. km (771 sq. miles); Lapland)

21 **Muddus**
   (492 sq. km (190 sq. miles); Lapland)

22 **Peljekaise**
   (146 sq. km (56 sq. miles); Lapland)

23 **Skuleskogen**
   (23·6 sq. km (9 sq. miles), Ångermanland)

24 **Töfsingdalen**
   (14 sq. km (5½ sq. miles); Härjedalen)

25 **Sonfjället**
   (27 sq. km (10 sq. miles); Härjedalen)

26 **Hamra**
   (0·3 sq. km (75 acres); Dalarna)

27 **Ängsö**
   (0·8 sq. km (200 acres); Uppland)

28 **Garphyttan**
   (1 sq. km (250 acres); Närke)

29 **Tiveden**
   (13·5 sq. km (5 sq. miles); Närke and Västergötland)

# National Parks in Scandinavia

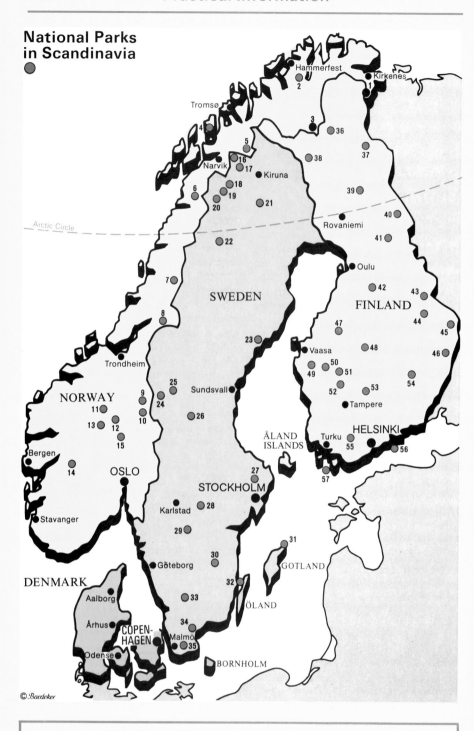

National Parks are large expanses of country, under state management, in which the natural landscape is as far as possible left undisturbed.

Norway, Sweden and Finland all have many National Parks. *Denmark* has no national parks, but a considerable number of smaller areas have been designated as *nature reserves*, to which the public has access (unlike the Danish *game reserves*, which are closed to the public).

30 **Norra Kvill**
(0·3 sq. km (75 acres); Småland)

31 **Gotska Sandön**
(36 sq. km (14 sq. miles); Gotland)

32 **Blå Jungfrun**
(0·7 sq. km (175 acres); Småland)

33 **Store Mosse**
(77·5 sq. km (30 sq. miles); Småland)

34 **Stenshuvud**
3·9 sq. km (1 sq. mile); Skåne)

35 **Dalby Söderskog**
(0·4 sq. km (100 acres); Skåne)

## FINLAND

36 **Lemmenjoki**
(2800 sq. km (1081 sq. miles); Lapland)

37 **Urho-Kekkonen-Nationalpark**
(2530 sq. km (977 sq. miles); Lapland)

38 **Pallas-Ounastunturi**
(500 sq. km (193 sq. miles); Lapland)

39 **Pyhätunturi**
(42 sq. km (16 sq. miles); Lapland)

40 **Oulanka**
206 sq. km (80 sq. miles); Oulu)

41 **Riisitunturi**
(76 sq. km (29 sq. miles); Lapland)

42 **Rokua**
(4 sq. km (1½ sq. miles) Oulu)

43 **Hiidenportti**
(40 sq. km (15 sq. miles); Oulu)

44 **Tiilikkajärvi**
(20 sq. km (8 sq. miles); Kuopio)

45 **Patvinsuo**
(100 sq. km (39 sq. miles); Northern Karelia)

46 **Petkeljärvi**
(6·3 sq. km (2½ sq. miles); Northern Karelia)

47 **Salamajärvi**
(55 sq. km (21 sq. miles); Central Finland)

48 **Pyhä-Häkki**
(12 sq. km (5 sq. miles); Central Finland)

49 **Lauhanvuori**
(26 sq. km (10 sq. miles); Vaasa)

50 **Kauhaneva-Pohjankangas**
(32 sq. km (12 sq. miles); Vaasa)

51 **Helvetinjärvi**
(21 sq. km (8 sq. miles); Häme)

52 **Seitseminen**
(31 sq. km (12 sq. miles); Häme)

53 **Isojärvi**
(19 sq. km (7 sq. miles); Häme)

54 **Linnansaari**
(21 sq. km (8 sq. miles); Mikkeli)

55 **Liesjärvi**
(6·3 sq. km (2½ sq. miles); Häme)

56 **Eastern Finnish Gulf National Park**
(5 sq. km (2 sq. miles); Kymi)

57 **South Western Skerries National Park**
(7 sq. km (3 sq. miles); S of Turku)

## Conservation

Large areas of Scandinavia, particularly in the north, are very sparsely populated and have preserved the natural landscape largely intact. In the climatic conditions of these areas, the ecological balance is very vulnerable to disturbance, since litter left by a careless visitor disintegrates more slowly than in warmer countries, and may indeed lie around for centuries. Accordingly, in Sweden, for example, concern for the environment is drummed into children from primary school on.

The "countryside code" regulating the conduct of visitors is about the same in all the Scandinavian countries. They must not, for example, take their car off the road, camp without the permission of the landowner (in Sweden, for a stay of over 24 hours), break off branches or twigs, or fish without permission. Great caution must be exercised in the lighting of open fires (which are, in general, prohibited in Norway between 15 April and 15 September), since in sparsely populated areas little can be done to fight forest fires and the short growing period means that vegetation takes a long time to recover from a fire.

# Fishing and hunting

## Fishing

The Scandinavian countries offer excellent fishing, both in fresh water and in the sea. In the sea, only the local fishermen are allowed to use nets. In fishing ports, it is often possible for visitors to go out with the fishermen in their boats to try their hand at deep-sea fishing. In the Baltic, fresh-water fish are also found in brackish water and in the sea just off the coast. – Since the regulations about close seasons and minimum sizes are complicated and subject to local variation, visitors should enquire locally about these matters.

### Denmark

*Fresh-water fish:* various species of trout, grayling, pike, perch, zander, a few salmon (in Jutland).

*Sea fish:* salmon, sea-trout, cod, coalfish, garfish, mackerel, turbot, plaice, flounder, dab, eel, pike, perch, whitefish. *Deep-sea fish:* shark, ray, sea-wolf.

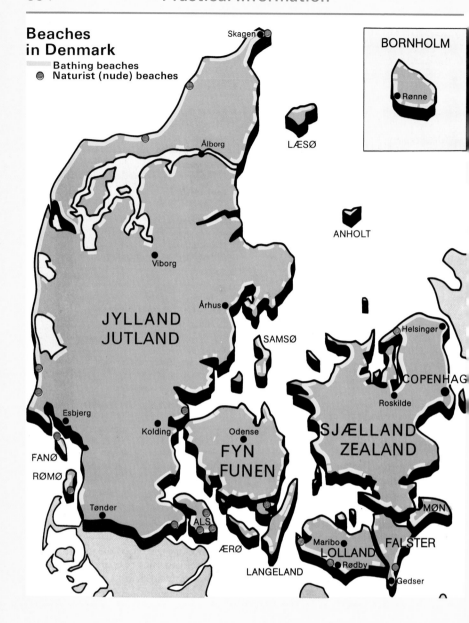

**Beaches in Denmark**

Bathing beaches
Naturist (nude) beaches

# The beaches of Denmark

The Danish coastline has a total length of 7400 km (4600 miles). The longest sandy **bathing beaches**, often sheltered by rings of dunes, extend almost continuously along the west coast of Jutland, from the islands of Rømø and Fanø in the south, to Denmark's northernmost tip at Skagen.

The best-known **bathing resorts** are found on the north coast of Zealand, the east coast of Falster and the southern tip of Bornholm. Bornholm is the only part of Denmark with any length of rocky coast, but it also has beaches of fine sand. On Mols and along the east coast of Jutland, the beaches are often fringed with woods. There are also excellent beaches on Funen and the neighbouring smaller islands.

Denmark has a number of beaches on which nude bathing is permitted (see map). Some of these are open to all, others only to members of a naturist organisation.

# Winter Sports Areas in Scandinavia

# Winter sports

In Norway, Sweden and Finland **lang-lauf** or **cross-country skiing** is by far the most popular form of skiing, but there are also some facilities for those who prefer *Alpine skiing*. – Denmark, with its flat topography and mild climate, offers little skiing, but there are artificial ice rinks in many towns.

**Permits required:** permits, daily or weekly, issued by fishing clubs, tourist offices and hotels (usually for hotel guests only). – Coastal fishing is free.

## Norway

*Fresh-water fish:* perch, pike, carp, bream, sturgeon, eel, char, grayling, salmon (usually 1 May to 1 September), trout.

*Sea fish:* cod, sea-trout, pollack, haddock, halibut, flounder, turbot, sea-wolf.

**Permits required:** state fishing licence and permit for the particular waters.

## Sweden

*Fresh-water fish:* various species of salmon and trout, pike, perch, char.

*Sea fish:* cod, flounder, sea-trout.

**Permits required:** fishing permit, obtainable in sports shops, tourist offices and hotels, and from vending machines at the fishing grounds. Group tickets for the larger districts are available.

For coastal fishing a free permit, available at local police stations, is necessary.

## Finland

*Fresh-water fish:* various species of trout, pike, perch, burbot, whitefish, zander, roach, char, grayling.

*Sea fish:* cod, flounder, sea-trout.

**Permits required:** fishing permit (for family), even required for coastal fishing, available at post offices, and permission from owner of fishing rights (fee).

# Hunting

In the southern parts of Scandinavia, the game is similar to that found elsewhere in Europe (deer, small game, game birds). Farther north, there are also elk. The elk season, however, usually lasts only a few weeks, and it is necessary to hire a local "gillie" or guide with an elkhound; a hunting permit is expensive. – Further information can be obtained from national tourist organisations.

# Winter Sports

## Norway

Norway has cross-country skiing, ski trekking and downhill skiing. In the larger skiing areas, there are several winter sports resorts.

1 **Oslo and surrounding area**
   (Oslo, Eggedal, Hurdal, Norefjell, Ringerike, Vikersund-Modum.)
2 **Kongsberg and Numedal**
   (Kongsberg, Flesberg and the eastern Blefjell, the Numedal as far as Dagali, Uvdal.)
3 **Telemark and Setesdal**
   (Telemark: Bolkesjø and Blefjell, Gautefall, Haukelifjell, Lifjell, Morgedal, Rauland, Vinje, the Rjukan area; Setesdal: Byglandsfjord, Vrådal-Kviteseid, Hovden, Våliosen, Åserdal.)
4 **Hallingdal and the Bergen railway**
   (Dagali-Skurdalen, Geilo-Ustaoset, Gol, Golsfjell, Hemsedal.)
5 **Valdres**
   (Fagernes area: Aurdal-Tonsåsen, Fagernes, Fjellstølen, Hovda-Sanderstølen, Vaset-Nøsen; Beito-

stølen area: Beitostølen and surrounding area; Vang/Filefjell area: Tyin and surrounding area, Eidsbugaren-Tyinholmen-Jotunheimen.)
6 **Western Norway**
   (Finse, Mjølfjell, Vatnahalsen, Voss, Oppheim, Seljestad, Standa, Sykkylven, Øtsta, Utvikfjell.)
7 **Vestoppland – Gjøvik**
   (Gjøvik, Toren, Lygnaseter, Synnfjell.)
8 **Gudbrandsdal and the Dovre railway**
   (Hamar and surrounding area; Lillehammer and surrounding area, Nordseter, Sjusjøen, Øyerfjell, Tretten; middle Gudbrandsdal, with Espedal, Kvam, Ringebu, Gausdal and Vinstra; northern Gudbrandsdal and Jotunheimen, with Bøverdalen, Sjodalen and Vågå; northern Gudbrandsdal and Rondane, with Høvringen, Mysuseter and Otta; northern Gudbrandsdal and Dovrefjell, with Bjorli, Dombås and Hjerrkinn.)
9 **Østerdal**
   (Atna, Engerdal, Elverun, Folldal, Os, Rena, Rendalen, Tynset.)
10 **Oppdal**
11 **Røros**
12 **Trondheim**
   and surrounding area
13 **Meråker**
14 **Grong**
15 **Lønsdal**
16 **Svolvær**
17 **Narvik**
18 **Bardu**
19 **Tromsø**
20 **Alta**
21 **Kautokeino**
22 **Karasjok**
23 **Skaidi**
24 **Skoganvarre**
25 **Levajok**
26 **Kirkenes**

## Sweden

There is skiing in Sweden from November to mid-May. There is ample skiing all over the country, from Småland in the south, to the far north of Lapland.
27 **Isaberg**
28 **Närke**
29 **Västmanland**
30 **Sunna**
31 **Lake Siljan**, with Leksand, Rättvik and Tällberg
32 **Sälen**
33 **Idre** and **Grövelsjön**
34 **Härjedalen**, with Vemdalsfjäll, Funäsdalen, Bruksvallarna, Tänndalen, Tännäs and Fjällnäs
35 **Sylarna**, **Storulvån** and **Blåhammaren**; Åre, Duved, Trillevallen
36 **Strömsund**
37 **Gäddede** and **Stora Blåsjön**
38 **Borgafjäll** and **Saxnäs**
39 **Vilhelmina**
40 **Storuman**
41 **Jokkmokk**
42 **Dundred**
43 **Abisko, Björkliden, Riksgränsen**

## Finland

Finland offers wide opportunities for cross-country skiing and ski trekking, with 35 cross-country skiing areas. The following is a selection of areas with facilities for both cross-country and downhill skiing.
44 **Lahti**
45 **Jyväskylä**, with Laajavuori
46 **Kuopio**, with Puijomäki
47 **Koli Hills**, with Lieksa
48 **Sotkamo**, with the Vuokatti sports institute
49 **Kuusamo – Ruka**
50 **Rovaniemi**, with Ounasvaara
51 **Kemijärvi**, with Suomutunturi
52 **Salla**, with Sallatunturi
53 **Kolari-Yllästunturi**
54 **Sodankylä**, with Luostotunturi
55 **Muonio**, with Olostunturi
56 **Pallastunturi area**
57 **Kilpisjärvi**, with Saanafjäll
58 **Saariselkä-Kaunispää**

# Calendar of Events

(A selection of interesting events)

**January**
**Norway**

| | |
|---|---|
| Ekeberg | Navigare Boat Show |

**Sweden**

| | |
|---|---|
| Malmö | Boat Show |

**Finland**

| | |
|---|---|
| Jyväskylä | Winter Festival |
| Kuopio | January Fair and Carnival |
| Tampere | International Short Film Festival |

**February**
**Norway**

| | |
|---|---|
| Geilo | Olympics for the Handicapped |
| Kongsberg | Kongsberg Fair |
| Røros | Fair, with ski race |
| Vikersund | International Ski-Flying Week |

**Sweden**

| | |
|---|---|
| Jokkmokk | Lapp Winter Fair (sale of handicrafts) |
| Arjeplog | Lapp Market |
| Gävle | International Motorcycle Ice Races |

**Finland**

| | |
|---|---|
| Helsinki | International Boat Show |
| Lahti, Vääksy | Skating Marathon |
| Hämeenlinna | Finlandia Cross-Country Ski Race |

**February–March**
**Sweden**

| | |
|---|---|
| Stockholm | International Boat Show |

**March**
**Norway**

| | |
|---|---|
| Lillehammer | Birkebeiner Ski Race |
| Oslo | Holmenkollen Ski Festival |
| Narvik | Winter Festival, with ski race |

**Sweden**

| | |
|---|---|
| Stockholm | Antiques Fair |
| Malmö | Malmex (stamp exhibition) |
| Norberg | Music Week |
| Gällivare | Lapp Market, with skiing contests |
| Dalarna | Vasa Run (cross-country ski race) |

**Finland**

| | |
|---|---|
| Tampere | Pirkka Ski Race |
| Inari | Reindeer Driving Competition |
| Rovaniemi | Winter Market |

**April**
**Sweden**

| | |
|---|---|
| Jönköping | Gunnar Nilsson Show (sports and race cars) |
| Helsingborg | Frimynt (coin and stamp exhibition) |
| Västerås | Nordic Cultural Festival |

**Finland**

| | |
|---|---|
| Naantali | Sleeping-Cap Carnival |
| Helsinki | Easter Festival (drama) |
| Kolari | International Winter Games (ski race) |

**30 April**
**Sweden**

| | |
|---|---|
| Throughout the country | Walpurgis Night |

**30 April to 1 May**
**Finland**

| | |
|---|---|
| Throughout the country | May Night |

**17 May**
**Norway**

| | |
|---|---|
| Throughout the country | Constitution Day (parades, fireworks, etc.) |

**May**
**Sweden**

| | |
|---|---|
| Jönköping | Scandinavian Game Fair |
| Råshult | Linnaeus Day |
| Älvkarleby | Waterfall Day |

**Finland**

| | |
|---|---|
| Valkeakoski | Helka Festival (folk events, processions) |

**May to June**
**Norway**

| | |
|---|---|
| Bergen | Bergen Festival (music, arts and drama) |

**6 June**
**Sweden**

| | |
|---|---|
| Throughout the country | Flag Day |

**7 June**
**Norway**

| | |
|---|---|
| Throughout the country | Norwegian Flag Day |

**15 June**
**Norway**

| | |
|---|---|
| Lofthus | Grieg Festival |

**22 to 23 June**
**Finland**

| | |
|---|---|
| Throughout the country | Midsummer Eve |

22 to 24 June
**Sweden**

| | |
|---|---|
| Throughout the country | Midsummer Festival |

23 June
**Norway**

| | |
|---|---|
| Throughout the country | Midsummer Eve |

June
**Norway**

| | |
|---|---|
| Harstad | North Norway Festival |
| Kongsberg | International Jazz Festival |

**Sweden**

| | |
|---|---|
| Anderstorp | Swedish Grand Prix (Formula 1) |
| Östersund | Expo Norr (trade fair) |
| Grisslehamn | Mail Rowing Race |

**Finland**

| | |
|---|---|
| Jyväskylä | Arts Festival (concerts, exhibitions, lectures) |
| Åland Islands | Mail Rowing Race |
| Kuopio | Dance and Music Festival |
| Oulu | Northern Finland Fair |
| Helsinki | Helsinki Day (concerts, open-air performances, entertainments) |
| Oulu | Tar-Burning Week |

June to July
**Denmark**

| | |
|---|---|
| Frederikssund | Viking Festival |

June to August
**Sweden**

| | |
|---|---|
| Many places | Local festivals |

June to September
**Sweden**

| | |
|---|---|
| Sjåne | Fair |
| Drottningholm | Festival performances in castle |

6 July
**Denmark**

| | |
|---|---|
| Many places | 6 July Festival (parades, fireworks, music, etc.) |

29 July
**Norway**

| | |
|---|---|
| Many places | Olsok Eve (St Olav's Day) |

July
**Denmark**

| | |
|---|---|
| Sandvig/Bornholm | Hammershus Festival (open-air performances) |
| Ebeltoft | Summer Festival |
| Odense | Hans Christian Andersen Festival |
| Holstebro | Nordlek (folk festival) |
| Rebild Hills | Rebild Festival |

**Norway**

| | |
|---|---|
| Stiklestad | Open-air Festival |
| Trondheim | St Olav's Days (plays in Cathedral) |

**Sweden**

| | |
|---|---|
| Helsingborg | Antiques Fair |
| Ronneby | Tosia Bonnada'n (folk festival) |
| Vilhelmina | Regional Folk Festival |
| Stockholm | Bellman Week |
| Sigtuna | Sigtuna Fair |
| Lycksele | Lapland Week |
| Halmstad | Salmon Festival |
| Trollhättan | Waterfall Day |
| Tärnaby | Border Festival |
| Söderhamn | Herring Festival |

Folk-dancing group at Rättvik on Lake Siljan

**Finland**

| | |
|---|---|
| Vaasa | Stundars Festival (folk dancing and music; regional specialties) |
| Lappeenranta, Imatra | Humppa Festival (Finnish dance music) |
| Sodankylä | Kuusrock (international rock festival) |
| Imatra | Imatra Week (folk festival) |
| Savonlinna | Opera Festival |

July to August
**Denmark**

| | |
|---|---|
| Vendsyssel | Music Festival (opera, classical, pop, folk) |
| Kalundborg | Lerchenborg Music Week |
| Bornholm | Bornholm Musical Festival |
| Copenhagen | Copenhagen Summer Festival (concerts) |

August
**Denmark**

| | |
|---|---|
| Odense | Fairytale Film Festival |
| Helsingør | Musical Festival |
| Rønne | Musical Festival in St Nicholas's Church |
| Ålborg | Musical Festival |

**Norway**

| | |
|---|---|
| Vinstra | Peer Gynt Festival (folk events, procession, etc.) |

**Sweden**

| | |
|---|---|
| Stockholm | St Erik's Fair (consumer goods) |
| Strängnäs | European Motorboat Championship on Lake Mälar |

**Finland**

| Turku | Music Festival; Turku Fair |
| Tampere | Summer Theatre |
| Helsinki | Helsinki Festival (concerts, opera, ballet, jazz, pop, exhibitions) |

**August to September**
**Denmark**

| Helsingør | Hamlet Festival in Kronborg Castle |

**September**
**Denmark**

| Århus | International Organ Festival |

**Sweden**

| Vesterås | Flax Harvest Festival (with folk events) |

**First working day in October**
**Norway**

| Oslo | Opening of Storting (with state procession) |

**10–11 November**
**Sweden**

| All over Skåne | Mårten Gås (St Martin's Day) |

**6 December**
**Finland**

| Throughout the country | Independence Day (celebrations, processions) |

A Swedish "St Lucia bride"

**13 December**
**Sweden**

| Throughout the country | St Lucia's Day (processions, etc.) |

**December**
**Norway**

| Many places | Christmas Fair |
| Oslo | Presentation of Nobel Peace Prize |

**Sweden**

| Many places | Christmas Fair |

# Statutory Public Holidays

**Denmark**
1 January
Maundy Thursday
(day before Good
Friday)
Good Friday
Easter Monday
Day of Repentance
(beginning of May)
Ascension
Whit Monday
(seventh after Easter)
5 June
(Constitution Day)
Christmas
(25 and 26 December)

**Norway**
1 January
Maundy Thursday
Good Friday
Easter Monday
1 May
17 May
(National Day)
Ascension
Whit Monday
25 and 26 December

**Sweden**
1 January
6 January (Epiphany)
Good Friday
Easter Monday
1 May
Ascension
Whit Monday
23 June
(Midsummer)
All Saints (last Sat.
in Oct. or first Sat.
in Nov.)
25 and 26 December

**Finland**
1 January
6 January or following
Saturday (Three Kings)
Good Friday
Easter Monday
Ascension
Whit Monday
Midsummer (Sat.
nearest 24 June)
All Saints (last Sat.
in Oct. or first Sat.
in Nov.)
6 December
(Independence Day)
25 and 26 December

# Shopping and souvenirs

All the Scandinavian countries excel in the field of *design*. Their designers not only produce the fine furniture of light-coloured wood for which these countries are famous, but also give a wide variety of everyday objects and craft products a modern and yet timeless stamp with their simple and functional lines. – It is worth remembering that the high Scandinavian value-added taxes can be avoided by having goods sent direct from the shop to a foreign address.

### Denmark

Porcelain (particularly the products of the Royal Manufactory in Copenhagen), silver, cutlery, toys, pewter, pipes and tobacco, aquavit.

### Norway

Knitwear (in colourful Norwegian patterns), wooden objects, pewter, enamel, brass articles, tapestries, toys, reindeer skins, reindeer antlers.

### Sweden

Glass (Orrefors), wooden objects, textiles (particularly children's clothes), stoneware, ceramics, pewter, reindeer skins.

### Finland

Silver and bronze jewelry and ornaments (sometimes based on ancient models), porcelain, ceramics, handwoven Ryivy carpets, glass, reindeer skins, reindeer antlers.

# Information

## Denmark

### Danish Tourist Board
(*Danmarks Turistråd*)
Head office:
H. C. Andersens Boulevard 22
DK-D1553 **Copenhagen** V;
tel. (01) 11 13 25.

Danish Tourist Board,
Sceptre House,
169–173 Regent Street,
**London** W1 R 8PY;
tel. (01) 734 2637–8.

Danish National Tourist Office,
75 Rockefeller Plaza,
**New York**, NY 10019;
tel. (212) 582 2802.

Danish National Tourist Office,
151 Bloor Street West, 8th floor,
**Toronto** M5S 1S4, Ontario;
tel. (416) 960 3305.

In the larger towns and resorts of Denmark, there are branch offices of the Danish Tourist Board. In writing to one of these offices, it is sufficient to address the letter to *Turistbureauet*, followed by the postal code and name of the town.

### Motoring organisations

**Forenede Danske Motorejere** (*FDM:* Federation of Danish Motorists),
Blegdamsvej 124,
DK-2100 **Copenhagen** Ø;
tel. (01) 38 21 12.

**Kongelig Dansk Automobil Klub** (*KDAK:* Royal Danish Automobile Club),
Frederiksberg Allé 41,
DK-1820 **Copenhagen** V;
tel. (01) 21 11 01.

### Embassies

**British Embassy**,
Kastelsvej 36–40,
DK-2100 **Copenhagen** Ø;
tel. (01) 26 46 00.

**United States Embassy**,
Dag Hammarksjölds Allé 24,
DK-2100 **Copenhagen** Ø;
tel. (01) 42 31 44.

**Canadian Embassy**,
Kr. Bernikowsgade 1,
DK-1105 **Copenhagen** K;
tel. (01) 12 22 99.

### Airlines

**Scandinavian Airlines System** (*SAS*),
SAS Building, Hammerichsgade,
DK-1611 **Copenhagen** V;
tel. (01) 59 66 22.

**British Airways**,
Vesterbrogade 2,
DK-1620 **Copenhagen** V;
tel. (01) 14 60 00.

### Danish State Railways

Representatives in the United Kingdom:
DFDS (UK) Ltd,
Mariner House, Pepys Street,
**London** EC3N 4BX.

# Norway

**Norway Travel Association**
(*Landslaget for Reiselivet i Norge*)
Head office:
Langkai 1,
N-**Oslo** 1;
tel. (02) 42 70 44.

Norwegian National Tourist Office
(Nortra),
20 Pall Mall,
**London** SW1Y 5NE;
tel. (01) 839 6255.

Norwegian-Swedish National Tourist
Office,
75 Rockefeller Plaza,
**New York**, NY 10019;
tel. (212) 582 2802.

There are branches of the Norway Travel
Association in the larger towns and tourist
resorts in Norway.

## Motoring organisations

**Norges Automobil Forbund** (*NAF:* Norwegian
Automobile Association),
Storgate 2–6,
N-**Oslo** 1;
tel. (02) 33 70 80.

**Kongelig Norsk Automobilklub** (*KNA:* Royal
Norwegian Automobile Club),
Parkveien 68,
N-**Oslo** 2;
tel. (02) 56 26 90.

## Embassies

**British Embassy,**
Thomas Heftyesgate 8,
N-**Oslo** 2;
tel. (02) 56 38 90–97.

**United States Embassy,**
Drammensveien 18,
N-**Oslo** 1;
tel. (02) 56 68 80.

**Canadian Embassy,**
Oscarsgate 20,
N-**Oslo** 3;
tel. (02) 46 69 55.

## Airlines

**Scandinavian Airlines System** (*SAS*),
SAS Building, Ruseløkkveien 6,
N-**Oslo** 2;
tel. (02) 42 99 70.
Holbergsgate 30,
N-**Oslo** 1;
tel. (02) 42 99 70.

**Braathens SAFE A/S,**
Ruseløkkveien 26,
N-**Oslo** 2;
tel. (02) 41 10 20.

**Widerøes Flyveselskap AS,**
Mustadsveien 1,
N-**Oslo** 2;
tel. 55 59 60
(booking through SAS).

**British Airways,**
Kronprinsesse Marthas Plass 1,
N-**Oslo** 2;
tel. (02) 41 87 50.

**Norwegian State Railways** (*NSB*)

21–24 Cockspur Street,
**London** SW1;
tel. (01) 930 6666.

# Sweden

**Swedish Tourist Board**
(*Sveriges Turistråd*)
Head office:
Hamngatan 27,
Box 7473,
S-10392 **Stockholm**;
tel. (08) 89 20 00.

Swedish National Tourist Office,
3 Cork Street,
**London** W1X 1HA;
tel. (01) 437 5816.

Norwegian-Swedish National Tourist
Office,
75 Rockefeller Plaza,
**New York**, NY 10019;
tel. (212) 582 2802.

**Swedish Tourist Association**
(*Svenska Turistföreningen*),
Birger Jarlsgatan 18,
Box 7615,
S-10394 **Stockholm**;
tel. (08) 22 72 00.

There are Swedish Tourist Board offices in
the larger Swedish towns and tourist
resorts.

## Motoring organisations

**Motormännens Riksförbund** (*M:* National Association of Motorists),
Sturegatan 32,
S-11436 **Stockholm**;
tel. (08) 7 82 38 00.

**Kungl. Automobil Klubben** (*KAK:* Royal Automobile Club),
Sturegatan 32
S-11436 **Stockholm**;
tel. (08) 67 05 80.

## Embassies

**British Embassy**,
Skarpögatan 6–8,
S-11527 **Stockholm**;
tel. (08) 67 01 40.

**United States Embassy**,
Strandvägen 101,
**Stockholm**;
tel. (08) 63 05 20.

**Canadian Embassy**,
Tegelbacken 4, 7th floor,
S-10323 **Stockholm**;
tel. (08) 23 79 20.

## Airlines

**Scandinavian Airlines System** (*SAS*),
Sveavägen 22,
S-11157 **Stockholm**;
tel. (08) 24 00 40 and 24 75 60.

**Linjeflyg AB**,
Fack,
S-16110 **Bromma**;
tel. (08) 24 00 20.

**British Airways**,
Norrmalmstorg 1,
**Stockholm**;
tel. (08) 23 39 00.

# Finland

## Finnish Tourist Board
(*Suomen Matkailun Edistämiskeskus*)
Head office:
Asemapäällikönkatu 12B,
SF-00520 **Helsinki**;
tel. (90) 14 45 11.

Finnish Tourist Board,
66–68 Haymarket,
**London** SW1 4RF;
tel. (01) 839 4048.

Finland National Tourist Office,
75 Rockefeller Plaza,
**New York**, NY 10019;
tel. (212) 582 2802.

There are Finnish Tourist Board offices in the larger Finnish towns and tourist resorts.

## Motoring organisation

**Finnish Automobile and Touring Club** (*Autoliitto*),
Kansakoulukatu 10,
SF-00100 **Helsinki**;
tel. (90) 6 94 00 22.

## Embassies

**British Embassy**,
Uudenmaankatu 16–20,
**Helsinki** 12;
tel. (90) 64 79 22.

**United States Embassy**,
Itainen Puistotie 14A,
**Helsinki**;
tel. (90) 17 19 31.

**Canadian Embassy**,
Pohjoisesplanadi 25B,
SF-00100 **Helsinki** 10;
tel. (90) 17 11 41.

## Airlines

**Finnair**,
Mannerheimintie 102
SF-00100 **Helsinki**;
tel. (90) 4 73 35 33.

**Scandinavian Airlines System** (*SAS*),
Pohjoisesplanadi 23,
SF-00100 **Helsinki**;
tel. (90) 17 56 11 and 8 22 19 04.

**British Airways**,
Keskuskatu 5,
**Helsinki**;
tel. (90) 65 06 77.

# Radio messages for tourists

In cases of serious emergency, the Scandinavian radio stations will broadcast messages for tourists. Information from motoring organisations and the police.

## International Telephone Dialling Codes

From the United Kingdom
| | |
|---|---|
| to **Denmark** | 010 45 |
| to **Norway** | 010 47 |
| to **Sweden** | 010 46 |
| to **Finland** | 010 358 |

From the United States and Canada
| | |
|---|---|
| to **Denmark** | 011 45 |
| to **Norway** | 011 47 |
| to **Sweden** | 011 46 |
| to **Finland** | 011 358 |

From **Denmark**
| | |
|---|---|
| to the United Kingdom | 009 44 |
| to the United States and Canada | 009 1 |

From **Norway**
| | |
|---|---|
| to the United Kingdom | 095 44 |
| to the United States and Canada | 095 1 |

From **Sweden**
| | |
|---|---|
| to the United Kingdom | 009 44 |
| to the United States and Canada | 009 1 |

From **Finland**
| | |
|---|---|
| to the United Kingdom | 990 44 |
| to the United States and Canada | 990 1 |

The zero (in Finland the 9) in the local dialling code should be omitted when dialling an international call.

# Emergency Calls

## Denmark

On the Danish motorways there are **emergency telephones** at intervals of 2 km ($1\frac{3}{4}$ miles).

Emergency calls (police, ambulance): throughout the country dial **000** (no coin required in public telephone boxes).

Breakdown assistance is also available from the FALCK and DAHU organisations.

## Norway

NAF emergency service in Oslo
(24-hour service): **(02) 33 70 80**

Police in Oslo: **(02) 11 00 11**

Accident service in Oslo: **(02) 20 10 90**

Outside Oslo there are no uniform numbers for calling the emergency services.

## Sweden

In case of breakdown, help can be obtained from the *Larmtjänst* which works in co-operation with the Swedish Automobile Club. The local telephone numbers of the club can be obtained from petrol (gas) stations, the police, etc.

Emergency calls (police, fire, ambulance) throughout the country: dial **9 00 00**.

## Finland

Throughout the day and night arrangements for the recovery of a vehicle and mechanical assistance can be obtained by dialling **6 94 04 96**. The oil companies also run a breakdown service throughout Finland (see telephone directory).

Breakdown service of the Finnish Automobile Club:
in Helsinki **90/6 94 00 22**

Police:
in Helsinki **002**

Help in case of accident:
in Helsinki **000**

(The letters Å, and Æ, Ø and Ö are treated in this Index as if they were A and O.)

# Baedeker's Travel Guides

"The maps and illustrations are lavish. The arrangement of information (alphabetically by city) makes it easy to use the book."
—*San Francisco Examiner-Chronicle*

What's there to do and see in foreign countries? Travelers who rely on Baedeker, one of the oldest names in travel literature, will miss nothing. Baedeker's bright red, internationally recognized covers open up to reveal fascinating A-Z directories of cities, towns, and regions, complete with their sights, museums, monuments, cathedrals, castles, gardens and ancestral homes—an approach that gives the traveler a quick and easy way to plan a vacation itinerary.

And Baedekers are filled with over 200 full-color photos and detailed maps, including a full-size, fold-out roadmap for easy vacation driving. Baedeker—the premier name in travel for over 140 years.

Please send me the books checked below:

☐ **Austria**...............................$14.95
0–13–056127–4

☐ **Caribbean**...........................$14.95
0–13–056143–6

☐ **Denmark**.............................$14.95
0–13–058124–0

☐ **Egypt**..................................$15.95
0–13–056358–7

☐ **France**.................................$14.95
0–13–055814–1

☐ **Germany**.............................$14.95
0–13–055830–3

☐ **Great Britain**.......................$14.95
0–13–055855–9

☐ **Greece**................................$14.95
0–13–056002–2

☐ **Greek Islands**......................$10.95
0–13–058132–1

☐ **Ireland**................................$14.95
0–13–058140–2

☐ **Israel**..................................$14.95
0–13–056176–2

☐ **Italy**....................................$14.95
0–13–055897–4

☐ **Japan**..................................$15.95
0–13–056382–X

☐ **Loire**.....................................$9.95
0–13–056375–7

☐ **Mediterranean Islands**..........$14.95
0–13–056862–7

☐ **Mexico**................................$14.95
0–13–056069–3

☐ **Netherlands, Belgium, and Luxembourg**...........................$14.95
0–13–056028–6

☐ **Portugal**..............................$14.95
0–13–056135–5

☐ **Provence/Côte d'Azur**.............$9.95
0–13–056938–0

☐ **Rhine**....................................$9.95
0–13–056466–4

☐ **Scandinavia**.........................$14.95
0–13–056085–5

☐ **Spain**..................................$14.95
0–13–055913–X

☐ **Switzerland**.........................$14.95
0–13–056044–8

☐ **Turkish Coast**.......................$10.95
0–13–058173–9

☐ **Tuscany**................................$9.95
0–13–056482–6

☐ **Yugoslavia**..........................$14.95
0–13–056184–3

Please turn the page for an order form and a list of additional **Baedeker Guides**.

A series of city guides filled with color photographs and detailed maps and floor plans from one of the oldest names in travel publishing:

Please send me the books checked below:

☐ **Amsterdam**......................$10.95
   0–13–057969–6

☐ **Athens**............................$10.95
   0–13–057977–7

☐ **Bangkok**..........................$10.95
   0–13–057985–8

☐ **Berlin**.............................$10.95
   0–13–367996–9

☐ **Brussels**..........................$10.95
   0–13–368788–0

☐ **Budapest**.........................$10.95
   0–13–058199–2

☐ **Cologne**..........................$10.95
   0–13–058181–X

☐ **Copenhagen**......................$10.95
   0–13–057993–9

☐ **Florence**..........................$10.95
   0–13–369505–0

☐ **Frankfurt**.........................$10.95
   0–13–369570–0

☐ **Hamburg**..........................$10.95
   0–13–369687–1

☐ **Hong Kong**.......................$10.95
   0–13–058009–0

☐ **Istanbul**...........................$10.95
   0–13–058207–7

☐ **Jerusalem**........................$10.95
   0–13–058017–1

☐ **London**............................$10.95
   0–13–058025–2

☐ **Madrid**............................$10.95
   0–13–058033–3

☐ **Moscow**...........................$10.95
   0–13–058041–4

☐ **Munich**............................$10.95
   0–13–370370–3

☐ **New York**.........................$10.95
   0–13–058058–9

☐ **Paris**..............................$10.95
   0–13–058066–X

☐ **Prague**............................$10.95
   0–13–058215–8

☐ **Rome**.............................$10.95
   0–13–058074–0

☐ **San Francisco**....................$10.95
   0–13–058082–1

☐ **Singapore**........................$10.95
   0–13–058090–2

☐ **Stuttgart**.........................$10.95
   0–13–058223–9

☐ **Tokyo**.............................$10.95
   0–13–058108–9

☐ **Venice**............................$10.95
   0–13–058116–X

☐ **Vienna**............................$10.95
   0–13–371303–2

**PRENTICE HALL PRESS**
Order Department—Travel Books
200 Old Tappan Road
Old Tappan, New Jersey 07675
In U.S. include $1 postage and handling for 1st book, 25¢ each additional book.
Outside U.S. $2 and 50¢ respectively.

Enclosed is my check or money order for $_____

NAME_____

ADDRESS_____

CITY_____STATE_____ZIP_____